Using Influencer Marketing as a Digital Business Strategy

Sandrina Teixeira
ISCAP, Polytechnic Institute of Porto, Portugal

Sara Teixeira
Polytechnic Institute of Porto, Portugal

Zaila Oliveira
Unichristus, Brazil & Unifametro, Brazil

Elnivan Souza
Christus University Center, Brazil

A volume in the Advances in Marketing, Customer Relationship Management, and E-Services (AMCRMES) Book Series

IGI Global
PUBLISHER of TIMELY KNOWLEDGE

Published in the United States of America by
IGI Global
Business Science Reference (an imprint of IGI Global)
701 E. Chocolate Avenue
Hershey PA, USA 17033
Tel: 717-533-8845
Fax: 717-533-8661
E-mail: cust@igi-global.com
Web site: http://www.igi-global.com

Library of Congress Cataloging-in-Publication Data

Names: Teixeira, Sandrina, 1975- editor. | Teixeira, Sara, editor. | Oliveira, Zaila, 1960- editor. | Souza, Elnivan, 1980- editor.
Title: Using influencer marketing as a digital business strategy / edited by Sandrina Teixeira, Sara Teixeira, Zaila Oliveira, Elnivan Souza.
Description: Hershey, PA : Business Science Reference, [2024] | Includes bibliographical references and index. | Summary: "This book seeks to explore influencer marketing which is a relevant topic for management and academia since influencers play an increasingly important role in the relationship of brands with their audiences. Given that this is a recent theme, the compilation of studies on this topic will serve as a basis for the development of more in-depth and specific scientific research, as well as contribute to assisting organizations in the process of identifying their brands and reaching their target"-- Provided by publisher.
Identifiers: LCCN 2023045032 (print) | LCCN 2023045033 (ebook) | ISBN 9798369305515 (hardcover) | ISBN 9798369305522 (paperback) | ISBN 9798369305539 (ebook)
Subjects: LCSH: Business--Data processing. | Marketing--Data processing.
Classification: LCC HF5548.2 .U77 2024 (print) | LCC HF5548.2 (ebook) | DDC 658/.05--dc23/eng/20231026
LC record available at https://lccn.loc.gov/2023045032
LC ebook record available at https://lccn.loc.gov/2023045033

This book is published in the IGI Global book series Advances in Marketing, Customer Relationship Management, and E-Services (AMCRMES) (ISSN: 2327-5502; eISSN: 2327-5529)

British Cataloguing in Publication Data
A Cataloguing in Publication record for this book is available from the British Library.

All work contributed to this book is new, previously-unpublished material. The views expressed in this book are those of the authors, but not necessarily of the publisher.

For electronic access to this publication, please contact: eresources@igi-global.com.

Advances in Marketing, Customer Relationship Management, and E-Services (AMCRMES) Book Series

Eldon Y. Li
National Chengchi University, Taiwan & California Polytechnic State University, USA

ISSN:2327-5502
EISSN:2327-5529

Mission

Business processes, services, and communications are important factors in the management of good customer relationship, which is the foundation of any well organized business. Technology continues to play a vital role in the organization and automation of business processes for marketing, sales, and customer service. These features aid in the attraction of new clients and maintaining existing relationships.

The Advances in Marketing, Customer Relationship Management, and E-Services (AMCRMES) Book Series addresses success factors for customer relationship management, marketing, and electronic services and its performance outcomes. This collection of reference source covers aspects of consumer behavior and marketing business strategies aiming towards researchers, scholars, and practitioners in the fields of marketing management.

Coverage

- Cases on CRM Implementation
- B2B marketing
- Mobile Services
- CRM strategies
- Text Mining and Marketing
- Web Mining and Marketing
- Data mining and marketing
- Online Community Management and Behavior
- Ethical Considerations in E-Marketing
- Electronic Services

IGI Global is currently accepting manuscripts for publication within this series. To submit a proposal for a volume in this series, please contact our Acquisition Editors at Acquisitions@igi-global.com or visit: http://www.igi-global.com/publish/.

The Advances in Marketing, Customer Relationship Management, and E-Services (AMCRMES) Book Series (ISSN 2327-5502) is published by IGI Global, 701 E. Chocolate Avenue, Hershey, PA 17033-1240, USA, www.igi-global.com. This series is composed of titles available for purchase individually; each title is edited to be contextually exclusive from any other title within the series. For pricing and ordering information please visit http://www.igi-global.com/book-series/advances-marketing-customer-relationship-management/37150. Postmaster: Send all address changes to above address.

Titles in this Series

For a list of additional titles in this series, please visit: www.igi-global.com/book-series

The Use of Artificial Intelligence in Digital Marketing Competitive Strategies and Tactics
Sandrina Teixeira (Centre for Organizational and Social Studies (CEOS), Porto Accounting and Business School, Polytechnic of Porto, Portugal) and Jorge Remondes (Centre for Organizational and Social Studies (CEOS), Porto Accounting and Business School, Polytechnic of Porto, Portugal)
Business Science Reference • © 2024 • 318pp • H/C (ISBN: 9781668493243) • US $250.00

The Rise of Blockchain Applications in Customer Experience
Mohammed Majeed (Tamale Technical University, Ghana) Kwame Simpe Ofori (International University of Grand Bassam, Cote D'Ivoire) George Kofi Amoako (Ghana Communication Technology University, Ghana) Abdul-Raheed Alolo (Tamale Technical University, Ghana) and Gideon Awini (Business School, University of Ghana, Ghana)
Business Science Reference • © 2024 • 304pp • H/C (ISBN: 9781668476499) • US $250.00

Effective Digital Marketing for Improving Society Behavior Toward DEI and SDGs
Inês Veiga Pereira (Accounting and Business School, Polytechnic of Porto, Portugal) Paulo Botelho Pires (Centre for Organizational and Social Studies, Polytechnic of Porto, Portugal) and José Duarte Santos (Accounting and Business School, Polytechnic of Porto, Portugal)
Business Science Reference • © 2024 • 330pp • H/C (ISBN: 9781668489840) • US $240.00

Sustainable Marketing, Branding, and Reputation Management Strategies for a Greener Future
Reason Masengu (Middle East College, Oman) Stanilas Bigirimana (Africa University, Zimbabwe) Option Takunda Chiwaridzo (University of Science and Technology, Beijing, China) Ruzive Bensson (Modern College of Business and Science, Oman) and Christina Blossom (Middle East College, Oman)
Business Science Reference • © 2023 • 670pp • H/C (ISBN: 9798369300190) • US $250.00

Origin and Branding in International Market Entry Processes
Carlos Francisco e Silva (Universidade Europeia, Portugal)
Business Science Reference • © 2023 • 298pp • H/C (ISBN: 9781668466131) • US $250.00

The Role of Brands in an Era of Over-Information
Ricardo Fontes Correia (Polytechnic Institute of Bragança, Portugal) Dominyka Venciūtė (ISM University of Management and Economics, Lithuania) and Bruno Miguel Sousa (Polytechnic Institute of Cávado and Ave, Portugal)
Business Science Reference • © 2023 • 257pp • H/C (ISBN: 9781668483510) • US $250.00

IGI Global
PUBLISHER of TIMELY KNOWLEDGE

701 East Chocolate Avenue, Hershey, PA 17033, USA
Tel: 717-533-8845 x100 • Fax: 717-533-8661
E-Mail: cust@igi-global.com • www.igi-global.com

Table of Contents

Preface xiii

Chapter 1
The Power of Influence: Unleashing the Potential of Influencer Marketing 1
Nitesh Behare, Balaji Institute of International Business, Sri Balaji University, Pune, India
Rashmi D. Mahajan, Balaji Institute of International Business, Sri Balaji University, Pune, India
Meenakshi Singh, Balaji Institute of International Business, Sri Balaji University, Pune, India
Vishwanathan Iyer, Balaji Institute of International Business, Sri Balaji University, Pune, India
Ushmita Gupta, Balaji Institute of International Business, Sri Balaji University, Pune, India
Pritesh P. Somani, Balaji Institute of International Business, Sri Balaji University, Pune, India

Chapter 2
Use of Influencers in Different Sectors of the Economy 37
Shikha Mittal, Raj Kumar Goel Institute of Technology, Ghaziabad, India

Chapter 3
How Influencers Can Leverage Performance in Business 58
Albérico Travassos Rosário, GOVCOPP, IADE, Universidade Europeia, Portugal

Chapter 4
All Users Are Equal, but Some Users Are More Equal Than Others: Exploring the Psychology of Users That Follow Social Media Influencers 89
Carla Sofia Ribeiro Murteira, School of Communication and Media Studies, Politécnico de Lisboa, Portugal & Institute for the Study of Literature and Tradition, NOVA University of Lisbon, Portugal
Ana Cristina Antunes, School of Communication and Media Studies, Politécnico de Lisboa, Portugal

Chapter 5
Virtual Influencers: The Irruption of Artificial Intelligence in Digital Influencers 112
Mario Sierra Martin, Universidad de Málaga, Spain
Alvaro Díaz Casquero, Universidad de Málaga, Spain
Marina Sánchez Pérez, Universidad de Málaga, Spain
Bárbara Rando Rodríguez, Universidad de Málaga, Spain

Chapter 6
Influencing the Influencers Through Co-Creation: Approaches to Successful Brand Strategies 129
Poornima Nair, Christ University, India
Sunita Kumar, Christ University, India

Chapter 7
The Intrinsic Property of a Representation in the Phygital Transformation: A (Meta) Influence as a Force With Magnitude and Direction in the Metaverse 147
Neli Maria Mengalli, Faculdade São Bernardo do Campo, Brazil
Antonio Aparecido Carvalho, Faculdade São Bernardo do Campo, Brazil

Chapter 8
Virtual Influencers: A Bibliometric Analysis 163
Belem Barbosa, University of Porto, Portugal

Chapter 9
Stimuli for the Use of Digital Influencers in the Culture Sector: An Analysis of the Portuguese Context 189
Nádia Patrícia Pinheiro Custódio, Technology and Management School of Oliveira do Hospital, Polytechnic Institute of Coimbra, Portugal
Nayra Leandro Miguel Martins, Technology and Management School of Oliveira do Hospital, Polytechnic Institute of Coimbra, Portugal & NECE-Research Center in Business Sciences, University of Beira Interior, Portugal

Chapter 10
TikTok Content Categories and User Engagement Behavior: Alisha Lehmann – Celebrity Athlete and Influencer 214
Sebastiano Mereu, Sports Business Research Academy, Switzerland

Chapter 11
Digital Marketing Tools and Market Trends in the Skincare Industry: Consumer Behavior and Sales Growth Insights 235
Lierni Castilla-Miguel, Universidad Pública de Navarra, Spain
Maria Elena Aramendia-Muneta, Universidad Pública de Navarra, Spain

Chapter 12
Digital Influencers and the Restaurant Sector 269
Alvaro Díaz Casquero, Universidad de Málaga, Spain
Eva María González Robles, Universidad de Málaga, Spain
Benjamín del Alcázar, Universidad de Málaga, Spain

Chapter 13
Changing Consumer Buyer Decision Process in the Context of Instamoms 288
Ece İpekoğlu, Yasar University, Turkey
Nilgün Gürkaynak, Izmir University of Economics, Turkey

Compilation of References 311

About the Contributors 362

Index 368

Detailed Table of Contents

Preface xiii

Chapter 1
The Power of Influence: Unleashing the Potential of Influencer Marketing 1
Nitesh Behare, Balaji Institute of International Business, Sri Balaji University, Pune, India
Rashmi D. Mahajan, Balaji Institute of International Business, Sri Balaji University, Pune, India
Meenakshi Singh, Balaji Institute of International Business, Sri Balaji University, Pune, India
Vishwanathan Iyer, Balaji Institute of International Business, Sri Balaji University, Pune, India
Ushmita Gupta, Balaji Institute of International Business, Sri Balaji University, Pune, India
Pritesh P. Somani, Balaji Institute of International Business, Sri Balaji University, Pune, India

This chapter provides an overview of influencer marketing, its evolution, development, and popularity in recent years. It emphasizes the significance and potential of influencer marketing for businesses in reaching and engaging their target audience. The chapter further explores different types of influencers, the role of influencers, and how to recognize the right influencers for a brand or target audience. It also explores various benefits of influencer marketing. The chapter also covers measuring and analyzing influencer marketing success through key performance indicators (KPIs), evaluating ROI, and tracking campaign performance using data to optimize future campaigns. This chapter also revealed challenges and risks associated with influencer marketing. Finally, emerging trends and the future outlook of influencer marketing, including new platforms, integration with other marketing strategies, and predictions for the field, are also explored.

Chapter 2
Use of Influencers in Different Sectors of the Economy 37
Shikha Mittal, Raj Kumar Goel Institute of Technology, Ghaziabad, India

With the advent of digital technologies, influencer marketing has acquired a key role in the social media approaches adopted by a growing number of companies operating in different sectors. Influencer marketing has grown with a startlingly rapid pace, and it has not just grown, but has helped in better product introduction with increased consumer and influencer communication. In the current scenario, undoubtedly, influencers will rule the digital space, and businesses will constantly come up with new strategies to utilize the influencing powers of these influencers. The author has selected seven different sectors—fashion and lifestyle, technology industry, travel and tourism industry, food and beverage, healthcare, finance sector, and entertainment and gaming—to study the importance of influencers and change they have made. This study examines the use of influencers in chosen sectors of the economy. It also aims to identify factors influencing consumers' behavior to generate revenue.

Chapter 3
How Influencers Can Leverage Performance in Business 58
Albérico Travassos Rosário, GOVCOPP, IADE, Universidade Europeia, Portugal

Influencers can indeed use their influence to boost business performance. Influencers and businesses can work together to market a company's goods or services to their subscriber base. Influencers can significantly affect sales and performance by endorsing goods or services and including their affiliate links in their content. Influencers and businesses can collaborate to produce sponsored content, in which the influencers create interesting and genuine posts or videos showcasing the brand's goods or services. By doing so, businesses can connect with the influencer's audience and use their power and inventive storytelling abilities. Businesses can benefit from this tactic by expanding their reach, increasing engagement, and boosting traffic to their websites and physical stores. For influencers to continue earning the trust of their audience, they must always be genuine and transparent in their collaborations. Influencers can influence business performance, so this study aims to review the bibliometrics literature using the Scopus database.

Chapter 4
All Users Are Equal, but Some Users Are More Equal Than Others: Exploring the Psychology of Users That Follow Social Media Influencers 89
Carla Sofia Ribeiro Murteira, School of Communication and Media Studies, Politécnico de Lisboa, Portugal & Institute for the Study of Literature and Tradition, NOVA University of Lisbon, Portugal
Ana Cristina Antunes, School of Communication and Media Studies, Politécnico de Lisboa, Portugal

The study of social influence in social media settings has gained significant importance in the last years due to the advent of the internet and the increase of social media users and followers of social media influencers (SMI). This chapter focuses on the followers' psychological experience by reviewing how SMIs are perceived by followers and what moves the users to follow SMIs. Users follow SMI in an attempt to obtain information, inspiration, and entertainment, therefore brands have the chance to promote their products and services based on an appealing communication that can be provided by the SMI. However, the SMIs' perceived credibility, trustworthiness, authenticity, and expertise can impact not just the interaction with followers but also the brand image. It is recommended that brands conduct a continuous and careful assessment of SMIs' communication style and followers' perceptions to improve followers' attitudes towards the brands and their purchase intentions.

Chapter 5
Virtual Influencers: The Irruption of Artificial Intelligence in Digital Influencers 112
Mario Sierra Martin, Universidad de Málaga, Spain
Alvaro Díaz Casquero, Universidad de Málaga, Spain
Marina Sánchez Pérez, Universidad de Málaga, Spain
Bárbara Rando Rodríguez, Universidad de Málaga, Spain

The digital revolution has fueled the rise of influencers who shape opinions and behaviors online. However, the arrival of virtual influencers, avatars generated by artificial intelligence, is transforming advertising. These avatars, like Lil Miquela, are run by brands and agencies, offer customization and flexibility, and pose fewer ethical risks. Although they are not always as effective as humans, they can be valuable in rational campaigns. In a world where artificial intelligence is growing, these virtual influencers are emerging as a powerful tool in marketing. This chapter explores its importance and evolution in society and marketing.

Chapter 6
Influencing the Influencers Through Co-Creation: Approaches to Successful Brand Strategies 129
Poornima Nair, Christ University, India
Sunita Kumar, Christ University, India

In today's technology-driven landscape, the internet and social media have seamlessly woven themselves into the fabric of both brands and consumers' lives. Among the arsenal of modern marketing strategies, influencer marketing has emerged as a formidable force. It bestows organisations the privilege of accessing extensive and dedicated online influencers and co-creation as a technique, making it one of the most potent tools in their marketing toolkit. This chapter focuses on the intricate art of how brands strategically harness the power of social media platforms and influencers to extend their reach far and wide, aiming to connect with as many consumers as possible. By forging these connections, brands aspire to cultivate a devoted and unwavering fan base, fostering long-term customer loyalty.

Chapter 7
The Intrinsic Property of a Representation in the Phygital Transformation: A (Meta) Influence as a Force With Magnitude and Direction in the Metaverse 147
Neli Maria Mengalli, Faculdade São Bernardo do Campo, Brazil
Antonio Aparecido Carvalho, Faculdade São Bernardo do Campo, Brazil

This chapter was written based on a qualitative methodology with reading reports and current articles at the time of writing. The objective was to highlight what (meta) influence is and how the (meta) influencer phygital can contribute to the brand. In the qualitative research, it was revealed that it is a prosperous field for marketing, mainly for influencer marketing; however, it is a new theme and lacks a lot of research. It was concluded that the metaverse is a reality that cannot be neglected, both in terms of the consumer's experience and the employee's experience, and the (meta)influencers are very familiar with the company's values, products, and services and are capable of making authentic and compelling recommendations.

Chapter 8
Virtual Influencers: A Bibliometric Analysis 163
Belem Barbosa, University of Porto, Portugal

Virtual influencers are rapidly gaining significance in the digital marketing realm. This study offers an overview of the fragmented landscape of virtual influencer research, addressing key contributions, themes, methodologies, and future directions. Employing a bibliometric analysis approach, the research examined 52 articles from the Scopus database, shedding light on the evolving field. Findings underscore a dispersed literature landscape that began in 2020, spanning 44 distinct outlets and involving 138 authors. The prevailing research primarily centers on general social media users' perceptions of virtual influencers, leaving substantial gaps in the study of actual followers. Many pieces of research exhibit a lack of methodological rigor and theoretical framework. As the discipline progresses, there is an emergent need for enhanced methodologies that focus on genuine followers and encompass broader managerial objectives. The prospects for subsequent research in this domain are vast and promising.

Chapter 9
Stimuli for the Use of Digital Influencers in the Culture Sector: An Analysis of the Portuguese Context 189
Nádia Patrícia Pinheiro Custódio, Technology and Management School of Oliveira do Hospital, Polytechnic Institute of Coimbra, Portugal
Nayra Leandro Miguel Martins, Technology and Management School of Oliveira do Hospital, Polytechnic Institute of Coimbra, Portugal & NECE-Research Center in Business Sciences, University of Beira Interior, Portugal

This chapter provides an overview of the current status of the cultural sector in Portugal and demonstrates how digital influencers can help this sector. It emphasizes the importance and potential of influencer marketing for companies in the cultural sector to reach and engage their target audience. The chapter provides an extensive literature review on the status quo of cultural marketing, relationship marketing, the cultural sector, the internet in the cultural sector, and digital influencers in the cultural sector. Finally, it highlights emerging trends and future prospects for influencer marketing in this sector.

Chapter 10
TikTok Content Categories and User Engagement Behavior: Alisha Lehmann – Celebrity Athlete and Influencer........ 214
Sebastiano Mereu, Sports Business Research Academy, Switzerland

This study investigates the impact of TikTok content categories on user engagement behavior on the official TikTok account of Alisha Lehmann. Analyzing 91 videos via multiple regression analysis, the research uncovers practical insights for content creators and marketers, as well as theoretical findings for academics. Notably, Alisha Lehmann's active professional life, showcasing her athletic prowess, emerged as the most influential category, driving engagement across views, likes, comments, saves, and shares. Videos emphasising her personal life through aesthetics also impacted video shares and saves to a certain degree. Additionally, non-active or non-sport professional life content garnered attention, especially in likes and comments. In contrast, TikTok games and promotional content had limited impact, emphasizing the importance of a balanced content strategy that integrates personal and professional aspects for athlete influencers. These findings provide guidance for optimizing online presence, aligning content with audience interests, and fostering brand loyalty on TikTok.

Chapter 11
Digital Marketing Tools and Market Trends in the Skincare Industry: Consumer Behavior and Sales Growth Insights 235
Lierni Castilla-Miguel, Universidad Pública de Navarra, Spain
Maria Elena Aramendia-Muneta, Universidad Pública de Navarra, Spain

The primary goal of the research is to investigate the efficiency of various digital marketing tools in the skincare industry, as well as to assess market trends and customer behavior in order to enhance sales. The study included a survey of 100 Spanish customers aged 18 to 64, and six regression models were developed to forecast sales growth based on various criteria. Transparency, sustainability, and personalized skincare products, as well as user-generated content and reviews, are highlighted as successful marketing methods to promote sales in the research. The study also emphasizes how age and gender play a significant role in this connection as well as the limited influence of influencer and celebrity marketing on skincare product sales. According to the findings, skincare firms should concentrate on developing transparent, environmentally friendly products that are customized to consumers' interests, using user-generated content and reviews in their marketing strategies to boost sales.

Chapter 12
Digital Influencers and the Restaurant Sector 269
Alvaro Díaz Casquero, Universidad de Málaga, Spain
Eva María González Robles, Universidad de Málaga, Spain
Benjamín del Alcázar, Universidad de Málaga, Spain

This chapter delves into digital influencers' influential role in reshaping restaurant industry communication, dissecting their evolution, categorizing types, and their pivotal role in gastronomic communication. Exploring strategies for optimizing influencer collaborations, scrutinizing trends, and spotlighting key platforms, it equips readers with a comprehensive understanding. Furthermore, it investigates influencers' profound impact on consumer behavior, serving as a practical guide with data-driven insights and examples. In today's digital age, this chapter underscores influencer collaborations' indispensable nature in the restaurant sector, emphasizing their potential for business success. Understanding and harnessing influencer power remains crucial for industry stakeholders as the culinary world evolves.

Chapter 13
Changing Consumer Buyer Decision Process in the Context of Instamoms 288
Ece İpekoğlu, Yasar University, Turkey
Nilgün Gürkaynak, Izmir University of Economics, Turkey

As an effective digital strategy, influencer marketing uses "influencers" on social media with their potential to deliver ideas to the masses. These people on social media are very attractive to consumers when making decisions. This research makes its theoretical contribution by combining marketing motherhood as a social construct as an instinctive process in social media. Within this context, mother influencers, called Instamoms, impact their followers by affecting their buyer decision process. This chapter aims to understand the impact of Instamoms on the buyer decision of their followers. The research concentrates on factors in how decisions in the process of mother followers can be shaped, affected, and harmonized toward the content of the Instamoms' posts, in terms the of influence that constitute the reference power, motherhood concept, and all other remaining factors that determine the buyer decision process.

Compilation of References 311

About the Contributors 362

Index 368

Preface

Influencer marketing has evolved into a pivotal strategy shaping the digital landscape. As the editorial team behind this comprehensive reference book, *Using Influencer Marketing as a Digital Business Strategy*, we have endeavored to dissect and analyze the multifaceted realm of influencers and their profound impact on contemporary business paradigms.

In today's digital milieu, these content creators wield immense power in shaping consumer behavior and brand perception. This compendium encapsulates a diverse array of critical topics essential to understanding and leveraging influencer marketing effectively.

From delineating the nuances of influencer typologies to exploring the intricate interplay between influencers, brands, and consumer intent, this book aims to serve as a beacon for both academia and industry professionals. By delving into the mechanisms of content creation, consumption habits, and the symbiotic relationship between influencers and their audiences, we aim to offer invaluable insights that transcend mere theoretical discourse.

Furthermore, in a rapidly evolving digital landscape, the metrics and methodologies of influencer marketing demand continual exploration. This compendium ventures into the realms of organic versus paid influencers, the spectrum from nano-influencers to the towering figures with expansive followings, and the pivotal role of influencers across various sectors of the economy.

From the emergence of metainfluencers to the intricacies of digital business models and the societal implications of digital transformation, this book presents a holistic panorama of influencer marketing's profound implications. It underscores the fusion of technological prowess with cultural influence and examines the ever-evolving digital trends that shape our interconnected world.

Intended for a wide spectrum of readers, ranging from researchers and executives to marketing agencies and aspiring scholars pursuing advanced degrees, this book aspires to be a definitive resource. It is our fervent hope that this compilation will not only inform but also inspire deeper exploration and nuanced discussions, serving as a catalyst for further groundbreaking research in this dynamic domain.

We extend our heartfelt gratitude to the contributors whose expertise and insights have enriched this compilation, and we invite readers to embark on a journey through the intricate tapestry of influencer marketing presented within these pages.

CHAPTER OVERVIEW

Chapter 1: The Power of Influence – Unleashing the Potential of Influencer Marketing

Written by Nitesh Behare, Rashmi D Mahajan, Meenakshi Singh, Vishwanathan Iyer, Ushmita Gupta, Pritesh P Somani, the first chapter serves as a foundational exploration into the world of influencer marketing. This chapter traces the evolution of influencer marketing, spotlighting its meteoric rise and undeniable impact in recent years. It elucidates the crucial role influencer marketing plays in enabling businesses to effectively engage their target audience, emphasizing its significance in the contemporary digital landscape.

Chapter 2: Use of Influencers in Different Sectors of the Economy

Authored by Shikha Mittal, this chapter serves as a comprehensive study highlighting the pervasive influence of influencer marketing across diverse sectors. It delves into the transformative impact of digital technologies, propelling influencer marketing to the forefront of social media strategies adopted by a myriad of companies operating in various industries.

Chapter 3: How Influencers Can Leverage Performance in Business

Authored by Albérico Rosário, this chapter explores how influencers can boost business performance. It outlines the collaborative strategies between influencers and businesses, emphasizing the impact of endorsements, affiliate links, and sponsored content. The study advocates for genuineness and transparency in collaborations to maintain trust with the audience. The chapter aims to review bibliometrics literature using the Scopus database to further understand the influence of influencers on business performance.

Chapter 4: All Users Are Equal, But Some Users Are More Equal Than Others – Exploring the Psychology of Users That Follow Social Media Influencers

Authored by Carla Murteira and Ana Antunes, this chapter delves into the profound psychological experiences of social media influencer (SMI) followers. Examining the perception of SMIs by their followers and the motivations driving users to follow them, the chapter explores the impact of SMIs' credibility, trustworthiness, authenticity, and expertise on both follower interactions and brand image. Brands are advised to conduct continuous assessments of SMIs' communication styles and followers' perceptions to enhance attitudes towards brands and influence purchase intentions.

Chapter 5: Virtual Influencers – The Irruption of Artificial Intelligence in Digital Influencers

Authored by Mario Sierra Martin, Alvaro Díaz Casquero, Marina Sánchez Pérez, and Bárbara Rando Rodríguez, this chapter explores the transformative impact of virtual influencers generated by artificial intelligence. Focusing on avatars like Lil Miquela, the chapter delves into their customization, flexibility, and reduced ethical risks compared to human influencers. It analyzes the importance and evolution of virtual influencers in society and marketing, positioning them as a powerful tool in the growing landscape of artificial intelligence.

Chapter 6: Influencing the Influencers Through Co-Creation Approaches to Successful Brand Strategies

Authored by Poornima Nair and Sunita Kumar, this chapter focuses on the strategic utilization of influencers and co-creation in modern marketing. It explores how brands strategically leverage social media platforms and influencers to extend their reach, connect with consumers, and cultivate long-term loyalty. The chapter aims to provide insights into the intricate art of influencer marketing, offering guidance for organizations to build strong connections with their target audience.

Chapter 7: The Intrinsic Property of a Representation in the Phygital Transformation – A (Meta) Influence as a Force With Magnitude and Direction in the Metaverse

Authored by Neli Mengalli and Antonio Carvalho, this chapter explores the concept of (meta) influence in the context of the phygital transformation and the metaverse. Based on a qualitative methodology, the chapter highlights the prosperous field for marketing, especially influencer marketing, in the metaverse. It emphasizes the importance of (meta) influencers who are familiar with company values and can make authentic recommendations, acknowledging the reality of the metaverse in both consumer and employee experiences.

Chapter 8: Virtual Influencers – A Bibliometric Analysis

Written by Belem Barbosa, this chapter embarks on an illuminating journey through the burgeoning domain of virtual influencers within the realm of digital marketing. This study represents an exhaustive overview, delving into the fragmented landscape of research dedicated to virtual influencers. Employing a bibliometric analysis approach, this chapter meticulously examines key contributions, prevalent themes, methodologies, and future trajectories within this evolving field.

Chapter 9: Stimuli for the Use of Digital Influencers in the Culture Sector – An Analysis of the Portuguese Context

Written by Nádia Custódio and Nayra Martins, this chapter provides an overview of the cultural sector in Portugal and demonstrates how digital influencers can contribute to its growth. Emphasizing the importance of influencer marketing for cultural companies to engage their target audience, the chapter reviews literature on cultural marketing, relationship marketing, and the role of influencers in the cultural sector. It concludes by highlighting emerging trends and future prospects for influencer marketing in this domain.

Chapter 10: TikTok Content Categories and User Engagement Behavior – Alisha Lehmann: Celebrity Athlete and Influencer

Authored by Sebastiano Mereu, this chapter investigates the impact of TikTok content categories on user engagement behavior, focusing on the account of Alisha Lehmann. Through multiple regression analysis of 91 videos, the research provides practical insights for content creators, marketers, and academics. It identifies categories that drive engagement, emphasizing the importance of balancing personal and professional aspects for athlete influencers and optimizing content to align with audience interests.

Chapter 11: Digital Marketing Tools and Market Trends in the Skincare Industry – Consumer Behavior and Sales Growth Insights

Written by Lierni Castilla-Miguel and Maria Elena Aramendia-Muneta, this chapter investigates the efficiency of digital marketing tools in the skincare industry. The study, based on a survey of 100 Spanish customers, develops regression models to forecast sales growth. Emphasizing transparency, sustainability, and personalized skincare products, the research highlights successful marketing methods and underlines the limited influence of influencer and celebrity marketing on skincare product sales.

Chapter 12: Digital Influencers and the Restaurant Sector

Authored by Alvaro Díaz Casquero, Eva González Robles, and Benjamín del Alcázar, this chapter explores the influential role of digital influencers in reshaping communication within the restaurant industry. It categorizes influencer types, delves into strategies for optimizing collaborations, and investigates the impact of influencers on consumer behavior. The chapter serves as a practical guide, providing data-driven insights and examples to highlight the indispensable nature of influencer collaborations for success in the dynamic restaurant sector.

Chapter 13: Changing Consumer Buyer Decision Process in the Context of Instamoms

Written by Ece İpekoğlu and Nilgün Gürkaynak, this chapter investigates the transformative impact of mother influencers, termed "Instamoms," on the buyer decision process. Combining marketing motherhood as a social construct with social media, the research analyzes how Instamoms influence decisions in the mother follower demographic. The exploration encompasses factors shaping, affecting, and harmonizing decisions towards Instamoms' content, emphasizing the reference power, motherhood concept, and other determinants of the buyer decision process.

IN SUMMARY

In the vast tapestry of influencer marketing, our compilation stands as a testament to the dynamic and ever-evolving landscape that shapes contemporary business paradigms. Through the collective efforts of diverse researchers and experts, this reference book illuminates the multifaceted facets of influencer marketing, offering insights, analyses, and foresight that reflect the pulse of this transformative realm.

From dissecting the psychology behind follower behavior to exploring the profound impact of influencers across various sectors, each chapter serves as a mosaic piece contributing to our collective understanding of this influential domain. The exploration of metrics, methodologies, and the rise of virtual influencers has unraveled uncharted territories, revealing both the immense potential and the notable gaps that pave the way for future exploration and advancement.

As editors, our journey through these chapters has unveiled the intricate dynamics between influencers, brands, and consumers. We've seen the transformative power wielded by influencers in reshaping consumer behavior, driving engagement, and fostering brand loyalty. Yet, we've also identified areas ripe for deeper investigation and refinement, beckoning scholars and practitioners to delve further.

This compilation stands as a beacon, not just for those seeking a comprehensive understanding of influencer marketing but for those eager to chart new territories, challenge existing paradigms, and redefine the future of this burgeoning field. It is a testament to collaboration, exploration, and the relentless pursuit of knowledge that propels industries forward.

In closing, we extend our gratitude to the diligent contributors whose expertise has enriched this compendium. It is our fervent hope that this reference book serves as a catalyst for thought-provoking discussions, innovative strategies, and groundbreaking research, propelling influencer marketing to greater heights and fostering a deeper understanding of its profound impact on the contemporary business landscape.

Sincerely,

Sandrina Teixeira
ISCAP, Polytechnic Institute of Porto, Portugal

Sara Teixeira
Polytechnic Institute of Porto, Portugal

Zaila Oliveira
Unichristus, Brazil & Unifametro, Brazil

Elnivan Souza
Christus University Center, Brazil

Chapter 1
The Power of Influence: Unleashing the Potential of Influencer Marketing

Nitesh Behare
https://orcid.org/0000-0002-9338-8563
Balaji Institute of International Business, Sri Balaji University, Pune, India

Vishwanathan Iyer
https://orcid.org/0009-0007-1469-2369
Balaji Institute of International Business, Sri Balaji University, Pune, India

Rashmi D. Mahajan
https://orcid.org/0000-0001-9082-6874
Balaji Institute of International Business, Sri Balaji University, Pune, India

Ushmita Gupta
https://orcid.org/0000-0002-6442-1248
Balaji Institute of International Business, Sri Balaji University, Pune, India

Meenakshi Singh
https://orcid.org/0009-0006-9505-8214
Balaji Institute of International Business, Sri Balaji University, Pune, India

Pritesh P. Somani
https://orcid.org/0000-0002-0039-0358
Balaji Institute of International Business, Sri Balaji University, Pune, India

ABSTRACT

This chapter provides an overview of influencer marketing, its evolution, development, and popularity in recent years. It emphasizes the significance and potential of influencer marketing for businesses in reaching and engaging their target audience. The chapter further explores different types of influencers, the role of influencers, and how to recognize the right influencers for a brand or target audience. It also explores various benefits of influencer marketing. The chapter also covers measuring and analyzing influencer marketing success through key performance indicators (KPIs), evaluating ROI, and tracking campaign performance using data to optimize future campaigns. This chapter also revealed challenges and risks associated with influencer marketing. Finally, emerging trends and the future outlook of influencer marketing, including new platforms, integration with other marketing strategies, and predictions for the field, are also explored.

DOI: 10.4018/979-8-3693-0551-5.ch001

INTRODUCTION TO INFLUENCER MARKETING

In today's digitally connected world, social media platforms have become entrenched in our daily lives. This paradigm shift in the digital world has given rise to a new form of marketing i.e. influencer marketing, which is transforming the way brands connect with their target audience. This social marketing approach enable brands to endorse their products, services, and ideas in more persuasive and authentic manner by harnessing the power of influential individuals. This innovative strategy includes partnering with social media influencers to endorse and showcase various offerings given by brand. With influencers, amassing substantial followings on social media platforms like Instagram, TikTok, Moj, Facebook, YouTube etc. brands are more and more distinguishing the value of partnering with them to create content that reverberates with their desired customer base (Venkatesh, Meleet, & Cholli, 2022). After collaborating with social media influencers, brands can tap into their conventional credibility and connection with their followers. Influencers have built authentic and organic relationships with their audience through relevant and appealing content, making them trusted sources of recommendations (Bansal, 2019). Through strategic collaborations, brands can leverage the influencer's reach, creativity, and influence their followers to effectively promote their products or services.

Influencer marketing delivers more organic and personalized approach to reaching targeted audience as compared to conventional advertising methods of brands (Leung, et al., 2022). By partnering with such influencer whose values, interests, and aesthetics align with their brand businesses can excellently engage with their target audience. The influencing ability of the influencer enables brands to connect with their targeted audience on a deeper level, which in turns fostering brand awareness, driving engagement and eventually leading to increased conversions with their targeted customers. Influencer marketing has arisen as a powerful tool for brands to navigate the digital landscape and connect with their target audience. By leveraging the influence and creativity of social media influencers, brands can establish genuine relations with their consumers, can also enhance their brand visibility and drive meaningful results in an increasingly competitive market.

On social media, Influencers have become influential figures amassing a large (fan) following through their contents. Their talent to associate with their followers on a personal level has recognized them as trustworthy individuals (Zhang & Mac, 2023). Influencers' distinct qualities make them an appealing alternative for companies trying to promote their products or services. Brands may effectively target their intended audience by engaging with influencers that cater to certain niches or demographics. Brands have recognized the ultimate potential of influencer marketing and are leveraging it to generate sponsored content of a brand, product reviews, and indications that showcase their offerings. Brands can make sure that their communication reaches the right audience, maximizing the impact of their marketing efforts through strategic partnerships with influencers. For instance, a fitness brand can collaborate with fitness influencers to endorse their products, effectively reaching individuals who have a keen interest in fitness and wellness (Pradhan, Kishore, & Gokhale, 2023).

Along with promoting products, influencers play significant role in creating brand awareness and intensifying the brand's reach to the targeted audience. Influencers have ability to share content which showcases a brand's values and other related information thereby creating a positive brand image which is predominantly relevant for younger generations who are more concerned about a brand's values and ethos, going beyond mere product features (Leung, 2022). In this socially connected world, social media influencers act as brand ambassadors, facilitating brands to establish a strong brand identity and connect with consumers who aligns with the brand's values. The effect of influencers goes beyond driving immediate sales. They have supremacy to influence consumer behaviour, comprising purchasing decisions and brand preferences. Their genuine and reliable endorsements hold significant influence over their followers, who often perceive them as reliable sources of information and guidance. This level of influence can result in long-term customer loyalty and advocacy, benefiting brands beyond individual campaigns.

The industry of influencer marketing is undergoing with significant growth, with brands progressively investing in this channel. Prognostications shows that influencer marketing industry will reach a value of $16.6 billion till the end of 2023, up from $13.8 billion in 2021 (Werner, 2023) (Maqbool, 2023). This growth of influencer marketing industry can be accredited to its efficiency and continued eminence of social media platforms, predominantly Facebook, Youtube, Moj, TikTok, ShareChat and Instagram. TikTok's rapid rise as one of the fastest-growing social media platform, boasting more than one billion monthly active users, has played substantial role in driving growth of influencer marketing. Brands are capitalizing on the platform's popularity by partnering with TikTok influencers to produce pleasing contents which reverberates with a younger audience. Meanwhile, Instagram remains most favored platform for influencer marketing, with eighty-nine percent of marketers considering it the most important platform for their influencer campaigns (Santora, 2023) (Ohio, 2022). With over one billion active users, Instagram remains a critical hub for influencers and companies to collaborate and produce content that effectively interacts with their target audience. (Bailis, 2021).

In recent years, India has seen a remarkable increase in the usage of social media and influencer marketing. According to research, the Indian influencer marketing sector is anticipated to rise to $75 million USD by 2025. (Bundhun, 2023). The rising number of social media users in India, which is predicted to reach 448 million by 2023, is driving this rise. (Equity, 2022) (Tondon, 2023). Another factor driving the rise of influencer marketing is the diminishing efficacy of traditional advertising. Traditional advertising platforms such as television commercials, print advertisements, and billboards are becoming less successful as individuals spend more time on social media. Influencer marketing has emerged as a viable alternative for brands searching for new methods to contact their target demographic. Celebrities and a few dedicated bloggers dominated the influencer marketing space a decade ago. Social media influencers are now well-known and dominate the industry at large. While their fan bases vary in size, these influencers have a significant impact. Their close-knit communities foster genuine connections, leading to increased trust and involvement. Working with digital artists and influencers, however, is a polished process for marketers. Another factor driving the rise of influencer marketing is the diminishing efficacy of traditional advertising. Traditional advertising platforms such as television commercials, print advertisements, and billboards are becoming less successful as individuals spend more time on social media. Influencer marketing has emerged as a viable alternative for brands searching for new methods to contact their target demographic. (Tiwari, 2022).

The influencer marketing industry is set to experience substantial growth, with an estimated compound annual growth rate of twenty five percent over the next five years (Basuroy, 2023). This growth trajectory is expected to propel the industry's value from Rs 900 crore in 2021 to Rs 2,200 crore by 2025 (BrandWagon, 2021) (Brand Equity, 2022). The projected rise can be attributed to several factors, including the increasing number of creators and the growing partnerships between brands and creators (Ching C., 2023). These collaborations aim to deliver captivating and relatable storytelling content to the target audience (Bhargava, 2021). A recent INCA influencer marketing survey revealed that hundred percent of marketing leaders identified influencer marketing as a high or top priority for their marketing calendar in 2023 (ANI, 2023).

Definition and Concept of Influencer Marketing

According to (Mailchimp, 2021), "Influencer marketing is a form of marketing that enables businesses to collaborate with individuals who have huge fan following for increased brand exposure". In other words, Influencer marketing is a powerful marketing approach which permits companies to partner with individuals who have a loyal following to enrich brand visibility. Through collaborations with social media influencer, companies can leverage credibility to encourage their products or services through social media content.

(SendPulse, 2021) mentioned that "Influencer marketing is a type of marketing that uses influencers to promote a brand to a larger market. Influencers are opinion leaders with a social fan following base. They appear as experts or trustworthy sources of information". Which means it is a dynamic marketing method which leverages credibility of individuals who promote brands to a wider audience. These influencers, who possess a significant social media following, are seen as trusted experts within their respective niches. By associating with influencers, brands can tap into their influence and reputation, effectively reaching and engaging with a larger market, while benefiting from the perception of authenticity and reliability that these influencers bring.

"Influencer Marketing is a hybrid of old and new marketing tools. It takes the idea of celebrity endorsement and places it into a modern-day content-driven marketing campaign" (Storai, 2023). The author also detailed that it signifies the integration of conventional and modern marketing strategies. It syndicates the concept of celebrity endorsements with modern content-driven campaigns. At its core, influencer marketing encompasses a brand partnering with virtual influencer to endorse their products or services. Nonetheless, its scope outspreads beyond tangible product promotion, with brands also leveraging influencers to heighten their brand recognition and overall attention in the market. By harnessing the reach and influence of these online personalities, brands can effectively tap into their audiences and establish a stronger presence in the digital landscape.

Basically, Influencer marketing is a strategic approach where brands work together with influential individuals, who have expanded credibility and trust with their followers, to create and dispense content which promotes the brand's offerings. The goal Influencer marketing is to tap into the influencer's reach and influence their fans followings to generate brand awareness, engagement, and increase sales. (Schaffer, 2022) in his vlog mentioned that "Influencer marketing is a marketing strategy of collaborating with social media users and other content creators who have influence over communities of varying sizes. This collaboration usually includes some sort of co-content creation or promotion of the brand by the influencer to their community".

Overview of the Rise and Popularity of Influencer Marketing in Recent Years

In last few years, the concept of influencer marketing has emerged profoundly and experienced an unprecedented popularity which helped in reshaping marketing communication. This increase in popularity can be attributed to several factors which include proliferation of social media platforms, the increasing trust and reliance on influencers for recommendations. The other important attributes such as decline in effectiveness of traditional advertising, the ability to boost brand awareness and drive sales, and creativity showcased in influencer-generated content. In addition, rise of micro-influencers, who have smaller but highly engaged audiences, has further contributed to the popularity of influencer marketing by posing a more targeted and niche approach. As a result, influencer marketing has become a vital and dynamic tool for brands to connect with their target audience, build credibility, foster meaningful engagement, and achieve their marketing objectives (Mathew, 2018).

According to the report of (SproutSocial, 2023) fifty-six percent of young buyers of America have made a purchase based on a social post from someone they follow. The industry itself has experienced considerable growth, reaching $16.4 billion in 2022, with projections to reach $21.1 billion in 2023, according to (Geyser, 2023). The effectiveness of influencer marketing is widely acknowledged, with eighty three percent of marketers considering it an effective form of marketing (SproutSocial, 2023). Furthermore, the report highlights that sixty-seven percent of marketers who have plan to increase their budgets for influencer collaborations in the upcoming year.

As per the (Rodrigue, 2023), the influencer market in the U.S. reached an impressive valuation which will showcase its significant impact whereas it is noteworthy to recognize its effectiveness because one out of four marketers currently utilize influencer marketing as part of their strategies. (Rodrigue, 2023) also states that the influence of influencers on social media is evident, as seventy-two percent of Gen Z and Millennials actively follow them. The prosperity of this industry continues with eighty-nine percent of marketers which are planning to increase their investment in influencer marketing in 2023, and an additional seventeen percent intending to venture into this realm for the first time.

Notably, fifty percent of the millennials reveal a higher level of trust in product recommendations from influencers compared to celebrities. The effectiveness of influencer marketing is widely acknowledged, as ninety-two percent of marketers believe in its power as an effective marketing form. Meanwhile, India's influencer marketing industry is predicted to experience a twenty five percent annual growth rate, reaching approximately $265 million by 2025 (Narula & Nangia, 2023). (Aslamova, 2023) in their research mentioned that globally, the number of social media users is projected to rise to around six billion by 2027, and according to a report from Mckinsey, Gen Z which occupy forty percent of market share spent more than three hours a day in viewing and creating content on social media. These customers are termed as the most "plugged in" generation to date (Aslamova, 2023).These statistics demonstrate the growing significance and positive sentiment surrounding influencer marketing as a valuable strategy for brands to engage their target audience and drive business results.

Many researches have proved that Influencer marketing campaigns are highly effective in targeting Generation Z. Throughout the globe, gen Z customers are spending much of their time on social media and they are most responsive to influencer marketing efforts (Martin, 2022) (Francis & Hoefel, 2018). Conversely, reaching older consumers can be more challenging as the percentage of followers of social media influencers decreases with age. Only twenty three percent of Millennials, sixteen percent of Gen X, and nine percent (Tabor, 2019) of Boomers follow influencers on social media (Monllos, 2023). Regularly conducting customer surveys can help to identify the influencers that resonate with brands' older audience. Additionally, women aged sixteen to twenty four are more likely to follow social media influencers compared to men, with one-third of women in this age group following influencers, compared to twenty five percent of men (Dopson, 2022) (Institute, 2019).

Potential of Influencer Marketing for Businesses

The global influencer market will achieve remarkable valuation (Dencheva, 2023), reflecting its substantial impact on marketing strategies and it can be evidenced by the fact that one in four marketers currently leverage influencer marketing to boost their marketing campaigns (Iskiev, 2023). On the other hand, Gen Z and Millennials have strong empathy for influencers, with seventy two percent actively following them on social media (Staff, 2019). One of the study also revealed that eighty nine percent of marketers who already engage in influencer marketing have plan to increase their investment in 2023 (Iskiev, 2023) whereas, for the first time this year, seventeen percent of businesses are planning to endeavour into influencer marketing (Iskiev, 2023). The key objective of many marketers in 2023 was to focus on generating sales and sales leads through influencer marketing, with thirty eight percent emphasizing this objective (Dencheva, 2023).

The other study reveals that Instagram remains the most prevalent social platform for influencer marketing in the United States, in which seventy-two percent of marketers utilizing it for their influencer campaigns in 2022 (Dencheva, 2023). For influencer campaigns, the use of Instagram is anticipated to amplify the reach by more than four percent in 2023. In 2023, products from Lifestyle and beauty category are emerged as most popular categories among global Instagram influencers. Additionally, eighty six percent of U.S. marketers enabled special tools for measuring effectiveness of their influencer marketing campaigns on Instagram, highlighting its effectiveness as a sales-driving platform (Dencheva, 2023). The other popular social platform, TikTok, is gaining traction as an influential platform, with forty-five percent of marketers utilizing it for influencer marketing campaigns in 2022 (Dencheva, 2023) and it is expected to grow by four percent in 2023. A TikTok video from a macro-influencer, receives an average of 38,517 views (Dencheva, 2023), indicating the platform's potential reach and engagement. On the other hand, on YouTube, twenty-eight percent of consumers reported that at least one virtual influencer, emphasizing platform's influence (Dencheva, 2023). Dance, music, and gaming arose as most popular categories for YouTube influencers in 2021. More Interestingly, micro-influencers of YouTube, unveiled highest engagement rates on the platform. Furthermore, YouTube endured the preferred platform for watching gaming influencers among users in the U.S. and Great Britain. According to (Rodrigue, 2023), in 2022, fifty two percent of businesses used Facebook for influencer marketing campaigns wherein Influencer videos accounted for sixty percent of video views on Facebook in the United States in the same year. These statistics give emphasis to the growing influence and popularity of influencer marketing across various platforms, showcasing its effectiveness in reaching and engaging with target audiences. (Zafar, Shahzad, Ashfaq, & Shahzad, 2023)

In 2022, a noteworthy portion of marketers, thirty-nine percent, had allocated ten to twenty percent of their marketing budget to influencer marketing (Dencheva, 2023). (Foster, 2022) in his report mentioned that ROI for influencer marketing was engendering an average of $6.50 in revenue for every $1 invested. The global market experienced a remarkable increase in influencer marketing, the spending was increased from $3.69 billion to $4.14 billion in 2022 (Dencheva, 2023). In 2021, the average price per post from a TikTok mega-influencer was $1,034, while an Instagram mega-influencer commanded a minimum of $1,200 per post. For sponsored videos, YouTube mega-influencers charged a minimum of $2,500 per video (Dencheva, 2023).

According to the research conducted by (Shepherd, 2023), eighty four percent of Instagram influencers are women, it highlights their prominent role in this industry. Contents related to lifestyle remains the most popular category among influencers which suggest the preferences of their audience (Campbell & Farrell, 2020). The impact of influencer marketing is particularly evident on Instagram, where eighty-seven percent of users have taken action after seeing a product. These statistics illustrate the widespread influence and effectiveness of influencer marketing in the modern business landscape. (Shepherd, 2023). Following infographics are self-explanatory and gives clear idea of most popular social media platform for Influencer Marketing.

UNDERSTANDING THE ROLE OF INFLUENCERS

Who Are Influencers? How to Define Influencers

Many authorities have differently defined influences. Some of them are listed below.

(Werner, 2023) defined influencer as an individual having the ability to influence consumer purchasing behaviours and decision-making due to their knowledge and relationship with their audience, who has a huge social media following and creates content that generates considerable engagement.

(Emeritus, 2022) described influencers as content creators with a large following and influence on social media platforms. These influencers build a recognized reputation by creating content on social media and showcasing their knowledge and credibility on a specific topic.

(Swan, 2018) in his blog defined influencer as a social media user that can have several hundred to several million followers who drive conversation and engagement around a particular topic, discussion, or niche area. Influencers have their fingers on the digital pulse or a highly-engaged and loyal audience.

According to (Sarah, 2019) An influencer is an individual who has above-average impact on a specific niche process. These influencers are normal people, who are connected to key roles of media outlets, consumer groups, industry associations or community tribes.

(Atisfyreach, 2020) defined influencer as an individual who has the power to affect purchase decisions of others because of his/her authority, knowledge, position, or relationship with his/her audience who has a following in a particular niche, which they actively engage with.

(Financial Dictonary, 2021) defined influencers as individuals who have power to impact customer purchase decisions of others because of their (real or perceived) authority, knowledge, position, or relationship. In other words, consumer spending, members of a peer group or reference group act as influencers.

Impact of Influencers on Consumer Behaviour

Influencers have a substantial impact on consumer buying behaviour because of their ability to build trust, establish reliability, and build relevant acquaintances with their audience. Here are some crucial ways in which influencers influence consumer behaviour:

1. **Authenticity and Trust:** Influencers often develop a sense of Authenticity and Trust with their followers through constant and honest content. Accordingly, recommendations and endorsements by influencers bring more weightage than traditional advertising. More likely, followers trust the opinion of an influencer they follow and perceive as genuine (Influencity, 2023).
2. **Suggesting Suitable Product/Service and creating Awareness:** As influencers have emotional connect with their followers hence they can help businesses to introduce new products or brands to their targeted audience, and influencers can act as a source of inspiration and discovery. By showcasing various products in their content and sharing personal experiences, influencers elevate awareness and generate interest among their followers (Gelati, Verplancke, & Frögren, 2022).
3. **Social Proof and Validation:** When any influencer endorses any product or service, it offers social proof to their followers. Normally, consumers are liable to look for validation from others before purchasing and this can create a perception of appeal and quality, influencing consumer behaviour (Cabeza Ramírez, Sánchez Cañizares, Santos Roldán, & FuentesGarcía, 2022).

4. **Personal Connection and Relatability:** Social Media Influencers regularly nurture personal connection with their followers by sharing relevant stories, their experiences, and lifestyles. This emotional connection between influencer and follower can influence consumer buying behaviour as followers can see themselves reflected in the influencer's content, making them more likely to trust and be influenced by their endorsements (Cabeza Ramírez, Sánchez Cañizares, Santos Roldán, & FuentesGarcía, 2022).
5. **Purchase Decision Support:** Influencers in their contents run valuable information, insights, and also give their reviews about products or services, assisting consumers to make decisions. Influencer's authentic thoughts and comprehensive evaluations about products or services can help consumers to assess 'pros and cons' of a product/service, and minimizing uncertainty associated with purchasing (Cabeza Ramírez, Sánchez Cañizares, Santos Roldán, & FuentesGarcía, 2022).
6. **Trendsetting and Aspiration:** in the social media industry, influencers often set trends and express popular culture. Their lifestyle, fashion choices, and product recommendations can form consumer preferences and aspirations. Consumers may endeavour to imitate influencers' lifestyles or adopt their favourite brands, leading to shifts in their buying behaviour.
7. **Engagement and Interaction:** Influencers foster active engagement with their followers, forming a sense of community and dialogue. This engagement with followers lets influencers to respond to their questions, offer additional information, and build honest relationships with their audience. Consumers feel more associated with the brand when interacting with an influencer, increasing the probability of purchase (Ao, Bansal, Pruthi, & Khaskheli, 2023).

It is essential to note that impression of influencers on consumer buying behaviour can differ subject to the factors like influencer's credibility, their niche expertise, demographics of the audience, and legitimacy of the collaboration between the influencer and the brand.

Different Types of Influencers and Their Respective Strengths

Many authors, researchers, vloggers, and bloggers have categorised influencers on some criteria such as type of influencers segments, number of followers they have, type of contents they float on social media, their demographics, and their engagement levels. Majorly influencers are classified on 'number of followers' they have under which they are classified as Mega Influencers, Macro Influencers, Micro Influencers and Nano Influencers. Let's discuss these types in detail

Mega or Celebrity Influencers

Individuals who have succeeded with high level of fame and popularity, often outside of social media platforms, normally termed as Mega or celebrity influencers. Typically, they are well-known personalities from sports industry, entertainment industry, or from other prominent fields. These influencers have considerable following (more than one million) and a noteworthy influence on their audience due to their celebrity status. This category of influencers may include athletes, actors, models, musicians, or public figures with a large fan base. Collaborating with mega or celebrity influencers can be tempting owing to their considerable fan following and wider reach but often comes with higher costs and may not always result in meaningful engagement or conversions. However, before collaborating with these types of influencers, it's important to consider whether their followers align with brands target market and whether their content resonates with brand values. It's essential to assess the authenticity, relevance and effectiveness of the partnership before deciding if mega or celebrity influencers are the right fit for brand's influencer marketing strategy. According to (Edwards, 2022), seventy one percent of influencers with 1,000 to 10,000 followers charge up to $100 for each Instagram post, and seventy seven percent of influencers with more than one million followers charge $1,000 or more (Enberg, 2021). Also, big influencers can't be community leaders that small influencers can since they don't have the same level of trust with their audience (Brooke, 2017).

Pros and Cons

These influencers have a major advantage with respect to their huge fan following and well- established reputation amongst their followers, which can offer instant brand recognition and exposure. Their relationship with brand or product/service can build a sense of prestige and legitimacy. Additionally, they always have wide media coverage and a robust online presence, which is allowing them to reach enormous audience across multiple platforms (Joshi, 2022).

Conversely, there are some drawbacks of these influencers to consider such as cost of collaborating with mega influencers can be exorbitant, which can be too much challenging for those with limited budgets or smaller brands to afford such partnerships. Moreover, their endorsement to their huge followers may result in less targeted audience, which means not all followers may align with the brand's target market. As mega influencers always work with several brands simultaneously, which can lead to a perception of artificiality and inauthenticity among their followers which can be another potential disadvantage (Wiley, 2023).

So, it's very critical for brands to carefully assess the fit between their brand values and the celebrity influencer's image and audience. Therefore, collaborations with mega influencers should line up with the brand's overall marketing strategy and goals, taking into consideration the target audience, budget, and long-term brand perception.

Macro-Influencers

Macro-influencers are such individuals who have a substantial following may range from 100,000 to one million followers (Nizri, 2022). These influencers are established personalities within their respective niches. They are also considered to be in the middle tier of influencers in terms of audience size and reach. These influencers can come from numerous fields like fashion, lifestyle, beauty, fitness, travel, and more. They have established themselves as reputable and influential figures within their respective niches and they also have ability to engage and influence their followers through their content. Popular vloggers, bloggers, content creators, pod casters, and social media personalities who have achieved considerable following and have potential to collaborate with brands for sponsored content or partnerships. As compared to Mega Influencers or celebrities, Macro-influencers have more targeted approach, as their followers usually share common interests. Collaborating with macro-influencers can offer substantial reach to the brand but it may still be fairly costly depending on the budget of the brands (Ismail, 2023).

Pros and Cons

Like Mega Influencers, Macro-influencers also offer numerous advantages for brands, such as diverse content creation, wider reach on social platform, amplified credibility, and capability to target precise demographics. Conversely, there are some drawbacks also to consider, for instance, higher costs of promotion, overlap between potential audience, and a smaller amount of personalized engagement. When associating with macro-influencers, brands should sensibly assess factors such as quality of content they are floating, engagement rates with their followers, demographics of their audience, and alignment with their brand values (Ismail, 2023).

Micro-Influencers

Micro-influencers are such individuals on social media platforms who have smaller but highly engaged fan following. Their followers may range from 10,000 to 100,000 (West, 2023). Normally, they have niche focus and they cater to particular interest groups or communities. The contents of micro-influencers revolve around definite topics like fitness, fashion, food, travel, or beauty. The influence of Micro-influencers lies in their skill to connect with their followers on a more personal level, nurturing trust and authenticity. Many studies have proven that Micro-influencers are seen as relatable and trustworthy figures (Borges-Tiago, Santiago, & Tiago, 2023), and their recommendations and endorsements carry weight among their dedicated followers. Because of their smaller audience size, micro-influencers can offer more targeted and specialized reach, making them attractive to brands looking for a more niche and engaged audience (Conde & Casais, 2023). Also, Micro influencers are more affordable than larger influencers but they are very effective in terms of interaction and engagement. Some studies have shown that micro-influencers have a sixty percent higher engagement rate than macro influencers, and can drive twenty percent more conversions for brand (Emplify, 2023). According to (Rodrigue, 2023) Micro-influencers can make sixty percent more engagement than macro influencers whereas forty four percent of marketers feels that it is less expensive than Mega and Macro Influencers. Out of the total influencer marketing industry, fifty-six percent marketers who invest in influencer marketing work with micro-influencers.

According to the recent study by (Treseler, 2021), micro influencers have two to five times followers' engagement rate which means more attention with less followers which micro-influencers can give their users. It can generate ten times more sales as compared to celebrities because of the attention they give to their followers whereas their contents have been shared twenty-two times than normal user reviews.

Pros and Cons

Micro-influencers, with their smaller yet greatly engaged followers and niche focus, offer benefits such as high engagement rates of their followers, cost-effectiveness and targeted reach (Ehlers, 2021). Micro-influencers are considered as relevant and reliable figures who can drive conversions for brands. Conversely, micro-influencers may have narrow reach for brands seeking broad audiences, entail more content management effort and present challenges in maintaining constant brand messaging when collaborating with multiple influencers.

Nano-Influencers

Individuals with small but highly engaged social media following, usually ranging from a few hundred to a few thousand followers are Nano-influencers. Many times, Nano-influencers aren't professional "influencers" in any way where most of their posts are based on content like photos of their friends, family, their pet's videos, memes and many more. These Nano-influencers are often everyday people who have developed a keen following within a specific community or niche. Most importantly, they are known for their legitimacy and honest connection with their audience. Usually, Nano-influencers have a peculiar and relevant approach to content creation, they always focus on the topics they are passionate about (Hutchinson, 2021). Since, Nano-influencers aren't in the business of regularly recommending products – or getting paid for their reviews – when they do post about a product or service, it often comes across as more authentic or genuine and their followers see them as trusted sources of information and recommendations. As compared to macro or micro-influencers Nano-influencers have a smaller reach, they compensate with higher engagement rates and stronger relationships with their followers. According to (Ethos, n.d.) impact of Nano influencers is more than sixty percent in their purchase decisions as compared to only twenty three percent for celebrities and influencers. Therefore, brands usually collaborate with Nano-influencers to tap into their highly targeted and loyal audience, which can help them in leveraging their authentic influence to promote products or services.

Pros and Cons

Nano-influencers offer several advantages, like their authenticity, cost-effectiveness, niche expertise and high engagement rates. Brands, while collaborating with Nano-influencers is very much cost-effective, mainly for brands with limited budgets. They often attain high engagement rates owing to their intensive attention on their audience. Conversely, Nano-influencers have very limited reach, so brands may require several collaborations for scalability where their quality and expertise can vary. Before proceeding for a collaboration, brands should cautiously assess factors like their engagement rates, demographics of their audience and alignment of brand when considering partnerships with Nano-influencers (Wibawa, Pratiwi, & Larasati, 2021).

Identifying the Right Influencers for Your Brand or Target Audience

For any business, identifying right influencers for targeted audience is a fundamental step in accomplishing a successful influencer marketing campaign. To find right influencers, brand should understand and evaluate a genuine connection with targeted audience and can effectually communicate brand's value and message to the followers (Burton, 2021). Identifying right influencers will capitalize on the impact of influencer marketing efforts. Following are some steps to identify right influencers:

1. **Setting up clear Goals and Targeted Audience:** firstly, brands need to clarify their marketing goals and clearly identify targeted audience. For the same, brand need to understand demographics, interests, and social behaviour of influencer and its followers to make sure a better alignment with potential influencers.

2. **Research Relevant to Niches:** second step is to identify the niches that are relevant to the brand and target audience. Search for influencers who are specialized in those niches and have expertise in your industry (Hayes, 2023).
3. **Evaluate Influencer Reach and Engagement:** It's Important to evaluate the reach and engagement of potential influencers. Because it will give us clarity on 'how far a promotion of brand can go'. It can be done by properly analysing number of followers, number of likes and comments they get on their contents and number of shares on their posts. Also, quantitative and qualitative analysis of audience engagement can be done before finalizing the influencer (Hayes, 2023).
4. **Evaluate Influencer Legitimacy and Credibility:** In influencer marketing Legitimacy and credibility are crucial factors. So, brands need to look for influencers who sustain genuine and transparent relationships with their followers.
5. **Review of Content Quality and Alignment:** Critically review their content, follower engagement and also feedback from their audience to device their authenticity. Quality of influencer's content can be assessed on some criteria like influencers' aesthetics, the way and effectiveness of their storytelling and their creativity. It's important to make sure that their contents must aligns with the brand values and desired image. It is also important to look for consistency in the type of content they generate and share and its relevance to the target audience.
6. **Analyse Past Brand Collaborations:** Review the influencers' past collaborations with other brands. It is important to determine whether they have effectively worked with similar brands or within your industry.
7. **Consider Influencer-Brand Fit:** Evaluating influencer's compatibility with the brand is also important. For brand promotion, considering influencer with huge followers is not important but it is also to be checked whether their personal brand aligns with your brand values, identity and target audience (Venciute, Mackeviciene, Kuslys, & Correia, 2023).
8. **Monitor Influencer Reputation:** Thorough a background check of potential influencers, it can be monitored. For monitoring the influencers' reputation brand has to consider their behaviour, reputation and any controversies that may affect brand's image or partnership (Venciute, Mackeviciene, Kuslys, & Correia, 2023).
9. **Leverage Influencer Tools and Platforms:** Utilize influencer marketing tools and platforms which can give detailed analytics, insights and data on influencers. Such tools can help in streamlining search and deliver valuable information to inform your decision-making.
10. **Establish Communication and Relationships:** Once potential influencers have been identified, reach out to them and initiate a conversation. Discuss your goals in details, brands expectations from influencer, and possible collaborations. Building a strong relationship with influencers can lead to more successful and authentic partnerships (Belanche, Casaló, Flavián, & Sánchez, 2021).

Along with the steps stated above, it's also essential to consider the engagement rate and audience demographics of potential influencers. Influencers who have high engagement rate, indicating an active and dedicated audience can be considered. Also, to assess demographics of their audience to confirm they align with target market in terms of location, age, interests, and purchasing power. The demographics analysis of influencers' audience will help to ensure that brand promotion reaches to the right people which can increase the chances of conversion from prospect to customers.

THE BENEFITS OF INFLUENCER MARKETING

Now, Influencer marketing is gradually popularising and widely accepted by businesses for their marketing communication. Collaborating with appropriate influencers can help to make online buzz about the company and brand. Moreover, Influencer marketing can reinforce brand's reputation, increase conversions and improve audience engagement. It is high time for marketers and businesses to recognize the significance of influencer marketing and take the advantage of it. Some of the benefits of Influencer marketing are listed below.

Amplified Brand Awareness

Influencer marketing is a trendy and powerful strategy for elevating brand awareness and reach where brands can tap into millions of potential consumers by associating with influencers who have huge followings. Unlike conventional advertising, influencer marketing allows for more genuine and engaging promotion to the targeted audience which is regularly receiving commercial advertisements. Influencer marketing is predominantly effective in reaching Millennials and Gen Z, who are extremely approachable for product information on social platforms (Grin, 2022). It also offers a less invasive way of interconnecting with customers, evading ad blockers and adopting a sense of trust. Brands must focus on generating relevant and meaningful content which can bring value to both influencers and their followers, helping to increase brand awareness.

Precise Targeting

For making any marketing communication to be successful, identifying and targeting the right audience is important. Though, it's always a meticulous process and entails detailed understanding of potential customers. Influencer marketing allows business to surpass this step as the hard work for the brands have already been done by influencers. Brands just need to ensure which influencer is more relevant to the brand's niche and their public persona aligns with brand's image. With influencer marketing campaigns, strategically brands can decide on influencers whose content aligns with their target audience which allows for precise targeting and also make sure that the brand's message reaches to the right audience (Grin, 2023).

Enhanced Credibility and Trust

Influencers have proficiency and trust in their relevant fields, which impressively influences their followers. The strong bond between influencer and their followers have nurtured with their followers which makes their recommendations highly reliable. Accordingly, when influencers recommend a brand or product/service, it doesn't reflect as conventional way of advertising rather as genuine and authentic advice. According to (Dean, 2015), significant percentage of YouTube viewers (seventy five percent) value the authenticity and relatability of influencers, with seventy percent of teenagers being more inclined to connect with influencers over traditional celebrities. Moreover, sixty percent of users prefer the product reviews provided by their favourite YouTubers over those of mainstream TV and movie stars. Such studies have already proven the influential power of influencers and their capability to influence consumer buying preferences and choices. (Engaiodigital, 2022).

Increased Audience Engagement

On social media, boosting engagement can be a perplexing task, specifically when influencers have huge followers but inadequate interaction though influencer marketing which can become a game-changer strategy for businesses. Working together with influencers will not only augment quality of brand's content but it will also make it more personalized to the interests of brands targeted audience. Additionally, when influencers share the content of a brand on their own social media platforms and if content resonates with them, they may even tag their friends or share it on their profiles, which significantly expands its reach (Sinha, 2023).

Win-Win Long-Term Partnerships

For any successful influencer marketing campaigns choosing right influencers is very important. Brands should select their relevant influencers based on their proficiency and target audience to upsurge sales and also establish long-term partnerships. By associating with right influencers, brands can earn immediate profits and achieve enduring brand awareness through relevant content sharing. Effective influencer partnerships create a win-win situation for both brands and influencers (BigCommerce, 2022).

Increased Conversions

The prime objective of any business is to lift sales and maximize their profits. Conversely, conventional methods of promotion many times fail to gain the attention of prospective customers who are more sceptical of claims made by the brand. These days, consumers significantly invest their time in exploring before making any final purchase decisions. Brands can leverage influencer marketing to figure out buying choices of customers and enrich conversions. A study by (Thorpe, 2019) revealed that thirty three percent of customers contemplate influencers as their most trustworthy sources for shopping advice. The study also emphasizes the efficiency of influencer marketing in lead generation, customer acquisition and growth in revenue. Indeed, according to (Grin, 2021) (Tulman, 2023), the return on investment for influencer marketing can reach upto 6.5 times which is very impressive rate of return for any business.

ROI and Bottom Line

For both, big brands and small businesses, Influencer marketing offers various benefits by providing amplified visibility and higher ROI as compared to other marketing channels. According to (Ed, 2022), fifty percent of marketers have faith in influencer marketing which delivers a higher ROI than other platforms, whereas forty-one percent of the consumers consider it to be on par with other channels (SocialSamosa, 2019) and activities focused on branding and engagement yield eight times more ROI than other campaigns (Smart Insights, 2019). A study by Burst Media revealed that when a brand spent one dollar on influencer marketing and in return, they are earning approximately $6.85 (Ed, 2022).

Cost-Effective

Businesses always face challenges by means of increasing cost of advertisement, influencer marketing can offer a cost-effective solution. As compared to the other advertising forms, functioning with influencers is fairly affordable. Influencer marketing allow brands to effectively compete on social media platforms like YouTube, Facebook, Linkedin, Instagram, etc. with an optimized strategy. Along with the benefits mentioned above, Influencer marketing have several benefits for businesses which may include ability to drive purchase decisions, adaptability for any business size and industry, save time on content creation and distribution and the potential to improve search engine rankings. It can also help business to tap into influencers' trust and influence over their followers which may lead to increase brand awareness and sales.

DEVELOPING AN INFLUENCER MARKETING STRATEGY

For harnessing potential of influencers, developing ingenious influencer marketing strategy is important to meet brand's marketing goals. This encompasses understanding your target audience, formulating clear objectives, researching and selecting relevant influencers, creating collaboration guidelines, and establishing a budget and compensation plan. Collaborating with influencers to produce authentic and engaging content, building and maintaining long-term relationships, monitoring its performance, and fulfilling regulations related to advertising are also critical (Upwork, 2022). Regular assessment and adjustments based on influencer marketing campaign results and consumer behaviour make sure the effectiveness and adaptability of their strategy. Flexibility and customization are key in maximizing the impact of influencer campaigns in the ever-evolving digital landscape.

MEASURING AND ANALYSING INFLUENCER MARKETING SUCCESS

For any business measuring and analysing attainment of influencer marketing campaigns is essential who are looking to optimize their strategies and make data-driven decisions. In today's competitive landscape, it is vital to determine ROI and to evaluate the impact of influencer collaborations as marketing budgets are examined critically. By implementing effective techniques of measurement and analysis, brands can gain valuable insights into key performance indicators (KPIs) like reach, conversions, engagement and effectiveness of overall campaign. These crucial insights empower brands to evaluate effectiveness of their partnerships with influencer. This performance evaluation can also identify areas for further improvement and enhance future strategies. Moreover, measuring and analysing success of influencer marketing allow brands to keep eye on the growth of their social media presence, measure sentiment towards brand and understand preferences of their targeted audience. By utilizing data-driven insights, brands can make informed decisions, optimize their efforts on influencer marketing, and they can also achieve maximum results from their partnerships. Following are some ways to measure and analyse success of Influencer Marketing (Anjali, Avhad, & Jaju, 2020).

Measure According to the Objectives of Your Influencer Campaign

It is important to formulate clear goals for campaigns of influencer marketing as it can help to understand whether this partnership is on right track or not. Many times, even for the same brand, goals may vary, like promoting a product, increasing brand awareness, improving brand reputation, increasing number of followers in the community or generating sales and leads. Even if a brand doesn't fully achieve their goals but the progress towards achieving set goals can still indicate that a successful campaign. Assessing results of the campaign allows you to recognize areas for improvement and polish the approach for future campaigns. Well defined planning and execution process of influencer marketing campaign ensures a strategic and effective results of the campaign (Fundafunda, 2023).

1. Choose Appropriate Influencer Marketing KPIs

There are various categories of influencer marketing metrics that a brand can choose from:

a. **Visibility indicators** (Han, Lee, & Masuda, 2022): Visibility indicators play a critical role in assessing the effectiveness of a campaign and understanding its reach. It can be done by understanding
   i. **The reach of influencers:** From this, a brand can understand number of unique followers and non-followers who have seen influencer's posts. These are organic viewers of influencers.
   ii. **Impressions obtained:** With the help of Impressions obtained on a content shared by influencer, a brand can see 'number of views of a particular post' (the same person can be exposed several times to the same publication) (Valat & Concannon, 2023), on which it can clearly understand the reach and visibility of influencer.

b. **Indicators of engagement:** These indicators provide insights into level of 'audience interaction and interest' in the contents shared by the influencer. Engagement indicator can be assessed on the following parameters. The number of reactions, including likes, favorites, and reposts, showcases the positive response and affinity towards the influencer's posts. Similarly, the number of comments reflects the level of engagement and allows for direct communication with the audience (Bonoboz, 2023).
   i. **Number of reactions:** likes, favourites, reposts, etc. showcases positive response and affinity towards the influencer's posts.
   ii. **Number of comments:** reflects the level of engagement and allows for direct communication with the audience.
   iii. **Number of shares:** indicate the willingness of the audience to spread the content further, increasing its reach and potential impact.
   iv. **Number of brand mentions:** when users mention name of the brand in their comments or posts, validate active engagement and brand awareness in the influencer marketing campaign.
   v. **Publication engagement rate:** can be calculated by comparing the number of engagements to the number of followers. This can help to gauge the overall engagement performance comparative to the size of the influencer's audience

c. **Community growth indicators:** Community growth indicators are indispensable for assessing the impact of influencer marketing campaigns on increasing brand's audience and attracting new followers. It is one of the vital indicators which helps to identify the number of new subscribers increased during the campaign period (Gahin & Paterson, 2003).

d. **Web traffic indicators:** These indicators include clicks generated by posts shared by influencer, number of new users visiting on the brands website, session duration, page views, and bounce rate. Web traffic indicators are crucial for evaluating the success of influencer marketing campaigns in driving traffic to a brand's website. Tracking these metrics helps to evaluate the level of engagement, interest, and effectiveness of influencer-driven content. Studying web traffic indicators can give valuable insights for optimizing marketing campaigns and refining user experience to accomplish desired marketing goals (Calibrate, 2023).

e. **Sales Indicators / Lead Generation**
   i. **Number of conversions:** reflects the actions taken by the audience, like, signing up for a newsletter, making a purchase, or filling out a form. This metric helps to determine the impact of marketing campaign on driving actual sales or generating leads.
   ii. **Influencer marketing ROI:** allows businesses to gauge profitability on their investment in collaborating with influencer, comparing cost of campaign vs revenue generated. With the help of ROI, businesses can understand campaign's bottom-line impact and can also help to optimize future marketing strategies.

f. **Awareness indicators**
   i. **Brand's voice against competitors:** refers to the percentage of online conversations and discussions associated with brand as compared to competitors. By benchmarking this metric, business can gauge the level of visibility and recognition the brand has achieved within its market.
   ii. **Key message penetration:** measures how well the brand's messages and its important points are being communicated and understood by the audience through influencer content. Monitoring these indicators can help to assess effectiveness of the campaign with respect to increasing brand visibility and delivering key messages to the target audience.

Measure the ROI of Your Influencer Marketing Campaigns

Measuring ROI of influencer marketing campaigns is essential to evaluate the effectiveness and success of your efforts. This evaluation can be done with the help of following:

1. Using UTM tracking

By using UTM (Urchin Tracking Module) parameters in the URLs shared by influencers, brand/business can easily track and analyse detailed metrics related to web traffic and its conversions. UTM parameters allow business to ascertain source, medium, and campaign linked with each click, allowing business to attribute website visits, conversions, and sales to particular influencers or campaigns (Wong, 2023). By evaluating these UTM-tracked metrics, business can also assess the impression of influencer marketing on website traffic, conversions, and user behaviour. The UTM data enables business to make data-driven decisions, optimize marketing campaigns, and also allocate resources efficiently to maximize ROI.

2. Promotional codes

Businesses may measure how many purchases were generated with these vouchers by distributing promo codes to influencers. Sharing various promo codes with each influencer allows you to track each influencer's specific performance (Valat & Concannon, 2023). These promotional codes allow businesses to easily track campaign results at a glance. Promo codes can also help business to understand the sales which is coming from influencers and sales that come from other marketing channels (Grin, 2021).

3. Compare to your own campaigns

Comparing performance of different campaign to other social media advertising campaigns can offer detailed insights on ROI. By studying metrics like cost per click, engagement or lead, business can assess effectiveness and cost-efficiency of each channel. This comparison will also help in allocating marketing budget effectively and identify trends for improvement. Regular tracking and measurement of metrics make sure reliable assessments of campaign's success and ROI within the overall marketing strategy.

4. Take into account the other benefits of influencer marketing

Influencer campaigns offer superfluous advantages beyond ROI analysis like they offer an opportunity to obtain new content created by influencers, that can be repurposed through various marketing channels like emails, social media, and websites, with prior agreement from the influencers. This content is often of high quality and authenticity, featuring personalities that resonate with your target audience. Moreover, influencer campaigns save time and money by outsourcing content creation to the influencers, freeing up resources for other marketing activities.

Get the Tools to Measure Your Influencer Campaigns

To effectively measure influencer campaigns, it's essential to have the right tools. Following are some well-known reliable tools for tracking and analysing the performance of influencer marketing efforts (Foy, 2023):

1. **Google Analytics:** Google Analytics is a free tool and ideal for tracking key performance indicators (KPIs) associated to the website like traffic and conversions.
2. **A spreadsheet (and a lot of patience):** With the help of spread sheet manual tracking of social media posts from influencers can be noted. A spreadsheet can be used to record comments, number of engagements, and endorsements received from the followers.
3. **Use an Influencer marketing platform:** Business can utilize dedicated influencer marketing platforms which can greatly abridge measurement process. These platforms automate data collection and provide comprehensive analytics on various KPIs, such as reach, mentions, impressions, sentiment, etc. These platforms also enable business to retrieve all influencer-generated content which can be challenging to track manually.

Create Marketing Campaign Report

Creating a marketing campaign report is vital for exploring influencer marketing efforts and validating their impression within the organization. Effectiveness can be evaluated either with a specific campaign report or time period report. A specific campaign report emphasis on objectives and allows for benchmarking against previously held campaigns, whereas a time period report tracks long-term results and evolution of key performance indicators (Belanche, Casaló, Flavián, & Sánchez, 2021).

According to (Valat & Concannon, 2023), Following metrics can be included in influencer campaign report.

1. **Detailed evaluation of each influencer:** number of posts, true reach, engagement rate
2. **Analyse particular posts by engagement, sales etc.**

3. **Evaluate audience reached:** age, location, gender and interests
4. **Study the mentions generated:** key trends, sentiment, increase in mentions
5. **Comparison**: to a past period, to a competitor, to a similar campaign.

OVERCOMING CHALLENGES AND MITIGATING RISKS

Overcoming challenges and mitigating risks is critical in maintaining integrity and effectiveness of the influencer marketing campaigns. Following are some key considerations for addressing common challenges and mitigating risks.

Transparency and Authenticity in Influencer-Brand Relationships

It is essential to make sure that influencers clearly disclose sponsored content to their audiences which helps to build trust and credibility amongst their followers. Brands should establish open communication channels with influencers, fostering a collaborative environment that encourages genuine and transparent partnerships. By highlighting the significance of authenticity and disclosure, brands can protect their reputation and maintain the trust of their target audience (Bang, 2023).

Managing Potential Risks and Controversies

Brands need to conduct thorough research and due diligence when partnering with influencers to minimalize potential risks and controversies. It can be done by evaluating past contents shared by influencer at their audience demographics, and any previous controversies associated with them. To limit this potential risk, business should establish clear guidelines and expectations for influencer behaviour and content creation to safeguard alignment with their brand values. Regular monitoring and evaluation of influencers' activities can help to identify and address any issues that may arise, protecting the brand from potential reputational damage.

Dealing With Influencer Fraud and Fake Engagement

Sometimes fake engagement and fraud by influencer are substantial challenges in influencer marketing. Therefore, in identifying signs of fraudulent activity, brands need to be vigilant in terms of exaggerated count of followers or inconsistent engagement rates. Third-party tools and platforms can offer detailed insights into authenticity of influencers' audience and also their engagement metrics can help to validate their credibility (Bang, 2023)

Clear Contracts and Agreements

Making clear agreements with influencers is important for keeping interests of both the parties' and mitigating potential risks. The agreements should clearly outline the content ownership, deliverables, compensation, expectations and disclosure requirements. Brands can frame clear rules and guidelines for influencer collaborations by having comprehensive agreement in place for reducing potential misunderstandings and disputes.

Continuous Monitoring and Evaluation

By continuous monitoring and evaluation of performance and behaviour of influencer throughout the marketing campaign are critical for managing risks efficiently. It's necessary for brands to regularly assess engagement rates, content quality and audience sentiment of influencers. By thoroughly monitoring influencers' activities, brands can promptly address any potential risk or issues. This proactive approach can help to protect reputation of a brand and allows for required adjustments to be made in real-time for optimizing the campaign's impact (Arora, Bansal, Kandpal, Aswani, & Dwivedi, 2019).

Diversify Your Influencer Pool

For any brand, depending on a single influencer can be risky. So, to minimize this risk, brands should diversify their pool of influencer. Brands can reach extensive audience and diminish the potential risk of relying on individual influencers by working with influencers from different niches, demographics, and follower sizes. Diversification can also help businesses to tap into diverse segments of their target market and boosts overall efficiency of efforts of their influencer marketing (Arora, Bansal, Kandpal, Aswani, & Dwivedi, 2019).

Stay Abreast of Industry Guidelines and Regulations

Like every industry, influencer marketing is also subject to different rules and regulations, industry guidelines and their best practices. Businesses must keep themselves updated on such guidelines and strictly adhere to them. These guidelines and regulations comprise of complying with data privacy regulations, disclosure requirements and advertising standards. Adhering to Industry Guidelines and Regulations not only protects the brand from legal risks but also helps to build trust and credibility with their audience. Brands should keep close eye on any changes in regulations and adjust their influencer marketing strategies accordingly (Michaelsen, et al., 2022).

Build Long-Term Relationships

Creating long-term relationships with influencers can bring several benefits to the business. Long-term relationship can foster trust, legitimacy, and deeper understanding between the brand and influencer. This leads to a reliable engagement of followers with the brand and their loyalty. Long-standing partnerships leverages the influencer's expertise and creativity effectively, which resulting in content that resonates with their audience. It also allows influencers to become sincere brand advocates, increasing engagement and trust. Long-term relationships allow brands to tap into the influencers' growth, expand their reach, and collaborate on innovative strategies. Largely, building long-term relationships of influencers and businesses fosters authentic content, strengthens their credibility and drives sustainable success in influencer marketing (Kashyap, 2023).

Ethics In Influencer Marketing

Ethics in influencer marketing is significant in maintaining transparency and trust. Influencers have accountability to reveal paid partnerships, ensuring their followers can distinguish sponsored content and genuine recommendations. Brands must also endorse ethical standards by encouraging products or services which align with their values and by respecting the realism and creative control of influencers (Chopra, 2023). Deceptive practices, such as fake followers or engagement, should be avoided to maintain the integrity of influencer marketing and foster genuine connections between influencers, brands, and their audience (Kuzminov, 2023). Building campaigns rooted in the principles of protection, equality, and respect while offering genuine value and communicating trustworthiness is essential. Transparent partnerships and clear disclosures help consumers make informed choices and reinforce trust, ultimately enhancing the ethical foundation of influencer marketing. (Nambakhsh, 2023).

EMERGING TRENDS AND FUTURE OUTLOOK

The Evolution of Influencer Marketing in the Ever-Changing Digital Landscape

In last few years, influencer marketing has experienced substantial changes and it will surely will continue to accustomed to ever-changing digital landscape. On the other hand, influencers are also exploring new ways to engage with their audience and create fascinating content as technology advances. Augmented Reality (AR), Live streaming, Virtual Reality (VR), and interactive contents are emerging trends in the Influencer Marketing which offer exciting opportunities for influencer collaborations. These innovative formats Influencer Marketing enable influencers to offer more immersive experiences, enhancing audience engagement and brand interactions (Phyllo, 2021).

Emerging Platforms and Formats for Influencer Collaborations

Though social media platforms like Facebook, Instagram and YouTube remain popular, new platforms are emerging as more feasible options for influencer marketing. For instance, TikTok, has gained substantial grip and offers a space for short video content and creative storytelling. Whereas, Twitch, a live streaming platform which was initially into gaming, is now becoming a hub for influencer collaborations, exclusively for brands targeting a younger demographic (Famesters, 2020). Brands should discover more opportunities to leverage unique features of these platforms and engage with their audiences in new and exciting ways. Emerging social media platforms and new formats for influencer collaborations are constantly reshaping the influencer marketing landscape, also offering new opportunities for brands to engage with their target audience. Here are some distinguished platforms and formats that are gaining traction (Phyllo, 2021):

1. **TikTok:** TikTok has exploded in popularity, particularly among younger demographics. The platforms short video format allows influencers to showcase their creativity, entertain their audience, and participate in viral challenges. Brands are leveraging TikTok influencers to create engaging and shareable content that aligns with their brand message. TikTok's algorithm-driven content discovery also presents an opportunity for brands to reach a wider audience.
2. **Instagram Reels:** Instagram's response to TikTok, Reels, has quickly gained popularity. These reels allow influencers to make short videos with several creative tools, effects and music. Brands can work together with influencers to generate engaging and entertaining reels which can showcase

their products or services and/or participate in trending challenges. The discoverability of reels in the Instagram offers brands with amplified visibility and exposure.

3. **Twitch:** Twitch was originally a built for gamers, later expanded to embrace a broader range of content categories. This USP of this platform is offer opportunities for live streaming product reviews, sponsored gameplay, unboxing sessions and interactive Q&A sessions. Real-time chat function of Twitch fosters direct interaction between influencers and their audience, creating an immersive and authentic experience.
4. **Podcasts:** Podcasts are becoming increasingly popular as a platform for influencers to offer in-depth debates and tales. Brands may collaborate with appropriate podcast hosts to sponsor episodes or participate as guests. Podcasts allow their users for more detailed conversations, brand storytelling and opportunity to reach highly engaged audience. Collaboration with Podcast provide an avenue for influencers to discuss and ratify products or services in more conversational and intimate manner (Atisfyreach, 2021).
5. **Virtual Events and Webinars:** Influencers are increasingly organising or participating in virtual events and webinars as remote work and virtual experiences become more prevalent. Brands and influencers may work together to co-host virtual panels, seminars, or keynote addresses. These collaborations allow influencers to offer their knowledge, interact with their audience in real time, and promote the brand's products or services to a captive online audience.
6. **AR and VR:** Augmented Reality (AR) and Virtual Reality (VR) are becoming more accessible, allowing influencers to create immersive and interactive experiences for their audience. Brands may work with influencers to create AR filters, lenses, or virtual try-on experiences that allow customers to engage with items in a virtual world. This engagement-driven structure improves the user experience and encourages product research, resulting in improved brand exposure and possible transactions.
7. **Niche Social Media Platforms:** While established platforms like Instagram and YouTube remain popular, niche social media platforms are gaining traction. Platforms like Clubhouse (audio-based social network), Lomotif (short video app), and Bilibili (Chinese platform for animation and gaming) cater to specific audiences and interests. Brands targeting these niche markets can collaborate with influencers who have a dedicated following on these platforms, ensuring a more targeted and engaged audience (Swat.io, 2022).

Integrating Influencer Marketing With Other Marketing Strategies

Influencer marketing alone can't bring revolutionary changes in marketing communication and customer engagement instead its future lies in its integration with other marketing practices. These days, brands are understanding the value of a holistic approach which integrate influencer marketing with social media advertising, content marketing and traditional marketing channels. Integrating influencer marketing with other marketing practices is a powerful approach which can intensify brand communication, customer engagement, also augment the reach of social marketing campaign, and create a cohesive brand experience across various channels. Here are some key considerations for effectively integrating influencer marketing with other marketing strategies:

1. **Content Marketing:** Influencer marketing and content marketing go hand in hand. Brands can leverage influencer collaborations to create compelling and authentic content that aligns with their

content marketing strategy. Influencer's expertise in storytelling and valuable insights can enhance the brand's content efforts. Brands may increase the reach and effect of their campaigns by reusing influencer-generated content across owned channels while keeping a consistent brand story. (EconomicTimes, 2023).

2. **Social Media Advertising:** Influencer marketing and social media advertising can complement each other to maximize effectiveness of the campaign. Brands can leverage influencers' engagement with their followers and their reach to intensify their social media ads. By integrating influencer endorsements for sponsored posts, brands can increase ad visibility, credibility and audience engagement. This integration allows for a seamless brand experience, where influencer-generated content supports and reinforces the messaging in social media ads (EconomicTimes, 2023).
3. **Public Relations (PR):** Influencer marketing may be included into public relations efforts to increase brand visibility and reputation. Collaborating with influencers that share the same values as the company and target audience may help build positive buzz and enhance brand perception. Influencers can act as brand advocates by attending media events, product launches, or brand activations, resulting in increased media coverage and a ripple effect throughout traditional PR channels. Brands may use the reach and credibility of influencers to convey their narrative, create connections with journalists, and generate earned media coverage.
4. **Event Marketing:** Integrating influencer marketing into event marketing techniques helps generate interest and buzz about brand events. Inviting influencers to brand events may increase attendance, engage the audience, and expand the event' s reach through influencer-generated content. Influencers can live-stream the event, offer behind-the-scenes footage, or develop event-related content, giving their followers with an immersive experience and promoting engagement.
5. **Influencer Affiliate Marketing:** Integrating influencer marketing into event marketing techniques helps generate interest and buzz about brand events. Inviting influencers to brand events may increase attendance, engage the audience, and expand the event's reach through influencer-generated content. Influencers can live-stream the event, offer behind-the-scenes footage, or develop event-related content, giving their followers with an immersive experience and promoting engagement (Warren, 2020).
6. **Influencer-Driven SEO:** Collaboration with influencers can help with search engine optimisation. Influencers may improve organic search visibility by creating keyword-rich content, collaborating on guest blog articles, or providing backlinks to the brand's website. Their content may drive traffic, increase consumer interaction, and increase social shares, so increasing the brand's online visibility and authority. (Warren, 2020).
7. **Cross-Promotion with Influencer Partners:** Brands and influencers can work together to promote one other's content or products. This method enables marketers to reach new sectors of their target market by tapping into the audience of influencers. Cross-promotion may take various forms, including co-created content, shoutouts and joint giveaways, resulting in mutually beneficial alliances and broadening the brand's reach. (SendPulse, 2021).

AI-Driven Influencer Marketing

Another future direction is the rise of AI-driven influencer marketing. AI tools can help brands to identify the most relevant influencers based on their audience demographics, engagement patterns, and content preferences. AI algorithms can also analyze campaign performance, identify trends, and optimize influencer selection and content strategies. Additionally, influencer marketing will continue to expand beyond traditional consumer brands. B2B companies, non-profit organizations, and even government entities are recognizing the potential of influencer marketing to reach and engage their target audiences effectively (Influencity, 2023).

Rise of User-Generated Content (UGC)

User-generated content will become more prevalent in influencer marketing strategies. Brands will actively encourage their audience to create and share content related to their brand, products, or campaigns. UGC offers a powerful way to amplify brand reach, enhance authenticity, and foster a sense of community among consumers (Beveridge, 2022).

Metaverse and the Future of Influencer Marketing

In the rapidly changing digital landscape, influencers are enthusiastically embracing the metaverse, a transformative realm reshaping the dynamics of marketing communication and branding. Within this digital cutting edge, brands are obligated to market digital products, predominantly in the purviews of beauty, luxury and fashion, using Non-Fungible Tokens (NFTs), that are composed to account for up to ten percent of these sectors' revenues by 2030 (Kolsquare, 2021).

A striking example of this transformation is Gucci's collaboration with Roblox for a virtual Gucci Garden event, which reached a staggering twenty million (Emeritus, 2022) users and saw digital handbags being sold for prices exceeding 4,000 USD (Kolsquare, 2021). Conversely, the metaverse is not just about commerce; it is redefining societal structures by placing emphasis on decentralization and individual ownership. (Sharma, 2022) This shift has comprehensive implications for influencers, potentially turning them into stakeholders in the brands they promote rather than mere endorsers. Concurrently, a new category of influencers i.e. "meta-influencers" is emerging, with Ai-Ailynn, an AI influencer, achieving an astonishing estimated worth of nearly fourteen billion USD (Kolsquare, 2021).

The metaverse heralds, a new era of influencer communication, enabling immersive experiences. Influencers specifically working in the segments like food, beauty and travel can now engage their followers in unique ways, leveraging Augmented Reality (AR) and Virtual Interactions (Aslamova, 2023). The metaverse presents immeasurable possibilities for influencer marketing and brand engagement, marking a ground-breaking shift in the digital landscape (Chadda, 2022).

CONCLUSION

In conclusion, the chapter underscores the remarkable impact that influencer marketing has had on modern businesses and their marketing strategies. It explores various facets of influencer marketing, from its origins to its current prominence in the digital landscape as well as the types of influencers and the degree of influence they exert. While mega-celebrity influencers can be powerful, micro-influencers with smaller, highly engaged audiences can offer more cost-effective and targeted marketing opportunities. Influencer marketing's effectiveness lies in the authenticity of the influencer's relationship with their audience. Consumers trust influencers who genuinely believe in and use the products or services they promote. Influencer marketing is not limited to one platform or niche. It has extended its reach to encompass various social media platforms, blogs, YouTube, and even emerging platforms like TikTok. This adaptability makes it a versatile tool for marketers.

Influencer marketing, unlike traditional advertising, facilitates precise monitoring of return on investment (ROI). Marketers may analyse campaign effectiveness by tracking engagement, conversion rates, and other crucial indicators. Building long-term relationships with influencers may be extremely advantageous to companies. These partnerships frequently produce larger payouts and more consistent returns over time. Influencer marketing evolves in tandem with digital technologies like as live streaming, augmented reality, and virtual reality, opening up new channels of interaction. The chapter also discussed the potential risks and controversies associated with influencer marketing, like managing potential risks and controversies, transparency and authenticity in influencer-brand relationships, dealing with influencer fraud and fake engagement, and the importance and necessity of clear contracts and agreements.

When performed intelligently and effectively, influencer marketing can be a powerful tool for business who are trying to engage with their target audiences in a genuine and engaging way. However, it is critical to understand that it is not a one-size-fits-all answer. Each campaign needs careful preparation, the identification of the appropriate influencers, and a thorough grasp of the target demographic. As we move forward in the ever-changing environment of digital marketing, influencer marketing will almost certainly remain a driving force, always adjusting to shifting consumer tastes and the introduction of new technology. Brands must stay educated, sincere, and devoted to creating meaningful connections with influencers and their audiences in order to realise their full potential. The power of influence in marketing is evident, and those that embrace it reap the benefits.

REFERENCES

ANI. (2023, Oct 19). *India's Influencer Marketing Industry to reach Rs. 2,200 crore by 2025 with increasing partnerships between Brands and Creators*. Retrieved Jun 06, 2023, from ANI: https://www.aninews.in/news/business/business/indias-influencer-marketing-industry-to-reach-rs-2200-crore-by-2025-with-increasing-partnerships-between-brands-and-creators20221019145522/

Anjali, C., Avhad, V., & Jaju, S. (2020, June). Influencer Marketing: An Exploratory Study to Identify Antecedents of Consumer Behavior of Millennial. *Business Perspectives and Research*, *9*(1), 77–91. doi:10.1177/2278533720923486

Ao, L., Bansal, R., Pruthi, N., & Khaskheli, M. B. (2023, February 02). Impact of Social Media Influencers on Customer Engagement and Purchase Intention: A Meta-Analysis. *Sustainability (Basel)*, *15*(03), 2744. Advance online publication. doi:10.3390u15032744

Arora, A., Bansal, S., Kandpal, C., Aswani, R., & Dwivedi, Y. (2019, July). Measuring social media influencer index- insights from facebook, Twitter and Instagram. *Journal of Retailing and Consumer Services*, *49*, 86–101. doi:10.1016/j.jretconser.2019.03.012

Aslamova, Y. (2023, Jan 7). *How Influencer Marketing will Change the Business Landscape in 2023*. Retrieved Jun 09, 2023, from Indianretailer.com: https://www.indianretailer.com/article/technology-e-commerce/digital-trends/how-influencer-marketing-will-change-business

Aslamova, Y. (2023, Mar 11). *How metaverse is powering influencer marketing for promoting brand campaigns*. Retrieved Sept 13, 2023, from https://www.financialexpress.com: https://www.financialexpress.com/business/blockchain-how-metaverse-is-powering-influencer-marketing-for-promoting-brand-campaigns-3005016/

Atisfyreach. (2020). *How Did Modern Day Influencers Become A Thing?* Retrieved Jun 08, 2023, from https://blog.atisfyreach.com/how-did-modern-day-influencers-become-a-thing/

Atisfyreach. (2021). *Take Your Influencer Campaigns To The Next Level With Podcasts*. Retrieved Sept 15, 2023, from https://blog.atisfyreach.com: https://blog.atisfyreach.com/take-your-influencer-campaigns-to-the-next-level-with-podcasts/

Bailis, R. (2021). *The State of Influencer Marketing: 10 Influencer Marketing Statistics to Inform Where You Invest*. Retrieved Jun 06, 2023, from BigCommerce: https://www.bigcommerce.com/blog/influencer-marketing-statistics/

Bang, M. (2023, Jun 7). *Authenticity in Influencer Marketing: Building Trust and Engagement with Audiences*. Retrieved Sept 15, 2023, from https://www.linkedin.com: https://www.linkedin.com/pulse/authenticity-influencer-marketing-building-trust-engagement-bang/

Bansal, P. (2019, May 27). *Why social media marketing has become a rage now*. Retrieved Jun 20, 2023, from The Satesman: https://www.thestatesman.com/business/why-social-media-marketing-has-become-a-rage-now-1502759272.html

Basuroy, T. (2023, Mar 20). *Value of influencer marketing industry in India from 2021 to 2022, with projections until 2026*. Retrieved Jun 03, 2023, from Statista: https://www.statista.com/statistics/1294803/india-influencer-marketing-industry-value/#:~:text=It%20was%20projected%20to%20grow,various%20kinds%20as%20of%202022

Belanche, D., Casaló, L. V., Flavián, M., & Sánchez, S. I. (2021, August). Understanding influencer marketing: The role of congruence between influencers, products and consumers. *Journal of Business Research, 132*, 186–195. doi:10.1016/j.jbusres.2021.03.067

Beveridge, C. (2022, Jan 13). *What is User-Generated Content? And Why is it Important?* Retrieved Sept 15, 2023, from https://blog.hootsuite.com/user-generated-content-ugc/

Bhargava, V. (2021, Dec 11). *Find The Best Fit: Your Beginner's Guide to Influencer Marketing*. Retrieved Jun 01, 2023, from shopify: https://www.shopify.com/in/blog/influencer-marketing

BigCommerce. (2022). *Discover New Leads and Brand Growth with Influencer Marketing*. Retrieved Sept 15, 2023, from https://www.bigcommerce.com: https://www.bigcommerce.com/articles/ecommerce/influencer-marketing/#types-of-influencer-marketing-opportunities-to-explore

Bonoboz. (2023, Aug 18). *Measure Success for Influencer Marketing Campaigns*. Retrieved Sept 15, 2023, from https://www.bonoboz.in/measure-success-for-influencer-marketing-campaigns/

Borges-Tiago, M. T., Santiago, J., & Tiago, F. (2023, March). Mega or macro social media influencers: Who endorses brands better? *Journal of Business Research, 157*, 1–12. doi:10.1016/j.jbusres.2022.113606

Brand Equity. (2022, Oct 20). *Influencer marketing industry in India to reach Rs 2,200 cr by 2025: Report*. Retrieved Jun 06, 2023, from Brand Equity.com: https://brandequity.economictimes.indiatimes.com/news/research/influencer-marketing-industry-in-india-to-reach-rs-2200-cr-by-2025-report/94990088

BrandWagon. (2021, Aug 17). *Influencer marketing industry size to reach Rs 2,200 crore in India by 2025: Report*. Retrieved Jun 06, 2023, from Financial Express: https://www.financialexpress.com/business/brandwagon-influencer-marketing-industry-size-to-reach-rs-2200-crore-in-india-by-2025-report-2332321/

Brooke, C. (2017). *Engaging the Long Tail, Engaging the Micro Influencer*. Retrieved Jun 10, 2023, from https://www.business2community.com/content-marketing-tips/engaging-long-tail-engaging-micro-influencer-01909491

Bundhun, R. (2023, Feb 27). *How the growth of social media is boosting India's influencers*. Retrieved Jun 26, 2023, from National News: https://www.thenationalnews.com/business/2023/02/27/how-the-growth-of-social-media-is-boosting-indias-influencers/

Burton, S. (2021, Jan 25). *The right fit: How to find influencers for your brand's marketing campaign*. Retrieved Sept 15, 2023, from https://sproutsocial.com/insights/how-to-find-the-right-influencers/

Cabeza Ramírez, L. J., Sánchez Cañizares, S. M., Santos Roldán, L. M., & Fuentes-García, F. J. (2022, November). Impact of the perceived risk in influencers' product recommendations on their followers' purchase attitudes and intention. *Technological Forecasting and Social Change*, *184*, 121997. Advance online publication. doi:10.1016/j.techfore.2022.121997

Calibrate, A. (2023, Jul 19). *Evaluating the Performance of Your Influencer Marketing Campaigns: Metrics and KPIs*. Retrieved Sept 15, 2023, from https://calibrate.thearena.ai/infohub/influencer-marketing-kpis

Campbell, C., & Farrell, J. R. (2020, August). More than meets the eye: The functional components underlying influencer marketing. *Business Horizons*, *63*(4), 469–479. doi:10.1016/j.bushor.2020.03.003

Chadda, R. (2022, Apr 30). *What metaverse means for influencer marketing?* Retrieved Sept 13, 2023, from https://www.financialexpress.com/business/brandwagon-what-metaverse-means-for-influencer-marketing-2508559/

Ching, C. (2023, March 23). *Here's How Much Instagram Influencers Make in 2023 (+ Free Report)*. Retrieved Jun 01, 2023, from Later: https://later.com/blog/instagram-influencers-costs/

Ching, C. (2023). *The power of Instagram influencer marketing: how to reach your target audience*. Retrieved Jun 03, 2023, from Plannthat: https://www.plannthat.com/instagram-influencer-marketing-2/

Chopra, S. (2023, Aug 25). *Ethics in Influencer Marketing*. Retrieved Sept 15, 2023, from https://www.dailypioneer.com/2023/columnists/ethics-in-influencer-marketing.html#:~:text=Ethical%20influencer%20marketing%20is%20not,genuine%20value%20and%20communicate%20trustworthiness.&text=Choose%20influencers%20who%20align%20with%20your%20brand's%20v

Conde, R., & Casais, B. (2023, March). Micro, macro and mega-influencers on instagram: The power of persuasion via the parasocial relationship. *Journal of Business Research*, *158*, 1–10. doi:10.1016/j.jbusres.2023.113708

Dean, K. (2015, Auyg). *The Role of Social Media Influencers*. Retrieved Jun 13, 2023, from https://www.manobyte.com/growth-strategy/the-role-of-social-media-influencers

Dencheva, V. (2023, Mar 21). *Influencer marketing spending in the United States from 2019 to 2024*. Retrieved Jun 02, 2023, from https://www.statista.com/statistics/1254039/influencer-marketing-spending-usa/

Dencheva, V. (2023). *Leading platforms used by marketers for influencer marketing in the United States from 2020 to 2025*. Retrieved Jun 01, 1, from https://www.statista.com/statistics/1092819/global-influencer-market-size/

Dencheva, V. (2023, Mar 15). *Share of marketing budgets spent on influencer marketing worldwide as of February 2023*. Retrieved Jun 01, 2023, from https://www.statista.com/statistics/268641/share-of-marketing-budgets-spent-on-digital-worldwide/

Dopson, E. (2022). *30+ Influencer Marketing Statistics You Should Know (2023)*. Retrieved Jun 13, 2023, from https://www.shopify.com/blog/influencer-marketing-statistics

EconomicTimes. (2023, Sept 7). *Social Media and Influencer Marketing for CMOs: Maximizing Brand Reach and Engagement*. Retrieved Sept 15, 2023, from https://economictimes.indiatimes.com/: https://economictimes.indiatimes.com/jobs/c-suite/social-media-and-influencer-marketing-for-cmos-maximizing-brand-reach-and-engagement/articleshow/103480616.cms?from=mdr

Edwards, G. (2022). *5 Reasons Why Macro & Mega Influencers May Not Be Good for Your Brand*. Retrieved Jun 09, 2023, from cipio.ai: https://blog.cipio.ai/5-reasons-why-macro-and-mega-influencers-may-not-be-good-for-your-brand

Ehlers, K. (2021, Jun 2). *Micro-Influencers: When Smaller Is Better*. Retrieved Sept 01, 2023, from FORBES: https://www.forbes.com/sites/forbesagencycouncil/2021/06/02/micro-influencers-when-smaller-is-better/?sh=24dbe848539b

Emeritus. (2022a). *Discover the Best Ways to Leverage Influencer Marketing for Your Brand*. Retrieved Jun 08, 2023, from https://emeritus.org/blog/digital-marketing-what-is-an-influencer/

Emeritus. (2022b, May 13). *Influencer Marketing Is Taking Advantage of The Metaverse! Are You Ready?* Retrieved Sept 13, 2023, from https://emeritus.org/blog/influencer-marketing-metaverse/

Emplify. (2023). *Micro influencers vs macro influencers: What's best for your business?* Retrieved Jun 12, 2023, from https://emplifi.io/resources/blog/micro-influencers-vs-macro-influencers?

Enberg, J. (2021, Nov 29). *Micro-influencers present macro opportunities*. Retrieved Jun 11, 2023, from Insider Intelligence: https://www.insiderintelligence.com/content/mirco-influencers-present-macro-opportunities

Engaiodigital. (2022). *What Is Influencer Marketing and Its Benefits*. Retrieved Jun 11, 2023, from https://engaiodigital.com/influencer-marketing/

Equity, B. (2022, Oct 20). *Influencer marketing industry in India to reach Rs 2,200 cr by 2025: Report*. Retrieved Jun 06, 2023, from Brand Equity: https://brandequity.economictimes.indiatimes.com/news/research/influencer-marketing-industry-in-india-to-reach-rs-2200-cr-by-2025-report/94990088

Ethos. (n.d.). *Nano-Influencers: Who, What, Why, When, and How to Engage Them.* Retrieved Jun 11, 2023, from https://www.ethos-marketing.com/blog/nano-influencers-social-media-marketing/#:~:text=Nano%2Dinfluencers%20are%20your%20everyday,from%20100%20to%20 10%2C000%20followers

Famesters. (2020). *What do TikTok and YouTube shorts have in common?* Retrieved Sept 15, 2023, from https://famesters.com: https://famesters.com/blog/tiktok-or-youtube-shorts-which-is-better-for-your-influencer-marketing/

Financial Dictonary. (2021). *Influencers.* Retrieved Jun 08, 2023, from https://indianmoney.com/financial-dictionary/i/influencers

Foster, J. (2022). *Why Influencer Marketing is Creating Huge Returns for Businesses.* Retrieved Jun 01, 2023, from https://www.convinceandconvert.com/digital-marketing/influencer-marketing-for-businesses/#:~:text=Influencer%20Marketing%20Delivers%20a%20Strong,failing%20to%20generate%20any%20revenue

Foy, P. (2023, Feb 25). *Influencer Marketing Metrics: 8 Key Metrics to Track Performance.* Retrieved Sept 15, 2023, from https://agencyanalytics.com/blog/influencer-marketing-analytics

Francis, T., & Hoefel, F. (2018, Nov 12). *'True Gen': Generation Z and its implications for companies.* Retrieved Jun 15, 2023, from McKinsey and company: https://www.mckinsey.com/industries/consumer-packaged-goods/our-insights/true-gen-generation-z-and-its-implications-for-companies

FundafundaC. (2023, April). Understanding social media influencer credibility, its components, and their individual effects on the purchase intentions of female Millennial consumers on Instagram. doi:10.13140/RG.2.2.34441.52328

Gahin, R., & Paterson, C. (2003, July). Community Indicators: Past, Present, and Future. *National Civic Review, 90*(4), 347–361. doi:10.1002/ncr.90406

Gelati, N., Verplancke, J., & Frögren, N. F. (2022, Dec). *The effect of influencer marketing on buying behavior ofyoung consumers.* Linköping University. Retrieved Sept 14, 2023, from https://liu.diva-portal.org/smash/get/diva2:1668422/FULLTEXT01.pdf

Geyser, W. (2023, Feb 7). *The State of Influencer Marketing 2023: Benchmark Report.* Retrieved Jun 06, 2023, from Influencer Marketing Hub: https://influencermarketinghub.com/influencer-marketing-benchmark-report/

Grin. (2021a). *Influencer Discount Codes & Affiliate Links – How and when to use them in your campaigns.* Retrieved Sept 15, 2023, from GRIN: https://grin.co/blog/influencer-discount-codes-affiliate-links-how-and-when-to-use-them-in-your-campaigns/

Grin. (2021b). *Why Influencer Marketing Is an Important Part of Today's Businesses.* Retrieved Jun 05, 2023, from GRIN: https://grin.co/blog/why-influencer-marketing/

Grin. (2022). *Psychology of Influence – The Reason for the Rise of Influencer Marketing.* Retrieved Sept 15, 2023, from GRIN: https://grin.co/blog/psychology-of-influence/

Grin. (2023). *6 Effective Ways to Reach Your Target Audience*. Retrieved Sept 15, 2023, from GRIN: https://grin.co/blog/reach-your-target-audience-more-effectively/

Han, H. S., Lee, J., & Masuda, H. (2022, January). mpacts of influencer attributes on purchase intentions in social media influencer marketing: Mediating roles of characterizations. *Technological Forecasting and Social Change, 174*(1), 121246. Advance online publication. doi:10.1016/j.techfore.2021.121246

Hayes, A. (2023, Apr 12). *Social Media Marketing (SMM): What It Is, How It Works, Pros and Cons*. Retrieved Sept 15, 2023, from https://www.investopedia.com: https://www.investopedia.com/terms/s/social-media-marketing-smm.asp

Hutchinson, A. (2021). *Nano Influencers: Who Are They and How to Work With Them [Infographic]*. Retrieved Jun 12, 2023, from https://www.socialmediatoday.com/news/nano-influencers-who-are-they-and-how-to-work-with-them-infographic/595048/

Influencity. (2023a, Apr 14). *The Impact of Influencer Marketing on Consumer Behavior and Purchase Decisions*. Retrieved Sept 14, 2023, from https://influencity.com: https://influencity.com/blog/en/the-impact-of-influencer-marketing-on-consumer-behavior-and-purchase-decisions

Influencity. (2023b, Aug 14). *The Future of Influencer Marketing: Leveraging AI for Enhanced Campaigns*. Retrieved Sept 15, 2023, from https://influencity.com: https://influencity.com/blog/en/the-future-of-influencer-marketing-leveraging-ai-for-enhanced-campaigns

Institute, D. M. (2019). *20 Surprising Influencer Marketing Statistics*. Retrieved Jun 15, 2023, from https://digitalmarketinginstitute.com/blog/20-influencer-marketing-statistics-that-will-surprise-you

Iskiev, M. (2023). *The HubSpot Blog's 2023 Marketing Strategy & Trends Report: Data from 1,200+ Global Marketers*. Retrieved Jun 05, 2023, from https://blog.hubspot.com/marketing/hubspot-blog-marketing-industry-trends-report?_ga=2.164494201.777083537.1669997995-495228435.1669997995&hubs_content=blog.hubspot.com%2Fmarketing%2Finfluencer-marketing-stats&hubs_content-cta=1%20in%204%20marketers

Ismail, K. (2023, Jun 21). *Types of Social Media Influencers: Mega, Macro, Micro or Nano*. Retrieved Sept 15, 2023, from CMSWIRE: https://www.cmswire.com/digital-marketing/social-media-influencers-mega-macro-micro-or-nano/

Joshi, K. (2022, Dec 22). *Discover the Best Ways to Leverage Influencer Marketing for Your Brand*. Retrieved Sept 15, 2023, from EMERITUS: https://emeritus.org/blog/digital-marketing-what-is-an-influencer/

Kashyap, M. N. (2023, Jul 03). *Build Long-Term Relationships with Influencers for Sustainable Campaign Success*. Retrieved Sept 15, 2023, from https://www.linkedin.com: https://www.linkedin.com/pulse/build-long-term-relationships-influencers-sustainable-campaign-success/

Kolsquare. (2021, Dec). *Will the metaverse shape the future of Influencer Marketing?* Retrieved Sept 13, 2023, from https://www.kolsquare.com: https://www.kolsquare.com/en/blog/will-the-metaverse-shape-the-future-of-influencer-marketing/

Kuzminov, M. (2023, Jan 30). *Social Responsibility And Ethics In Influencer Marketing*. Retrieved Sept 15, 2023, from https://www.forbes.com: https://www.forbes.com/sites/forbesagencycouncil/2023/01/30/social-responsibility-and-ethics-in-influencer-marketing/?sh=5b028f15685c

Leung, F. &. (2022). Online influencer marketing. *Journal of the Academy of Marketing Science, 50*(5). doi:10.1007/s11747-021-00829-4

Leung, F. F., Gu, F. F., Li, Y., Zhang, J., & Palmatier, R. W. (2022). Influencer Marketing Effectiveness. *Journal of Marketing, 86*(5), 1-23.

Mailchimp. (2021). *What Is Influencer Marketing?* Retrieved Jun 07, 2023, from mailchimp: https://mailchimp.com/resources/what-is-influencer-marketing/#:~:text=Influencer%20marketing%20is%20a%20form,promotes%20their%20products%20or%20services

Maqbool, F. I. (2023). *Influencer Marketing: A Rising Trend for Brands*. Retrieved Jun 06, 2023, from Rising Kashmir: http://risingkashmir.com/influencer-marketing-a-rising-trend-for-brands

Martin, M. (2022, Aug 30). *24 Gen Z Statistics That Matter to Marketers in 2023*. Retrieved Jun 15, 2023, from HootSuite: https://blog.hootsuite.com/gen-z-statistics/

Mathew, J. (2018, July 30). *Understanding Influencer Marketing And Why It Is So Effective*. Retrieved Jun 01, 2023, from Forbes: https://www.forbes.com/sites/theyec/2018/07/30/understanding-influencer-marketing-and-why-it-is-so-effective/?sh=a27ccb471a94

Mehra, C. (2022, May 24). *Rise Of Influencer Marketing: Creators To Commerce*. Retrieved Jun 04, 2023, from Business World: https://www.businessworld.in/article/Rise-Of-Influencer-Marketing-Creators-To-Commerce-/24-05-2022-429999/

Michaelsen, F., Collin, L., Jacob, C., Goanta, D. C., Kettner, D. S., Bishop, D. P., . . . Yesiloglu, D. S. (2022). *The impact of influencers on advertising and consumer protection in the Single Market*. European Parliament. Retrieved Sept 15, 2023, from https://www.europarl.europa.eu/RegData/etudes/STUD/2022/703350/IPOL_STU(2022)703350_EN.pdf

Monllos, K. (2023, Apr 21). *More brands choose Boomer, Gen X influencers, as 'older audiences can be just as impactful' as young ones*. Retrieved Jun 14, 2023, from DIGIDAY: https://digiday.com/marketing/more-brands choose older-influencers-as-older-audiences-can-be-just-as-impactful-as-young-ones/

Nambakhsh, C. (2023, July 9). *Ethical Influencer Marketing: Navigating Disclosure, Transparency, And Responsibility*. Retrieved Sept 15, 2023, from https://blog.ainfluencer.com: https://blog.ainfluencer.com/ethical-influencer-marketing/

Narula, R., & Nangia, A. (2023, May 23). *India attempts to reel in influencer marketing*. Retrieved Jun 06, 2023, from ManagingIP: https://www.managingip.com/article/2bp81m226pjlycqrzjrb4/expert-analysis/local-insights/india-attempts-to-reel-in-influencer-marketing#:~:text=India's%20influencer%20marketing%20industry%20is,in%2C%20an%20influencer%20marketing%20platform

Nizri, E. (2022, Mar 1). *Macro-Influencers vs. Micro-Influencers: The Great Social Media Debate*. Retrieved Sept 15, 2023, from Forbes: https://www.forbes.com/sites/forbestechcouncil/2022/03/01/macro-influencers-vs-micro-influencers-the-great-social-media-debate/?sh=5673f745286f

Ohio. (2022). *How to Market to Instagram Influencers: Understanding the Influencer Business Model and Analytics*. Retrieved Jun 06, 2023, from Ohio University: https://onlinemasters.ohio.edu/instagram-influencers/

Phyllo. (2021). *The Evolution of Influencer Marketing*. Retrieved Sept 15, 2023, from https://www.getphyllo.com/post/the-evolution-of-influencer-marketing

Pradhan, B., Kishore, K., & Gokhale, N. (2023, February). Social Media Influencers and Consumer Engagement: A Review and Future Research Agenda. *International Journal of Consumer Studies*, *47*(6), 2106–2130. Advance online publication. doi:10.1111/ijcs.12901

Rodrigue, E. (2023). *31 Influencer Marketing Stats to Know in 2023*. Retrieved Jun 06, 2023, from https://blog.hubspot.com/marketing/influencer-marketing-stats

Santora, J. (2023, Jan 11). *Key Influencer Marketing Statistics to Drive Your Strategy in 2023*. Retrieved Jun 06, 2023, from Influencer Marketing Hub: https://influencermarketinghub.com/influencer-marketing-statistics/

Sarah, D. (2019). *What is Influencer Marketing? Here's How Influencer Marketing Works*. Retrieved Jun 08, 2023, from https://www.getcarro.com/blog/what-is-influencer-marketing

Schaffer, N. (2022, Dec 5). *What is Influencer Marketing? A Definition and Guide to Successful Influencer Collaborations*. Retrieved Jun 03, 2023, from https://nealschaffer.com/what-is-influencer-marketing/

SendPulse. (2021a). *Cross-Promotion*. Retrieved Sept 15, 2023, from https://sendpulse.com: https://sendpulse.com/support/glossary/cross-promotion

SendPulse. (2021b). *Influencer Marketing*. Retrieved Jun 08, 2023, from https://sendpulse.com/support/glossary/influencer-marketing

Sharma, V. (2022, Apr 20). *How Influencer Marketing is Going to Change in the Age of Metaverse?* Retrieved Sept 13, 2023, from https://www.indianretailer.com/article/technology/digital-trends/how-influencer-marketing-is-going-to-change-in-the-age-of-metaverse.a7899

Shepherd, J. (2023, May 15). *28 Essential Influencer Marketing Statistics You Need to Know in 2023*. Retrieved Jun 05, 2023, from Social Shepherd: https://thesocialshepherd.com/blog/influencer-marketing-statistics

Sinha, M. (2023, Jun 13). Augmented Reality: New Future of Social Media Influencer Marketing. *Vision The Journal of Business Perspective*. doi:10.1177/09722629221147124

Smart Insights. (2019). *80% of marketers find influencer marketing effective*. Retrieved JUn 14, 2023, from https://www.smartinsights.com/online-pr/influencer-marketing-effectiveness/

SocialSamosa. (2019). *Data: 89% marketers say Instagram is important to their influencer marketing strategy*. Retrieved Jun 14, 2023, from https://www.socialsamosa.com/2019/02/report-influencer-marketing-statistics-2019/

SproutSocial. (2023, Apr 17). *What is influencer marketing: How to develop your strategy*. Retrieved Jun 01, 2023, from SproutSocial: https://sproutsocial.com/insights/influencer-marketing/

Staff, M. C. (2019). *The Influencer Report*. Retrieved Jun 05, 2023, from https://pro.morningconsult.com/analyst-reports/influencer-report

Storai. (2023, Jan 17). *Making Influencer Marketing Click*. Retrieved JUn 07, 2023, from https://www.globallinker.com/bizforum/article/making-influencer-marketing-click/91904#/overlay/signup/articleview/91904

Swan, G. (2018, Apr 20). *What Is Influencer Marketing & Why It Matters | A Brand's Guide*. Retrieved Jun 08, 2023, from https://tinuiti.com/blog/influencer-marketing/what-is-influencer-marketing/

Swat.io. (2022, Nov 8). *6 Social Media Niches with Potential – How to Reach Your Target Group through Niche Platforms*. Retrieved Sept 15, 2023, from https://swat.io/en/strategize/social-media-niche-platforms/

Tabor, E. (2019, Dec 19). *Can You Really Market To Gen X And Baby Boomers On Social Platforms?* Retrieved Jun 15, 2023, from Forbes: https://www.forbes.com/sites/forbesagencycouncil/2019/12/19/can-you-really-market-to-gen-x-and-baby-boomers-on-social-platforms/?sh=7ea08ae55741

Thorpe, J. (2019, Nov 18). *The Influence of Influencers: New Research Unveiled*. Retrieved Jun 09, 2023, from gen.video: https://www.gen.video/blog/the-influence-of-influencers-new-research-unveiled

Tiwari, S. (2022, Nov 4). *Influencer marketing and its contribution to the creator economy of India*. Retrieved Jun 06, 2023, from https://etinsights.et-edge.com/influencer-marketing-and-its-contribution-to-the-creator-economy-of-india/

Tondon, R. (2023, Mar 18). *GenZs and the influencer market: Using social media to build business empires*. Retrieved Jun 06, 2023, from Economic Times: https://economictimes.indiatimes.com/jobs/fresher/genzs-and-the-influencer-market-using-social-media-to-build-business-empires/articleshow/98750919.cms?from=mdr

Treseler, J. (2021, Mar 23). *What is a micro influencer anyway?* Retrieved Jun 11, 2023, from Crunchylinks: https://crunchylinks.com/what-is-a-micro-influencer-anyway/

Tulman, S. (2023, Jan 2). *The ROI of Influencer Marketing*. Retrieved Jun 05, 2023, from Business2Community: https://www.business2community.com/online-marketing/roi-influencer-marketing-2-01787448#u65UTYdmZEZkKgMX.97

Upwork. (2022, Dec 7). *How To Build an Efficient Influencer Marketing Strategy*. Retrieved Sept 15, 2023, from https://www.upwork.com/en-gb/resources/influencer-marketing strategy

Valentina Dencheva. (2023, Jan 6). *Average price per post of TikTok influencers worldwide in 2021, by number of followers*. Retrieved Jun 05, 2023, from Statista: https://www.statista.com/statistics/1251177/price-per-post-tiktok-influencers-worldwide/

Venciute, D., Mackeviciene, I., Kuslys, M., & Correia, R. F. (2023, November). The role of influencer–follower congruence in the relationship between influencer marketing and purchase behaviour. *Journal of Retailing and Consumer Services*, *75*, 103506. Advance online publication. doi:10.1016/j.jretconser.2023.103506

Venkatesh, R., Meleet, M., & Cholli, D. N. (2022). Influencer Marketing in Recent Times. *International Journal of Engineering Research & Technology (Ahmedabad), 11*(07), 292–296. Retrieved June 11, 2023, from https://www.ijert.org/research/influencer-marketing-in-recent-times-IJERTV11IS070172.pdf

Warren, J. (2020, Apr 27). *Affiliate Marketing for Influencers: How to Make Money on Instagram*. Retrieved Sept 15, 2023, from https://later.com/blog/affiliate-marketing-for-influencers/

Werner, G. (2023a, Feb 7). *The State of Influencer Marketing 2023: Benchmark Report*. Retrieved Jun 06, 2023, from Influencer Marketing Hub: https://influencermarketinghub.com/influencer-marketing-benchmark-report/

Werner, G. (2023b, Mar 24). *What is an Influencer? Social Media Influencers Defined* [Updated 2023]. Retrieved Jun 08, 2023, from https://influencermarketinghub.com/what-is-an-influencer/

West, C. (2023). *Micro-influencer marketing guide: Facts and uses*. Retrieved Jun 11, 2023, from https://sproutsocial.com/insights/microinfluencer-marketing/

Wibawa, R. C., Pratiwi, C. P., & Larasati, H. (2021). The Role of Nano Influencers Through Instagram as an Effective Digital Marketing Strategy. *Advances in Economics, Business and Management Research, 198*, 233-238. Retrieved Jun 12, 2023, from https://www.researchgate.net/publication/358878321_The_Role_of_Nano_Influencers_Through_Instagram_as_an_Effective_Digital_Marketing_Strategy

Wiley, D. (2023, Mar 13). *Why Smaller Influencers Outshine Mega-Influencers in The Age of Social Media*. Retrieved Jun 12, 2023, from Forbes: https://www.forbes.com/sites/forbesagencycouncil/2023/03/13/why-smaller-influencers-outshine-mega-influencers-in-the-age-of-social-media/?sh=1cbce1ac4090

Wong, L. (2023, Aug 3). *How to Use UTM Parameters to Track Social Media Success*. Retrieved Sept 15, 2023, from https://blog.hootsuite.com/how-to-use-utm-parameters/

Zafar, A. U., Shahzad, M., Ashfaq, M., & Shahzad, K. (2023, May). Forecasting impulsive consumers driven by macro-influencers posts: Intervention of followers' flow state and perceived informativeness. *Technological Forecasting and Social Change, 190*, 122408. Advance online publication. doi:10.1016/j.techfore.2023.122408

Zhang, Y., & Mac, L. (2023). Social media influencers: The formation and effects of affective factors during online interactions. *International Journal of Consumer Studies, 47*(5), 1824–1837. Advance online publication. doi:10.1111/ijcs.12957

ADDITIONAL READING

Deng, F., Lin, Y., & Jiang, X. (2023, November). Influence mechanism of consumers' characteristics on impulsive purchase in E-commerce livestream marketing. *Computers in Human Behavior, 148*, 107894. Advance online publication. doi:10.1016/j.chb.2023.107894

Jha, A. K., & Ray, S. (2023, November 7). Influencer recommendation system: Choosing the right influencer using a network analysis approach. *Marketing Intelligence & Planning, 41*(8), 1197–1212. doi:10.1108/MIP-04-2023-0149

Kim, H., & Park, M. (2024, January). When digital celebrity talks to you: How human-like virtual influencers satisfy consumer's experience through social presence on social media endorsements. *Journal of Retailing and Consumer Services*, *76*, 103581. Advance online publication. doi:10.1016/j.jretconser.2023.103581

Mero, J., Vanninen, H., & Keränen, J. (2023, January). B2B influencer marketing: Conceptualization and four managerial strategies. *Industrial Marketing Management*, *108*, 79–93. Advance online publication. doi:10.1016/j.indmarman.2022.10.017

Syed, T. A., Mehmood, F., & Qaiser, T. (2023, July). Brand–SMI collaboration in influencer marketing campaigns: A transaction cost economics perspective. *Technological Forecasting and Social Change*, *192*, 122580. Advance online publication. doi:10.1016/j.techfore.2023.122580

Zhou, Q., Li, B., Li, H., & Lei, Y. (2024, January). Mere copycat? The effects of human versus human-like virtual influencers on brand endorsement effectiveness: A moderated serial-mediation model. *Journal of Retailing and Consumer Services*, *76*, 103610. Advance online publication. doi:10.1016/j.jretconser.2023.103610

Zhou, S., Blazquez, M., McCormick, H., & Barnes, L. (2021, September). How social media influencers' narrative strategies benefit cultivating influencer marketing: Tackling issues of cultural barriers, commercialised content, and sponsorship disclosure. *Journal of Business Research*, *134*, 122–142. doi:10.1016/j.jbusres.2021.05.011

KEY TERMS AND DEFINITION

Engagement Rate (ER): The engagement rate (ER) in influencer marketing is a measure of how actively an audience engages with an influencer's material. Audience engagement can take the form of actions such as likes, comments, shares, and saves for the influencer's content.

Influencer: Influencer is an individual who may have huge fan following ad can influence the purchasing decisions and/or opinions of others due to their knowledge, authority, position, or relationship with their audience, especially on social media platforms.

Influencer Affiliate Marketing: Influencer Affiliate Marketing is a collaborative marketing strategy where influencers promote a brand in exchange of a commission for driving traffic or sales to a brand's products through unique affiliate links provided to them.

Influencer Fraud and Fake Engagement: These are dishonest activities or practices in which influencers or their followers manipulate engagement metrics (for instance likes, comments or number of followers) to create a manipulated impression of popularity or engagement.

Influencer Legitimacy and Credibility Evaluation: It is the process of assessing an influencer's trustworthiness, authenticity, and expertise within their niche to ensure they align with a brand's values and goals.

Influencer Marketing: Influencer marketing is a form of marketing that enables businesses to collaborate with individuals (who are popular on social media) who have a significant and engaged following to promote a brand, product or service to their audience.

Influencer Reach and Engagement Evaluation: It is an evaluation of the size of an influencer's audience (reach) and the amount of interaction generated by their content (engagement), crucial for brands to determine the potential impact of a collaboration.

Social Proof: It is a psychological phenomenon that refers to the tendency for people to follow the actions of others. It is commonly used in influencer marketing to build trust by highlighting others' positive experiences.

Virtual Influencer: A virtual influencer is a fictional character (computer-generated or AI-powered persona) designed to interact with and engage audiences on social platforms.

Chapter 2
Use of Influencers in Different Sectors of the Economy

Shikha Mittal
https://orcid.org/0000-0002-1092-1765
Raj Kumar Goel Institute of Technology, Ghaziabad, India

ABSTRACT

With the advent of digital technologies, influencer marketing has acquired a key role in the social media approaches adopted by a growing number of companies operating in different sectors. Influencer marketing has grown with a startlingly rapid pace, and it has not just grown, but has helped in better product introduction with increased consumer and influencer communication. In the current scenario, undoubtedly, influencers will rule the digital space, and businesses will constantly come up with new strategies to utilize the influencing powers of these influencers. The author has selected seven different sectors—fashion and lifestyle, technology industry, travel and tourism industry, food and beverage, healthcare, finance sector, and entertainment and gaming—to study the importance of influencers and change they have made. This study examines the use of influencers in chosen sectors of the economy. It also aims to identify factors influencing consumers' behavior to generate revenue.

USE OF INFLUENCERS IN DIFFERENT SECTORS OF THE ECONOMY

Influencers are becoming more and more common, and they have an impact on customer attitudes, perceptions, preferences, decisions and choices. A McKinsey study found that Gen Z, a group of people between the ages of 16 and 26, currently represents 40% of customers. They are recognized as the most "plugged in" generation to date since they spend three hours every day reading and posting content on social media. This has prompted firms to update their marketing plans in order to meet the needs of the new generation. As per (Bastrygina & Lim, 2023) Influencers are average people who, through their digital channel or page, have built an online presence from the ground up and, in the process, gained a substantial following. Influencers differ from traditional celebrities or public figures in this regard because the former rely on their current jobs (such as acting, singing, or politics) to gain popularity and influence.

DOI: 10.4018/979-8-3693-0551-5.ch002

Influencers started appearing in the start of 2000s, and ever since, influencing has developed from a part time involvement to a lucrative full-time job. There is a constantly expanding group of online users who want to become Influencers since influencer marketing has become so alluring. Influencers are now using their exposure and popularity to advance their careers in traditional media, including the film and television industries.

Three categories can be defined for Influencers based on the followers of Influencers: micro-influencer, meso-influencer, and macro-influencers. As per (Lou & Yuan, 2019) from marketing perspective, influencer serves two primary goals with their posts: They helps in increasing the interest of their followers in a specific products or service. This process of increasing the interest is done in a way along with increasing the buy intention of the followers, it also helps in the attractiveness of Influencers as a category expert. These posts have details of a category and have recommendation about a specific product or service elaborating the features, these posts give information to the followers and make them familiar with the product of service. The use of appealing ways and posturing, gives the Influencers edge and conveys their aesthetic value and beauty during the process.

Scholars have explained Influencers in numerous ways. Influencers are the new age endorsers who are not affiliated to any brand or service, who helps in creating interest of followers in a service or products with the help of their social media posts (Freberg, Graham, McGaughey, & Freberg, 2011). According to (Abidin, 2016) Influencers are a set of microcelebrities, who use social media as a tool to share exciting glance of the rare opportunities that come their way. By carefully managing their online image, these Influencers may influence followers and public opinion. Influencers are the one who have accumulated a large following and these are accepted as trustworthy consumers in various categories, (Ye, Hudders, De Jans, & De Veirman, 2021). Influencers, according to (Ge & Gretzel, 2018) are people with whom a consumer is connected via social network and have significant impact on that consumer's behavior. Influencers are persons who, due to their personal social image, develop and encourage an association with the followers and can make the followers feel enlightened, amused, and can impact the follower's viewpoint, and behavior, according to (Dhanesh & Duthler, 2019).

Combining all these definitions and looking at the Influencers from the marketing viewpoint, Influencers are the people who build and sustain a personal image and a fan following on the social media through their posts. They represent their posts with their personality and Lifestyle in a way that it promotes goods, services, idea, place and people they associate with, they can impact the follower's attitude (Choice, perception, behaviour, preferences etc.) in positive and negative way. In this study we will look at the impact of Influencers on different sectors. Also, will study the popularity of different platforms and return based on the investment done by the brands. Certainly, future of the Influencer marketing is bright and new trends are evolving in influencer marketing, we will also touch upon the new trends in this arena.

LITERATURE REVIEW

As social media has become part of daily life in past few years and popularity of other media forms like print and television has reduced. This change has compelled business to look social media as another potential form of interaction with customers (Colliander & Erlandsson, 2015). Followers have confirmed that they trust the influencer and the content provided by the Influencers on social media platforms (Kapitan & Silvera, 2016). Influencer marketing industry has raised up from 1.7B$ in 2016 to a whooping 16.4B$ in 2022 in USA, according to Statista-2022. Followers consider the Influencers to be dependable, genuine and expert. Increasing impact of social media has forced organizations to use Influencers as a part of overall marketing strategy. With the advent to social media, it has become a simple and direct form to interact with target consumer (Bakker, 2018).

With platforms like Facebook, Instagram and TikTok becoming increasingly popular with each passing day, social media has also become an integral part of marketing tools in marketing mix. These platforms are used by the Influencers for posting their content. Partnership of companies with the Influencers give not only marketing exposure to companies, but also helps in developing a strong relationship with consumers (Borchers, 2019). Influencers can be instrumental for an organization to communicate with the consumer. Influencers can play the role of an intermediary by sharing sponsored content, a content developer and distributor, an event organizer and a counsellor. In the past companies used to have a large team for these roles and now Influencers are doing these activities in more better way (Hudders, De Jans, & De Veirman, 2021). (Pöyry, Reinikainen, & Luoma-Aho, 2022) studied influencer role as components of marketing communication processes. Use of endorsers for promotion of a product in not new concept for a company but increasing popularity of social media channels has pushed organizations to change the marketing strategies to use the Influencers. Companies are connecting with Influencers to build content and create a connection with target customer in partnership with company. (Sundermann & Raabe, 2019) studied the impact of Influencers content for the viewpoint of companies, consumer and influencer, they observed that 13% of overall internet users and approx. 50% of the teenagers have high impact of the Influencers and have used the product or services proposed by the influencer. They also studied that most of the organizations are using or planning to use the Influencers, even almost half of the companies have a separate department to manage Influencers.

The message from the Influencers is perceived as coming from a fellow social media member who converses with and shares content with other users in their own language. Additionally, when earning consumers' trust, Influencers have the potential to stand out from the sea of advertisements and form lasting bonds with them. This is because the concept of trustworthiness is crucial when evaluating an influencer's capacity to persuade consumers to purchase a good or service and to alter their attitudes. Since their primary objective while working with an organization is to encourage a purchase, Influencers have a significant role in the decision-making process (Evans, Phua, Lim, & Jun, 2017).

Influencers have the power to sway people's opinions while promoting an organization's brand image. In addition, prior research has shown that the influencer can play a variety of roles within an organization, depending on the objectives of the cooperation including that of content creator, public figure, and content distributor (Borchers & Enke, 2021). According to (Bakker, 2018) audiences are less receptive to traditional media than they once were. They now turn to Influencers for reliable, real information. Therefore, to enhance revenue and return on investment, the majority of sectors have incorporated Influencers into their promotional strategies. What is the impact of the influencer marketing on different sectors? Therefore, the use of Influencers and the functions they can perform in all areas of the economy are essential research topics, especially a study of the impact of Influencers in different sectors. Out of numerous sectors, we have selected 7 sectors to study the impact of Influencers. Fashion & Lifestyle sector, Technology Industry, Travel & Tourism Industry, Food & Beverage sector, Healthcare sector, Finance sector and Entertainment & Gaming sector to study the impact of Influencers using different platform.

MAJOR PLATFORMS FOR INFLUENCER MARKETING: INSTAGRAM, YOUTUBE, TIKTOK, FACEBOOK

More than 2,000 global brands in 2022[1] survey it was found that around 80 percent use Instagram for influencer marketing, 56 percent of participating brands using TikTok platform for influencer marketing campaigns as per study in 2023.

As social media is where most influencer marketing efforts are conducted, choosing the right social media platform is crucial to the campaign's success. According to eMarketer with 76.7% of marketers using Instagram to collaborate with Influencers and creators, it is the most popular channel for influencer marketing. Instagram's robust return on investment (ROI) can be attributed to its popularity with influencer marketers. According to a HubSpot report, 30% of marketers get the highest return on investment for influencer marketing while using the platform. Facebook is in second place, being used by 58% of marketers. Following this, TikTok (50% of marketers use it) and YouTube (44.2% of marketers use it). While Twitter and Snapchat lagging way behind. In terms of influencer marketing ROI, YouTube and Facebook are tied, with 20% of marketers claiming that they receive the highest ROI from both platforms.

Figure 1. The most common channel used by influencers (eMarketer)

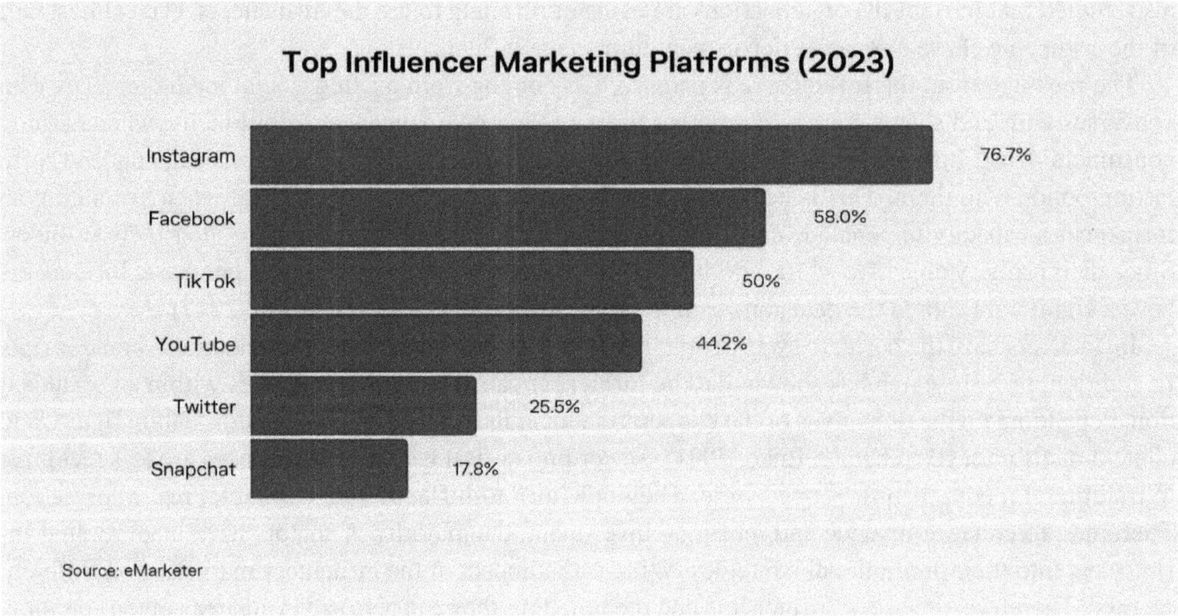

ADVANTAGES OF INFLUENCERS

1. **Authenticity -** Using influencer, a brand can create real resonance through their audience by allowing them to convey their brand message.

2. **Trust & Credibility -** Consumers are no longer as responsive to advertising as they earlier were. Consumers rely on evidence from others rather than being persuaded to buy instead. They are more eager to learn about brands. Influencers and their followers have developed a positive and respectful bond. People therefore trust their advice and ideas.
3. **Niche opportunities -** With so many interests, it's easier to find tighter niches for, ex there are thousands of models on digital platforms promoting all sorts of clothes and then there will be niches within swimwear or lingerie or plus sizes. The cost of working with a highly niched influencer might be higher but the likely return is also far higher.
4. **Relevance -** A brand can tap into a vertical market that aligns with their brand. An influencer that focuses on beauty makeup tutorials is an ideal fit for a lipstick brand but not for a car manufacturer. It helps convey the brand story in a unique way and through the lens of Influencers often depicting similar types to those of their typical audience.
5. It can create a great return on investment rather than other forms of advertising media; research has suggested as much as 11 times more. The results are often quicker too. A campaign could be turned around in less than a week with imminent results linked to a strong call to action (CTA).
6. **Boost search engine optimization (SEO) -** If an influencer is promoting a brand and sharing websites or landing pages these are powerful backlinks.
7. Influencers can be a great source for community. For ex- Marques Brownlee has over 11 million subscribers on YouTube and regular reviews different products; therefore, his impartial advice is highly valued. (www.youtube.com/user/marquesbrownlee (archived at https://perma.cc/2DYZ-AF53)).
8. **To Enhance brand visibility -** The majority of social media Influencers have millions of followers, including the 50 Influencers on Instagram with the most followers, who collectively have more than 2.5 billion. Despite the widespread use of ad blockers and the inherent mistrust of overt advertisements, influencer marketing gives firms a practical, unobtrusive method of connecting with consumers.
9. **Cost-effective & Saves Time** - The size of the audience and the particular niche are major determinants of an influencer's price. Brands now have a completely new potential to compete on social media platforms like YouTube and Instagram using a more effective and optimized strategy as a result of Influencers.
10. **Vast Posting Opportunities on Social Platforms -** Influencers are skilled at engaging with the target audience on the content they publish about any sector its products or services because they communicate with their fans almost every day.
11. **Suitable for all Industries -** Influencers tend to be subject matter experts in their respective professions, such as healthcare, sports, technology, travel, media & entertainment etc. For instance, a low-cost, optimized technique is better suited for small firms. For larger businesses, it will be smart to choose a comprehensive strategy that involves a higher expenditure to engage with celebrities or other authorized brands. The size of the audience and the particular niche have a big impact on how much an influencer cost. Brands now have a completely new potential to compete on social media platforms like YouTube and Instagram using a more effective and optimized strategy.

INDUSTRIES THAT BENEFIT FROM INFLUENCERS

Influencer marketing is very important in promotional mix strategy making for brands to differentiate, but it varies with type of sectors. Below are the important sectors that benefited majorly from influence marketing-

Fashion and Lifestyle Industry

The fashion and Lifestyle industries, which are both quite active on Instagram, stand to gain a great deal from influencer marketing. Influencers enable the fashion and lifestyle industries to relate to consumers while leveraging the power of social media and real people to create successful campaigns. By following celebrities on social media sites like Facebook, Instagram, and TikTok, customers typically become aware of the necessity for a product in the early stages of the purchasing process. Buyers also used blogs to study the things they were thinking about buying. Influencers help the fashion and lifestyle sectors by increasing brand accessibility and relatability. A successful campaign depends on promoting sales, providing prizes, and choosing the appropriate Influencers depending on the target audience and company values.

Instead of high-profile celebrities, users of various media platforms hunt for people they can relate to personally. As a result, they frequently follow these people and consume their content consistently. This led to the development of influencer marketing as many companies exploited it to their advantage to advertise products to customers in a more genuine way. Fashion Influencers are undoubtedly the most popular and followed users on the social media site Instagram, making them excellent targets for brands and companies looking to advertise their goods through a distinctive way to a specific customer base.

For instance, Dior and the influencer marketing firm Buttermilk collaborated to win the Gold Award for the Best Beauty Campaign at the 2020 Influencer Marketing Awards. The advertising campaign was

Figure 2. Beauty campaign by Dior's forever foundation
Source: https://influencermarketinghub.com/influencer-marketing-examples/

created to commemorate the debut of Dior's Forever Foundation, a collection of 67 different foundation shades.

By displaying the numerous shades offered, the advertisement aims to raise awareness of the new Dior Forever Foundation on a global scale. They also intended to highlight the product's variety by having an ambassador for each shade. Making branded material that could be reused on Dior's owned channels was another marketing goal. In the end, 67 Influencers were chosen for the campaign, and they all matched one of Dior's 67 shades. The Influencers responded by publishing one post each day for 67 days straight. The combined audience reach of the 67 Influencers was 2.66 million. Additionally, their postings generated 592K engagements and 1.85M impressions.

Technology Sector

The present digital world includes Influencers, and social media users also rely on technology or a gadget of some kind to connect. The younger generation is the perfect target market for influencer marketing of contemporary technologies. It is simple to sell products like phones, tablets, and headphones with the aid of influencer marketing. It is an excellent marketing tool since Influencers may use it to promote software and apps by showing how to utilise them. Influencers share stories about how your technology solved a problem, improved their life, or provided a unique benefit. This can lead to deeper engagement and a stronger emotional connection with the audience.

Figure 3. Microsoft's collaboration with Instagram influencer
Source: https://www.grynow.in/blog/influencer-marketing-for-tech-brands.html

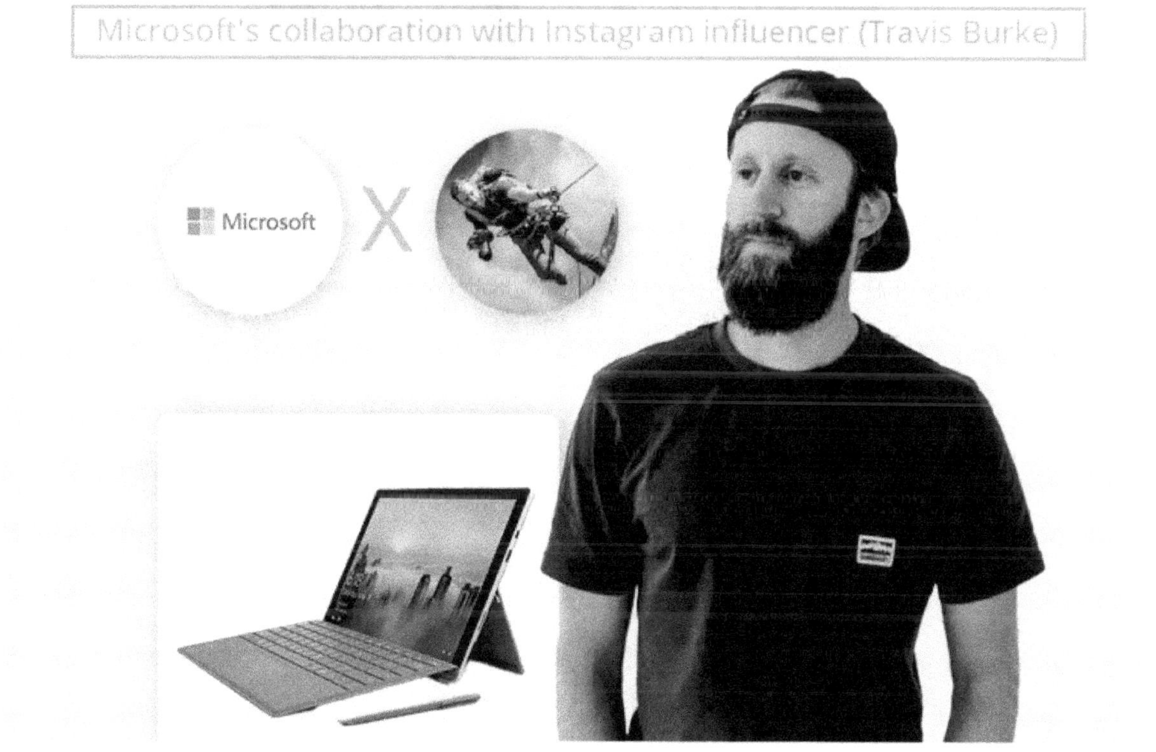

Microsoft's collaboration with Instagram influencer and adventurer, Travis Burke, perfectly illustrates this strategy. Burke used the Surface Pro 4 during his adventures and shared stories about how the device made his life easier.

Another important use of Influencers is to leverage product demonstration. Influencers can show how to use the product, explain its unique features, and highlight its benefits in a practical, easy-to-understand manner. Tech influencer Unbox Therapy (Lewis Hilsenteger) regularly demonstrates tech products on his YouTube channel. For example, when Dyson released its new V11 vacuum, Unbox Therapy created a detailed hands-on video that allowed viewers to see the product in action and understand its benefits, which boosted its appeal significantly.

Another use of Influencers in Technology sector is to engage in continuing collaboration. A single post from an influencer might not have a lasting impact. However, a continued collaboration, where the influencer repeatedly showcases the benefits of your product, can build trust and credibility over time. By carefully selecting Influencers, developing authentic relationships, and creating strategic, engaging content, tech brands can enhance their visibility, drive engagement, and ultimately, grow their customer base.

Figure 4. Lewis Hilsenteger tech influencer with unbox therapy on his YouTube channel
Source: https://www.grynow.in/blog/influencer-marketing-for-tech-brands.html

Figure 5. Samsung's #withGalaxy campaign on Instagram
Source: https://www.grynow.in/blog/influencer-marketing-for-tech-brands.html

Tech consumers appreciate aesthetics and design, so high-quality visuals should also be used in campaigning. Whether it's stunning photos of your product, or slick, well-produced videos, make sure your visuals reflect the quality and innovation of your tech brand.

Samsung's #withGalaxy campaign on Instagram is an excellent example. The campaign uses stunning images taken by users and Influencers with their Samsung Galaxy phones, emphasizing the superior camera quality and showcasing the product's capabilities through attractive visuals. By pinpointing the right creators, nurturing authentic relationships, and continuously monitoring and refining their strategy, tech brands can exploit Influencers to boost their brand visibility and customer engagement.

Travel and Tourism Sector

The Indian Travel & Tourism sector is one of the nation's fastest-growing economic sectors in India. This sector has a big impact on employment, propels regional growth, and boosts the performance of sectors that are strongly associated. The visitor exports from India's tourism and hospitality sector are predicted to reach $50.9 billion by 2028, up from $28.9 billion in 2018. In addition, it is expected that by 2028, there would be 30.5 million foreign tourists arriving in India.

One of the segments that is significantly impacted by Influencers is the travel and tourism industry. Influencers and business owners alike are increasingly interested in Instagram. Instagram stands apart from the competition because to a range of multimedia-based features like posts, stories, Live, and IGTV. It gives travel Influencers the high-resolution social look they require. Influencer marketing's predicted market size increased from just $1.7 billion in 2016 to $16.4 billion in 2022. Additionally, it is anticipated that this will increase by a further 29% to an estimated $21.1 billion in 2023[2]. Influencers are now an essential part of the industry's marketing strategy, benefiting the travel and tourism sector most due to the user-generated content (UGC) engagement rate of 50%.

Ex- With her page @travelstoriesbyus, Jinali Sutariya is currently one of the fastest growing travel Influencers in India. In order to generate engaging material that will genuinely entice people to plan a desired trip, Influencers in India are exploring ways to further use technology such as augmented reality (AR) and virtual reality (VR). She is working on this with her Instagram collaborator, Malav Jhaveri. This technology will give yet another degree of confidence for anyone considering a trip to India by enabling potential consumers to experience what a specific destination looks and feels like before they even purchase their ticket. These are some strategies for utilizing Influencers in the tourism and travel sector.

Influencers are one of the important part of the Instagram tourism ecosystem. Influencers often travel to different destinations and share photos and videos of their experiences with their followers. For example, many businesses are using Instagram to create photo and video content that showcases their destinations and attractions. This content is being used to inspire potential customers to book a trip. The most recent FIFA World Cup is a prime example of how influential travelers were able to collaborate with five-star hotels, restaurants from around the world, retail centers, and sports organizers. Influencers can also be used to promote cooperation in the travel and tourism sectors. Travel enthusiasts are constantly looking for recommendations and specialized destinations, creating chances for Influencers to market domestic travel, authentic local experiences, and wellness and health travel.

Influencers' journey stories have a significant part in bringing viewers closer to the location when they are either invited to international events or opt to travel independently. Their specialty also aids in focusing on particular marketing alliances, hence boosting revenue for all parties. Overall, the tourism industry's revival and new method of operating following the epidemic presents Influencers with a variety of unique opportunities for engagement.

Food and Beverage Sector

The food and beverage business can increase sales by using Influencers. In the modern world, when 85% of consumers believe user-generated content to be more persuasive than branded material, collaborating with Influencers who are not tied to your brand has emerged as a successful marketing tactic for the food and beverage sector. For every dollar spent on influencer advertising, restaurants and fast-food chains made $6.50, according to a 2019 study.

This illustrates the influencer marketing's potential to affect the sector's revenue. Pepsi designed limited edition packaging and the hashtag "Say It with Pepsi" in an effort to boost sales at Walgreens. They believed social media involvement would be the best marketing, even for in-store purchases, because they wanted to appeal to millennials. The goal of the campaign was to show that adding the specially packaged Pepsi emoji bottles—available only at Walgreens—to your summertime activities made them all more enjoyable.

The 200 Pepsi emojis were an example of distinctive organic content created by known Influencers, who subsequently shared it with their Millennial-era following. Original blog posts, photographs, and branded videos were among the shared materials. In order to help them have an enjoyable summer adventure, it drove the teenagers to Walgreens and Duane Reade outlets to purchase Pepsi Emoji bottles.

The effectiveness of all the content that these key Influencers had produced and shared was then examined by Pepsi. Again, they were focusing on Millennials. They chose the best-performing things and arranged for 40 secondary Influencers to promote it with their audiences. 26,000 more people clicked on the shared information as a result of the second step. Two Twitter parties honoring #SayItWithPepsi and the Pepsi Emoji bottles marked the culmination of the campaign. In the end, the Say It with Pepsi campaign generated 46 million impressions and more than 50,000 interactions with the campaign's content.

Healthcare Sector

The healthcare sector has seen significant growth in the post-Covid period. The Indian healthcare sector is one of the largest sectors in terms of both revenue & employment. The popularity of Doctor Influencers on Instagram has increased as more users turn to their Instagram feeds for reliable health People are now more conscious of their physical and emotional health than before the devastating waves of the pandemic. To aid India in maintaining its health, numerous brands have emerged to offer food and fitness programs. The popularity of Instagram healthcare Influencers has increased as more users turn to their Instagram feeds for reliable health advice and suggestions. As a result, influencer marketing for the healthcare industry has grown, and prominent Indian doctors who are Influencers have been landing partnerships with companies that provide sincere healthcare related goods and services.

Tata 1mg, a healthcare platform used influencer for its Calcium tablet Influencers like Arjun Bijlani who're Fitness athlete and posts about Fitness and Health took part in the campaign. He spoke with ease about how the 1mg product improved his way of life. The audiences were paying attention to the brand, but they were also associating their Influencers journeys with 1mg, which had a significant impact on sales and brand equity.

Digital channels are used by Influencers to tell their followers about their health issues and provide advice. Healthcare sector is in a constant state of flux, and the significance of healthcare Influencers has never been more paramount. These Influencers hold power in shaping public opinion, guiding purchasing decisions, and influencing policymakers. However, with the abundance of information available, identifying the right Influencers can be a daunting task. With the help of AI, healthcare companies can efficiently analyze data and identify the most relevant Influencers for their specific needs.

In the healthcare industry, there are several types of Influencers who play a crucial role in shaping decisions and driving change. These key players include Key Opinion Leaders (KOLs), Key Online Influencers (KOls), Digital Opinion Leaders (DOLs), and Patient Influencers.

Key Opinion Leaders (KOLs) are highly respected and influential experts in their respective medical fields. They are often physicians or researchers who are well-respected by their peers and have published extensively in their field. KOLs have the power to influence medical research, drug development, and clinical practice.

Figure 6. Tata 1mg. with Arjun Bijlani fitness athlete
Source: https://collab-deals.medium.com

Key Online Influencers (KOIs) are a new type of influencer that has arisen as a result of the growth of social media. They include bloggers, Influencers, and podcasters that have built large followings and can influence healthcare decisions through their online presence.

Digital Opinion Leaders (DOLs) are a diverse group of Influencers, including patient advocates, online communities, and disease-specific organizations. They use their influence to advocate for patients and provide support and information to those affected by a particular disease or condition.

Finally, patient influencer is an individual who frequently write or post on social media about their healthcare experiences and perspectives. They offer a unique perspective on healthcare and can provide valuable insights to healthcare companies and professionals.

Real-world examples of companies that have leveraged AI for healthcare Influencers identification:

1. Pfizer found key opinion leaders (KOLs) in the field of oncology by using machine learning (ML) and natural language processing (NLP) methods. By analyzing scientific publications, clinical trial data, and social media activity, the company was able to identify and classify KOLs based on their

expertise and influence. This approach led to more targeted engagement with KOLs and ultimately contributed to the successful launch of a new oncology product.

2. Gilead Sciences, a pharmaceutical company, used social network analysis (SNA) to identify and map the relationships between healthcare Influencers in the field of infectious diseases. By analyzing online interactions, conference attendance, and other data sources, the company was able to identify key opinion leaders and Influencers in the field. This approach helped the company to more effectively engage with KOLs and develop more targeted educational materials and marketing campaigns.
3. Spark Therapeutics, Inc., a biotech startup, used predictive analytics to identify healthcare Influencers in the field of gene therapy. By analyzing historical data on healthcare influences behaviour and preferences, the company was able to develop a model to predict which KOLs were most likely to support its products and research. This approach led to more successful collaborations with KOLs and ultimately helped to drive the company's growth and success.

AI-driven healthcare Influencers identification has proven to be a powerful tool for pharma companies looking to engage with the right experts and Influencers in their fields. By leveraging the latest AI techniques and best practices, these companies are able to effectively identify and engage with KOLs, leading to better outcomes for patients and the industry as a whole.

Finance Sector

Influencers play a powerful role in creating trust among investors. Millennials and members of Generation Z are more conscious of their personal money and actively seek out information. Influencers enables finance companies to connect with the appropriate audiences through storytelling of relatable every-day financial experiences - the questions, concerns, ideas, actions, and successes - on a human-to-human level, while leveraging the connections creators have established with their audiences to build credibility and, in the end, drive brand awareness and consideration. The finance sector is creating waves with the new and enhanced approachable tone towards bridging the gap to financial dialogues thanks to viral movements like FinTok and StockTok.

Generally, consumer require financial information on things mentioned below:

The fact that India's top Influencers have more YouTube followers than both modern broking companies like Zerodha, Groww, Upstox, and 5Paisa as well as more established ones like IIFL, Kotak Securities, ICICI Direct, and Angel Broking demonstrates their popularity. Even well-known western Influencers with thousands, or at most three to four lakhs, of followers include Anthony O'Neal, My Fab Finance,

Table 1. Different age groups with their different financial goals

Gen Z	Millennials	Gen X	Baby Boomers
Investing	Investing	Retirement	Investing
Budgeting	Saving for an emergency	Investing	Fraud ID protection
Financing large purchases	Building savings	Savings	Retirement
saving for an emergency	Budgeting	Saving for an emergency	Building savings
Building savings	Credit score management		

Figure 7. American Express with Cariss Alvarado influencer
Source: https://confluencr.com/influencer-marketing-guide-for-finance-brands/

Mr. Money Moustache, The Budgetnista, and Mrs. Dow Jones. But not even close to the ten lakh (or million) that their Indian counterparts did. Due to their rising popularity in India, top broking companies are hiring these YouTube celebrities to connect with potential investors.

Indian Influencers have benefited financially from the large subscriber count, especially those with one million or more fans. A financial influencer, like those in the other categories, has several income streams, such as Google adverts, collaborations, and partnerships, even if their videos are free to see. The combined income from all of these streams may reach lakhs. According to one estimate, the monthly amount is higher than Rs 15 lakh.

Gen Z and Millennials specifically seek for financial advice on social networks, according to a Qualtrics and Credit Karma study, which found that 56%[3] of the fintech industry is leveraging influencer marketing to their benefit. Additionally, 51% of Gen Z acknowledge taking financial advice from a stranger online, demonstrating the greater effect Influencers have on this generation.

American Express has worked with many Influencers, including Lead Amex Ambassadors, to promote its Pay It, Plan It payment plan service. Clariss Alvarado, who has more than 385K followers, was one of those Influencers.

The influencer campaign We Count on You was launched on YouTube, Facebook, Instagram, and Twitter for Ex-Tata Capital by the financial services division of the Tata Group. Through Influencers like Atul Khatri, Pranav Sapra, and Gunjan Shouts, the campaign seeks to increase consumer satisfaction.

Entertainment and Gaming Sector

India uses media and entertainment apps on mobile devices 82% of the time. Live events, animation and VFX, and online gaming are predicted to drive India's media and entertainment sector's 10.5% CAGR growth to $34.62 billion by 2025. India ranks fourth in "ICT Services Exports". The OTT, gaming, animation, and VFX sectors are predicted to drive India's Media & Entertainment sector's 10-12% CAGR growth to $55-70 Bn by 2030.

The Entertainment & gaming industry has caught onto the trend of influencer marketing. Through creating engaging content that their followers will love, gaming & entertainment Influencers help brands promote their products and services. One of the biggest, most original, and creative industries in the contemporary tech world we live in is the gaming sector. It is regarded as one of the most interesting sectors in the world due to its impact on social, technological, and entertainment improvements. Gaming Influencers in India work across a number of digital channels and have global fan bases. While some people upload quick videos to Instagram, others choose to watch long-form YouTube films.

Bollywood celebrities and Influencers collaborated fairly in 2020 to promote the movie "Dil Bechara." Influencers from diverse fields were involved in the marketing campaign for the late actor Sushant Singh Rajput's final film. It was advertised by CarryMinati, a well-known Indian YouTuber with a sizable fan base. He highlighted the movie and urged his audience to watch it in one of his videos. His genuine presentation of his adoration for Sushant Singh Rajput struck a chord with his fans.

One more famous influencer in Indian music industry was deployed to promote the song "Paani Paani" by Badshah and Jacqueline Fernandez in 2021. The song was released on the music label Saregama India's YouTube channel, which was already popular among youth. To promote this song, a brilliant marketing strategy was deployed, including an online dance challenge, "PaaniPaaniDanceChallenge." The challenge was promoted on various social media platforms, including Instagram and TikTok, where fans were asked to create and share their dance covers of the song.

With the largest penetration of gaming influencer followers among both active (25%) and heavy (33%) gamers, India stands out from the rest of the world. China and Indonesia report having a large number of followers who are gaming influencers, closely following India.

The famous "Slime" and "Kinetic Sand" toys, which swiftly became vital for any child due to their distribution by influencers on YouTube, are among the most well-known toys marketed in recent years. After being acquired by Amazon in 2014, the video game broadcasting service Twitch generated an estimated $2.3 billion in revenue in 2020 and averaged 2.84 million concurrent viewers in 2021. An example is the crazy time game by Evolution. The game was released in 2020, based on the company's successful outing with the Dream Catcher money wheel. However, the power of YouTubers quickly boosted the acceptability of crazy time by players. Various YouTubers played the game and won, showing the whole process on their channels. This attracted a significant number of viewers who subsequently turned into players of the game. Influencers promote products by sharing reviews, tutorials, and other related content, engaging millions of followers. Due to the time and money investments gamers put in, they are inclined to seek reassurance from reliable sources which are the influencers. Gaming companies use this to influence the decision-making of their target audience.

According to a survey by Sequoia India and BCG, India's gaming sector represents 1% of the overall gaming business making it less than that of the US and China. However, because to the mobile first phenomena, it is now making $1.5 billion in sales and is projected to increase to over $5 billion by 2025.

E-sports players and content producers both exist on a global scale. The various India Gaming Federation's CEO, Roland Landers, explains that "those who create content around all kinds of games—casual, card, and fantasy games—are earning money through ads and sponsorships." Some people who make content live stream it, while others make videos, and still others do both. According to a survey by EY FICCI, there were approximately 390 million online gamers in India in 2021, with 90 to 100 million of them playing every day. By 2023, it is predicted that there will be over 450 million players online.

There will probably be a significant increase of gaming influencers as a result of all of this growth. Even brand-new gamer streaming services are beginning to emerge, joining the likes of Twitch, Steam, YouTube Gaming, and other well-known ones.

MEASURE OF INFLUENCER MARKETING SUCCESS

All type of industries use engagement rate, reach and conversions to measure the effectiveness of their influencer marketing campaigns:

Rate of Engagement: The level of interaction between the audience and the content is measured by the engagement rate.

Reach: The amount of people who have viewed the material is referred to as reach.

Conversions: Conversions measure the number of people who have taken action, such as making a purchase, after seeing the content.

In 2019[4] and previous years, the emphasis on influencer marketing measurement was evenly distributed among various campaign goals, but Conversion/Sales was the least-supported factor. Conversions/

Figure 8. Measure of influencer marketing success
Source: https://influencermarketinghub.com/influencer-marketing-benchmark-report/

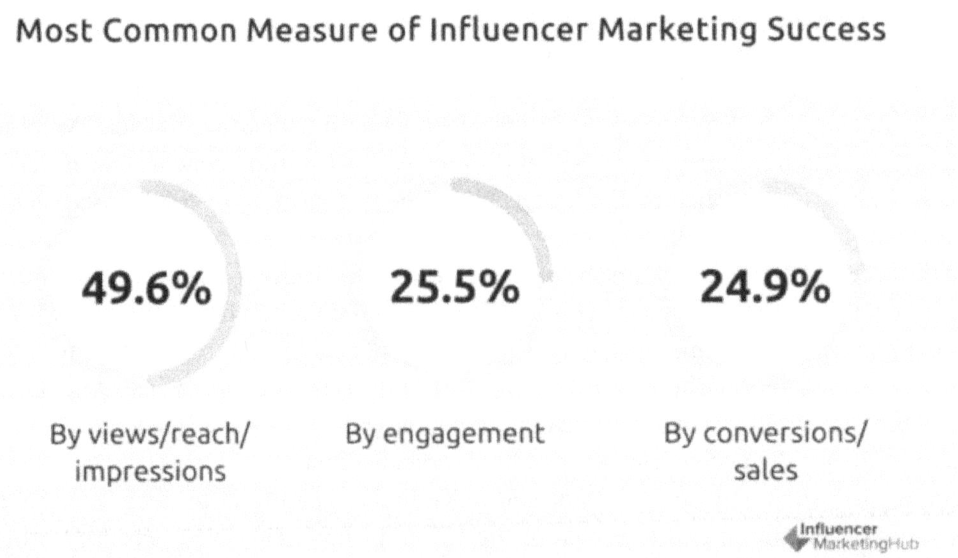

Figure 9. Framework of measuring success of an influencer marketing

Sales, on the other hand, began to take a clear, indisputable lead in 2020, and this trend persisted in 2021 and 2022.

But this year, 49.6% of our respondents said they assess an influencer marketing campaign's effectiveness based on views, reach, and impressions, 25.5% on engagement or clicks, and only 24.9% on conversions and sales. This is a significant change from last year, when 24.2% of respondents were interested in views/reach/impression and 42.3% said that the best way to evaluate a campaign was by how many conversions or sales it generated.

Though measurement of success of a marketing campaign is measured at later stage, but during the whole campaign we need to check whether each step is aligned with the goal we want to achieve. As each step need planning and evaluation based on the goal. Right from the Research & planning to defining the Goal & budget we allocate to the campaign.

Defining the campaign based on the target customer to deciding upon the platform to be used and outreach the influencers. Creating the content based on the message we want to give, tracking the campaign execution. Till most important evaluation and optimization, each step needs planning and measurement in order to make a campaign successful.

THE FUTURE OF INFLUENCER MARKETING

With the changing environment of marketing in India Influencer marketing has come up as a powerful marketing strategy. Influencer marketing has come a long way, how it impacts the consumer behavior. Impact of influencer marketing along with the study of live shopping trends and its impact has been discussed below.

The influencer marketing market in India was estimated to be worth about 12 billion Indian rupees as of 2022[5]. Over the next five years, it is anticipated to increase at a compound annual growth rate of 25%. The market value of related sector was projected to reach 28 billion Indian rupees by 2026. As in 2022, almost 55 million urban Indians were direct users of various influencers. Companies that use influencer marketing are more likely to be successful, particularly if they can build a strong and lasting relationship with creators. There will undoubtedly be significant changes to the influencer marketing sector as new technologies are developed and attitudes shift.

INFLUENCER MARKETING AND BRAND

In India, influencer marketing is highly effective because followers regard influencers as credible advisors. One of the key elements influencing the rising impact of influencer marketing is the change in customer behavior. Traditional advertising methods like print or television ads are attracting consumers' attention have fade. Influencers may now directly sell things through their posts and stories, bridging the gap between influence and purchase, which has increased the potential of influencer marketing. People are increasingly turning to social media and online content for guidance, inspiration, and information. Influencers have gained their fans' respect and credibility as well as a loyal and active following by consistently creating informative and approachable content.

LIVE SHOPPING TREND

With brands and influencers using live streams to highlight products, respond to viewer questions, and encourage in-person purchases, India is adopting the international trend of live shopping. By providing customers with a novel and dynamic way to search for, engage with, and purchase goods, this trend is altering the face of e-commerce. Live shopping combines the power of video content, real-time engagement, and social effects to provide a dynamic and engaging buying experience that appeals to a variety of consumers. Live shopping is expected to become more and more prevalent in the retail industry during the next few days.

CONCLUSION

Influencers are recognized by their sizable, committed, and loyal social media audience. They are regarded as experts in their fields, and their followers frequently hold them in high regard in the industries we choose, including fashion & lifestyle, technology, travel & tourism, food & beverage, healthcare, finance, and entertainment & gaming. Due to a number of factors, using influencers as a potent advertising strategy has become obvious. First of all, influencers have developed a devoted and active fan base that allows marketers to use their authority and influence. Second, influencers are adept at producing relatable, authentic content that connects with their audience and amplifies corporate messages. Last but not least, influencers provide a way for firms to target certain, specialized parts of the population and hone their marketing strategies. Different industries can capitalize on this trust, establish credibility, and legitimately market their goods or services by collaborating with influencers. Greater engagement rates, greater conversion rates, and improved brand sentiment demonstrate the benefit. According to research, Instagram is the most widely utilized platform by influencers, followed by Facebook, TikTok, Twitter, Snapchat, and YouTube.

REFERENCES

Abidin, C. (2016). Visibility labour: Engaging with Influencers' fashion brands and# OOTD advertorial campaigns on Instagram. *Media International Australia, Incorporating Culture & Policy*, *161*(1), 86–100. doi:10.1177/1329878X16665177

Bakker, D. (2018). Conceptualising influencer marketing. *Journal of Emerging Trends in Marketing and Management, 1*(1), 79-87.

Bastrygina, T., & Lim, W. M. (2023). Foundations of consumer engagement with social media influencers. *International Journal of Web Based Communities*, *19*(2-3), 222–242. doi:10.1504/IJWBC.2023.131410

Borchers, N. S., & Enke, N. (2021). Managing strategic influencer communication: A systematic overview on emerging planning, organization, and controlling routines. *Public Relations Review*, *47*(3), 102041. doi:10.1016/j.pubrev.2021.102041

Colliander, J., & Erlandsson, S. (2015). The blog and the bountiful: Exploring the effects of disguised product placement on blogs that are revealed by a third party. *Journal of Marketing Communications*, *21*(2), 110–124. doi:10.1080/13527266.2012.730543

Dhanesh, G. S., & Duthler, G. (2019). Relationship management through social media influencers: Effects of followers' awareness of paid endorsement. *Public Relations Review*, *45*(3), 101765. doi:10.1016/j.pubrev.2019.03.002

Evans, N. J., Phua, J., Lim, J., & Jun, H. (2017). Disclosing Instagram influencer advertising: The effects of disclosure language on advertising recognition, attitudes, and behavioral intent. *Journal of Interactive Advertising*, *17*(2), 138–149. doi:10.1080/15252019.2017.1366885

Ge, J., & Gretzel, U. (2018). Emoji rhetoric: A social media influencer perspective. *Journal of Marketing Management*, *34*(15–16), 1272–1295. doi:10.1080/0267257X.2018.1483960

Kapitan, S., & Silvera, D. H. (2016). From digital media influencers to celebrity endorsers: Attributions drive endorser effectiveness. *Marketing Letters*, *27*(3), 553–567. doi:10.100711002-015-9363-0

Lin, H. C., Bruning, P. F., & Swarna, H. (2018). Using online opinion leaders to promote the hedonic and utilitarian value of products and services. *Business Horizons*, *61*(3), 431–442. doi:10.1016/j.bushor.2018.01.010

Lou, C., & Yuan, S. (2019). Influencer marketing: How message value and credibility affect consumer trust of branded content on social media. *Journal of Interactive Advertising*, *19*(1), 58–73. doi:10.1080/15252019.2018.1533501

Magno, F., & Cassia, F. (2018). The impact of social media influencers in tourism. *Anatolia*, *29*(2).

Mediakix. (2019). *The CMO's Guide to Influencer Marketing*. Mediakix.

Paço, A., & Oliveira, S. (2017). Influence marketing in the fashion and beauty industry. *Estudos em Comunicação*, *1*(25), 119–136. doi:10.20287/ec.n25.v1.a07

Pöyry, E., Reinikainen, H., & Luoma-Aho, V. (2022). The role of social media influencers in public health communication: Case COVID-19 pandemic. *International Journal of Strategic Communication, 16*(3), 469–484. doi:10.1080/1553118X.2022.2042694

Shan, Y., Chen, K. J., & Lin, J. S. (2020). When social media influencers endorse brands: The effects of self-influencer congruence, parasocial identification, and perceived endorser motive. *International Journal of Advertising, 39*(5), 590–610. doi:10.1080/02650487.2019.1678322

Sundermann, G., & Raabe, T. (2019). Strategic communication through social media influencers: Current state of research and desiderata. *International Journal of Strategic Communication, 13*(4), 278–300. doi:10.1080/1553118X.2019.1618306

Ye, G., Hudders, L., De Jans, S., & De Veirman, M. (2021). The value of influencer marketing for business: A bibliometric analysis and managerial implications. *Journal of Advertising, 50*(2), 160–178. doi:10.1080/00913367.2020.1857888

ADDITIONAL READING

De Veirman, M., Cauberghe, V., & Hudders, L. (2017). Marketing through Instagram influencers: The impact of number of followers and product divergence on brand attitude. *International Journal of Advertising, 36*(5), 798–828. doi:10.1080/02650487.2017.1348035

Djafarova, E., & Rushworth, C. (2017). Exploring the credibility of online celebrities' Instagram profiles in influencing the purchase decisions of young female users. *Computers in Human Behavior, 68*, 1–7. doi:10.1016/j.chb.2016.11.009

Fornell, C., & Larcker, D. F. (1981). Evaluating structural equation models with unobservable variables and measurement error. *JMR, Journal of Marketing Research, 18*(1), 39–50. doi:10.1177/002224378101800104

Freberg, K., Graham, K., McGaughey, K., & Freberg, L. A. (2011). Who are the social media influencers? A study of public perceptions of personality. *Public Relations Review, 37*(1), 90–92. doi:10.1016/j.pubrev.2010.11.001

Joshi, Y., Lim, W. M., Jagani, K., & Kumar, S. (2023). Social media influencer marketing: Foundations, trends, and ways forward. *Electronic Commerce Research*, 1–55. doi:10.100710660-023-09719-z

Ye, G., Hudders, L., De Jans, S., & De Veirman, M. (2021). The Value of Influencer Marketing for Business: A Bibliometric Analysis and Managerial Implications. *Journal of Advertising, 50*(2), 160–178. doi:10.1080/00913367.2020.1857888

KEY TERMS AND DEFINITIONS

Baby Boomers: Baby Boomers refers to the people of the period when population increased very rapidly. As on 2023, age group of people between the ages of 57-75 years in U.S.

Digital Channels: Digital channels are platforms which are used to send the information to target audiences in digital form (Websites, Mobile apps etc). These majorly include social media, search engines and websites.

Gen X: This generation is successor of baby boomers and are predecessor of Gen-Y (Millennial's) Generation X is a group of people between the ages of 41-56 years, as in 2023.

Gen Z: Generation Z is a group of people between the ages of 16 and 26, as in 2023. Gen Z is known for working, shopping, dating, and making friends online. This generation is highly active on internet and social media.

Influencer Marketing: In this marketing strategy, companies collaborate with a influencer having varied number of followers. Here companies co-create content with influencer for communication with his followers for promotion of a product or services.

Macro-Influencers: An influencer with followers count in between 1,00,000 to 10,00,000 is called macro influencer.

Meso-Influencer: An influencer with followers count in between 10,000 to 1,00,000 is called meso influencer.

Micro-Influencer: An influencer with followers count in between 1,000 to 10,000 is called micro influencer.

Millennial: Gen Y, or Millennials, are a group of people between the ages of 25 and 40 years, as in 2023. This generation falls between Gen X and Gen Y.

ROI: ROI stands for return on investment. This is the calculation of the revenue generated against the money spent on digital marketing.

ENDNOTES

1. https://www.mckinsey.com/featured-insights/mckinsey-explainers/what-is-influencer-marketing#/
2. https://www.thehansindia.com/hans/opinion/news-analysis/travel-tourism-makes-a-come-back-784440
3. https://timesofindia.indiatimes.com/blogs/voices/how-is-the-fintech-industry-using-influencer-marketing-to-their-advantage/
4. https://influencermarketinghub.com/influencer-marketing-benchmark-report/
5. https://www.statista.com/statistics/1294803/india-influencer-marketing-industry-value/

Chapter 3
How Influencers Can Leverage Performance in Business

Albérico Travassos Rosário
https://orcid.org/0000-0003-4793-4110
GOVCOPP, IADE, Universidade Europeia, Portugal

ABSTRACT

Influencers can indeed use their influence to boost business performance. Influencers and businesses can work together to market a company's goods or services to their subscriber base. Influencers can significantly affect sales and performance by endorsing goods or services and including their affiliate links in their content. Influencers and businesses can collaborate to produce sponsored content, in which the influencers create interesting and genuine posts or videos showcasing the brand's goods or services. By doing so, businesses can connect with the influencer's audience and use their power and inventive storytelling abilities. Businesses can benefit from this tactic by expanding their reach, increasing engagement, and boosting traffic to their websites and physical stores. For influencers to continue earning the trust of their audience, they must always be genuine and transparent in their collaborations. Influencers can influence business performance, so this study aims to review the bibliometrics literature using the Scopus database.

INTRODUCTION

With the increasing competition in global marketplaces, marketers are fighting for attention by placing advertisements everywhere. They are developing marketing techniques based on the best ways to influence modern consumers. Influencer marketing has emerged as one way of achieving this goal (Tanwar et al., 2022). This technique enables businesses to use "normal people" with a large online presence to drive brand messages and promote their products and services. In this case, influencers are paid to create posts and publish them on their social media platforms, thus creating brand awareness and recommending specific products and services to their audiences (Edwards et al., 2022). For this marketing technique to work, the influencers must seamlessly include the sponsored products or services in their editorial content and encourage their audiences to engage with the content (Amaro & Scheepers, 2023). The ef-

DOI: 10.4018/979-8-3693-0551-5.ch003

fectiveness of influencer marketing is often based on these opinion leaders' relatability with their target audiences. For instance, unlike celebrities, influencers are more accessible and live a life their audiences relate to or admire. They often share most aspects of their lives with their audiences, thus building loyal and highly-engaged followers. This enables them to promote products, services, or places, often based on their experiences and interests. As a result, influencers can help improve business performance.

The influencer marketing industry has seen significant growth in recent years. For instance, Tanwar et al. (2022) found that this sector has grown by US$3.2 billion since 2019, with more than 60 influencer marketing agencies entering the market within a year. In addition, influencer marketing has been associated with a higher return on investment (ROI) than traditional marketing strategies. For example, Johansen and Guldvik (2017) indicate that influencer marketing ROI is 11 times higher than other forms of traditional digital marketing. Similarly, Tanwar et al.'s (2022) research suggests that the ROI for every $1 spent on influencer marketing is $5.78. Moreover, the researchers suggest that 80% of marketers find influencer marketing effective, while 60% expected an increase in influencer marketing in 2019. Similarly, Johansen and Guldvik (2017) indicate that 82% of consumers are more likely to purchase products or services based on influencer advice. In addition, 92% of consumers nowadays trust recommendations from people more than brands, contributing to the success of influencer marketing and electronic word of mouth (e-WOM). Besides, most people find influencers more knowledgeable, credible, and believable. Collaborating with influencers helps marketing managers leverage their reach and audience through valuable content to sell and promote products and services to targeted audiences more likely to purchase. This study aims to review the bibliometrics literature using the Scopus database to demonstrate how influencers can improve business performance.

The article is structured as follows: The introduction tells us about the topic and its importance, as well as the objective of the investigation. In the methodology approach of the methodological process, in the distribution of publications, we analyze their nature from a theoretical perspective; they embroider the subjects and results found in the articles, and, finally, the main conclusions, theoretical implications, and future lines of investigation are presented.

METHODOLOGICAL APPROACH

The researcher employed a systematic bibliometric literature review (LRSB) methodology to identify relevant resources and integrate findings. The LRSB method was selected since it enables researchers to identify, collect, and analyze a vast amount of scholarly literature on how influencers can improve business performance. It encourages the researcher to employ rigorous search strategies, including predefined search terms and inclusion/exclusion criteria. In addition, LRSB helps identify emerging research trends, key concepts, and topics within a specific field or research area, thus providing valuable insights into the evolution of knowledge and developments in the particular field of study.

The search process began with identifying the database. In this study, the Scopus database was selected based on Baas et al. (2020) description of the database as a trustworthy platform for accessing high-quality, curated content.

The LRSB greatly aided in filtering the most pertinent and high-quality sources for analysis and reporting. As a result, this methodology can be effectively employed to decipher and map the accumulated scientific knowledge and emerging variations within a well-established subject (Rosário, et al., 2023; Rosário & Dias, 2023; Rosário & Dias, 2022; Rosário, et al., 2021).

Table 1. Process of systematic LRSB

Fase	Step	Description
Exploration	Step 1	formulating the research problem
	Step 2	searching for appropriate literature
	Step 3	critical appraisal of the selected studies
	Step 4	data synthesis from individual sources
Interpretation	Step 5	reporting findings and recommendations
Communication	Step 6	presentation of the LRSB report

Source: Rosário and Dias (2023); Rosário and Dias (2022)

Hence, bibliometric analysis holds the potential to illuminate its progress and integration in business settings, while also identifying potential hurdles. The LRSB review process encompasses three distinctive phases and six sequential steps (see Table 1), as proposed by Rosário, et al., 2023; Rosário and Dias (2023); Rosário and Dias (2022); Rosário, et al. (2021).

Throughout this investigation, we utilized the esteemed Scopus database, renowned for its remarkable reputation in the scientific and academic realm, as our primary source of indexed scholarly documents. However, it is important to note that our study is constrained by its exclusive reliance on the Scopus decomposition database, thereby neglecting other valuable scientific and academic resources. Our comprehensive literature search was conducted exclusively on peer-reviewed scientific and academic documents published between 2019 and 2023.

The researcher used the keyword "influencer" for the initial search, identifying 7,522 documents. However, most of these sources did not match the research topic, prompting the researcher to add the keyword "performance" to narrow the document results to the most relevant. As a result, the number of documents found was reduced to 598. The search was further limited to the subject area "Business, Management, and Accounting," further limiting the documents found to 170. Filtering the search to publications published between 2019- August 2023 reduced the results to 110 (N=110), which were integrated into the final reporting Table 2.

Finally, content and theme analysis techniques were used to identify, analyze and report the various documents as proposed by Rosário and Dias (2023); Rosário (2021); Rosário and Dias (2022); Rosário et al. (2021).

Table 2. Screening methodology

Database Scopus	Screening	Publications
Meta-search	keyword: Influencer	7522
First Inclusion Criterion	keyword: Influencer, Performance	598
Eligibility criteria	keyword: Influencer, Performance Limit to Subject Area: Business, Management, and Accounting	170
Final Screening	keyword: Influencer, Performance Limit to Subject Area: Business, Management, and Accounting Publication year: 2019-August 2023	110

Source: own elaboration

The 110 scientific and/or academic documents indexed in Scopus are later analyzed in a narrative and bibliometric way to deepen the content and possible derivation of common themes that directly respond to the research question (Rosário & Dias, 2023; Rosário, 2021; Rosário & Dias, 2022; Rosário et al., 2021). Of the 110 selected documents, 85 Articles; 11 are Books chapter; 6 Conference papers; 3 Reviews; 3 are Conference reviews; and 2 Books.

PUBLICATION DISTRIBUTION

Peer-reviewed articles on how influencers can leverage performance in business 2019 - August 2023. The year 2021 had the highest number of peer-reviewed publications on the subject, reaching 29. Figure 1 summarizes the peer-reviewed literature published until August 2023. The publications were sorted out as follows: The publications were sorted out as follows: Springer Proceedings In Business And Economics (6); Developments In Marketing Science Proceedings Of The Academy Of Marketing Science (6); Journal Of Business Research (3); International Journal Of Scientific And Technology Research (3); Industrial Marketing Management 3; with 2 publications (Management For Professionals 2

Journal Of Digital And Social Media Marketing; Journal Of Cleaner Production; International Journal Of Advertising; Business Horizons; Benchmarking; Asia Pacific Journal Of Marketing And Logistics); and the remaining publications with 1.

In Table 3 we analyze the Scimago Journal & Country Rank (SJR), which registers the Journal Of Marketing in the position of best quartile and H index per publication, which is the most cited publication with 10,800 (SJR), Q1 and H Index 268.

There is a total of 43 publications in Q1, 16 in Q2 and 10 in Q3 and 7 in Q4. Publications from best quartile Q1 represent 49% of the publications on titles; best quartile Q2 represents 18%, best quartile Q3 represents 11%, and best Q4 represents 13% of each of the titles of 87 publications. Finally, 11 publications still do not have data available, representing 13% of publications. As shown in Table 3, the significant majority of publications are in the best quartile Q.

Figure 1. Documents by year

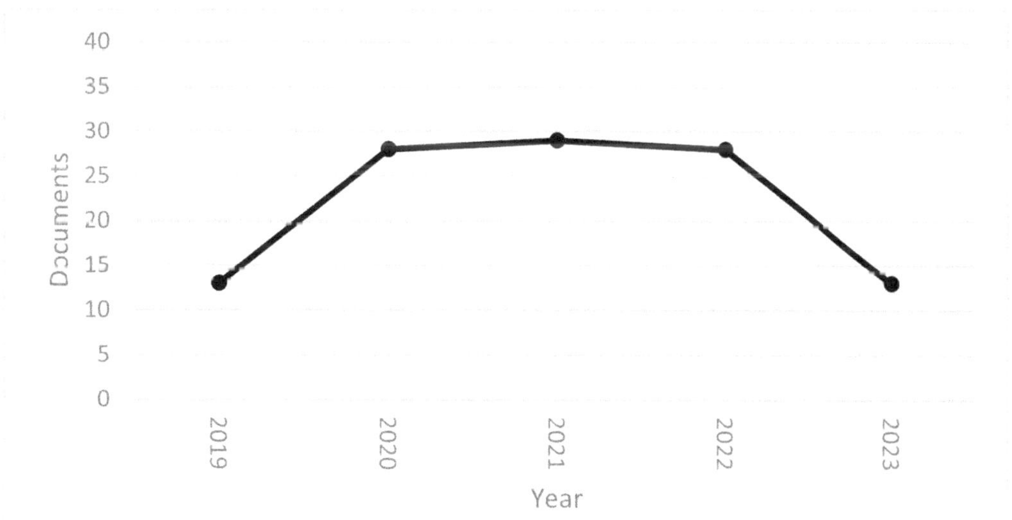

Table 3. Scimago journal and country rank impact factor

Title	SJR	Best Quartile	H Index
Journal Of Marketing	10,800	Q1	268
Strategic Management Journal	8,500	Q1	318
Developments In Marketing Science Proceedings Of The Academy Of Marketing Science	6,250	Q1	194
Academy Of Management Perspectives	4,840	Q1	148
Journal Of Interactive Marketing	4,090	Q1	120
Journal Of Human Resources	3,340	Q1	118
Journal Of Business Research	2,900	Q1	236
Information And Management	2,690	Q1	182
Omega United Kingdom	2,680	Q1	160
Industrial Marketing Management	2,660	Q1	161
Technological Forecasting And Social Change	2,640	Q1	155
International Journal Of Operations And Production Management	2,620	Q1	155
Journal Of Advertising	2,610	Q1	126
Journal Of Interactive Advertising	2,510	Q1	15
International Journal Of Contemporary Hospitality Management	2,500	Q1	113
Business Horizons	2,480	Q1	106
Gender Work And Organization	2,240	Q1	88
International Journal Of Advertising	2,080	Q1	74
Current Issues In Tourism	2,060	Q1	94
Journal Of Cleaner Production	1,980	Q1	268
Journal Of Services Marketing	1,580	Q1	119
Electronic Markets	1,550	Q1	49
Public Relations Review	1,430	Q1	96
Journal Of Product And Brand Management	1,430	Q1	97
Journal Of Air Transport Management	1,400	Q1	88
Management Review Quarterly	1,330	Q1	27
International Journal Of Tourism Research	1,300	Q1	75
Journal Of Enterprise Information Management	1,240	Q1	75
Benchmarking	1,190	Q1	74
Journal Of Economic Behavior And Organization	1,180	Q1	129
Financial Innovation	1,170	Q1	36
Journal Of Brand Management	1,090	Q1	62
International Journal Of Bank Marketing	1,090	Q2	96
International Transactions In Operational Research	1,060	Q1	61
IEEE Transactions On Engineering Management	1,000	Q1	103
Asia Pacific Journal Of Marketing And Logistics	0,990	Q1	57
Business Process Management Journal	0,920	Q1	90

continued on the following page

Table 3. Continued

Title	SJR	Best Quartile	H Index
Utilities Policy	0,910	Q1	59
Gender In Management	0,910	Q1	61
Journal Of Business And Industrial Marketing	0,850	Q1	78
Journal Of Competitiveness	0,800	Q1	32
Foundations And Trends In Entrepreneurship	0,790	Q1	36
Journal Of Asia Business Studies	0,740	Q1	27
Big Data Research	0,710	Q2	33
Corporate Communications	0,650	Q2	66
Competitiveness Review	0,650	Q2	34
Publications	0,630	Q1	21
European Journal Of Training And Development	0,620	Q2	65
Journal Of Modelling In Management	0,580	Q2	37
Measuring Business Excellence	0,560	Q2	49
Information Technology And Management	0,530	Q2	42
Administrative Sciences	0,530	Q2	28
Cogent Business And Management	0,520	Q2	32
Corporate Reputation Review	0,460	Q2	69
Industrial And Commercial Training	0,440	Q2	38
Worldwide Hospitality And Tourism Themes	0,420	Q2	28
Uncertain Supply Chain Management	0,350	Q3	23
International Journal Of Knowledge Management	0,350	Q2	27
Information Resources Management Journal	0,330	Q2	45
International Journal Of Business Excellence	0,320	Q3	23
Journal Of Transport And Supply Chain Management	0,310	Q3	8
Recherche Et Applications En Marketing	0,300	Q3	12
South African Journal Of Business Management	0,280	Q3	20
Innovative Marketing	0,250	Q3	19
Acrn Journal Of Finance And Risk Perspectives	0,240	Q3	5
International Journal Of Value Chain Management	0,230	Q3	15
International Journal Of Technology Marketing	0,230	Q3	15
Asian Journal Of Business And Accounting	0,220	Q3	15
South Asian Journal Of Business And Management Cases	0,200	Q4	8
International Journal Of Business Performance Management	0,180	Q4	23
International Journal Of Electronic Finance	0,150	Q4	20
Fashion Style And Popular Culture	0,150	Q2	4
Eurasian Studies In Business And Economics	0,130	Q4	8
Contributions To Management Science	0,130	Q4	18

continued on the following page

Table 3. Continued

Title	SJR	Best Quartile	H Index
Revue Internationale De Droit Economique	0,120	Q4	8
Journal Of Applied Business Research	0,120	Q4	29
International Journal Of Scientific And Technology Research	0	-*	26
International Journal Of Recent Technology And Engineering	0	-*	27
Springer Proceedings In Business And Economics	-*	-*	-*
Management For Professionals	-*	-*	-*
Journal Of Digital And Social Media Marketing	-*	-*	-*
Where Authentic Leaders Dare From Professional Competence To Inspiring Leadership	-*	-*	-*
Routledge Companion To Advertising And Promotional Culture Second Edition	-*	-*	-*
Proceedings Of The International Conference On Electronic Business Iceb	-*	-*	-*
In Search Of Business Models In Social Entrepreneurship Concepts And Cases	-*	-*	-*
Digital Business	-*	-*	-*
Atas Da Conferencia Da Associacao Portuguesa De Sistemas De Informação	-*	-*	-*

Note: *data not available.
Source: own elaboration

The subject areas covered by the 110 scientific and/or academic documents were: Limited to Business, Management and Accounting (111); Social Sciences (27); Economics, Econometrics and Finance (23); Decision Sciences (14); Computer Science (14); Engineering (10); Environmental Science (6); Psychology (3); Energy (2); Materials Science (1); and Chemical Engineering (1).

The most cited article was "Advancing social media driven sales research: Establishing conceptual foundations for B-to-B social selling," by Ancillai et al. (2022) with 80 citations published in Industrial Marketing Management 2,660 (SJR), the best quartile (Q1) and with an H index (161), this article he has

Figure 2. Evolution of citations between ≤2013 and 2023

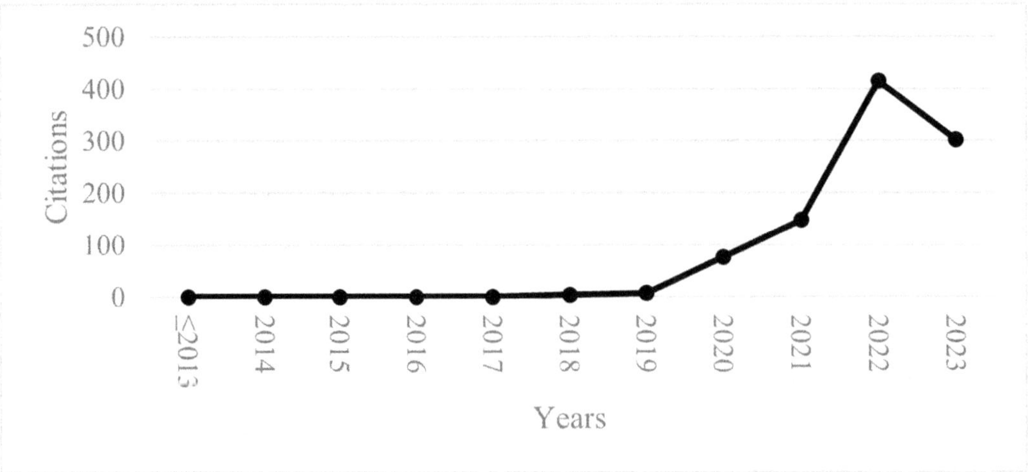

Figure 3. A network of all keywords

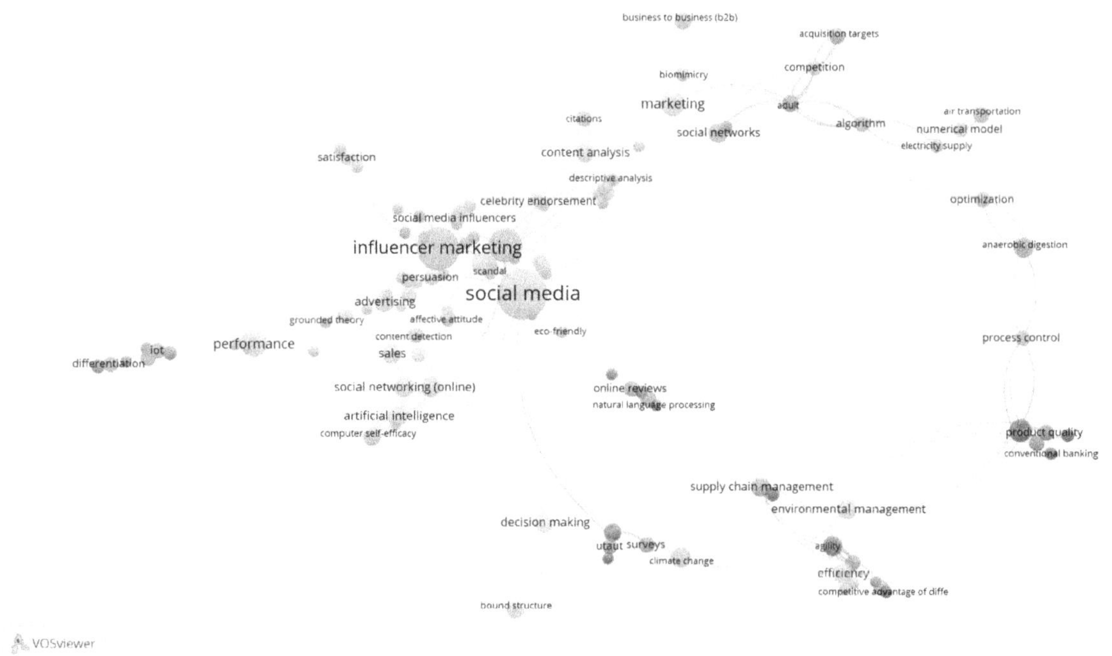

“research approach and conceptualize social selling and its key facets based on a systematic literature review and a field study involving thought leading social selling professionals.”

In Figure 2, we can analyze the evolution of citations of the documents published until August 2023. The number of citations shows a positive net growth with R2 of 61% for the period ≤2013-2023, with 2022 reaching 414 citations.

The h-index was used to ascertain the productivity and impact of the published work based on the largest number of articles included that had at least the same number of citations. Of the documents considered for the h-index, 16 have been cited at least 16 times.

Citations of all scientific and/or academic documents from the period ≤2013 to August 2023, with a total of 949 citations of the 110 documents 43 were not cited. The 74 self-citations of documents in the period ≤2013 to August 2023.

This investigation is based on a bibliometric study that was carried out to research and discover indicators of the evolution and dynamics of scientific and/or academic information in published articles based on the main keywords (Figure 3).

The results were extracted from VOSviewe, a scientific software, which aims to find and identify the main search keywords “Influencer, Performance.”

To conduct this study, a survey was carried out based on scientific and/or academic documents addressing how influencers can leverage performance in Business. Figure 4 allows examining the linked keywords with the aim of highlighting the keywords network that appears together/linked in each scientific article, leading to the recognition of the studied topics and the identification of trends in future research. Finally, in Figure 5, a profusion of bibliographic coupling is presented, including a unit of analysis of the cited references.

Figure 4. A network of linked keywords

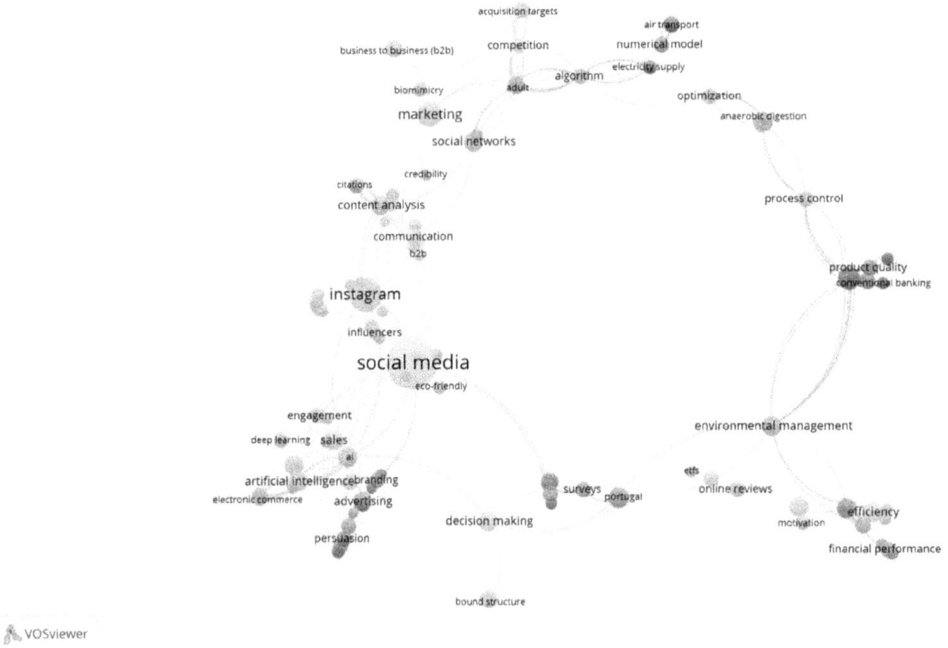

Figure 5. A network of bibliographic coupling

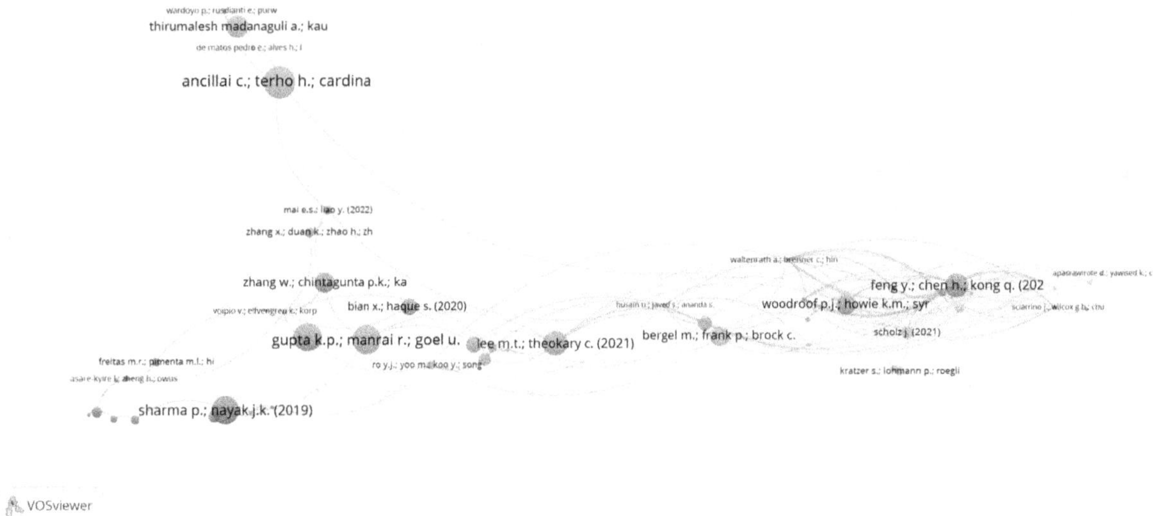

THEORETICAL PERSPECTIVES

Leveraging influencers and incorporating influencer marketing into a brand's marketing techniques can help improve business performance. In the modern digital world, influencers can influence consumer purchasing decisions and attitudes toward a brand or product (Falasca & Helgesson, 2021). This is because influencers spend time creating content relatable to their target audiences, which helps build trust and establish their status as opinion leaders (Amyx et al., 2020; Guo et al., 2021).

Thus, collaborating with influencers through sponsored content or affiliate programs can help businesses improve brand awareness and increase sales (Asare-Kyire et al., 2019). This section explores the definition and role of influencers and influencer marketing in business, how they can be leveraged to improve performance, and their potential challenges.

Defining Influencer Marketing and Influencers

An influencer is an individual with a significant following and influence over a specific audience. Alshahrani et al. (2021) define influencers as content creators who produce valuable and creative content on social media platforms to attract a substantial network of people. These individuals usually publish content to showcase their expertise, knowledge, and personality in a particular field or niche. In addition, influencers build trans-parasocial relations, which Hudders and Lou (2023, p.152) describe as a "more interactive, reciprocal, and co-created relationship" between influences and their followers. Influencers usually expose their private lives, engage their followers, and respond to their comments and direct messages, which helps establish intimate bonds (Guo et al., 2023).

As a result, most followers perceive influencers as their friends and often have a positive bias toward them and their recommendations. Moreover, most followers consider influencers as a source of inspiration since they inform them about new trends, brands, and products (Zhu & Westphal, 2021; Yu & de Barnier, 2022). For example, a fashion blogger typically shares fashion-related content, which may include new trendy styles or brands. The consistency makes them trustworthy, and they are often considered experts in their specific niche. The trust, high engagement, and position influencers have as experts enable them to provide value to marketers (Balestra et al., 2023). In this case, marketers can collaborate with influencers to create sponsored content, which helps improve brand awareness or promote products and services. This collaboration allows marketers to leverage influencers' authority and reach to communicate with potential customers.

Influencer marketing is the marketing strategy used to collaborate with influencers to promote brands, products, and services to their audiences. Jain (2021, p.77) defines influencer marketing as "a process of discovering and engaging individuals who have influence over a certain target demographic or media in order to be part of a brand's campaign to improve reach, sales, or engagement?" Businesses use tactics such as monetary rewards, gifts, and travel sponsorships to motivate influencers to endorse their products and services, thus leveraging their large follower base (Feng et al., 2021).

Marketers leverage influencers' credibility, expertise, and reach to create authentic, engaging content that resonates with their followers. Influencer marketing is more effective when businesses prioritize identifying and establishing partnerships with influencers whose audience aligns with their target market (Gray, 2022; Sciarrino et al., 2020). Collaborating with influencers provides a more organic and personalized approach to marketing by leveraging the influence and trust that influencers have established with their audience. As a result, influencer marketing is increasingly becoming more popular and effective than traditional marketing strategies since it incorporates relationship marketing approaches.

Role of Influencers in Business

Influencers allow companies to improve their business performance by enhancing brand awareness or increasing sales. Embracing influencer marketing enables businesses to leverage their large follower base, thus providing an opportunity to expand the brand's audience reach (Apasrawirote et al., 2022; Harrison et al., 2023). In addition, influencers have loyal followers who are more likely to follow their recommendations and guidance. In this aspect, influencers can use sponsored content to encourage followers to purchase certain products or services from an endorsed brand (Balasubramanian, 2022). This technique can help increase the company's revenues and expand its customer base.

Brand Advocacy and Promotion

Influencers act as brand advocates by promoting products, services, or brands to their audience. Influencer endorsements serve as social proof, with their audiences perceiving the endorsements as a means of validating a brand's quality and reliability (Chen et al., 2019). Moreover, influencers create awareness and generate brand interest through authentic content and personal recommendations (Dam & Pillai, 2021; de Bruin et al., 2021).

Some influencers, such as those in the makeup industry, often provide in-depth reviews and demonstrations of products or services they have used or experienced (Husain et al., 2021). In this case, they give opinions on a brand and explain the benefits of using its products, thus effectively influencing purchasing decisions.

Content Creation and Storytelling

Influencers are skilled content creators who understand how to engage their audience through captivating storytelling. Hudders and Lou (2023) explain that influencers have the talent to seamlessly include sponsored products or services in their editorial content in ways that resonates with their target audiences. They create relatable and authentic content that may consist of stories about their personal experiences, anecdotes, and narratives about the brand and its products (Feng et al., 2021). These storytelling and content creation abilities enable businesses to leverage their creativity for brand collaborations.

Targeted Marketing and Audience Segmentation

Influencers have the advantage of having a niche-specific audience. As a result, they adequately understand their audience's interests, preferences, and demographics (Freitas et al., 2020). This allows businesses to target their marketing efforts more precisely by partnering with influencers who align with their target market (Arduini & Paoloni, 2020). For example, a bank can collaborate with influencers sharing content around finances and investments (Illia et al., 2021). Businesses can achieve higher engagement and better results by selecting influencers whose audience matches their ideal customer profile.

Product Feedback and Market Insights

Collaborating with influencers provides businesses with valuable feedback and insights about their products or services. Influencers can share their experiences and provide feedback on the brand's offerings, helping companies to understand their strengths, weaknesses, and areas for improvement (Bühlmann et al., 2021).

In addition, companies can monitor engagement, comments, and questions posed by the influencer's followers regarding the promoted products and services (Chen et al., 2022; Carmona et al., 2020). Such valuable information can help understand customer sentiments and address concerns or issues.

Leveraging Key Performance Metrics

Influencer marketing is characterized by multiple key metrics that provide valuable insights into the performance and impact of influencer campaigns.

Tracking and analyzing these metrics can enable businesses to make data-driven decisions that help improve their influencer marketing strategies and enhance overall business performance.

Reach and Impressions

Reach and impressions are crucial metrics that help companies assess the potential audience size reached by collaborating with an influencer. Reach represents the number of unique individuals exposed to an influencer's content, while impressions measure the number of times the content has been viewed (Gräve, 2019). By monitoring these metrics, businesses can assess the effectiveness of their campaign in terms of brand visibility and awareness.

Engagement Rate

The engagement rate measures the level of interaction and engagement an influencer's content receives from their audience. It includes metrics such as likes, comments, shares, and saves (Chinnasamy & Tahrim, 2019; Monica, 2019). A higher engagement rate indicates that the content resonates well with the audience since interesting content is more likely to provoke reactions and attitudes toward the influencer marketing campaign (Gräve, 2019). Therefore, businesses can analyze engagement rates to assess the level of audience interest and involvement with the brand. This helps in understanding the relevance and effectiveness of the influencer's content in driving audience engagement.

Conversion Rate

Conversion rate measures the percentage of individuals who take a desired action after being exposed to an influencer's content. It could include purchasing promoted products, signing up for a newsletter, or downloading an app (Chu et al., 2022). Tracking conversion rates helps businesses determine the effectiveness of influencer campaigns in driving conversions and achieving their desired goals (Zeren & Gökdağlı, 2020; Wilson & Arroyo, 2022). This metric helps identify which influencers or content types successfully drive tangible results.

Return on Investment (ROI)

ROI measures the profitability and returns generated from an influencer campaign compared to the investment. Marketing research shows that influencer marketing has higher ROI than traditional marketing techniques (Tanwar et al., 2022). The ROI metric considers the costs of collaborating with influencers, such as fees, products, or services provided (Jat et al., 2023). Thus, calculating the ROI enable businesses to assess the financial impact of their influencer marketing efforts and make informed decisions on budget allocation and campaign optimization.

Benefits of Using Influencers to Improve Business Performance

Marketing managers can leverage influencers to improve business performance. For instance, influencer marketing allows businesses to expand their reach and access a loyal fanbase built by the influencers using valuable content. They can target this audience to promote a brand, products, and services (Wardoyo et al., 2019; Jhang-Li & Liou, 2023). Moreover, collaborating with influencers enable the business to track and analyze audience feedback on certain offers or campaign messaging. Monitoring this feedback can help modify marketing strategies and improve products or services to match customer needs (Thirumalesh Madanaguli et al., 2021). This section of the literature review incorporates findings from multiple studies to illustrate how leveraging influencers can result in improved business outcomes.

Customer Engagement Value

Collaborating with influencers can aid businesses' efforts to generate customer engagement value. This is because influencers prioritize creating authentic connections and fostering meaningful interactions with their audience, which drive engagement (Abo ElHamd et al., 2022). Through their relatable content, engaging storytelling, and trusted recommendations, influencers can captivate their followers.

As a result, their audiences are more likely to perceive a promoted product or service as a genuine endorsement (Apasrawirote et al., 2022; Kaleka & Morgan, 2019). Moreover, influencers often share their experiences and opinions, which resonate with their audience, creating a sense of trust and credibility. As a result, Bergel et al. (2019) explain that their followers are more likely to engage with content or show interest in promoted brands, thus enabling brands to extend their reach to potential new customers. Therefore, partnering with influencers can help businesses tap into influencers' existing networks, increasing brand exposure and opening up opportunities for customer engagement and interaction on a larger scale.

One unique characteristic of influencer marketing is its approach to fostering conversations and interactions with the audience. Influencers engage with their followers through comments, direct messages, and social media interactions, which helps create a sense of community and strengthen the relationship between them and their audience (Chinnasamy & Tahrim, 2019; Monica, 2019). Businesses can participate in these conversations by collaborating with influencers to answer customer inquiries and gather feedback (Khaleeli et al., 2021).

Customers will more likely feel heard and valued when their favourite influencer and the brand actively respond to their comments or messages, leading to increased customer engagement (Waltenrath et al., 2022). In addition, these conversations and interactions allow followers to share their experiences, reviews, or creative content featuring the brand, thus igniting a wave of customer engagement.

Social Selling

Social selling is the process of leveraging social media platforms to engage with potential customers, build relationships, and ultimately drive sales. Most internet users perceive influencers as trusted authorities within their respective niches, thus valuing their opinions and recommendations (Ancillai et al., 2019). In this case, an influencer's endorsement of a product or service conveys trust and credibility. Businesses can leverage this trust to promote their offerings (Kahr et al., 2021; Kratzer et al., 2019). Moreover, influencers' recommendations and endorsements help build brand credibility, making it more likely for their audience to consider purchasing the products or services (Guha & Majumdar, 2021).

This is especially effective when influencers frequently share their experiences and opinions on products or services they have used or tried (Lin & Chang, 2020). The knowledge enables them to provide in-depth reviews, showcase product features, and highlight the benefits. These influencers' product recommendations and reviews create a level of authenticity and relatability that can drive social selling.

Customer Purchase Intentions and Decisions

Influencers are trusted figures with a loyal following that values their perspectives about products, services, brands, and trends. As a result, their content can significantly influence customer purchase intentions since the followers are more likely to consider and trust the influencer's endorsement (Yeo et al., 2022). Johansen and Guldvik (2017, p.27) define purchase intentions as "an individual's conscious plan to make an effort to purchase a brand." According to these authors, the influencers' impacts on consumers' purchase decisions can be explained using the AIDA model. It incorporates four key stages, i) an advertisement is published which attracts the audience (A-attraction), ii) it arouses consumer interests (I), iii) the message encourages the consumer to desire the promoted product or service (D), and iv) it encourages them to take a certain action (A). Content shared by influencers helps improve consumer knowledge about a product, leading to the desire to purchase and use the products or services (Li et al., 2023; Singh et al., 2021).

Since influencers are often considered "friends" due to their relatability, their followers are more likely to buy products or services they constantly use. This creates an opportunity for marketing managers to leverage this inclination to promote a brand's offerings and improve its performance.

Emotional Brand Trust and Attachment

Influencers build their following based on authenticity and relatability by sharing their personal experiences, values, and preferences. As a result, they create a sense of psychological closeness with their followers, which helps build trust and emotional attachment (Bian & Haque, 2020). Zhang and Choi (2022) explain that influencers' ability to share personal opinions on social media about issues affecting society and willingness to engage with audiences through comments helps create emotional connections, enhancing their persuasiveness. Emotional attachment is directly connected to people's consumption behaviors (Lee & Theokary, 2021; Zhang et al., 2021). For instance, emotionally involved consumers have stronger brand loyalty, which benefits the company. Most followers perceive the influencer as trusted, making them more open to establishing emotional brand trust (Vani et al., 2020). In addition, their storytelling capabilities enable them to create and share content that engages and captivates their audience. These stories evoke emotions, experiences, and aspirations (Rach, 2023). As a result, businesses that leverage influencers' storytelling as a marketing approach have higher chances of establishing an emotional brand attachment and trust with the audience. This can increase sales and help create and maintain long-term relationships with new and existing customers.

Corporate Reputation

Incorporating influencer marketing into a company's overall marketing strategy can help improve its corporate reputation. Influencers can be brand advocates, promoting and endorsing a company's values, products, or services (Soltani et al., 2023; Ro et al., 2021). Their positive endorsement and association with the brand can significantly impact corporate reputation. For example, when influencers publicly support a company and its offerings, their followers perceive the brand positively (Sudaryanto et al., 2022; Lamola, 2022). Moreover, influencers often position themselves as experts or thought leaders within their niche, allowing marketing managers to leverage their knowledge and expertise to enhance a brand's reputation (Zhao & Zhang, 2019). By collaborating with respected and recognized influencers for their expertise, brands can tap into their credibility and association (Ribbink et al., 2022). Besides, influencers are known for their authenticity and the trust they have built with their audience. As a result, their partnerships with different companies are often perceived as an authentic endorsement, thus fostering trust in the company and improving its reputation.

In times of crisis or reputation challenges, influencers can help businesses mitigate the damage and regain consumer trust. For instance, they can lend their support, provide positive testimonials, or share their personal experiences to counteract negative perceptions. (Ahmed et al., 2021). Their influential reach and credibility can contribute to rebuilding and strengthening the corporate reputation during challenging times. In addition, companies can improve their reputation by leveraging influencers to promote social causes, sustainability, and corporate social responsibility (CSR) communication (Stone, 2020; Dalla-Pria & Rodríguez-de-Dios, 2022). They can partner with influencers who align with their values and CSR initiatives to amplify their efforts and enhance their reputation as socially responsible entities (Rickaby et al., 2020). This approach can help influence consumers' perceptions and attitudes towards the brand and its offers through the generated positive associations. However, it is crucial for marketing managers to thoroughly screen the influencers before initiating the partnership to ensure that they achieve the desired goals (Borchers et al., 2022). For instance, if the goal is to promote CSR initiatives, the influencers selected should be known for advocating for sustainability or its related concepts. This approach helps avoid potential backlash and campaign failure.

Affiliate Marketing

Affiliate marketing involves a partnership program in which brands pay influencers based on their sales. Syrdal et al. (2023) describe it as a performance-based approach that enables companies to trace a sale to a specific influencer, ensuring they only pay for results. As a result, affiliate marketing with influencers provides a cost-effective advertising model for businesses (Mohr, 2019). Instead of paying upfront for traditional advertising campaigns, companies pay influencers a commission based on the sales or conversions generated through their affiliate links. According to Mangio and Di Domenico (2022), affiliate marketing is one of the main forms of digital marketing, generating up to 15% of global digital media revenues. Influencers often specialize in specific niches or industries, attracting followers with similar interests. Businesses can collaborate with influencers in their industries whose followers align with the brand's target market, thus ensuring that their marketing efforts are highly targeted and relevant (Pandey & Chawla, 2019; Presler, 2022). In this regard, influencers can help businesses connect with their ideal customer base, increasing the chances of attracting qualified leads and improving conversion rates. This targeted marketing approach saves businesses time and resources by focusing on the right audience, thus maximizing their ROI.

Consumer Brand Attitudes

Brand attitudes can influence consumer behavior, purchasing decisions, and brand loyalty. For instance, positive brand attitudes increase customers' likelihood of considering, choosing, and advocating for a brand (Nafees et al., 2021). In addition, consumers with positive brand attitudes are more likely to engage with the brand and share positive experiences, contributing to customer retention, word-of-mouth marketing, and long-term business growth (Mai & Liao, 2022; De Bernardi & Azucar, 2020). Influencers can influence consumer brand attitudes through authentic content and genuine recommendations. This approach is especially effective if the influencers' recommendations are considered unbiased and reliable, which helps build consumer trust in a brand (Pattnaik & Tripathy, 2022). In addition, influencers create content that resonates with their audience on a personal level, thus building authenticity and relatability (Horning, 2020; Scholz, 2021). The real-life experiences, stories, and use cases incorporated in their content make the brand more relatable to the audience. This relatability helps consumers form positive brand attitudes as they see the brand aligning with their values, lifestyle, or aspirations, which increases the likelihood of creating stronger brand affinity and loyalty.

Entering Foreign Marketplaces

Businesses can leverage influencers to enter targeted foreign markets. Influencers in foreign markets possess in-depth knowledge of local consumer preferences, cultural nuances, and market trends, which can help gain valuable insights and better understand the target market (Wang, 2023). In addition, influencers can guide adapting marketing strategies, product localization, and understanding of consumer behavior (Zhang et al., 2020; Smith, 2019). This localized expertise helps businesses make informed decisions and tailor their approach to the specific foreign market, increasing the chances of success (Voipio et al., 2020). Moreover, influencers have established audiences in foreign markets, allowing businesses to access a ready-made customer base. Collaborating with influencers with a significant following and influence within the target market will enable firms to establish a presence, generate brand awareness, and gain traction. As a result, they can introduce their brand and products to the local audience quickly.

Further, consumers in different regions worldwide have varying information consumption and communication styles. For example, the use of slang influences language use in different countries (Lee & Theokary, 2021). Therefore, brands targeting new markets must understand these differences and leverage localized content and messaging. Influencer marketing provides an effective tool for creating localized content that aligns with the target market's preferences and cultural context (Dall Jensen et al., 2019; de Matos Pedro et al., 2020). Marketing managers can engage influence to adapt the brand's messaging, storytelling, and visuals to ensure they resonate with the local audience, thus facilitating deep connections with target consumers (Singh & Kottath, 2022). Finally, partnering with influencers in foreign markets helps leverage their influence to generate positive word-of-mouth and social proof (Doratiotto et al., 2023). When influencers share their positive experiences with the brand, their followers are likelier to trust and consider the brand when purchasing. This social proof helps build brand credibility and accelerates business performance in foreign markets.

Considerations When Selecting an Influencer for Collaboration

The effectiveness of an influencer marketing campaign hugely requires selecting the most appropriate influencers whose values, styles, and personal brand match the company's. For instance, a fashion brand's influencer marketing campaign is more likely to generate higher ROI if featured influencers create fashion content (Brewster & Sklar, 2022). This is because such influencers provide targeted audiences, which increases the likelihood of influencing the audience's purchasing intentions and brand attitudes. This section explores the various factors marketing managers must consider before partnering with an influencer.

Influencer Transparency

Influencer transparency determines their openness and honesty in content creation and brand partnerships. The ongoing advocacy for disclosures in sponsored content drives the need to assess influencers' transparency (Woodroof et al., 2020). Consumers are increasingly demanding that influencers inform them when products or services in their content are sponsored. De Cicco et al. (20211) indicate that consumers respond negatively to disguised commercial intent. As a result, the authors encourage influencer marketers and marketing managers to embrace prominent disclosures, which increases ad recognition and perceived transparency. Besides, transparency builds trust and ensures the influencer's recommendations and endorsements are genuine and authentic (Drenten et al., 2020). Therefore, brands should look for influencers who disclose their sponsored or paid content, indicating transparency to their audience.

Influencer Credibility

Influencer credibility refers to the trustworthiness and expertise of the influencer within their niche or industry. Evaluate an influencer's credibility by considering their knowledge, experience, and reputation (Wiedmann & von Mettenheim, 2020). Followers are more likely to take advice from influencers who have established themselves as experts or thought leaders in their respective fields. In this regard, marketing managers should assess an influencer's track record of delivering valuable content and engaging with their audience meaningfully (Gupta et al., 2019; Dutta et al., 2021). Collaborating with credible influencers enhances the brand's credibility, as their endorsement lends authenticity and authority to the promoted products or services.

Influencer Reach and Authenticity

An influencer's reach and authenticity can significantly impact the outcomes of the influencer marketing campaign. These aspects can be evaluated through metrics such as follower count, engagement rate, and demographics to ensure alignment with the target market (Sewpersadh, 2020). For instance, influencers with a higher follower base are likelier to have a greater reach, meaning that the promoted brand, products, or services are more likely to be seen by a larger audience (Shen et al., 2022; Schmid & Dowling, 2022). In addition, influencers with genuine connections with their followers create authentic, relatable content, increasing engagement (Brewster & Sklar, 2022). Thus, collaborating with influencers with both reach and authenticity helps ensure the brand message reaches the right audience and resonates with them at a personal level.

Challenges of Using Influencers to Improve Business Performance

Despite the opportunities and benefits of using influencers in digital marketing strategies, influencer marketing poses various challenges which hinder adoption and lower outcomes. This section integrates findings from multiple studies to identify and explain common challenges associated with influencer marketing.

Compliance and Disclosure

Adhering to advertising regulations and disclosure guidelines when working with influencers can be complex. For instance, De Cicco et al. (20211) acknowledge the importance of disclosure in building transparency and positive consumer behavioral response. However, the stud also notes that ad disclosures can have the opposite effect by causing resistance, leading to negative consumer attitudes and reducing their behavioral intentions to purchase from the brand or share the content. Ad disclosures' positive and potentially negative impacts create uncertainties, which can discourage influencers and brands from disclosing the partnership (Saternus et al., 2022). However, some countries have advertising regulations to ensure transparency and protect consumers from deceptive practices (Tzoulia, 2019; Sharma & Nayak, 2019). Failure to comply with these regulations can lead to legal issues, and they may face penalties and fines. In addition, non-compliance can erode consumer trust and damage the brand's reputation.

Identifying the Right Influencers

Identifying influencers for a marketing campaign can be daunting. The process requires thorough research and evaluation to ensure values, audience demographics, and content style alignment. However, the influencer landscape is vast and diverse with influencers specializing in various niches, industries, and content types (Gil-Quintana & Vida de León, 2021). This diversity makes it challenging to identify influencers who align perfectly with the brand's values, target audience, and messaging. In addition, influencers have their values, interests, and personal brand identities, which may not align with the brand's mission, message, and values (McMullan, 2023; Momani, 2021). Furthermore, aligning audience demographics can be challenging as it requires a detailed analysis of follower demographics, engagement rates, and other relevant metrics (Provance et al., 2022). Understanding the influencer's audience and ensuring it aligns with the target market is crucial for effective communication and achieving desired business outcomes. Consequently, finding influencers whose personal brands and content genuinely resonate with the brand's identity requires extensive research and evaluation.

Maintaining Influencer Authenticity

Balancing brand messaging and preserving the influencer's authenticity can be challenging. Influencers have unique voices, personal experiences, and genuine opinions, which help attract and engage their audience (Lascity, 2023). Consequently, businesses collaborating with influencers may face the challenge of ensuring that the brand messaging is effectively communicated while allowing the influencer to maintain their authentic voice and content style (Choobchain et al., 2019; Cicala & Zhang, 2020). Overly controlling the content or diluting the influencer's unique voice can lead to a lack of credibility and audience disengagement. When the content feels scripted or excessively promotional, it can erode the audience's trust in the influencer and the brand (Aleixo et al., 2021). Therefore, the established partnership between the influencer and a brand must respect their creativity and unique approach to content creation (Dutta et al., 2020). Therefore, businesses must balance providing guidance and creative direction while allowing the influencer the freedom to express their creativity and maintain their unique style.

CONCLUSION

Influencer marketing involves partnering with social media influencers to leverage their reach and audience to convey a brand's message or promote products and services. Influencers often publish authentic, relatable content on various social media platforms, which helps them build a targeted, loyal audience. In addition, they engage with their followers and share personal stories and experiences, which help create a sense of closeness and emotional attachment. Consequently, their endorsements, recommendations, and reviews are often considered trustworthy and can influence purchasing decisions. Therefore, incorporating influencer marketing into a company's marketing strategy can help improve business performance and enhance its competitive edge. However, achieving this goal requires marketing professionals to monitor and track key performance metrics, including reach, impressions, engagement and conversion rates, and ROI. These metrics help assess the effectiveness of an influencer marketing campaign by providing critical insights such as the number of people reached through a specific post, the rate of engagement through likes, comments, and shares, and the financial outcomes of the campaign.

Influencer marketing presents various benefits and opportunities to improve a company's performance. For instance, collaborating with influencers can help generate customer engagement value and facilitate social selling. Influencers are skilled storytellers who prioritize engaging with their audiences to build trust and emotional connections. As a result, they often create opportunities for their followers to share experiences and provide opinions and unique perspectives regarding brands and their products and services. As a result, businesses partnering with influencers can leverage this opportunity to gather data on exceptional customer feedback, which can be used to improve their offers or branding strategies. In addition, influencers can shape consumer decision-making through in-depth reviews and unbiased opinions. For example, an influencer can publish content showcasing a product's benefits and potential drawbacks, which helps consumers make informed purchasing decisions. Modern consumers prefer peer recommendations over company-generated promotional messages. Thus, it has become increasingly important for businesses to collaborate with influencers whose branding, values, and content align with theirs.

Despite the benefits of leveraging influencers to improve business performance, influencer marketing faces multiple challenges which undermine its effectiveness. For instance, some companies struggle with adhering to advertising regulations and disclosure guidelines. This challenge can cause reputational damage and result in negative financial impacts. In addition, identifying the right influencers whose content styles, self-branding, values, and messaging align with a brand's can be challenging. Most influencers establish their strong personal brands through authentic content and interactions, which may not always match a company's marketing approach. Therefore, brands partnering with influencers must find ways to contribute to sponsored content creation without undermining their authenticity and relatability while also complying with appropriate regulations and guidelines.

The rise of influencers has had a significant impact on business performance, both in theory and practice. Here are some of the main theoretical and practical implications of how influencers can leverage business performance: (i) Influencers have the ability to reach large audiences through their social media platforms. By partnering with influencers, businesses can tap into their established following and gain exposure to a wider range of potential customers. This increased reach can lead to higher brand awareness and visibility; (ii) Influencers often have a loyal and engaged fan base that trusts their recommendations. When an influencer promotes a product or service, it can lend credibility and authenticity to the brand. This trust can positively impact consumers' perceptions and increase their likelihood of engaging with the business; with a niche or target audience that aligns with their content and brand. This allows businesses to strategically choose influencers who cater to their desired customer segment. By partnering with influencers with a similar target audience, businesses can ensure their marketing efforts are directed toward a relevant and interested group of potential customers; (iii) they have the ability to engage with their audience on a personal level, creating a sense of community and fostering interaction. By leveraging influencers, businesses can encourage customer engagement, such as comments, likes, shares, and direct interactions with the brand. This can increase brand loyalty, customer satisfaction, and long-term customer relationships; (iV) Influencer marketing allows businesses to track and measure the impact of their collaborations. With the help of analytics tools and tracking systems, businesses can monitor metrics such as reach, engagement, conversions, and sales attributed to influencer campaigns. This data-driven approach enables businesses to evaluate their influencer partnerships' return on investment (ROI) and make informed decisions for future marketing strategies. Influencers have transformed the marketing landscape, providing businesses with new avenues to connect with consumers and drive business performance. Businesses can tap into their reach, credibility, and engagement by strategically leveraging influencers to enhance brand visibility, target specific audiences, and achieve measurable results.

In the future, researchers may explore several lines of research on how influencers can leverage business performance. Here are some potential areas of focus: (i) Current research primarily focuses on short-term outcomes such as immediate sales or brand awareness. Future studies may investigate the long-term effects of influencer marketing on business performance. This could involve examining customer loyalty, repeat purchases, and the sustainability of influencer-driven growth; (ii) Developing robust models to attribute business outcomes to influencer marketing efforts will be crucial. Researchers may explore advanced statistical and machine learning techniques to accurately measure the contribution of influencers to sales, customer acquisition, and brand equity. This would help businesses allocate resources more effectively and optimize their influencer marketing strategies; (iii) The ethical implications of influencer marketing are gaining prominence. Future research may delve into the ethical challenges associated with influencer endorsements, disclosure practices, and the potential for deceptive marketing practices. Understanding the ethical dimensions of influencer marketing will help shape industry guidelines and best practices. Overall, future research on how influencers can leverage business performance will likely encompass a broader scope, accounting for long-term effects, advanced measurement techniques, industry-specific considerations, ethical aspects, and the evolving landscape of influencer marketing.

ACKNOWLEDGMENT

I want to express gratitude to the Editor and the Arbitrators. They offered extremely valuable suggestions or improvements. The GOVCOPP Research Center of the University of Aveiro supported the author.

REFERENCES

Abo ElHamd, E., Shamma, H., Saleh, M., & Elkhodary, E. (2022). Customer engagement value: Process, limitations and future research. *Journal of Modelling in Management, 17*(4), 1144–1176. doi:10.1108/JM2-12-2020-0319

Ahmed, R. R., Streimikiene, D., & Zheng, X. (2021). The impact of proactive environmental strategy on competitive and sustainable development of organizations. *Journal of Competitiveness, 13*(4), 5–24. doi:10.7441/joc.2021.04.01

Aleixo, A. M., Leal, S., & Azeiteiro, U. M. (2021). Higher education students' perceptions of sustainable development in Portugal. *Journal of Cleaner Production, 327*, 129429. Advance online publication. doi:10.1016/j.jclepro.2021.129429

Alshahrani, M., Zhu, F., Mekouar, S., Alghamdi, M. Y., & Liu, S. (2021). Identification of top-K influencers based on upper confidence bound and local structure. *Big Data Research, 25*, 100208. Advance online publication. doi:10.1016/j.bdr.2021.100208

Amaro, L., & Scheepers, C. B. (2023). Exploring the nexus between microlevel and contextual influencers on women leaders' paradox mindset. *Gender in Management, 38*(1), 36–56. doi:10.1108/GM-11-2021-0335

Amyx, D., Alford, B., Zmich, L. J., Amyx, J., Mertz, B., & Sumlin, C. (2020). The study of different factors affecting salesperson deviance: An abstract. In *Marketing Opportunities and Challenges in a Changing Global Marketplace: Proceedings of the 2019 Academy of Marketing Science (AMS) Annual Conference* (pp. 113-114). Springer International Publishing. 10.1007/978-3-030-39165-2_47

Ancillai, C., Terho, H., Cardinali, S., & Pascucci, F. (2019). Advancing social media driven sales research: Establishing conceptual foundations for B-to-B social selling. *Industrial Marketing Management, 82*, 293–308. doi:10.1016/j.indmarman.2019.01.002

Apasrawirote, D., Yawised, K., Chatrangsan, M., & Muneesawang, P. (2022). Short-form video content (SVC) engagement and marketing capabilities. *Asian Journal of Business and Accounting, 15*(2), 221–246. doi:10.22452/ajba.vol15no2.8

Arduini, S., & Paoloni, P. (2020). The IT strategy in the luxury sector: The case of a fashion company. *Springer Proceedings in Business and Economics*, 211-226. 10.1007/978-3-030-46874-3_12

Asare-Kyire, L., Zheng, H., & Owusu, A. (2019). An empirical examination of the influencers of the premature decline of African clusters: Evidence from textile clusters in Ghana. *South African Journal of Business Management, 50*(1). Advance online publication. doi:10.4102ajbm.v50i1.318

Baas, J., Schotten, M., Plume, A., Côté, G., & Karimi, R. (2020). Scopus as a curated, high-quality bibliometric data source for academic research in quantitative science studies. *Quantitative Science Studies*, *1*(1), 377–386. doi:10.1162/qss_a_00019

Balasubramanian, S. (2022). A review of the pre-merger performance of select public sector banks in India using key performance indicators. *Springer Proceedings in Business and Economics*, 73-86. 10.1007/978-981-19-4892-3_5

Balestra, S., Sallin, A., & Wolter, S. C. (2023). High-ability influencers? the heterogeneous effects of gifted classmates. *The Journal of Human Resources*, *58*(2), 633–665. doi:10.3368/jhr.58.4.0920-11170R1

Bergel, M., Frank, P., & Brock, C. (2019). The role of customer engagement facets on the formation of attitude, loyalty and price perception. *Journal of Services Marketing*, *31*(7), 890–903. doi:10.1108/JSM-01-2019-0024

Bian, X., & Haque, S. (2020). Counterfeit versus original patronage: Do emotional brand attachment, brand involvement, and past experience matter? *Journal of Brand Management*, *27*(4), 438–451. doi:10.105741262-020-00189-4

Borchers, N. S., Hagelstein, J., & Beckert, J. (2022). Are many too much? examining the effects of multiple influencer endorsements from a persuasion knowledge model perspective. *International Journal of Advertising*, *41*(6), 974–996. doi:10.1080/02650487.2022.2054163

Brewster, M. L., & Sklar, M. (2022). 'Brand, community, lifestyle': Fashioning an authentic, body positive influencer brand on Instagram. *Fashion, Style & Popular Culture*, *9*(4), 501–521. doi:10.1386/fspc_00158_1

Bühlmann, C. H., Mickan, B. S., Tait, S., Renton, M., & Bahri, P. A. (2021). Lactic acid from mixed food wastes at a commercial biogas facility: Effect of feedstock and process conditions. *Journal of Cleaner Production*, *284*, 125243. Advance online publication. doi:10.1016/j.jclepro.2020.125243

Carmona, J., Delcoure, N., & Fernandez, F. H. (2020). Social media sentiment, tariffs, and international equity pricing. *International Journal of Electronic Finance*, *10*(1-2), 93–115. doi:10.1504/IJEF.2020.110298

Chen, J., Frankwick, G. L., & Zhang, Z. (2022). *Adopting artificial intelligence to manage a turbulent environment: An abstract*. doi:10.1007/978-3-030-89883-0_61

Chen, J., Tsao, S., & Chyou, J. (2019). Investigating the key factor of virtual personal brand in e-commerce: A case study of "myhomes". *Proceedings of the International Conference on Electronic Business (ICEB)*, 263-271. Retrieved from www.scopus.com

Chinnasamy, S., & Tahrim, A. M. (2019). New media and social influencer engagement on lifestyle and political content. *International Journal of Recent Technology and Engineering*, *8*(3), 3526–3541. doi:10.35940/ijrte.C5274.098319

Choobchain, S., Momtaz, A. M., & Farhadian, H. (2019). Gender differences of farmers in conflict with climate change. *International Journal of Scientific and Technology Research*, *8*(7), 359–363. www.scopus.com

Chu, M., Zhou, G., & Wu, W. (2022). *Data envelopment analysis on relative efficiency assessment and improvement: Evidence from Chinese bank branches*. doi:10.1007/978-3-030-94036-2_9

Cicala, J., & Zhang, Z. (2020). *Does technological self-efficacy decrease new salesperson job insecurity: An abstract*. doi:10.1007/978-3-030-39165-2_110

Dall Jensen, R., Ravn, S., & Krogh Christensen, M. (2019). Identification and development of talent in surgery: A scoping study across the performance domains of surgery, sport, and music. *European Journal of Training and Development*, *43*(3-4), 272–305. doi:10.1108/EJTD-07-2018-0070

Dalla-Pria, L., & Rodríguez-de-Dios, I. (2022). CSR communication on social media: The impact of source and framing on message credibility, corporate reputation and WOM. *Corporate Communications*, *27*(3), 543–557. doi:10.1108/CCIJ-09-2021-0097

Dam, L. B., & Pillai, D. (2021). Crafting virtual community of indigenous entrepreneurs: Case in social entrepreneurship. *South Asian Journal of Business and Management Cases*, *10*(1), 111–120. doi:10.1177/2277977921991916

De Bernardi, P., & Azucar, D. (2020). *The role of universities in harnessing entrepreneurial opportunities*. Retrieved from www.scopus.com doi:10.1007/978-3-030-33502-1_2

de Bruin, L., Roberts-Lombard, M., & de Meyer-Heydenrych, C. (2021). The interrelationship between internal marketing, employee perceived quality and customer satisfaction–a conventional banking perspective. *Cogent Business and Management*, *8*(1), 1872887. Advance online publication. doi:10.1080/23311975.2021.1872887

De Cicco, R., Iacobucci, S., & Pagliaro, S. (2021). The effect of influencer–product fit on advertising recognition and the role of an enhanced disclosure in increasing sponsorship transparency. *International Journal of Advertising*, *40*(5), 733–759. doi:10.1080/02650487.2020.1801198

de Matos Pedro, E., Alves, H., & Leitão, J. (2020). Assessing the citations of articles on intellectual capital: What are the "influencers"? *International Journal of Knowledge Management*, *16*(2), 30–51. doi:10.4018/IJKM.2020040103

Doratiotto, K., Vidal Vieira, J. G., da Silva, L. E., & Fávero, L. P. (2023). Evaluating logistics outsourcing: A survey conducted with Brazilian industries. *Benchmarking*, *30*(3), 788–810. doi:10.1108/BIJ-06-2021-0341

Drenten, J., Gurrieri, L., & Tyler, M. (2020). Sexualized labor in digital culture: Instagram influencers, porn chic and the monetization of attention. *Gender, Work and Organization*, *27*(1), 41–66. doi:10.1111/gwao.12354

Dutta, G., Kumar, R., Sindhwani, R., & Singh, R. K. (2020). Digital transformation priorities of India's discrete manufacturing SMEs – a conceptual study in perspective of industry 4.0. *Competitiveness Review*, *30*(3), 289–314. doi:10.1108/CR-03-2019-0031

Dutta, K., Sharma, K., & Goyal, T. (2021). Customer's digital advocacy: The impact of reviews and influencers in building trust for tourism and hospitality services. *Worldwide Hospitality and Tourism Themes*, *13*(2), 260–274. doi:10.1108/WHATT-09-2020-0123

Edwards, J., Miles, M. P., D'Alessandro, S., & Frost, M. (2022). Linking B2B sales performance to entrepreneurial self-efficacy, entrepreneurial selling actions. *Journal of Business Research*, *142*, 585–593. doi:10.1016/j.jbusres.2021.12.074

Falasca, K., & Helgesson, E. (2021). Revolving around roles – public affairs practitioners as democratic enablers or as hired guns. *Public Relations Review*, *47*(1), 101923. Advance online publication. doi:10.1016/j.pubrev.2020.101923

Feng, Y., Chen, H., & Kong, Q. (2021). An expert with whom i can identify: The role of narratives in influencer marketing. *International Journal of Advertising*, *40*(7), 972–993. doi:10.1080/02650487.2020.1824751

Freitas, M. R., Pimenta, M. L., Hilletofth, P., Jugend, D., & Oprime, P. C. (2020). Demand management: The role of cross-functional integration in a context of political turbulence. *Asia Pacific Journal of Marketing and Logistics*, *32*(3), 817–839. doi:10.1108/APJML-11-2018-0473

Gil-Quintana, J., & Vida de León, E. (2021). Educational influencers on Instagram: Analysis of educational channels, audiences, and economic performance. *Publications / MDPI*, *9*(4), 43. Advance online publication. doi:10.3390/publications9040043

Gräve, J. F. (2019). What KPIs are key? Evaluating performance metrics for social media influencers. *Social Media + Society*, *5*(3). doi:10.1177/2056305119865475

Gray, A. (2022). How behavioral science can improve influencer marketing campaigns. *Journal of Digital and Social Media Marketing*, *10*(1), 61–68. www.scopus.com

Guha, S., & Majumdar, S. (2021). In search of business models in social entrepreneurship: Concepts and cases. In Search of business models in social entrepreneurship: Concepts and cases (pp. 1-291) doi:10.1007/978-981-16-0390-7

Guo, L., Wang, W., Wu, Y. J., & Goh, M. (2021). How much do social connections matter in fundraising outcomes? *Financial Innovation*, *7*(1), 79. Advance online publication. doi:10.118640854-021-00293-7

Guo, Q., Cheng, S., & Zhao, P. (2023). How to introduce a livestreaming channel: A case of the hotel at a fixed capacity. *International Transactions in Operational Research*, itor.13259. Advance online publication. doi:10.1111/itor.13259

Gupta, K. P., Manrai, R., & Goel, U. (2019). Factors influencing adoption of payments banks by Indian customers: Extending UTAUT with perceived credibility. *Journal of Asia Business Studies*, *13*(2), 173–195. doi:10.1108/JABS-07-2017-0111

Harrison, J. S., Ho, V. T., Bosse, D. A., & Crilly, D. (2023). A configurational theory of generalized exchange in stakeholder-oriented firms. *The Academy of Management Perspectives*, *37*(1), 16–36. doi:10.5465/amp.2022.0034

Horning, D. L. (2020). *Sports marketing special session: Ice hockey consumers: Who cares about women recreational players? An abstract*. doi:10.1007/978-3-030-42545-6_25

Hudders, L., & Lou, C. (2023). The rosy world of influencer marketing? Its bright and dark sides, and future research recommendations. *International Journal of Advertising*, *42*(1), 151–161. doi:10.1080/02650487.2022.2137318

Husain, U., Javed, S., & Ananda, S. (2021). Digital marketing as a game changer strategy to enhance brand performance. *International Journal of Technology Marketing*, *15*(2-3), 107–125. doi:10.1504/IJTMKT.2021.118226

Illia, L., Colleoni, E., & Meggiorin, K. (2021). How infomediaries on twitter influence business outcomes of a bank. *International Journal of Bank Marketing*, *39*(5), 709–724. doi:10.1108/IJBM-08-2020-0414

Jain, V. (2021). An overview on social media influencer marketing. *South Asian Journal of Marketing & Management Research*, *11*(11), 76–81. doi:10.5958/2249-877X.2021.00112.0

Jat, M., Jajja, M. S. S., ur Rehman, A., & Farooq, S. (2023). Manufacturer's contexts, supply chain risk management, and agility performance. *IEEE Transactions on Engineering Management*, 1–13. doi:10.1109/TEM.2023.3234050

Jhang-Li, J., & Liou, J. (2023). An analysis of operating strategy for a video live streaming platform: Advertisement, advertorial, and donation. *Information Technology Management*. Advance online publication. doi:10.100710799-023-00387-x PMID:36742341

Johansen, I. K., & Guldvik, C. S. (2017). *Influencer marketing and purchase intentions: how does influencer marketing affect purchase intentions?* [Master's thesis]. https://openaccess.nhh.no/nhh-xmlui/bitstream/handle/11250/2453218/masterthesis.PDF?sequence=1

Kahr, M., Leitner, M., Ruthmair, M., & Sinnl, M. (2021). Benders decomposition for competitive influence maximization in (social) networks. *Omega*, *100*, 102264. Advance online publication. doi:10.1016/j.omega.2020.102264

Kaleka, A., & Morgan, N. A. (2019). How marketing capabilities and current performance drive strategic intentions in international markets. *Industrial Marketing Management*, *78*, 108–121. doi:10.1016/j.indmarman.2017.02.001

Khaleeli, M., Faisal, R., & Anwar, S. (2021). The effect of green marketing, green supply chain and green human resources on business performance: Balanced scorecard approach. *Uncertain Supply Chain Management*, *9*(1), 133–138. doi:10.5267/j.uscm.2020.11.001

Kratzer, S., Lohmann, P., Roeglinger, M., Rupprecht, L., & zur Muehlen, M. (2019). The role of the chief process officer in organizations. *Business Process Management Journal*, *25*(4), 688–706. doi:10.1108/BPMJ-07-2017-0192

Lamola, K. X. T. (2022). Employees' aptitudes and trepidations for the adoption of enterprise application architecture for supply chain management in small and medium enterprises: A case of Capricorn district municipality. *Journal of Transport and Supply Chain Management*, *16*. Advance online publication. doi:10.4102/jtscm.v16i0.708

Lascity, M. E. (2023). Contour of masculinity: Reading bros in popular culture and fashion branding. In The Routledge companion to advertising and promotional culture: Second edition (pp. 197-208) doi:10.4324/9781003124870-21

Lee, M. T., & Theokary, C. (2021). The superstar social media influencer: Exploiting linguistic style and emotional contagion over content? *Journal of Business Research*, *132*, 860–871. doi:10.1016/j.jbusres.2020.11.014

Li, G., Tang, P., & Feng, J. (2023). How streamer channels influence luxury brand sales in live streaming commerce: An empirical study. *Asia Pacific Journal of Marketing and Logistics*. Advance online publication. doi:10.1108/APJML-01-2023-0096

Lin, C., & Chang, K. (2020). Establishing the service evaluation and selection system for emerging culture festival events using the hybrid MCDM technique. *Current Issues in Tourism*, *23*(18), 2240–2272. doi:10.1080/13683500.2019.1665628

Mai, E. S., & Liao, Y. (2022). The interplay of word-of-mouth and customer value on B2B sales performance in a digital platform: An expectancy value theory perspective. *Journal of Business and Industrial Marketing*, *37*(7), 1389–1401. doi:10.1108/JBIM-05-2021-0269

Mangio, F., & Di Domenico, G. (2022). All that glitters is not real affiliation: How to handle affiliate marketing programs in the era of falsity. *Business Horizons*, *65*(6), 765–776. doi:10.1016/j.bushor.2022.07.001

McMullan, K. (2023). A checklist for managers to enhance influencer partnerships and avoid potential pitfalls. *Business Horizons*, *66*(4), 443–452. doi:10.1016/j.bushor.2022.09.003

Mohr, J. J. (2019). A marketing perspective on innovation. *Foundations and Trends in Entrepreneurship*, *15*(3-4), 431–479. doi:10.1561/0300000085-4

Momani, A. M. (2021). A modified technology acceptance theory to assess social commerce technology adoption. *Information Resources Management Journal*, *34*(2), 43–62. doi:10.4018/IRMJ.2021040103

Monica, R. (2019). Factors influencing work engagement and its impact on task performance. *International Journal of Business Excellence*, *17*(1), 97–129. doi:10.1504/IJBEX.2019.096913

Nafees, L., Cook, C. M., Nikolov, A. N., & Stoddard, J. E. (2021). Can social media influencer (SMI) power influence consumer brand attitudes? the mediating role of perceived SMI credibility. *Digital Business*, *1*(2), 100008. Advance online publication. doi:10.1016/j.digbus.2021.100008

Pandey, S., & Chawla, D. (2019). Engaging m-commerce adopters in India: Exploring the two ends of the adoption continuum across four m-commerce categories. *Journal of Enterprise Information Management*, *32*(1), 191–210. doi:10.1108/JEIM-06-2018-0109

Pattnaik, S., & Tripathy, S. K. (2022). The effect of organizational justice on employee performance in the Indian public sector units: The role of organizational identification. *Benchmarking*. Advance online publication. doi:10.1108/BIJ-08-2021-0508

Presler, J. L. (2022). You are who you eat with: Academic peer effects from school lunch lines. *Journal of Economic Behavior & Organization*, *203*, 43–58. doi:10.1016/j.jebo.2022.08.029

Provance, T. W., Ramisetty, S. B., Urick, M. J., & Wieczorkowski, K. A. (2022). Building and evolving a culture of excellence: A conceptual exploration. *Measuring Business Excellence*, *26*(2), 197–209. doi:10.1108/MBE-05-2021-0067

Rach, M. (2023). Louis Vuitton, Cristiano Ronaldo and Lionel Messi. the greatest marketing stunt of the century, or just hype driven vanity-metrics? *Springer Proceedings in Business and Economics*, 290-297. 10.1007/978-3-031-31836-8_28

Ribbink, D., Pun, H., & Yan, T. (2022). Revenue sharing bids of a loss-averse supplier for a new product development contract: A multi-method investigation. *International Journal of Operations & Production Management*, *42*(12), 1853–1877. doi:10.1108/IJOPM-01-2022-0006

Rickaby, M. A., Glass, J., & Fernie, S. (2020). Conceptualizing the relationship between personal values and sustainability—A TMO case study. *Administrative Sciences*, *10*(1), 15. Advance online publication. doi:10.3390/admsci10010015

Ro, Y. J., Yoo, M., Koo, Y., & Song, J. H. (2021). The roles of learning orientation: Structural determinants for improving knowledge sharing with committed and satisfied employees. *Industrial and Commercial Training*, *53*(1), 60–76. doi:10.1108/ICT-10-2019-0094

Rosário, A., Moniz, L., & Cruz, R. (2021). Data Science Applied to Marketing: A Literature Review. *Journal of Information Science and Engineering*, *37*(5), 1067-1081. doi:10.6688/JISE.202109_37(5).0006

Rosário, A. T., & Dias, J. C. (2022). Sustainability and the Digital Transition: A Literature Review. *Sustainability (Basel)*, *14*(7), 4072. doi:10.3390u14074072

Rosário, A. T., & Dias, J. C. (2023). How Industry 4.0 and Sensors Can Leverage Product Design: Opportunities and Challenges. *Sensors (Basel)*, *23*(3), 1165. doi:10.339023031165 PMID:36772206

Rosário, A. T., Lopes, P. R., & Rosário, F. S. (2023). Influencer Marketing in the Digital Ecosystem. In R. Bansal, S. Qalati, & A. Chakir (Eds.), *Influencer Marketing Applications Within the Metaverse* (pp. 132–166). IGI Global. doi:10.4018/978-1-6684-8898-0.ch009

Saternus, Z., Weber, P., & Hinz, O. (2022). The effects of advertisement disclosure on heavy and light Instagram users. *Electronic Markets*, *32*(3), 1351–1372. doi:10.100712525-022-00546-y

Schmid, Y., & Dowling, M. (2022). New work: New motivation? A comprehensive literature review on the impact of workplace technologies. *Management Review Quarterly*, *72*(1), 59–86. doi:10.100711301-020-00204-7

Scholz, J. (2021). How consumers consume social media influence. *Journal of Advertising*, *50*(5), 510–527. doi:10.1080/00913367.2021.1980472

Sciarrino, J., Wilcox, G. B., & Chung, A. (2020). Measuring the effectiveness of peer-to-peer influencer marketing in an integrated brand campaign. *Journal of Digital and Social Media Marketing*, *8*(1), 85–95. www.scopus.com

Sewpersadh, N. S. (2020). Governing board attributes as profitability influencers under endogeneity: An econometric analysis in south Africa. *ACRN Journal of Finance and Risk Perspectives*, *8*(1), 133–151. doi:10.35944/jofrp.2019.8.1.009

Sharma, P., & Nayak, J. K. (2019). Understanding memorable tourism experiences as the determinants of tourists' behavior. *International Journal of Tourism Research*, *21*(4), 504–518. doi:10.1002/jtr.2278

Shen, R., Liu, D., Wei, X., & Zhang, M. (2022). Your posts betray you: Detecting influencer-generated sponsored posts by finding the right clues. *Information & Management*, *59*(8), 103719. Advance online publication. doi:10.1016/j.im.2022.103719

Singh, A., Jenamani, M., Thakkar, J. J., & Rana, N. P. (2021). Propagation of online consumer perceived negativity: Quantifying the effect of supply chain underperformance on passenger car sales. *Journal of Business Research*, *132*, 102–114. doi:10.1016/j.jbusres.2021.04.027

Singh, P., & Kottath, R. (2022). Influencer-defaulter mutation-based optimization algorithms for predicting electricity prices. *Utilities Policy*, *79*, 101444. Advance online publication. doi:10.1016/j.jup.2022.101444

Smith, R. (2019). Where authentic leaders DARE: From professional competence to inspiring leadership. In Where authentic leaders DARE: From professional competence to inspiring leadership (pp. 1-115) doi:10.4324/9780429243158

Soltani, M., Veer, E., de Vries, H. P., & Kemper, A. J. (2023). "Did you see what happened?" how scandals are shared via social media. *Corporate Reputation Review*. Advance online publication. doi:10.105741299-023-00165-z

Stone, D. (2020). Type of board and sustainability reporting. *Journal of Applied Business Research*, *36*(5), 229–240. doi:10.19030/jabr.v36i5.10361

Sudaryanto, S., Courvisanos, J., Dewi, I. R., Rusdiyanto, R., & Yuaris, J. R. (2022). Determinants of purchase intention during COVID-19: A case study of skincare products in east java. *Innovative Marketing*, *18*(1), 181–194. doi:10.21511/im.18(1).2022.15

Syrdal, H. A., Myers, S., Sen, S., Woodroof, P. J., & McDowell, W. C. (2023). Influencer marketing and the growth of affiliates: The effects of language features on engagement behavior. *Journal of Business Research*, *163*, 113875. doi:10.1016/j.jbusres.2023.113875

Tanwar, A. S., Chaudhry, H., & Srivastava, M. K. (2022). Trends in influencer marketing: A review and bibliometric analysis. *Journal of Interactive Advertising*, *22*(1), 1–27. doi:10.1080/15252019.2021.2007822

Thirumalesh Madanaguli, A., Kaur, P., Bresciani, S., & Dhir, A. (2021). Entrepreneurship in rural hospitality and tourism. A systematic literature review of past achievements and future promises. *International Journal of Contemporary Hospitality Management*, *33*(8), 2521–2558. doi:10.1108/IJCHM-09-2020-1121

Tzoulia, E. (2019, July). 'Influencer Marketing' on Social Media: Consumer Protection Issues from the Perspective of EU Law. In *Tzoulia, European Legal Forum (EuLF)* (pp. 29-38). Academic Press.

Vani, M., Sankaran, H., & Praveen Kumar, S. (2020). To explore the relationship between emotional intelligence and transformational leadership and their effect on organizational culture. *International Journal of Scientific and Technology Research*, *9*(1), 990–992.

Voipio, V., Elfvengren, K., & Korpela, J. (2020). In the bowling alley: Acceptance of an intelligent packaging concept in European markets. *International Journal of Value Chain Management, 11*(2), 180–197. doi:10.1504/IJVCM.2020.106825

Waltenrath, A., Brenner, C., & Hinz, O. (2022). Some interactions are more equal than others: The effect of influencer endorsements in social media brand posts on engagement and online store performance. *Journal of Interactive Marketing, 57*(4), 541–560. doi:10.1177/10949968221096591

Wang, N. (2023). Influencer marketing strategies in foreign marketplaces. *Springer Proceedings in Business and Economics*, 86-90. 10.1007/978-3-031-31836-8_11

Wardoyo, P., Rusdianti, E., & Purwantini, S. (2019). Salesforce performance of rural bank: The impact of sales training and experience selling. *International Journal of Scientific and Technology Research, 8*(9), 1079–1087. www.scopus.com

Wiedmann, K., & von Mettenheim, W. (2020). *An adaptation of the source credibility model on social influencers: An abstract.* doi:10.1007/978-3-030-42545-6_65

Wilson, J. A. J., & Arroyo, L. (2022). Conceptualizing performative Instagram influencer and user relationships – through advertising and sponsored brand content. *International Journal of Business Performance Management, 23*(3), 257–284. doi:10.1504/IJBPM.2022.123859

Woodroof, P. J., Howie, K. M., Syrdal, H. A., & VanMeter, R. (2020). What's done in the dark will be brought to the light: Effects of influencer transparency on product efficacy and purchase intentions. *Journal of Product and Brand Management, 29*(5), 675–688. doi:10.1108/JPBM-05-2019-2362

Yeo, S. F., Tan, C. L., Kumar, A., Tan, K. H., & Wong, J. K. (2022). Investigating the impact of AI-powered technologies on Instagrammers' purchase decisions in digitalization era–A study of the fashion and apparel industry. *Technological Forecasting and Social Change, 177*, 121551. Advance online publication. doi:10.1016/j.techfore.2022.121551

Yu, S., & de Barnier, V. (2022). *Social attachment theory and the relationship between satisfaction, luxury brand attachment, and influencer attachment: A focus on young Chinese online consumers under quarantine: An abstract.* doi:10.1007/978-3-030-95346-1_50

Zeren, D., & Gökdağlı, N. (2020). Influencer versus celebrity endorser performance on Instagram. *Springer Proceedings in Business and Economics*, 695-704. 10.1007/978-3-030-36126-6_77

Zhang, W., Chintagunta, P. K., & Kalwani, M. U. (2021). Social media, influencers, and adoption of an eco-friendly product: Field experiment evidence from rural china. *Journal of Marketing, 85*(3), 10–27. doi:10.1177/0022242920985784

Zhang, X., & Choi, J. (2022). The importance of social influencer-generated contents for user cognition and emotional attachment: An information relevance perspective. *Sustainability (Basel), 14*(11), 6676. doi:10.3390u14116676

Zhang, X., Duan, K., Zhao, H., Zhao, Y., Wang, X., & de Pablos, P. O. (2020). Can cooperation drive the success of suppliers in B2B crowdsourcing innovation projects? A large scale data perspective. *Industrial Marketing Management, 90*, 570–580. doi:10.1016/j.indmarman.2019.09.011

Zhao, H., & Zhang, N. (2019). Who is the main influencer on safety performance of dangerous goods air transportation in China? *Journal of Air Transport Management*, *75*, 198–203. doi:10.1016/j.jairtraman.2018.11.001

Zhu, D. H., & Westphal, J. D. (2021). Structural power, corporate strategy, and performance. *Strategic Management Journal*, *42*(3), 624–651. doi:10.1002mj.3239

ADDITIONAL READING

Adamson, B., Dixon, M., & Toman, N. (2012). The end of solution sales. *Harvard Business Review*, *90*(7-8). www.scopus.com

Andzulis, J., Panagopoulos, N. G., & Rapp, A. (2012). A review of social media and implications for the sales process. *Journal of Personal Selling & Sales Management*, *32*(3), 305–316. doi:10.2753/PSS0885-3134320302

Brodie, R. J., Fehrer, J. A., Jaakkola, E., & Conduit, J. (2019). Actor engagement in networks: Defining the conceptual domain. *Journal of Service Research*, *22*(2), 173–188. doi:10.1177/1094670519827385

Leeflang, P. S. H., Verhoef, P. C., Dahlström, P., & Freundt, T. (2014). Challenges and solutions for marketing in a digital era. *European Management Journal*, *32*(1), 1–12. doi:10.1016/j.emj.2013.12.001

Moore, J. N., Hopkins, C. D., & Raymond, M. A. (2013). Utilization of relationship-oriented social media in the selling process: A comparison of consumer (B2C) and industrial (B2B) salespeople. *Journal of Internet Commerce*, *12*(1), 48–75. doi:10.1080/15332861.2013.763694

Reinartz, W., Krafft, M., & Hoyer, W. D. (2004). The customer relationship management process: Its measurement and impact on performance. *JMR, Journal of Marketing Research*, *41*(3), 293–305. doi:10.1509/jmkr.41.3.293.35991

Trainor, K. J. (2012). Relating social media technologies to performance: A capabilities-based perspective. *Journal of Personal Selling & Sales Management*, *32*(3), 317–331. doi:10.2753/PSS0885-3134320303

Wang, Y., Hsiao, S., Yang, Z., & Hajli, N. (2016). The impact of sellers' social influence on the co-creation of innovation with customers and brand awareness in online communities. *Industrial Marketing Management*, *54*, 56–70. doi:10.1016/j.indmarman.2015.12.008

KEY TERMS AND DEFINITIONS

Brand Advocacy: Brand advocates promote the business through word of mouth. Their positive reviews about the company's products or services help to promote the company to new customers.

Business Performance: The results of a company measured using a series of metrics known as key performance indicators (KPIs).

Corporate Social Responsibility (CSR): Describes the voluntary contribution of companies to sustainable development that goes beyond legal requirements.

Electronic Word of Mouth (e-WOM): Consumers' information sharing and exchange about a product or company via the Internet, social media, and mobile communication.

Influencers: The individual who has the power to affect the purchase decisions of others because of his/her authority, knowledge, position, or relationship with his or her audience.

Relationships: Is a marketing strategy with the goal of maximizing profits by building strong relationships with customers and increasing their satisfaction with products and services.

Return on Investment (ROI): Is a performance measure used to evaluate the efficiency or profitability of an investment or compare the efficiency of a number of different investments.

Storytelling: The interactive art of using words and actions to reveal the elements and images of a story while encouraging the listener's imagination.

Chapter 4
All Users Are Equal, but Some Users Are More Equal Than Others:
Exploring the Psychology of Users That Follow Social Media Influencers

Carla Sofia Ribeiro Murteira
School of Communication and Media Studies, Politécnico de Lisboa, Portugal & Institute for the Study of Literature and Tradition, NOVA University of Lisbon, Portugal

Ana Cristina Antunes
https://orcid.org/0000-0001-8983-2062
School of Communication and Media Studies, Politécnico de Lisboa, Portugal

ABSTRACT

The study of social influence in social media settings has gained significant importance in the last years due to the advent of the internet and the increase of social media users and followers of social media influencers (SMI). This chapter focuses on the followers' psychological experience by reviewing how SMIs are perceived by followers and what moves the users to follow SMIs. Users follow SMI in an attempt to obtain information, inspiration, and entertainment, therefore brands have the chance to promote their products and services based on an appealing communication that can be provided by the SMI. However, the SMIs' perceived credibility, trustworthiness, authenticity, and expertise can impact not just the interaction with followers but also the brand image. It is recommended that brands conduct a continuous and careful assessment of SMIs' communication style and followers' perceptions to improve followers' attitudes towards the brands and their purchase intentions.

DOI: 10.4018/979-8-3693-0551-5.ch004

INTRODUCTION

Social life is fueled by argument, conflict, and controversy, always in an attempt to influence other individual's thoughts, feelings, and behaviors. Social influence among individuals has long and critical importance for human evolution, socialization, and day-to-day interaction in society via persuasion mechanisms. Building on the fact that the real or imagined presence of others impacts and influences our own behavior and attitudes (Hogg & Vaughan, 2014), it is not surprising that Social Influence processes can be transferred from real-world settings to online settings, such as Social Media, to foster human connection but also conformity among Social Media users.

Social media's popularity has skyrocketed in the last few years and this trend is expected to continue in the near future. Indeed, the number of social media users worldwide is expected to grow from 4.59 billion in 2022 to 5.85 billion users in 2027 (Statista, 2023). Given social media's demand in daily activities (Duffett, 2017), we can expect that social media is related to countless effects on its users, namely on the way they get informed about global and local news, their exposure to advertising, and the way they seek for information in general (e.g., Ganguly, 2015; Gottfried & Shearer, 2016). Social Networking Sites (SNS) are changing and redefining how people respond to and engage with worldwide information. Despite the worldwide changing and challenging times for the quality of communicated information, companies and institutions have found the new Holy Grail Cup full of communication opportunities between brands and consumers. To respond to the skeptical opinions regarding the traditional forms of marketing, Influencer marketing has been raised to provide the much-needed connection between brands and consumers has increased in the last years. As the terminology suggests, Influencer marketing is based on the investment on influencers to develop forms of branded communication and content close to their followers (Yodel, 2017), these forms of communication seem to lead to a more organic, authentic and direct contact with potential consumers than traditional advertising (Talavera, 2015), thus the popularity of Influencer marketing is been growing exponentially (Bevilacqua & Del Giudice, 2018). Since influencer marketing is based on the interaction between users in SNS, it is important to note that not all social media users are equal, some of them have gained the power to influence other users' behaviors, while others just joined the crew and followed the lead.

In this chapter we propose to review and discuss the psychology of users who follow other users in Social Media, focusing on the perception that users form towards influencers and the motives and reasons to follow them. In the first part, we provide some background concepts by presenting the relevance of influencer marketing for brands and for digital marketing strategy. Then we proceed to a literature review on the definition of Social Media Influencer (SMI), their main characteristics, and their communication styles to influence other users. In the second part, we proceed to the main goals of the chapter which is to provide a literature review on the motives and reasons behind following the SMI, and how the SMI is perceived by their followers. We conclude this chapter, by providing some insights on marketing strategy assessment and possible solutions that can be adopted to improve the influencer marketing effectiveness for brands based on the motives to follow and perception about the SMIs. In the end, some knowledge and research shortcomings are identified to point to future research avenues regarding SMI and marketing strategy.

INFLUENCER MARKETING AND BRANDS DIGITAL MARKETING STRATEGY

According to the latest data from Influencer Marketing Hub Benchmark Report (2023), which gathered information from more than 3500 marketing agencies, brands, and other professionals all over the world, influencer marketing is expected to grow to be worth $21.1 billion in 2023. Moreover, more than 80% of them intended to dedicate a budget to influencer marketing in 2023, while 67% intended to increase their influencer marketing spending in 2023. There are several reasons behind this huge brand investment in influencer marketing, which according to Influencer Marketing Hub (2023) has been growing steadily in the last years.

In the current landscape, consumers have grown not only skeptical of traditional brand-centered advertising but are also empowered to circumvent it, given its perceived intrusiveness and disruption (e.g., Antunes et al., 2022; Peng, 2023). Consumers possess the ability to proactively skip commercials or employ ad-blocking software, creating a more challenging environment for brands to connect with their target audience. Additionally, the rapid adoption and growing popularity of social media changed the relationship and the balance of power between consumers and brands (e.g., Lamberton & Stephen, 2016) and generated new communication dynamics (e.g., Vrontis et al., 2021). Nowadays, consumers have been turning to social media aiming for closer and more transparent communication and new ways to connect and relate to brands (e.g., San-Miguel et al., 2018; Taillon et al., 2020).

In response to this dynamic, brands are pivoting toward digital marketing strategies that leverage the benefits of word-of-mouth while sidestepping the limitations of conventional advertising methods, including avoidance and resistance. One of these strategies is influencer marketing. This strategy can be defined as "the art and science of engaging people who are influential online to share brand messaging with their audiences in the form of sponsored content" (Sammis et al., 2016, p. 7). It represents a marketing strategy where marketers and advertisers use social media influencers to endorse products, brands, organizations, or ideas on their social media profiles, bridging the gap between brands and their targets (e.g., Hudders et al., 2021). Influencers have the ability to reshape the way consumers engage with products and services through their relatable, approachable, and perceived as authentic persona on social media platforms (Taillon et al., 2020).

SMIs represent a potent and substantial advertising avenue that can rival or even surpass the effectiveness of brand advertising and celebrity endorsements and provide an effective way to reach audiences who may otherwise bypass brand messages (e.g., Rosengren & Campbell, 2021; Schouten et al., 2020). As Duffy (2020) noted "Influencer brand endorsements are integrated into their existing arsenals of visual, textual, and/or narrative content, their persuasive communication is understood as more "authentic" or "organic" than traditional paid advertising".

Social media influencers have highly specific and engaged audiences, allowing brands to target niche markets effectively. This turns influencer marketing into a cost-effective and viable alternative for brand managers to quickly reach more targeted and specific market segments (e.g., Phua et al., 2017; Taillon et al., 2020; Vrontis et al., 2021). As SMIs are not only content producers but also community managers (Campbell & Farrell, 2020), through influencer marketing brands can build communities around their products or services (e.g., Rundin & Colliander, 2021). Influencers can foster engagement and conversation among their sizable community of followers, strengthening the brand's relationship with its audience in a natural and organic way.

As brands have recognized the persuasive sway that social media influencers wield over their followers, influencer marketing is now a commonly used strategy (Hudders et al., 2021). Besides, their strategic use has been identified as a key to the success of many of the fastest-growing brands of the past decade (Rundin & Colliander, 2021). Therefore, in the ever-evolving landscape of digital marketing, it is not surprising that influencer marketing is now considered one of the most relevant digital marketing strategies available and frequently used on its own or along with other digital marketing strategies by marketers and advertisers. Since influencers seem to figure as a fundamental part of digital marketing strategy, in the following section we depict the concept of Social Media Influencer (SMI), their characteristics, and communication styles.

Social Media Influencers

A social media influencer (SMI) is a digital content creator who disseminates compelling content on a regular basis. These online personalities have the ability to attract keep and influence other user's attention and behavior through the development of valuable and engaging digital content, such as videos, stories, images, reviews, reels, etc., across one or several social media platforms (e.g., Varsamis, 2018). Due to the perceived quality of their communication, these content creators reached a status of expertise in a specific subject, and have gathered a significant number of followers that interact with the SMI's content (De Veirman et al., 2017; Haenlein et al., 2020; Hudders & Lou, 2022; Lou & Yuan, 2019).

The ability to create and share compelling content based on their daily lives, adventures, and experiences, as well as opinions and beliefs through personal disclosure and storytelling (Andò, 2016; Leung et al., 2022), probably facilitate the development of a singular brand persona on social networking sites (SNS) (Antunes & Murteira, 2023; Duffy, 2020; Lou, 2021). The building of this brand persona shows paramount importance in the process of attracting and growing the number of followers. Considering that SMI has the capability to influence other peoples' opinions, attitudes, and behaviors towards a specific subject (Geyser, 2022), the created content should be on a specific knowledge or topic domain to help in the development of a brand persona on SNS (Antunes & Murteira, 2023; Duffy, 2020; Lou, 2021).

Building upon a sense of intimacy, accessibility, proximity, and relatability, SMIs are able to create rapport and forge emotional bonds and parasocial relationships with their followers, which facilitates SMI's capability to influence the followers' attitudes and lifestyles (e.g., Abidin, 2015; Ferberg et al., 2011; Karhawi, 2017; Lee et al., 2021; Marwick, 2016). Thus, it is not surprising that these online personalities count with several followers, and become a source of interest, advice, and influence for other SNS's users that follow them (e.g., Ruiz Gomez, 2018; Vrontis et al., 2021). They become important to those who rely on them to learn about new information in general, but also, regarding brands, services, or products (Geyser, 2022; Klear, 2022; Lou & Yuan, 2019). Nevertheless, it is worth noting that not all SMI show the same range of influence.

The social recognition achieved by the SMIs is largely dependent on their status, audience size, influence, and social media behaviors (Ruiz-Gómez, 2019; Sicilia & Lopez, 2023). Several criteria have been applied to distinguish and classify SMI into categories, those criteria range from the platform used by the influencers, the product category they are experts in, the perceived authenticity, accessibility, expertise, social capital, and even their age. Therefore, one could say that it seems that classifying SMIs is not a straightforward task. Nevertheless, the most popular classification and probably the easier criteria to measure, lies in their popularity in SNS, which is the number of followers. Based on the number of followers, SMI can be categorized as mega-influencers, macro-influencers, meso-influencers (Boerman,

Table 1. Relation between the type of influencer and the number of followers.

Type of Influencer	Number of followers
Celebrity – influencer	More than 1.000.000 followers (Campbell & Farrell, 2020; Ruiz-Gómez, 2019)
Mega – influencer	More than 1.000.000 followers (Campbell & Farrell, 2020; Ruiz-Gómez, 2019)
Macro – influencer	More than 1.000.000 followers (Boerman, 2020) Between 100.000 and one 1.000.000 followers (Campbell & Farrell, 2020; De Veirman et al., 2017; Ruiz-Gómez, 2019)
Meso - influencer	between 10.000 and 1.000.000 followers (Boerman, 2020)
Micro – influencer	Up to 99.000 followers (Ruiz-Gómez, 2019) Between 10.000 and 100.000 followers (De Veirman et al., 2017; Campbell & Farrell, 2020) Up to 10.000 followers (Boerman, 2020)
Nano – influencer	Less than 10.000 followers (Campbell & Farrell, 2020)

2020) micro-influencers, nano-influencers (Campbell & Farrell, 2020; Ruiz-Gómez, 2019; Zarei et al., 2020), and celebrities (Campbell & Farrell, 2020), see Table 1.

SMI have built a significant follower base towards which they can promote brands, products, and services. This endorsement marketing draws potential customers' attention, leads to positive word-of-mouth (WOM), generates consumer engagement, and drives sales through the cooperation between brands and SMIs (e.g., Masuda et al., 2022; Zniva et al., 2023). Therefore, SMIs are a fundamental piece in this interactive marketing era due to the bi-directional value creation for influencers and the active customer connection, engagement, participation, and interaction (Wang, 2021). Nevertheless, not all influencers produce the same effect or are perceived in the same way by their followers or other SNS' users. Celebrities, Mega-influencers, and Macro-influencers are perceived as influencers characterized by high expertise and high cultural capital (Zarei et al., 2020). However, despite being the ones that gathered the largest number of followers, it is interesting to notice that micro-influencers are perceived as more authentic, genuine, and reachable compared with them (Campbell & Farrell, 2020). Also, it is the micro-influencer and nano-influencer that reach better engagement rates with their followers or other users from all categories of influencers (Campbell & Farrell, 2020; Zarei et al., 2020). The following section deepens the social influence phenomena to explain the arise of a SMI.

Social Influence

Social influence is critical for individual interaction once the real or implied presence of others impacts our own behavior and attitudes (Hogg & Vaughan, 2014), thus one could say that social influence is facilitated by the behavioral synchronization, interpersonal coordination, and uniformity of behavior among individuals when they are in groups (Koban, Rammoorthy, & Konvalinka, 2019). Considering the biological importance of synchronization and interpersonal coordination for improved communication, fitness, social cohesion, bonding, and affiliation (Duranton & Gaunet, 2016; Koban et al., 2019; Murteira, 2023; Scott-Phillips, 2008), it is not surprising that synchronization and interpersonal coordination processes that move social influence are strongly present in human interaction, even in online settings, such as Social Media, to foster human connection and testify the phenomena of following social media users.

Table 2. Type of persuasion communication strategies used in communication based on French and Raven (1959) and Raven (1965).

Source of Power	
Reward Power	Give or promise rewards for compliance behaviors and attitudes.
Coercive Power	Threatening of punishments in case of non-compliance.
Informational Power	Belief that the influencer has a stronger source and amount of information than influenced individuals.
Expert Power	Belief that the influencer has a greater expertise, experience and knowledge than influenced individuals.
Legitimate Power	Belief that the influencer is authorized by a recognized power structure.
Referent Power	Identification with, attraction towards, or respect towards the source of influence.

Nevertheless, it is important to recognize that the act and ability to influence others is a demonstration of power. While it is well accepted that the capability to grasp users' attention is dependent on good quality, attractive, interactive, and informative content (Ruiz-Gómez, 2019; Ki & Kim, 2019), it is also clear that the capability to retain flowers and influence their behaviors and attitudes is dependent on a good interaction with them. The quality of communication and the structure of an argument are the keys to guiding users' attention and facilitating persuasion. In generic terms, we can say that there are six forms of perceived social power that have been identified (French & Raven, 1959; Raven, 1965) and may explain the influencing outcomes based on the elements provided in persuasive communications. Table 2 lists and defines each of the sources of power that can be used by SMI in order to facilitate their persuasive communication.

Certainly, not all forms or sources of power can be found in just one SMI, although some sources of power desirably should not be found, namely the Coercive Power. Coercive Power is associated with a threatening discourse aiming to guide users to follow the SMI ideas, this type of discourse can develop fear and conforming behaviors among SMI followers to avoid any sort of punishment from a real or imagined entity. Therefore, one could say that Coercive Power discourses can be damaging to the SMI image and the brands associated with the SMI.

SMI's communication strategy to influence their followers and gather new followers can be based on Reward Power, Informational Power, Expert Power, Legitimate Power, and Referent Power. Having in mind the influencer marketing strategy, the Reward Power could be any form of SMI communication where the follower could receive some sort of benefit provided by the SMI, this can include discount codes, voucher discounts, product free samples, etc., that can be used by the follower to complete the purchase. Informational Power consists of the delivery of practical and useful information regarding a brand or product, this can include product reviews, product unboxing experiences, product sharing, etc.. Expert Power and Legitimate Power are characterized by any form of communication that is developed by a SMI that is based on their meritocratic abilities, this can include SMIs that are recognized professionals in a subject that is related to the topic of influence. Referent Power is based on the followers' perception towards the SMI, several variables can contribute to improve the SMI perceived attractiveness, nevertheless, it seems important to guarantee a good congruency and resemblance between the influencer and the message conveyed to improve persuasion. Mettenheim and Wiedmann (2021) suggest three forms of congruency: the perceived congruency between the product and brand with the SMI, the perceived congruency between the SMI and the real self of the follower, and the perceived congruency between the SMI and the ideal self of follower. The presence of these forms of congruency is associated with a more efficient combination between the SMI and a brand (Belanche et al., 2021a) that can increase the Referent Power of persuasion of an SMI.

Reward Power Information Power, Referent Power and in some cases, Expert Power and Legitimate Power are the key social power strategies used by SMI to drive communication with followers and other social media users. Once Celebrities, Mega-influencers, and Macro-influencers are perceived as influencers characterized by high expertise and high cultural capital (Zarei et al., 2020), then we can infer that they possess strong social Information Power and perhaps in some cases Expert Power. On the other hand, micro-influencers are perceived as authentic, genuine, and reachable (Campbell & Farrell, 2020), while micro-influencers and nano-influencers reach better engagement rates (Campbell & Farrell, 2020; Zarei et al., 2020), which is suggestive of a strong social Referent Power for influencers with a lower number of followers. While Reward Power can be applied across all categories of SMI, Expert Power and Legitimate Power are limited to SMI abilities and academic knowledge.

The communication power used by the SMI will strongly influence follower's perception of the quality of content but also on the SMI's main characteristics. Nonetheless, it is key to consider that follower's motivation to follow SMI can in itself impact their perception regarding the SMI communication style and credibility, thus in the next section we will explore the motives behind following SMI before exploring the way followers perceive SMIs.

Motivation to follow Social Media Influencers

What drives human behavior has been one the most debated topics since antiquity. Theories of motivation were developed across several human social sciences with the goal of predicting what moves human behaviors. As expected, it is in marketers' and consumer researchers' best interest, to learn about the motives underlying the following SMIs, since these motives may offer cues to improve the communication between the brand and consumers via SMI (Babin, Harris, & Murray, 2018).

Motivation has received several definitions over time from scholars from different fields of knowledge. Broadly speaking, motivation refers to the reasons underlying individuals' behavior to reach a predetermined goal (Babin, Harris, & Guay et al., 2010; Solomon, 2018). However, other authors expand the definition of motivation to a psychological drive force that moves individuals towards a specific behavior that is kept over time (Kimmel, 2018), or to a set of energetic forces that can start in or out of individuals to drive their behaviors (Pina e Cunha et al., 2006). Despite some differences between authors on the understanding of motivation, we can say that all definitions suggest that motivation is a psychological construct inherent to each individual that can be understood as the motives behind individuals showing behaviors in response to their needs.

One of the most relevant research streams in influencer marketing is related to the followers' psychological processes when exposed to SMIs (e.g., Vrontis et al., 2021), such as the followers' perceptions of SMIs and their motives for following digital influencers. Both psychological processes, motivation, and perception, are relevant for understanding why and how followers start and why they continue to follow digital influencers. Yet, while there is ample evidence of how SMIs are perceived by their communities, there is a limited understanding of their followers' motives. Albeit understudied, understanding the motivational processes of followers is a relevant issue, attending to its potential impact on the effectiveness of influencer marketing, considering the followers' consumer journeys (Lee et al., 2021).

Followers have their own motives to follow, usually related to needs that are satisfied by influencers or because SMIs support them in the achievement of their own goals and objectives. Rosengren and Campbell (2021) add that followers also respond to influencers based on their inferred motives, although those motives can be shaped by the influencers themselves.

One thing worth noticing is that motivation to follow SMI can be driven by intrinsic vs. extrinsic reasons and utilitarian vs. hedonic reasons. Intrinsic motivation refers to a driving force for individuals to engage in a specific behavior due to the inherent satisfaction that can be derived from the activity in itself, this motivation manifests as a form of personal enjoyment, interest, or pleasure when following the SMI; whereas extrinsic motivation refers to the reasons for engaging in a behavior to earn rewards or avoid punishments, such as winning discounts or avoiding not being informed about the last trends (Deci, Koestner, & Rya, 1999; Lai, 2011). On the other hand, we can say individuals' behavior is driven by a utilitarian motivation when it implies acquiring a product or information regarding a brand that will help the follower to accomplish something that they need, whereas a behavior can be driven by a hedonic motivation when it implies that the follower will experience something emotionally gratifying when following an SMI (Babin, Harris, & Murray, 2018). In all cases, individuals' behavior aims to fulfill their needs.

So far, the limited evidence is consensual that young adults tend to follow SMIs to be entertained, as this is an enjoyable way to pass their time but are also motivated to seek information and gain more knowledge on products, brands, and trends, as they consider SMIs as experts in a particular domain (Croes & Bartels, 2021; Djafarova & Rushworth, 2017; Kühn & Riesmeyer, 2022; Morton, 2020).

One of the few pioneering studies that explored followers' motives was developed by Morton (2020), who adopted an exploratory approach to this topic. By interviewing 30 Mexican young adults aged 20–25 years old, she identified five motives for following SMIs: information, inspiration, communication, entertainment, and surveillance. Indeed, one of the reasons to follow is because SMIs share information about relevant and interesting topics (such as new products, new fashion trends, and useful ideas for daily life). Producing inspiring content related to some aspect of followers' lives or sharing content that can make a positive impact on society is another motive registered. Communication motive seems to be also related to the need of belonging and inclusion: this motive arises when significant people, such as friends or family already follow a given influencer and talk about their content, and the individual begins to follow that SMI to take part in these conversations. Followers also look for entertainment, as they follow to pass their time and entertain themselves with SMIs humorous content. Finally, surveillance refers to the expressed to see how SMIs live their daily lives.

A qualitative study by Kühn and Riesmeyer (2022), who interviewed 36 German young adults aged 14-27 years old, found that they intentionally followed SMIs from different fields driven by inspiration and information needs (on specific topics), as well as by entertainment, and pastime. Similarly, to the conclusions of Morton's (2020) study, they consciously follow them because these SMIs a) stand for topics in which they are interested, b) are perceived as experts on specific topics, and serve as sources of information for both familiar and new areas of interest of their followers, c) provide entertainment and help their followers pass their time in an agreeable manner. In the specific case of fitness influencers, they also motivate their followers by acting as role models and by encouraging them to do sports. An interesting finding is that the gratification of motives is constantly questioned when the SMI content is consumed, but when the aforementioned needs are no longer satisfied by the SMI, these young German followers decide to unfollow.

One must note that the set of motives and needs presented by SMI followers is more diverse, as other studies, using quantitative approaches in different countries, suggest. According to a study by Ki et al. (2020) with 325 U.S. consumers, the influential power of SMIs comes from the emotional bond and attachment forged with their followers, who perceive them as human brands that fulfill their needs for ideality (via displaying inspiration), relatedness (through similarity and enjoyability) and competence (by curating informative content).

Building on the Uses and Gratifications Theory to explain why young Dutch people (16-25 years old) follow social influencers on YouTube, Croes and Bartels (2021) identified six motives. information sharing, cool and new trends, relaxing entertainment, companionship, boredom/habitual pass time, and information seeking. Their findings suggest that relaxing entertainment and boredom/habitual pass time were the most relevant drivers of their followers. The single different motive identified – companionship, that is, following because seeking companionship and not being lonely – seems to be a less relevant motive.

Departing from the same theory, Lee et al. (2021) identified four unique consumer motivations for following SMIs on Instagram: authenticity, consumerism, creative inspiration, and envy. That is, they follow Instagram influencers because they are genuine, open, and relatable but also because these followers seek brand information (consumerism) and to be creatively inspired by these SMIs. The fourth motive – envy - suggests that these U.S. Instagram users aged 18 to 29 are also driven by aspirational and emotional motives. These motives seem to be significantly related to trust: the more one follows Instagram influencers because of their authenticity and brand information, the more the followers are more likely to trust their brand-related posts. Additionally, consumerism and envy seem to have a positive impact on the frequency of purchasing SMI-recommended brands.

The diverse set of motives identified in the literature are summarized in Table 3.

Table 3. Motives for following SMI.

Motives for following	Some key references
Entertainment	Croes and Bartels (2021); Djafarova and Rushworth (2017); Kühn and Riesmeyer (2022);
Passing time	Croes and Bartels (2021); Djafarova and Rushworth (2017); Kühn and Riesmeyer (2022);
Information (seeking/sharing)	Croes and Bartels (2021); Ki et al. (2020); Kühn and Riesmeyer (2022); Morton (2020)
Trendy	Shoenberger & Kim (2022)
Inspiration	Ki et al. (2020); Morton (2020); Kühn and Riesmeyer (2022); Lee et al. (2022); Shoenberger & Kim (2022)
Uniqueness of the SMI	Shoenberger & Kim (2022)
Communication	Morton (2020)
Surveillance	Morton (2020)
Relatedness	Ki et al. (2020)
Companionship	Croes and Bartels (2021)
Authenticity	Lee et al. (2022)
Envy	Lee et al. (2022)
Consumerism	Lee et al. (2022)

As a final comment, we warrant researchers and practitioners to take these motives with caution. So far, the studies that have tried to uncover reasons, motives, or needs for following SMIs focused on Western young adults, mainly from the US or Europe, who follow SMIs on Instagram. Besides, a significant part of these studies fall under the broad category of qualitative research, implying that the findings are not generalizable. Therefore, more studies are warranted on other social networks (e.g., TikTok, YouTube) with participants from other cultures. A transcultural perspective is also welcomed. While the limited evidence available focuses on Gen Z, the literature remains silent on the fundamental forces that drive other generations, for instance, Millennials, to follow digital influencers. Further research could widen the current frame of reference by drawing on larger samples and addressing followers of different ages and demographic profiles.

Perception of Social Media Influencers

Followers' perception of the SMIs is paramount to defining all the recurring interactions and understanding other psychological processes of the followers, such as cognitive processes, attitudes, or decision-making processes. Perception is a subjective, personal interpretation of reality, not the reality itself. Additionally, there is a certain amount of ambiguity and imprecision about social objects (people) and this, according to Moscovici (1976), makes it possible for people to have different perceptions and adopt different positions regarding these social objects. Thus, followers can perceive differently the same influencer.

Several other features of the perception process must be taken into account: besides being an active and selective process, perception is also temporal (Cuesta, 2000). Perception variation throughout time is relevant: not only influencers change (as very few things about people never change) (Cook, 2021), but the followers' perception of a given influencer may also change throughout time. Therefore, perception is not static nor enduring and followers' perception can be altered both by changes in the influencer, in the follower, or in the wider context.

The context is relevant when we are addressing followers' perception of SMI since social perceivers are heavily influenced by their social (and more broad) environments (Fiske & Taylor, 2021). For this purpose, we can say that a) the type of digital platform and its affordances, b) the emergence and popularity of other influencers or even other types of influencers (e.g., virtual influencers), c) the influence of other members of the followers' community or even d) the wider social media ecosystem, together or separately, can alter how a given influencer is perceived by a certain follower. Regarding the SNS, the followers' interactions and experiences with SMI are contingent upon the characteristics of social media platforms (Lou et al., 2023). There is evidence that followers interact and engage differently with an influencer depending on the platform (Arora et al., 2019) and that SMI communities and practices vary widely across platforms and sectors (e.g., Duffy, 2020). Additionally, followers' perception of each influencer may vary cross-platform, which may be modeled by the shared contents and fueled by the underlying digital dynamics of platforms, and their affordances and algorithms (e.g., Bucher & Helmond, 2018; Cotter, 2019). As algorithms and technological affordances of SNS change over time, so must influencer practices change (e.g., Cotter, 2019; Lou et al., 2023), spreading their winds of change upon followers' perceptions.

Several authors (e.g., Ruiz-Gomez, 2019; Sokolova & Kefi, 2019) highlight the ephemeral nature of attention in social media: in what Fairchild (2007) called an Attention Economy, attention is considered the most valuable commodity, capturing and maintaining the audience's attention. This poses increasing challenges for digital influencers, as they are confronted with an ever-changing number of other influencers that dispute users' attention. In this context, new or emergent influencers in SNS can influence people's perception of already existing influencers.

Other people have a major role in shaping one's psychological processes. Indeed, as Garcia-Marques, Ferreira, and Garrido (2017) underscore, the cognitions, judgments, and behaviors of others during social interactions can have an impact on the processes involved in person perception, as well as in information processing and retrieval related to social cognition. Considering influencers as the most influential and visible members of their communities, SMIs play a key role in setting the agenda for conversations and shaping the flow of information within the community (e.g., Lutkenhaus et al., 2019). Yet, other community members, that is, followers, also interact and comment on the influencers' posts. As followers they are engaged within the community, they also engage with each other more intensely (e.g., Lutkenhaus et al., 2019). As a community, followers frequently hold similar views on certain topics and are exposed to a narrower range of information and content, frequently similar to their ideas and beliefs, reinforcing them, a phenomenon commonly referred to as 'echo chambers' (Karlsen et al., 2017). Also, when they voice their opinions and comments, they usually receive positive and similar feedback, seeing their beliefs reinforced and amplified through communication (Chen, 2022), creating 'filter bubbles', that is, self-reinforcing systems that isolate individuals from diverse ideas, beliefs, or content (Areebe et al, 2023; Rowland, 2011). The filter bubble effect and echo chambers shape their members' perspectives, including their SMI perception.

Taking the former arguments, one can say that followers' perceptions of SMI are plural, dynamic, and deeply intertwined with what goes on in the influencer-follower relationship and its context. Yet, the extant literature transversely depicts a more stable portrait of how influencers are perceived by their followers, emphasizing some core features. A common procedure in research involves distinguishing them from celebrities. For this purpose, Gräve (2017) examined what were the main differences in followers' perception of influencers vs. traditional celebrities. He concluded that celebrities were evaluated more favorably, although this difference diminished for high levels of familiarity and even reversed when SMIs were perceived as more trustworthy and similar to their followers. According to Schouten et al. (2020), audiences reveal a higher similarity and wishful identification with SMI when compared with celebrities. Additionally, celebrities and influencers seem to occupy distinct positions in their followers' minds, with familiarity shaping the perceived trustworthiness, expertise, and likeability of both groups (Gräve & Bartsch, 2022). Familiarity seems to play an important role: in their study, celebrities scored significantly higher on these variables than SMI. Yet, as the level of familiarity increased, the differences became not significant (for trust and likeability) or the evaluations of influencers became more positive than evaluations of celebrities (on perceived expertise).

In their seminal study, Freberg et al. (2011) found that SMIs were perceived as outspoken, smart, ambitious, productive, and poised. Yet, one must take into account that Freberg et al. (2011) did not resort to followers' perceptions, relying instead on the perception of college students. In her exploratory study, Morton (2020) identifies four main characteristics assigned to influencers by their Mexican followers, who perceived these SMI as (a) 'normal' (ie not public celebrities) (b) sharing their daily lives with their followers; (c) famous because of the content they post; and (d) collaborating with companies, as they are paid to promote brands and products.

The profuse literature on followers' perception of SMIs derives from the studies of celebrities' endorsements from the previous century. Not surprisingly, research endeavors on the endorsement effects of SMI upon their communities focused on the perceived characteristics with a significant impact on their followers' customers' journeys. In this sense, the literature has suggested that SMI share several

Table 4. The most common perceived characteristics attributed to SMI

Perceived characteristics	Definition	Some key citations
Credibility	Source credibility refers to the degree to which a target audience evaluates as credible a message source, to determine the expertise and knowledge of the source who recommends a product or service (Djafarova & Rushworth, 2017; Ohanian, 1990).	Belanche et al. (2021b); Breves et al. (2019); Djafarova and Rushworth (2017); Lou and Yuan (2019); Reinikainen et al. (2020); Schouten et al. (2020); Sokolova and Kefi (2020); Xiao et al. (2018); Uzunğlu and Kip (2014); Weismueller et al. (2020)
Expertise	Expertise refers to consumer perception of the source's knowledge and experience in a given domain (Hovland & Weiss, 1951). According to Erdogan (1999), expertise can be defined as the degree to which an individual is perceived as experienced, knowledgeable, qualified and, in general, a valid source for the receiver.	Djafarova and Rushworth (2017); Hughes et al. (2019); Ki and Kim (2019); Li and Peng (2021); Trivedi and Sama (2020)
Trustworthiness	While trust is defined as "a willingness to rely on an exchange partner in whom one has confidence" (Moorman et al., 1992, p. 315), trustworthiness refers to the perceived reliability, dependability and honesty of an endorser (Erdogan, 1999).	Balaban et al. (2022); Lou and Yuan (2019); Masuda et al. (2022); Schouten et al. (2020); Uzunoğlu and Kip (2014)
Atractiveness	Attractiveness refers to the extent to which an endorser is perceived as classy, sexy and beautiful (Erdogan, 1999). Physical and social attractiveness can be distinguished, with social attractiveness referring to the likeability of a speaker (Sokolova & Kefi, 2020).	Lou and Yuan (2019); Ki and Kim (2019); Masuda et al. (2022); Sokolova and Kefi (2020); Trivedi and Sama (2020)
Authenticity /genuineness	Perceived authenticity has generally been understood as a person (or a brand) being perceived to be true to one's self (Luoma-Aho et al., 2019). Across the literature, according to Beverland and Farrely (2010), authenticity encapsulates what is genuine, real, and/or true.	Kapitan et al. (2022); Luoma-Aho et al. (2019); Pöyry et al. (2019); Zniva et al. (2023)

characteristics, being considered credible experts, trustworthy, genuine, attractive, unique, popular, close to their followers, and similar to them (e.g., De Veirman et al., 2017; Djafarova & Rushworth, 2017; Lou & Yuan, 2019; Luoma-Aho et al., 2019; Sokolova & Kefi, 2020). Table 4 lists the most common perceived characteristics attributed to SMI by their followers, including a brief definition of each one.

Credibility was one of the most studied aspects of celebrities' endorsements (e.g., Erdogan, 1999; Ohanian, 1990). When compared with traditional celebrities, influencers are perceived as more credible, especially among younger audiences (e.g., Lou & Yuan, 2019; Trivedi & Sama, 2020). Yet, as many scholars alert, they are perceived as credible information sources within their domains of expertise and interest, not in all areas (e.g., Hudders et al., 2021; Schouten et al., 2020). As SMIs are perceived as experts in particular domains, their opinions and attitudes on those specific areas are relevant to their audiences, turning them into opinion leaders (Carter, 2016) in the social media context. Next to being considered as experts, the creation of an authentic identity is central to defining influencers (e.g., Carter, 2016; Hudders et al., 2021) and for their exercise of influence upon their communities of followers. SMIs craft authentic 'personal brands' via SNS (Hearn & Schoenhoff, 2016), embedding their communicative practices with flashes of authenticity. Asserting authenticity has a wide impact on their followers' perception: SMIs are considered more sincere or trustworthy sources of information and advice (Duffy, 2020). It also allows them to distinguish from other influencers by offering something relatively unique to their followers (Cotter, 2019).

Audiences have come to consider popular social media influencers as credible, attractive, and trusted opinion leaders (e.g., De Veirman et al., 2017; Djafarova & Rushworth, 2017; Lou & Yuan, 2019). As ordinary yet popular social media users, influencers that also perceived as more similar to their followers, who identify more with them than mainstream celebrities (e.g., Janssen et al., 2022; Lou, 2021; Schouten et al., 2020). Perceived endorser credibility, trustworthiness, and expertise as well as identification with the influencer, which derives from perceived similarity and wishful identification, seem to be important drivers of influencer endorsement effects (Janssen et al., 2022), thus increasing their value for brands and stimulating the use of influencer marketing.

SOLUTIONS AND RECOMMENDATIONS

Every marketing communication is an opportunity for brands to work on brand awareness and customers' attitudes towards the brand. Besides promoting products and services, influencer marketing can also facilitate the development of positive attitudes and raise market awareness towards the brand, however, not all SMIs may successfully achieve these goals. The success of influencer marketing is probably dependent on the SMI's persuasive abilities, but also on the way the SMIs' are perceived by social media users. By learning on how followers react to different SMIs' communication styles, brands can better elaborate their influencer marketing strategies. Based on research insights, brands can select the SMIs that show a better congruency with the products and brands but also select the SMI that show a better congruency with their customers. To increase SMIs' communication effectiveness, it is suggested that brands develop case studies close to their customers regarding the SMIs that represent the brand. It is always in brand's best interest to select the SMI that better matches the interests and the values of the brand, therefore conducting market studies on how those SMIs are perceived by their followers is fundamental to assess if their communication provides good quality information to their followers, but also to assess if their communication is credible, authentic, trustworthy and original. SMIs that are associated with positive characteristics tend to keep their followers and attract new ones, this is particularly important for brands for two distinct reasons. First, the interaction between SMI and followers can contribute to an open dialogue where business insights about customers' needs can arise, thus it provides the chance for brands to learn about their customers' expectations and about their frustrations, which can facilitate the development and improvement of services and products; second, after some time the SMIs' positive characteristics are associated with the brand in itself due to Classical Conditioning Learning mechanisms which help in the development of positive attitudes towards the brand (for more information regarding the Theory of Classical Conditioning see Babin, Harris, & Murray, 2018; Solomon, 2018), thus it is on brand best interest to detect the SMIs that produce positive perceptions close to their followers, but it is fundamental to also detect the ones that produce negative perceptions to prevent some brand damage. On the other hand, the assessment of the motives behind following SMI facilitates the understanding regarding the type of communication that is preferred by followers, which allied with the SMIs perceived characteristics facilitates the selection of an SMI that shows congruency with the brand but also their followers.

The advance of Artificial Intelligence will certainly offer simplified ways to assess followers' opinions and perceptions of SMIs. Nevertheless, it seems relevant to run qualitative and quantitative research on the comments produced by SMIs' followers to assess their valence, their suggestions, and their needs.

FUTURE RESEARCH DIRECTIONS

While the knowledge regarding the SMIs' characteristics is well developed, the same is not true for the motives to follow SMIs. Nevertheless, both topics of research show methodological shortcomings related to the universe of individuals that were gathered to run the studies. The studies that focused on the perception of SMIs and the studies that intended to uncover reasons, motives, or needs for following SMIs were mainly conducted among Western young adults from the US or Europe who follow SMIs on Instagram. Future research should expand their universe of individuals by focusing on other populations and other social networks (e.g., TikTok, Youtube). The call for transcultural research is particularly important for marketing strategies since different cultures and values can contribute to different perceptions of SMIs and motives to follow them. Moreover, the age gap that exists in these studies is particularly concerning, since these studies mainly draw conclusions about individuals from Gen Z, thus it remains unclear if the same conclusions cloud be applied to other generations, which can negatively impact the design of marketing strategies targeting other age generations rather than Gen Z.

CONCLUSION

Influencer marketing is on the rise, as it seems that future marketing strategies will adopt SMI as a reliable source of communication between the brand and customers. The relatively less expensive form of communication, compared with traditional marketing and advertising techniques also pushes the development and investment in influencer marketing across several brands. Followers underline motivations and perception of SMI seem to be fundamental to gather a stronger audience, nevertheless it is important that research their avenues to the understanding of communication and persuasion strategies used by SMI on the effectiveness of message communication, comprehension and behavioral change in SMIs' followers. SMI may not just help brands communicate information, in fact, they may also have a role in the production of knowledge close to customers that may inform brands regarding customers' behaviors and expectations, opening with this new form of product research directly close to their own costumers.

REFERENCES

Abidin, C. (2015). Communicative intimacies: Influencers and perceived interconnectedness. *Ada: A Journal of Gender. New Media, and Technology*, *8*, 1–16.

Andò, R. (2016). The ordinary celebrity: Italian young vloggers and the definition of girlhood. *Film. Fashion & Consumption*, *5*(1), 123–139. doi:10.1386/ffc.5.1.123_1

Antunes, A. C., Miranda, S., & Gama, A. (2022). The (not so) secret life of senior social media influencers: An analysis of the top five 'granfluencers' on Instagram. In I. Saur-Amaral, S. Filipe, & T. Aragonez (Eds.), *Proceedings of ICIEMC 2022 - International Conference on Innovation and Entrepreneurship in Marketing and Consumer Behaviour* (pp. 30-39). UA Editora.

Antunes, A. C., & Murteira, C. (2023). *Can macroinfluencers have an impact on the customers' journey of their followers? Acciones y reacciones ante-la manipulación social: redes sociales, publicidad y marketing*. Dykinson S. L.

Areeb, Q. M., Nadeem, M., Sohail, S. S., Imam, R., Doctor, F., Himeur, Y., Hussain, A., & Amira, A. (2023). Filter bubbles in recommender systems: Fact or fallacy-A systematic review. *Wiley Interdisciplinary Reviews. Data Mining and Knowledge Discovery*, *13*(6), 1512. doi:10.1002/widm.1512

Arora, A., Bansal, S., Kandpal, C., Aswani, R., & Dwivedi, Y. (2019). Measuring social media influencer index-insights from Facebook, Twitter and Instagram. *Journal of Retailing and Consumer Services*, *49*, 86–101. doi:10.1016/j.jretconser.2019.03.012

Babin, B. J., Harris, E. G., & Murray, K. B. (2018). *CB8: Consumer behavior*. Cengage Learning.

Balaban, D., Mucundorfeanu, M., & Naderer, B. (2022). The role of trustworthiness in social media influencer advertising: Investigating users' appreciation of advertising transparency and its effects. *Communications*, *47*(3), 395–421. doi:10.1515/commun-2020-0053

Belanche, D., Casaló, L. V., Flavián, M., & Ibáñez-Sánchez, S. (2021a). Understanding influencer marketing: The role of congruence between influencers, products and consumers. *Journal of Business Research*, *132*, 186–195. doi:10.1016/j.jbusres.2021.03.067

Belanche, D., Casaló, L. V., Flavián, M., & Ibáñez-Sánchez, S. (2021b). Building influencers' credibility on Instagram: Effects on followers' attitudes and behavioral responses toward the influencer. *Journal of Retailing and Consumer Services*, *61*, 102585. doi:10.1016/j.jretconser.2021.102585

Beverland, M., & Farrelly, F. (2010). The Quest for authenticity in consumption: Consumers' purposive choice of authentic cues to shape experienced outcomes. *The Journal of Consumer Research*, *36*(5), 838–856. doi:10.1086/615047

Bevilacqua, J., & Del Giudice, E. (2018). *Why brands need to utilize influencer marketing in 2018*. St Joseph Communications. https://stjoseph.com/insight/influencer-marketing-2018-infographic/

Boerman, S. C. (2020). The effects of the standardized instagram disclosure for micro- and meso-influencers. *Computers in Human Behavior*, *103*, 199–207. doi:10.1016/j.chb.2019.09.015

Breves, P., Liebers, N., Abt, M., & Kunze, A. (2019). The perceived fit between Instagram influencers and the endorsed brand. *Journal of Advertising Research*, *59*(4), 440–454. doi:10.2501/JAR-2019-030

Bucher, T., & Helmond, A. (2018). The affordances of social media platforms. In J. Burgess, A. Marwick, & T. Poell (Eds.), *The SAGE handbook of social media* (pp. 233–253). Sage. doi:10.4135/9781473984066.n14

Campbell, C., & Farrell, J. R. (2020). More than meets the eye: The functional components underlying influencer marketing. *Business Horizons*, *63*(4), 469–479. doi:10.1016/j.bushor.2020.03.003

Carter, D. (2016). Hustle and Brand: The sociotechnical shaping of influence. *Social Media + Society*, *2*(3), 1–12. doi:10.1177/2056305116666305

Chen, J. (2022). Research on the echo-chamber effect. *Advances in Social Science, Education and Humanities Research, 638*, 874–877.

Cook, M. (2021). *Perceiving others: The psychology of interpersonal perception*. Routledge. doi:10.4324/9781003173908

Cotter, K. (2019). Playing the visibility game: How digital influencers and algorithms negotiate influence on Instagram. *New Media & Society, 21*(4), 895–913. doi:10.1177/1461444818815684

Croes, E. A., & Bartels, J. (2021). Young adults' motivations for following social influencers and their relationship to identification and buying behavior. *Computers in Human Behavior, 124*, 106910. doi:10.1016/j.chb.2021.106910

Cuesta, U. (2000). *Psicología social de la communicación*. Ediciones Cátedra.

De Veirman, M., Cauberghe, V., & Hudders, L. (2017). Marketing through Instagram influencers: The impact of number of followers and product divergence on brand attitude. *International Journal of Advertising, 36*(5), 798–828. doi:10.1080/02650487.2017.1348035

De Veirman, M., Cauberghe, V., & Hudders, L. (2017). Marketing through Instagram influencers: The impact of number of followers and product divergence on brand attitude. *International Journal of Advertising, 36*(5), 798–828. doi:10.1080/02650487.2017.1348035

Deci, E. L., Koestner, R., & Ryan, R. M. (1999). A meta-analytic review of experiments examining the effects of extrinsic rewards on intrinsic motivation. *Psychological Bulletin, 125*(6), 627–668. doi:10.1037/0033-2909.125.6.627 PMID:10589297

Djafarova, E., & Rushworth, C. (2017). Exploring the credibility of online celebrities' Instagram profiles in influencing the purchase decisions of young female users. *Computers in Human Behavior, 68*, 1–7. doi:10.1016/j.chb.2016.11.009

Duffett, R. (2017). Influence of social media marketing communications on young consumers' attitudes. *Young Consumers, 18*(1), 19–39. doi:10.1108/YC-07-2016-00622

Duffy, B. E. (2020). Social media influencers. In K. Ross, I. Bachmann, V. Cardo, S. Moorti, & M. Scarcelli (Eds.), *International encyclopedia of gender, media, and communication*. Wiley-Blackwell. doi:10.1002/9781119429128.iegmc219

Duranton, C., & Gaunet, F. (2016). Behavioural synchronization from an ethological perspective: Overview of its adaptive value. *Adaptive Behavior, 24*(3), 181–191. doi:10.1177/1059712316644966

Erdogan, B. Z. (1999). Celebrity endorsement: A literature review. *Journal of Marketing Management, 15*(4), 291–314. doi:10.1362/026725799784870379

Fairchild, C. (2007). Building the authentic celebrity: The "Idol" phenomenon in the attention economy. *Popular Music and Society, 30*(3), 355–375. doi:10.1080/03007760600835306

Fiske, S. T., & Taylor, S. E. (2021). *Social cognition: From brains to culture* (4th ed.). Sage.

Freberg, K., Graham, K., McGaughey, K., & Freberg, L. A. (2011). Who are the social media influencers? A study of public perceptions of personality. *Public Relations Review*, *37*(1), 90–92. doi:10.1016/j.pubrev.2010.11.001

French, J. R., Raven, B., & Cartwright, D. (1959). The bases of social power. *Classics of Organization Theory, 7*(311-320), 1.

Ganguly, S. (2015). Why social media advertising is set to explode in the next 3 years. *Marketing Land*. https://marketingland.com/social-media-advertising-setexplode-next-3-years-121691

Garcia-Marques, L., Ferreira, M. B., & Garrido, M. (2017). Processos de influência social [Social influence processes]. In J. Vala & M.B. Monteiro (Coord.), Psicologia social (pp. 245-300). Fundação Calouste Gulbenkian.

Geyser, W. (2022, July 27). *What is an influencer? Social media influencers defined* [Updated 2022]. Influencer Marketing Hub. https://influencermarketinghub.com/what-is-an-influencer/#toc-0

Gottfried, J., & Shearer, E. (2016). *News use across social media platforms 2016*. Pew Research Center. https://www.journalism.org/2016/05/26/news-use-acrosssocial-media-platforms-2016/

Grävc, J.-F. (2017). Exploring the perception of influencers vs. traditional celebrities: Are social media stars a new type of endorser? In *Proceedings of the 8th International Conference on Social Media & Society*. Association for Computing Machinery. 10.1145/3097286.3097322

Gräve, J.-F., & Bartsch, F. (2022). #Instafame: Exploring the endorsement effectiveness of influencers compared to celebrities. *International Journal of Advertising*, *41*(4), 591–622. doi:10.1080/02650487.2021.1987041

Guay, F., Chanal, J., Ratelle, C. F., Marsh, H. W., Larose, S., & Boivin, M. (2010). Intrinsic, identified, and controlled types of motivation for school subjects in young elementary school children. *The British Journal of Educational Psychology*, *80*(4), 711–735. doi:10.1348/000709910X499084 PMID:20447334

Haenlein, M., Anadol, E., Farnsworth, T., Hugo, H., Hunichen, J., & Welte, D. (2020). Navigating the new era of influencer marketing: How to be successful on Instagram, TikTok, & Co. *California Management Review*, *63*(1), 5–25. doi:10.1177/0008125620958166

Hogg, M. A., & Vaughan, G. M. (2014). *Social Psychology* (7th ed.). Pearson Education Limited.

Hovland, C. I., & Weiss, W. (1951). The influence of source credibility on communication effectiveness. *Public Opinion Quarterly*, *15*(4), 635–650. doi:10.1086/266350

Hudders, L., De Jans, S., & De Veirman, M. (2021). The commercialization of social media stars: A literature review and conceptual framework on the strategic use of social media influencers. *International Journal of Advertising*, *40*(3), 327–375. doi:10.1080/02650487.2020.1836925

Hudders, L., & Lou, C. (2022). A new era of influencer marketing: Lessons from recent inquires and thoughts on future directions. *International Journal of Advertising*, *42*(1), 1–5. doi:10.1080/02650487.2022.2031729

Hughes, C., Swaminathan, V., & Brooks, G. (2019). Driving brand engagement through online social influencers: An empirical investigation of sponsored blogging campaigns. *Journal of Marketing*, *83*(5), 78–96. doi:10.1177/0022242919854374

Influencer Marketing Hub. (2023). *The state of influencer marketing 2023: Benchmark report*. https://influencermarketinghub.com/influencer-marketing-benchmark-report/

Janssen, L., Schouten, A. P., & Croes, E. A. (2022). Influencer advertising on Instagram: Product-influencer fit and number of followers affect advertising outcomes and influencer evaluations via credibility and identification. *International Journal of Advertising*, *41*(1), 101–127. doi:10.1080/02650487.2021.1994205

Kapitan, S., van Esch, P., Soma, V., & Kietzmann, J. (2022). Influencer marketing and authenticity in content creation. *Australasian Marketing Journal*, *30*(4), 342–351. doi:10.1177/18393349211011171

Karhawi, I. (2017). Influenciadores digitais: conceitos e práticas em discussão. *Revista Communicare, 17*, 46-61.

Karlsen, R., Steen-Johnsen, K., Wollebæk, D., & Enjolras, B. (2017). Echo chamber and trench warfare dynamics in online debates. *European Journal of Communication*, *32*(3), 257–273. doi:10.1177/0267323117695734 PMID:28690351

Ki, C. W., Cuevas, L. M., Chong, S. M., & Lim, H. (2020). Influencer marketing: Social media influencers as human brands attaching to followers and yielding positive marketing results by fulfilling needs. *Journal of Retailing and Consumer Services*, *55*, 102133. doi:10.1016/j.jretconser.2020.102133

Ki, C. W. C., & Kim, Y. K. (2019). The mechanism by which social media influencers persuade consumers: The role of consumers' desire to mimic. *Psychology and Marketing*, *36*(10), 905–922. doi:10.1002/mar.21244

Kimmel, A. J. (2018). *Psychological foundations of marketing: The keys to consumer behavior* (2nd ed.). Routledge. doi:10.4324/9781315436098

Klear. (2022). *2022 State of influencer marketing report*. https://klear.com/reports/2022-state-of-influencer-marketing-report/

Koban, L., Ramamoorthy, A., & Konvalinka, I. (2019). Why do we fall into sync with others? Interpersonal synchronization and the brain's optimization principle. *Social Neuroscience*, *14*(1), 1–9. doi:10.1080/17470919.2017.1400463 PMID:29091537

Kühn, J., & Riesmeyer, C. (2022, Mai). *More than just advertising - An explorative study of young adults' motives for following social media influencers* [Posterpräsentation]. Poster presentation at the International Communication Association (ICA), Paris.

Lai, E. R. (2011). Motivation: A literature review. *Person Research's Report*, *6*, 40–41.

Lamberton, C., & Stephen, A. T. (2016). A thematic exploration of digital, social media, and mobile marketing: Research evolution from 2000 to 2015 and an agenda for future inquiry. *Journal of Marketing*, *80*(6), 146–172. doi:10.1509/jm.15.0415

Lee, J. A., Sudarshan, S., Sussman, K. L., Bright, L. F., & Eastin, M. S. (2021). Why are consumers following social media influencers on Instagram? Exploration of consumers' motives for following influencers and the role of materialism. *International Journal of Advertising*, *41*(1), 78–100. doi:10.1080/02650487.2021.1964226

Leung, F., Zhang, J., Gu, F., Li, Z., & Palmatier, R. (2022). Does influencer marketing really pay off? *Harvard Business Review*. https://hbr.org/2022/11/does-influencer-marketing-really-pay-off

Li, Y., & Peng, Y. (2021). Influencer marketing: Purchase intention and its antecedents. *Marketing Intelligence & Planning*, *39*(7), 960–978. doi:10.1108/MIP-04-2021-0104

Lou, C. (2021). Social media influencers and followers: Theorization of a trans-parasocial relation and explication of its implications for influencer advertising. *Journal of Advertising*, 1–18.

Lou, C. (2022). Social media influencers and followers: Theorization of a Trans-Parasocial relation and explication of its implications for influencer advertising. *Journal of Advertising*, *51*(1), 4–21. doi:10.1080/00913367.2021.1880345

Lou, C., Taylor, C. R., & Zhou, X. (2023). Influencer marketing on social media: How different social media platforms afford influencer–follower relation and drive advertising effectiveness. *Journal of Current Issues and Research in Advertising*, *44*(1), 60–87. doi:10.1080/10641734.2022.2124471

Lou, C., & Yuan, S. (2019). Influencer marketing: How message value and credibility affect consumer trust of branded content on social media. *Journal of Interactive Advertising*, *19*(1), 58–73. doi:10.1080/15252019.2018.1533501

Luoma-Aho, V., Pirttimäki, T., Maity, D., Munnukka, J., & Reinikainen, H. (2019). Primed authenticity: How priming impacts authenticity perception of social media influencers. *International Journal of Strategic Communication*, *13*(4), 352–365. doi:10.1080/1553118X.2019.1617716

Lutkenhaus, R. O., Jansz, J., & Bouman, M. P. (2019). Tailoring in the digital era: Stimulating dialogues on health topics in collaboration with social media influencers. *Digital Health*, *5*, 1–11. doi:10.1177/2055207618821521 PMID:30729023

Marwick, A. (2016). You may know me from Youtube: (Micro-)celebrity in social media. In P. D. Marshall & S. Redmond (Eds.), A companion to celebrity (pp. 333-350). Wiley.

Masuda, H., Han, S. H., & Lee, J. (2022). Impacts of influencer attributes on purchase intentions in social media influencer marketing: Mediating roles of characterizations. *Technological Forecasting and Social Change*, *174*, 121246. doi:10.1016/j.techfore.2021.121246

Moorman, C., Zaltman, G., & Deshpandé, R. (1992). Relationships between providers and users of market research: The dynamics of trust within and between organizations. *JMR, Journal of Marketing Research*, *29*(3), 314–328. doi:10.1177/002224379202900303

Morton, F. (2020). Influencer marketing: An exploratory study on the motivations of young adults to follow social media influencers. *Journal of Digital & Social Media Marketing*, *8*(2), 156–165.

Moscovici, S. (1976). *La psychanalyse: Son image et son public* [Psychoanalysis: Its image and public]. Presses Universitaires de France.

Murteira, C. (2023). *Facial mimicry in social relations. Género y educación ante-la manipulación de la comunicación*. Dykinson S. L.

Ohanian, R. (1990). Construction and validation of a scale to measure celebrity endorsers' perceived expertise, trustworthiness, and attractiveness. *Journal of Advertising*, *19*(3), 39–52. doi:10.1080/00913367.1990.10673191

Peng, C. (2023). Influencer marketing: Statistics and skepticism. *Open Journal of Business and Management*, *11*(2), 744–754. doi:10.4236/ojbm.2023.112040

Phua, J., Jin, S. V., & Kim, J. J. (2017). Gratifications of using Facebook, Twitter, Instagram, or Snapchat to follow brands: The moderating effect of social comparison, trust, tie strength, and network homophily on brand identification, brand engagement, brand commitment, and membership intention. *Telematics and Informatics*, *34*(1), 412–424. doi:10.1016/j.tele.2016.06.004

Pöyry, E. I., Pelkonen, M., Naumanen, E., & Laaksonen, S.-M. (2019). A call for authenticity: Audience responses to social media influencer endorsements in strategic communication. *International Journal of Strategic Communication*, *13*(4), 336–351. doi:10.1080/1553118X.2019.1609965

Raven, B. H. (1965). Social influence and power. In I. D. Steiner & M. Fishbein (Eds.), *Current studies in social psychology* (pp. 371–382). Holt, Rinehart & Winston.

Raven, B. H., & French, J. R. P. (1958). Legitimate power, coercive power, and observability in social influence. *Sociometry*, *21*(2), 83–97. doi:10.2307/2785895

Reinikainen, H., Munnukka, J., Maity, D., & Luoma-Aho, V. (2020). 'You really are a great big sister'—Parasocial relationships, credibility, and the moderating role of audience comments in influencer marketing. *Journal of Marketing Management*, *36*(3–4), 279–298. doi:10.1080/0267257X.2019.1708781

Rosengren, S., & Campbell, C. (2021). Navigating the future of influencer advertising: Consolidating what is known and identifying new research directions. *Journal of Advertising*, *50*(5), 505–509. doi:10.1080/00913367.2021.1984346

Rowland, F. (2011). The filter bubble: What the internet is hiding from you. *Portal (Baltimore, Md.)*, *11*(4), 1009–1011.

Ruiz-Gomez, A. (2019). Digital fame and fortune in the age of social media: A classification of social media influencers. *aDResearch ESIC, 19*, 8-29.

Rundin, K., & Colliander, J. (2021). Multifaceted influencers: Toward a new typology for influencer roles in advertising. *Journal of Advertising*, *50*(5), 548–564. doi:10.1080/00913367.2021.1980471

Sammis, K., Ng, J., Pomponi, S., & Lincoln, C. (2015). *Influencer marketing for dummies*. For Dummies.

SanMiguel, P., Guercini, S., & Sádaba, T. (2018). The impact of attitudes towards influencers amongst millennial fashion buyers. *Studies in Communication Sciences*, *18*(2), 439–460.

Schouten, A. P., Janssen, L., & Verspaget, M. (2020). Celebrity vs. influencer endorsements in advertising: The role of identification, credibility, and product-endorser fit. *International Journal of Advertising*, *39*(2), 258–281. doi:10.1080/02650487.2019.1634898

Scott-Phillips, T. C. (2007). The social evolution of language, and the language of social evolution. *Evolutionary Psychology*, *5*(4), 147470490700500405. doi:10.1177/147470490700500405

Sicilia, M., & López, M. (2023). What do we know about influencers on social media? Toward a new conceptualization and classification of influencers. In C. L. Wang (Ed.), *The Palgrave handbook of interactive marketing* (pp. 393–622). Palgrave Macmillan Cham. doi:10.1007/978-3-031-14961-0_26

Sokolova, K., & Kefi, H. (2020). Instagram and YouTube bloggers promote it, why should I buy? How credibility and parasocial interaction influence purchase intentions. *Journal of Retailing and Consumer Services*, *53*, 1–9. doi:10.1016/j.jretconser.2019.01.011

Solomon, M. (2018). *Consumer behavior- Buying, having, and being* (12th ed.). Pearson Education.

Statista. (2023). *Number of social media users worldwide from 2017 to 2027*. https://www.statista.com/statistics/278414/number-of-worldwide-social-network-users/

Taillon, B. J., Mueller, S. M., Kowalczyk, C. M., & Jones, D. N. (2020). Understanding the relationships between social media influencers and their followers: The moderating role of closeness. *Journal of Product and Brand Management*, *29*(6), 767–782. doi:10.1108/JPBM-03-2019-2292

Talavera, M. (2015). 10 reasons why influencer marketing is the next big thing. *Adweek*. https://www.adweek.com/digital/10-reasons-why-influencer-marketing-is-thenext-big-thing/

Trivedi, J., & Sama, R. (2020). The effect of influencer marketing on consumers' brand admiration and online purchase intentions: An emerging market perspective. *Journal of Internet Commerce*, *19*(1), 103–124. doi:10.1080/15332861.2019.1700741

Uzunoğlu, E., & Kip, S. M. (2014). Brand communication through digital influencers: Leveraging blogger engagement. *International Journal of Information Management*, *34*(5), 592–602. doi:10.1016/j.ijinfomgt.2014.04.007

Varsamis, E. (2018). Are social media influencers the next-generation brand ambassadors? *Forbes*. https://www.forbes.com/sites/theyec/2018/06/13/are-social-mediainfluencers-the-next-generation-brand-ambassadors/#2d8b9e82473d

von Mettenheim, W., & Wiedmann, K. P. (2021). The complex triad of congruence issues in influencer marketing. *Journal of Consumer Behaviour*, *20*(5), 1277–1296. doi:10.1002/cb.1935

Vrontis, D., Makrides, A., Christofi, M., & Thrassou, A. (2021). Social media influencer marketing: A systematic review, integrative framework and future research agenda. *International Journal of Consumer Studies*, *4*(45), 617–644. doi:10.1111/ijcs.12647

Wang, C. L. (2021). New frontiers and future directions in interactive marketing: Inaugural Editorial. *Journal of Research in Interactive Marketing*, *15*(1), 1–9. doi:10.1108/JRIM-03-2021-270

Weismueller, J., Harrigan, P., Wang, S., & Soutar, G. N. (2020). Influencer endorsements: How advertising disclosure and source credibility affect consumer purchase intention on social media. *Australasian Marketing Journal*, *28*(4), 160–170. doi:10.1016/j.ausmj.2020.03.002

Xiao, M., Wang, R., & Chan-Olmsted, S. M. (2018). Factors affecting YouTube influencer marketing credibility: A heuristic-systematic model. *Journal of Media Business Studies*, *15*(3), 188–213. doi:10.1080/16522354.2018.1501146

Yodel, G. (2017). What is influencer marketing? *Huffpost*. https://www.huffingtonpost.com/global-yodel/what-is-influcnermarketing_b_10778128.html

Zarei, K., Ibosiola, D., Farahbakhsh, R., Gilani, Z., Garimella, K., Crespi, N., & Tyson, G. (2020). Characterizing and detecting sponsored influencer posts on Instagram. *ASONAM 2020: IEEE/ACM International Conference on Advances in Social Networks Analysis and Mining*, 327-331.

Zniva, R., Weitzl, W., & Lindmoser, C. (2023). Be constantly different! How to manage influencer authenticity. *Electronic Commerce Research*, *23*(3), 1485–1514. doi:10.100710660-022-09653-6

ADDITIONAL READING

Antunes, A. C., & Murteira, C. (2023). *Can macroinfluencers have an impact on the customers' journey of their followers? Acciones y reacciones ante-la manipulación social: redes sociales, publicidad y marketing*. Dykinson S. L.

Fennis, B. M., & Stroebe, W. (2021). *The psychology of advertising* (3rd ed.). Psychology Press.

Gupta, S. (2021). How people buy online: The psychology behind consumer behaviour. *Sage (Atlanta, Ga.)*. Advance online publication. doi:10.4135/9789354793066

Kahle, L. R., Lowrey, T. M., & Huber, J. (Eds.). (2022). *APA handbook of consumer psychology*. American Psychological Association. doi:10.1037/0000262-000

Lou, C., & Yuan, S. (2019). Influencer marketing: How message value and credibility affect consumer trust of branded content on social media. *Journal of Interactive Advertising*, *19*(1), 58–73. doi:10.1080/15252019.2018.1533501

Trivedi, J., & Sama, R. (2020). The effect of influencer marketing on consumers' brand admiration and online purchase intentions: An emerging market perspective. *Journal of Internet Commerce*, *19*(1), 103–124. doi:10.1080/15332861.2019.1700741

Vrontis, D., Makrides, A., Christofi, M., & Thrassou, A. (2021). Social media influencer marketing: A systematic review, integrative framework and future research agenda. *International Journal of Consumer Studies*, *4*(45), 617–644. doi:10.1111/ijcs.12647

Wang, C. L. (2021). New frontiers and future directions in interactive marketing: Inaugural Editorial. *Journal of Research in Interactive Marketing*, *15*(1), 1–9. doi:10.1108/JRIM-03-2021-270

KEY TERMS AND DEFINITIONS

Attitude: Evaluation of an object that impacts the way individuals feel, think, and behave.

Consumerism: Conscious consuming behaviour that is based on economic, social, cultural, and environmental responsibility.

Motivation: Reasons underlying individuals' behavior to reach a predetermined goal.

Perception: Subjective and personal interpretation of reality.

Persuasion: Influencing process to change individuals' beliefs and behaviors.

Social Influence: Social process where the presence of imaged presence of others impacts individuals' behavior, believes, or attitudes.

Social Media Influencer: Digital content creator who disseminates compelling content on a regular basis.

Chapter 5
Virtual Influencers:
The Irruption of Artificial Intelligence in Digital Influencers

Mario Sierra Martin
Universidad de Málaga, Spain

Alvaro Díaz Casquero
Universidad de Málaga, Spain

Marina Sánchez Pérez
Universidad de Málaga, Spain

Bárbara Rando Rodríguez
Universidad de Málaga, Spain

ABSTRACT

The digital revolution has fueled the rise of influencers who shape opinions and behaviors online. However, the arrival of virtual influencers, avatars generated by artificial intelligence, is transforming advertising. These avatars, like Lil Miquela, are run by brands and agencies, offer customization and flexibility, and pose fewer ethical risks. Although they are not always as effective as humans, they can be valuable in rational campaigns. In a world where artificial intelligence is growing, these virtual influencers are emerging as a powerful tool in marketing. This chapter explores its importance and evolution in society and marketing.

INTRODUCTION

The digital era has undergone a significant upheaval in recent years, and the role of the influencer has proven to be an extraordinary phenomenon. According to recent data (Smith, 2021), the number of people consuming and creating online content has seen a substantial increase, with over 3.6 billion active users on social media worldwide. Furthermore, it has been observed that many of these influencers are capable

DOI: 10.4018/979-8-3693-0551-5.ch005

of profoundly impacting the opinions, purchasing decisions, and even the behavior of their followers. According to a market study (Johnson et al., 2022), 72% of consumers trust product recommendations made by influencers they follow. These influencers have become experts in shaping trends and influencing societal opinions through their loyal follower communities. This phenomenon has transformed the dynamics of digital communication and marketing.

In the last decade, with the growth of social networks such as Facebook or Instagram, these content creators have become very popular among companies to promote their brands (Bergkvist & Zhou, 2016). They give credibility to the message that the company wants to convey (Kamins, 1989) and improve its appearance thanks to the image that these influencers have in the eyes of their followers (Louie & Obermiller, 2002; McCracken, 1989).

However, in recent times, technology has continued to evolve and part of the market has been changing. Specifically, these popular influencers that we have been getting to know could be overshadowed by the arrival of those already known as Virtual Influencers. These are avatars with the appearance or features of human beings that are generated by a computer and are turning the advertising industry upside down (Franke, C., et al. 2022).

These digital characters are assigned to profiles on social networks and can be directed by digital agencies or brands (Guthrie, 2020). They are able to create communities of loyal followers, just like human influencers, and brands are increasingly interested in them (Hugh & Leung, 2022). These avatars can take on a variety of appearances, from beings that appear to be mere caricatures to characters that are almost impossible to distinguish if they are human beings. Virtual influencers can range from imaginary cartoon-like beings to incredibly realistic characters that are almost impossible to distinguish from real humans in everyday life (Aggarwal & McGill, 2007; Delbaere, 2011).

An example of this is the influencer Lil Miquela, who has been able to reach almost 3 million followers on Instagram, and has managed to collaborate with such important brands as Bershka, Prada or Alexander McQueen. It has been generated by Brud, a company dedicated to artificial intelligence located in Los Angeles that has also created other virtual influencers such as Bermuda or Blawko.

If brands want to collaborate with these influencers, they must carefully evaluate their characteristics, especially taking into account ethical and social issues.

Virtual influencers have numerous advantages that make them so special and unique: first of all, one of the aspects to highlight about this type of influencer is personalization. What do we mean by this? Virtual influencers have a peculiarity. What distinguishes them from the influencers that we are used to seeing on networks and is the case of adaptation of these to the target audience that we want to attract. For example: we can create a virtual influencer with a certain appearance, with a specific skin color, their height and clothing, in addition to their location and behavior (Guthrie, 2020; Sands, 2022). However, it must be taken into account that a representation that is too fictitious or unrealistic of the standards we are used to seeing can achieve the opposite result (Franke, C., et al. 2022).

On the other hand, another of the advantages of having a virtual influencer is flexibility, this means that by working with this type of influencer we avoid concerns such as fatigue, hunger, location problems, etc. (Appel, 2020).

Comparing working with real influencers (Pradhan, 2023), collaborations with virtual influencers take on lower risks related to involvement in scandals and unethical behavior (Guthrie, 2020).

The novel concept of virtual influencers also raises concerns about the transparency and authenticity of the recommendations and opinions promoted by these influencers. It is essential to always make it clear that they are fictional entities. Lack of authenticity is the main issue that brands may encounter.

When the companies themselves, creators of these virtual influencers, control their image and actions, followers may struggle to differentiate between genuine recommendations and a marketing strategy.

These ethical issues emphasize the importance of regulation and self-regulation in the virtual influencer industry (Smith, 2020; García-Gavilán et al., 2021).

There is concern about the difficulty certain populations have in detecting that virtual influencers are not real people, and this concern is based on cognitive and comprehension factors.

In these cases, the lack of experience and limited exposure to technology can hinder the discernment ability of these populations, further emphasizing the importance of regulation and education in the virtual influencer industry to protect consumers of all ages (Smith, 2020)

Moreover, as previously emphasized, it is imperative to consistently clarify the artificial nature of these virtual entities. Failure to do so can raise ethical and moral concerns, potentially resulting in a loss of trust among followers (Brown & Martinez, 2022). Such trust issues can have adverse effects on brand collaborations and partnerships (Smith & Johnson, 2021). Therefore, transparency regarding the virtual influencer's synthetic identity is essential to maintain credibility and avoid negative repercussions within the industry.

Regarding their role in digital marketing, these influencers perform a similar function to that of human influencers. They are dedicated to advertising on their social networks, collaborating with large and small brands, whether to promote products, gain buzz for a launch or a campaign or to spread a specific message. They make sponsorship posts and stories for which companies pay, and this is agreed with a contract that is signed with the company in charge of their profiles or with the individual who maintains them, if they do not belong to a company.

Although these influencers could be more effective on some social media platforms than on others, it should be noted that today they are not given as much credibility and are not as effective as human influencers and people do not perceive them as close because many publications and content that they share. However, there are reasons why companies use them as they would not otherwise exist. Studies suggest that when the message is rational and does not appeal to the emotional side, they can be as effective as human influencers, and are more predictable and easier to direct and with greater flexibility in different market segments, something that can be very useful for brands. (Ozan Ozdemir, Bora Kolfal, Paul R. Messinger & Shaheer Rizvib, 2023).

We are living in an era of exponential growth in the field of artificial intelligence. This 2023 may be a year where we fully explore the potential of artificial intelligence and begin to integrate it into our work practices, so these virtual influencers that years ago we could see as something too unusual, today can be perceived as something normal. Tools like ˝Chat GPT˝ become valuable to both content creators and brands and their communications teams, so it may be that these digital avatars are seen as a way to harness the power of AI to their benefit.

We cannot determine what will happen in the future, however, we have no doubt that this type of influencer will be decisive in the change in companies' strategy to advertise their products (Sands et al, 2022). In addition to all this, virtual influencers are very powerful tools for companies since they are capable of creating consumer trends among certain segments, so we predict that they will continue to be used due to their power of influence.

The objectives of this book chapter are (1) contextualize the figure of virtual influencers, (2) determine their importance for the marketing sector, (3) understand the evolution and (4) know the future implications of these figures in the society.

BACKGROUND

The Figure of the Virtual Influencer: Current Situation

As a result of the technological development suffered in the last era, virtual influencers have been growing exponentially and are increasingly common on social networks. (Miao et al., 2022; Davenport et al., 2020). Currently, we can define virtual influencers as robotic figures attributed to specific characters created by individuals or companies. (Guthrie, 2020; Sands et al., 2022a). Being a type of influencer directed by companies, they are adapted to the needs of the market countless times, virtual influencers establish relationships and have a life as complete as a human being can have (Hugh et al., 2022; Leung et al., 2022a), this makes a character appear close, so much so that they can create needs for consumers, which is why companies have seen a great business opportunity using these characters to increase their sales. Companies like Balenciaga or Samsung have already started interacting with virtual influencers to promote their products. (Conti et al., 2022; Guthrie, 2020), in addition to the fact that they can be represented in numerous ways, from cartoon characters to hyperrealistic recreations that look like human beings, this is due to the evolution of artificial intelligence and the great perfection in creation of these avatars. (Adtraction, 2020; Miao et al., 2022). Virtual influencers known as hyperrealists are created through CGI technologies that make them so unmistakably human, so much so that it is difficult to distinguish them, in addition to sharing content from their personal and social lives. A clear example is a virtual influencer known as Imma, she usually appears in fashion shows, participates in commercial photo shoots as one more. Virtual influencers represented as drawings or animals, avatars that do not resemble human beings, are created through 2D or 3D, so they usually make a clear distinction between the virtual and real world. Their content is related to specific topics such as advice, an example is Good Advice Cupcake which focuses on entertaining stories.

Virtual influencers have proven to be highly impactful in advertising and consumer influence. Brands employ a straightforward strategy when utilizing them: harnessing human-like characteristics and exerting precise control over their personas. This approach aims to establish relatability among consumers, leading them to identify with these virtual figures and, to some extent, overlook their non-human nature, thereby reaping the associated benefits (Conti et al., 2022).

Virtual influencers have numerous advantages that make a difference with respect to human influencers: the first aspect to highlight is personalization, this means that companies can "build" the perfect virtual influencer for their campaign or brand, for example: In case you need a virtual influencer of a specific skin color, age, appearance, height or clothing, it is possible because it is not a human being and can be created from scratch (Guthrie, 2020; Sands, 2022), on the other hand, we must highlight the flexibility that virtual influencers have, they do not have to stop to rest or eat, if you need a place to be at a specific time, it is, we avoid any problem of this style. (Appell, 2020). In addition to the reduction of risk that companies run when using these influencers since they are not related to external problems, ideals or unethical behavior. (Guthrie, 2020). On the other hand, highlighting the property, this means that these avatars belong to companies or agencies, so they can only get involved with the companies that they see fit, thus avoiding conflicts of interest. (Conti et al., 2022; Mustak et al., 2023). Automation is a good aspect that benefits companies since the tasks of publishing content, responding to messages... are done automatically thanks to the help of AI, so we should not worry if our influencer responds to the doubts of our clients or No. (Sands et al., 2022a).

However, getting involved with the avatars known as virtual influencers is not all advantages, they have some drawbacks such as: the lack of humanity in these avatars means that many people do not feel identified with them despite their hyperrealism, to such an extent. point that can even cause rejection. (Kamoonpuri and Sengar, 2023; Rajaobelina et al., 2021).

In 2021, virtual influencers began to evolve on social networks, platforms such as Instagram, YouTube or TikTok, so much so that they gained a large number of followers and were able to "influence" their followers about their opinions or trends. This is why brands have begun to interact and create campaigns with them to promote their products or services. This type of alliance with virtual influencers has led to distrust on the part of consumers in brands due to the suspicion of lack of transparency. Virtual influencers have changed the way of marketing, in which they are in charge of using these platforms correctly to positively influence society and raise awareness.

As a consequence of the power of influence that these avatars possess, they have a great responsibility and have to be able to take the risks that they may have when creating such an impact on their followers and on society in general.

This is where we pause to consider how virtual influencers can make a positive contribution to society through their publications, revealing their way of life, their environment, and their perspectives on various topics to promote significant messages and essential social changes. These messages encompass diverse domains, including fashion and even politics, allowing brands to engage with those avatars that share similar ideals.

This type of influencer must learn to communicate like a human to reach customers (Arsenyan & Mirowska; Conti et al.,2021) this is possible because virtual influencers rely on machine learning programs to provide personalized messages and thus target your followers on social media. (Conti et al.,2021; Deng & Jiang, 2019) To achieve greater interest from its followers and increasingly reach more people. In addition, it is supported by real people, thus ensuring perfection on the part of the virtual influencers, which is one of the characteristics that stand out about these avatars.

We can assert that trust plays a pivotal role for virtual influencers in their mission to connect with people and convey emotions. This is supported by a study conducted by Ying Qu, who sought to investigate the necessary conditions for people to trust virtual influencers more than humans. Qu stated that the mere fact that these avatars are created by companies tends to make consumers distrust their intentions (Hudders et al., 2021). On the other hand, they found that distrust increases significantly as the avatar's appearance becomes more human-like (Mori, 1970; Mori et al., 2012). Consequently, they concluded that if a virtual influencer is accompanied by a virtual friend or partner, it elicits the same level of trust as a human influencer. However, if this influencer is hyperrealistic and placed in a genuine environment, trust diminishes, as humans tend to perceive it as excessively real and contrived, leading to a sense of opacity and a lack of authenticity.

In conclusion, while virtual influencers are currently on the rise, consumers tend to have more negative reactions and place less trust in virtual influencers compared to human influencers. This is because these avatars are perceived as hyper-realistic machines rather than human beings. As a result, they lack mental characteristics such as empathy or cognitive-affective processing, which in turn engender fear and distrust (Arsenyan and Mirowska, 2021; Sands et al., 2022; Go and Sundar, 2019).

Evolution of the Influencer Figure

The revolution in the digital age has turned upside down in recent years and with the constant advances in artificial intelligence technology we have witnessed the recent rise of figures known as virtual influencers. These avatars are artificial, computer-created constructs and generate the same type of content as their human counterparts in the realm of online influence, as noted in Stein's 2022 study. Research has shown that these influencers can forge more connections. effective and meaningful with digital audiences than human influencers (Arsenyan & Mirowska, 2021).

It was in 2016 when the first AI-generated avatars began to be seen on Instagram. These characters have a humanoid appearance, with human features, characteristics and personalities, some more realistic, such as Lil Miquela (@lilmiquela) who was the first virtual influencer, or Shudu (@shudu.gram), and others with a more similar to that of a cartoon as is the case of Kizuna AI (@aichannel_official) or Noonouri (@noonoouri). In both cases they have been created by humans with the help of artificial intelligence and have brought about a new panorama in advertising. These avatars have the ability to promote a wide variety of products and services through their official profiles on social networks, interacting with their followers in a similar way to how a human influencer would, as studies such as Conti's have already shown (2022).

These characters can be controlled by companies, such as the aforementioned Lil Miquela, an American avatar with Brazilian and Spanish roots, which is controlled by Brud, a company dedicated to artificial intelligence based in California, USA, and which after seeing the success that Lil harvested decided to create two more avatars with which Lil Miquela could interact and create more content, in addition to also turning them into virtual influencers, who were Ronald F. Blawko (@blawko22) and Bermuda (@bermudaisbae). On the other hand, they can be controlled by an individual, such as the African digital supermodel Shudu who is controlled by Cameron-James Wilson. Something to note about these influencers is that a large part of these virtual characters have been hired by major fashion brands and high-end beauty products, such as Chanel, Burberry, Dior, Prada, Versace, Marc Jacobs, Louis Vuitton and Calvin Klein., so these avatars, in addition to advertising on their social networks, have also starred in large campaigns, which is why they have quickly adapted to different media (CITES).) Jhawar, A., Kumar, P., Sanjeev Varshney, S., 2023)

Its beginnings were in 2016 when they started a current known as the trend of "virtual youtubers" or "Vtubers". In this phenomenon of digital avatars, designed with highly realistic appearance and behavior, they began to make their presence in YouTube videos and also in live broadcasts (Miao et al., 2022; Zhou, 2020). At the same time, in April of that same year, Lil Miquela appeared on Instagram, created by Brud with the aim of becoming an "it girl" and earning her first collaborations with the makeup brand Color Pop or the clothing company Bornxraised.

However, when they began to gain more popularity it was from 2018 thanks to social networks such as Instagram or Facebook, and that was when the first large campaigns began to take place (Moustakas et al., 2020). This year the first influencers appeared with an appearance more similar to that of a cartoon than of a human being, such as the already named Kizuna AI, a Japanese virtual influencer dedicated to video games who began her career with videos on YouTube or Noonouri, focused on the area fashion and beauty. On the other hand, once again it was Miquela who achieved a great collaboration by jumping to another media outlet and doing a shoutout for V Magazine. That same year, digital supermodel Shudu Gram also made the leap and did a collaboration with Cosmopolitan magazine. In addition, she collaborated with the luxury brand Balenciaga through a photographic campaign where the digital supermodel wore the brand's creations and posed in completely digital and personalized environments. This collaboration blurred the boundaries between digital and reality, innovating and challenging everything we knew about fashion so far. He made it clear that these digital creators were not only used to promote products, but that they were capable of reinterpreting fashion. It was also in 2018 when Shudu did a collaboration for the luxury brand Balmain. The campaign was with other virtual influencers of different races, created by the same author of Gram, Cameron-James Wilson, with the aim of promoting diversity in the fashion world in every way.

In 2019, these avatars made the leap to television through a controversial Calvin Klein advertisement that starred supermodel Bella Hadid and one of the best-known virtual influencers that we have already mentioned before, Lil Miquela. The ad was for the #MyTruth #MyCalvins campaign, and ended with a kiss between the protagonists, for which both the brand and Bella and Miquela were accused of "queerbating", a term that refers to the strategy used by writers and filmmakers. to attract the LGBTI audience by developing a fictional plot of romance between characters of the same gender. Although this announcement led to a large amount of criticism, it meant an increase in the popularity of Lil Miquela, and therefore, also that of virtual influencers, since the announcement was broadcast in several countries and helped them to become known among the people who do not use social networks.

Starting in 2020 and thanks to the pandemic, the agreement between virtual influencers and companies accelerated, since they were not limited in time and space like the rest of the world was as they were characters generated by artificial intelligence. Brands took advantage of this and a huge demand arose for these avatars.

In 2023 we have been able to see how these virtual influencers have transferred to more interactive experiences. The popular game Fornite has collaborated with the famous American streamer Richard Tyler Blevins, popularly known as Ninja. This collaboration consisted of the creation of a playable character who has the same physical features as the famous streamer.

In short, over the years we have witnessed the constant evolution of these digital avatars, each one with its own personality and style. Some have been able to move forward quickly, capturing the attention of audiences and brands, and others have progressed more slowly, even falling behind. Despite the initial perceptions of strangeness, novelty, and even rejection by some part of society, today we can firmly and confidently affirm that the figure of virtual influencer has taken root and consolidated in our current society.

What was once something atypical and foreign to the normal, is today accepted by a large majority and has been considered another element of digital culture. These avatars are no longer an experiment or a curiosity and have made their presence as influencers so normal and similar to the human influencers to which we are already so accustomed.

The journey of these virtual figures over the last few years has been proof of the adaptation, acceptance and transformation that society is experiencing. What started as a curiosity has become an influential figure for our society, demonstrating that the integration of technology in our lives is something that is in continuous and constant evolution, and this is just one example.

Virtual Influencers as an Advertising Tool

In the contemporary digital era in which we live, advertising has also undergone great transformations. Virtual influencers have emerged as prominent players in the current business scenario, and their impact is especially evident when it comes to reaching young audiences. Like their human counterparts, these digital avatars play a crucial role in mobilizing and persuading this particular demographic, whose attitudes and behaviors are increasingly being influenced by digital platforms and trends.

Young people are often drawn to the feeling of innovation and novelty, and virtual influencers can channel this attraction towards themselves and simultaneously towards specific products and services. According to a recent study (García et al., 2023), it has been observed that virtual influencers have an impressive reach, connecting with over 2.5 billion young people worldwide. Like regular influencers, these avatars have the ability to mobilize this demographic group to fulfill their acquisition desires, whether related to products, brands, or even lifestyle.

A great advantage of virtual influencers that can be decisive for brands is the versatility they offer. You can choose to follow the values, style and even a specific personality that matches what your brand wants to convey and the message you want to give in the campaign, adapting to the target audience you want to address.

On the other hand, they can offer a greater level of control in the campaign and work without needing to rest, without suffering physical wear and tear. Furthermore, people who participate on social media platforms show their particular tastes in specific topics. Virtual profiles and their agencies take advantage of this to create content that reflects these interests, exploring various aspects such as lifestyle, fashion or video games. By examining followers closely, messages can be developed. campaigns and social behaviors that incorporate brands as protagonists, thus creating a bond between avatars and their followers, with the aim of creating a community.

All this translates into an increase in interest from the economic point of view of brands towards virtual influencers.

To check the effectiveness of these influencers as an advertising tool, we are going to see a study carried out by Rodrigo Martín, et al., (2021) Luis Rodrigo Martín, Isabel Rodrigo Martín and Daniel Muñoz Sastre, by the University of Valladolid, Spain.

To carry out this research, they chose the virtual Influencer Lil Miquela, who we have already talked about previously. The last four months of 2020 were selected, analyzing a total of 122 publications.

According to the study itself, 85% of these publications contain some advertising reference, something that makes it a reference in commercial advertising. The remaining 15% focus on turning Lil Miquela into a friendly character, so that her followers perceive her as someone normal, similar to human influencers.

Another aspect that stands out is that the majority of their publications are of the avatar alone, only 25% of them appear accompanied either by another virtual influencer or by a human influencer or a celebrity. This serves to add realism to your account and even increase its popularity.

In the analysis, they observed how various industries opt for the @lilmiquela profile as a platform to promote their products or services, with a wide range of sectors. However, there is one that stands out above the rest: the fashion sector, especially with regard to clothing, occupies a remarkably predominant position.

50% of commercial publications focus on the field of fashion. In a second position, although with a significantly lower percentage of 17%, is the sector related to art, creators and designers. 12% of the publications are linked to the jewelry sector, while 9% correspond to the footwear and accessories sector.

On the other hand, another point that stands out is that in Lil Miquela's commercial publications they can refer to several trademarks at the same time. In the same publication you can tag different brands in different clothing items, jewelry, makeup... Therefore, within the 104 commercial publications, it mentions 151 references, of which there are 84 different brands.

Within these brands, there are luxury brands such as Dior or Prada, but they are mostly small fashion companies generally located in the US. On the other hand, the study indicates that despite the fact that there are many commercial brands that have used the profile, less than half do so on a regular basis.

After the study by Luis Rodrigo Martín, Isabel Rodrigo Martín and Daniel Muñoz Sastre have reached the following conclusions:

Digital avatars have effectively consolidated their role as an advertising tool. They introduce brands in their publications organically, they do not limit themselves to inserting them in their description, but they also tag them. They present products and services to their audience just as traditional influencers do.

On the other hand, the power of virtual influencers goes beyond promoting brands, these avatars have the ability to shape trends. Thanks to their ability to adapt and their great versatility, they are the ideal agents to promote the latest fashions, trends and lifestyle.

Finally, they have shown that they can create an authentic bond with their community of followers. Despite being computer-generated characters, they have managed to develop unique personalities that attract the audience, which strengthens the relationship with their followers and increases their ability to influence and therefore increases the effectiveness of their advertising activity.

Ultimately, digital avatars are redefining the advertising and marketing landscape. Their ability to promote brands and influence their followers makes them essential for those brands that want to connect with a more modern audience that is more connected to networks. As the years go by, they will most likely play an increasingly important role in the communications and marketing industry.

To end this section, we are going to see some cases in which virtual influencers have led successful campaigns:

- Shudu Gram has collaborated with luxury jewelry brands such as Swarovski or Bvlgari, presenting exclusive jewelry pieces. Thanks to the fact that these campaigns are developed in completely digital environments, they can be edited so that the details of the jewels stand out.
- Noonouri runs campaigns through her Instagram account with Dior Beauty. Through video tutorials made digitally, she creates artistic and eye-catching looks to promote the brand's products and while explaining how to use and apply them properly.
- Lil Miquela collaborated with the technology brand Samsung in a campaign in which the avatar interacted with the brand's devices, exposing how technology improved her life and sharing the following message: "I myself am a product of technology, so I can relate to Samsung in a MUCH more literal way than most people."
- Japanese virtual influencer Imma collaborated with Amazon Fashion to promote her clothing collection, promoting diversity and inclusion with garments available on the Amazon platform. The campaign not only featured clothing, but also highlighted how digital fashion and virtual influences can complement and broaden the reach of online shopping options.

METHODOLOGY

As we have mentioned previously, society is in a moment of technological boom, in addition to strong development in terms of artificial intelligence and the way in which this influences society. We carried out a bibliographic review of the last 3 years, with the aim of investigating whether society is ready or if it is at the right time for virtual influencers to fear the replacement and have the power to "influence" changes in behavior and consumption of their followers and society in general.

To do this, this study aims to analyze the current situation regarding virtual influencers. The literature search was conducted on the Web of Science platform. A total of 230 articles were identified from 2020 to 2023.

The search was performed using paired combinations with the "and" connector. The procedure is summarized in the following table:

Database: Web of Science

Combinations: Virtual Influencer "and" Digital Marketing

Virtual influencer "and" Artificial Intelligence
Influencer "and" Virtual Influencer

File Types: All types of indexed references were used (publications, books, conference proceedings, articles, etc.).

Publication Areas: All publication areas were considered.

The first study, conducted by Kim EA, Kim D, E Z and Shoenberger H in 2023, titled as "The Next Hype in Social Media Advertising: Examining the Effectiveness of Brand Endorsement of Virtual Influencers", in which discusses the essential differences between virtual influencers vs. human influencers.

Virtual influencers have taken advantage of the advantages and journey of human influencers to reach consumers. This study states that 58% of respondents follow at least one virtual influencer and 35% of respondents have already purchased a product promoted by these avatars. (The Influencer Marketing Factory, 2022), however, consumers continue to prefer humans as it transmits more social signals and therefore more trust. This research affirms that the credibility of the message is an important antecedent of the attitude of the message, they concluded that "a credible message improves liking for advertisements and generates favorable advertising attitudes."

As a conclusion of the study, IVs are capturing the attention of users of these platforms; however, in general, participants showed more positive attitudes regarding the advertisements announced by HVIs. Instagram posts that showed sponsorship disclosure obtained a lower perception of the credibility of the message than those posts without disclosure, however, at the moment in which the sponsorship was revealed, the credibility of the message was extremely low in both cases, which led to non-significant mediation.

In this second study recently conducted by Huajun Li, Yuqiu Lei, Qi Zhou in June 2023, titled how: "Can you feel without being human? Comparing the effectiveness of virtual and human influencer endorsements", examines consumer responses to virtual influencers such as perceived trust and engagement intent (for example, intention to like, comment and follow), we should add that these results are focused on the IV and not on the brand. In addition to addressing the theory of perception, in which we can state that if a being or object that lacks a mind is perceived, consumers trust them less. (Rapp et al., 2021).

However, if we take into account the concept of "experience", it tends to be equivalent to or superior to that of humans since, as it is about advanced technology, they are perceived as more reliable in providing information, compared to humans.

Once the research has been carried out, it is determined that interaction and participation in social networks is a crucial factor to evaluate the effectiveness of support (Ren et al., 2023).

Comments and likes have been engagement measures to analyze the thoughts and feelings of consumers. That is why they have concluded that the number of comments in the category of experience, agency and perception of the profiles of the IVs are significantly higher than in the profiles of the HVIs, therefore, consumers talk more about the mental perception of the IV than on that of the HVI.

However, upon further investigation, they were able to verify that the emotional orientation of the comments of virtual influencers receive significantly less positive emotion and higher negative emotion. This means that: although consumers seem to be more active with virtual influencers through the number of "likes" and comments, these comments are more negative.

After verifying the negative effects in terms of the promotion of products or services by these avatars, companies ask themselves: what can we do to reduce these negative effects?

There is no doubt that virtual influencers are booming, just like the metaverse, all of this has great potential for development and application, however, this type of research reaches social media platforms, so the impact caused on the metaverse could be totally different, if being a live broadcast it would have a different reception.

On the other hand, depending on the type of product to be promoted, it has a different impact, for example: foods need more sensory signals to have credibility.

In conclusion, we can affirm that virtual influencers are a reality today and that society is accepting this new form of communication. The incorporation of these influencers raises questions from professionals in the sector. As technology advances, virtual influencers are gaining more and more strength and offer consistent advantages to represent a brand. It is clear that human and virtual influencers will coexist together. The ecosystem generated around social networks will continue to provide service to brands since society is something that continues to demand. For some experts, the culmination will take place when the fusion between virtual characters and voice assistants takes place.

CONCLUSION

Importance of Virtual Influencers for the Marketing Sector

In the digital era that we find ourselves in, social networks have revolutionized the way in which people consume content, interact with the digital medium and base their purchasing decisions on the impacts received on their platforms.

The arrival of virtual influencers designed by artificial intelligence (AI) is one of the new trends that has been gaining market share.

Among the different advantages that virtual influencers provide, we can highlight the implications that they can have for the marketing sector.

1. Without geographical barrier.

Virtual influencers stand out for their ability to generate content without geographical and cultural limitations. Compared to conventional or human influencers who usually have an audience limited by geographical factors, this is not a problem for virtual influencers, since they do not have border limitations or the logistical problems associated with traveling or settling in different places. (Johnson, 2020)

This advantage goes further when artificial intelligence allows it to adapt to various cultures and contexts. Virtual influencers can learn and understand trends in regions, cultural preferences and even language. Generating more relevant content adapted to the geographical area. (Harrys and Smith, 2019)

From the point of view of marketing for agencies or companies, being able to generate communication campaigns without geographical barriers allows you to offer a more globalized product.

2. Personal opinions.

Creating profiles in the digital world through artificial intelligence makes it possible to control the "personal" opinions of influencers, providing a clear advantage over conventional human influencers.

One of the main features of virtual influencers is the ability to control and adapt opinions, unlike human influencers whose opinions can change according to personal factors. Virtual influencers can be programmed to express coherent opinions aligned with the brand's personality. Facilitating the generation of a message aligned with the brand's values. (Johnson, 2022)

Thanks to this feature, we avoid controversies and conflicts (Harris and Lee, 2019) that occur on different occasions when a brand hires a human influencer and they lead a life far from the values that the brand promises to its audience. (Smith, 2021)

By being generated by AI, if the brand wishes, it can guarantee a constant representation of the brand over time. But it is also feasible to modify the "personality" of the influencers to adapt to current trends and remain competitive. (Garcia, 2020)

3. Timelessness.

This value is possibly one of the biggest milestones in the field of influencer marketing.

Constant availability is one of the most valued characteristics by companies and brands when it comes to virtual influencers. These can be programmed to interact with your followers at any time, regardless of day or time, which generates a more loyal and effective brand-audience relationship. In addition, when programmed by artificial intelligence, they can respond to several comments at the same moment.

For global brands or companies, having a virtual influencer allows you to be connected at any time of the day, a clear advantage over human influencers, who are subject to being available at a certain time slot that changes depending on the region of the world where they live or work the human influencer. With AI-generated influencers, availability is 24/7, allowing campaigns to reach audiences in different time zones without restrictions. (Garcia, 2021)

This constant availability allows companies to obtain greater reach, since they can use different time slots to try to reach different audience segments, thus increasing the probability of obtaining greater engagement from the campaign. (Harris and Lee, 2019)

4. Physical and psychological risk.

One of the main implications that having virtual influencers generated by artificial intelligence can have for marketing is aversion to both physical and psychological risk.

Virtual influencers, unlike their human counterparts, are not subject to the physical and psychological risks linked to live events, intense social interactions, and potential negative situations online (Rodríguez, 2023)

Guaranteeing emotional stability is synonymous with achieving a more consistent representation of the brand. Ensuring that impulsive emotions do not influence the digital behavior of virtual influencers encourages a faithful representation aligned with the brand. (Rodriguez, 2023)

The possible crises that can harm the work of a human influencer disappear when working with virtual influencers, thus helping to minimize the risk of damaging the brand image (Thompson, 2023)

Sometimes communication campaigns disseminate activities that involve a certain physical risk; when working with virtual influencers, aversion to physical risk ensures physical integrity in live events. (Thompson, 2023)

5. Personalization

Lastly, there is the implication in marketing, the personalization capacity of virtual influencers, which helps to achieve greater relevance and authenticity in online interactions.

Using artificial intelligence to personalize the brands' message and even the influencer's appearance allows brands or companies to better adapt to the needs or preferences of the audience. (Miller, 2023)

This capability allows virtual influencers to be shaped to better reach specific audiences, ensuring that content is relevant and engaging to different demographic groups. (Miller, 2023)

Thanks to personalization, virtual influencers can guarantee that the message is consistent with the brand's identity and values, promoting trust and authenticity. (Collins, 2023)

Furthermore, given the possible changes that may be required in the communication campaign, working with virtual influencers facilitates the change, thus ensuring relevance in a constantly evolving environment. (Collins, 2023). Ensuring that the online message represents the brand culture. (Miller, 2023)

DISCUSSION

The emergence of virtual influencers in recent years has sparked significant interest and debate within the realms of marketing and digital communication. This section aims to discuss key insights and implications drawn from existing literature on virtual influencers.

Authenticity and Trust: One central point of discussion revolves around the authenticity and trustworthiness of virtual influencers compared to human influencers. While some argue that virtual influencers may lack the genuine human touch, studies suggest that they can still foster a strong sense of trust and connection among their followers (Liang et al., 2022). This trust often stems from their consistent persona and image, which can be meticulously controlled and maintained.

Brand Collaborations: Virtual influencers have become a sought-after asset for brand collaborations due to their ability to promote products seamlessly. The literature highlights the effectiveness of virtual influencers in driving consumer engagement and purchase intentions (Smith & Johnson, 2021). Brands can leverage the creativity and versatility of virtual influencers to create unique and captivating marketing campaigns.

Demographic Targeting: Virtual influencers offer a valuable opportunity for precisely targeting specific demographics, particularly younger audiences. This precision in demographic targeting is supported by the ability to customize virtual influencers to align with the preferences and interests of the target group (García et al., 2023).

Ethical Considerations: The rise of virtual influencers also raises ethical concerns, such as transparency about their artificial nature and the potential for misleading audiences (Brown & Martinez, 2022). Ethical guidelines and regulations are still evolving in response to these concerns.

Future Trends: As technology advances, virtual influencers are likely to become even more sophisticated. Incorporating AI-driven conversational abilities and enhanced realism may open up new avenues for interaction and engagement (Johnson & Li, 2024). Additionally, the exploration of virtual influencers in various industries beyond fashion and cosmetics remains an exciting area of future research.

In conclusion, the discussion surrounding virtual influencers is multifaceted, touching on authenticity, trust, brand collaborations, demographic targeting, ethical considerations, and future trends. While virtual influencers offer unique advantages, it is essential for both researchers and marketers to continue exploring their impact and ethical implications as they continue to reshape the digital landscape.

FUTURE IMPACT OF VIRTUAL INFLUENCERS ON SOCIETY

Present throughout the world and with millions of followers on their accounts, virtual influencers are expected to have an even greater impact in the future. How this emerging trend looks for the future:

Transformation of the way of consumption: These virtual influencers are altering the way in which consumers make and make purchasing decisions. In the future, it is proposed that these virtual influencers will have a lot of weight in consumers' shopping basket choices. What awaits companies? They will have to adapt and modify their marketing strategies to take advantage of this trend, so that they can collaborate to promote their products and services.

New forms of communication: Virtual influencers are transforming the communication industry. Possibly, in the future we will be able to see virtual characters starring in movies and television shows.

Ethics: Although they gain strength and have increasingly more "human" behavior, ethical debates will arise that will call into question transparency and authenticity, which can affect companies that work with these virtual influencers.

In short, it is likely that we will increasingly interact with avatars of Artificial Intelligence in our daily lives. Without a doubt, the future of Artificial Intelligence that awaits us is exciting and has infinite possibilities, but it must be treated carefully and regulated so that it can be guaranteed that both human influencers and virtual influencers coexist.

With all this, the trend indicates that the digital marketing strategies of the following years will be marked, to a large extent, by virtual influencers.

REFERENCES

Appel, G., Grewal, L., Hadi, R., & Stephen, A. T. (2020). The future of social media in marketing. *Journal of the Academy of Marketing Science*, *48*(1), 79–95. Advance online publication. doi:10.100711747-019-00695-1 PMID:32431463

Bergkvist, L., & Zhou, K. Q. (2016). Celebrity endorsements: A literature review and research agenda. *International Journal of Advertising*, *35*(4), 642–663. Advance online publication. doi:10.1080/02650487.2015.1137537

Brown, L., & Martinez, C. (2022). Ethical Considerations in the Use of Virtual Influencers. *Journal of Digital Ethics*, *8*(2), 123–140.

Collins, M. (2023). Authentic communication through customizable virtual influencers. *Communication Studies Quarterly*, *12*(3), 53–67.

Delbaere, M., Michael, B., & Phillips, B. J. (2021). Social media influencers: A route to brand engagement for their followers. *Psychology and Marketing*, *38*(1), 101–112. Advance online publication. doi:10.1002/mar.21419

Franke, C., Groeppel-Klein, A., & Müller, K. (2022). Consumers' Responses to Virtual Influencers as Advertising Endorsers: Novel and Effective or Uncanny and Deceiving? *Journal of Advertising*. Advance online publication. doi:10.1080/00913367.2022.2154721

García, A., Smith, J., & Johnson, M. (2023). Virtual Influencers: Targeting Youth Audiences in the Digital Age. *Digital Marketing Journal*, *15*(1), 45–60.

García-Gavilán, S., López-González, H., & Acosta-Vargas, P. (2021). Virtual Influencers: A New Challenge in the Ethical Dilemma of Advertising. In Marketing and Smart Technologies (pp. 175-183). Springer.

Guthrie, S. (2020). Virtual influencers More human than humans. In Influencer marketing (Vol. 1). Academic Press.

Jhawar, A., Kumar, P., & Varshney, S. (2023). The emergence of virtual influencers: A shift in the influencer marketing paradigm. *Young Consumers*, *24*(4), 468–484. Advance online publication. doi:10.1108/YC-05-2022-1529

Johnson, A., & Li, S. (2024). The Future of Virtual Influencers: Trends and Implications for Marketing. *Journal of Digital Marketing*, *20*(3), 213–230.

Kamins, M. A. (1989). Celebrity and Noncelebrity Advertising Advertising in a two-sided context. *Journal of Advertising Research*, *29*(3).

Kim, E., Kim, D., Zihang, E., & Shoenberger, H. (2023). The next hype in social media advertising: Examining virtual influencers' brand endorsement effectiveness. *Frontiers in Psychology*, *14*, 1089051. Advance online publication. doi:10.3389/fpsyg.2023.1089051 PMID:36949930

Kim, H., & Park, M. (2023). Virtual influencers' attractiveness effect on purchase intention: A moderated mediation model of the Product–Endorser fit with the brand. *Computers in Human Behavior*, *143*, 107703. Advance online publication. doi:10.1016/j.chb.2023.107703

Kim, M., & Baek, T. H. (2023). Are Virtual Influencers Friends or Foes? Uncovering the Perceived Creepiness and Authenticity of Virtual Influencers in Social Media Marketing in the United States. *International Journal of Human-Computer Interaction*, 1–14. Advance online publication. doi:10.1080/10447318.2023.2233125

Leung, F. F., Gu, F. F., & Palmatier, R. W. (2022). Online influencer marketing. *Journal of the Academy of Marketing Science*, *50*(2), 226–251. Advance online publication. doi:10.100711747-021-00829-4

Li, H., Lei, Y., Zhou, Q., & Yuan, H. (2023). Can you sense without being human? Comparing virtual and human influencers endorsement effectiveness. *Journal of Retailing and Consumer Services*, *75*, 103456. Advance online publication. doi:10.1016/j.jretconser.2023.103456

Liang, X., & ... . (2022). Authenticity and Trust in Virtual Influencers: A Comparative Study. *Journal of Consumer Behaviour*, *17*(4), 345–360.

Louie, T. A., & Obermiller, C. (2002). Consumer response to a firm's endorser (dis) association decisions. *Journal of Advertising*, *31*(4), 41–52. Advance online publication. doi:10.1080/00913367.2002.10673684

McCracken, G. (1989). Who is the Celebrity Endorser? Cultural Foundations of the Endorsement Process. *The Journal of Consumer Research*, *16*(3), 310. Advance online publication. doi:10.1086/209217

Miller, S. (2023). Personalization in virtual influencers: A strategic approach in influence marketing. *Journal of Digital Marketing*, *8*(1), 38–50.

Ozdemir, O., Kolfal, B., Messinger, P. R., & Rizvi, S. (2023, August). Human or virtual: How influencer type shapes brand attitudes. *Computers in Human Behavior*, *145*, C. doi:10.1016/j.chb.2023.107771

Pradhan, D., Kuanr, A., Anupurba Pahi, S., & Akram, M. S. (2023). Influencer marketing: When and why gen Z consumers avoid influencers and endorsed brands. *Psychology and Marketing*, *40*(1), 27–47. Advance online publication. doi:10.1002/mar.21749

Rodrigo-Martín, L., Rodrigo-Martín, I., & Muñoz-Sastre, D. (2021). Los Influencers Virtuales como herramienta publicitaria en la promoción de marcas y productos. Estudio de la actividad comercial de Lil Miquela. *Revista Latina de Comunicación Social*, *79*(79), 69–90. Advance online publication. doi:10.4185/RLCS-2021-1521

Rodriguez, E. (2023). Aversión al riesgo en influencers virtuales: Un análisis en el marketing de influencia. *Journal of Digital Marketing*, *7*(2), 45–56.

Sands, S., Campbell, C. L., Plangger, K., & Ferraro, C. (2022). Unreal influence: Leveraging AI in influencer marketing. *European Journal of Marketing*, *56*(6), 1721–1747. Advance online publication. doi:10.1108/EJM-12-2019-0949

Smith, J. (2020). The Ethics of Influencer Marketing. *Journal of Business Ethics*, *167*(3), 605–618.

Smith, J. (2021). The State of Social Media in 2021. Social Media Today. Johnson, A., Brown, L., & Martinez, C. (2022). The Influence of Digital Influencers on Consumer Behavior. *JMR, Journal of Marketing Research*, *45*(2), 123–140.

Smith, R., & Johnson, K. (2021). Brand Collaborations with Virtual Influencers: An Analysis of Effectiveness. *JMR, Journal of Marketing Research*, *28*(2), 89–105.

Thompson, M. (2023). Virtual influencers and their risk aversion: Implications for ethics in technology. *Ética y Tecnología, 12*(1), 68-80.

ADDITIONAL READING

Choi, M., Choi, Y., & Lee, H. (2023). Gen Z Travelers in the Instagram Marketplace: Trust, Influencer Type, Post Type, and Purchase Intention. *Journal of Hospitality & Tourism Research (Washington, D.C.)*, 10963480231180938. Advance online publication. doi:10.1177/10963480231180938

Gerlich, M. (2023). The Power of Virtual Influencers: Impact on Consumer Behaviour and Attitudes in the Age of AI. *Administrative Sciences*, *13*(8), 178. Advance online publication. doi:10.3390/admsci13080178

Haikel-Elsabeh, M. (2023). Virtual Influencers versus Real Influencers Advertising in the Metaverse, Understanding the Perceptions, and Interactions with Users. *Journal of Current Issues and Research in Advertising*, *44*(3), 252–273. Advance online publication. doi:10.1080/10641734.2023.2218420

Mouritzen, S. L. T., Penttinen, V., & Pedersen, S. (2023). Virtual influencer marketing: The good, the bad and the unreal. *European Journal of Marketing*. Advance online publication. doi:10.1108/EJM-12-2022-0915

Ozdemir, O., Kolfal, B., Messinger, P. R., & Rizvi, S. (2023). Human or virtual: How influencer type shapes brand attitudes. *Computers in Human Behavior*, *145*, 107771. Advance online publication. doi:10.1016/j.chb.2023.107771

KEY TERMS AND DEFINITIONS

Artificial Intelligence (AI): Is an interdisciplinary discipline of computing that is dedicated to creating systems and programs capable of carrying out tasks that normally require human intelligence, such as learning, reasoning, problem solving, and decision making.

Consumer Perception: Cognitive process through which consumers acquire, interpret and organize the information received based on previous impressions and evaluations that influence their decisions and purchasing behavior.

Fornite: Fortnite is an online multiplayer video game developed by Epic Games. It features a Battle Royale mode where up to 100 players compete to be the last person or team standing, and a cooperative “Save the World” mode where players fight against hordes of monsters. The game is known for its colorful, cartoonish graphics and extensive customization options for characters.

Queerbating: Strategy used by writers, filmmakers, video game developers... which is based on developing a romantic plot with characters of the same gender in order to attract an LGTBI audience.

Vtubers: “Vtubers” stands for “Virtual YouTubers” and refers to content creators who use animated digital avatars, typically in 2D or 3D, to interact with their audience on platforms like YouTube and Twitch. These avatars enable creators to maintain anonymity or adopt a digital persona while engaging with viewers. Vtubers are popular for a wide range of content, from gaming to discussions and music.

Chapter 6
Influencing the Influencers Through Co-Creation:
Approaches to Successful Brand Strategies

Poornima Nair
https://orcid.org/0000-0001-9259-291X
Christ University, India

Sunita Kumar
https://orcid.org/0000-0002-0628-1873
Christ University, India

ABSTRACT

In today's technology-driven landscape, the internet and social media have seamlessly woven themselves into the fabric of both brands and consumers' lives. Among the arsenal of modern marketing strategies, influencer marketing has emerged as a formidable force. It bestows organisations the privilege of accessing extensive and dedicated online influencers and co-creation as a technique, making it one of the most potent tools in their marketing toolkit. This chapter focuses on the intricate art of how brands strategically harness the power of social media platforms and influencers to extend their reach far and wide, aiming to connect with as many consumers as possible. By forging these connections, brands aspire to cultivate a devoted and unwavering fan base, fostering long-term customer loyalty.

INTRODUCTION

This chapter aims to explore the concept of co-creation as a powerful tool for successful brand strategies in today's digital era. Specifically, the chapter will focus on the role of influencers and how brands can effectively collaborate with them through co-creation to enhance brand reach, engagement, and brand loyalty. The aim is to explore and analyse the concept of co-creation as a collaborative approach to influence influencers and its role in successful brand strategies.

DOI: 10.4018/979-8-3693-0551-5.ch006

In Today's world, Continuous and meaningful interaction between various stakeholders and the brands would lead to a cycle of learning where brands constantly keep themselves updated on the consumer's needs and modify their products or services to meet the consumer's expectations (Ind & Coates, 2013). The nature of consumer and brand relations has changed as a consequence of the widespread use of digital innovations by customers (Horakova et al., 2022). Identifying branding strategies most appropriate for brands has been a priority for brand managers, but with the advent of the digital era, where the presence of both the brand and the consumers on social media platforms has become a given, it has become even more crucial. Consumers are no longer passive receivers of information and are more than willing to be active participants in the brand's various activities (Prahalad & Ramaswamy, 2004). Consumers' position in conventional power structures has undergone a fundamental change as a result of the widespread connectedness made possible by the growth of social media (Evans, 2019). Nowadays, people are at the core of value creation since they are the ones who are changing the world and advancing it (Ramaswamy & Ozcan, 2014), and as a result, it becomes imperative to understand consumers on a continuous basis and find ways to keep them constantly engaged to the brand through various means which are effective. With the extensive use of social media and the boom of social media influencers, brands have to involve the right influencers to engage their target customers effectively. Past researchers have delved into the efficiency of influencer marketing and how their followers view them (Audrezeta et al., 2020; Ki & Kim, 2019), but a scarce number of studies have been conducted on the role that influencers play in co-creating value, specifically co-creating brands. And there is little research on how influencer marketing affects the consumer-brand connection (Schouten et al., 2019). The Indian influencer market was worth more than 12 billion Indian rupees in the year 2022, with an estimated growth of up to 28 billion in the year 2026 (Statista,2023). Influencer marketing has become an indispensable instrument to businesses in India, as relatable content helps foster genuine bonds with consumers. They have a substantial effect on consumer choice and product research. (Statista,2023). The majority of Indians on social media are tech-savvy and relatively young, and many of them follow at least one social media influencer. Furthermore, a sizable portion of these users primarily rely on social networks for their online brand research (Statista,2023). The Influencer Marketing Report 2022 was released by Influencer. In highlighted the fact that influencer marketing has become an important part of digital marketing strategy for big brands and that approximately 61 per cent of brands have acknowledged the fact that the influencer market has the power to attract new customers and increase the customer base of the brands (Brandequity. com,2022). Indian markets are complex because of the vast diversity, especially when it comes to the languages that are spoken in various parts of the country, there are over 210 million internet users who access content in regional tongues. Hence, brands are collaborating with influencers who create content in regional languages to connect to the maximum number of audiences (Forbes,2022).

The chapter will delve into the benefits and challenges associated with this approach, highlighting best practices. The chapter will provide valuable insights for marketers, brand managers, and researchers interested in leveraging co-creation to influence influencers and achieve their brand objectives. This will primarily involve a systematic literature review, including academic articles, industry reports, and case studies. The chapter will explore the benefits and challenges associated with co-creation in influencer-brand collaborations. It will examine how co-creation can enhance brand reach, increase consumer engagement, and foster long-term brand loyalty. The discussion will also address potential pitfalls and provide recommendations for implementing effective co-creation strategies.

BACKGROUND

Social Media

Internet users accounted for 5.18 billion people globally as of April 2023, out of which 4.8 billion people used social media (Statista,2023). Social media is a collection of Internet-based programs that expand upon the conceptual and technical underpinnings of Web 2.0 and permit the generation and exchange of content generated by the users (Kaplan & Haenlein, 2010). The prevalence of social networking sites is a swiftly expanding trend in today's corporate world, which has influenced both marketing and innovation efforts (Hollebeek et al., 2014). A variety of new ways to interact, communicate with, and involve customers have been made possible by the rise of social media(Nambisan & Baron, 2007). Through social media, businesses can establish relationships with current and potential customers and create communities that actively work together to identify issues and find solutions (Tsimonis &.Dimitriadis,2014). Social media platforms are frequently utilised by customers to share their experiences with brands. Social media has evolved into a social trendsetter in the current digital age as people spend a growing amount of time online. The majority of consumers today get their information predominantly through social media platforms, which are also one of the most effective marketing tools for fashion brands (Chu & Seock, 2020). Consumers now predominantly communicate their ideas on social media, whether they are positive or negative. This has given marketers a new avenue through which to communicate with their target market and gives them another tool with which to distinguish their customers' buying experiences (Journée & Weber, 2016). With the advent of social media, individuals now have the ability to both use and promote brands (Lamberton & Stephen, 2016). Given the scale and speed of the dispersion of information on the internet, some contributors draw a large audience, form a fan following, and serve as a resource for their followers, becoming social media influencers (SMIs) (Vrontis et al., 2021), and because of the popularity they gain, for a lot of content creators, this becomes their choice of career (Makrides et al., 2020). One of the extremely popular social media platforms, Instagram has helped fashion enthusiasts become well-known and successful, in part because of the aesthetic appeal of the platform's filters and its ability to connect with a large audience (Jin et al., 2019). Fashion firms have become interested in the rise of fashion bloggers, or people who share style advice and present certain items and brands through their blogs and social media profiles (Paton, 2014); with the growing popularity and credibility of the influencers in the market, brands are even more keen on being associated with influential influencers.

Influencers

Using a social setting and conducted in a more professional manner, influencer marketing is a development of the original notion of word-of-mouth advertising (M & K, 2017). One of the fastest-growing subfields of marketing is influencer marketing, which is also a major focus of marketing research (Boerman, 2020;Lou & Yuan,2019). Influencer endorsements are a popular technique used by brands to promote their content(Ooi et al,2023).Building beautiful and engaging social media profiles has helped a lot of individuals attain online popularity during the past ten years, as evidenced by a sizable number of followers(Hudders et al., 2021). Influencers are an innovative category of opinion leaders who have grown as an outcome of the mushrooming number of social media opportunities. A social media influencer is one of the celebrity endorsers that numerous organizations engage on Instagram. A social media influencer is an individual who gradually built up a sizable social media following by creating relevant content on the subject of interest, such as such areas as travel, sports, food, beauty, and fashion (Lou & Yuan, 2019). Specifically, Social media fashion influencers (SMFIs) are people whose high established credibility, which in turn results in high trust and relationships with their followers (Jin & Ryu,2019). Influencers promote or create content about products or services that align with their personality, as only genuineness and truthful endorsements will legitimacy with their followers (Bora Semiz & Paylan, 2023) and SMFIs have shifted the focus of basic marketing strategies from only exposure to content to participation in the process (Lang & Armstrong, 2016). And they may be active on one or many social media platforms and may be called Instagrammers, blogger or even a YouTuber (Brito et al., 2020). They occupy a position between celebrities and friends. Influencers could be characterized as "microcelebrities" who made their own achievements possible (Evans et al., 2017). There have been some researchers who claim that consumers consider social media influencers as more trustworthy sources than traditional celebrities like actors, athletes etc. (Weinswig, 2016). Through the social media content created by them, social media influencers (SMIs) have the ability to engage with their followers and affect how they see brands (De Veirman et al., 2017). The focus has shifted from goods to services to ultimately focusing on being customer-centric, which means learning and continuously collaborating with them(Vargo & Lush, 2004), where continuous and meaningful involvement is not only a necessity but also something that brands look forward to. Brands rarely succeed in meaningfully interacting with consumers on social media (Kapitan & Silvera, 2016). Higher sales, reduced price sensitivity, loyalty to the brand, and greater profitability are all outcomes of a good consumer-brand relationship (Aaker & Joachimsthaler, 2000). And what better way to engage customers than being associated with social media influencers who themselves use the products or services and then share their opinion to their followers. By engaging influencers to promote their products and services to customers who already favour their image or point of view, brands are able to take advantage of these powerful ties (Rakuten, 2019). Influencers on various social media platforms influence consumer behaviour; it motivates followers to interact and participate in the co-creation process with the influencers and also recommend those accounts to their friends and family (Casaló et al., 2020).

Co-Creation

Consumers today, despite having a plethora of choices, are either confused or dissatisfied. For managers, value creation and growth have taken centre stage. Consumers increasingly aim to exert their influence on all aspects of the business. With access to the internet and social media, they want to co-create the offering provided by the brands (Prahalad & Ramaswamy, 2004). Most businesses aim to develop products and services that are desired and relevant to both present and potential clients(Ind et al., 2019). Brands have come to understand that it's essential to increase social engagement(Kumar & Pansari, 2016). Companies have acknowledged the need to strengthen their social engagement in the current, global, and dynamic marketplace, which is defined by rising consumer power (Kumar & Pansari, 2016). The process by which an experience is generated by involving the efforts of both a provider and a consumer is known as co-creation (Prahalad & Ramaswamy, 2004), and in the case of social media influencers, brands involve them so as to be able to connect with the consumers in a more personal manner and increase their engagement in the branding process. The act of "engaging" can be understood as the interactive experiences that customers co-created with other actors (Lusch &Vargo, 2010). Co-creation has been adopted to explore how networks create brand meaning (Vallaster & Von Wallpach, 2013, Ramaswamy & Ozcan, 2016). Currently, a developing perspective emphasises that sharing personal experiences with others and users' capacity to assign their own interpretations, experiences, and contexts are vital for value creation (Kim & Choi, 2019). Co-creation is a benefit achieved from combining resources through activities and relationship-building with collaborators in the customer's service network (McColl-Kennedy et al., 2012).Past researches have concluded that co-creation activities improves the experiences that consumers derive out of the interaction with the brands (Sugathan & Ranjan,2019).

Customer Engagement

Customers today demand more from brands than just the sale of a product, confirming the transition from transactional to relationship marketing, a major shift that is evident in the recent past (Vivek et al., 2012; Islam et al., 2019). More and more, marketers refer to engagement as an all-encompassing term for marketing tactics that give organisations that employ engagement techniques a competitive advantage (Baldus et al., 2015). Customer engagement (CE) has also been included by the Marketing Science Institute (2020) in the priority list again for the period from 2020 to 2022 as the importance of CE in building brand loyalty among customers was clearly identified.Customers' identification and regular encounters with a company are indicators of customer engagement (Behnam et al., 2021). Customer engagement was proposed to be a concept comprising of constructs like identification, interaction, attention, enthusiasm absorption, etc (So et al.,2016). With the growing use of technology, client engagement frequently takes place in online settings (Venkatesan, 2017). Customers become involved when they browse for information about products, promotions, and brand or organisation news; when they use online services to purchase products or services; when they download brand- or product-related apps or promotional coupons; and so forth (Baldus et al., 2015).

Collaboration With Influencers

Influencer marketing is one of the major growth areas in digital marketing, but finding these influencers in massive data sets is a never-ending difficulty (Harrigan et al., 2021). More than 70% of buyers are reportedly more likely to buy a personally recommended good or service (Hubspot, 2019). Brands are very interested in social media influencers (SMIs). They have the huge advantage of possessing an extensive network and, consequently, a broad audience for the brand since they are regarded by customers as being personal, real, and reliable sources of information (Djafarova & Rushworth, 2017). Collaboration with the right kind of influencers becomes imperative for brands as user-generated content is unpredictable and completely out of the brand's control (UGC), and hence, they identify the right kind of influencers who can create content that aligns with the brand marketing strategies (Davcik et al., 2021). Fashion firms often use two distinct types of accounts to execute their social media campaigns, namely official brand pages and accounts of social media influencers chosen by the brands (Jin et al., 2021). In contrast to conventional word-of-mouth marketing, influencer marketing gives advertisers more visibility into and control over the results of their marketing efforts. Marketers may see how many times their items have been seen, liked, commented on, and shared by influencers (De Veirman et al., 2017).Fashion and beauty firms have incorporated influencer marketing into their strategies to the point where brands and agencies are now paying influencer experts and using web platforms just for the goal of finding and authenticating influencers (Neff, 2019). The way in which influencer marketing works is quite different from that of normal endorsements of any kind, as the influencers create and post content that is meant for people who follow them on social media platforms and are interested in their day-to-day lives and personal opinions about brands (Jin & Phua, 2014). Fashion firms have discovered that working with human ambassadors in branding promotions favours association with the endorsing source (Jin et al., 2021). Influencers on social media (SMIs) substantially impact consumers' purchase behaviour (Nam & Dân, 2018). Choosing the right fit of influencers to collaborate with is extremely crucial for the brands because it not only impacts the reputations and following of the influencers but also negatively reflects on the reputation of the brand. There are other criteria when choosing an influencer that aligns with the brand's ideology and, apart from inauthenticity, another point that the brand needs to keep in mind is unethical influencers who fake their followers' numbers and engagement rates (Mediakix, 2019). An industry report by TapInfluence (2019) indicates that the return on investment is approximately eleven times higher than any other form of traditional marketing strategies or channels.

Brand Strategies

Branding encompasses the strategic efforts to cultivate a desired perception and reputation for a product, service, individual, location, or entity. This multifaceted process entails standing out from competitors, generating awareness and a distinct identity, and cultivating a favourable reputation (Healey, 2010; Sammut-Bonnici, 2015)). Conversely, Keller (2013) has directed attention to the procedure of crafting an unparalleled and identifiable persona for a product, service, or organization. This is frequently achieved through the integration of a distinct name, logo, design, and messaging, all aimed at fostering a potent and affirmative perception within the consumer psyche.

Branding strategies focus on competitive positioning, value chain development, and brand equity management (Gunarso et al., 2015). Competitive brand positioning involves identifying a distinct market space and cognitive location in consumers' minds (Strömberg, 2015). Value chain development includes product innovation, design, and market development through pricing, distribution, and marketing communications [5]. Brand equity refers to the assets and liabilities associated with a brand. In healthcare, branding is important for differentiating providers and managed care companies, and its value lies in integrating it into operational structures and strategies. Brands and branding have become key concepts in marketing, management, and strategy, with research focusing on corporate, consumer, cultural, and critical perspectives.

The transformation of branding and consumer engagement brought about by the rise of social media is a dynamic phenomenon that underscores the evolving nature of business strategies. The concept of two-way communication and engagement stands at the forefront of this evolution, as social media platforms have shifted the paradigm from one-sided brand messaging to a participatory and interactive model. Consumers are no longer passive recipients but active contributors to the brand narrative, influencing perceptions through their engagement in the form of comments, shares, and user-generated content. This shift underlines the power of collaboration in shaping brand identities and fostering a deeper sense of connection (Kaplan & Haenlein, 2010; Mangold & Faulds, 2009). Now, authenticity and storytelling emerge as critical cornerstones in this new branding landscape. Social media's unique platform allows brands to showcase genuine stories and values, cultivating emotional bonds with consumers. However, the discerning nature of modern users necessitates a high degree of authenticity. In a digital ecosystem where inauthenticity is easily detected, brands must tread carefully to avoid insincere attempts at branding that could lead to user distrust and disengagement (Vargo & Lusch, 2004; Escalas & Bettman, 2005)

Visual branding and content strategy have emerged as integral components within this new paradigm. The visual nature of social media platforms places emphasis on compelling imagery and videos as primary tools for brand communication. Consistency in visual branding across diverse platforms bolsters brand recognition and recall, serving as a silent ambassador that speaks to the brand's essence, irrespective of the digital touchpoint (Avery et al., 2010; Kim & Ko, 2012).The era of social media also witnesses the ascendancy of influencer marketing and brand endorsement as a potent means of amplifying brand reach. Collaborations with influencers allow brands to harness the established follower base of these individuals, leveraging their credibility and resonance. Crucially, the effectiveness of such partnerships hinges on the alignment of brand values with those of the influencer, ensuring a seamless fusion of authenticity and advocacy (Belch & Belch, 2012; Abidin, 2016).

User-generated content and community building underscore the power of involving consumers in the brand creation process. Brands actively encourage users to generate and share content related to their products, fostering a sense of belonging and camaraderie. In this participatory approach, user-generated content not only serves as a testament to social proof but also resonates as authentic endorsements from consumers themselves. Real-time marketing and agility in response to dynamic trends underscore the fast-paced nature of the social media landscape. Brands now have the capacity to seize upon real-time events and trends to craft timely and relevant marketing content. To remain effective in this environment, brands must exhibit nimbleness in their responses and adaptability to the fluid digital currents. Leveraging data analytics for personalisation signifies the intersection of technology and consumer-centricity. Brands can now tap into consumer insights to tailor content, enhancing the overall consumer experience. The result is a more meaningful interaction that resonates with individual preferences, effectively driving engagement and loyalty.

However, as social media provides a plethora of opportunities, it equally exposes brands to potential risks. Effective crisis management is crucial in this context, as the same platforms that facilitate engagement can also amplify crises. Brands must be prepared to manage crises transparently, swiftly mitigating damage to brand reputation while maintaining open lines of communication. Navigating global reach while respecting cultural sensitivities is the final frontier of this discussion. Social media, with its borderless reach, enables brands to transcend geographical confines. Yet, this expansion requires cultural astuteness and localization to resonate effectively with diverse audiences while honouring local norms and values. In summation, the integration of branding within the sphere of social media introduces a multi-faceted landscape where agility, authenticity, and community building converge. As brands navigate this dynamic terrain, an understanding of these aspects stands crucial in sculpting effective strategies that foster meaningful engagement and enduring resonance with the digital audience(Hofstede, 1980; Lu & Lu, 2014).

Brand Loyalty

Organisations continually attempt to attract new clients and keep their current ones. Every organisation must prioritize attracting and keeping devoted clients (Singh et al., 2012). Maintaining strong connections with consumers has become crucial for any firm in this fiercely competitive market (Tabaku & Zerellari,2015). One of the key topics of marketing study for a very long time has been establishing and sustaining brand loyalty (Chaudhuri & Halbrook, 2001). Brand loyalty is the strongly held intention of the consumers to continue purchasing a particular brand in the future regardless of external circumstances (Chaudhuri & Holbrook, 2001). Building strong relationships with customers helps increase a brand's market share (Palmatier et al., 2006). A biased response or a specific tendency to buy a particular brand by a consumer while buying/choosing a product among all the other options available in the market, and such a decision is made by the consumer over a period of time consistently by a decision-making unit which need not, necessarily be the actual purchaser but influences the decision and the brands are chosen by the consumers based on their personal criteria which ultimately leads to commitment towards the brand are the basic requirements mentioned by Jacoby and Chestnut (1978). Brand loyalty is a vitally important component of competitive advantage. Brand loyalty benefits businesses by increasing sales, market share, and profitability, and helping them expand or at least maintain their position in the market (Keller,2008). High brand loyalty is a resource that promotes market share expansion, high returns on investment, and, eventually, high brand equity (Kha,2008). In the digital era, where social media marketing is prevalent, and almost everyone has access to it, consumers have greater power and means to share their knowledge and ideas among themselves. Such conversations lead to increased brand awareness, positively impact brand recall and also have a positive impact on brand loyalty (Gunelius, 2011).

PROPOSED MODEL

The proposed conceptual model, as shown in Fig 1, is based on the literature review of past researchers and constructs are sourced from other relevant literature. The development in the recent past in the area of research in marketing and service is shedding light on the fact that the demarcation made between the brands and the customers is blurring (Jaakkola & Alexander, 2014), and customers are no more passive participants but active in each stage of marketing and branding. In the past decade, with the rise of various social media platforms as one of the primary sources of interaction information regarding products and services and with the rise of social media influencers as an important part of brands' marketing strategy, the current study will help in gaining an in-depth view of how brands identify the right fit of influencers and engage them to promote their products or services to their target audiences in the process co-creating brands not only with the influencers themselves but also actively engaging consumers in the

Figure 1. Proposed conceptual model

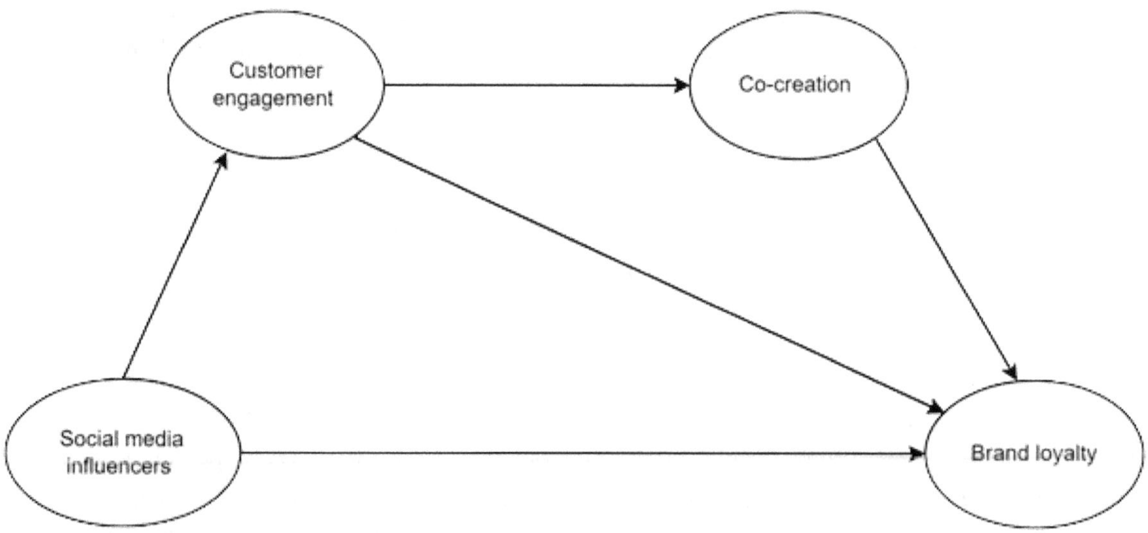

process. The concept of social media influencers and consumer engagement has gained importance in the recent past, and a number of studies have been conducted on the same. Still, the majority of them have been done separately (Pradhan et al., 2023). The concept of "customer engagement" (CE) refers to a recent effort to group together many different ways that customers act aside from transactions that can impact the business (Brodie et al. 2011; Van Doorn et al. 2010). The possibility of involving customer communities and customers in "coproduction" or "co-creation" to improve business performance or customer value is of great interest (Chan et al., 2010). Uncertainty still exists regarding the recurrent effects of CE on the value co-creation by a multitude of people in a network system (Brodie et al., 2013).

DISCUSSION AND CONCLUSION

Discussion

The basic main aim of this chapter was to get a thorough understanding of the relationship between the various variables, namely social media influencers, customer engagement, and brand loyalty and the effect that co-creation has on the dependent variable. Thanks to the rise of influencer marketing, customer engagement approaches, co-creation, and their combined effects on brand loyalty, the modern marketing landscape has seen a significant change in the way that both consumers and companies engage. Customer engagement is simply explained as a firm's conscious attempt to encourage, empower, and evaluate a customer's voluntary participation in its marketing functions beyond a basic economic transaction (Harmeling et al., 2017). Customer brand engagement entails connecting to a brand through continuous interaction (Mollen & Wilson,2010). Chang et al. (2017), in their research, posited that an essential basis for a long-term relationship between the brand and the customer is customer engagement with the brand. And continuous and long-term relationship is likely to result in loyalty towards the brand. Loyalty is a customer's unwavering dedication to using or purchasing a specific service or good (Oliver,1999).

In conclusion, Influencers on social media have developed into formidable platforms for brand communication and serve as dependable links for brands and their audiences. Influencer marketing has become an extremely effective tool for fashion firms looking for deeper interaction with their target audience. Past Research has also repeatedly shown that influencers offer a successful means to increase consumer involvement. Influencers are seen as relatable and trustworthy, which makes it easier for customers to interact with the brands or goods they recommend. Influencers and customers work together during the co-creation process, which has shown to be effective in increasing customer engagement. A sense of ownership emerges when brands empower consumers to be involved actively in the creation process of their favourite products. In the fashion business, where customers are looking for ways to express themselves, this can be especially effective. Co-creation can result in active consumer participation in product design, going beyond passive consumption and strengthening customer loyalty.Customer engagement is greatly influenced by the mutually beneficial, authentic relationship that exists between influencers and their followers. The findings suggest that buyers are more likely to be associated with the influencers who engage with a brand's goods or services in an honest manner. It is impossible to sufficiently emphasize the influencer's significance in closing the gap between brands and their consumers. Businesses may effectively engage customers on a personal level by tapping into the authenticity and credibility that influencers bring to the table through the relationships they create with their audiences. A complex and dynamic relationship that significantly impacts contemporary marketing strategies is the interaction between social media influencers, the customers and the level of co-creation activities that the customers take part in, which ultimately leads to a strong base of loyal customers. Influencer-driven customer engagement facilitates meaningful encounters, dialogues, and emotional ties beyond simple transactions. These interactions serve as the foundation of co-creation, in which consumers actively contribute to the creation of goods, services, and brand identities. Participation in co-creation activities leads to a sense of belonging and ownership, it leads to a deeper engagement on the part of the customer, and the customers like to be consistently involved with the brand and contribute to its growth. Because influencers serve as relatable brand ambassadors who share the values and passions of their followers, influencer marketing offers brands an exceptional opportunity to establish long-lasting relationships with their customers. The ultimate goal of brands does not just stop at creating and maintaining a customer base but also creating a strong base of loyal customers. Brands that actively encompass influencers in the co-creation process, pay attention to consumer opinions, and place a high value on real relationships are likely to experience consistent feedback that increases engagement and loyalty and leads to consistent and sustainable growth. It takes a structured, customer-focused approach to effectively integrating social media influencers, consumer interaction, co-creation, and brand loyalty. Brands can build long-lasting brand loyalty and maintain their position in the ever-changing marketing environment by embracing the collaborative power of influencers, encouraging real customer involvement, and fostering co-creation. Influencers are crucial to the development and promotion of new products in the fashion industry, illustrating the intersection of co-creation and influencer marketing. Influencers frequently bring their original ideas and originality to the co-creation process, establishing a cooperative effort that appeals to their audience. Products that satisfy consumer tastes and complement the influencer's personal brand are the result of this dual strategy, which adds an additional dimension of authenticity. A vital goal of marketing campaigns is brand loyalty, which evolves organically from the relationships between influencers, involvement of the customers in the marketing and branding process, and co-creation. Stronger emotional ties are often formed between a brand and engaged consumers who actively participate in the co-creation process facilitated by the influencers they trust and follow. This ingrained commitment frequently results in advocacy, recurring business, and long-lasting client connections. Brands that realise this potential and take advantage of this strong bond that can be formed have the opportunity to grow their consumer base, build brand loyalty and advocacy, and accomplish long-term success.

Implications of the Study

The importance of social media channels and influencers as a medium of reaching consumers is undeniable and sufficiently established in various past research and the current chapter. The current chapter will help brand managers understand the importance of an appropriate selection of influencers who create content that aligns with the brand's core vision. Involving influencers in the marketing strategies will create a devoted customer base and enable consumer interactions and active participation. A few of the benefits that brand managers can gain out of engaging customers with the help of influencers through the process of co-creation are a wider customer base and an increase in awareness of the brand, easy access to consumer insights, efficient and quick feedback both from the influencers and consumers, influencer marketing can be used as a differentiator in the highly competitive market, brands aiming for sustainability can align themselves with influencers who create content on the same lines and this will provide more authenticity to their initiatives.

REFERENCES

Aaker, D. A., & Joachimsthaler, E. A. (2000). The Brand Relationship Spectrum: The Key to the Brand Architecture Challenge. *California Management Review*, *42*(4), 8–23. doi:10.1177/000812560004200401

Abidin, C. (2016). Visibility labour: Engaging with influencers' fashion brands and #OOTD advertorial campaigns on Instagram. *Media International Australia, Incorporating Culture & Policy*, *161*(1), 86–100. doi:10.1177/1329878X16665177

Audrezet, A., De Kerviler, G., & Moulard, J. G. (2020). Authenticity under threat: When social media influencers need to go beyond self-presentation. *Journal of Business Research*, *117*, 557–569. doi:10.1016/j.jbusres.2018.07.008

Avery, J., Steenburgh, T. J., Deighton, J., & Caravella, M. (2010). Adding bricks to clicks: Predicting the patterns of online and offline information search. *Marketing Science*, *29*(2), 294–308.

Baldus, B. J., Voorhees, C. M., & Calantone, R. J. (2015). Online brand community engagement: Scale development and validation. *Journal of Business Research*, *68*(5), 978–985. doi:10.1016/j.jbusres.2014.09.035

Behnam, M., Hollebeek, L. D., Clark, M., & Farabi, R. (2021). Exploring customer engagement in the product vs. service context. *Journal of Retailing and Consumer Services*, *60*, 102456. doi:10.1016/j.jretconser.2021.102456

Belch, G. E., & Belch, M. A. (2012). *Advertising and promotion: An integrated marketing communications perspective*. McGraw-Hill Education.

Boerman, S. C. (2020). The effects of the standardized Instagram disclosure for Micro- and Meso-influencers. *Computers in Human Behavior*, *103*, 199–207. doi:10.1016/j.chb.2019.09.015

Bora Semiz, B., & Paylan, M. (2023, November 13). ali. (2023). A study on the mediating effect of brand trust between perceived legitimacy of influencers and attitude toward brand: Evidence from Turkey. *Asia Pacific Journal of Marketing and Logistics*, *35*(9), 2181–2197. Advance online publication. doi:10.1108/APJML-08-2022-0702

Brand Equity. (2022). https://brandequity.economictimes.indiatimes.com/news/research/influencer-marketing-industry-in-india-to-reach-rs-2200-cr-by-2025-report

Breazeale, M., Fritzsche, D. J., & Wells, W. D. (2009). A study of advertising message content on liking of the brand: The moderating role of the degree of consumer involvement. *Journal of Advertising*, *18*(2), 43–51.

Brito, P. Q., Brandão, A., Gadekar, M., & Castelo-Branco, S. (2020). Diffusing fashion information by social media fashion influencers: Understanding antecedents and consequences. *Journal of Fashion Marketing and Management*, *24*(2), 137–152. doi:10.1108/JFMM-09-2019-0214

Brodie, R. J., Hollebeek, L. D., Jurić, B., & Ilić, A. (2011). Customer engagement: Conceptual domain, fundamental propositions, and implications for research. *Journal of Service Research*, *14*(3), 252–271. doi:10.1177/1094670511411703

Brodie, R. J., Ilic, A., Juric, B., & Hollebeek, L. (2013). Consumer engagement in a virtual brand community: An exploratory analysis. *Journal of Business Research, 66*(1), 105–114. doi:10.1016/j.jbusres.2011.07.029

Casaló, L. V., Flavián, C., & Ibáñez-Sánchez, S. (2020). Influencers on Instagram: Antecedents and consequences of opinion leadership. *Journal of Business Research, 117*, 510–519. doi:10.1016/j.jbusres.2018.07.005

Chan, K. W., Yim, C. K., & Lam, S. S. K. (2010). Is Customer Participation in Value Creation a Double-Edged Sword? Evidence from Professional Financial Services across Cultures. *Journal of Marketing, 74*(3), 48–64. doi:10.1509/jmkg.74.3.048

Chang, S. W., & Fan, S. H. (2017). Cultivating the brand-customer relationship in Facebook fan pages: A study of fast-fashion industry. *International Journal of Retail & Distribution Management, 45*(3), 253–270. doi:10.1108/IJRDM-05-2016-0076

Chaudhuri, A., & Holbrook, M. B. (2001). The chain of effects from Brand Trust and brand affect to brand performance: The Role of Brand Loyalty. *Journal of Marketing, 65*(2), 81–93. doi:10.1509/jmkg.65.2.81.18255

Chu, S., & Seock, Y. (2020). The power of social media in fashion advertising. *Journal of Interactive Advertising, 20*(2), 93–94. doi:10.1080/15252019.2020.1802955

Coombs, W. T. (2007). Protecting organization reputations during a crisis: The development and application of situational crisis communication theory. *Corporate Reputation Review, 10*(3), 163–176. doi:10.1057/palgrave.crr.1550049

Davcik, N. S., Langaro, D., Jevons, C., & Nascimento, R. (2021). Non-sponsored brand-related user-generated content: Effects and mechanisms of consumer engagement. *Journal of Product &amp. Journal of Product and Brand Management, 31*(1), 163–174. doi:10.1108/JPBM-06-2020-2971

De Veirman, M., Cauberghe, V., & Hudders, L. (2017). Marketing through Instagram influencers: The impact of number of followers and product divergence on brand attitude. *International Journal of Advertising, 36*(5), 798–828. doi:10.1080/02650487.2017.1348035

Djafarova, E., & Rushworth, C. (2017). Exploring the credibility of online celebrities' Instagram profiles in influencing the purchase decisions of young female users. *Computers in Human Behavior, 68*, 1–7. doi:10.1016/j.chb.2016.11.009

Escalas, J. E., & Bettman, J. R. (2005). Self-construal, reference groups, and brand meaning. *The Journal of Consumer Research, 32*(3), 378–389. doi:10.1086/497549

Evans, M. (2019, September 23). Five key traits defining connected consumers in 2019. *Forbes*. https://www.forbes.com/sites/miche lleevans1/2019/09/23/five-key-trait s-defining-connected-consumers in-2019/#6b1b97e622df

Evans, N. J., Phua, J., Lim, J., & Jun, H. (2017). Disclosing Instagram influencer advertising: The effects of disclosure language on advertising recognition, attitudes, and behavioral intent. *Journal of Interactive Advertising, 17*(2), 138–149. doi:10.1080/15252019.2017.1366885

Forbes. (2022). https://www.forbesindia.com/articlc/bharatiya-vidya-bhavan039s-spjimr/the-evolution-of-influencer-marketing

Gunelius, S. (2010). *30-minute social media marketing: Step-by-step techniques to spread the word about your business: Social media marketing in 30 minutes a day*. McGraw Hill Professional.

Harmeling, C. M., Moffett, J. W., Arnold, M. J., & Carlson, B. D. (2017). Toward a theory of customer engagement marketing. *Journal of the Academy of Marketing Science*, *45*(3), 312–335. doi:10.100711747-016-0509-2

Harrigan, P., Daly, T. M., Coussement, K., Lee, J., Soutar, G. N., & Evers, U. (2021). Identifying influencers on social media. *International Journal of Information Management*, *56*, 102246. doi:10.1016/j.ijinfomgt.2020.102246

Healey, M. (2010). *Branding: A guide to creating successful brands*. Macmillan International Higher Education.

Hennig-Thurau, T., Malthouse, E. C., Friege, C., Gensler, S., Lobschat, L., Rangaswamy, A., & Skiera, B. (2010). The impact of new media on customer relationships. *Journal of Service Research*, *13*(3), 311–330. doi:10.1177/1094670510375460

Hofstede, G. (1980). Culture's consequences: International differences in work-related values. *Sage (Atlanta, Ga.)*.

Hollebeek, L. D., Glynn, M. S., & Brodie, R. J. (2014). Consumer brand engagement in social Media: Conceptualization, scale development and validation. *Journal of Interactive Marketing*, *28*(2), 149–165. doi:10.1016/j.intmar.2013.12.002

Horáková, J., Uusitalo, O., Munnukka, J., & Jokinen, O. (2022). Does the digitalization of retailing disrupt consumers' attachment to retail places? *Journal of Retailing and Consumer Services*, *67*, 102958. doi:10.1016/j.jretconser.2022.102958

Hubspot. (2019). *71% more likely to purchase based on social media referrals*. https://blog. hubspot.com/blog/tabid/6307/bid/30239/71-More-Likely-to-Purchase-Based-onSocial-Media-Referrals-Infographic.aspx

Hudders, L., Jans, S. D., & Veirman, M. D. (2021). The commercialization of Social Media Stars: A Literature Review and conceptual framework on the strategic use of Social Media influencers. *Social Media Influencers in Strategic Communication*, 24–67. doi:10.4324/9781003181286-3

Hutter, K., Hautz, J., Dennhardt, S., & Füller, J. (2013). The impact of user interactions in social media on brand awareness and purchase intention: The case of MINI on Facebook. *Journal of Product and Brand Management*, *22*(5/6), 342–351. doi:10.1108/JPBM-05-2013-0299

Ind, N., & Coates, N. (2013). The meanings of co-creation. *European Business Review*, *25*(1), 86–95. doi:10.1108/09555341311287754

Ind, N., Coates, N., & Lerman, K. (2019). The gift of co-creation: What motivates customers to participate. *Journal of Brand Management*, *27*(2), 181–194. doi:10.105741262-019-00173-7

Islam, J. U., Hollebeek, L. D., Rahman, Z., Khan, I., & Rasool, A. (2019). Customer engagement in the service context: An empirical investigation of the construct, its antecedents and consequences. *Journal of Retailing and Consumer Services*, *50*, 277–285. doi:10.1016/j.jretconser.2019.05.018

Jaakkola, E., & Alexander, M. (2014). The role of customer engagement Behavior in Value Co-Creation. *Journal of Service Research*, *17*(3), 247–261. doi:10.1177/1094670514529187

Jacoby, J., & Chestnut, R. W. (1978). *Brand Loyalty: Measurement and Management*. John Wiley & Sons.

Jin, S. A., Muqaddam, A., & Ryu, E. (2019). Instafamous and social media influencer marketing. *Marketing Intelligence & Planning*, *37*(5), 567–579. doi:10.1108/MIP-09-2018-0375

Jin, S. A., & Phua, J. (2014). Following celebrities' tweets about brands: The impact of Twitter-Based electronic Word-of-Mouth on consumers' source credibility perception, buying intention, and social identification with celebrities. *Journal of Advertising*, *43*(2), 181–195. doi:10.1080/00913367.2013.827606

Jin, S. A., Ryu, E., & Muqaddam, A. (2021). I trust what she's #endorsing on Instagram: Moderating effects of parasocial interaction and social presence in fashion influencer marketing. *Journal of Fashion Marketing and Management*, *25*(4), 665–681. doi:10.1108/JFMM-04-2020-0059

Jin, S. V., & Ryu, E. (2019). Celebrity fashion brand endorsement in Facebook viral marketing and social commerce: Interactive effects of social identification, materialism, fashion involvement, and opinion leadership. *Journal of Fashion Marketing and Management*, *23*(1), 104–123. doi:10.1108/JFMM-01-2018-0001

Journée, R., & Weber, M. (2016). Co-creation of Experiences in Retail: Opportunity to innovate in retail business. In Springer proceedings in business and economics (pp. 391–404). doi:10.1007/978-3-319-29058-4_31

Kapitan, S., & Silvera, D. H. (2016). From digital media influencers to celebrity endorsers: Attributions drive endorser effectiveness. *Marketing Letters*, *27*(3), 553–567. doi:10.100711002-015-9363-0

Kaplan, A. M., & Haenlein, M. (2010). Users of the world, unite! the challenges and opportunities of social media. *Business Horizons*, *53*(1), 59–68. doi:10.1016/j.bushor.2009.09.003

Keller, K. L. (2008). *Strategic Brand Management: Building, Measuring and Managing Brand Equity* (3rd ed.). Pearson Prentice Hall.

Keller, K. L. (2013). *Strategic brand management: Building, measuring, and managing brand equity*. Pearson.

Kha, B. M. (2008). Consumers And Their Brands: Deciphering Dimensions Of Loyalty. *International Journal of Business Insights & Transformation*, *2*(1).

Ki, C., & Kim, Y. (2019). The mechanism by which social media influencers persuade consumers: The role of consumers' desire to mimic. *Psychology and Marketing*, *36*(10), 905–922. doi:10.1002/mar.21244

Kim, A. J., & Ko, E. (2012). Do social media marketing activities enhance customer equity? An empirical study of luxury fashion brand. *Journal of Business Research*, *65*(10), 1480–1486. doi:10.1016/j.jbusres.2011.10.014

Kim, J., & Choi, H. (2019). Value Co-creation through social media: A case study of a start-up company. *Journal of Business Economics and Management*, *20*(1), 1–19. doi:10.3846/jbem.2019.6262

Kozinets, R. V. (2002). The field behind the screen: Using netnography for marketing research in online communities. *JMR, Journal of Marketing Research*, *39*(1), 61–72. doi:10.1509/jmkr.39.1.61.18935

Kumar, V., & Pansari, A. (2016). Competitive Advantage through Engagement. *JMR, Journal of Marketing Research*, *53*(4), 497–514. doi:10.1509/jmr.15.0044

Lamberton, C., & Stephen, A. T. (2016). A Thematic Exploration of Digital, Social Media, and Mobile Marketing: Research Evolution from 2000 to 2015 and an Agenda for Future Inquiry. *Journal of Marketing*, *80*(6), 146–172. doi:10.1509/jm.15.0415

Lang, C., & Armstrong, C. M. (2016). Personal attributes: Influences on clothing disposal reasons and frequency. *Journal of Family and Consumer Sciences*, *108*(3), 41–47. doi:10.14307/JFCS108.3.41

Leissner, J., Pidun, U., & Krafft, M. (2019). Corporate crisis management in the digital age: A framework and cases from the automotive industry. *International Journal of Research in Marketing*, *36*(3), 435–456.

Lou, C., & Yuan, S. (2019). Influencer Marketing: How message value and credibility affect consumer trust of branded content on social media. *Journal of Interactive Advertising*, *19*(1), 58–73. doi:10.1080/15252019.2018.1533501

Lu, X., & Lu, L. (2014). Beyond demographics: Using psychographics and social networking to predict consumer intentions. *Journal of Advertising Research*, *54*(3), 282–295.

Lusch, R. F., & Vargo, S. L. (2010). SD logic: Accommodating, integrating, transdisciplinary. *Grand Service Challenge, 23.*

M, S., & K, S. (2017). Impact of influencers in consumer decision process: the fashion industry. *SCMS Journal of Indian Management*, 14–30.

Makrides, A., Vrontis, D., & Christofi, M. (2020). An empirical study on the importance of electronic word of mouth in the concierge industry: The case of Cyprus. In *Exploring the Power of Electronic Word-of-Mouth in the Services Industry* (pp. 265–287). IGI Global. doi:10.4018/978-1-5225-8575-6.ch015

Mangold, W. G., & Faulds, D. J. (2009). Social media: The new hybrid element of the promotion mix. *Business Horizons*, *52*(4), 357–365. doi:10.1016/j.bushor.2009.03.002

Marketing Science Institute. (2020, May 7). MSI announces 2020-22 research priorities. *MSI at the ARF*. Available at https://www.msi.org/articles/2020-22-msi-research-pri orities-outline-marketers-top-concerns/

McColl-Kennedy, J. R., Vargo, S. L., Dagger, T. S., Sweeney, J., & Van Kasteren, Y. (2012). Health care customer value cocreation practice styles. *Journal of Service Research*, *15*(4), 370–389. doi:10.1177/1094670512442806

Mediakix. (2019). *Influencer marketing 2019 industry benchmarks.* Retrieved from: bit. ly/3pNFLXs

Mollen, A., & Wilson, H. (2010). Engagement, telepresence and interactivity in online consumer experience: Reconciling scholastic and managerial perspectives. *Journal of Business Research*, *63*(9-10), 919–925. doi:10.1016/j.jbusres.2009.05.014

Nam, L. G., & Dân, H. T. (2018). Impact of social media influencer marketing on consumer at ho Chi Minh City. *International Journal of Social Sciences and Humanities Invention*, *5*(5), 4710–4714. doi:10.18535/ijsshi/v5i5.10

Nambisan, S., & Baron, R. A. (2007). Interactions in virtual customer environments: Implications for product support and Customer Relationship Management. *Journal of Interactive Marketing*, *21*(2), 42–62. doi:10.1002/dir.20077

Neff, J. (2019). *How to succeed with influencers: brand playbook*. AdAge. Available at: https://adage.com/article/cmo-strategy/succeed-influencers/316313

Ooi, K. B., Lee, V. H., Hew, J. J., Leong, L. Y., Tan, G. W. H., & Lim, A. F. (2023). Social media influencers: An effective marketing approach? *Journal of Business Research*, *160*, 113773. doi:10.1016/j.jbusres.2023.113773

Palmatier, R. W., Dant, R. P., Grewal, D., & Evans, K. R. (2006). Factors influencing the effectiveness of relationship marketing: A meta-analysis. *SSRN Electronic Journal*. doi:10.2139/ssrn.904647

Pradhan, B., Kishore, K., & Gokhale, N. (2023). Social Media influencers and consumer engagement: A review and future research agenda. *International Journal of Consumer Studies*, *47*(6), 2106–2130. Advance online publication. doi:10.1111/ijcs.12901

Prahalad, C. K., & Ramaswamy, V. (2004). Co-creation experiences: The next practice in value creation. *Journal of Interactive Marketing*, *18*(3), 5–14. doi:10.1002/dir.20015

Rakuten. (2019). *2019 Influencer marketing global survey consumers*. Retrieved from: bit.ly/2WD9ebL

Ramaswamy, V., & Ozcan, K. (2016). Brand value co-creation in a digitalized world: An integrative framework and research implications. *International Journal of Research in Marketing*, *33*(1), 93–106. doi:10.1016/j.ijresmar.2015.07.001

Sammut-Bonnici, T. (2015). *Brand and branding. Wiley Encyclopedia of Management*, 1–3. doi:10.1002/9781118785317.weom120161

Schouten, A. P., Janssen, L., & Verspaget, M. (2019). Celebrity vs. Influencer endorsements in advertising: The role of identification, credibility, and Product-Endorser fit. *International Journal of Advertising*, *39*(2), 258–281. doi:10.1080/02650487.2019.1634898

Scott, D. M. (2016). *The new rules of marketing and PR: How to use social media, online video, mobile applications, blogs, news releases, and viral marketing to reach buyers directly*. John Wiley & Sons.

Singh, J. J., Iglesias, O., & Batista-Foguet, J. M. (2012). Does having an ethical brand matter? the influence of consumer perceived ethicality on trust, affect and loyalty. *Journal of Business Ethics*, *111*(4), 541–549. doi:10.100710551-012-1216-7

So, K. K. F., King, C., Sparks, B. A., & Wang, Y. (2016). The role of customer engagement in building consumer loyalty to tourism brands. *Journal of Travel Research*, *55*(1), 64–78. doi:10.1177/0047287514541008

Statista. (2023a). https://www.statista.com/statistics/1294803/india-influencer-marketing-industry-value

Statista. (2023b). https://www.statista.com/topics/9189/influencer-marketing-in-india

Statista. (2023c). https://www.statista.com/statistics/617136/digital-population-worldwide

Strömberg, P. (2015). Theming. The Wiley Blackwell Encyclopedia of Consumption and Consumer Studies, 1–5. doi:10.1002/9781118989463.wbeccs228

Sugathan, P., & Ranjan, K. R. (2019). Co-creating the tourism experience. *Journal of Business Research*, *100*, 207–217. doi:10.1016/j.jbusres.2019.03.032

Tabaku, E., & Zerellari, M. (2015). Brand loyalty and loyalty programs; a literature review. *Romanian Economic Business Review*, *10*(2), 87.

TapInfluence. (2019). *Earn 11x higher sales ROI with influencer marketing in your digital marketing tech stack j TapInfluence*. available at: https://www.tapinfluence.com/tp_resource/nielsen-casestudy/

Tsimonis, G., & Dimitriadis, S. (2014). Brand strategies in social media. *Marketing Intelligence & Planning*, *32*(3), 328–344. doi:10.1108/MIP-04-2013-0056

Vallaster, C., & Von Wallpach, S. (2013). An online discursive inquiry into the social dynamics of multi-stakeholder brand meaning co-creation. *Journal of Business Research*, *66*(9), 1505–1515. doi:10.1016/j.jbusres.2012.09.012

Van Doorn, J., Lemon, K. N., Mittal, V., Nass, S., Pick, D., Pirner, P., & Verhoef, P. C. (2010). Customer Engagement Behavior: Theoretical foundations and research directions. *Journal of Service Research*, *13*(3), 253–266. doi:10.1177/1094670510375599

Vargo, S. L., & Lusch, R. F. (2004). Evolving to a New Dominant Logic for Marketing. *Journal of Marketing*, *68*(1), 1–17. doi:10.1509/jmkg.68.1.1.24036

Venkatesan, R. (2017). Executing on a customer engagement strategy. *Journal of the Academy of Marketing Science*, *45*(3), 289–293. doi:10.100711747-016-0513-6

Vrontis, D., Makrides, A., Christofi, M., & Thrassou, A. (2021). Social media influencer marketing: A systematic review, integrative framework and future research agenda. *International Journal of Consumer Studies*, *45*(4), 617–644. doi:10.1111/ijcs.12647

Weinswig, D. (2016). Influencers are the new brands. *Forbes*. https://www.forbes.com/sites/deborahweinswig/2016/10/05/celebritys-are-the-new-brands/#66ad98a37919

Yovcheva, Z., & Buhalis, D. (2017). Analysing travel experiences: The potential of social media data. *Current Issues in Tourism*, *20*(1), 1–19.

ADDITIONAL READING

Bu, Y., Parkinson, J., & Thaichon, P. (2022). Influencer marketing: Sponsorship disclosure and value co-creation behaviour. *Marketing Intelligence & Planning*, *40*(7), 854–870. doi:10.1108/MIP-09-2021-0310

Jha, A. K., & Ray, S. (2023). Influencer recommendation system: Choosing the right influencer using a network analysis approach. *Marketing Intelligence & Planning*. doi:10.1108/MIP-04-2023-0149

Lv, J., Yang, R., Yu, J., Yao, W., & Wang, Y. (2023). Macro-influencers or meso-influencers, how do companies choose? *Industrial Management & Data Systems*. doi:10.1108/IMDS-05-2022-0310

Romero-Rodriguez, L. M., & Castillo-Abdul, B. (2023). Toward state-of-the-art on social marketing research in user-generated content (UGC) and influencers. *Journal of Management Development*, *42*(6), 425–435. doi:10.1108/JMD-11-2022-0285

Tiwari, A., Kumar, A., Kant, R., & Jaiswal, D. (2023). Impact of fashion influencers on consumers' purchase intentions: Theory of planned behaviour and mediation of attitude. *Journal of Fashion Marketing and Management: An International Journal*. doi:10.1108/JFMM-11-2022-0253

KEY TERMS AND DEFINITIONS

Brand Strategies: Strategy to engage customers and build brand equity through various social media platforms involving influencers.

Co-Creation: Collaboration between brands and influencers to increase consumer engagement.

Collaboration: Constant suggestion and interaction between the brands and their chosen social media influencers for improving branding and marketing strategies.

Customer Engagement: Involvement of customers in the process of co-creating fashion products.

Customer Loyalty: Building customer loyalty through co-creation and collaboration.

Influencers: Individuals with more than 5000 followers on social media platforms and having expertise in the area of fashion.

Social Media: Various platforms on the internet are accessible to consumers and brands for constant interaction.

Chapter 7
The Intrinsic Property of a Representation in the Phygital Transformation:
A (Meta) Influence as a Force With Magnitude and Direction in the Metaverse

Neli Maria Mengalli
https://orcid.org/0000-0002-3782-3807
Faculdade São Bernardo do Campo, Brazil

Antonio Aparecido Carvalho
Faculdade São Bernardo do Campo, Brazil

ABSTRACT

This chapter was written based on a qualitative methodology with reading reports and current articles at the time of writing. The objective was to highlight what (meta) influence is and how the (meta) influencer phygital can contribute to the brand. In the qualitative research, it was revealed that it is a prosperous field for marketing, mainly for influencer marketing; however, it is a new theme and lacks a lot of research. It was concluded that the metaverse is a reality that cannot be neglected, both in terms of the consumer's experience and the employee's experience, and the (meta)influencers are very familiar with the company's values, products, and services and are capable of making authentic and compelling recommendations.

INTRODUCTION

In times when the knowledge society coexists with artificial intelligence in interactions that involve anxiety, fear, insecurity, and fascination and among the not-so-well-formulated questions that have well-structured answers. People look for images with commands and they return images that they do

DOI: 10.4018/979-8-3693-0551-5.ch007

not know the source. The exhibition, on social networks, shows where work is, what people think about work and what contributions work makes to people's lives.

Bulz (2023, p. 19) wrote that the knowledge society is moving towards a still consciousness society. The author demonstrates a social and collective consciousness that tends to be linked to a social identity shared with people from diverse cultures. In the article, it is informed about a (re) research of the past and the future for innovative social change, which consists of conceptual surveys and a praxis proposal, that is, the knowledge society is admitted, however, the society of consciences is evident and that investigations are necessary to know to what extent (meta) influencers are part of these societies and (cyber) societies of knowledge and conscience.

The certainty is that there is a revolution in the history and culture of humanity that includes the phygital transformation, because it includes the physical and the digital concomitantly, and Mengalli, Carvalho and Galvão (2023, p. 40) wrote that digital influencers [phygital transformation] mobilize in consumption, that is, culture and society have new agents [phygital influencers] both in the generation of content authorship and in the presence and phygital representation.

The revolution can be like the evolution of business and the presentation and representation of the brand based on strategies with disruptive technologies that make it possible to work with creativity and competitiveness in the present and future market in contemporary times. The global economy is changing every day with phygital Marketing, artificial intelligence and the metaverse. It is known that natural intelligences transform business and Bulz (2023, p. 20) highlights the planetary, the possible innovative technology revolution and industrial transformations.

The author's approach is (inter), (trans) and (multi) disciplinary in the third millennium and is a challenge to reduce the social gap between humanity's aspirations and everyday social limitations and such confrontation is related to technological expansion and is historical. Creativity shows humanity and the desire for human representation, but it is not enough to generate it computationally.

Vincent (2020) wrote about the Neon project (Samsung) and showed that each avatar can maintain conversations with users and display "emotions and intelligence". Models that have human likenesses also have expressions, dialogue, and emotions. The customization of each avatar is adapted to different tasks, according to the understanding of the developer and designer.

In the report, the newsperson expresses the possibility of licensing or signing to have a Neon as service representatives and shows that Neons can be financial consultants, health care providers, concierge, news program anchors, spokespersons, or actors of movie theater. In the text, there was mention of companions and friends. Paid human representations are friends or companions by subscription or licensing.

The Unreal Engine makes it possible for people to create realistic characters and informs that the (pre) definitions of metahumans are based on (pre) existing scans of real people with the most different facial, skin, hair, eyes, or body characteristics. It is possible to refine the metahumans created with the most different potentialities offered by the company. Developers or designers, using software, make human representations available in games or immersive worlds for companies or consumers.

Four-dimensional human representation and influence on digital media through drawings or avatars are people's desires and brands are looking for influencers who enable recurring revenue for them. It is known that representations are not only people, but characters. Mengalli, Carvalho and Galvão (2023, p. 37, 40) wrote about immersive retail, luxury shopping platforms in the metaverse, and Ayayi and Timo, digital human influencers, that is, they showed that there are ecosystems in the metaverse, and the representations are researched as trends for immersive experiences, like the Alibaba DAMO Academy, for example.

Influencer Marketing is in the metaverse, and new concepts of influence change the immersive market. Karabacak and Güngör (2023, p. 184) wrote about Kyra, a (meta) influencer with the ability to produce content based on programming with artificial intelligence.

The intrinsic property of a representation in the phygital transformation promotes a (meta) influence as a force with magnitude and direction in the metaverse and in this chapter it will be possible to understand the ecosystem that enhances the existence of a (meta) influencer in phygital Marketing strategies.

This chapter approaches one of the most current themes nearby phygital influence, therefore, it tends to be a contribution for the market, for developers, for designers, for those interested in the subject and for the academy for research and investigations. The objective is to highlight what (meta) influence is and how the (meta) phygital influencer can contribute to the brand. The career will be one of the elements unveiled in the chapter. It is a qualitative study. The chapter's audience is undergraduate and graduate academics, researchers, brand and agency managers, executives, influencers, and those interested about (meta) influence. The division of this chapter has background, focus of the chapter, directions for future research, solutions and recommendations, and final considerations.

BACKGROUND: THE COMPOSITION OF THE THEME WITH THE RESEARCHED REALITY AND WITH FACTS

When reading the book's proposal, which had as its motto the use of influencer marketing as a digital business strategy, the word strategy shone and seemed to be a way forward but needed other people's experience or should it be a way to combine existing methods to achieve certain purposes or goals. It is possible to think, in the chapter proposal in line with the book, on the experience or skills and abilities of others to design an art with the vision of strategic planning, that is, to look to the future to portray a present with a depth of a decade and a half.

Even though στρατηγική [strategy] can remember an army with leadership, in non-militarized contexts, strategy, in influencer Marketing, can be the planning and execution for the use of animate and inanimate resources to achieve organizational purposes from influencers. As an action plan in digital or phygital business, it is a conscious action that needs stories and, with the advancement of immersive spaces, influencers are metaverses together with the brand's consumers.

In the medium term, the strategy may be within the scope of digital business, however, in the long term, the business is phygital even if the name of the immersive world is not metaverse, as happened with Second Life, for example. The book proposal produced the continuity of research on the metaverse ecosystem with the reasoning and actions that required preparation with the term (meta) phygital influencer. The defined plan started with social networks, continued with digital humans, and reflected about (meta) influencers, businesses and brands in a strategy that presented an elevated level of difficulty, because in the market influence is strong on social networks.

In social networks, the number of followers is one of the metrics. Influencers are often inspired by other digital influencers with certain differences. The legacy of the older influencer makes it possible for new influencers to differentiate. Digital influencers, for example, have journeys exposed on social networks to have more followers.

There is also public encouragement for experiences in the metaverse along with the digital influencer through key features, Kyra, for example, in the article "Real or Robotic?": Kyra, Who Claims to Be

India's First Meta-Influencer, Leaves Internet Confused (2022), she was described as a dream chaser, model and traveler. It is possible to generate empathy with the audience.

There are news articles about digital influencers, personification of digital humans for constructive collaboration with the brand's audience and the connection of digital influencers with social networks and the metaverse, however academic investigations are still few. In the academic search engine, the term meta-influencer returned with six results between the years 2022 and 2023.

It is known that influencer marketing platforms create digital influencers through developers and designers or people can create their own digital representations, although it is not recommended, because the studies of professionals allow a greater accuracy for the Marketing of people and brands. Creators and people at phygital Marketing customize the character's digital and phygital life with rich details to increase followers and generate empathy. Virtual influencers have real lives in the phygital present. Meeting a fan can be a way of getting closer.

Social media bubbles tend to flow to the entrance of physical worlds, in other words, digital influencers with more popularity and at unique moments generate empathy with real people. Such practice is a phygital experience, because the presence of the digital influencer is embedded in the physical universe. Face-to-face, televised, or social media events can promote phygital experiences.

There are spaces to (co) create ideas like these, such as Area 2071, which is an ecosystem that brings together government entities, private companies, and startups from all over the planet to give life to ideas that tend to transform the future. Participants receive prizes and can have their startup accelerated. Regarding virtual reality, participants had the opportunity, according to the report Area 2071: Your Invitation to Be a Part of Creating the Future. (2020, p. 51), to incubate in a hub and have interaction between the most different actors to validate or not ideas and prototypes, that is, the participants had the opportunity to evaluate the technologies and network.

It is noteworthy that digital solutions are not magic, nor do they appear as magic tricks, they are tested and pivoted countless times by people in startups, they require a lot of research and testing by research academies of companies or brands, they are worked on by companies in reports with authorities on the subject and unite research with teaching and extension activities in higher education institutions. In terms of consumption, the consumer experience is important for the business and phygital influencers engage more people for brands.

Brands generate phygital appearances as promotional opportunities to bring the brand closer to the public. The digital influencer is within reach of potential consumers. There is tangibility in events, because it reinforces the curiosity of fans, whether of the brand or the digital influencer. The connection generation has phygital activations that tend to attract, in addition to attention, new audiences. Digital influencers who make phygital appearances at fashion shows, for example, collaborate with the brand's success through phygital experiences.

Finally, digital influencers are booming. Creating content with phygital characters impacts consumers in the metaverse. Usually, phygital influence tends to occur with demand for character creation with history and with agencies that create content for brands. However, what if the content was created in conjunction with a digital influencer who was a student at a higher education institution or a collaborator of the brand?

Influencer Marketing can be enhanced with the experience of the influencer in the brand. Fauser, et al. (2023, p. 30) analyzed three digital influencers in three different countries. Lu (Magalu), in Brazil, Nobody Sausage, in Portugal, and Miquela Sousa, in the United States. Lu and Miquela are operated by LuizaLabs and Brud at Dapper Labs, respectively. The authors wrote that the analyzed influencers had marketing value and, with unique characteristics of influence, positioned brands favorably in the eyes of consumers.

It was considered a Marketing strategy with virtual influencers, although the implications for the buying and selling process in the phygital era require further research. In the comparison made by the authors, information was sought about the attitudes and behaviors of consumers in relation to virtual influencers. There was a comparison of virtual influencer Marketing in relation to traditional Marketing with human influencers.

Some conclusions of the article were potential for reflection on the (meta) phygital influencer or phygital influencer who works in the organization, because, according to Fauser, et al. (2023, p. 34), virtual influencers were perceived as a mixture of the virtual and the real that attracted generation Z by the inference of the authors as to liking the feeling of the unpredictable in the virtual world and some participants expressed openness to purchases of promoted products by virtual influencers. The reservation that participants had regarding authenticity could be mitigated if the phygital influencer worked at the institution.

The verisimilitude of the created content is based on the daily life of the brands and the followers can get to know the daily life of the brand with the work of the influencers. The link of (meta) influence is the collaborator who is a digital influencer in metaverse. It is possible to have a profile on social networks, but in immersive experiences, there may be the possibility of being a brand ambassador.

Brand employees have not used to talking about brands on social media, nor do brands select employees to talk about on social media. The panorama, in the chapter, is the metaverse through reports from corporations that studied the phenomenon of the metaverse in companies, in addition to highlighting the opportunities in each number shown.

The Delimitation of (Meta) Influence as the Force and as the Direction for the Metaverse

In a Gartner press release (2022), Gartner's vice president of research stated that suppliers are creating ways for users of immersive universes to replicate lives in digital worlds. It is inferred that the metaverse hype modifies business plans for the phygital transformation and the research executive's statement makes sense for the existence of (meta) phygital influencers as ambassadors of companies in the metaverse, after all, in the aforementioned press release, it is stated that by 2026, 25% of people will spend at least one hour a day in the metaverse whether for work, educational and social activities, shopping or entertainment.

In the McKinsey report (2022, p. 7) Value Creation in the Metaverse: The Real Business of the Virtual World, the metaverse is a reality and the top five corporate use cases are the campaigns or Marketing initiatives, learning and development for employees, immersive meetings, events or conferences and product design or digital burgeoning. Regarding influencer Marketing, it was understood that the development of contents is changing, and it was noticed that, in the report, such a change is a good omen for the growth of the metaverse, because innovative and engaging experiences are related to users who are the creators.

Readers may feel the absence of more real examples, but company reports do not list the phygital meta-influencer as an accounting asset for the brand in the income statements for the year. This statement is a precursor to more future research in the accounting area, for example, because having the influence of a brand ambassador is a financial asset for the company when there is the attraction of more consumers to the brand.

It is noticed that the potential for virtual or phygital influencers in the metaverse for phygital interaction with followers and for the evolution of stories that have the real, digital and phygital as a junction designed by knowledge and artificial intelligence that expand the functions in the most different spaces and in the various formats. Until 2023, it can be inferred that the metaverse was still in an evolutionary stage and when searching for a virtual influencer in the Virtual Humans space and when studying each text referring to influencer Marketing, it was understood that there are opportunities and challenges for business, because, at every moment, new virtual influencers are created in the world with the most different stories and with the most varied digital influencer marketing strategies, the phygital scenarios are constantly evolving.

Donald and Mouratidau (2022, p. 3) wrote that a sustainable career can be understood as a dynamic and flexible process that develops over time and it is linked to a commitment to learning and to the generation of personal resources through experiences that make meaning possible for the employee. The authors highlighted three elements of a sustainable career: people, context, and time. In contemporary times, it is inferred that (meta) influencers can have sustainable careers if there is flexibility, learning and experiences as resources generated for the meaning and (re) meaning of phygital influence.

By involving the employee in the demands of the phygital influencer, there will be preparation, work by the influencer Marketing team and will involve time, context, and formation of the employee's representation in relation to the image of the business and the brand. Social representations require training to be recognized for the impact on consumers' decision-making process. According to Koay et al. (2023, p. 2), there are other influencers, in addition to social media influencers, which include metaverse influencers and all gain strength in the advertising world.

It is inferred that (meta) influencers are emerging and have the potential to revolutionize the way influencer Marketing operates to find who represents the brand or business, in addition to modifying the formats and means of advertisements and presence. In the authors' conclusion, at the junction of the development of the metaverse and the preparation of people, including mentally and technologically, to enter immersive worlds, companies tend to collaborate with influencers in the metaverse in Marketing campaigns.

The (meta) influencer needs development and a growth mindset to have a sustainable career, it is not a representation at the service of Marketing, since it is a human being with phygital experiences. It is not possible to forget that everything must be consistent with reality, because the promotion of balance, mental and environmental health in everyday life is the duty of both the company and the employee.

According to Mengalli and Carvalho (2024, in press) the employee is the subject of his own career, in sustainability, the employee is in tune with the ethical values, beliefs and purposes of the company and takes care of his own professional trajectory with emotional stability so that, in the market, it is possible to demonstrate personal values closely linked to knowledge. The awareness and actions of the employee and the brand need to be coherent.

The expertise of the collaborator impacts the brand and tends to impact the brand's public. There are still challenges for thinking and acting in the global context, because it is necessary to expand the purposes of companies and ethics to the detriment of purely financial results. A (meta) influencer, in the organization, adds value to the business and reskilling enables personal and professional redirections. In Brazil, an investment company had as a (meta) influencer a brand collaborator who engaged people through social networks that used the verb to explain in the third person singular and the first name of the (meta) influencer in juxtaposition.

In the InfoMoney Magazine article, MoneyLab (2021) showed an excerpt from the (goal) influencer's speech that stated that she understood much of what she did as a financial educator and in doing so she listened to people's difficulties and found simple and easy solutions to solve people's problems regarding investment. The (meta) influencer engaged people to invest and created a certain credibility in relation to the investment company's brand through social networks. There are no details in publications about how the collaborator and (meta) influencer relationship occurred.

It is known that, in digital, the company had projection and the (goal) influencer became a partner of the company. From the digital to the phygital that unites the physical with the virtual, it is possible to understand the importance of the (meta) phygital influencer in the context of the organization, because it is the person who lives the mission, vision, values and purposes of the business and the representation in the metaverse ecosystem enhances the company's reach. People know about digital influencers, influencers in relation to the brands' strategy, the intention, habits, and customs of both the influencer and customers or consumers and social ecosystems and influencers, who people still do not know is the routine of phygital (meta) influencers.

The media usually brings the history and background of influencers. In the first decades of the 21st century, most influencers were digital. Another Brazilian example of a (meta) influencer shows a chief strategist at an investment company who combined the team's knowledge so that together they were able to bring the best ideas and content to an audience that followed the (meta) influencer who, years later, he became head of digital content at another investment firm.

In the institutional article "Prazer, Betina Roxo: Conheça a Nova Estrategista Chefe da Rico" (2020), the company praises the employee with a bit of history, a vision of the whole that can impact investment decisions. Years later, IstoÉ Dinheiro Magazine (2022) reported that the head of content had funny stories experienced in the financial market and that she gave tips for those who were starting to invest money, as well as having the mission to lead more people to the world of finance.

The first (meta) digital influencer needed upskilling to work and to engage people and the second had knowledge about the subject and needed reskilling to master the contents in virtual spaces. In a world with phygital transformations, there is an alteration in the types of content of influencers and influencer Marketing metrics are changing to verify reach in digital and phygital media, metrics for influencers organically and driven by paid modes. It is known that companies can opt for (nano) influencers or influencers with more followers according to their Marketing strategies.

It is noticed the growth in the use of influencers in the most diverse sectors of the economy and the market begins to look at the (meta) influencer and includes him or her in digital business models. Communication and digital Marketing are transforming society in the digital scope. According to Gartner's press release (2022), there is a prediction that 25% of people will spend at least one hour a day in the metaverse in 2026.

If people are in the metaverse, influencers must be there, and phygital (meta) influencers must also be in the immersive worlds. However, upskilling and reskilling are necessary for a better four-dimensional representation. The technological and recursive skills of influencers must be phygital. The roles of influencers change cultures, societies, histories, and physical economies. The trend incorporates the physical and the digital to be phygital, so the phygital (meta) influencer is represented in the real world and in the virtual universe and on platforms that unite the two elements: physical and digital.

The (meta) influencers as professionals of the companies are representations that are within the scope of the organization and the new business models must include this phygital representation, including remuneration. The market for influencers has expanded in recent years and organizations are starting to look inside the company and at (intra) entrepreneurs. Brands and consumers often turn to the stars and celebrities to promote products and services.

In China, research, and development academies, such as Alibaba Damo Academy, use digital humans to increase sales on major marketplaces, and on Singles Day, a (meta) human representative, Timo, assists consumers with shopping in the metaverse. It could be an innovation, a brand collaborator being the (meta) influencer, because he would know the products and tell a little about the product's history. It stands out that people like storytelling.

The era of (meta) influencers or internal influencers is the present and the future in digital Marketing. Owners or partners often provide a powerful force for companies and people like to know the story and how they managed to make money with the brand. In the new business models, companies tend to promote employees as partners in the company, so it makes perfect sense for collaborating partners to represent the organization on social networks or in immersive spaces.

In Brazil, investment companies made it possible for internal influencers to have space and time to talk about the organization's theme with the public and potential public to demystify investments. Thinking about sustainable careers for (meta) influencers and the mitigation of human varnish emerges, because it includes communication and creativity to enhance adherence to the brand and the strengthening of ties with the organization.

QUALITATIVE STUDY AND EVIDENCE OF (META) REPRESENTATION FOR PHYGITAL TRANSFORMATION

In this chapter, what is (meta) influence it was evidenced with recent texts and with examples of (meta) influencers who collaborated with companies in the investment area. It is known that (meta) influence has digital predominance, however, with advances in the metaverse and digital humans that represent brands in immersive worlds, phygital (meta) influencers have potential for Marketing in terms of contribution to brands. Career is one of the elements present in the chapter, even though the legislation does not show how the (meta) influencer's relationships with the brand occur, since the current contracts are usually employment or partnership ties.

In the research, the career was supporting and evidenced the human varnish in labor relations, and it was noticed that careers are more sustainable both for employees and for brands, because employees transcend functions and engage people for the business. The relationships between influencer Marketing and virtual humans, digital humans and phygital humans were investigated in articles and texts to situate the representations of (meta) influencers as contributions to brands.

According to Taylor, Bogdan and DeVault (2016, p. 8) qualitative research aims to build theory and it should be noted that the research design was flexible (Marshall and Rossman, 2011, apud Taylor, Bogdan and DeVault, 2016, p. 8), in the beginning, the studies had investigation questions and, with the countless readings, the learning and appropriation of the theme (re) signified the subject in a holistic way, after all, examining the different theories allow countless perspectives and unexpected and new insights.

Meta-Influencer was investigated in search engines to complete what it was searched and, in 2023, only two texts were found, however the theme that emerges is influencers and not meta-influencers. In the conclusion of Koay, et al. (2023, p.52), influencers of social networks play a significant role in the decision-making process of consumers and the authors mention the existence of influencers of pets and influencers of the metaverse that have visibility in the world of advertising and that revolutionize how companies advertise brands and products.

The authors stated that, when the metaverse is more developed and people are more prepared with technological infrastructure and mentally to enter the metaverse, companies will have more influencers in the metaverse in Marketing campaigns. Karabacake and Güngör (2023, p. 194) wrote that the metaverse will transform people's life practices and add that there are new experiences in the areas of business, education, entertainment, development, and Marketing and emphasize new opportunities in Marketing activities of influence. In conclusion, the authors wrote that the metaverse provides opportunities for brands to develop updated and alternative modes of advertising formulas and methods.

In other years, the meta-influence theme appears in the results, however there is no evidence of meta-influencers. The expressions "Influencer Marketing", "Virtual Human", "Digital Human", and "Phygital Human" were searched in academic search engines, however the meta-influence subject was not contained.

META-INFLUENCE AND THE POSSIBILITIES OF FUTURE RESEARCH

It was noticed that researchers recognize that the metaverse is changing and will change influencer Marketing and advertising, as well as businesses and brands, however influencers, whether virtual, digital or phygital, are creations that are not parts of the companies, that is, the company's ambassadors in the metaverse are still not found searches, at least, in the English language, although it is known that the word metaverse was coined in the 90s of the twentieth century by the American writer Neal Stephenson (1959 -).

Bell (2022) wrote that the metaverse seems to be an innovative word, but the idea is not so new and mentioned that it is necessary to look beyond the work Snow Crash that Stephenson (2000) baptized the immersive space of metaverse. The metamorphosis for businesses that intended to combine virtual worlds within the scope of digital media with online games and extended realities must be placed in research so that they do not seem like just opportunities without the sides to be unveiled.

The sense of presence as a quality of the metaverse needs further studies for (meta) influencers because the billions to be invested involve physical commerce and the jobs of designers, developers and collaborators with companies and brands in immersive spaces. The Consumer Electronics Show (2022, 2023) made it possible for people to think about beauty for avatars and the combined smells of perfumes. Thus, software and hardware must be studied to be developed.

From technological infrastructures, advertising and influencer Marketing, researchers may be able to locate phygital meta-influencers to study this trend for both brands and employees in sustainable careers and in constructive collaboration with organizations to engage people for the business the consumer experience is phygital in immersive worlds.

It is believed that physical and digital influencers are history and leave a legacy for phygital meta-influencers, because the careers and professions of the future are changing in the present, just as the human varnish needs to be evidenced for business with communication and with creativity. Repetitions at work are in the process of being replaced by programming in artificial intelligence and by machines considered to be intelligent, allowing humans to interact with robots and mechanizations.

As the market for influencers grows and the values get higher, saturation and skepticism occur among consumers and clients, because the content appears as sponsored by the companies and the verisimilitude becomes fragile. Investigations must be conducted to understand how companies seek new ways of connecting with audiences in media that combine the physical with the digital and how they understand the work of internal influencers or (meta) influencers.

It is not envisaged that artificial intelligences can be meta-influencers, because they will not be hired by companies, nor will they be part of the human resources staff, therefore, the intrinsic property of a representation in the phygital transformation as a (meta) influence as a force with magnitude and direction in the metaverse lack much new research both in the area of Marketing and in the area of business and law in the metaverse. One does not believe in utopias, but, without research, dystopias can be written as a way of denouncing an existing reality to readers. It is believed in upskilling and reskilling employees to represent brands.

SOLUTIONS AND RECOMMENDATIONS: POSSIBILITIES OF REFLECTION FOR ADVANCEMENT

In the upskilling and reskilling movement and based on the sustainable behavior of human beings with their own careers, success stories with sustainability tend to occur with strategies for implementing corporate or public policies. The theme of sustainability and governance tend to emerge in initiatives, because the future of the brand has environmental and social governance in organizations based on the formation of human beings and their own four-dimensional phygital representation and the options regarding the careers people will have during their lives.

It is known that people will still need time to get used to the combination of physical or digital work in immersive worlds, however it is a reality that will not go backwards, and legislation must insert the constitutional rights provided for in the world of work. Although there are reservations about the type of content produced, it must be admitted that there is a tendency for the market to grow despite the difficulties and the benefits should be studied in research to gain knowledge of the relationships between the works and how they are impacting society. and (cyber) society.

Understanding Employee Value Proposition - EVP - or value proposals for employees as a mix of benefits and rewards that can be offered by companies to (meta) influencers based on the financial returns brought by employee-ambassadors not only in productivity and performance, but people and sales engagements. In an interview with the company VendaMais, the largest shareholder of Magazine Luiza which owns the digital influencer Lu, in Brazil, she answers the question about the importance of the seller at Magazine Luiza with the information that everyone in the company, is and says they are sellers, and everyone is proud to be a seller.

The businesswoman said in the interview that she usually says that people are always selling, no matter if they are sellers, doctors, or dentists. She compliments those who learn to sell never again have problems in life, because if you become unemployed, they will always have something to sell. The businesswoman uses the physical context in her speech and has a virtual influencer in the company, adding that the metaverse and influencer Marketing are realities, therefore, the attributions of contemporary Marketing will have more responsibilities in the future.

Karabacake and Güngör (2023, p. 194) wrote that influencer Marketing activity evidence metaverse brands with the connection of the physical and digital world and that influencer agencies connect new audiences in the metaverse, in addition to all developments will significantly affect influencer Marketing in the metaverse and will bring new and current research questions.

FINAL CONSIDERATIONS

It is concluded that, for a long time, organizations were concerned with the type of content that collaborators produced, and freedom was very restricted. The policies still exist, however, with the need to have the collaborators as a brand ambassador, some changes were made and have the internal support of the Marketing teams to show empathy with the consumer. Some companies created and included in their business models the representation of collaborators as (meta) influencers.

Even though the cases of Kyra, Lu (Magalu), Miquela Sousa and Betina Roxo were highlighted, among other examples, the certainty was that it is known to many Marketing teams that Influencer Marketing is a reality for social networks and that immersive experiences do not escape the concerns and actions of brands, however company reports do not include the phygital (meta) influencer or insights due to labor legislation issues.

The explicit and the real exist, but the implicit in positions, salaries and legislation prevails in phygital influencer Marketing. Many experts, to meet the demands of the metaverse, speak or write bricolages of labor, tax, commercial, corporate law, among many branches of law, to inform that the metaverse ecosystem can be brought to real courts. It is not that this conclusion is superficial, there is the part of the research that has evidence and cannot put the researchers' desires in the text. The certainty that the objective of the chapter has been achieved is that the term (meta) influence and how the (meta) phygital influencer are expressed in this text and in research, reports and examples have shown that the (meta) phygital influencer can contribute to the brand in metaverse ecosystem.

The parts that need to be highlighted require future research in the areas of psychology, human resources, computer science, the various branches of law, among many areas that involve human beings and business, because, as in the section referring to in future research, it is not intended that artificial intelligences will be phygital meta-influencers, but that people from companies can be brand ambassadors in immersive universes, therefore, the demand for upskilling and reskilling is legitimate, as well as more research into human qualifications.

There were many reflections for the creation of the phygital (meta) influencer and Fauser, et al. (2023, p. 34) wrote that virtual influencers pleasure generation Z, therefore, consumers born after 2010 tend to seek new sensations and experiences both in consumer experiences and in employee experiences. In the Gartner press release (2022), there is evidence of the prediction that 25% of people, in 2026, will spend at least one hour a day in the metaverse and, in the McKinsey report (2022, p. 7), a of the corporate uses of the metaverse is in the Marketing area, it is inferred that phygital (meta) influencers are not far from reality.

(Meta) influencers are very familiar with the company's values, products and services and can make authentic and convincing recommendations, as Costa (2023) wrote for a Brazilian newspaper and mentioned that internal influencers have a better understanding of the company's public, which enables the personalization of the advertising message for greater effectiveness and consumption of products or services.

As written in the background of this chapter, companies can start with digital business in the medium term, but, in the future that needs the strategy, brands must leave the phygital meta-influencer well evidenced in the Marketing plan for the phygital experience of customers. If not for execution, the writing in the plan should be for research or training and development demands that involve upskilling and reskilling.

Depending on the company's strategy, one or more internal influencers may have contact with the organization's public. It is possible to have a team of internal influencers to diversify the speeches and contents in the most different Marketing channels that include the metaverse ecosystems. It is known that the costs for acquiring consumers and customers increase over the years, competition is usually great.

The identification of the internal influencer is careful, and the training enables skills, knowledge, and charisma to adapt people to be (meta) influencers of the brands. Legal and compliance teams are the best stakeholders for the journey of (meta) influencers on brands in contracts. Research, within the scope of law, must be conducted to locate whose audience is built, whether from (meta) influencers or companies.

The (meta) influencer trend is a reality and strategies must be based on research and reports from specialized companies for the best adaptation to the market and society. It is believed that the movement of millions of dollars will place both Marketing and the areas of law for the strategies of organizations..

REFERENCES

Alibaba Damo Academy. (n.d.). https://damo.alibaba.com/

Area 2071: Your Invitation to Be a Part of Creating the Future. (2020). Dubai Future Foundation. https://area2071.ae/wp-content/uploads/2021/05/AREA-2071-Report.pdf

Bell, G. (2022). *The Metaverse is a New Word for an Old Idea*. Massachusetts Institute of Technology. https://www.technologyreview.com/2022/02/08/1044732/metaverse-history-snow-crash/

Bulz, N. (2023). *The Terrestrial Rational Subject – A Finite Being – Eliciting the 'Towards Infinite' Tentation and Tension. Does a Universal Consciousness be Comprehended by a Rational Subject?* https://papers.ssrn.com/sol3/papers.cfm?abstract_id=4392715

Consumer Electronics Show. (n.d.). https://www.ces.tech/.

Costa, A. (2023). *A era dos Metainfluencers ou influenciadores internos*. Gazeta do Povo. https://www.gazetadopovo.com.br/vozes/voce-amanha/a-era-dos-metainfluencers-ou-influenciadores-internos/

Donald, W. E., & Mouratidou, M. (2022). Preparing for a Sustainable Career: Challenges and Opportunities. *GiLE Journal of Skills Development, 2*(2), 3-5. https://insight.cumbria.ac.uk/id/eprint/6647/

Fauser, S. (2023). Virtual Influencer Marketing and its Impact on Customer Purchase Behaviour. *International Journal of Business and Applied Social Science, 9*(6). doi:10.33642/ijbass.v9n6p4

Gartner Predicts 25% of People Will Spend at Least One Hour Per Day in the Metaverse by 2026. (2022). Gartner Inc. Press Release. Newsroom. https://www.gartner.com/en/newsroom/press-releases/2022-02-07-gartner-predicts-25-percent-of-people-will-spend-at-least-one-hour-per-day-in-the-metaverse-by-2026

HumansV. (n.d.). https://www.virtualhumans.org/category/research

Karabacak, Z. İ., & Güngör, İ. (2023). The Metaverse as Influencer Marketing Platform: Influencer-Brand Collaborations of Par3ıs Hilton with 'Superplastic', 'Bohoo', and 'Levi's'. *Etkileşim, 6*(11), 176–199. doi:10.32739/ctkilcsim.2023.6.11.194

Koay, K. Y. (2023). Social Media Influencer Marketing: Commentary on the Special Issue. *Journal of Internet Commerce, 22*(1), S1-S3. https://www.tandfonline.com/doi/full/10.1080/15332861.2022.2128277

Luiza Helena - O que é que a Luiza tem? (n.d.). VendaMais. https://vendamais.com.br/luiza-helena-o-que-e-que-a-luiza-tem/

Mengalli, N. M., & de Carvalho, A. A. (2024). Environmental, Social and Corporate (Human) Governance in Phygital Transformation: Industry 5.0 with Paradigm Shifts, Disruptions and the Metaverse. In Organizational Management Sustainability in VUCA Contexts. IGI Global. https://doi.org/doi:10.4018/979-8-3693-0720-5

Mengalli, N. M., de Carvalho, A. A., & Galvão, S. M. (2023). Metaverse Ecosystem and Consumer Society 5.0: Consumer Experience and Influencer Marketing in Phygital Transformation. In R. Bansal, S. Qalati, & A. Chakir (Eds.), *Influencer Marketing Applications Within the Metaverse* (pp. 33–56). IGI Global. doi:10.4018/978-1-6684-8898-0.ch003

MoneyLab. (2021). *Do Zero à Educação Financeira: Como Ana Laura Magalhães se Tornou Sócia da XP.* InfoMoney. https://www.infomoney.com.br/onde-investir/como-uma-ex-atendente-de-telemarketing-virou-socia-da-xp/

Prazer, B. R. (2020). *Conheça a Nova Estrategista Chefe da Rico.* https://riconnect.rico.com.vc/analises/prazer-betina-roxo/

"Real Or Robotic?": Kyra, Who Claims to Be India's First Meta-Influencer, Leaves Internet Confused. (2022). https://www.ndtv.com/offbeat/real-or-robotic-kyra-who-claims-to-be-indias-first-meta-influencer-leaves-internet-confused-3048975

Roxo, B. (2022). *da XP, dá dicas de como investir seu dinheiro.* IstoÉ Dinheiro. https://istoedinheiro.com.br/betina-roxo-da-xp-da-dicas-de-como-investir-seu-dinheiro/

Stephenson, N. (2000). *Snow Crash.* Bantam Books.

Taylor, S. J., Bogdan, R., & DeVault, M. L. (2016). *Introduction to Qualitative Research Methods: A Guidebook and Resource. Wiley.* Unreal Engine. https://www.unrealengine.com/en-US/metahuman

Value Creation in the Metaverse: The Real Business of the Virtual World. (2022). McKinsey Company. https://www.mckinsey.com/~/media/mckinsey/business%20functions/marketing%20and%20sales/our%20insights/value%20creation%20in%20the%20metaverse/Value-creation-in-the-metaverse.pdf

Vincent, J. (2020). Samsung's 'Artificial Humans' are Just Digital Avatars. *The Verge.* https://www.theverge.com/2020/1/7/21051390/samsung-artificial-human-neon-digital-avatar-project-star-labs

ADDITIONAL READING

B'chir, H. B., Erragcha, N., & Bchir, S. (2023). How Will Influencer Marketing Change in the Metaverse? In R. Bansal, S. Qalati, & A. Chakir (Eds.), *Influencer Marketing Applications Within the Metaverse* (pp. 13–32). IGI Global. doi:10.4018/978-1-6684-8898-0.ch002

Bansal, R., & Pruthi, N. (2023). Avatar-Based Influencer Marketing: Demystifying the Benefits and Risks of Marketing Through Virtual Influencers. In R. Bansal, S. Qalati, & A. Chakir (Eds.), *Influencer Marketing Applications Within the Metaverse* (pp. 78–86). IGI Global. doi:10.4018/978-1-6684-8898-0.ch005

Devi, S., & Kohli, G. (2023). A Lead or a Dread?: Employee Influencer as Brand Co-Creator. In R. Bansal, S. Qalati, & A. Chakir (Eds.), *Influencer Marketing Applications Within the Metaverse* (pp. 241–253). IGI Global. doi:10.4018/978-1-6684-8898-0.ch015

Kouchih, A., & Mataa, H. (2023). The Potential of Influencer Marketing in the Emerging Metaverse. In R. Bansal, S. Qalati, & A. Chakir (Eds.), *Influencer Marketing Applications Within the Metaverse* (pp. 57–77). IGI Global. doi:10.4018/978-1-6684-8898-0.ch004

Kumar, P., Oberoi, S., & Jaitly, R. (2023). Impact of Social Media Influencers on Consumer Engagement and Its Consequences in the Emerging Environment of Metaverse. In R. Bansal, S. Qalati, & A. Chakir (Eds.), *Influencer Marketing Applications Within the Metaverse* (pp. 225–240). IGI Global. doi:10.4018/978-1-6684-8898-0.ch014

Rodrigues, P., Sousa, A., Borges, A. P., Brochado, A., & Barbosa, I. (2023). Human(oid): Virtual Social Media Influencers. In R. Bansal, S. Qalati, & A. Chakir (Eds.), *Influencer Marketing Applications Within the Metaverse* (pp. 1–12). IGI Global. doi:10.4018/978-1-6684-8898-0.ch001

Rosário, A. T., Lopes, P. R., & Rosário, F. S. (2023). Influencer Marketing in the Digital Ecosystem. In R. Bansal, S. Qalati, & A. Chakir (Eds.), *Influencer Marketing Applications Within the Metaverse* (pp. 132–166). IGI Global. doi:10.4018/978-1-6684-8898-0.ch009

Saini, S., & Bansal, R. (2023). Power of Social Media Influencer Credibility on the Influence of Brand Attitude. In R. Bansal, S. Qalati, & A. Chakir (Eds.), *Influencer Marketing Applications Within the Metaverse* (pp. 167–177). IGI Global. doi:10.4018/978-1-6684-8898-0.ch010

Tyagi, S., Srivastava, A. K., Dubey, A., & Sharma, D. (2023). Metaverse Is the Future of Influencer Marketing. In R. Bansal, S. Qalati, & A. Chakir (Eds.), *Influencer Marketing Applications Within the Metaverse* (pp. 102–116). IGI Global. doi:10.4018/978-1-6684-8898-0.ch007

KEY TERMS AND DEFINITIONS

Future: It is the time that follows the present and has several interconnected sets of facts and phenomena that are related and intersect to create new sets and conjunctures. Time is included, as is expectation and prospecting of scenarios through data culture. This is what did not happen, in Latin, "futurum" (article [the] and noun [future]) and "futurus" (prospect). It is what will be, what was not and what is to come. If the suffix "ism" is added to the noun, there is futurism, which is a state, a doctrine, a principle or even a condition.

Human Varnish: Term brought to the business area and linked to professions that need physical work or continuous use of computational resources that can be supported by artificial intelligence bases. Although there is social interaction to perform functions, professions with these characteristics tend, in the future, to have artificial intelligence to support or to perform most of the human function. The professional in the area tends to be necessary regarding decisions involving elements that only exist in human beings. Communication and creativity are evidence that humans can transform careers sustainably and in immersive worlds with the skills and abilities that can connect business brands with human strategic intelligence to people who want more service tips or of the products that the companies offer. Content from people who work at the companies and generate empathy with people who are not so fluent in using the products or services. The presentation of the working day usually generates empathy with the people who follow the influencers.

Marketing: It is an area that includes a process for identifying consumers and for creation and (co) creation that includes communication and distribution of a product or service for the best user, client, or consumer experience. It is part of business management as a science and as creation of values for the consumer market by offering services, experiences, or products to the brand's audience. It is an area that provide the energy to the brand's profits.

(Meta) Influencer: An influencer who belongs to the business and represents the organization as an ambassador in accordance with the company's purposes, mission, vision, and values. It is a character that represents the brand. Stories, identity, and resources are branded based on the core values of the business. It includes creativity in the brand's operations, tactics, and strategy. It can take on a meta-human format and add effects based on artificial intelligence as an editorial and communication strategy. The meta-influencer leads the brand towards a contemporary style of communication on social media and immersive worlds.

Metaverse: It is a word created in a work of fiction that had its concept strengthened over the years since the 90s of the 20th century. As a platform, they are new and face technological and recursive problems for insertion into the daily lives of the population, mainly non-(cyber) citizens. They tend to be open source and operationalized via blockchain. There are challenges in the ecosystem and advances under the concept of a phygital universe that transcends the current world wide web [2023]. It can be part of the future imagined for the world wide web with the potential to transform consumption through immersive experiences, because it is a collective phygital environment that allows interaction between meta-humans and between meta-humans and brands. It is used in business, games, events, entertainment, tourism and in the educational area, such as metaversities. The world wide web can stop being a screen that separates the physical world from the digital universe and become a space for immersive experiences.

Phygital Transformation: It is a term coming from the business world and highlights the combination of the physical and the digital. It is based on interfaces and context to be situated and related to the industry, society, and consumption 5.0. In the user and consumer journey, there are processes that change over time and space, which highlights the dissociation of reality and virtuality. In the integration of physical and digital, emotions, feelings, behaviours, and intelligence, whether artificial or emotional, mix in the consumer's experience with the brand and affect the phygital journey through strategic decisions and meaning.

Sustainable Career: It combines mental health, happiness, time management, productivity, performance, and the possibility of being a company ambassador in a physical or digital way or even in the combination of both, phygitally. Mental health becomes a public health issue when it is not reflected as a center of sustainability. Work activities can show the harm to human life and careers need to be fully sustainable, including the possibility of representing the brand with knowledge about the brand's products or services. Some people are happy to contribute on social networks or in the metaverse. The happiness element is present in studies that have conclusions about the contribution of happiness in the employee's professional life. Neural connections relate to health, well-being, feelings, emotions, actions, and recognition. The represented productivity can be through performance and deliveries, it is related to the management of enjoyment and work time and can also be measured with the presentation of the business on digital or phygital platforms. Sustainable employability is contained in the sustainable career, just as the sustainable career is at the intersection of mental health, happiness, and time management. Personal life influences the professional and the professional trajectory interferes in people's way of life. The employee's experience and the consumer's experience tend to come together, given the classifications given by the global consultancy Great Place to Work, for example.

Chapter 8
Virtual Influencers: A Bibliometric Analysis

Belem Barbosa
https://orcid.org/0000-0002-4057-360X
University of Porto, Portugal

ABSTRACT

Virtual influencers are rapidly gaining significance in the digital marketing realm. This study offers an overview of the fragmented landscape of virtual influencer research, addressing key contributions, themes, methodologies, and future directions. Employing a bibliometric analysis approach, the research examined 52 articles from the Scopus database, shedding light on the evolving field. Findings underscore a dispersed literature landscape that began in 2020, spanning 44 distinct outlets and involving 138 authors. The prevailing research primarily centers on general social media users' perceptions of virtual influencers, leaving substantial gaps in the study of actual followers. Many pieces of research exhibit a lack of methodological rigor and theoretical framework. As the discipline progresses, there is an emergent need for enhanced methodologies that focus on genuine followers and encompass broader managerial objectives. The prospects for subsequent research in this domain are vast and promising.

INTRODUCTION

In recent years, the integration of virtual and augmented reality technologies with social media platforms has catalyzed the rise of virtual influencers, which can be defined as "computer-generated characters or avatars designed and maintained by experts and digital agencies that help brands appeal to and reach desirable target groups effectively through their digital personalities" (Audrezet & Koles, 2023, p. 353). In the literature, the term "virtual influencers" is frequently used interchangeably with related concepts such as "computer-generated influencer" (e.g., Block & Lovegrove, 2021; Mrad et al., 2022), "virtual avatar" (e.g., de Brito Silva et al., 2022), and "social bot" (e.g., Choong & Wang, 2023). However, "virtual influencer" seems to be the most accepted terminology. Robinson (2020) stresses that virtual influencers are neither humans nor robots; rather, they are fictional characters whose representations are computer-generated. They are controlled by artificial intelligence (Sands et al., 2022) and often mimic

DOI: 10.4018/979-8-3693-0551-5.ch008

the appearance, actions, and behaviors of human beings (Choudhry et al., 2022; da Silva Oliveira & Chimenti, 2021; Franke et al., 2023; Ham, Li, et al., 2023; Mirowska & Arsenyan, 2023). Moustakas et al. (2020) stress that, even when their virtual nature is disclosed, virtual influencers frequently exhibit human emotions in their posts and interactions with social media users.

According to Lou et al. (2022), there are six motivations for following virtual influencers: novelty, information, entertainment, surveillance, esthetics, and integration and social interaction. Available data underscores consumers' interest in virtual influencers. For instance, in the US, it was estimated that over half of the consumers had followed a virtual influencer in 2022 (Dencheva, 2023b). Notably, Adult Gen Z exhibited the most pronounced affinity, with 75% of them following these digital influencers (Dencheva, 2023b). The primary reason behind following these influencers was content and storytelling (Dencheva, 2023a), with platforms like YouTube and Instagram emerging as the primary hubs for such engagements.

Ham, Li, et al. (2023) stress that the advertising and entertainment sectors are pioneering the use of virtual humans in the digital realm. However, and like their human counterparts, the most popular virtual influencers frequently advertise a myriad of product categories, from fashion and beauty items, to automobiles, food, and tourism experiences. Interestingly, there are diverse strategies employed within virtual influencers. Some are owned directly by brands, such as Lu do Magalu, created for Magazine Luiza in 2009, who boasts millions of followers on both Instagram and TikTok. In contrast, there are virtual influencers like Miquela Sousa (@lilmiquela), created by Brud, who collaborate with major brands and also have millions of followers on Instagram and TikTok. Furthermore, certain virtual influencers have carved out niche positions aligned with specific consumer values; for instance, Noonoouri promotes veganism and sustainable fashion and maintains a notable online presence.

Collaborating with virtual influencers offers companies several advantages. Virtual influencers are customizable (de Brito Silva et al., 2022; Mouritzen et al., 2023) and provide enhanced control over their digital presence (Conti et al., 2022; da Silva Oliveira & Chimenti, 2021; de Brito Silva et al., 2022; Franke et al., 2023; Mouritzen et al., 2023; Moustakas et al., 2020). While deceptive practices among traditional influencers pose reputational risks for collaborating brands, virtual influencers mitigate these risks. Additionally, virtual influencers provide more flexibility that human influencers (Conti et al., 2022; Mouritzen et al., 2023). Their absence of physical constraints allows for versatile brand representations in diverse scenarios. It can also reduce costs (de Brito Silva et al., 2022; Franke et al., 2023), including related to logistics and campaign preparation. Virtual influencers also offer automation and ownership advantages (Mouritzen et al., 2023). Moreover, they are especially appealing to the younger audiences (Audrezet & Koles, 2023; Bringé, 2023; Jhawar et al., 2023) and can enable companies to engage with those segments more effectively. According to Statista, virtual influencers provide relevant engagement rates, as for example Lu of Magalu, who has over 6 million followers, 0.26 percent of which interacted with her posts on average. Lil Miquela had in 2022 an engagement rate of 1.4%.

Arsenyan and Mirowska (2021) argue that virtual influencers have the potential to cater to the same user engagement needs as human influencers on social media platforms. Virtual influencers can assist users in forming and displaying their personal identity, particularly in the context of social media's public nature. Furthermore, they offer a unique diversion, presenting an alternate yet familiar reality, enhancing the immersive experience. Interactions with virtual influencers can simulate genuine social interactions, potentially leading to perceived intimate or parasocial relationships. This interaction can also fulfill the need for autonomy, as users consciously choose to engage with virtual content, thereby ensuring a genuine interaction experience.

Virtual influencers as shown as particularly effective in building brand image and brand awareness (Lou et al., 2022) and brand trust (Choi et al., 2023). However, some studies suggest that, compared their human counterparts, virtual influencers have limited ability to foster purchase intentions (Lou et al., 2022), namely due to lack of perceived authenticity (Laszkiewicz & Kalinska-Kula, 2023; Lou et al., 2022) and low perceived similarity (Lou et al., 2022) and lower credibility than human influencers (Ozdemir et al., 2023). Franke et al. (2023) and Ozdemir et al. (2023) found that human influencers outperformed virtual ones in endorsement and ad evaluations. However, virtual influencers brought a sense of novelty and brand innovation, though the duration of this effect is uncertain. Choudhry et al. (2022) found that followers tend to find virtual influencers less trustworthy than human influencers, except in areas like technology, music, games, and art. In a study focused on cosmetic brand advertising, Franke et al. (2023) agrees with this view, suggesting that virtual endorsers fit better with technical items than with personal ones like cosmetics.

Virtual influencers may exhibit various levels of anthropomorphism, i.e., can be visually similar to humans or have a clear non-human appearance. In the case of anthropomorphism, Franke et al. (2023) found that consumers often struggle to discern virtual from human influencers. Although it is expected that human traits of virtual influencers may affect their credibility and persuasiveness, the findings in the literature are inconsistent. Kim et al. (2023) found that users view virtual influencers with human traits as credible endorsers. However, a study by Cornelius, Leidner and Bina (2023) suggest that less realistic virtual influencers can be more credible and more persuasive.

Despite the significant interest from both organizations and academics, virtual influencers are a relatively new phenomenon. Previous studies have consolidated literature digital influencers, including systematic literature reviews (e.g., Joshi et al., 2023; Pradhan et al., 2023; Vrontis et al., 2021) and bibliometric analyses (e.g., Fernández-Prados et al., 2021; Neves et al., 2019). However, virtual influencers have clear specificities compared to human influencers and are expected to significantly transform what we know on influencer marketing. Research in this area remains limited and is particularly fragmented. The development of the literature on the topic would benefit of a general overview of research scope and trends. The need for a more holistic understanding is evident, especially when considering the opportunities and challenges posed by this digital marketing strategy. Recognizing the need to provide an overview of the state of the art, da Silva Oliveira and Chimenti (2021) claim to have conducted the first systematic literature review. However, from the 32 publications that they have considered, only two focused on virtual influencers. More recently, Laszkiewicz and Kalinska-Kula (2023) published a systematic literature review that focused on journal articles on virtual influencers, but their analysis included only journal articles, and included only five articles published after 2022. Moreover, the methodological approaches adopted in the field were not explored by extant research.

Given the need in the literature for a bibliometric approach to virtual influencer literature, his chapter aims to further consolidate fragmented views on the topic and identify prevailing trends in existing literature. The following research questions (RQ) were defined:

RQ1: Which are the journals, institutions, countries, and researchers that have most contributed to virtual influencer research?
RQ2: What are the key research themes in virtual influencer research?
RQ3: What are the prominent methodological approaches in virtual influencer research?
RQ4: What are the future research directions for virtual influencers?

The remainder of the article is organized as follows. The next section presents the method adopted in the bibliometric study, followed by the findings. Theoretical and managerial implications derived from the study are highlighted in the solutions and recommendations section. Then the chapter suggests future research directions and ends with the general conclusion.

METHOD

Given the main aim and the research questions defined for this chapter, adopted a bibliometric analysis approach. Bibliometric analysis is particularly useful to reveal temporal dynamics, highlight the main contributors, provide a longitudinal overview of a particular research topic, to discern the research strategies adopted by extant literature, and consequently to help identify research gaps and avenues for future research.

This study sourced data from Scopus, a leading database for top-tier academic journal and proceedings content. Scopus database has been employed in several prior bibliometric reviews, namely in the social media research domain (e.g., Donthu et al., 2021; Fernández-Prados et al., 2021; Neves et al., 2019). It should be noted that some studies retrieve data from other databases, namely Web of Science (e.g., Goyal et al., 2021). However, this research found that, at the time of data extraction (July 11th, 2023), Web of Science only returned 22 results for the topic "virtual influencer", while Scopus returned 57. So, it was concluded that Scopus was the preferred database for this research, as it offered a more comprehensive overview of the topic. The search process is summarized in Table 1. The table is inspired in the Preferred reporting items for systematic reviews and meta-analysis (PRISMA) flowchart, adapted to a table format. As noted, of the 57 records found in the Scopus database, 52 were considered for the bibliometric analysis.

After screening and identified the records to be included in the analysis, data was further explored using the Biblioshiny, a interactive web interface provided by Bibliometrix. This is a tool that provides resources to comprehensive data analyses particularly recommended for bibliometric analyses of the literature (Aria & Cuccurullo, 2017). Further analyses related to methodological approaches were coded and summarized in a spreadsheet. A summary of the data records is presented in Table 2.

Table 1. Data gathered and procedures

Stages	Records	Procedures
Identification	Records identified through Scopus database: N = 57	• Search query: "virtual influencer" • Fields: Title, Abstract, Keywords • Date of search: July 11th, 2023
Screening	Exclusions: • Publications not about virtual influencers = 4 • Records that were not publications = 1	Analysis of title and abstract to identify duplicates and articles beyond the scope of the study
Eligibility	No article was excluded.	Full-text articles were assessed for eligibility.
Records Included	Studies included in the bibliometric analysis: N = 52	

Source: Developed by the author.

Table 2. Synthesis of the publications (in alphabetical order of the first author)

Authors and Year	Main topic	Approach	Method	Population	Sample	Data Analysis
Arsenyan and Mirowska (2021)	Human and virtual influencers' behaviors and users' reactions	QUANT	Netnography	Influencers' posts and users' comments	1011 posts 231014 comments	Content analysis, ANOVA
Audrezet and Koles (2023)	Consumer perspectives Consumer segmentation	QUAL	Interviews	Social media users	42 social media users, Ages: 19-45	Thematic content analysis
Awdziej et al. (2021)	Perceived credibility of virtual influencer	QUANT	Experimental design	Social media users	246 management students	t-Test
Block and Lovegrove (2021)	Virtual influencer as a strategy of public relations	QUAL	Case study	Virtual influencers	Lil Miquela	n.a.
Brachtendorf (2022)	Virtual influencers in fashion culture	QUAL	Case study	Virtual influencers	Lil Miquela	n.a.
Chiu and Ho (2023)	Source credibility of traditional celebrity, micro-celebrity, and virtual influencers) – and impact on emotional attachment and purchase intention	QUANT	Survey	Generation Z	581 young social media users, Ages: 18-24	Path analysis
Choi et al. (2023)	Gen Z travelers' trust in Instagram marketplace and virtual influencers	Mixed	Interviews & Experiments	Gen Z travelers	15 interviewees & 1216 survey respondents	ANCOVA
Choong and Wang (2023)	Social bots in the public relations context	Conceptual / Theoretical	n.a.	n.a.	n.a.	n.a.
Choudhry et al. (2022)	Followers' motivations, perceptions, and concerns	QUAL	Interviews	Virtual influencer followers	30 consumers from 16 countries, Ages: 14-16	Data-driven thematic content analysis
Conti et al. (2022)	Comprehensive reflection on virtual influencers	n.a.	Netnography & survey	n.a.	360	n.a.
Cornelius, Leidner and Benbya (2023)	Factors explaining credibility of virtual influencers	QUANT	Experimental design	Social media users	885	Path analysis
Cornelius, Leidner and Bina (2023)	Perceptions towards different levels of humanness (visual appearance) of virtual influencers	QUANT	Experimental design	Social media users	623	MANCOVA
da Silva Oliveira and Chimenti (2021)	Categorization of virtual influencers to facilitate management decisions	Mixed	Netnography & Interviews	Professional experts	8 experts (interviews), 4 virtual influencers - 497 posts	Data-driven thematic content analysis
de Brito Silva et al. (2022)	Typologies of anthropomorphic virtual influencers, their benefits and risks	Mixed	Online non participant observation	Anthropomorphic virtual influencers	5 virtual influencers, 55 post	Descriptive statistics, Semiotic analysis

continued on following page

Table 2. Continued

Authors and Year	Main topic	Approach	Method	Population	Sample	Data Analysis
Deng and Jiang (2023)	Compare users' appearance anxiety associated with virtual and human influencers	QUANT	Experimental design	Young consumers	178, Ages: 18-35	t-Test, ANOVA, Path analysis
Ferrari and McKelvey (2022)	Conceptualize hyperproduction associated with artificial intelligence	Conceptual / Theoretical	Case study (illustrations)	n.a.	n.a.	n.a.
Franke et al. (2023)	Compare the appeal of virtual vs. human influencers and analyze the effect of perceived congruence with advertised products	QUANT	Experimental design	Consumers	560 female consumers	Path analysis. ANOVA, ANCOVA
Ham, Li, et al. (2023)	Perceived anthropomorphism and authenticity of virtual influencers in mixed reality	QUANT	Experimental design	Gen Z social media users	242 college students	ANCOVA, multiple Regression analysis, Binary logistic regression.
Ham, Shah, et al. (2023)	Consumers' motivations to follow and engage with virtual influencers	QUANT	n.a.	n.a.	n.a.	n.a.
Hofeditz et al. (2023)	Virtual influencers' virtues and its effect on user engagement	QUAL	Netnography	Mega and macro virtual influencers	100 most recent posts of 10 virtual influencers	Data-driven content analysis
Jayles et al. (2020)	Impact of incorrect information provided by virtual influencers	QUANT	Experimental design	n.a.	180	Regression
Jhawar et al. (2023)	Determinants of user acceptance of virtual influencers (parasocial interaction and source credibility)	Conceptual / Theoretical	Case study (illustrations)	Virtual influencers	2	n.a.
Kim et al. (2023)	Effects of human-like virtual influencers vs. anime-like virtual influencers on message credibility and attitudes	QUANT	Survey	Social media users	364 female Instagram users	Confirmatory factor analysis
Kim and Park (2023)	Virtual influencers' attractiveness and users' purchase intentions	QUANT	Experimental design	Instagram users	250, Age: 18-34	ANOVA, Path analysis
Laszkiewicz and Kalinska-Kula (2023)	Assess the literature on virtual influencers	Conceptual / Theoretical	Systematic literature review	n.a.	35 journal articles	Content analysis
Liu and Lee (2022)	Social orientation and virtual influencer endorsement failure	QUANT	Experimental design	Social media users	380	ANOVA, MANOVA

continued on following page

Table 2. Continued

Authors and Year	Main topic	Approach	Method	Population	Sample	Data Analysis
Lopez et al. (2023)	The impact of virtual influencer authenticity on brand credibility, brand engagement and purchase intention	QUANT	Experimental design	n.d.	n.d.	n.d.
Lou et al. (2022)	Followers' motivations and potential effects on consumer behaviors	QUAL	Interviews	Virtual influencer followers	26, Ages: 20-28	Theory-driven and data-driven thematic content analysis
Mirowska and Arsenyan (2023)	How empathy affects reactions to virtual vs. human influencers	QUANT	Experimental design	Social media users	214 university students	Stepwise regression
Miyake (2023)	Raciality and gender within the context of virtual influencer	QUAL	Netnography	Virtual influencer	1 virtual influencer, 325 posts on Instagram	Textual analysis
Mouritzen et al. (2023)	Conceptualization of virtual influencer marketing	Conceptual / Theoretical	Literature review	n.a.	n.a.	n.a.
Moustakas et al. (2020)	Marketing effectiveness of virtual influencers	QUAL	Interviews	Marketing experts	6 marketing experts	Data-driven content analysis
Mrad et al. (2022)	Components of virtual influencer identities perceived by followers and relational outcomes	QUAL	Interviews	Followers of virtual influencers	37	Data-driven content analysis
Nissen et al. (2023)	Perceptions and evaluations of virtual vs. human influencers	QUANT	Survey & EEG study	Social media users	149 Instagram users & 22 University students	Linear regression
Oosterom et al. (2023)	Virtual influencers in fashion marketing	Conceptual / Theoretical	Literature review	n.a.	n.a.	n.a.
Ozdemir et al. (2023)	Effect of virtual vs. human influencers on brand attitudes	QUANT	Experimental design	Social media users	1734	MANOVA, Mediation analysis
Park et al. (2021)	Effect of single vs. multiple social actors (virtual and human)	QUANT	Netnography	Comments on virtual influencer posts	2036 posts, 364053 comments	Sentiment analysis, t-Test
Robinson (2020)	Ontology and ethics of virtual influencers	Conceptual / Theoretical	Literature review	n.a.	n.a.	n.a.
Rodrigo Martín et al. (2022)	Virtual influencers' use of political communication techniques	Mixed	Case study	Virtual influencer	1	n.a.
Rodrigo-Martín et al. (2021)	Virtual influencers' commercial activity	Mixed	Case study	Virtual influencer	1	n.a.
Rossi and Rivetti (2023)	Perceptions and attitudes regarding virtual influencers	QUAL	Focus groups	Gen Z and Gen Y	2 focus groups, 16 females, Age:18-41	Data-driven content analysis

continued on following page

Table 2. Continued

Authors and Year	Main topic	Approach	Method	Population	Sample	Data Analysis
Sakuma et al. (2023)	Persuasiveness of human vs. virtual influencers	QUANT	Experimental design	Social media users	318	ANOVA, Multiple regression analysis
Sands et al. (2022)	Consumer reactions to virtual influencers	QUANT	Survey	Social media users	2160	Percentages
Sookkaew and Saephoo (2021)	Factors that explain virtual influencer popularity	Conceptual / Theoretical	n.a.	n.a.	n.a.	n.a.
Stein et al. (2022)	Compare users' parasocial interactions with virtual vs. human influencers	QUANT	Experimental design	Social media users	179	t-Test, Path analysis
Suprawan and Pojanavatee (2022)	Users' engagement with virtual influencers	QUANT	Survey	Social media users	230	Structural equation modeling
Um (2023)	Determinants of users' evaluation of virtual influencer advertising	QUANT	Survey	Social media users	179 college students	Multiple regression analysis
Xie-Carson et al. (2023)	Effect of source and content attributes on engagement with virtual influencers in the tourism context	QUANT	Survey	Social media users	309	Discrete choice modeling
Yang, Chuenterawong, Lee and Chock (2023)	Anthropomorphism in CSR endorsement	QUANT	Experimental design	Social media users	202	ANOVA, Path analysis
Yang, Chuenterawong, Lee, Tian, et al. (2023)	Effect of humanness and interactivity on persuasive CSR	QUANT	Experimental design	Social media users	219	MANCOVA, Path analysis
Yap and Ismail (2022)	Determinants of purchase intentions in the context of virtual influencer marketing	QUANT	Survey	Social media users	450	Multiple regression analysis
Zelenskaya and Rundle-Thiele (2022)	Example of virtual influencer for an environmental project	n.a.	Case study	n.a.	n.a.	n.a.
Zhang and Ren (2022)	Anthropomorphism and product type effects on attitude toward advertising made by virtual influencers	QUANT	Experimental design	n.a.	n.a.	n.a.

FINDINGS

Research on virtual influencers is a rapidly emerging field. The inaugural scientific publications on the topic appeared in 2020 with three articles. This number more than doubled in both 2021 and 2022. Impressively, in just the first half of 2023, the field saw a surge with 29 publications (Table 3). It is also

Table 3. Number of publications and mean citations

Year	2020	2021	2022	First Semester of 2023
Number of publications	**3**	**6**	**16**	**27**
Citable years	4	3	2	1
Mean citation per publication	20.3	14.2	4.8	0.9
Mean citations per year	5.1	4.7	2.4	0.9

Source: Developed by the author.

Table 4. Document types and authorship characteristics

Document Types	Number of Publications
Journal article	37
Book chapter	4
Conference paper	10
Review	1
Average citations per document	4.7
Authorship	
Total number of authors	138
Single-authored documents	4
Co-Authors per document	3.0
Percentage of international co-authorships	26,9

Source: Developed by the author.

demonstrated that the topic shows an interesting potential to generate citations, especially the seminal works on the topic.

As shown in Table 4, the most common publication types on virtual influencers are research articles (n = 37) and conference papers (n = 10). Most research on virtual influencers involves co-authorship, with only 5 single authored documents found. The average number of co-authors per document is 2.9. More than a quarter of the publications resulted from international collaboration. It's noteworthy that the high number of authors associated with the current literature indicates a strong interest in exploring this new phenomenon.

The bibliometric analysis also evidenced that the research has been conducted in various locations. Considering the country of the corresponding author, USA (n = 7) and Australia (n = 6) have been the most prolific countries publishing research on virtual influencers (Table 5). Other countries that stand out in number of publications are France, Germany, and South Korea, with 4 publications each. Furthermore, the seven countries most represented accounted for more than half of the publications on virtual influencers.

In examining the affiliations most frequently represented in virtual influencer literature, it becomes evident that authors hail from a diverse range of locations. No single university has published more than two articles during the analyzed period. All affiliations with more than one article published are presented in Table 6.

Table 5. Countries of the corresponding author most represented in the literature

Country	Number of Publications	Percent
Australia	6	11.5
USA	6	11.5
France	4	7.7
Germany	4	7.7
South Korea	4	7.7
Canada	3	5.8
China	3	5.8
Brazil	2	3.8
India	2	3.8

Source: Developed by the author.

Table 6. Affiliations most represented in the literature

Affiliation	Number of Publications
Ewha Womans University	2
Griffith University	2
Middlesex University Dubai	2
Neoma Business School	2
Rennes School of Business	2
University of Phayao	2
University of Valladolid	2
University of Virginia	2
Université de Toulouse - Paul Sabatier (UPS)	2

Source: Developed by the author.

Lastly, the publications on virtual influencers are dispersed across various journals and outlets (see Table 7). While 44 distinct outlets have contributed to this research, seven sources, each publishing two or more articles on the topic, have collectively accounted for one-fourth of the total publications to date (i.e., 15 out of 52).

As a summary, this analysis concluded that Research on virtual influencers began in 2020 and has witnessed exponential growth, particularly in the first half of 2023. This topic not only holds significant citation potential, especially for its foundational works but also showcases a trend towards collaborative research, with the majority of publications stemming from co-authorships. The USA and Australia lead as the predominant countries in this domain, but the research landscape is geographically diverse, with notable contributions from France, Germany, and South Korea. Universities globally contribute to the discourse without any single institution dominating the publications. Additionally, the body of work on virtual influencers is spread across a myriad of journals and outlets, with a select few accounting for a

Table 7. Sources of the publications

Sources	Number of Publications
Proceedings of the Annual Hawaii International Conference on System Sciences	3
Australasian Journal of Information Systems	2
Computers In Human Behavior	2
Developments In Marketing Science: Proceedings of The Academy of Marketing Science	2
International Journal of Human Computer Studies	2
Journal Of Advertising	2
Journal Of Interactive Advertising	2
Lecture Notes in Computer Science (Including Subseries Lecture Notes in Artificial Intelligence and Lecture Notes in Bioinformatics)	1
The Palgrave Handbook of Interactive Marketing	1
Business Horizons	1
Conference On Human Factors in Computing Systems - Proceedings	1
Digital Fashion Innovations: Advances in Design, Simulation, And Industry	1
Distinction	1
European Journal of Marketing	1
Fashion, Style and Popular Culture	1
Frontiers in Computer Science	1
Frontiers in Psychology	1
IEEE Communications Magazine	1
IMX 2022 - Proceedings of the 2022 ACM International Conference on Interactive Media Experiences	1
Innovative Marketing	1
International Conference on Cyber Security and Protection of Digital Services, Cyber Security 2020	1
International Journal of Advanced Computer Science and Applications	1
International Journal of Consumer Studies	1
International Journal of Internet Marketing and Advertising	1
Journal of Consumer Culture	1
Journal of Digital and Social Media Marketing	1
Journal of Hospitality and Tourism Research	1
Journal of Promotion Management	1
Journal of Retailing and Consumer Services	1
Journal of the Royal Society Interface	1
Marketing Intelligence and Planning	1
New Media and Society	1
Proceedings of the 10th European Conference on Social Media, ECSM 2023	1
Proceedings of the 2021 15th International Conference on Ubiquitous Information Management and Communication, Imcom 2021	1
Proceedings of the Acm on Human-Computer Interaction	1
Public Relations Inquiry	1

continued on following page

Table 7. Continued

Sources	Number of Publications
Revista Latina de Comunicacion Social	1
Revista Mediterranea de Comunicacion	1
Sage Open	1
Social Network Analysis and Mining	1
Studies in Australasian Cinema	1
Sustainability (Switzerland)	1
Tourism Management	1
Young Consumers	1

Source: Developed by the author.

significant proportion of the total publications. Hence, these results underscore the widespread academic interest and the fragmentation of the research that has been published.

Most Cited Publications

The leading publications on virtual influencers are detailed in Table 8. As of the data retrieval date, some of these works have amassed two-digit citation counts and maintain an average yearly citation rate above 5. Notably, this list encompasses articles from the foundational year of 2020 (Moustakas et al., 2020; Robinson, 2020), as well as significant contributions from the subsequent two years.

The article with most impact so far was published by the International Journal of Human-Computer Studies in 2021. Arsenyan and Mirowska (2021) compared users' affective reactions to posts on Instagram by three types of digital influencers: human, a human-like virtual, and an anime-like virtual influencer. The study's findings suggest that virtual agents could effectively replace traditional influencers. However, human-like virtual influencers received fewer positive reactions and consistently garnered more negative responses than the anime-like virtual influencer. Hence, the authors concluded that overemphasizing humaneness of virtual influencers can lead to negative perceptions and therefore overly anthropomorphic virtual influencers should be avoided.

Table 8. The most cited publications on virtual influencers

Paper	Total Citations	Total Citations per Year
Arsenyan and Mirowska (2021)	41	13,67
Robinson (2020)	32	8,00
Moustakas et al. (2020)	22	5,50
da Silva Oliveira and Chimenti (2021)	16	5,33
Conti et al. (2022)	13	6,50
Sands et al. (2022)	13	6,50
Stein et al. (2022)	12	6,00

Source: Developed by the author.

Robinson (2020) published one of the oldest articles on virtual influencers, exploring the topic from an ontological and ethical perspective. According to the author, this was the first article theorizing the phenomenon. Robinson (2020) argued that, since the distinction between virtual and human influencers may be negligible, virtual influencers pose significant questions regarding the ethical formation of identity and its potential impact on maintaining core social values, such as trust, in digital realms. Based on the discussion of the topic, the author suggests that virtual influencers present both theoretical and empirical challenges. Theoretical concerns address the true nature and ethical considerations of these digital characters, the role of social media platforms in regulating them, and individual responsibilities in presenting truthful online identities. Empirically, the author suggests that further studies are needed on users' attitudes towards online fictional identities, their impact on platform trustworthiness, and the brands they represent.

Another seminal work on virtual influencers, authored by Moustakas et al. (2020), explored the perspectives of marketing experts on the effectiveness of virtual influencers, emphasizing challenges, opportunities, and success factors perceived in this social media marketing strategy. The study identified the main challenges as the lack of authenticity, relatability, and risks posed to brands. It also highlighted anthropomorphism and storytelling as primary opportunities and success factors. Moreover, the research suggested that an animated virtual influencer might be a less risky strategy, emphasizing that transparency is crucial for anthropomorphism.

da Silva Oliveira and Chimenti (2021) made a first attempt to offer a systematic literature review on virtual influencers. However, by the time they conducted their research, they found only two articles (i.e., Moustakas et al., 2020; Robinson, 2020) that focused on virtual influencers. Hence, their analysis comprised mostly articles on human influencers, although a few of them mentioned virtual influencers. Through netnography and expert interviews, it was confirmed that virtual influencers, like their human counterparts, are characterized by attractiveness. While authenticity poses a significant challenge for virtual influencer strategies, controllability emerges as a primary advantage over human influencers. Anthropomorphism's potential impact on users sparks considerable debate, and the scalability of virtual influencers is highlighted as a significant benefit.

Three recent papers, published in 2021, are amongst the most cited. Conti et al. (2022) provided an overview of the phenomenon, by combining secondary data analysis, netnography, and a survey. According to Conti et al. (2022) the main advantages of virtual influencers are flexibility, exclusivity, brand safety, and brand innovation. They also suggest that the main risks posed by virtual influencers are triggering unrealistic expectations on users, being unrelatable, authenticity, trust, and transparency issues, and considerable costs.

Sands et al. (2022) also delve into the opportunities and challenges associated with virtual influencers. Based on their literature review, they underscore the capacity of virtual influencers to humanize, standardize, and scale customer service, enhance advertising strategies—including native ads—and emulate brand ambassadors in novel digital realms such as the metaverse. Furthermore, they highlight the potential roles of virtual influencers in cultivating brand communities and the augmented control avenues available for brand-owned influencers. Conversely, challenges encompass addressing consumer apprehensions and subversion, achieving realistic beauty portrayals, fostering authenticity, and navigating prospective legal and ethical directives.

Stein et al. (2022) conducted an experiment to compare users' reactions to human and virtual influencers,

Participants exhibited analogous parasocial responses to both human and virtual influencers. Notably, while initial findings indicated enhanced parasocial interactions with the virtual influencer, this advantage was attenuated due to perceptions of diminished human-likeness and relatability. The authors concluded that virtual influencers' novelty contributes to parasocial responses similar to human influencers. However, they may face a humanness limit and be seen as lacking authenticity, leading to an expected erosion of users' engagement.

It is interesting to note that the seven most cited articles on virtual influencers primarily center around three principal trends.

Anthropomorphism is a prominent theme, with studies like Arsenyan and Mirowska (2021) investigating the degree of human likeness in virtual influencers and the audience's response to varying degrees of such representations. This dimension was further elaborated on by Stein et al. (2022) who studied users' reactions to virtual versus human influencers, particularly in the context of parasocial interactions.

Ethical and authenticity concerns are another major focal point. Robinson (2020) delved deep into the ontological and ethical considerations surrounding virtual influencers, highlighting the profound implications they might have for identity formation and the preservation of core social values in digital spaces. These concerns were echoed in the findings of Sands et al. (2022) and Conti et al. (2022), both of whom identified challenges related to authenticity, trust, and transparency.

Marketing Effectiveness of virtual influencers forms a crucial axis of investigation across the most cited articles. Moustakas et al. (2020) conducted an in-depth exploration of marketing experts' perspectives on the effectiveness, challenges, and opportunities presented by virtual influencers. This was complemented by the work of Sands et al. (2022), which scrutinized the potential of virtual influencers in various digital marketing contexts, emphasizing both their unique advantages and associated risks.

The seven most cited articles on virtual influencers also showcase a rich tapestry of research methodologies and foci, indicative of a field that is both diverse and fragmented. Arsenyan and Mirowska (2021) and Stein et al. (2022) took a comparative analysis approach, directly juxtaposing human and virtual influencers to discern nuanced audience responses. Meanwhile, Robinson (2020) embarked on a theoretical and ethical exploration of the subject, pondering the ontological intricacies and the ethical challenges virtual influencers present. Shifting gears to a business perspective, Moustakas et al. (2020) provided an expert opinion and marketing perspective, gathering insights from seasoned marketing professionals. Literature reviews formed the backbone of research for both da Silva Oliveira and Chimenti (2021) and Sands et al. (2022), albeit the former faced a dearth of specific literature on the topic. lastly, a mixed methods research approach was employed by Conti et al. (2022), interweaving multiple research methods for a holistic comprehension of the virtual influencer phenomenon. The variety in methodologies and thematic concerns evident in this sample substantiates the assertion that the current literature on virtual influencers is both diverse and fragmented.

Most Prolific Authors

Collaborative efforts appear to be a dominant trend among the leading authors in the field. Table 9 presents the authors who have published more than one publication included in this bibliometric analysis. Confirming the high incidence of collaborations, all authors with more than one publication on virtual influencers collaborated with a team. It is interesting to note that the results of these collaborations are mostly concentrated in 2023.

Table 9. The most prolific authors on virtual influencer literature

Authors	Number of Publications	Publications
Arsenyan, J Mirowska, A	2	(Arsenyan & Mirowska, 2021; Mirowska & Arsenyan, 2023)
Chock, TM Chuenterawong, P Lee, H Yang, J	2	(Yang, Chuenterawong, Lee, & Chock, 2023; Yang, Chuenterawong, Lee, Tian, et al., 2023)
Cornelius, S Leidner, DE	2	(Cornelius, Leidner, & Benbya, 2023; Cornelius, Leidner, & Bina, 2023)
Eastin, MS Ham, J Shah, P	2	(Ham, Li, et al., 2023; Ham, Shah, et al., 2023)
Muñoz-Sastre, D Rodrigo-Martín, I Rodrigo-Martín, L	2	(Rodrigo-Martín et al., 2022; Rodrigo-Martín et al., 2021)

Source: Developed by the author.

Methodological Approaches in the Virtual Influencer Literature

Research on virtual influencers has seen a diverse range of methodological approaches, as evident from the data presented in Table 10. The most commonly adopted method is quantitative (N = 28), indicating a preference for empirical, data-driven insights in the field, namely founded on the previous contributions by the influencer marketing literature. Qualitative research (N = 10), which provides in-depth, nuanced insights, is also frequently adopted, given the novelty of the topic and the scarce literature on the specificities of virtual influencers. Theoretical or conceptual approaches (N = 8) are also well represented in the sample, offering foundational perspectives and frameworks, laying the groundwork for empirical exploration. There are also 5 studies that have employed mixed methods, combining both qualitative and quantitative strategies for a comprehensive understanding. This array of methodologies underscores the multifaceted nature of virtual influencer research.

The literature on virtual influencers also utilized a diversity of methods (Table 11). Experimental design (N = 18) stands out as the predominant method, suggesting a strong inclination towards controlled research setups in the field, namely, to compare virtual influencers with human influencers, and to explore typologies of virtual influencers, particularly their anthropomorphism. Surveys (N = 8) and

Table 10. Methodological approaches of virtual influencer research

Adopted Method	Number of Publications
Theoretical or conceptual	8
Quantitative	28
Qualitative	10
n.a.	2
Mixed method	5

Source: Developed by the author. Notes: Some publications adopted a combination of methods.

Table 11. Methods adopted by virtual influencer research

Adopted Method	Number of Publications
Experimental design	18
Survey	8
Interviews	6
Netnography, online non-participant observation, and social media data mining	6
Case study	5
Literature review	4
n.a.	3
Article with illustrations (informal case study)	2
Focus groups	1
EEG study	1

Source: Developed by the author. Notes: Some publications adopted a combination of methods.

interviews (N = 6) are also frequently conducted, underlining the importance of direct feedback and in-depth understanding from stakeholders. The population of such studies is most frequently social media users, but participants also include virtual influencers' followers and marketing experts. Meanwhile, the use of netnography, online non-participant observation, and social media data mining (N = 6) reflect the digital native nature of virtual influencers and the growing data freely available (e.g., posts, comments, reactions). Other methods also present in the literature, albeit less frequently chosen, include case studies, illustrations, focus groups, and EEG studies. The diversity of these methods suggests the comprehensive and multidimensional nature of investigations into virtual influencers.

It can be concluded that, in examining virtual influencers, research showcases a broad methodological spectrum. Predominantly empirical and data-driven, studies lean heavily on quantitative methods, with experimental designs being especially prevalent. While qualitative approaches provide nuanced understanding due to the topic's novelty, the use of mixed methods and diverse research techniques like netnography highlights the digital essence of virtual influencers. Overall, the diverse research methods reflect the depth and multifaceted explorations within virtual influencer studies.

With respect to the methodological procedures in virtual influencer literature, several aspects highlighted in Table 2 within the Method section merit attention. Firstly, in terms of study populations, a majority of the studies investigating attitudes and various facets of consumer behavior target general social media users, often sourced from the college student demographic. While students might align closely with the typical audience of virtual influencers and indeed represent a portion of their followers, it's crucial to emphasize that many researched topics would be more appropriately studied among participants with prior experience with virtual influencers—namely, their actual followers. The potential drawbacks of using a study population of prospective rather than experienced followers appear to be inadequately emphasized in the abstracts and conclusions, which might lead to misinterpretation of findings.

Secondly, basic methodological approaches prevail. Quantitative studies often lean on bivariate analyses (e.g., ANOVA) in lieu of employing more robust analysis techniques (e.g., structural equation modeling). This oversight could detrimentally affect the quality of insights and pave the way for misconceptions, especially when the inherent limitations of these methodologies aren't sufficiently underscored. A similar challenge is evident in qualitative research; many studies lack robust support and in-depth discussion of the categories—whether they are data-driven or theory-driven—utilized in content analyses.

Lastly, a scant number of publications leverage a well-defined theoretical framework to steer their empirical investigations. This omission could potentially diminish the overall significance and impact of such works.

Emerging Areas of Research on Virtual Influencers

To conclude this bibliometric analysis of research on virtual influencers, the publications were coded in terms of the main areas they focus on. A synthesis of the findings is presented in Table 12.

Table 12. Focal areas of research

Focal Areas / Topics / Themes	Number of Publications
Motivations, perceptions, attitudes, and engagement of consumers with virtual influencers	24
Applications and examples of virtual influencers	13
Virtual vs. Human influencers	12
Virtual influencers' anthropomorphism	9
Impact of virtual influencer advertising on consumer intentions	7
Conceptual considerations on virtual influencers	5

Source: Developed by the author. Note: Some publications account for more than one topic.

The analysis of virtual influencer research, as outlined in Table 12, showcases a multi-dimensional focus within the field. Most prominently, studies on consumer interactions with virtual influencers, encompassing aspects like motivations, perceptions, and engagement, dominate (N = 24). This highlights the critical importance placed on understanding consumer dynamics with virtual entities. A close examination of the comparison between virtual and human influencers (N = 12) reflects the need to gauge the efficacy and potential challenges of virtual influencers against traditional influencers, providing a new direction of research within the digital influencer literature. The application-centric research on virtual influencers is also gaining traction, with several studies (N = 13) dedicated to its real-world implementations. It should be noted, however, that the case studies chosen are often repetitive, with for instance several articles exploring the case of Lil Miquela (e.g., Block & Lovegrove, 2021; Brachtendorf, 2022; Rodrigo-Martín et al., 2021). Given the diversity of approaches in virtual influencer marketing, several articles delve into anthropomorphic features of these characters (N = 9), by exploring the impacts of virtual influencers that resemble as humans in comparison to others that look like avatars or dolls. Exploratory and foundational conceptual considerations (N = 5) are also flourishing, justified by the novelty and uncanny nature of virtual influencers. In essence, the academic landscape on virtual influencers is both diverse and evolving, with the potential for further nuanced investigations.

As expected, the predominant emphasis of current research is on consumer interactions with virtual influencers. However, these studies often adopt an exploratory stance, delving into motivations for following such influencers, users' attitudes, and engagement behaviors. Yet, there remains a significant gap in understanding the effectiveness of virtual influencers and their broader impacts as a marketing strategy.

FUTURE RESEARCH DIRECTIONS

Despite the current success and interest on virtual influencers, Statista points out several aspects that may limit their future growth (Dencheva, 2023c), particularly the expenses associated with virtual influencers, due to the need for advanced skills and technology, and the issues in virtual influencers' perceived credibility, as consumers increasingly value authenticity and virtual influencers may seem less genuine than their human counterparts. As such, managers need insights from research to assist them in defining and controlling their virtual influencer marketing strategies.

The literature so far provides relevant contributions on social media users' perspectives and behaviors regarding virtual influencers. Extant literature conceptualizes the phenomenon, presents in detail relevant case studies, and often adopts experimental design approaches to control certain variables (e.g., virtual influencers' characteristics) to better assess its effects on consumers.

This chapter helps identify the primary research gaps in the literature on virtual influencers. As detailed in Table 13, current research delves into aspects related to the characteristics of virtual influencers, the reactions of followers, and the outcomes of the strategy. While the diverse range of contributions is a positive facet of this evolving research field, it is evident that apart from the conceptualization of virtual influencers and the motivations and perceptions of social media users, all other topics require deeper investigation and exploration.

Table 13. Current virtual influencer research, research gaps, and methodological recommendations

Current Virtual Influencer Research		
Virtual Influencers	**Followers**	**Outcomes**
Conceptualization	Motivations	Impact on consumers' intentions
Virtual influencer characteristics: Anthropomorphism	Perceptions, Attitudes, Engagement	Effectiveness as digital marketing and brand strategy
Virtual influencers vs. Human influencers	Followers' characteristics	Typologies of products
Research Gaps		
Explore the typologies of virtual influencers	Focusing on followers instead of social media users in general	Wider range of virtual influencer marketing outcomes: knowledge, emotions, involvement, and purchases
	Address specific segments of followers, by exploring relevant segmentation criteria	
Methodological Recommendations		
Prioritize actual influencer followers over general social media users. Shift from basic to more robust and comprehensive analysis techniques. Incorporate clear, well-defined theoretical underpinnings.		

Source: Developed by the author.

Recently, Laszkiewicz and Kalinska-Kula (2023) introduced a comprehensive model that suggests examining certain aspects of virtual influencers (e.g., anthropomorphism) and mediating conditions (e.g., type of product) to elucidate their effectiveness in shaping consumer attitudes and perceptions. This chapter further recommends that future research on the outcomes of virtual influencer strategies should extend beyond merely examining attitudes and perceptions. Instead, it should address the primary objectives typically set by managers. As highlighted by Pereira et al. (2023) social media campaigns generally pursue four main objectives: fostering interaction and involvement, disseminating information, evoking emotions, and promoting sales. Therefore, the outcomes resulting from virtual influencers might span knowledge acquisition, emotional responses, user engagement, and sales — each of which deserves thorough investigation.

As emphasized in earlier sections, future research should prioritize examining followers' behaviors, rather than focusing solely on general social media users, which have predominantly been the research subjects thus far. Additionally, future studies should account for the intricacies of consumer segments, delving deeper into specific consumer traits that might influence their behavior on social media platforms, particularly in their role as followers of influencers. Therefore, it's recommended that subsequent research considers pertinent segmentation criteria, such as psychographic attributes and lifestyles, and concentrates on distinct follower segments. The same applies to virtual influencers, who have a myriad of characteristics that are expected to impact on their followers' behaviors, and therefore should be explored by future research.

Furthermore, and given the methodological concerns observed in virtual influencer research, future studies should be more discerning in participant selection, ensuring a representation of actual influencer followers rather than a broad social media user base. Adopting more robust and comprehensive analysis methods will enhance the validity and depth of insights. Additionally, incorporating a clear theoretical framework is crucial to anchor the research and elevate its academic and practical significance. Addressing these gaps will fortify the credibility and relevance of ensuing studies in this domain.

The ability to identify research trends in virtual influencer marketing can be enriched by examining the extensive body of existing research on influencer marketing. This includes pivotal systematic reviews that have pinpointed crucial research gaps. Hudders et al. (2021) categorized research into three clusters: sources, message, and audience. Notably, the emerging literature on virtual influencers reflects these areas, with studies spanning the key topics identified. The research gaps outlined by Hudders et al. (2021) concerning the strategic use of social media influencers are also pertinent to the realm of virtual influencer marketing. For instance, they emphasize outcomes such as message attention, awareness, knowledge, attitudes, and behaviors—recommendations that resonate with those from our bibliometric analysis. Vrontis et al. (2021) offer an exhaustive list of antecedents of social media influencer marketing. This encompasses source characteristics, psychological factors like enjoyability and inspiration, and content attributes such as quality and hedonic value—all of which can be applied to virtual influencer research. Vrontis et al. (2021) also underscore the need to bolster theoretical underpinnings, listing an array of theories and models to guide investigations. Furthermore, they advocate for methodological enhancements, spanning improved sampling to more advanced experimental designs. These recommendations dovetail with the insights from our current bibliometric study on virtual influencers.

CONCLUSION

Although the field of research on virtual influencers is nascent, having only commenced in 2020, it is experiencing swift expansion. The emergence of virtual influencers on social media platforms has catalyzed multidisciplinary inquiries since that year. This heterogeneity in scholarly investigation, highlighted in the bibliometric analysis, indicates that this research domain is poised for sustained growth. Drawing upon the prevailing trends discerned from the extant literature—encompassing methodological modalities and predominant themes—this study furnishes pivotal insights to scaffold future academic pursuits in this realm.

To conclude the chapter, this section revisits the research questions posed in the introduction. In response to **RQ1** (Which are the journals, institutions, countries, and researchers that have most contributed to virtual influencer research?), it's evident that while countries like Australia, USA, France, Germany, and South Korea emerge as primary contributors, the landscape of affiliations, journals, and individual researchers is notably fragmented. Of the 52 publications, 44 are in distinct outlets. A prevalent trend of co-authorship exists, with 4 authors co-authoring at least two articles in the sample. Notably, certain articles, owing to their citation counts, have the potential to shape future research in this domain. Nevertheless, the overarching conclusion is the pronounced fragmentation of the literature, with no single authors, institutions, or journals emerging as dominant contributors.

Regarding the prominent methodological approaches in virtual influencer research (**RQ3**), it was found that, despite an interesting array of qualitative (e.g., interviews) and quantitative (e.g., experiments) methods, most studies focus on general social media users, particularly college students, rather than actual followers, leading to potential misinterpretations. Methodologies often rely on basic analysis techniques, lacking depth in both quantitative and qualitative approaches. Additionally, many studies don't utilize a solid theoretical framework, compromising their impact and significance.

This chapter offers insights into the primary research themes in virtual influencer research (**RQ2**) and on the future research directions (**RQ4**). The current literature on virtual influencers provides insights into how social media users perceive and interact with these digital entities. While the research presents valuable case studies and experimental designs, notable gaps persist. Emphasis has mainly been on the basic conceptualization of virtual influencers and user motivations, leaving other vital areas underexplored. It's evident that research should expand beyond just examining user attitudes to cover broader managerial objectives, including fostering interactions, sharing information, evoking emotions, and driving sales.

One significant oversight is the heavy reliance on general social media users as study subjects, rather than focusing on actual followers of these influencers. Future studies should delve deeper into specific consumer segments and their unique traits. From a methodological standpoint, there's a need for more careful participant selection, advanced analysis techniques, and a stronger grounding in theoretical frameworks. When compared to traditional influencer marketing research, parallels in trends and gaps emerge, emphasizing the applicability of broader influencer marketing insights to the realm of virtual influencers.

As we delve deeper into virtual influencer research, the future looks bright, filled with exciting opportunities for discovery and growth.

REFERENCES

Aria, M., & Cuccurullo, C. (2017). bibliometrix: An R-tool for comprehensive science mapping analysis. *Journal of Informetrics*, *11*(4), 959–975. doi:10.1016/j.joi.2017.08.007

Arsenyan, J., & Mirowska, A. (2021). Almost human? A comparative case study on the social media presence of virtual influencers. *International Journal of Human-Computer Studies*, *155*, 102694. Advance online publication. doi:10.1016/j.ijhcs.2021.102694

Audrezet, A., & Koles, B. (2023). Virtual influencer as a brand avatar in interactive marketing. In The Palgrave Handbook of Interactive Marketing (pp. 353-376). doi:10.1007/978-3-031-14961-0_16

Awdziej, M., Plata-Alf, D., & Tkaczyk, J. (2021, Sep 22-24). *Real or Not, Doesn't Matter, As Long As You Are Hot: Exploring the Perceived Credibility of an Instagram Virtual Influencer* [Extending boundaries: The impact of the digital world on consumers and marketing]. Regional Conference of the European-Marketing-Academy, Warsaw, Poland.

Block, E., & Lovegrove, R. (2021). Discordant storytelling, 'honest fakery', identity peddling: How uncanny CGI characters are jamming public relations and influencer practices. *Public Relations Inquiry*, *10*(3), 265–293. doi:10.1177/2046147X211026936

Brachtendorf, C. (2022). Lil Miquela in the folds of fashion: (Ad-)dressing virtual influencers [Article]. *Fashion, Style & Popular Culture*, *9*(4), 483–499. doi:10.1386/fspc_00157_1

Bringé, A. (2023). *The rise of virtual influencers and what it means for brands*. Forbes. Retrieved October 26 from https://www.forbes.com/sites/forbescommunicationscouncil/2022/10/18/the-rise-of-virtual-influencers-and-what-it-means-for-brands/

Chiu, C. L., & Ho, H. C. (2023). Impact of Celebrity, Micro-Celebrity, and Virtual Influencers on Chinese Gen Z's Purchase Intention Through Social Media. *SAGE Open*, *13*(1). Advance online publication. doi:10.1177/21582440231164034

Choi, M., Choi, Y., & Lee, H. (2023). Gen Z Travelers in the Instagram Marketplace: Trust, Influencer Type, Post Type, and Purchase Intention. *Journal of Hospitality & Tourism Research (Washington, D.C.)*. Advance online publication. doi:10.1177/10963480231180938

Choong, J., & Wang, M. B. (2023). Disruptive and destructive? A typology of social bots in public relations. *Journal of Digital and Social Media Marketing*, *10*(4), 312–325.

Choudhry, A., Han, J., Xu, X., & Huang, Y. (2022). "I felt a little crazy following a 'doll'": Investigating real influence of virtual influencers on their followers. *Proceedings of the ACM on Human-Computer Interaction*. doi:10.1109/MCOM.001.2100786

Cornelius, S., Leidner, D. E., & Benbya, H. (2023). Credibility of Virtual Influencers: The Role of Design Stimuli, Knowledge Cues, and User Disposition. *Proceedings of the Annual Hawaii International Conference on System Sciences*. doi:10.3127/ajis.v25i0.3223 de Brito Silva, M. J., de Oliveira Ramos Delfino, L., Alves Cerqueira, K., & de Oliveira Campos, P. (2022). Avatar marketing: A study on the engagement and authenticity of virtual influencers on Instagram. *Social Network Analysis and Mining*, *12*(1), 130. Advance online publication. doi:10.100713278-022-00966-w

Dencheva, V. (2023a). *Reasons why consumers follow virtual influencers in the United States as of March 2022*. Statista. Retrieved October 26 from https://www.statista.com/statistics/1302739/reasons-consumers-follow-virtual-influencers-us/

Dencheva, V. (2023b). *Share of consumers who follow at least one virtual influencer in the United States as of March 2022, by age group*. Statista. Retrieved October 26 from https://www.statista.com/statistics/1304080/consumers-follow-virtual-influencers-age-us/

Dencheva, V. (2023c). *Virtual influencers - statistics & facts*. Statista. Retrieved October 26 from https://www.statista.com/topics/9805/virtual-influencers/#topicOverview

Deng, F. Y., & Jiang, X. (2023). Effects of human versus virtual human influencers on the appearance anxiety of social media users. *Journal of Retailing and Consumer Services*, *71*, 103233. Advance online publication. doi:10.1016/j.jretconser.2022.103233

Donthu, N., Kumar, S., Pandey, N., Pandey, N., & Mishra, A. (2021). Mapping the electronic word-of-mouth (eWOM) research: A systematic review and bibliometric analysis. *Journal of Business Research*, *135*, 758–773. doi:10.1016/j.jbusres.2021.07.015

Fernández-Prados, J. S., Lozano-Díaz, A., Bernal-Bravo, C., Muyor-Rodríguez, J., & IEEE. (2021, Mar 27-29). Influencers and Social Media: State of the Art and Bibliometric Analysis. *9th International Conference on Information and Education Technology (ICIET), Electr Network.*

Ferrari, F., & McKelvey, F. (2022). Hyperproduction: A social theory of deep generative models. *Distinktion : Scandinavian Journal of Social Theory*. Advance online publication. doi:10.1080/1600910X.2022.2137546

Franke, C., Groeppel-Klein, A., & Müller, K. (2023). Consumers' Responses to Virtual Influencers as Advertising Endorsers: Novel and Effective or Uncanny and Deceiving? *Journal of Advertising*, *52*(4), 523–539. doi:10.1080/00913367.2022.2154721

Goyal, S., Hu, C. H., Chauhan, S., Gupta, P., Bhardwaj, A. K., & Mahindroo, A. (2021). Social Commerce: A Bibliometric Analysis and Future Research Directions. *Journal of Global Information Management*, *29*(6), 1–33. Advance online publication. doi:10.4018/JGIM.293291

Ham, J., Li, S., Shah, P., & Eastin, M. S. (2023). The "Mixed" Reality of Virtual Brand Endorsers: Understanding the Effect of Brand Engagement and Social Cues on Technological Perceptions and Advertising Effectiveness. *Journal of Interactive Advertising*, *23*(2), 98–113. doi:10.1080/15252019.2023.2185557

Ham, J., Shah, P., & Eastin, M. S. (2023). Do You Think I'm Real? A Mixed Reality Approach to the Effects of the Virtual Influencer Engagement on Attitude and Brand Attachment: An Abstract. In *Developments in Marketing Science: Proceedings of the Academy of Marketing Science* (pp. 73-74). Academic Press.

Hofeditz, L., Erle, L., Timm, L., & Mirbabaie, M. (2023). How Virtuous are Virtual Influencers? - A Qualitative Analysis of Virtual Actors' Virtues on Instagram. *Proceedings of the Annual Hawaii International Conference on System Sciences*.

Jayles, B., Escobedo, R., Cezera, S., Blanchet, A., Kameda, T., Sire, C., & Theraulaz, G. (2020). The impact of incorrect social information on collective wisdom in human groups: The impact of incorrect social information on collective wisdom in human groups. *Journal of the Royal Society, Interface*, *17*(170), 20200496. Advance online publication. doi:10.1098/rsif.2020.0496 PMID:32900307

Jhawar, A., Kumar, P., & Varshney, S. (2023). The emergence of virtual influencers: A shift in the influencer marketing paradigm. *Young Consumers*, *24*(4), 468–484. doi:10.1108/YC-05-2022-1529

Joshi, Y., Lim, W. M., Jagani, K., & Kumar, S. (2023). Social media influencer marketing: Foundations, trends, and ways forward. *Electronic Commerce Research*. Advance online publication. doi:10.100710660-023-09719-z

Kim, E., Kim, D., Zihang, E., & Shoenberger, H. (2023). The next hype in social media advertising: Examining virtual influencers' brand endorsement effectiveness. *Frontiers in Psychology*, *14*, 1089051. Advance online publication. doi:10.3389/fpsyg.2023.1089051 PMID:36949930

Kim, H., & Park, M. (2023). Virtual influencers? attractiveness effect on purchase intention: A moderated mediation model of the Product-Endorser fit with the brand. *Computers in Human Behavior*, *143*, 107703. Advance online publication. doi:10.1016/j.chb.2023.107703

Laszkiewicz, A., & Kalinska-Kula, M. (2023). Virtual influencers as an emerging marketing theory: A systematic literature review. *International Journal of Consumer Studies*, *47*(6), 2479–2494. Advance online publication. doi:10.1111/ijcs.12956

Liu, F., & Lee, Y. H. (2022). Unveiling Behind-the-Scenes Human Interventions and Examining Source Orientation in Virtual Influencer Endorsements. *IMX 2022 - Proceedings of the 2022 ACM International Conference on Interactive Media Experiences*. 10.1145/3505284.3529962

Lou, C., Kiew, S. T. J., Chen, T., Lee, T. Y. M., Ong, J. E. C., & Phua, Z. (2022). Authentically Fake? How Consumers Respond to the Influence of Virtual Influencers. *Journal of Advertising*. Advance online publication. doi:10.1080/00913367.2022.2149641

Mirowska, A., & Arsenyan, J. (2023). Sweet escape: The role of empathy in social media engagement with human versus virtual influencers. *International Journal of Human-Computer Studies*, *174*, 103008. Advance online publication. doi:10.1016/j.ijhcs.2023.103008

Miyake, E. (2023). I am a virtual girl from Tokyo: Virtual influencers, digital-orientalism and the (Im)materiality of race and gender. *Journal of Consumer Culture*, *23*(1), 209–228. doi:10.1177/14695405221117195

Mouritzen, S. L. T., Penttinen, V., & Pedersen, S. (2023). Virtual influencer marketing: The good, the bad and the unreal. *European Journal of Marketing*. Advance online publication. doi:10.1108/EJM-12-2022-0915

Moustakas, E., Lamba, N., Mahmoud, D., & Ranganathan, C. (2020). Blurring lines between fiction and reality: Perspectives of experts on marketing effectiveness of virtual influencers. *International Conference on Cyber Security and Protection of Digital Services, Cyber Security 2020*. doi:10.1108/MIP-12-2021-0423

Neves, S., Barbosa, B., & Carlos, V. (2019, May09). Digital Influencers: A Bibliometric Analysis. *Proceedings of the International Workshop Tourism and Hospitality Management.*

Nissen, A., Conrad, C., & Newman, A. (2023). Are You Human? Investigating the Perceptions and Evaluations of Virtual Versus Human Instagram Influencers. *Conference on Human Factors in Computing Systems – Proceedings*.10.1145/3544548.3580943

Ozdemir, O., Kolfal, B., Messinger, P. R., & Rizvi, S. (2023). Human or virtual: How influencer type shapes brand attitudes. *Computers in Human Behavior*, *145*, 107771. Advance online publication. doi:10.1016/j.chb.2023.107771

Park, G., Nan, D., Park, E., Kim, K. J., Han, J., & del Pobil, A. P. (2021, Jan 04-06). Computers as Social Actors? Examining How Users Perceive and Interact with Virtual Influencers on Social Media. *International Conference on Ubiquitous Information Management and Communication-IMCOM.*

Pereira, I., Barbosa, B., & Vale, V. T. (2023). An Integrated View on Social Media Marketing Actions and Their Expected Impacts on Consumer Behavior. *Management and Marketing for Improved Retail Competitiveness and Performance*, 303-319.

Pradhan, B., Kishore, K., & Gokhale, N. (2023). Social media influencers and consumer engagement: A review and future research agenda. *International Journal of Consumer Studies*, *47*(6), 2106–2130. Advance online publication. doi:10.1111/ijcs.12901

Robinson, B. (2020). Towards an Ontology and Ethics of Virtual Influencers. *AJIS. Australasian Journal of Information Systems*, *24*. Advance online publication. doi:10.3127/ajis.v24i0.2807

Rodrigo-Martín, I., Muñoz-Sastre, D., & Rodrigo-Martín, L. (2022). Virtual influencers as opinion leaders and their use in political communication technics. *Revista Mediterranea de Comunicacion*, *13*(1), 251–266. doi:10.14198/MEDCOM.20751

Rodrigo-Martín, L., Rodrigo-Martín, I., & Muñoz-Sastre, D. (2021). Virtual influencers as an advertising tool in the promotion of brands and products. Study of the commercial activity of lil miquela. *Revista Latina de Comunicacion Social*, *2021*(79), 69–90. doi:10.4185/RLCS-2021-1521

Rossi, C., & Rivetti, F. (2023). Virtual Influencer Marketing: Is It Effective in Engaging Younger Generations? *Proceedings of the 10th European Conference on Social Media, ECSM 2023*. 10.3389/fcomp.2023.1043342

Sands, S., Ferraro, C., Demsar, V., & Chandler, G. (2022). False idols: Unpacking the opportunities and challenges of falsity in the context of virtual influencers. *Business Horizons*, *65*(6), 777–788. doi:10.1016/j.bushor.2022.08.002

Sookkaew, J., & Saephoo, P. (2021). "Digital Influencer": Development and Coexistence with Digital Social Groups. *International Journal of Advanced Computer Science and Applications*, *12*(12), 326–332. doi:10.14569/IJACSA.2021.0121243

Stein, J. P., Breves, P. L., & Anders, N. (2022). Parasocial interactions with real and virtual influencers: The role of perceived similarity and human-likeness. *New Media & Society. New Media & Society*. Advance online publication. doi:10.1177/14614448221102900

Suprawan, L., & Pojanavatee, S. (2022). What causes social media users to engage and mimic virtual influencers? The role of self-congruity. *Innovative Marketing*, *18*(4), 148–160. doi:10.21511/im.18(4).2022.13

Um, N. (2023). Predictors Affecting Effects of Virtual Influencer Advertising among College Students. *Sustainability (Basel)*, *15*(8), 6388. Advance online publication. doi:10.3390u15086388

Vrontis, D., Makrides, A., Christofi, M., & Thrassou, A. (2021). Social media influencer marketing: A systematic review, integrative framework and future research agenda. *International Journal of Consumer Studies*, *45*(4), 617–644. doi:10.1111/ijcs.12647

Xie-Carson, L., Magor, T., Benckendorff, P., & Hughes, K. (2023). All hype or the real deal? Investigating user engagement with virtual influencers in tourism. *Tourism Management*, *99*, 104779. Advance online publication. doi:10.1016/j.tourman.2023.104779

Yang, J., Chuenterawong, P., Lee, H., & Chock, T. M. (2023). Anthropomorphism in CSR Endorsement: A Comparative Study on Humanlike vs. Cartoonlike Virtual Influencers' Climate Change Messaging. *Journal of Promotion Management*, *29*(5), 705–734. doi:10.1080/10496491.2022.2163041

Yang, J., Chuenterawong, P., Lee, H., Tian, Y., & Chock, T. M. (2023). Human versus Virtual Influencer: The Effect of Humanness and Interactivity on Persuasive CSR Messaging. *Journal of Interactive Advertising*, *23*(3), 275–292. Advance online publication. doi:10.1080/15252019.2023.2189036

Yap, Y. R., & Ismail, N. (2022). Factors of virtual influencer marketing influencing Generation Y consumers' purchase intention in Malaysia. *International Journal of Internet Marketing and Advertising*, *17*(3-4), 437–458. doi:10.1504/IJIMA.2022.126735

Zelenskaya, M., & Rundle-Thiele, S. (2022). Wildlife Watcher Kylie: Co-designing a virtual ambassador for the Koala Watch programme. *Studies in Australasian Cinema*, *16*(2-3), 93–108. doi:10.1080/17503175.2022.2148413

Zhang, L., & Ren, J. (2022). Virtual Influencers: The Effects of Controlling Entity, Appearance Realism and Product Type on Advertising Effect. In Lecture Notes in Computer Science (including subseries Lecture Notes in Artificial Intelligence and Lecture Notes in Bioinformatics) (Vol. 13337 LNCS, pp. 298-305). Springer.

KEY TERMS AND DEFINITIONS

Bibliometric Analysis: Research technique that considers quantitative aspects of a body of literature (e.g., citations) and the characteristics of the publications (e.g., authors, affiliations, country) to provide a comprehensive overview of the state of the art and identify its main trends.

Biblioshiny: Online tool for comprehensive bibliometric analyses that uses the bibliometrix package in R.

Digital Influencer: Social media user and content producer, who is seen by their large number of followers as an expert in a certain topic (e.g., fashion, lifestyle, well being). Digital influencers have emerged as an essential digital marketing strategy to shape and influence consumers' knowledge, attitudes, and behaviors.

Social Media Influencer: The same as digital influencer.

Social Media Marketing: A digital marketing strategy that uses social media (e.g., social networking sites) to interact with their target audiences and achieve diverse digital marketing objectives (e.g., reach, engagement, sales).

Virtual Influencer: Computer-generated social media influencer.

Chapter 9
Stimuli for the Use of Digital Influencers in the Culture Sector:
An Analysis of the Portuguese Context

Nádia Patrícia Pinheiro Custódio
Technology and Management School of Oliveira do Hospital, Polytechnic Institute of Coimbra, Portugal

Nayra Leandro Miguel Martins
https://orcid.org/0000-0001-7177-3375
Technology and Management School of Oliveira do Hospital, Polytechnic Institute of Coimbra, Portugal & NECE-Research Center in Business Sciences, University of Beira Interior, Portugal

ABSTRACT

This chapter provides an overview of the current status of the cultural sector in Portugal and demonstrates how digital influencers can help this sector. It emphasizes the importance and potential of influencer marketing for companies in the cultural sector to reach and engage their target audience. The chapter provides an extensive literature review on the status quo of cultural marketing, relationship marketing, the cultural sector, the internet in the cultural sector, and digital influencers in the cultural sector. Finally, it highlights emerging trends and future prospects for influencer marketing in this sector.

INTRODUCTION

This chapter aims to describe and demonstrate the numerous benefits of digital influencers in the cultural sector. To provide context, various perspectives on related topics are analysed, such as cultural marketing, marketing communication actions, marketing actions in cultural institutions and the cultural sector in Portugal. It then explores the theme of digital influencers in the cultural sector and the advantages they can bring to organisations in the sector. This chapter has academic implications, as there are not many

DOI: 10.4018/979-8-3693-0551-5.ch009

scientific studies analysing digital influencers in the cultural sector in Portugal; and practical implications, as it serves as a guide for companies and entrepreneurs in the cultural sector who still have doubts about the effectiveness and efficiency of using digital influencers in their business.

Contextualising the Topic

Marketing is of significant importance to institutions in the cultural sector, not only to build loyalty among visitors who already visit the institution, but also to attract new visitors (Pais, 2016). In recent years, the socio-cultural context has been changing continuously, which is reflected in consumer practices (Bardhi & Eckhardt, 2017; Schmitt, 2019). Consequently, marketing research has started to consider an alternative approach as a possibility to investigate consumption as a cultural practice.

The Ministry of Culture is responsible for the cultural sector in Portugal, but there are also public and private initiatives (Santos, B., 2021). Culture is a factor of cohesion and national identity. Today, it is a generator of wealth, employment and quality of life and, at the same time, an instrument for Portugal's affirmation in the international community (Governo da República Portuguesa, n.d.).

According to the 'Survey of the Cultural Practices of the Portuguese 2020', coordinated by José Machado Pais, Pedro Magalhães and Miguel Lobo Antunes, in the 12 months prior to the pandemic only 28 per cent of those surveyed visited museums and 11 per cent art galleries. The survey involved a sample of 2,000 people randomly selected from the resident population in Portugal aged 15 or over. This shows that there is still little interest in cultural spaces among the Portuguese.

Some of the most common marketing actions designed for cultural spaces are publications on social networks, on the institution's own website, in newspapers and magazines. There are also other, more creative actions, such as establishing partnerships with schools and universities, developing *QR codes* with digital art distributed around the city in which the institution is located and organising competitions for the target audience (Santos, B., 2021).

It is important to analyse the adherence and derived behaviour of the Portuguese in order to understand what aspects can be improved in the cultural sector, so that they feel more encouraged to attend institutions in this sector. This topic is therefore relevant because it helps to understand how digital influencers can contribute to increasing adherence, frequency of visits and interest in cultural institutions, a gap that is still visible in the country.

BACKGROUND

Cultural Marketing

Marketing is a social activity that involves planning and implementing prices, promotions and publicising a product or service, and is present in a variety of areas in order to find solutions to consumer problems. Culture is a source of knowledge that encompasses scientific, technological, economic, religious and artistic aspects. Cultural marketing helps cultural management by providing tools and techniques that improve relationships with the public (Santos, B., 2021).

The concept of cultural marketing originated in the 60s. At first, it proved complicated to implement marketing in the cultural field, but it began to be accepted and gain weight in cultural organisations, along with the need that arose for them to stand out from the competition and develop their attractiveness to the target audience (Mariñelarena, 2015, as cited in Santos, B., 2021; Paço & Pinto, 2019). Thus, marketing should not be seen as an enemy to art, but rather as an asset for it to reach its audiences more efficiently (Paço & Pinto, 2019; Garcia, 2018).

Cultural marketing is the dimension of marketing applied to various artistic disciplines and cultural products, with a large scope for action in the cultural industry (Ramírez, 2013, as cited in Santos, B., 2021; Yanaze, 2020). Unlike other companies, where the main focus is on making a profit, cultural organisations are more concerned with visitor satisfaction and loyalty, with a view to disseminating culture (Garcia, 2018).

Initially, cultural products were promoted by the artists themselves in order to sell their products to institutions in the sector, and this approach can be considered marketing (Kolb, 2013 as cited in Santos, B., 2021).

Cultural marketing is often confused with event marketing, due to the sponsorship/mecenage technique where companies associate themselves with cultural activities as a communication and brand image building strategy to get closer to their audiences (Reichelt & Boller, 2016, as cited in Santos, B., 2021), as is the case with MEO Marés Vivas, a music festival associated with MEO, a telecommunications company. Thus, cultural marketing can also be associated with event promotion, in order to better target market strategies to keep a recognised event going over time (Rocha, 2018). Nowadays, the support given by companies to sport, the environment, society and culture is a differentiating factor from the competition, as it is becoming increasingly important to open up horizons beyond the organisation itself (Yanaze, 2017).

According to Reis (2003) and Garcia (2018), the cultural marketing process encompasses the state, which establishes cultural policies and economies; cultural producers, who draw up cultural projects; intermediaries and cultural institutions, where activities, exhibitions and shows are organised (with cultural marketing in this case as a way of reaching the target audience) and private initiative, which has an increasingly notorious influence, with companies using culture to increase their notoriety and improve their image by supporting events (Santos, B., 2021).

Cultural marketing has naturally developed more and more over time and is used by various elements of culture, ranging from artists to companies, and has shown a very significant importance in this sector (Vaz et al., 2018). It fosters better management of organisations in the cultural sector, as it involves planning that leads to alignment in the organisation's strategy (Santos, B., 2021).

Cultural marketing is an articulation between culture and art and government and business interests (Cardoso, 2006, as cited in Rocha, 2018; Tavares, 2019). In this way, it is a means of promoting the organisation's image, fostering relationships with the target audience by associating the brand with artistic and cultural products (Yanaze, 2020). It also helps to distinguish the brand and the social positioning of the organisation, with the appeal to cultural actions being a differentiating element. This type of marketing aims to satisfy the cultural needs of a specific audience, with characteristics that correspond to their tastes and expectations, associating this action with the corresponding organisation, which makes the audience feel touched (Augusto & Yanaze, 2010, as cited in Rocha, 2018; Pereira, 2015). Cultural marketing applied to events allows them to be valorised and gives them a diversified vision (Damascena, Oliveira & Melo, 2012, as cited in Rocha, 2018).

There is some dissonance when it comes to the definition of cultural marketing by authors (Reis, 2003; Rocha, 2018; Santos, B., 2021), and cultural marketing is a term that causes some confusion in its definition (Yanaze, 2017). These differences can be clarified by the types of cultural marketing defined by Machado Neto (2010), mentioned in Freitas (2019): end cultural marketing, which is carried out by organisations with the aim of promoting culture as their end activity, in which case the process begins with the design of the product, rather than with the demands of the market (Garcia, 2018); cultural marketing as a means, which is practised by organisations that don't have culture as their main activity, but use cultural marketing as a means to promote themselves, such as a bank that supports art galleries, exhibitions or cultural houses, which carries out cultural marketing, but its main marketing activity focuses on banking and financial products (Yanaze, 2017); and mixed cultural marketing, which has aspects of the two types mentioned above, thus being an organisation or event of a cultural nature with the collaboration of a company from another sector (Freitas, 2019).

Relationship Marketing

The concept of relationship marketing arises from the articulation between industrial marketing and services marketing, and presents a different approach to transactional marketing. This is aimed at customer satisfaction, loyalty and building and maintaining long-term relationships with customers, in order to achieve the objectives of all those involved, with a mutual exchange of promises (Brito, 2011, as cited in Parente, 2018; Freitas, 2019). It therefore focuses on strategies developed to foster customer loyalty (Demo et al., 2021).

The origins of relationship marketing date back to the 1980s, marking the transition between transactional marketing, centred on sales, and relational marketing, focused on customer relationships. This change was brought about by the need for companies to stand out from the competition and respond to growing consumer demands (Scussel et al., 2017; Pinto, 2019). Until then, long-term relationships and customer loyalty were put on the back burner (Figueiredo et al., 2022). In addition, relationship marketing contributes to the creation of value for organisations by managing customer relationships through the use of data and information systems. In this way, customer behaviour is understood with a view to individualisation and the creation of new strategies (Demo et al., 2021; Figueiredo et al.,2022).

With the emergence of relationship marketing, the traditional marketing mix has been replaced by strategies that involve more involvement and interaction with the public (Brito, 2011 as cited in Parente, 2018). Thus, establishing long-term relationships is less costly and requires less effort to acquire customers (Kotler, 1998, as cited in Parente, 2018; Pinto, 2019).

Relationship marketing has become more relevant in the organisational world with the evolution of information technology, and has been incorporated into the strategy of organisations in an integrated way, thus improving relationships with customers. Customer Relationship Management (CRM) then emerged, combining relationship marketing with the potential of information technology to improve customer knowledge and develop marketing strategies. However, it is important to emphasise that relationship marketing and CRM are not the same thing; relationship marketing is a broader concept that encompasses CRM, which manifests itself as one of the strategies of relationship marketing (Demo et al., 2021).

Relationship marketing has proved to be the most prevalent aspect of marketing today. It allows the relationship with customers to be prioritised over the product, so that there is interaction with them to build the firm and lasting relationship that is desired (Andersen, 2005, as cited in Figueiredo et al., 2022; Pinto, 2019). Furthermore, establishing this empathetic relationship with consumers allows brands to have a constant competitive advantage and differentiate themselves from the rest (Alves, 2019).

Relationship Marketing in Arts and Culture Centres

Performing arts centres must have a programme that meets the expectations of the audience, as well as hosting quality and attractive shows, in order to allow for the sustainability and visibility of the organisation. The success of these institutions depends not only on attracting new spectators, but also on retaining the audiences that already attend them. In this sector, marketing must incite a high level of involvement with the visitor. It is therefore important to have a relationship marketing strategy that fosters audience loyalty, i.e. a sense of attachment to the services of performing arts centres and consequent regular attendance. To communicate events of this type, it is important to have integrated communication planning that links various techniques, including new media, in particular social networks, which encompass new ways of sharing information (Freitas, 2019).

To create loyalty among the public, marketing can involve interactions, customer service, exchanges of information and funding, the creation of interdependence, commitment and trust, which is why it is classified as relationship marketing. It seeks to create relationships rather than incite transactions, so that the same customer repeats transactions, or in this case, visits the centres several times, and not just with the focus of attracting new visitors. The maintenance and frequency of existing visitors is often taken for granted, which means that they are only paid attention to when there is a problem, such as a complaint (Freitas, 2019).

When visitor loyalty is achieved, they can help increase the visibility of the institution, contributing to its economy, social cohesion, cultural identity and the sustainability of the space (Freitas, 2019).

Subscriptions, such as newsletters, are a technique that shows good results for performing arts centres, but it is important to take into account the cost of acquiring new subscribers, retaining them, the duration of the subscription and its growth rate. In addition, they don't cater for the group of visitors who only want to buy a ticket for a particular show (Freitas, 2019).

Artistic products stand out from the rest because their marketing mix involves careful planning of the marketing strategy that combines the organisation's social, financial and artistic objectives. Marketing activity thus involves promises, expectations and an exchange of values that reveals itself in satisfaction, commitment, trust, interdependence and loyalty (Freitas, 2019).

Marketing Communication Actions

Marketing communication is the set of all the tools that carry a message to the target audience, through which organisations seek to inform, persuade and remind consumers about their brands and products (Kotler & Keller 2012, as cited in Saraiva, 2019). Communication is made up of messages that are planned by the company and unplanned messages that arise through its customers (Saraiva, 2019).

Traditional media (e.g. television and radio) continue to be important in communicating with consumers and have adapted to the new developments that are emerging. However, the focus of marketing is on people, which means that digital is playing an increasingly significant role in organisations' marketing communication strategies. More than technological change, behavioural change must be analysed, and this constant adaptation is more than just an option, it is essential to ensure the survival of companies (Torres, 2018).

Nowadays, communication plays a fundamental role within organisations, being a strategic tool for differentiating themselves from the competition, as well as for developing a perception of value (Rocha & Trevisan, 2018; Mazieri et al., 2018). The messages that an organisation communicates must be consistent with what it actually does and with its values, as this is the only way to convey transparency, credibility and trust (Rocha & Trevisan, 2018).

Many companies have focussed their activity on just one or two communication tools, although new media are increasingly being developed, consumers are becoming more sophisticated and the number of markets is increasing, requiring specific approaches (Kotler & Keller, 2006).

Communication through a single medium is no longer sufficient, given that different audiences are or are becoming present on different channels. It is necessary to understand these audiences, the media they use most and their preferred ways of interacting with the organisation. Selecting the media, as well as understanding the relationship between the public and them, is a very important stage in integrated communication planning. By getting to know the media, it is possible to realise the return and results that can be obtained from each of them (Rocha & Trevisan, 2018).

Integrated communication planning is based on three elements: the core messages (mission, vision and values), knowledge of the public and an integrated vision of the communication tools (Rocha & Trevisan, 2018). It should include three stages: the pre-plan, which involves understanding the organisation (strengths and weaknesses), the market (opportunities and threats), the public, consumers, brand positioning and the organisation's objectives; the plan, which incorporates the objectives, strategies, techniques and tools for each communication action; and the post-plan, where the performance metrics for each action/tool are established in order to measure, compare and analyse, thus reviewing the actions (Rocha & Trevisan, 2018). Consumers create barriers to receiving the message, so it is important that marketing communication includes various techniques and tools to encourage a reaction in the consumer.

The corporate communication process is no longer unilateral, as the recipient has become active and is also a sender. It is therefore important to listen to the public in order to meet their needs, desires and expectations, without neglecting the transparency and ethics of communication actions (Gil, 2017).

Digital Marketing

The Internet is a global network of interconnected computer networks, comprising millions of private networks, public institutions, companies and other organisations. There are three roles to play on the Internet: content provider (information, entertainment, etc., practically everyone is one nowadays); user, who accesses the content and exchanges data over the network; and the technological infrastructure, which is the support for the previous two (hardware and software) (Santos, B., 2021).

Internet use has been on the rise in recent years, with the highest rates of use in the younger and more educated age groups (100 per cent in the 15-24 age group), according to the "Survey of the Cultural Practices of the Portuguese 2020", drawn up by the Institute of Social Sciences.

The internet is a space where people can gather information to make decisions, by comparing and checking the various offers available. That said, organisations must closely monitor their audience in order to stand out from the competition (Alves et al., 2017; Rocha, 2018).

Information technologies have enabled public relations and communication activities in organisations to evolve and have fostered consumer influence on the image of organisations. Thus, customer relations and loyalty are increasingly important so that customers can form favourable opinions of the organisation (Alves, 2019; Freitas, 2019; Tavares, 2019; Cezar, 2019).

The power that digital communication holds today is something that companies cannot ignore. It is essential to continuously monitor the internet in order to visualise what audiences feel, share and need through the various digital tools and how what they say can affect the image and reputation of organisations (Gil, 2017).

With the evolution of information and communication technologies, digital marketing has emerged, consisting of a cluster of marketing actions carried out using digital channels to publicise their products in order to build customer loyalty and acquire new ones. On the internet, control no longer belongs to companies, but to consumers (Castro et al., 2019; Torres, 2018; Torres, 2010, as cited in Saraiva, 2019).

Digital marketing enables closer and more frequent contact with consumers, through tools such as CRM. This should not replace traditional marketing, but should be planned strategically in collaboration with it. Traditional marketing is more relevant in the organisation's initial phase of making itself known and arousing interest, while digital marketing allows the relationship to develop and increase proximity. Thus, the combination must be designed to create rewarding experiences for consumers (Kotler et al., 2017, as cited in Freitas, 2019).

According to Chleba (1999), as cited in Castro et al. (2019), digital marketing has seven strengths: personalisation, interactivity, integration, globalisation, approximation, convergence and democratisation of information. The advantages of digital marketing include: low cost, no real space limit, speed and ease of access (Kotler, 2000, as cited in Castro et al., 2019).

When planning and developing digital marketing actions, there are certain points that must be taken into account: having the consumer's consent to interact with them; preserving the user, making their experience the best it can be; being transparent; thinking about groups of people, i.e. reaching the minds and hearts of consumers and not just their computers; working in stages, i.e. although the aim is to reach thousands, you have to think about the unit; knowing how to listen to consumers and give due importance to their interactions; being direct, objective and simple (Torres, 2018).

It's important for companies to keep an eye on new developments and digital services to think about how they can be integrated and benefit their digital marketing strategy, as is the case with augmented reality and artificial intelligence, which are paving the way for marketing 5.0 (Torres, 2018).

Digital marketing is currently a means for companies to seek a competitive advantage. In addition, it has several benefits, such as: direct communication; greater publicity for the product, service or brand; the possibility for companies to get to know and relate to consumers; stimulating new business; and increasing market share (Saraiva, 2019).

It's no longer a question of whether consumers are connected, but when, where and how they connect. They have changed their purchasing behaviour and now have a variety of tools at their disposal that allow them to search, analyse, compare and decide (Torres, 2018; Filho, 2001, as cited in Saraiva, 2019).

One factor to take into account in the digital universe is generational, and consumers can be divided into three groups. The first is the digital immigrants, made up of people born before 1980, and marketing actions aimed at them should consist of a balance between traditional and digital. The second is the millennium generation, made up of people born between 1981 and 1996, where digital marketing should be a priority. The third group are the digital natives (or generation Z), born after 1997, who see the online universe, the internet and mobile technology as something innate and are permanently connected. This group ignores traditional media, either out of ignorance or practicality, so in this case marketing should be entirely digital, with the exception of some complementary traditional actions (Torres, 2018).

The internet has helped companies progress immensely by promoting communication and exponentially improving the interaction and relationship between companies and customers/potential customers (Saraiva, 2019).

Social Networks

Social networks are websites/applications where people can create an account, where they register their personal details, develop profiles and can thus establish relationships with other people through friends lists, sending messages and posting photos and videos (Torres, 2009, as cited in Castro et al., 2019; Santos, B., 2021).

The role of the media has been altered by the resonance of social networks (Souza-Leão et al., 2022; Paiva et al., 2017), which are increasingly becoming a strategic resource for promoting brands, products and services (McQuarrie et al., 2013; Uzuñoglu & Kip, 2014). Such platforms not only allow for instant feedback on the level of interaction and reach of the content produced for their media, but also allow users to form direct and interactive relationship channels (Van Dijck, 2013). Social networks are exponents of the possibilities for new marketing strategies based on communication practices which, among other factors, legitimise the role of digital influencers in this context (Sette & Brito, 2020; Zanette et al., 2013).

They have increasingly been used by people to increase their contacts, share ideas and connect with people from different regions and locations, marking a radical change in the way they communicate (Castro et al., 2019; Torres, 2018). Social networks thus create a sense of closeness with the rest of the people and are platforms that are constantly changing (Torres, 2018). Social networks have internal rules for users, who become adept at using them through their experience and interaction with them. However, the internal rules are also constantly changing, due to the corrections and evolutions that arise with the use of social media (Torres, 2018).

In today's technological universe, social networks are very important tools for a brand to build customer loyalty, publicise its products, expand its reach, gain momentum and increase its sales (Castro et al., 2019). Social networks are spaces for the joint creation of content, interaction and information sharing, where the consumer is both receiver and sender (Torres, 2009, as cited in Castro et al., 2019; Torres, 2018). Thus, social networks allow companies to establish a closer connection with the public, where immediate feedback can be obtained. They also make it possible to collect relevant data about the consumer, such as location, behaviour and preferences, quickly and at low cost (Gil, 2013, as cited in Castro et al., 2019; Torres, 2018). In this way, companies can define their strategies according to consumers' needs and desires.

Marketing via social media allows for a great level of reach (Fabrício, 2011, as cited in Castro et al., 2019). However, it must be well planned, and it is important to avoid mass messages, as there is a high probability that the user will block the brand and it will no longer be possible to establish contact through this medium. Social networks are also an excellent medium for *word of mouth*, reaching potential audiences through loyalty (Garcia, 2018). It is important to emphasise that each social network has a different audience, so the selection of the network to use must also be well thought out (Torres, 2018).

Companies can also use this network to their advantage, transmitting short, attractive information and thus becoming part of a simple but powerful digital community where thousands of purchasing decisions are made (Castro et al., 2019). Twitter is thus a space where consumers can feel closer to brands and interact with them (Vaz, 2010, as cited in Saraiva, 2019). Lucena and Oliveira (2021), as cited in Saraiva (2019), state that this social network is suitable for organisations that want to engage in bold digital marketing in relation to their customers, because, for example, it provides information that a product has been launched, so users don't have to go to the organisation's website to find out.

Social networks are playing an increasingly important role in organisational communication as a means of customer relations, due to their ability to share information at much lower costs than traditional media. When there is an investment in social media, the results presented improve significantly, as it brings more efficiency and benefits in communication, interactivity and business processes (Alves, 2019; Freitas, 2019; Tavares, 2019; Cezar, 2019).

Website

When applied to companies, websites can serve various communication purposes, such as gathering information about their customers, publicising information, maintaining relations with investors and strengthening and enhancing the company's identity (Truell et al., 2005, as cited in Rodrigues, 2021).

It is important to consider that the consumer's experience on the website encompasses their browsing through the various pages, not just the first one, so they must feel satisfied as a result of a positive experience in order to return (Rodrigues, 2021).

Usability is one of the factors to take into account when designing a website. It consists of how easily the user can communicate with a website or application, even if they have never been told how. It is one of the main factors taken into account in evaluation, and determines the success of a website (Sari & Rochimah, 2018, as cited in Rodrigues, 2021).

In addition, it is also relevant to consider the website's performance and design attributes, such as ease of use, adequate navigation, improved layout and structure and good speed, in order to attract and hold customers' attention (Gul et al., 2020, as cited in Rodrigues, 2021). In an increasingly competitive organisational world, a website can be a fundamental aspect of standing out from the competition (Rodrigues, 2021).

The website can be a tool for increasing customer confidence in an organisation, through the quality of the information it provides, as well as the reliability and credibility conveyed by the website itself (Rodrigues, 2021). To evaluate a website, there are metrics that can assess certain elements, provided by the website itself, which are very relevant to understanding the functionality of the website and its users (Rodrigues, 2021).

When developing a website, the concepts of usability and user experience should be combined with design to ensure that the user achieves what they want in an intuitive and pleasant way. The user experience is influenced by ease of navigation, interactivity, whether the navigation is intuitive or not, among other factors (Santos, B., 2022).

A well-designed aesthetic will capture the public's interest and confidence in browsing the website. Website design must be in line with the brand's values, identity and objectives, but above all it must prioritise the user experience, because only by thinking about the customer can a brand achieve its objectives (Santos, B., 2022; Selas, 2022).

E-Mail Marketing

Email marketing is an online means of communication that sends messages via email addresses for commercial purposes. It is a form of direct marketing and has benefits such as low cost, practicality of sending and ease of viewing by recipients on devices connected to the internet (Panigrahi, 2016, as cited in Akamine, 2018; Saraiva, 2019). There are several software that make email marketing easier, such as E-goi, Sendinblue, 1and1Mail and SendBlaster (Akamine, 2018).

Email is an already widespread means of communication that is older and more durable than other online media, such as social networks (Panigrahi, 2016, as cited in Akamine, 2018). At the beginning of the internet, email was the main means of online communication, as it quickly replaced faxes, as well as presenting itself as a competitor to the telephone and post office. Although it continues to be an efficient means of online communication, other more direct means have emerged that have captured a significant part of the email audience. Most studies show that the younger population considers email to be an outdated medium and interacts more frequently through instant messaging, such as Messenger and WhatsApp (Torres, 2018).

The newsletter is part of email marketing and aims not only to publicise the organisation's products and services, but also to add value to the relationship with the recipient. It is thus characterised by sending messages that aim to inform, entertain and benefit the recipient (Panigrahi, 2016, as cited in Akamine, 2018). It makes it possible to evaluate its effectiveness by checking how many emails have been opened, deleted and how many clicks the links in the messages have had (O'Neil, 2016, as cited in Akamine, 2018).

The Cultural Sector

"Culture is a factor of cohesion and national identity. Today, it is a generator of wealth, employment and quality of life and, at the same time, an instrument for Portugal's affirmation in the international community." (Government of the Portuguese Republic, n.d.).

The concept of culture is defined in the "Declaration of Mexico on Cultural Policies" (UNESCO, 1982), as referred to in the document "Culture and Development: Cultural Projects and the 2030 Agenda" (Gama, 2020), as a set of distinctive elements, both spiritual and material, intellectual and affective, that characterise a particular social group or society. It encompasses literature, the arts, values, ways of life, beliefs, fundamental rights and traditions. In addition to its capital importance, culture is also of significant importance for sustainable development and the transformation of the world, and should therefore be seen as an essential element for society (Gama, 2020; Alves, 2019; Santos, M., 2021).

The same document refers to the 2010-2012 Culture Satellite Account, which defines culture as a set of goods, services and human activities that have the function of producing, disseminating, commercialising, preserving, regulating or educating symbolic content (Gama, 2020).

This concept demonstrates three fundamental characteristics: it relates to expressions, it is based on the creation and communication of symbols and it is also generally associated with intellectual property rights (Instituto Nacional de Estatística, 2016, p. 9, as cited in Gama, 2020).

On a global level, interest in culture increased considerably after the Second World War, given that people are more receptive to this area in safe circumstances and this period brought more stability in economic and social terms. This has led to an increased desire to make the best use of free time, which adds strength to the cultural sector (Parente, 2018).

General cultural attractions include archaeological, historical and architectural assets and engineering works. Specific cultural attractions include art, crafts, museums, gastronomy, monuments, fairs, events, exhibitions, sports complexes and festivals (Parente, 2018).

In the cultural sector, it is very important to value the visitor's experience to ensure that they will continue to visit the centre. To do this, cultural centres must try to get to know their visitors as well as possible and adapt to them, creating unique experiences. Unlike most companies, whose main objective is to make a profit, cultural institutions seek to satisfy their visitors in order to democratise culture (Freitas, 2019). Cultural institutions house objects, goods and collections and are spaces for the production and sharing of knowledge, enjoyment and development (Tavares, 2019).

Cultural Sector in Portugal

In Portugal, the cultural sector is the responsibility of the Ministry of Culture, which aims to enhance and preserve cultural heritage, promote artistic creation, disseminate culture and, together with the Ministry of Foreign Affairs, publicise Portuguese culture and language internationally. The Directorate-General for the Arts (DGARTES) is the organisation in charge of coordinating and implementing support policies for the arts, which highlights one of the Ministry of Culture's objectives, to qualify artistic creation. At a regional level there are five bodies, the Direção Regional da Cultura Norte, Centro, Lisboa e Vale do Tejo, Alentejo and Algarve, whose function is to monitor and supervise the cultural institutions supported by the government (Santos, B., 2021).

In addition to the cultural initiatives under the Ministry of Culture, there are other public initiatives, usually municipal, such as museums, libraries, theatres and equipment for fairs and exhibitions; or private, such as theatres, cinemas, television channels, radio and galleries run by independent professionals (Santos, B., 2021). There has been an increase in cultural initiatives in Portugal, which has created new opportunities in the economic and environmental fields, and in the requalification of spaces, among others (Alves, 2019).

The most recent figures released by the National Statistics Institute show that 187,700 people were employed in the cultural sector in 2021, representing 3.9% of total employment. With regard to companies, the most recent final figures show that in 2020 there were 64,559 companies in the cultural and creative sector (a decrease of 1.5% on the previous year). This sector generated a turnover of 5.9 billion euros (-15.6%) and a Gross Value Added (GVA) of 2.2 billion euros, a decrease of 13.6% on the previous year. Preliminary figures for 2021 show that the total number of companies increased by 6 per cent to 68,456 and turnover grew by 14.1 per cent to 6.7 billion euros. Gross Value Added reached 2.5 billion euros, representing an increase of 15.3% compared to 2020 (Instituto Nacional de Estatística, 2022).

Cultural Practices of the Portuguese

The Institute of Social Sciences of the University of Lisbon, with funding from the Calouste Gulbenkian Foundation, produced the "Survey of Cultural Practices 2020", which focused on the resident population in Portugal, including the Autonomous Regions, aged 15 and over. This survey confirmed the weaknesses of the cultural practices of the Portuguese, despite the fact that in some situations the country shows similarities to other European countries (Antunes et al., 2020). The main reasons for these weaknesses are a lack of time, interest and money, the latter reinforced by the National Statistics Institute, which reveals that in 2018 Portuguese families spent 21.2 per cent less per year on cultural activities than in 2012. However, the district of Coimbra shows greater consumption in the cultural sector, fuelled by the city's history, size and student population, the latter representing a third of the population (Freitas, 2019).

Museums, Historical Monuments, Archaeological Sites, and Art Galleries

One of the cultural groups studied by the "Survey of the Cultural Practices of the Portuguese 2020", prepared by the Institute of Social Sciences, were museums, historical monuments, archaeological sites and art galleries. The 12 months before the start of the pandemic were investigated, so as not to jeopardise the results of these spaces having been closed. 31% of those surveyed had visited historical monuments,

28% had been to museums, 13% had visited archaeological sites and 11% had been to art galleries, most of whom had travelled to another municipality to do so.

When it came to motivations for visiting these sites, the historical importance of the space was the strongest among those surveyed (40 per cent), followed by social motivations, namely for socialising, the aesthetics of the space and its works and recommendations from family, friends or others, the latter being the predominant reason in the 25 to 34 age group. With a smaller percentage, there was also the intention to deepen their knowledge of the area in question, recommendations from guides and itineraries, opinions and images from social networks, on an outing or for leisure, advertising, the visit having been organised by the parish council, town hall or school, reviews from professionals and the institution's website. The social component of visits is significantly emphasised, as only 4% of respondents go to these venues alone, while 65% go accompanied by family members, 27% with their partner or friends and 8% with their school.

Among the reasons given for not making the visits, the most noteworthy are lack of time, mentioned by 39 per cent of respondents, lack of interest (more common among respondents with lower levels of education), high prices and lack of proximity, reasons also mentioned by Cashman (2010), as cited in Paço and Pinto (2019).

With regard to the frequency of visits to these institutions, the majority of respondents say they visit them once or twice a year. This survey also showed that the frequency of visits to these cultural venues is significantly related to the level of education: 70% of respondents with higher education have visited these venues, a percentage that decreases with the level of education. With regard to professional status, students stand out, with 58 per cent of them having visited these cultural venues. In terms of age, there was a predominance of younger people, between 15 and 24 years old, almost 50 per cent. In the work by Santos, M., (2021), "Public satisfaction in cultural communication: the case of the Convento São Francisco", it was also found that individuals with higher education qualifications are the ones who most often attend the institution, and in this case the working population stands out.

With regard to the price of tickets for access to these cultural spaces, 57 per cent of respondents paid for a normal ticket, 18 per cent were exempt from paying, 12 per cent visited during a period when access was free and 7 per cent received a discount on their ticket. The type of ticket is related to the age group, with the normal ticket predominating in the 45 to 54 age group and the discounted ticket in the 15 to 24 age group.

Another study by Freitas (2019) also states that the most decisive factors for visiting museums and art galleries are age, income, race, education, previous experiences, general preferences, the theme of the exhibition and family responsibilities.

Live Shows, Festivals, and Popular Celebrations

The "Survey on the Cultural Practices of the Portuguese 2020", drawn up by the Institute of Social Sciences, concluded that in this area, local festivals and celebrations were the events most frequented by those surveyed (38%), followed by live music concerts, theatre plays and the circus. The lowest percentages correspond to more erudite shows, namely classical music, ballet or classical dance and opera.

Of the live music concerts attended, pop and rock were the most popular (14 per cent). The younger age groups attended more hip hop and rap, the 55 to 64 age group Latin American music and the over 65s classical, traditional, folk and fado music (Antunes et al., 2020). With regard to the motivating factors for attending music concerts, there are two basic ones: utility and hedonism. Concerts should have a utilitarian facet that satisfies physical needs and an experiential one, both social and personal. The utilitarian dimension refers to the fulfilment of functional goals, such as strengthening family or social ties. Thus, to make the decision to attend a concert, people evaluate its tangible and intangible factors and its emotional benefits. The hedonism related to a concert is evaluated taking into account its emotional value and its entertainment capacity, this dimension being more significant than the utilitarian one (Freitas, 2019). As far as music festivals are concerned, they offer the possibility of providing new experiences, adventures and emotions to those who enjoy them (Alves, 2019).

With regard to dance, 5 per cent of respondents attended ballet or classical dance shows and 6 per cent attended shows of other types of dance, such as contemporary dance, ethnic or folkloric dance, street dance and African dance. The group aged 15 to 24 attended more street dance and African dance shows, those aged 45 to 54 contemporary dance and those over 65 ethnic or folkloric dance (Antunes et al., 2020). Lopes (2013) emphasises that the dance genre that stands out the most is contemporary dance, followed by classical dance.

In the area of theatre, the 35 to 44 age group stands out, followed by the youngest group, aged 15 to 24. With regard to the genres of this art form and referring to the last theatre they attended, 3% was contemporary theatre, 3% was revue theatre and 3% was musical theatre (Antunes et al., 2020).

The reasons why respondents don't attend live shows, festivals and local celebrations include lack of time, especially in the 25 to 54 age group, lack of interest, difficulty understanding the show and lack of company, predominantly in the over 65 age group (Antunes et al., 2020).

The streaming of films and live shows on the Internet was more popular during the pandemic crisis. The content most sought after by respondents once a week or more was films (20%), followed by concerts, local festivals and celebrations, dance styles other than ballet, theatre and classical music. This type of entertainment was more popular among respondents with higher education, aged 15 to 24 and 35 to 44 (Antunes et al., 2020).

Walmsley (2011) states that emotional, social, spiritual and intellectual motivations are the ones that most influence going to a show. The benefits that stand out the most are entertainment, learning, socialising with friends and contact with famous artists (Paço & Pinto, 2019).

Marketing Actions in Cultural Institutions

In his project on the Imaginarius Creation Centre, Santos, B., (2021) highlights the importance of having an employee at the centre responsible for planning and creating content for social networks, making them more dynamic and fostering the connection with the public. He also mentions the importance of planning and scheduling publications.

Another action that could also be developed is establishing partnerships with other institutions, such as schools and universities (Santos, B., 2021; Garcia, 2018). Santos, B., (2021) also presents as an action the creation of *QR codes* with digital art representing the centre spread throughout the city in which it is located, namely next to other cultural venues. In order to promote a large-scale event taking place in the centre, it is worth highlighting the creation of *billboards* that encourage people to post creative photos on social media, with a view to choosing the most creative one to be awarded with exclusive merchandising for the event (Santos, B., 2021). In addition to mupis, posters placed outside, in places such as schools, universities and libraries, among others, are another means of advertising outside the cultural centre (Pereira, 2015).

In a more traditional vein, Santos, B., (2021) proposes publicising the centre's activities in local magazines and newspapers. Word of mouth is also highlighted, i.e. promoting the space and its services to potential clients through people who have already experienced it, such as the centre's employees. Thus, an agreement is proposed with the public to share their experience of the centre on their social networks, in order to increase its market coverage (Santos, B., 2021; Alves et al., 2017). Other marketing actions include buying words on Google Ads, sending newsletters, satisfaction surveys, joining national and international cultural networks and taking part in cultural fairs (Santos, B., 2021; Santos, M., 2021).

As a means of promoting cultural events, there are some examples mentioned by Rocha (2018) to publicise the Salão do Livro do Piauí event, such as television adverts, both commercial and on university television, radio, billboards in strategic locations such as avenues, roundabouts and university entrances. But this project mentions that the best way to publicise the event is word of mouth, i.e. the public itself sharing information about the event. Other means of promotion mentioned are local newspapers and leaflets. The author says that since the event is large and annual, its image is already established among its participants, fostering trust and confidence in its organisation. As such, this solidified image allows participants to remain loyal and new audiences to be attracted (Rocha, 2018).

Offers and discounts are another action that can be taken by cultural institutions, for visitors who have subscribed to loyalty programmes, for example (Paço & Pinto, 2019). The development of the organisation's merchandising is also another means of communication pointed out to cultural institutions (Garcia, 2018).

The Internet in the Cultural Sector

The Internet encompasses the most varied areas, and cultural activities are no exception. According to Antunes et al. (2020), 15% of respondents search the Internet for information on music, cinema, books and shows at least once a week. Around half look for this type of information at least somewhat regularly. In addition, 20 per cent disseminated cultural content of their own creation and 25 per cent interacted on cultural topics with posts and likes on social networks or other digital groups once or several times a month. These results show the importance and potential of the digital universe in increasing adherence to culture (Antunes et al., 2020; Alves, 2019).

The digital universe has been particularly important during the pandemic, as it has spurred the development of the cultural sector, which has adapted its events and exhibitions to the online world, through streaming platforms, digital art or virtual visits to venues (Santos, B., 2021). It is also important in the cultural sector for organisations to keep up with technology, adapting their ways of communicating with the public (Santos, M., 2021; Moreno, 2019, as cited in Nunes, 2021).

The digital world has allowed many cultural institutions to introduce online audio guides, for example, which visitors can download to their smartphones (Remelgado, 2014). Podcasts are another means of using the internet in these organisations. They consist of publishing audio content that can be subscribed to and downloaded. They can include complementary information about exhibitions or events and help attract new audiences (Remelgado, 2014).

Another online tool adopted by cultural institutions is the QR code, which consists of a barcode that links physical objects with digital information. These have advantages such as low costs, ease of use, the practicality of being associated with mobile devices and their small size, which makes them easy to integrate into the cultural space. It also allows accessibility for communities with special needs (Remelgado, 2014). This tool can be used in a variety of ways, such as placing digital art, readable with a QR code, around the city and in cultural spaces (Santos, B., 2021).

Virtual tours are another digital element used by various cultural institutions that not only allow those who cannot physically visit the space to visit, but also complement the experience of those who do (Remelgado, 2014). Also within the digital universe can be the development of an institution app (Tavares, 2019).

According to the questionnaire carried out as part of the article "Museum Communication on Websites and Social Media as a Way of Attracting Visitors", 60 per cent of respondents know information about museums through websites and social media (Nunes, 2021). The presence of cultural institutions in the digital universe makes it possible to strengthen their image, visibility and reach, bring them closer to visitors and potential visitors and even make it easier for people to be producers of culture (Remelgado, 2014; Brunello, 2020; OMC, 2012, as cited in António, 2021).

DIGITAL INFLUENCERS IN THE CULTURAL SECTOR

Influencer marketing was born before social networks, as was seen, for example, in the presence of public figures in brand adverts. However, social networks have added another dimension to this type of marketing, allowing closer and more interactive contact with followers on a daily basis (Costa, 2022).

The resonance of social networks has given a new meaning to the role of the media (Pedroni, 2016; Sette & Brito, 2020). Social networks have had a major impact on reducing barriers to social participation and debate, since they belong to the public sphere and allow different stakeholders to participate in the production of media texts (Paiva et al., 2017).

Influencers are figures who showcase their lives on social networks, where they create a profile and publish content. The growth of social networks and the awareness of video as a format that is easy to consume online have been factors that have fuelled the development of digital influencers. Considering the media agents that influence various consumption practices (including cultural consumption), digital influencers have achieved increasing notoriety (Cotter, 2019). Called 'micro-celebrities', they emerge from the connection with specific audiences, whose relationships are created by two important aspects (Cotter, 2019; Kapitan & Silvera, 2015):

-the affective and sensory stimuli they emanate (e.g. authenticity/attractiveness); and
-their information capacity (e.g. expertise in certain subjects).

Traditional celebrities often maintain a protocol distance from their audience, while digital influencers make massive use of the interactive potential of new media technologies to create interest and maintain a close relationship with their target audience (Hearn, 2008; Pedroni, 2016).

Thus, the concept that was initially seen as a hobby has become a profession. Most followers end up following influencers on a daily basis (Firmino, 2022; Camargo et al., 2017). Digital influencers are present on a variety of formats and platforms, such as Instagram, Twitter, TikTok and Youtube. The content they publish is varied and can range from dance challenges, product tests, demonstrations of their daily lives, among others (Firmino, 2022). According to Traackr company, there are at least ten types of digital influencers: the authority, the activist, the celebrity, the connector, the analyst, the expert, the journalist, the insider, the disruptor and the one whose name is a kind of brand (Camargo et al., 2017).

For a good performance, it's important to have personality, a good set, good lighting and sound design, and practice (Capricho, 2016, as cited in Camargo et al., 2017).

Influencers have achieved their status as trusted agents in the transmission of information through their activity of filtering the information that travels the web and reaches various audiences, and through their own attributes of reputation, credibility and prestige. This is only maintained by constantly producing content and developing and maintaining a relationship with followers (Almeida, 2022).

According to Costa (2022), digital influencers can be classified as:

-Top Celeb, if they have a high number of followers and a high engagement rate, but their content doesn't have a specific focus. They are relevant for generating brand awareness and recognition, but not necessarily for increasing sales;
-Fit Celeb, those who have a large number of followers but whose content is focused on one segment. Their followers are interested in learning about specific subjects and themes;
-Authority, those who are references on certain subjects, considered to be 'experts', ideal for generating brand awareness;
-Trendsetter, more focused on businesses with an environmental and/or social cause, generating credibility through their values;
-Micro-influencers, with a smaller number of followers, are important in humanising the brand and bringing it closer to the public, as they can generate a lot of engagement.

We now know that digital influencers have a great capacity to influence public behaviour and opinion. For this reason, companies from a wide range of sectors have come to regard them as potential ambassadors for their products and services (Magno & Cássia, 2018; Uzuñoglu & Kip, 2014). This is because they are able to win over a large number of people, have a specialised language for market segments, and are viewed with authority, influencing the habits and behaviours of their followers. Influence comes from network participation, media convergence and, above all, the proximity and interaction that influencers have with their audience. They are thus able to promote the success of a brand. Their achievements or the controversies they get involved in often end up making the news (Firmino, 2022; Youpix, 2016, as cited in Camargo et al., 2017). According to data presented by the company Meio&Mensagem (2016) in Infobase Interativa, influencers are of equal or greater importance than a 30-second advert on prime-time television (Camargo et al., 2017). The characteristics of influencers end up being transferred to brands, whether positive or negative.

As several studies have shown (Sudha & Sheena, 2017; Uzuñoglu & Kip, 2014), consumers trust influencers more than the brand's own promotional activities. Once companies realised this, influencers began to be used as a means of marketing communication, as a way of building consumer trust and credibility (Gardner, 2005; Sudha & Sheena, 2017). According to Cafferky (1999), as cited in Costa (2022), more than 80 per cent of people consider recommendations from professionals, family and/or friends when purchasing products or services. Digital influencers are already classified as the second largest source of information for making purchasing decisions (the first being family and friends). According to a survey by Opinion Box, 71 per cent of Instagram users follow at least one digital influencer, and 58 per cent of respondents said they had already bought a product recommended by an influencer (Costa, 2022).

In 2017, the Brazilian Association of Digital Agents - Abradi developed the Code of Conduct for Digital Agencies in Hiring Influencers, in order to establish guidelines for digital influencers and the adverts shared on social networks. It states that it is essential to encourage transparency, making it clear that the publications made by contracted influencers are advertising and that they are paid or benefit from it (Araujo, 2023).

Digital influencers dictate fashion and behaviour, share knowledge, give tips and engage their audiences in a variety of ways. Culturally speaking, they have become increasingly important, especially in the post-pandemic context, as the cultural sector has been one of the hardest hit during this period. Professionals and supporters of the cultural sector have taken advantage of social media platforms such as Instagram, TikTok, Facebook, YouTube and so on, to become influencers and also establish partnerships, to create content and deliver it to their target audience.

Cultural institutions can therefore use digital influencers to promote their events, exhibitions and activities, resulting in a greater number of visitors, their loyalty and also greater profitability. This is also a beneficial tool because it is low-cost, highly visible and yields positive results (Costa, 2022). Influencers can thus share videos and photographs documenting their experience at the institution, in order to build a more personal and authentic image of the space, fostering interest among followers (Araujo, 2023).

Culture-orientated digital influencers are able to provide information in a more didactic way and in a language that is more similar to what their audience uses on a day-to-day basis. Various topics are covered in this content, such as music, history, the country's culture, the arts and cinema. The influencers in this niche are always up to date with all the news that encompasses the concept of culture.

The importance of cultural influencers is precisely the ease with which they can transmit information to a large number of people simultaneously. Publications are created in an objective manner, focused on delivering as much relevant material as possible to the public.

Influencers are often appreciated for their trustworthiness and authenticity (Childers et al., 2018; McQuarrie et al., 2013; Sette & Brito, 2020; Uzuñoglu & Kip, 2014), attracting consumers in search of identity projects with which they identify (McQuarrie, et al., 2013), and affecting their choices and interests based on the personal influence they exert on other individuals in their network (Sette & Brito, 2020; Zanette, et al., 2013), and affecting their choices and interests based on the personal influence they exert on other individuals in their network (Sette & Brito, 2020; Zanette, et al., 2013) - which the marketing literature has agreed to consider word-of-mouth communication (Godey et al., 2016; Zanette, et al., 2013).

However, it is clear that in Portugal the use of digital influencers in the cultural sector is still in its infancy (whether due to a lack of knowledge, experience or cultural aspects). Given all of the above, the Portuguese cultural sector could pay attention to the new possibilities that influencers provide, in order to boost the country's various cultural activities.

EMERGING TRENDS AND FUTURE RESEARCH DIRECTIONS

In recent years, influencer marketing has undergone substantial changes and will certainly continue to be accustomed to the ever-changing digital landscape. On the other hand, influencers are also exploring new ways of engaging with their audiences and creating fascinating content as technology advances. Among the various trends, we can highlight three that are very present in the Portuguese context:

- **Augmented Reality (AR) and Virtual Reality (VR):** these technologies are becoming more accessible, allowing influencers to create immersive and interactive experiences for their audiences. Companies in the cultural sector can collaborate with influencers to develop AR filters, lenses or test virtual experiences that allow users to interact with people, bands and products in a virtual environment. This engagement-orientated format enhances and facilitates the user experience, leading to greater recognition and proximity. An excellent example of this trend in the Portuguese context is Symphony[1] - an immersive audiovisual experience that provides a journey through emotions and music, with the aim of bringing classical music closer to all types of audiences. The viewer has the opportunity to feel and understand classical music as if they were one of the musicians in the orchestra. Through this unique experience, you can enjoy the compositions of Beethoven, Mahler and Bernstein, performed by the great conductor Gustavo Dudamel and the more than 100 musicians of the prestigious Mahler Chamber Orchestra. This experience is itinerant and recently took place at the Casa da Música square, in the city of Porto in Portugal, from 2 June to 12 July 2023, a partnership between the "la Caixa" Foundation and the Casa da Música.

- **Metaverse:** this network of virtual worlds, created in 3D, into which several users can enter simultaneously via various platforms, Virtual Reality being the most immersive. The first Portuguese media organisation to arrive at Metaverso is RFM[2], in a space prepared to experience radio from the inside. To access it, users can use a computer, mobile phone or tablet, and for a more immersive experience they can wear VR glasses. In this experience, the user can enter and explore the RFM spaces in Metaverso.
- **Podcasts:** podcasts continue to grow in popularity, providing a platform for influencers to share in-depth discussions and stories. Companies can partner with influencers who host relevant podcasts to sponsor episodes or participate as guests. This format allows for more in-depth conversations, brand storytelling and the opportunity to reach a highly engaged audience. Podcast collaborations provide a way for influencers to discuss and endorse cultural products or services in a more conversational and intimate way. A great example of the success of a cultural-historical podcast in Portugal is 'O Sargento da Cela 7', a six-part series that is part of Observador's Podcast Plus, which tells the first-person story of António Lobato, the Portuguese soldier who spent the longest time as a prisoner of war. It is also the story of the secret operation to rescue him, which the Estado Novo dictatorship always denied.

In view of the above, it is expected that these trends will become increasingly common, especially in the cultural sector, and that these future prospects will be more present in everyday life.

FINAL COMMENTS

In today's context, influencer marketing in the cultural sector has emerged as a powerful tool for effectively reaching and engaging your target audience. During the Covid-19 pandemic, this trend gained alarming proportions that continue to be present in our daily lives. It turns out that many companies were taken by surprise and failed to implement these innovations in a timely manner and ended up going bankrupt. But those that have managed to implement and are still implementing, end up achieving more engagement, more user-generated content (UGC), more recurring word-of-mouth and consequently, better financial results.

The content of this chapter shows the growing importance of digital influencers today, as well as their ability to move audiences and influence behaviour, so the cultural sector should not ignore this very effective means of communication. It is therefore important to exploit it in its various formats in order to increase the effectiveness of the institutions' communication.

Especially in the Portuguese context, there is still a reluctance to accept the legitimacy of digital influencers, and the cultural sector is no different. It is hoped that with this chapter, more researchers and managers will become interested in this topic in the cultural sector and that knowledge will be even more widespread, regardless of social class, purchasing power and other characteristics of the population in general.

In terms of practical implications, this chapter can serve as a guide for companies and entrepreneurs in the cultural sector who still have doubts about the effectiveness and efficiency of using digital influencers in their business. By accessing the information contained here, they will realise the relevance of these professionals today, especially in attracting and retaining audiences from the younger generations. In addition, you will be able to see the current panorama of cultural institutions in Portugal in general and, with this, gain a competitive advantage by differentiating yourself through the use of digital influencers. This is made possible by the fact that the chapter takes an in-depth look at the various stimuli and benefits of the services of these professionals.

The main limitation found in the development of this chapter is related to the fact that there are not many scientific studies on the impact of digital influencers in the cultural sector, specifically in Portugal. This absence makes it difficult to compare the performance of organisations that have used influencers with those that have not. In this way, this research manages to reduce this existing gap somewhat, thus reinforcing its major contribution. Another limitation to be highlighted is the descriptive nature of the research, since it was limited to describing the phenomenon studied and demonstrating the advantages associated with encouraging its spread.

For future research, we suggest using a quantitative approach to analyse the topic, where it would be possible to collect primary data through questionnaires and interviews. It would be interesting to obtain information from customers of cultural institutions and also from the managers of these establishments, in order to understand why they are reluctant and afraid to use digital influencers. Another suggestion for future research would be to make a comparison between Portuguese cultural institutions and those in other cultural contexts, where the use of digital influencers is much more widespread and generally accepted. In this way, it would be possible to verify the real gains of their use and encourage the Portuguese scenario.

REFERENCES

Akamine, A. (2018). *Responsive regulation of the practice of e-mail marketing in Brazil* [Bachelor's thesis]. University of Brasília. https://bdm.unb.br/handle/10483/22306

Almeida, M. (2022). Booktubers, literature and cyberculture: mediation and circulation of cultural information. *Configurações- Revista Ciências Sociais, 29*. https://journals.openedition.org/configuracoes/15110

Alves, B. (2019). *Music Festivals as Cultural Spaces* [Master's thesis, University of Lisbon]. Repository of the University of Lisbon. http://hdl.handle.net/10451/40826

Alves, F., Costa, H. & Perinotto, A. (2017). Instagram as a tool for customer loyalty: Photography, Social Media and Tourism. *Marketing & Tourism Review*, *2*(2). .4562 doi:10.29149/mtr.v2i2

António, I. (2021). *Strategic Communication in Public Cultural Institutions: A Communication Plan for the Cinemateca Portuguesa - Cinema Museum* [Master's thesis]. ISCTE Repository - University Institute of Lisbon. http://hdl.handle.net/10071/24417

Antunes, M. (2020). *Survey of the Cultural Practices of the Portuguese 2020, Summary of Results*. ICS Studies and Reports.

Araujo, N. (2023). The image of a tourist destination as a tool for digital influencers. *Tourism, Society & Territory, 5*(1). https://periodicos.ufrn.br/revtursoter/article/view/32044

Bardhi, F., & Eckhardt, G. M. (2017). Liquid consumption. *The Journal of Consumer Research, 44*(3), 582–597. doi:10.1093/jcr/ucx050

Brunello, L. (2020). *Strategic Communication Planning for Museums*. LinkedIn.

Camargo, I., Estevanim, M., & Silveira, S. (2017). Participatory and convergent culture: the scenario that favours the birth of digital influencers. *Revista Communicare, 17*. https://www.researchgate.net/publication/327120381_Convergent_and_participatory_culture_the_scene_that_favours_the_uprising_of_digital_influencers_Cultura_participativa_e_convergente_o_cenario_que_favorece_o_nascimento_dos_influenciadores_digitais

Castro, D., Junior, F., & Lopes, S. (2019). Social networks as a tool for marketing: the vision of a company in the city of Palmas - TO. *Revista Humanidades e Inovação, 6*(12). https://revista.unitins.br/index.php/humanidadeseinovacao/article/view/1555

Cezar, L. (2019). *Communication and Marketing in the Public Sector: different approaches to the Brazilian reality*. Public Management Collection, v. 03. National School of Public Administration (Enap) and Brazilian Society of Public Administration (SBAP). http://repositorio.enap.gov.br/handle/1/4279

Childers, C. C., Lemon, L. L., & Hoy, M. G. (2018). #Sponsored #Ad: Agency perspective on influencer marketing campaigns. *Journal of Current Issues and Research in Advertising, 40*(3), 258–274. doi:10.1080/10641734.2018.1521113

Costa, P. (2022). *Social networks and digital influencers in the promotion of tourist destinations from the point of view of advertising agents: a case of Natal/RN, Natal/RN 2022* [Bachelor's thesis, Federal University of Rio Grande do Norte]. Institutional Repository of the Federal University of Rio Grande do Norte. https://repositorio.ufrn.br/handle/123456789/48961

Cotter, K. (2019). Playing the visibility game: How digital influencers and algorithms negotiate influence on Instagram. *New Media & Society, 21*(4), 895–913. doi:10.1177/1461444818815684

Demo, G., Lima, T., Scussel, F., Miranda, P., & Moreno, L. (2021). Relationship Marketing in the Consumer Market: Scientific Production Profile and Research Agenda. *Future Studies Research Journal: Trends and Strategies, 13*(2), 179–202. doi:10.24023/FutureJournal/2175-5825/2021.v13i2.569

FigueiredoE.RibeiroC.PassosC.PereiraP. (2022). Relationship marketing in university libraries: a literature review. *Gestão E Desenvolvimento*, (30), 289-316. https://doi.org/ doi:10.34632/gestaoedesenvolvimento.2022.11342

Firmino, I. (2022). *Influenciador digital: emblema da indústria cultural, Goiânia 2022* [Master's dissertation, Federal University of Goiás]. Federal University of Goiás Digital Library of Theses and Dissertations. https://repositorio.bc.ufg.br/tede/handle/tede/12399

Freitas, I. (2019). *A influência das caraterísticas do Centro Cultural na Satisfação e na Laldade: O Caso do Centro de Artes e Espectáculos da Figueira da Foz* [thesis, Coimbra School of Education and Oliveira do Hospital School of Technology and Management]. Common Repository. http://hdl.handle.net/10400.26/31150

Gama, M. (2020). *Culture and Development: Cultural projects and the 2030 Agenda Phase 1, Portugal, 1st quarter 2020.* Observatory of Communication and Culture Policies Centre for Communication and Society Studies University of Minho.

Garcia, C. (2018). *Marketing in Portuguese contemporary dance companies - Case studies: CiM Companhia de Dança, Companhia de Dança de Almada and Quorum Ballet* [Master's dissertation]. Iscte - University Institute of Lisbon. http://hdl.handle.net/10071/18789

Gardner, S. (2005). *Buzz marketing with blogs for dummies*. Wiley Publishing Inc.

Gil, P. (2017). *Comunicação pública e públicos em questão* (1st ed., Vol. 2). Vertentes conceptuais e metodológicas. PPGCOM UFMG. https://www.researchgate.net/publication/342786807_Uma_rota_para_teoria_e_pratica_em_comunicacao_publica_a_argumentacao_como_luta_civica_por_reconhecimento_respeito_e_justica

Godey, B., Manthiou, A., Perdezoli, D., Rokka, J., Aiello, G., Donvito, R., & Singh, R. (2016). Social media marketing efforts of luxury brands: Influence on brand equity and consumer behaviour. *Journal of Business Research*, *69*(12), 5833–5841. doi:10.1016/j.jbusres.2016.04.181

Governo da República Portuguesa. (n.d.). *Cultura*. https://www.historico.portugal.gov.pt/pt/o-governo/arquivo-historico/governos-constitucionais/gc19/os-temas/cultura/cultura.aspx#:~:text=A%20cultura%20%C3%A9%20um%20fator%20de%20coes%C3%A3o%20e,para%20a%20afirma%C3%A7%C3%A3o%20de%20Portugal%20na%20comunidade%20internacional.

Hearn, A. (2008). Meat, mask, burden: Probing the contours of the branded "self". *Journal of Consumer Culture*, *8*(2), 197–217. doi:10.1177/1469540508090086

Kapitan, S., & Silvera, D. H. (2015). From digital media influencers to celebrity endorsers: Attributions drive endorser effectiveness. *Marketing Letters*, *27*(3), 553–567. doi:10.100711002-015-9363-0

Kotler, P., & Keller, K. L. (2006). *Marketing for the 21st Century*. Pearson Prentice Hall.

Lopes, M. (2013). *20th Edition of the Almada Dance Fortnight: an analysis of the audiences of dance performances* [Master's dissertation, Lusófona University of Humanities and Technologies]. Lusófona Scientific Repository. http://hdl.handle.net/10437/5295

Magno, F., & Cássia, F. (2018). The impact of social media influencers in tourism. *Anatolia*, *29*(2), 288–290. doi:10.1080/13032917.2018.1476981

Mazieri, M., Queiroz, M., Queiroz, R., & Yanaze, M. (2018). Conceptual model for evaluating marketing communication in consumer goods franchises. *Revista Brasileira de Marketing*, *17*(2), 2018. doi:10.5585/remark.v17i2.3978

McQuarrie, E. F., Miller, J., & Phillips, B. J. (2013). The megaphone effect: Taste and audience in fashion blogging. *The Journal of Consumer Research*, *40*(1), 136–158. doi:10.1086/669042

National Statistics Institute. (2022). *Culture Statistics - 2021*. Lisbon: INE. https://www.ine.pt/xurl/pub/18212178

Nunes, R. (2021). *Communication strategies of cultural institutions for Generation Z* [Master's dissertation, University of Aveiro]. University of Aveiro Institutional Repository. http://hdl.handle.net/10773/32616

Paço, A., & Pinto, C. (2019). *Strategic marketing planning in cultural centres. Actions to attract and retain audiences at the São João National Theatre*. IS Working Paper. 3rd Series, No. 77. https://www.researchgate.net/publication/370067739_Planeamento_estrategico_de_Marketing_em_equipamentos_culturais

Pais, M. (2016). *A Comunicação no Contexto das Organizações Culturais O caso do Centro Cultural de Belém* [Master's Degree Internship Report in Communication Sciences - Strategic Communication, Faculty of Social Sciences and Humanities, Universidade Nova de Lisboa]. Universidade Nova Repository. http://hdl.handle.net/10362/19659

PaivaA. L.GarciaA. S.AlcântaraV. C. (2017). Discursive disputes about corruption in Brazil: A discursive-critical analysis on Twitter. *Revista de Administração Contemporânea, 21*(5), 627-647. http://dx.doi.org/doi:10.1590/1982-7849rac2017160163

Parente, A. (2018). *The importance of relationship marketing in the management of cultural attractions* [Master's thesis, Polytechnic Institute of Viana do Castelo]. IPVC Scientific Repository. http://hdl.handle.net/20.500.11960/2010

Pedroni, M. (2016). Meso-celebrities, fashion, and the media: How digital influencers struggle for visibility. Film. *Fashion and Consumption*, *5*(1), 103–121. doi:10.1386/ffc.5.1.103_1

Pereira, I. (2015). *A Comunicação do CCB- As Estratégias de Comunicação* [Master's dissertation]. Repository of Iscte - University Institute of Lisbon. http://hdl.handle.net/10071/10636

Pinto, C. (2019). *The influence of branding and communication on brand attachment and consumer behaviour: a Super Bock case study* [Master's thesis, University of Minho]. RepositóriUM- University of Minho. https://hdl.handle.net/1822/64223

Reis, A. (2003). *Cultural marketing and cultural funding*. https://garimpodesolucoes.com.br/wp-content/uploads/2016/02/Marketing-Cultural-e-Financiamento-da-Cultura-Garimpo-de-Solu%C3%A7%C3%B5es.pdf

Remelgado, A. (2014). *Communication Strategies in Museums - Management Tools in Museological Institutions* [PhD thesis]. Open Repository of the University of Porto. https://hdl.handle.net/10216/109315

Rocha, M., & Trevisan, N. (2018). *Integrated Marketing Communication* (1st ed.). Marketing in Modern Times Collection. Saraiva Educação. https://books.google.pt/books?id=FnCwDwAAQBAJ&lpg=PT11&dq=a%C3%A7%C3%B5es%20de%20comunica%C3%A7%C3%A3o%20de%20marketing%20&lr&hl=pt-BR&pg=PT3#v=onepage&q=a%C3%A7%C3%B5es%20de%20comunica%C3%A7%C3%A3o%20de%20marketing&f=false

Rocha, P. (2018). *Cultural marketing: market strategies based on a case study of the Piauí Book Fair (Salipi)* [PhD thesis]. Fernando Pessoa University Institutional Repository. http://hdl.handle.net/10284/6489

Rodrigues, F. (2021). *Projeto Sonae - Análise da Usabilidade do Website MO* [Master's thesis, Instituto Superior de Contabilidade e Administração do Porto]. Scientific Repository of the Polytechnic Institute of Porto. http://hdl.handle.net/10400.22/19929

Santos, B. (2021). *Organizações de apoio cultural - o caso do Imaginarius Centro de Criação analisado sob o prisma do marketing* [Master's thesis, Instituto Superior de Administração e Gestão]. Open Access Scientific Repositories of Portugal. http://hdl.handle.net/10400.26/36610

Santos, M. (2021). *Audience satisfaction in cultural communication: the case of the São Francisco Convent* [Master's thesis, University of Minho]. RepositóriUM- University of Minho. https://hdl.handle.net/1822/79278

Saraiva, P. (2019). Digital Marketing: The Use of Social Media as a Communication Channel in Fashion Retail in Barbalha-CE. Id on Line - Multidisciplinary and Psychology Journal. https://idonline.emnuvens.com.br/id

Schmitt, B. (2019). From atoms to bits and back: A research curation on digital technology and agenda for future research. *The Journal of Consumer Research*, *46*(4), 825–832. doi:10.1093/jcr/ucz038

Scussel, F. B. C., de la Martinière Petrol, M., Semprebon, E., & Da Rocha, R. A. (2017). What is relationship marketing? A proposal for a unifying concept. *Revista de Ciências da Administração*, *19*(48), 9–23. doi:10.5007/2175-8077.2017v20n48p9

Selas, D. (2022). *The importance of user experience evaluation and usability testing in website development: the Diffuse.TV case* [Master's thesis, University of Beira Interior]. uBibliorum- Digital Repository of the University of Beira Interior. http://hdl.handle.net/10400.6/13271

Sette, G., & Brito, P. Q. (2020). To what extent are digital influencers creative? *Creativity and Innovation Management*, *29*(51), 90–102. doi:10.1111/caim.12365

Souza-Leão, A. L. M., Moura, B. M., & Nunes, W. K. S. (2022). All in one: Digital influencers as pop culture marketers. *Revista Brasileira de Gestão de Negócios*, *24*(2), 247–274. doi:10.7819/rbgn.v24i2.4167

Sudha, M., & Sheena, K. (2017). Impact of influencers in consumer decision process: The fashion industry. *SCMS Journal of Indian Management, 14*(3), 14-30. https://www.scms.edu.in/uploads/journal/articles/article_12.pdf

Tavares, S. (2019). *Complexo Cultural Ferreira de Castro: Comunicação Estratégica do Valor Cultural* [Master's thesis, University Institute of Lisbon]. Iscte Repository, University Institute of Lisbon. http://hdl.handle.net/10071/19620

Torres, C. (2018). *The digital marketing bible* (2nd ed.). Novatec Editora Ltda. https://books.google.pt/books?id=uDN7DwAAQBAJ&lpg=PT4&dq=a%C3%A7%C3%B5es%20de%20comunica%C3%A7%C3%A3o%20de%20marketing%20&lr&hl=pt-BR&pg=PT2#v=onepage&q&f=false

Uzuñoglu, E., & Kip, S. M. (2014). Brand communication through digital influencers: Leveraging blogger engagement. *International Journal of Information Management*, *34*(5), 592–602. doi:10.1016/j.ijinfomgt.2014.04.007

Van Dijck, J. (2013). *The culture of connectivity: A critical history of social media*. OUP. doi:10.1093/acprof:oso/9780199970773.001.0001

Vaz, G., & Venâncio, M. (2018). Marketing, dissemination, action and cultural mediation in public archives. *RACIn, 6*(1), 1-29. https://eds.s.ebscohost.com/eds/pdfviewer/pdfviewer?vid=1&sid=d94c4ea1-b6ef-4d42-9118-20334a11b610%40redis

Walmsley, B. (2011). Why people go to the theatre: A qualitative study of audience motivation. *Journal of Customer Behaviour*, *10*(4), 335–351. doi:10.1362/147539211X13210329822545

Yanaze, M. (2017). *Marketing and Communication Management* (2nd ed.). Saraiva Educação. https://books.google.pt/books?id=eSprDwAAQBAJ&lpg=PT6&dq=a%C3%A7%C3%B5es%20de%20comunica%C3%A7%C3%A3o%20de%20marketing%20&lr&hl=pt-BR&pg=PT4#v=onepage&q=a%C3%A7%C3%B5es%20de%20comunica%C3%A7%C3%A3o%20de%20marketing&f=false

Yanaze, M. (2020). *Marketing and Communication Management* (3rd ed.). Saraiva Educação. https://books.google.pt/books?id=es4iEAAAQBAJ&lpg=PT6&dq=cultural%20marketing&lr&hl=pt-BR&pg=PP1#v=onepage&q=cultural%20marketing&f=false

Zanette, M. C., Brito, E. P. Z., & Coutinho, M. (2013). New influentials: An exploratory study on blogs. *Journal of Direct, Data and Digital Marketing Practice*, *15*(1), 36–46. doi:10.1057/dddmp.2013.45

ADDITIONAL READING

Hu, L., Min, Q., Han, S., & Liu, Z. (2020). Understanding followers' stickiness to digital influencers: The effect of psychological responses. *International Journal of Information Management*, *54*, 102169. doi:10.1016/j.ijinfomgt.2020.102169

Jiménez-Castillo, D., & Sánchez-Fernández, R. (2019). The role of digital influencers in brand recommendation: Examining their impact on engagement, expected value and purchase intention. *International Journal of Information Management*, *49*, 366–376. doi:10.1016/j.ijinfomgt.2019.07.009

Silva, M. J. D. B., Farias, S. A. D., Grigg, M. K., & Barbosa, M. D. L. D. A. (2020). Online engagement and the role of digital influencers in product endorsement on Instagram. *Journal of Relationship Marketing*, *19*(2), 133–163. doi:10.1080/15332667.2019.1664872

Torres, P., Augusto, M., & Matos, M. (2019). Antecedents and outcomes of digital influencer endorsement: An exploratory study. *Psychology and Marketing*, *36*(12), 1267–1276. doi:10.1002/mar.21274

Wielki, J. (2020). Analysis of the role of digital influencers and their impact on the functioning of the contemporary on-line promotional system and its sustainable development. *Sustainability (Basel)*, *12*(17), 7138. doi:10.3390u12177138

KEY TERMS AND DEFINITIONS

Core Messages (Mission, Vision, and Values): Mission statements describe an organization's reason for existence, vision statements describe the ideal state that the organization wants to achieve, and values statements list the principles that guide and direct the organization and its culture.

Customer Relationship Management (CRM): This term was created to define an entire class of information systems or tools that automate customer contact functions.

Digital Immigrants: A digital immigrant is a person born before the widespread adoption of computers and has had to adopt digital technology later in life. In other words, is a person who was born before it was common to use things such as personal computers and mobile phones.

Digital Natives: A digital native is a person who grew up with the presence of digital technology or in the information age. Having grown up in information technologies (IT) presence, digital natives are comfortable with and fluent in technology.

Gross Value Added (GVA): It is defined as the value that producers have added to the goods and services they have bought. When they sell their wares, producers' income should be more than their costs, and the difference between the two is the value they have added.

Millennium Generation: The millennial generation is defined as anyone born between 1981 and 1996, which means anyone between the ages of 24 and 39 in 2020. This age range, like other generational cohorts, is chosen for statistical analysis of certain trends rather than being a strict identifier.

Traditional Media: Traditional media consists of all forms of communication used before the internet age, including radio, TV, newspaper, magazines, and billboards. This means it refers to various forms of mass media communication that existed before the internet.

User-Generated Content: User-generated content (also known as UGC or consumer-generated content) is original, brand-specific content created by customers and published on social media or other channels. UGC comes in many forms, including images, videos, reviews, a testimonial, or even a podcast.

ENDNOTES

1 https://fundacaolacaixa.pt/pt/exposicao-itinerante-symphony

2 https://rfm.sapo.pt/metaverso

Chapter 10
TikTok Content Categories and User Engagement Behavior:
Alisha Lehmann – Celebrity Athlete and Influencer

Sebastiano Mereu
https://orcid.org/0000-0003-2607-1782
Sports Business Research Academy, Switzerland

ABSTRACT

This study investigates the impact of TikTok content categories on user engagement behavior on the official TikTok account of Alisha Lehmann. Analyzing 91 videos via multiple regression analysis, the research uncovers practical insights for content creators and marketers, as well as theoretical findings for academics. Notably, Alisha Lehmann's active professional life, showcasing her athletic prowess, emerged as the most influential category, driving engagement across views, likes, comments, saves, and shares. Videos emphasising her personal life through aesthetics also impacted video shares and saves to a certain degree. Additionally, non-active or non-sport professional life content garnered attention, especially in likes and comments. In contrast, TikTok games and promotional content had limited impact, emphasizing the importance of a balanced content strategy that integrates personal and professional aspects for athlete influencers. These findings provide guidance for optimizing online presence, aligning content with audience interests, and fostering brand loyalty on TikTok.

INTRODUCTION

The rise of influencer marketing has transformed the landscape of digital marketing and social media engagement, with platforms like TikTok playing a pivotal role in reshaping how individuals interact with brands and public figures (Haenlein et al., 2020; Brooks et al., 2021). This chapter explores the intricate relationship between content categories on TikTok and user engagement behaviors (Abidin, 2020), specifically on the official TikTok account of Alisha Lehmann, a renowned celebrity athlete and

DOI: 10.4018/979-8-3693-0551-5.ch010

influencer. In an age where influencers and brands wield great power on social media, understanding how the different types of content affect the way users behave upon consuming such content becomes crucial (Newman et al., 2013; Dolan et al., 2015; Doyle et al., 2020).

As the boundaries between celebrity and influencer blur, empirical research is essential to comprehend how content categories influence user behavior on TikTok (Zuo & Wang, 2019; Su et al., 2020; Barta et al., 2023). This study is motivated by the need to provide empirical evidence and insights into the specific content categories that drive user engagement on the platform, enabling a more informed and strategic approach to influencer marketing. Thus, the research objectives of the chapter include (1) investigating the influence of individual content categories on Alisha Lehmann's official TikTok account and (2) identifying which content categories exhibit the strongest impact on user engagement and to what extent, allowing for more effective content strategy recommendations.

To achieve the above-mentioned objectives, multiple regression analysis is chosen to examine the causal relationships between TikTok content categories and user engagement behaviors, because it enables the investigation of the combined effect of multiple independent variables, i.e., content categories, on dependent variables, i.e., user engagement behaviors (Vale & Fernandes, 2018; Saunders et al., 2023). This statistical approach provides a comprehensive understanding of the causal relationships between content categories and user engagement, ensuring a more robust and accurate analysis of Alisha Lehmann's TikTok account dynamics. Based upon the collected data and its respective analysis, the chapter discusses theoretical findings and practical implications that enable content creators and marketers to craft adequate influencer marketing strategies in the context of an athlete.

BACKGROUND TO THE RESEARCH

Content and User Behavior

Influencer marketing leverages the social media influence of individuals with large and engaged followings to promote their own or a collaborating brand's products or services by reaching a targeted audience (Haenlein et al., 2020; Leban & Voyer, 2020). Influencers can harness their credibility and social media reach to effectively drive brand awareness, engagement, and sales of products or services they promote directly or indirectly (Sokolova & Kefi, 2020). New facets added by social media have also enhanced the way people are entertained, inform themselves, or escape day-to-day routines, which has enabled influencers and brands alike to choose from a wider spectrum of marketing and communication channels to achieve respective business objectives (Kietzmann et al., 2011; Batra & Keller, 2016; Appel et al., 2020).

Social media has further transformed the way viewers consume and experience spectator sports (Sanderson, 2011). Fans can engage with their favorite athletes and teams through various social media channels to feel close to them before, during, and after a main event, e.g., a game of basketball or a football match (Sutera, 2013). Such user engagement can be encouraged through different kinds of media contents, which may be informative, affective, social, or aesthetic in nature (Chen et al., 2021; Gómez-Suárez & Veloso, 2020). These characteristics form the foundation of a brand experience, which can foster fan satisfaction and loyalty (Schmitt, 1999; Brakus et al., 2009; Pine & Gilmore, 2020). Consequently, social media experiences are characterized by what is published on a given channel through content that may follow a conscious or unconscious strategic categorization by an athlete or brand (Hu et al., 2014; Geurin-Eagleman & Burch, 2016). At the same time, the various types of content that support these experiences, seek to achieve an array of communication and engagement objectives (Baetzgen & Tropp, 2013; Batra & Keller, 2016).

Content categories can drive uses and gratifications for users to follow an athlete or brand on social media and to engage in specific behaviors (Whiting & Williams, 2013). The uses and gratifications theory can be a valid choice for the categorization of media contents in mass communication (Blumler & Katz, 1974). However, various studies propose an adaptation of its categories to the context of the respective research or business application (e.g., Cvijikj & Michahelles, 2013; De Vries et al., 2014; Dolan et al., 2016; Geurin-Eagleman & Burch, 2016; Vale & Fernandes, 2018). This might include combining or excluding certain categories or altering them to fit the given context.

Although TikTok, the social media platform to be examined in this research, is often portrayed as mainly being used for entertainment purposes (Zuo & Wang, 2019; Su et al., 2020), extant literature suggests that the platform offers a wider range of content types (Basch et al., 2021; Huebner, 2022; Jiang et al., 2022). This is a legitimate argument given that TikTok content is created and consumed by more than 1 billion monthly active users worldwide in July 2023 (Datareportal, 2023). Furthermore, it can be argued that the degree to which video content is attractive to its targeted audience may be influenced by factors such as a video's visual appeal, emotional reference, informative value, or engaging properties (Newman et al., 2013; Yang & Kang, 2021).

The proactive conceptualization and planning of social media content for different categories can help influencers coordinate the creation of their content more efficiently and effectively (Klimsa, 2017). Moreover, strategically organizing and delivering different types of content across a variety of communication channels helps content creators maintain consistency in how a story is told to the target audience and, hence, strengthens associations with fans (Fetchko et al., 2018). Yet, content creators should examine how audiences use available communication channels and respectively deliver the type of content appropriate for a specific channel; not all content categories might be suitable for all channels or to achieve all marketing and communication objectives (Batra & Keller, 2016; Ryan, 2020).

Celebrity Athletes as Influencers

An athlete with celebrity appeal can be considered a high-profile sports figure and can leverage their fame, achievements, and personal brand to influence and engage with a larger and more dedicated following on social media platforms (Sanderson, 2011; Geurin-Eagleman & Burch, 2016). They might have achieved celebrity status due to their exceptional skills, accomplishments, and public recognition within their respective sports (Arai et al., 2014; Brooks et al., 2021), and their influence can extend beyond their athletic performance, as they often have significant impact on their fans' lifestyle choices, product preferences, and even societal views (Andrews et al., 2015; Mahmoudian et al., 2021).

The appeal of social media for celebrity athletes is manifold. Social media provides a direct and unfiltered avenue of communication to connect with fans on a personal level (Sutera, 2013; Brooks et al., 2021). By sharing behind-the-scenes glimpses of their training routines, daily lives, and moments of triumph, these athletes humanize themselves and forge emotional connections with followers (Geurin-Eagleman & Burch, 2016). This authenticity fosters loyalty and a sense of relatability, which can be challenging to achieve through traditional media channels (Sanderson, 2011; Mahmoudian et al., 2021).

Social media also empowers influencers to control their narrative (Zhou et al., 2021). Celebrity athletes can address rumors, controversies, or misconceptions promptly and directly, ensuring that their side of the story reaches the public accurately (Sanderson, 2011). This control over their online presence contributes to shaping and preserving their image, both on and off the field (Sutera, 2013; Arai et al., 2014).

Additionally, social media offers unparalleled reach and engagement (Datareportal, 2023). Influencers have by definition a certain influence on their fanbases, which can span the globe, and platforms like Instagram, YouTube, and TikTok enable them to reach their audience with less effort as compared to traditional media (Leban & Voyer, 2020). Through engaging content like videos, photos, and live streams, influencers can maintain a constant presence and interact with fans in real time (Ryan, 2020). This active engagement fosters a sense of community and belonging among followers, who feel acknowledged and valued by their idols through parasocial interaction (Sanderson, 2011; Sokolova & Kefi, 2020).

From a business perspective, social media provides lucrative opportunities for brand collaborations and endorsements (Von Felbert & Breuer, 2020). Celebrity athletes are highly sought-after by brands aiming to tap into their credibility, authenticity, and extensive reach (Haenlein et al., 2020; Leban & Voyer, 2020; Leo & von Kuczkowski, 2020). These partnerships can be mutually beneficial, since celebrity athletes as influencers can monetize their platforms while promoting products or causes they genuinely support (Brooks et al., 2021).

These arguments determine that social media's appeal for celebrity athlete lies in its capacity for personal connection, image control, global reach, active engagement, and commercial opportunities. Through social media platforms, athletes extend their influence beyond the sports arena, impacting fans' lives, influencing trends, and fostering a community that revolves around shared interests and admiration.

TikTok and Influencer Marketing for a Celebrity Athlete

Investigating TikTok in the context of influencer marketing can be a legitimate and intriguing academic pursuit. TikTok has rapidly emerged as a powerful player in the social media landscape, boasting more than 1 billion users worldwide by July 2023 (Datareportal, 2023). This extensive reach makes it a compelling platform for influencer marketing, as influencers on TikTok can engage vast and diverse audiences, influencing consumer behaviors and preferences (Darmatama & Erdiansyah, 2021; Barta et al., 2023). TikTok has also reshaped the influencer marketing paradigm. Unlike other platforms, it offers a more dynamic video content format, which challenges influencers and marketers to create impactful messages in mere seconds (Zuo & Wang, 2019). Similarly, TikTok's algorithmically personalized, diverse, and easily consumable content fosters a continually intriguing user experience (Abidin, 2020). This shift demands new and innovative strategies (Haenlein et al., 2020), making it an attractive area for academic exploration.

With this in mind, Alisha Lehmann, a professional women's football player and internet celebrity from Switzerland, can be considered an interesting and viable subject to base this research on, as she counts 9.7 million followers and 78.9 million likes on her TikTok channel alone as of 30 August 2023; also, she collaborates with a variety of companies and brands as an influencer or ambassador (alishalehmann7 on TikTok, 2023). As a celebrity athlete, Alisha Lehmann holds a high level of influence and appeal to a broad audience, extending beyond sports enthusiasts (Geurin, 2017). Investigating her presence on TikTok provides valuable insights into how these individuals leverage their fame in the influencer marketing sphere. TikTok's short-form video format challenges celebrity athletes to engage with their audience in a more personal and creative way, differing from traditional sports coverage (Dakroub et al., 2023). Understanding how these athletes adapt their content and brand collaborations on this platform can shed light on evolving influencer marketing strategies (Su et al., 2020). Moreover, athlete endorsements and partnerships on TikTok can significantly impact their personal brands and sponsorships (Haenlein et al., 2020). Analyzing these interactions can contribute to an understanding of the broader sports marketing landscape, shedding light on how influencer marketing is transforming the sports industry (Sanderson, 2011; Leo & von Kuczkowski, 2020). Therefore, exploring the TikTok activities of a celebrity athlete is a legitimate and intriguing subject for academic study in influencer marketing due to their vast reach, the unique nature of TikTok's content, and its implications for sports marketing and branding.

THEORETICAL BACKGROUND

The following sections define the terms social media content categories and user engagement behavior, discuss their importance in regard to influencer marketing, and explore the associations between the two elements. The resulting discussion offers the theoretical foundation upon which the investigation of this study is based.

Social Media Content Categories

Social media content categories are distinct thematic divisions or topics that individuals, brands, influencers, and other creators use to classify and structure the content they share on various social media platforms (Hu et al., 2014). This may happen consciously or unconsciously. These categories serve as organizational frameworks, allowing for the systematic presentation of different types of content to cater to diverse audience interests (Newman et al., 2013; Ryan, 2020). By encompassing a range of subjects within a single profile, content creators can deliver a well-rounded experience to their followers; for example, an athlete might post content that relates to their personal life, professional life, to the athlete's sport, other sports, a repost from a post previously posted by someone else, etc. (Geurin-Eagleman & Burch, 2016).

The influence of social media content categories on engagement behavior can be significant, as categories enable creators to tailor their content to specific segments of their audience, enhancing relevance and resonance (Dolan et al., 2016). Followers are more likely to engage with posts that align with their interests and motivations, resulting in higher likes, comments, shares, and saves (Vale & Fernandes, 2018). Moreover, content categories establish a sense of predictability in posting schedules, encouraging followers to return during specific times to engage with anticipated content (Klimsa, 2017).

Distinct content categories also broaden audience engagement by catering to various preferences within a single account (Newman et al., 2013). This prevents content from becoming monotonous and appeals to a wider range of followers, thereby promoting a more engaged and active community (Sutera, 2013). Similarly, offering various types of content may lead to deeper interaction and discussion around specific subjects (Sanderson, 2011). Followers with a keen interest in a particular category are more likely to participate in meaningful conversations, thereby fostering a sense of community and belonging (Kietzmann et al., 2011).

Analyzing engagement patterns within different content categories yields valuable insights into audience preferences and behavior; creators can identify which categories generate the most engagement, helping them refine their content strategy and optimize their posting schedule (Vale & Fernandes, 2018). This data-driven approach enhances the overall quality of content and its ability to spark interactions (Ryan, 2020).

The algorithms that decide which pieces of content are shown in a user's social media feed often reward content with higher engagement by granting it increased visibility (Hubspot, 2023). Consistent engagement within specific content categories can therefore boost the overall reach and discoverability of an account's posts. This mechanism further underscores the importance of delivering content that resonates strongly with the audience (Kietzmann et al., 2011).

It can therefore be reasoned that social media content categories serve as a strategic tool for organizing and delivering a variety of content types, thus influencing different engagement behaviors. By offering targeted content, broadening audience engagement, fostering community, providing insights, and aligning with algorithmic mechanisms, content categories enhance the overall user experience, deepen audience connections, and contribute to the success of content creators and brands in the dynamic landscape of social media (Newman et al., 2013; Na et al., 2020). This leads to the proposed TikTok content categories applied in this study, which are defined and explained in Table 1.

Table 1. Definitions of content categories for this study

Content Category	Definition and Explanation
Active personal life	TikTok videos in this category capture moments of the celebrity athlete's everyday experiences, from daily routines to hobbies and interests. These videos may showcase the athlete's interactions with friends and family, their creative pursuits, or even their leisure activities, offering viewers an authentic glimpse into their personal world beyond their professional life or online persona (Geurin-Eagleman & Burch, 2016). Such content fosters a sense of relatability and connection with the persons as fans get to see the more genuine and unfiltered aspects of their life (Arai et al., 2014; Sokolova & Kefi, 2020).
Aesthetic personal life	These TikTok videos emphasize a celebrity athlete's aesthetics over showcasing their general active personal or professional life by focusing on visually appealing content, such as fashionable looks, stylish photoshoots, or poses with a sensual or alluring undertone; furthermore, these videos may prioritize aesthetics, visual storytelling, and creative editing techniques to present a polished and curated image (Kim & Sagas, 2014; Barta et al., 2023). Viewers can expect to see an emphasis on the athlete's fashion sense, visual self-presentation, or overall aesthetic preferences, with the aim to inspire or captivate their audience through visual attraction (Sokolova & Kefi, 2020).
Active athlete life	This category features TikTok videos that capture moments from an athlete's sports competitions, training sessions, or on-the-field performances. Respective videos may offer highlights of their athletic prowess, key achievements, or memorable game moments, providing fans with an exciting and immersive look into their professional journey (Geurin-Eagleman & Burch, 2016). This type of content can provide viewers with an understanding of the athlete's commitment, expertise, and the hurdles they encounter in their sports career (Arai et al., 2014).
Non-active or non-sport athlete life	TikTok videos that portray a celebrity athlete in a non-active, non-sport situation in their professional life typically may feature behind-the-scenes glimpses of their off-field experiences, such as interviews, media appearances, or moments from their daily life as a sports personality. Such videos can provide insights into their personality, interests, or off duty activities, allowing fans to connect with them on a more personal level beyond their athletic endeavors (Sanderson, 2011; Arai et al., 2014). The videos might show the athlete engaging in discussions, charity work, promotional events, or other aspects of their professional career outside of the physical demands of their sport (Sutera, 2013).
TikTok games	TikTok videos in this category present the celebrity athlete playing interactive TikTok games by engaging with popular challenges, trends, or games within the platform. The videos may highlight the athlete's sense of humor, creativity, and ability to participate in the TikTok community's viral trends, which includes taking on various challenges, participating in duets, or attempting fun and lighthearted activities that resonate with TikTok's interactive and entertaining nature (Zuo & Wang, 2019; Su et al., 2020).
Promotion of or information about products and services	This category presents the celebrity athlete promoting or informing about specific products or services they are involved with. In these videos, the person typically shows or explains the benefits and features of the endorsed items in a relatable and engaging manner; this could include product demonstrations, endorsements, or testimonials that highlight the athlete's personal connection to the brand or service (Haenlein et al., 2020; Brooks et al., 2021). The athlete might use a call-to-action in the video or its copy to encourage viewers to have a closer look at the promoted product or service and, ultimately, make the purchase (Yocco, 2016).

User Engagement Behaviors

Ryan (2020) emphasizes the significance of user engagement behaviors in social media by defining social media as "the umbrella term for web-based software and services that allow users to come together online and exchange, discuss, communicate and participate in any form of social interaction" (p. 220). Vale and Fernandes (2018) dive deeper into these characteristics and propose a framework outlining three tiers of engagement on social media. The first level, which is the most common, is consumption. This involves basic and passive behaviors like viewing posts, watching videos, and reading comments. The second level, termed contribution, entails more active interactions such as liking, commenting, saving, and sharing. These actions demand greater effort than mere consumption and demonstrate heightened user interest in the product or brand. The third tier, creation, necessitates the most effort. It involves the active generation and sharing of user-generated content related to a brand or product. This type of content, such as informative reviews and commentary, has the potential to encourage other users to engage in consumption, contribution, and creation.

Based upon these features, athletes should recognize the importance of the different types of engagement on social media due to the impact on their personal brand, audience connection, and overall effectiveness as influencers (Sutera, 2013). Engagement behaviors encompass a range of interactions, as mentioned above, with a strong emphasis on discussions and further interests that occur around shared content (Kietzmann et al., 2011). Such interactions go beyond mere follower count, reflecting genuine interest and connection. High fan engagement on social media signals a strong and active fanbase, bolstering an athlete's credibility and influence (Na et al., 2020; Sokolova & Kefi, 2020). Moreover, engagement algorithms on platforms prioritize content that generates more interaction, amplifying the reach of posts and attracting a wider audience (Ryan, 2020).

For celebrity athletes, engagement behaviors offer a unique opportunity to forge a deeper connection with fans, given that direct interaction can foster a sense of intimacy, allowing followers to feel acknowledged and valued (Sanderson, 2011; Fetchko et al., 2018). This emotional bond translates to increased loyalty and advocacy, as engaged fans are more likely to champion the athlete's endeavors, from competitions to endorsement campaigns (Mahmoudian et al., 2021). Additionally, engagement behaviors provide valuable insights into audience preferences and opinions (Vale & Fernandes, 2018). Celebrity athletes can gather feedback, refine their content strategy, and tailor their messaging for better resonance (Sutera, 2013).

Table 2. Definitions of user engagement behaviors for this study

Engagement Behavior	Definition
Views	TikTok video views refer to the count of how many times a video has been watched by users on the TikTok platform.
Likes	TikTok video likes represent the number of times users have tapped the "heart" icon to express their appreciation or approval of a particular video on the TikTok platform.
Comments	TikTok comments are written responses or reactions from users in the form of text that are posted with a video to express thoughts, opinions, or engage in discussions directly or indirectly related to the content.
Saves	TikTok video saves refer to the action users take to bookmark or save a video for later viewing within their TikTok account.
Shares	TikTok video shares indicate the number of times a video has been shared by users to their own TikTok profiles, with other users, or other social media platforms, expanding its reach to a broader audience.

In the competitive landscape of influencer marketing, brands seek influencers with not only a large following, but also active engagement (Haenlein et al., 2020). Strong engagement ensures that promotional content reaches a receptive audience, driving better results for both the athlete and the partnering brands (Brooks et al., 2021). Understanding and fostering engagement behaviors on social media is indispensable for athlete influencers, as it nurtures authenticity, expands reach, cultivates loyalty, and optimizes collaboration with brands, all of which are pivotal for sustained success in the dynamic world of influencer marketing (Sutera, 2013; Arai et al., 2014; Haenlein et al., 2020; Mahmoudian et al., 2021). Accordingly, users' engagement behaviors applied in this study are defined in Table 2.

Research Question and Conceptual Model

The discussion above established the theoretical foundation for the research question guiding this study, which is defined as follows: "How do individual TikTok content categories, including (1) active personal life, (2) aesthetic personal life, (3) active athlete life, (4) non-active or non-sport athlete life, (5) TikTok games, and (6) promotion of or information about products and services, influence user engagement behaviors, such as (a) video views, (b) likes, (c) comments, (d) saves, and (e) shares, on the official TikTok account of celebrity athlete and influencer Alisha Lehmann?" Figure 1 offers a visual representation of the conceptual framework and the posited associations.

Figure 1. Conceptual model

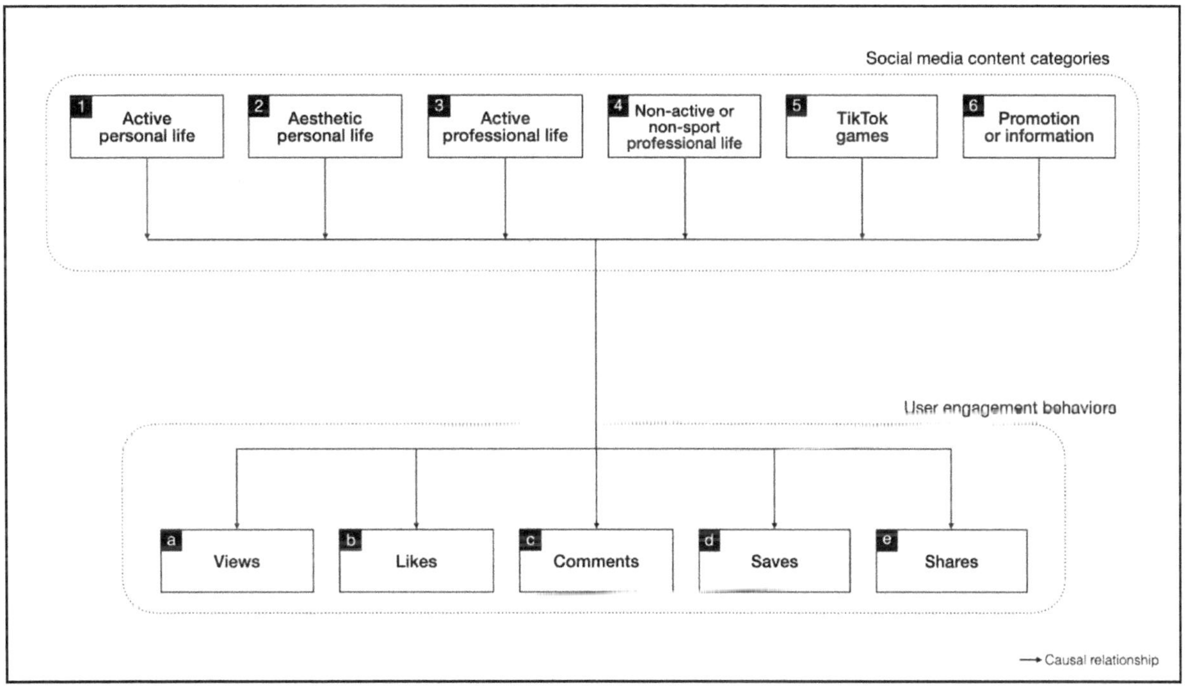

METHODOLOGY

This study includes the categorization of video content through thematic coding and a multiple regression analysis to investigate associations between the categorized content and users' engagement behaviors. Data was collected from a sample of 91 TikTok videos published on Alisha Lehmann's official TikTok account between 30 June 2022 and 12 August 2023. All videos that were published within the mentioned timeframe, were manually categorized, i.e., coded, according to the discussion in the theoretical background section. Additionally, user engagement behavior metrics for the sampled videos, including the number of views, likes, comments, saves, and shares for each video, were documented in the same spreadsheet on 19 August 2023. All values were standardized, i.e., converted to the same scale, to allow for an accurate analysis of the proposed associations. A multiple regression analysis was then applied in SPSS to measure the causal relationships between the defined variables. A step-by-step explanation of the data collection and standardization process is offered in the following section.

Data Collection and Standardization Process

Step 1: Preparing the spreadsheet. The first step of the data collection process includes preparing a spreadsheet in which all necessary data is recorded. For this study, it includes the following columns: Video date (i.e., when the video was posted), content URL (i.e., the URL under which the specific TikTok video can be accessed), copy of the post (i.e., the text that complements the video), info (i.e., information about the content in the video that helps the researchers categorize the video; a possible categorization, i.e., thematic code, that refers to one of the defined social media content categories in Table 1, is added in this column, which will then be used in the formal categorization of each video that follows in Step 3), channel followers (i.e., the number of followers at the time of posting the respective video), the number of video likes, saves, shares, comments, and views. The columns are mainly chosen based on the technical features available for user engagement behaviors on a respective social media platform, as discussed in the previous section.

Step 2: Access and recording of the necessary values. All videos that need to be analyzed in the research are accessed, ideally in reverse-chronological order to keep better track of the recorded data. While accessing each video, the above-mentioned data is recorded in the spreadsheet. All data can be retrieved from the access page of each individual video, except for the number of channel followers at the time of posting the video. Certain websites offer easy and free access to the evolution of channel followers. For this study, the website socialblade.com was utilized. If such data cannot be found on third-party websites, further research needs to be undertaken and approximate values need to be calculated for each post on its posting date.

Step 3: Extension of the spreadsheet with video content categories and recording of respective values. The spreadsheet is extended with columns that represent the final content categories. This formal categorization is based upon the respective information recorded in the info column in Step 1. If the previously recorded information, i.e., the thematic content analysis, is unclear or lacks important details, the respective video should be viewed again and additional details should be recorded. Finally, each video is attributed to a content category code (Saunders et al., 2023). For this research, the defined content categories include the following: active personal life, aesthetic personal life, active athlete life, non-active or non-sport athlete life, TikTok games, and promotion or information. The coding is done by recording the value "1" in the content category column which is sought to best represent what the video displays or conveys; the value "0" is recorded in all other content category columns; this process is repeated for each video. With this, all data necessary to analyze the assumed causal relationships is recorded.

Step 4: Normalization of engagement behavior values. Values recorded for engagement behaviors on each video need to be normalized, as they vary in strength according to the number of channel followers on the date the video was published (Cvijikj & Michahelles, 2013). Therefore, additional columns are created, specifically for each normalized engagement behavior value. This is done by dividing the original engagement behavior value, e.g., video likes, by the number of channel followers on the date of publishing the video. In the case at hand, the names of the columns for the normalized engagement behavior value include the ending '_ratio' to better visualize the meaning of the column.

Step 5: Standardization of content category and normalized engagement behavior values. Standardizing data for regression analysis ensures the fair treatment of variables with different scales and units (Saunders et al., 2023). The mean and standard deviation should be calculated for each variable, i.e., all content categories and all engagement behaviors, using Excel functions such as AVERAGE and STDEV, placing these calculations at the bottom of each respective column. Next, new columns for each variable that needs to be standardized are created. The Excel formula STANDARDIZE can be used to standardize all respective values. This process is repeated for all variables that are to be included in the regression analysis. Once this step is completed, the regression analysis can be undertaken.

Step 6: Multiple regression analysis to assess causal relationships between content categories and engagement behaviors. Following the methodological examples of Cvijikj and Michahelles (2013), Vale and Fernandes (2018), and Doyle et al. (2020), the hypothesized causal relationships presented above were investigated through a multiple regression analysis. Regression analysis is a valid choice for evaluating causal relationships between social media content categories and user engagement behaviors, as it quantifies how changes in content types relate to changes in engagement metrics; by examining the statistical significance of these relationships, empirical evidence of causation is offered, aiding researchers in understanding the impact of different content categories on user engagement (De Vries et al., 2012). This method allows for precise modeling, control of confounding factors, and robust statistical inferences, making it a legitimate and widely accepted approach in social media research for investigating causality (Vale and Fernandes, 2018; Saunders et al., 2023).

DATA ANALYSIS

This research applies an exploratory approach to investigate the causal relationships between video content categories and users' engagement behaviors on a celebrity athlete's TikTok channel. Because of that, a pragmatic and context-sensitive methodology regarding statistical significance is employed to maintain the credibility of the findings. A detailed explanation is offered in the following sections.

Statistical Significance

Statistical significance levels, i.e., the *p*-value, are typically set at 0.05 (5%), 0.01 (1%), or 0.001 (0.1%) and play a critical role in hypothesis testing within scientific research (Saunders et al., 2023). However, setting such a threshold without considering the context of the study can lead to several issues (Argamon, 2017). For one, it is essential to recognize that the above-mentioned significance levels are an arbitrary convention and not all research questions or disciplines require the same level of confidence (Berry, 2016). Some fields, such as medical research, may demand a more stringent threshold to minimize the risk of false positives, while others, like social sciences, may allow for a higher level of error to avoid missing potentially important effects (Argamon, 2017).

Thus, it can be argued that in exploratory research in a marketing and communications context, such as this study, a higher *p*-value might be acceptable, as it can lead to the discovery of novel findings. For instance, Lew (2016) explains that one of the two types of *p*-values "shows what the data say" (p. 3), which is the technical aim of this study. Similarly, and in support of the previous argument, Tong (2019) suggests that "exploratory analysis of data from a confirmatory study (sub-sequent to the completion of the preplanned analysis) should also be entertained, for the purpose of hypothesis *generation* rather than hypothesis *testing*" (p. 256, italics in original).

Consequently, while the above-mentioned significance levels are common benchmarks, their application is deemed inappropriate within the specific context of this exploratory study. Therefore, a flexible and context-aware approach to determining statistical significance is applied in the respective data analysis and discussion to ensure the reliability and validity of the presented findings.

Results

Of the 91 videos analyzed for this study, 25 (27%) were categorized as active personal life, 18 (20%) as aesthetic personal life, 13 (14%) as active athlete life, 13 (14%) as non-active or non-sport athlete life, 11 (12%) as TikTok games, and 11 (12%) as promotion of or information about products and services. This suggests a stronger emphasis on videos about Alisha Lehmann's personal life followed by videos about her life as an athlete. Findings resulting from the multiple regression analysis of the variables discussed above focus on the statistical significance levels of all tested causal relationships, of which a visualization is provided in Figure 1, and an overview is offered in Table 3. Results show that videos related to Alisha Lehmann's active professional life have by far the strongest statistical significance in relation to video views (R3a, p<.001; β=.441), likes (R3b, p<.001; β=.462), comments (R3c, p=.003; β=.362), saves (R3d, p=.002; β=.365), and shares (R3e, p=.002; β=.363) compared to all other content categories. The second-strongest degree of statistical significance is found in videos that portray her personal life from an aesthetic perspective, with influence on video shares (R2e, p=.128; β=.184) and saves (R2d, p=.261; β=.135). Videos about Alisha Lehmann's non-active or non-sport professional life offer the third-strongest level of statistical significance. Within the category, the strongest impact is found on video likes (R4b, p=.292; β=.118) and on comments (R4c, p=.365; β=.106); the other engagement behaviors are impacted to a similarly weak degree in the following order: views (R4a, p=.427; β=.089), saves (R4d, p=.437; β=.091), and shares (R3e, p=.449; β=.088). Next, again, videos of Alisha Lehmann's personal life with emphasis on aesthetics are found to influence video likes (R2b, p=.524; β=.073) and comments (R2c, p=.599; β=.063) to a comparably weak degree; in comparison, this content category's effect on video views (R2a, p=.881; β=.017) can be considered very weak. Videos in which

Alisha Lehmann plays TikTok games all have a considerably weak or close to no impact on engagement behavior in the following order: video comments (R5c, p=.706; β=.043), likes (R5b, p=.785; β=.030), saves (R5d, p=.871; β=.019), views (R5a, p=.921; β=.011), and shares (R5e, p=.952; β=.007). Similarly, videos that promote or inform about products endorsed by Alisha Lehmann have a noticeably weak or close to no influence on video shares (R6e, p=.799; β=.029), likes (R6b, p=.883; β=-.016), saves (R6d, p=.963; β=-.005), views (R6a, p=.984; β=-.002), and comments (R6c, p=.984; β=-.002). The video content category active personal life was excluded from the analysis due to collinearity issues. Based on these results, it can be summarized that active professional life has the most significant impact on engagement behaviors, followed by aesthetic personal life and non-active or non-sport professional life. The content categories TikTok games and promotion and information have a considerably weaker and even inconsiderable degree of statistical significance compared to the previously mentioned categories, and videos from Alisha Lehmann's active personal life need to be revisited to better understand what caused the variable to be excluded from the analysis.

Excluded Content Category Variable

SPSS excluded the videos from the content category active personal life from the undertaken multiple regression analysis due to collinearity issues, as collinearity indicates a strong linear relationship between two or more independent variables; this occurred, because it became difficult for the regression model to distinguish the unique contributions of each variable, leading to unstable and unreliable coefficient estimates (Field, 2018; Saunders et al., 2023). To maintain the integrity of the regression analysis and ensure meaningful results, SPSS automatically excluded the highly collinear variable.

DISCUSSION

The subsequent discourse provides insights into the presented outcomes in Table 3 while presenting theoretical findings and practical implications.

Theoretical Findings

Results of this study suggest that videos on Alisha Lehmann's official TikTok account, featuring her as a popular, young, female footballer being active in her professional life, wield by far the most significant, positive influence on her followers. This is indirectly supported by Geurin-Eagleman and Burch's (2016) study on how Olympic athletes' present themselves on Instagram, which found that the most popular content category based on follower likes were Instagram photos of an athlete's professional life. Similarly, a study by Doyle et al. (2022) suggests that social media content centered around athletic performance garners higher levels of consumer engagement compared to other types of content.

Moreover, the respective videos from Alisha Lehmann's active professional life serve as a source of inspiration and empowerment for her followers, who might see her as a representative of the contemporary, successful European female football player. This is comparable to how the media crafted Neymar Jr.'s identity in his early professional years, presenting him as the modern representation of "futebol-arte" within the "mulatto nation" (Andrews et al., 2016). Nevertheless, in the case at hand, Alisha Lehmann's

Table 3. Regression analysis results

Causal Relationship	IV	DV	*p*	*β*	*Information*
R1a	Active personal life	Views	n/a	n/a	Excluded from analysis due to collinearity issues
R1b		Likes			
R1c		Comments			
R1d		Saves			
R1e		Shares			
R2a	Aesthetic personal life	Views	.881	.017	-
R2b		Likes	.524	.073	
R2c		Comments	.599	.063	
R2d		Saves	.261	.135	
R2e		Shares	.128	.184	
R3a	Active professional life	Views	<.001	.441	-
R3b		Likes	<.001	.462	
R3c		Comments	.003	.362	
R3d		Saves	.002	.365	
R3e		Shares	.002	.363	
R4a	Non-active or non-sport professional life	Views	.427	.089	-
R4b		Likes	.292	.118	
R4c		Comments	.365	.106	
R4d		Saves	.437	.091	
R4e		Shares	.449	.088	
R5a	TikTok games	Views	.921	.011	-
R5b		Likes	.785	.030	
R5c		Comments	.706	.043	
R5d		Saves	.871	.019	
R5e		Shares	.952	.007	
R6a	Promotion or information	Views	.984	-.002	-
R6b		Likes	.883	-.016	
R6c		Comments	.984	-.002	
R6d		Saves	.963	-.005	
R6e		Shares	.799	.029	

Note. IV: independent variable, DV: dependent variable, *p*: strength of statistical significance, *β*: standardized regression coefficient.

image is crafted by herself through her social media posts and presence, as she controls her own social media channels and reaches millions of followers while circumventing traditional media outlets.

By showcasing her dedication, skills, and commitment to her profession as an athlete, she not only fosters admiration, but also motivates her followers to become more engaged and share their views and their interest with others online (Sutera, 2013). As they watch her being active in her life as an athlete, they can connect on a deeper level with her professional journey, feeling a sense of shared aspiration and pride in her achievements, which strengthens their loyalty and compels them to watch her videos repeatedly (Mahmoudian et al., 2020). These arguments contradict the argument by Abidin (2021), who notes that TikTok prefers post-based virality over persona-based fame. The contradiction is further supported by this study's results showing that videos in the category non-active or non-sport professional life have a relatively significant and positive influence on video likes and comments. This implies that Alisha Lehmann's followers are interested in her life as an athlete in general. Furthermore, videos in the category aesthetic personal life have a relatively significant and positive influence on video shares and saves. This supports the notion that Alisha Lehmann's followers are interested in a holistic presentation of her persona, an argument posited by Arai et al. (2014) and Geurin-Eagleman and Burch (2016).

Videos that are categorized as promotional or informational are found to have a statistically insignificant influence on any of the investigated engagement behaviors in this study. It can be reasoned that TikTok users are generally motivated to use the platform for the pursuit of entertainment and self-expression, and less to gather information or receive promotional messages (Zuo & Wang, 2019). Nevertheless, this does not mean that Alisha Lehmann's followers are not influenced to purchase a promoted product by these videos; it simply means that her followers do not interact with the videos, but the purchase intention might still be affected (Darmatama & Erdiansyah, 2021).

Similarly, videos showing how Alisha Lehmann plays TikTok games, have a weak or irrelevant statistical significance on users' engagement behaviors. This contradicts the general notion that TikTok emphasizes entertainment over other video categories (Zuo & Wang, 2019; Su et al., 2020). However, this argument should be considered within a broader context. TikTok games offer just one facet of the platform's entertainment possibilities, i.e., interactive challenges or activities within a specific setting that users can participate in (TikTok, 2023).

Practical Implications

The findings of this study highlight the importance of prioritizing TikTok content related to a celebrity athlete's active professional life. In this case, Alisha Lehmann's videos related to her life as an athlete garnered the highest statistical significance in terms of user engagement behavior, i.e., video views, likes, comments, saves, and shares. This suggests that fans and followers are highly engaged when athletes like her provide glimpses into their training routines, matches, and behind-the-scenes moments on social media (Sutera, 2013; Geurin-Eagleman & Burch, 2016). For content creators and athletes seeking to increase their online presence and engagement, focusing on sharing their professional journey and accomplishments can be an effective strategy on TikTok.

The second most significant content category was videos emphasizing aesthetics in the personal life of Alisha Lehmann. These videos have a notable impact on video shares and saves, although they may not have the same level of engagement as those related to her professional life. This finding suggests that viewers are interested in telling others about or revisiting videos showing personal aspects of a female athlete's life outside of their sport, especially with emphasis on visually appealing content, such as trendy outfits, chic photoshoots, or poses with an enticing allure (Sokolova & Kefi, 2020). While visually appealing aesthetics can contribute significantly to shaping a brand experience (Brakus et al., 2009; Pine & Gilmore, 2020), celebrity athletes such as Alisha Lehmann must be mindful of ethical concerns associated with sexually suggestive content. Such content has the potential to overly emphasize physical attractiveness, potentially overshadowing the athlete's athletic achievements and perpetuating stereotypes (Kim & Sagas, 2014).

Videos related to Alisha Lehmann's non-active or non-sport professional life also had a certain degree of statistical significance, particularly in terms of likes and comments. This indicates that viewers are interested in her broader career and pursuits as a celebrity athlete beyond her work on the pitch. Similar content creators should therefore consider to share behind-the-scenes glimpses of their off-field experiences, such as interviews, media appearances, moments from their daily life as a sports personality or other professional endeavors, as it can enhance their follower engagement and brand presence (Sanderson, 2011; Arai et al., 2013). With the above in mind, content creators should conceptualize and plan their contents to strike a balance between showcasing the influencer's professional and personal sides, thereby offering content that covers a broader range of interests and, thus, pleases a wider target audience (Baetzgen & Tropp, 2013; Hu et al., 2014).

On the other hand, TikTok games and promotional content demonstrated considerably weaker or even close to no effect on engagement behaviors. TikTok games, while entertaining, did not significantly drive likes, comments, saves, views, or shares. Similarly, videos promoting or informing about products endorsed by Alisha Lehmann had limited or no influence. For marketers and content creators, this suggests that these content categories may not be as effective for generating engagement on TikTok compared to other types of content. However, further research should be undertaken on these videos' importance in the context of a holistic brand experience. Pine and Gilmore (2020) and Schmitt (1999) suggest that a brand experience is based upon an aesthetic, emotional, cognitive, and behavioral dimension and can foster loyalty. Thus, it can be argued that the entertaining nature of TikTok games videos and the informational nature of promotional videos might add a certain indirect value to the holistic brand experience, even if only subliminal and without direct causal effect on engagement behavior.

CONCLUSION

This study answers the research question, "How do individual TikTok content categories, including (1) active personal life, (2) aesthetic personal life, (3) active athlete life, (4) non-active or non-sport athlete life, (5) TikTok games, and (6) promotion of or information about products and services, influence user engagement behaviors, such as (a) video views, (b) likes, (c) comments, (d) saves, and (e) shares, on the official TikTok account of celebrity athlete and influencer Alisha Lehmann?" by analyzing 91 TikTok videos published on Alisha Lehmann's official TikTok account between 30 June 2022 and 12 August 2023 through a multiple regression analysis. The analysis sheds light on the impact of various content categories on follower engagement and offers theoretical and practical implications for academics, students, content creators, and marketers. Notably, Alisha Lehmann's active professional life, exemplified by videos showcasing her athletic prowess, emerged as the most influential content category, eliciting the highest levels of user engagement in terms of views, likes, comments, saves, and shares. This underscores the importance of athletes and content creators prioritizing content related to their professional journey and accomplishments as a means to foster admiration, motivation, and audience loyalty. The second most significant content category was videos highlighting Alisha Lehmann's personal life through aesthetics or aesthetically, which notably impacted video shares and saves. While these videos may not match the engagement levels of videos showcasing her active professional life, they underline the value of providing a holistic representation of an athlete's persona, including their personal style and lifestyle, to engage a broader audience. Additionally, videos presenting Alisha Lehmann's non-active or non-sport professional life had a certain degree of significance, particularly regarding likes and comments, suggesting that viewers are interested in a celebrity athlete's broader career pursuits beyond sports. However, TikTok games and promotional content demonstrated limited or close to no impact on engagement behaviors, signaling that these content categories may not be as effective for driving user interaction on the platform. Nevertheless, these categories could indirectly contribute to the overall brand experience, a multidimensional concept encompassing aesthetics, emotions, cognition, and behavior, which can foster brand loyalty and should not be underestimated. Ultimately, content creators and marketers should consider these findings when crafting content strategies, aiming to strike a balance between presenting an athlete's professional and personal aspects while remaining mindful of ethical considerations. The data from this study provides valuable insights into optimizing online presence and engagement on TikTok, aligning content with audience interests, and ensuring a more comprehensive representation of celebrity athletes.

LIMITATIONS AND FUTURE RESEARCH

The research at hand focuses on the official TikTok account of one influencer, i.e., celebrity athlete Alisha Lehmann; hence, its findings cannot be generalized. They solely offer insights into her content and the behavior of her followers. In order to generalize the offered findings, the study should be replicated with further and different athletes. Also, the study included all videos that were published in the time period 30 June 2022 to 12 August 2023 and neglected videos that were published before that. Possibly, more accurate results may be drawn from including further videos in the analysis. A major limitation is the exclusion of videos related to Alisha Lehmann's active personal life from the analysis due to collinearity issues. Although it is an interesting technical finding in itself, it implies that there may be complexities or overlaps in the way the given content categories are defined. Further exploration is needed to understand why this category was excluded. Lastly, the study applies a rather pragmatic approach to statistical significance by assessing significance levels according to their absolute *p*-values without setting fixed levels at 5%, 1%, or 0.1%, as it is traditionally the case. This may not necessarily be a limitation of the study, but a possibly unconventional characteristic that needs consideration and should be investigated in future research.

REFERENCES

Abidin, C. (2020). Mapping internet celebrity on TikTok: Exploring attention economies and visibility labours. *Cultural Science Journal*, *12*(1), 77–103. doi:10.5334/csci.140

alishalehmann7 on TikTok. (2023). *Alisha Lehmann official TikTok account.* https://tiktok.com/@alishalehmann7

Andrews, D. L., Lopes, V. B., & Jackson, S. J. (2015). Neymar: sport celebrity and performative cultural politics. *A Companion to Celebrity*, 421-439. doi:10.1002/9781118475089.ch23

Appel, G., Grewal, L., Hadi, R., & Stephen, A. T. (2020). The future of social media in marketing. *Journal of the Academy of Marketing Science*, *48*(1), 79–95. doi:10.100711747-019-00695-1 PMID:32431463

Arai, A., Ko, Y. J., & Kaplanidou, K. (2013). Athlete brand image: Scale development and model test. *European Sport Management Quarterly*, *13*(4), 383–403. doi:10.1080/16184742.2013.811609

Argamon, S. E. (2017). Don't strengthen statistical significance—Abolish it. *American Scientist*. https://www.americanscientist.org/blog/macroscope/dont-strengthen-statistical-significance-abolish-it

Baetzgen, A., & Tropp, J. (2013). *Brand Content: Die Marke als Medienereignis*. Schäffer-Poeschel.

Barta, S., Belanche, D., Fernández, A., & Flavián, M. (2023). Influencer marketing on TikTok: The effectiveness of humor and followers' hedonic experience. *Journal of Retailing and Consumer Services, 70*, 103149. doi:10.1016/j.jretconser.2022.103149

Basch, C. H., Yalamanchili, B., & Fera, J. (2022). Climate change on TikTok: A content analysis of videos. *Journal of Community Health, 1-5*(1), 163–167. Advance online publication. doi:10.100710900-021-01031-x PMID:34545460

Batra, R., & Keller, K. L. (2016). Integrating marketing communications: New findings, new lessons, and new ideas. *Journal of Marketing, 80*(6), 122–145. doi:10.1509/jm.15.0419

Berry, D. A. (2016). P-values are not what they're cracked up to be. Supplemental material to the ASA statement on p-values and statistical significance. *The American Statistician, 70*(2).

Blumler, J. G., & Katz, E. (1974). *The Uses of Mass Communications: Current Perspectives on Gratifications Research* (Vol. 3). Sage Annual Reviews of Communication Research.

Brakus, J. J., Schmitt, B. H., & Zarantonello, L. (2009). Brand experience: What is it? How is it measured? Does it affect loyalty? *Journal of Marketing, 73*(3), 52–68. doi:10.1509/jmkg.73.3.052

Brooks, G., Drenten, J., & Piskorski, M. J. (2021). Influencer celebrification: How social media influencers acquire celebrity capital. *Journal of Advertising, 50*(5), 528–547. doi:10.1080/00913367.2021.1977737

Chen, X., Jiao, C., Ji, R., & Li, Y. (2021). Examining customer motivation and its impact on customer engagement behavior in social media: The mediating effect of brand experience. *SAGE Open, 11*(4). Advance online publication. doi:10.1177/21582440211052256

Cvijikj, I. P., & Michahelles, F. (2013). Online engagement factors on Facebook brand pages. *Social Network Analysis and Mining, 3*(4), 843–861. doi:10.100713278-013-0098-8

Dakroub, R., Koles, B., Issa, H., & Jens, B. (2023). Instagram users' motives of social media engagement with female athletes. *The International Journal of Sport and Society, 14*(2), 173–199. doi:10.18848/2152-7857/CGP/v14i02/173-199

Darmatama, M., & Erdiansyah, R. (2021). The influence of advertising in TikTok social media and beauty product image on consumer purchase decisions. In *International Conference on Economics, Business, Social, and Humanities (ICEBSH 2021)* (pp. 888-892). Atlantis Press. 10.2991/assehr.k.210805.140

Datareportal. (2023). *Digital 2023 July Global Statshot Report (slide 164)*. https://datareportal.com

De Vries, L., Gensler, S., & Leeflang, P. S. (2012). Popularity of brand posts on brand fan pages: An investigation of the effects of social media marketing. *Journal of Interactive Marketing, 26*(2), 83–91. doi:10.1016/j.intmar.2012.01.003

Dolan, R., Conduit, J., Fahy, J., & Goodman, S. (2016). Social media engagement behaviour: A uses and gratifications perspective. *Journal of Strategic Marketing*, *24*(3-4), 261–277. doi:10.1080/0965254X.2015.1095222

Doyle, J. P., Su, Y., & Kunkel, T. (2022). Athlete branding via social media: Examining the factors influencing consumer engagement on Instagram. *European Sport Management Quarterly*, *22*(4), 506–526. doi:10.1080/16184742.2020.1806897

Fetchko, M. J., Roy, D. P., & Clow, K. E. (2018). *Sports marketing*. Routledge. doi:10.4324/9781315175614

Field, A. (2018). Discovering statistics using IBM SPSS statistics. *Sage (Atlanta, Ga.)*.

Geurin, A. N. (2017). Elite female athletes' perceptions of new media use relating to their careers: A qualitative analysis. *Journal of Sport Management*, *31*(4), 345–359. doi:10.1123/jsm.2016-0157

Geurin-Eagleman, A. N., & Burch, L. M. (2016). Communicating via photographs: A gendered analysis of Olympic athletes' visual self-presentation on Instagram. *Sport Management Review*, *19*(2), 133–145. doi:10.1016/j.smr.2015.03.002

Gómez-Suárez, M., & Veloso, M. (2020). Brand experience and brand attachment as drivers of WOM in hospitality. *Spanish Journal of Marketing-ESIC*.

Haenlein, M., Anadol, E., Farnsworth, T., Hugo, H., Hunichen, J., & Welte, D. (2020). Navigating the New Era of Influencer Marketing: How to be Successful on Instagram, TikTok, & Co. *California Management Review*, *63*(1), 5–25. doi:10.1177/0008125620958166

Hu, Y., Manikonda, L., & Kambhampati, S. (2014). What we instagram: A first analysis of instagram photo content and user types. *Proceedings of the international AAAI conference on web and social media, 8*(1), 595-598. 10.1609/icwsm.v8i1.14578

Hubspot. (2023). *6 Social Media Algorithms Marketers Need to Know About in 2023*. https://blog.hubspot.com/marketing/how-algorithm-works-facebook-twitter-instagram

Huebner, E. J. (2022). TikTok and museum education: A visual content analysis. *International Journal of Education through Art, 18*(2), 209-225. doi:10.1386/eta_00095_1

Jiang, Y., Jin, X., & Deng, Q. (2022). *Short video uprising: How# BlackLivesMatter content on TikTok challenges the protest paradigm*. https://doi.org//arXiv.2206.09946 doi.10.48550

Kietzmann, J. H., Hermkens, K., McCarthy, I. P., & Silvestre, B. S. (2011). Social media? Get serious! Understanding the functional building blocks of social media. *Business Horizons*, *54*(3), 241–251. doi:10.1016/j.bushor.2011.01.005

Kim, K., & Sagas, M. (2014). Athletic or sexy? A comparison of female athletes and fashion models in Sports Illustrated swimsuit issues. *Gender Issues*, *31*(2), 123–141. doi:10.100712147-014-9121-2

Klimsa, P. (2017). *Digitale Medienprodukte: Grundlagen der Medienproduktforschung* (Vol. 1). BoD–Books on Demand.

Klug, D., Qin, Y., Evans, M., & Kaufman, G. (2021, June). Trick and please. A mixed-method study on user assumptions about the TikTok algorithm. In *Proceedings of the 13th ACM Web Science Conference 2021* (pp. 84-92). 10.1145/3447535.3462512

Leban, M., & Voyer, B. G. (2020). Social media influencers versus traditional influencers: Roles and consequences for traditional marketing campaigns. In S. Yesiloglu & J. Costello (Eds.), *Influencer Marketing: Building Brand Communities and Engagement* (pp. 26–42). Routledge. doi:10.4324/9780429322501-4

Leo, M., & von Kuczkowski, A. (2020). *Kaufen Sie Ronaldo: Wie Facebook, Instagram und Google den Profifußball verändern*. Die Werkstatt.

Lew, M. J. (2016). Three inferential questions, two types of p-value. Supplemental material to the ASA statement on p-values and statistical significance. *The American Statistician, 70*(2).

Mahmoudian, A., Sadeghi Boroujerdi, S., Mohammadi, S., Delshab, V., & Pyun, D. Y. (2021). Testing the impact of athlete brand image attributes on fan loyalty. *Journal of Business and Industrial Marketing, 36*(2), 244–255. doi:10.1108/JBIM-10-2019-0464

Na, S., Kunkel, T., & Doyle, J. (2020). Exploring athlete brand image development on social media: The role of signalling through source credibility. *European Sport Management Quarterly, 20*(1), 88–108. doi:10.1080/16184742.2019.1662465

Newman, T., Peck, J., Harris, C., & Wilhide, B. (2013). *Social media in sport marketing*. Holcomb Hathaway.

Omar, B., & Dequan, W. (2020). Watch, share or create: The influence of personality traits and user motivation on TikTok mobile video usage. *International Association of Online Engineering*. https://www.learntechlib.org/p/216454/

Pine, B. J., & Gilmore, J. H. (2020). *The Experience Economy: Competing for customer time, attention, and money*. Harvard Business Review Press.

Ryan, D. (2020). *Understanding digital marketing: A complete guide to engaging customers and implementing successful digital campaigns*. Kogan Page Publishers.

Sanderson, J. (2011). *It's a whole new ballgame: How social media is changing sports*. Hampton Press.

Saunders, M., Lewis, P., & Thornhill, A. (2023). *Research methods for business students*. Pearson education.

Schmitt, B. (1999). Experiential marketing. *Journal of Marketing Management, 15*(1-3), 53–67. doi:10.1362/026725799784870496

Sokolova, K., & Kefi, H. (2020). Instagram and YouTube bloggers promote it, why should I buy? How credibility and parasocial interaction influence purchase intentions. *Journal of Retailing and Consumer Services, 53*, 101742. doi:10.1016/j.jretconser.2019.01.011

Su, Y., Baker, B. J., Doyle, J. P., & Yan, M. (2020). Fan engagement in 15 seconds: Athletes' relationship marketing during a pandemic via TikTok. *International Journal of Sport Communication, 13*(3), 436–446. doi:10.1123/ijsc.2020-0238

Sutera, D. (2013). *Sports fans 2.0: How fans are using social media to get closer to the game*. Scarecrow Press.

TikTok. (2023). *Gaming on TikTok*. https://www.tiktok.com/creators/creator-portal/en-us/how-to-level-up-your-gaming-content/creating-gaming-content-on-tiktok/

Vale, L., & Fernandes, T. (2018). Social media and sports: Driving fan engagement with football clubs on Facebook. *Journal of Strategic Marketing*, *26*(1), 37–55. doi:10.1080/0965254X.2017.1359655

Von Felbert, A., & Breuer, C. (2020). How the type of sports-related endorser influences consumers' purchase intentions. *International Journal of Sports Marketing & Sponsorship*, *22*(3), 588–607. doi:10.1108/IJSMS-01-2020-0009

Whiting, A., & Williams, D. (2013). Why people use social media: A uses and gratifications approach. *Qualitative Market Research*, *16*(4), 362–369. doi:10.1108/QMR-06-2013-0041

Yang, K. C., & Kang, Y. (2021). Predicting the relationships between narrative transportation, consumer brand experience, love and loyalty in video storytelling advertising. *Journal of Creative Communications*, *16*(1), 7–26. doi:10.1177/0973258620984262

Yocco, V. S. (2016). *Design for the mind: Seven psychological principles of persuasive design*. Manning.

Zhou, S., Blazquez, M., McCormick, H., & Barnes, L. (2021). How social media influencers' narrative strategies benefit cultivating influencer marketing: Tackling issues of cultural barriers, commercialised content, and sponsorship disclosure. *Journal of Business Research*, *134*, 122–142. doi:10.1016/j.jbusres.2021.05.011

Zuo, H., & Wang, T. (2019). Analysis of Tik Tok user behavior from the perspective of popular culture. *Frontiers in Art Research*, *1*(3), 1–5. doi:10.25236/FAR.20190301

ADDITIONAL READING

Frederick, E. L., Lim, C. H., Clavio, G., & Walsh, P. (2012). Why we follow: An examination of parasocial interaction and fan motivations for following athlete archetypes on Twitter. *International Journal of Sport Communication*, *5*(4), 481–502. doi:10.1123/ijsc.5.4.481

Janssen, L., Schouten, A. P., & Croes, E. A. (2022). Influencer advertising on Instagram: Product-influencer fit and number of followers affect advertising outcomes and influencer evaluations via credibility and identification. *International Journal of Advertising*, *41*(1), 101–127. doi:10.1080/02650487.2021.1994205

Smith, L. R., & Sanderson, J. (2015). I'm going to Instagram it! An analysis of athlete self-presentation on Instagram. *Journal of Broadcasting & Electronic Media*, *59*(2), 342–358. doi:10.1080/08838151.2015.1029125

Su, Y., Guo, X., Wegner, C., & Baker, T. (2023). The new wave of influencers: Examining college athlete identities and the role of homophily and parasocial relationships in leveraging name, image, and likeness. *Journal of Sport Management*, *37*(5), 371–388. doi:10.1123/jsm.2022-0192

Yuan, S., & Lou, C. (2020). How social media influencers foster relationships with followers: The roles of source credibility and fairness in parasocial relationship and product interest. *Journal of Interactive Advertising*, *20*(2), 133–147. doi:10.1080/15252019.2020.1769514

KEY TERMS AND DEFINITIONS

Alisha Lehmann: A Swiss professional women's football (soccer) player and internet celebrity.

Celebrity Athlete: A sports figure who has achieved fame and recognition beyond their athletic accomplishments, often garnering widespread media attention and a substantial fan following.

Influencer: A person who utilizes their online presence and credibility within a particular niche or industry to persuade and shape the opinions, choices, or actions of their audience, often in the context of marketing and promotion.

Internet Celebrity: A person who has gained significant fame, recognition, or a large following primarily through their activities and content on the internet, often across various online platforms and social media.

Social Media Content Categories: Distinct thematic topics or subjects under which posts and media are organized and shared on social platforms.

TikTok: A popular social media platform that allows users to create, share, and discover short-form videos.

User Engagement Behavior: Interactive actions and reactions of users, such as views, likes, comments, saves, and shares, that indicate their level of involvement and interest with posted content on social platforms.

Chapter 11
Digital Marketing Tools and Market Trends in the Skincare Industry:
Consumer Behavior and Sales Growth Insights

Lierni Castilla-Miguel
Universidad Pública de Navarra, Spain

Maria Elena Aramendia-Muneta
https://orcid.org/0000-0001-6167-3194
Universidad Pública de Navarra, Spain

ABSTRACT

The primary goal of the research is to investigate the efficiency of various digital marketing tools in the skincare industry, as well as to assess market trends and customer behavior in order to enhance sales. The study included a survey of 100 Spanish customers aged 18 to 64, and six regression models were developed to forecast sales growth based on various criteria. Transparency, sustainability, and personalized skincare products, as well as user-generated content and reviews, are highlighted as successful marketing methods to promote sales in the research. The study also emphasizes how age and gender play a significant role in this connection as well as the limited influence of influencer and celebrity marketing on skincare product sales. According to the findings, skincare firms should concentrate on developing transparent, environmentally friendly products that are customized to consumers' interests, using user-generated content and reviews in their marketing strategies to boost sales.

DOI: 10.4018/979-8-3693-0551-5.ch011

INTRODUCTION

Due to technological advancements, the skincare products industry is a highly competitive and continually expanding sector. To keep ahead of the competition, businesses must examine new market trends and the efficiency of digital marketing techniques. In this regard, the primary goal of this research is to investigate the efficacy of various digital marketing methods in the skincare products business, as well as to examine market trends and customer behavior.

The Spanish skincare market has grown steadily in recent years due to factors like increased disposable incomes and growing consumer interest in health and wellness. In fact, the skincare industry in Spain was 8.2 billion euros in 2021, with a growth of +7.8%. (Stanpa, 2021). This, together with the fact that digital marketing is growing by leaps and bounds, being one of the main ways to reach customers, makes this the right time to make a more detailed analysis of what are the market trends, and which are the most effective marketing tools.

Accordingly, this paper focuses on how to enhance skincare product sales by analyzing consumer behavior and preferences toward various product features such as transparency, personalization, and sustainability. Furthermore, the effectiveness of various marketing strategies, such as influencer marketing, celebrity endorsement, user-generated content, and reviews, in increasing skincare product sales is examined.

Although little research has been done on digital marketing as a marketing tool and its effectiveness and there is also research on skincare market trends, there is no specific research that analyzes in depth the specific marketing tools for this sector and the effect of the current trends. Furthermore, the analyses performed, while not conducted many years ago, may be out of date due to the rapidly evolving market. As a result, it is critical to keep industry trends and customer behavior analyses up to date so that businesses may select the most effective marketing techniques.

The limitations of the actual literature have led brands to lack guidance on the effectiveness of these tools and consumer preferences. Through this analysis, cosmetic companies and brands can acquire the necessary knowledge to take informed decisions about the strategies for their products, taking into account their effectiveness and depending on the segment they want to target.

The study aims to evaluate the effect of marketing strategies on the consumer's buying behavior of skincare products. Therefore, the general objective is to investigate the variables that influence consumers to buy skincare products and the impact of different marketing strategies. For that matter, the specific objectives are to analyze if sustainability, personalization, and transparency are factors increasing skincare product sales and the effect of different marketing strategies on the sales of this kind of product.

The study emphasizes the value of user-generated content and reviews, personalized skincare products, transparency, sustainability, and user-generated content as successful marketing methods to boost sales. On the contrary, it highlights the little impact celebrity and influencer marketing has on purchases of skincare products as well as the significance of age and gender in this connection.

Finally, the study remarks on the effectiveness of understanding consumer preferences and behaviors when developing effective marketing strategies in the highly competitive skincare industry. The study's findings can assist skincare firms in making educated decisions to better their marketing strategies and, as a result, increase sales in the competitive skincare sector.

EVOLUTION OF SKINCARE PRODUCT MARKETING

Marketing is the process of generating, communicating, and providing value to consumers to fulfill their wants and expectations (Kotler et al., 2017). This concept highlights the necessity of understanding consumer needs and delivering products and services that meet those demands using various tools and tactics.

Marketing dates to ancient times when traders and merchants employed numerous ways of promoting their goods. However, modern marketing as we know it today emerged in the early 1920s, driven by the rise of mass production and the necessity for enterprises to stand out in a crowded market.

Edward Bernays had a key role in the evolution of modern marketing. He considered that it should be focused on understanding consumer psychology and then using that information to generate convincing messages that can affect consumers (Bernays, 1928). Since then, the use of psychology to influence consumer behavior has been a fundamental component of marketing.

During the 1950s and 1960s, marketing experienced a considerable transformation as a result of the emergence of the marketing concept. This principle prioritized customer interests and needs by suggesting that businesses should focus on providing value for them over simply selling goods (Levitt, 1960). As an outcome, various methods and strategies were developed in response to this shift including market research intended to more precisely identify desirable niches or audiences to target.

Furthermore, the advancement of digital technology in the last 50 years has had a significant effect on marketing. The markets now have an extensive variety of tactics to engage and converse with their clients due to the internet and social media which also facilitate gathering data about consumers for analysis and shaping appropriate marketing strategies that will boost sales. Consequently, revolutionary marketing approaches have emerged.

Over the past few decades, advances in technology and society have had an impact on the skincare industry. Customers' buying behaviors regarding cosmetics have undergone a shift recently. This change is due to more people understanding that artificial compounds could harm both skin and the environment; therefore, natural component products are becoming increasingly popular leading to an increase in demand for them. Consequently, this situation gives rise to innovative marketing strategies like eco-friendly packaging or previously unavailable treatments primarily driven by customer preferences towards cosmetic goods today.

In addition, Spain's skincare industry is full of competition. Many companies both native and foreign engage in a battle for dominance of the market, catering to consumers at every level from those preferring more affordable options such as Nivea or Garnier up to luxury brands like Yves Saint Laurent, Clinique, or Estée Lauder. This can be seen illustrated by price competitiveness coupled with aggressive promotional tactics designed to grab customer attention which include a range of advertising efforts along with influencer marketing initiatives alike.

Also in Spain, as in many other countries, social media has become a crucial channel for skincare brand marketing, with platforms like Instagram and TikTok giving companies a chance with younger consumers and increasing brand recognition. Influencer marketing has gained in popularity, with firms collaborating with social media influencers to promote their products and reach a large audience. Spanish influencers including such as Teresa Bass, María Pombo, Alexandra Pereira, and Rocio Osorno have participated in skincare brand partnerships in order to promote products to their followers.

Regulation is also an important consideration for skincare brands operating in Spain. The European Union has strict regulations governing the safety and labeling of cosmetic products, and brands must ensure that their products comply with these regulations to avoid fines or legal action (European Commission, 2023).

NEW TRENDS OF SKINCARE PRODUCTS AND SETTING HYPOTHESES

As already mentioned, the skincare sector has grown significantly in recent years, and skincare product marketing has evolved in accordance. Consumers are more aware of the components, and they seek brands to their specific demands. As a result, skincare companies are promoting their products differently, with a focus on personalization, sustainability, and transparency.

Transparency

Transparency is becoming more popular in the skincare industry, with customers increasingly seeking honesty and authenticity from firms. This trend is being pushed by factors such as the rise of social media and e-commerce, which have increased customer access to product information and reviews while also raising consumer awareness of green and unethical production techniques.

Transparency is being incorporated into brand marketing initiatives by offering clear and concise information about their products and ingredients. This includes publishing the entire ingredient list, the sourcing and manufacturing procedures, and any testing or certifications that the product has received. Some brands additionally provide information about their products' environmental and social impact, such as their carbon footprint or support for ethical sourcing techniques (Mamun et al., 2020).

Brands like The Ordinary have made transparency a core part of their brand identity, emphasizing their commitment to providing clear and honest information about their products (Montemayor, 2022). This company offers detailed product descriptions and ingredient lists on its website, as well as a glossary of skincare terms to help consumers make informed choices.

Brands are implementing transparency into their marketing by answering freely and honestly to consumer comments and concerns, in addition to offering information about their products. This includes responding to bad reviews and complaints, as well as providing consumers with information and resources to assist them in making informed decisions.

Transparency in skincare marketing helps consumers while also assisting brands in building trust and reputation. According to Label Insight, 94 percent of consumers are more inclined to remain loyal to a company that provides transparency (Label Insight, 2016).

However, there are difficulties for firms when it comes to establishing openness in skincare marketing. It may be time-consuming and expensive to provide detailed information regarding ingredients and manufacturing procedures, so businesses must make sure that their claims are true and verifiable. Additionally, the skincare sector is controlled by a complicated network of laws and norms, which can make it challenging for firms to manage the legal system.

Based on this information, the first hypothesis of the analysis will be to see if transparency in skincare products increases sales. The first hypothesis is:

H1: Transparency in skincare products will lead to an increase in sales.

Personalization

Consumers demand solutions that address their own skin concerns and needs, and companies have responded by providing personalized skincare routines. One way marketers are doing this is by analyzing customer data and developing individualized skincare routines depending on their skin type, age, and other specific criteria.

Brands such as L'Oréal or Neutrogena are using AI algorithms to analyze customer data and create personalized skincare routines based on factors such as skin type, age, and lifestyle habits. For example, L'Oréal uses AI to create a custom skincare formula based on a customer's skin analysis, environmental factors, and daily routines (Dominguez, 2022).

However, worries regarding privacy and data protection are generated by the employment of AI technology to analyze client data (Infosecurity Magazine, 2019). Brands must make sure they are following data protection laws and are open and honest about their data-gathering procedures.

According to Grand View Research, the worldwide customized skincare market will be worth USD 48.65 billion by 2028, expanding at 8.0% CAGR from 2023 to 2030, (Grand View Research, 2021). This expansion is being driven by rising demand for individualized skincare products as well as the availability of technology that allows businesses to give personalized solutions to their clients.

Specific skincare routines not only provide tailored solutions to customers but also increase customer engagement and loyalty. According to a Deloitte analysis, personalized skincare is an effective strategy for firms to differentiate themselves from the competition and strengthen consumer relationships (Deloitte, 2019). Brands may create a sense of exclusivity and make their customers feel valued and understood by offering individualized items.

In order to check if personalized skincare products affect these products' sales, the second hypothesis is settled:

H2: Personalized skincare products will lead to an increase in sales.

Sustainability

Another skincare marketing trend is sustainability. Consumers are becoming more conscious of the environmental effects of their purchases, and they choose eco-friendly and sustainable items. Sustainability is becoming a crucial driver of purchasing decisions in the skincare business, according to a McKinsey & Company analysis (McKinsey & Company, 2021).

Eco-friendly ingredients are one way firms are incorporating sustainability into their marketing efforts. Some companies, for example, use organic or plant-based components that are environmentally produced and biodegradable. Others utilize reused or recycled packaging materials, such as recycled plastic or biodegradable materials like bamboo or paper (Morgan, 2020). Lush, for example, has made sustainability a central component of their corporate identity, highlighting its dedication to eco-friendly ingredients, packaging, and manufacturing procedures (Latana, 2021).

In addition, brands are also focusing on sustainable production practices regarding the production process. For example, some brands are implementing sustainable farming practices, such as regenerative agriculture or sourcing from small-scale farmers (Morgan, 2020). Others are using renewable energy sources in their production facilities, such as solar or wind power (Morgan, 2020).

Implementing sustainable methods in skincare marketing, on the other hand, might present some problems for brands. Sustainable products and packaging may be more expensive than standard alternatives, and green manufacturing techniques may necessitate significant investment. Brands must strike a balance between their sustainability ambitions and their budgetary limits, while also ensuring that their efforts are genuine and transparent to consumers.

For the analysis of sustainable skincare products the following hypotheses have been stated:

H3: Sustainable skincare products will lead to an increase in sales.

MARKETING TOOLS IN THE SKINCARE INDUSTRY AND SETTING HYPOTHESES

In the very competitive skincare market, several companies compete for customers' attention. Companies are always examining and enhancing their marketing strategies to stand out in this crowded industry. Celebrity endorsement, influencer marketing, customer reviews, and user-generated content are just a few of the ongoing marketing strategies that have become increasingly popular in the skincare industry in recent years. Skincare companies use these approaches to interact with customers, foster trust, and increase sales.

Celebrity Endorsement

Celebrity endorsement is a marketing tactic used by businesses to advertise their goods or services by asking famous people to do so. Skincare businesses may boost brand recognition and earn credibility by collaborating with a celebrity. This is because celebrities have a vast fan base of admirers who view them as gurus on beauty and skincare.

The skincare sector often uses celebrity endorsement. One of the most common ways is through social media. These companies often use celebrities with large followings on platforms such as Instagram, Twitter, and Facebook to promote their products by opting to pay them for sponsored posts, where a celebrity uploads a photo or video to promote a product, or product placements, where a celebrity includes a product in their skincare routine and shares it with their followers.

Traditional forms of advertising, including print and television commercials, also employ celebrity endorsements. Famous people are frequently used by firms as brand ambassadors, whereby the celebrity serves as the brand image and is highlighted in promotional materials (Xiong et al., 2021). Given that customers have a strong association between the celebrity and the company thanks to this form of endorsement, it may be extremely powerful.

Spanish skincare brands like Natura Bissé, Germaine de Capuccini, and MartiDerm have all collaborated with celebrities to promote their products. For example, MartiDerm has partnered with Spanish football player Alexia Putellas, who has a large social media following, to promote their skincare products. This partnership has helped this brand to gain more visibility and attract new customers (Martín, 2021).

In the Spanish skincare market, celebrity endorsement may boost sales and brand recognition. According to a Statista Global Consumer Survey, Spanish consumers are likely to buy things recommended by their favorite celebrities since they tend to trust their recommendations (Mena Roa, 2022). For instance, L'Oréal witnessed a rise in sales when Eva Longoria promoted the brand's skincare products (Ad Age, 2020).

However, there are risks for celebrity sponsorship. A celebrity endorsement may be expensive, and not every star is a suitable fit for every company. In addition, if the celebrity endorser gets involved in a scandal or issue, there is a chance of bad publicity.

The actress Paula Echevarria, who formerly served as an Olay brand ambassador, can serve as an illustration of this. In 2019, Paula shared a picture on Instagram where it was apparent that she had altered her figure using editing tools. This caused a lot of controversy on social media, and fans criticized the actress heavily since they believed that this technique encouraged unhealthy and impossible beauty standards (Mujerhoy, 2019). The actress's reputation as well as the brand suffered as a result, which may have influenced Olay product sales.

Influencer Marketing

In the skincare sector, influencer marketing often entails collaboration with individuals who have a sizable fan base on social media sites like Instagram, YouTube, and TikTok. These influencers frequently provide content that highlights the skincare items they use daily, share their opinions on the items, and offer guidance on how to have healthy, radiant skin. This kind of material is compelling and has a great potential for attracting customers and convincing them to buy the products (Aramendia-Muneta, 2015; Xiong et al., 2021).

Another method skincare companies may collaborate with influencers is through the development of sponsored content, in which an influencer posts or creates a video supporting a product. The law states that users need to be aware when they are seeing promoted or paid material, so the influencer needs to add some element like #ad o similar while promoting (Velasco, 2019). The skincare company may reach a bigger audience and increase brand recognition thanks to this sort of relationship.

The advantage of influencer marketing over traditional advertising in the skincare industry is that it is less expensive. Skincare companies may work with micro-influencers, who have a more limited but highly engaged following, and pay them less than a celebrity endorser would. Influencer marketing may also provide more authentic content and higher engagement rates since influencers are frequently seen as more accessible and reliable than conventional celebrities.

One benefit of influencer marketing in the Spanish skincare industry is that it enables businesses to connect with a larger and more varied audience. Skincare brands may collaborate with Spanish influencers from various areas, whose following represent the diversity of the nation. This may be especially useful when advertising goods that address certain skin issues or types.

The potential of unfavorable publicity if the influential endorser is implicated in a scandal or controversy is one of the key drawbacks. Furthermore, there is a risk that the influencer's material will not fit with the brand's values or messaging. Furthermore, Spanish consumers are becoming more cautious and critical of influencer marketing, which can lead to skepticism and distrust if the material does not look authentic (Lastra, 2022). The following hypothesis is thus proposed:

H4: Celebrity endorsements and influencer marketing do not impulse sales of skincare products

User-Generated Content

User-generated content (UGC) has developed into a powerful marketing strategy in the cosmetics industry. Due to the expansion of social media channels, customers are sharing their experiences with skincare products more than ever before. This trend has led to businesses embracing user-generated content to sell their goods and have more direct interactions with consumers.

UGC refers to any content contributed by users rather than the brand itself. This can include consumer-created social media postings, reviews, and even videos. According to surveys, 85 percent of customers believe UGC is more powerful than brand-created content (Oladipo, 2022). This is because UGC is perceived as more genuine and trustworthy. Consumers may observe the effects of the product on actual individuals rather than relying just on the brand's promises.

Skincare brands have taken advantage of this trend by incorporating UGC into their marketing strategies. For example, Natura Bissé, a popular skincare brand in Spain, has used UGC as a key part of its marketing strategy. The company encourages its followers to share their experiences and results on its social networks using the hashtag #NaturaBisse.

UGC is now being used by other businesses in their marketing initiatives. For instance, the L'Oréal-owned skincare line Kiehl's includes a section on their website titled "Customer Favorites.". Reviews and ratings left by users who have bought and tried the items are included in this area. Additionally, the company encourages users to use the hashtag #kiehls when posting their experiences on social media.

It is also used through channels other than TikTok or Instagram. A great example of how a typical retail firm may change its marketing approach to incorporate user-generated content is Sephora. Customers of Sephora may interact with one another and share their own beauty experiences, advice, and suggestions on a website called the Beauty Insider Community (Rice, 2019). With the help of this UGC-based strategy, this firm has been able to develop a devoted following of clients who love to spread the word about their favorite cosmetics.

Finally, since it enables companies to interact with customers on a more personal level, user-generated content (UGC) has been effectively employed in skincare marketing. Instead of depending just on the assertions made by the company, customers may see how the product performs on real people. By enabling customers to connect with others who are curious about skincare, UGC provides a feeling of community around the company.

In order to analyze the relation between user-generated content and the increase in sales of skincare products, the next hypotheses have been settled:

H5: User-generated content is an effective marketing strategy that increases sales.

Customer Reviews

Customer reviews in the skincare industry can give useful information about the efficacy and quality of products as perceived quality is one of the most significant factor in influencing consumers' purchase intention in this sector (Lee et al., 2019). These reviews can help skincare firms find areas for development and alter their marketing strategy accordingly. Furthermore, these ratings can assist businesses in identifying trends in consumer preferences and adjusting their product ranges to better match customer wants.

Offering incentives to customers who submit reviews, like discounts or free samples, is one method skincare companies may use to promote user feedback. Customers are motivated to return to the business by this, which also encourages them to submit reviews.

The public display of client evaluations on a company's website or social media platforms is another way skincare businesses can use them as a marketing tactic. Companies may increase their credibility with targeted buyers and demonstrate the value and efficiency of their products by showing favorable

Table 1. Summary of hypotheses settled

	Hypotheses
1	H1: Transparency in skincare products will lead to an increase in sales.
2	H2: Personalized skincare products will lead to an increase in sales.
3	H3: Sustainable skincare products will lead to an increase in sales.
4	H4: Celebrity endorsements and influencer marketing do not impulse sales of skincare products
5	H5: User-generated content is an effective marketing strategy that increases sales.
6	H6: Skincare product reviews increase sales.

client feedback. Furthermore, skincare companies can leverage customer reviews by incorporating them into their advertising campaigns. This can be done through social media posts or paid ads, where the company can highlight positive reviews from satisfied customers.

For next hypothesis will be analyzed in order to see the relation between skincare products and sales if confirmed:

H6: Skincare product reviews increase sales.

A summary of all hypotheses can be seen in Table 1.

MODERATING EFFECT: GENDER AND AGE GROUP

Numerous studies have been conducted recently on gender differences in social networks and internet usage. Men and women often employ the same platforms, yet there are substantial behavioral and motivational variations between the groups.

First, the majority of people who buy cosmetics and personal care items are women. In Spain, for instance, women account for 59% of the market, compared to men's 41% (Gómez-Salgado et al., 2020) This is also demonstrated by the fact that they are more active than males in the following accounts and profiles linked to personal care and beauty on social media. Moreover, women spend more time on social media than males do, and they use the internet more frequently (7%) now (Marketing News, 2018)

Additionally, there is a big difference between how men and women of different age groups utilize social networks. According to investigations, 1.7%of women and 1.2% of males between 13–17 years, use social networks. In contrast, just 4.7% of males and 6.2%of women in the 55 to 64 age range have social media profiles (García, 2021). However, the proportion between the males and females is more equal in the 25–34 age bracket.

In terms of how people consume beauty-related content, males prefer videos and tutorials on websites like YouTube, while women typically look for advice and suggestions on blogs, forums, and social media. Additionally, compared to males, women often post more social media material on self-care and beauty (Twenge & Martin, 2020).

METHODOLOGY

Analyzing the impact of digital marketing strategies on consumer behavior concerning skincare products is a topic of great interest from both academic and business perspectives. The skincare industry is highly competitive and digital marketing has become a critical tool for companies to reach and engage with their target audience. Therefore, understanding how these strategies influence consumer behavior is essential for companies to optimize their marketing efforts, increase sales and gain a competitive advantage.

In addition, the skincare industry is dynamic and continually evolving, with new products and trends appearing regularly. Digital marketing is a powerful platform for companies to present their products to consumers and educate them on the benefits of their offerings. By analyzing the effectiveness of these strategies, companies can stay abreast of the latest industry trends and adapt their marketing efforts accordingly. In that line, this research will also analyze how sustainability, transparency and personalization are affecting consumers' behavior towards skincare products.

Due to the nature of the study, the most appropriate research design is conclusive. This method aligns with the objectives of the paper, that is testing hypotheses to finally reach conclusions used as input for decision making. Quantitative data will be collected through statistical techniques, to be later analyzed.

Sampling Method

The target population of the research consists of Spanish citizens of legal age. According to INE, 39,415,017 people over eighteen years old resided in Spain in April 2023. To narrow this wide universe, the sampling frame of the study is made up of Spanish individuals from 18 to 64 years old. This range of age has the biggest consumption of skincare products, hence it is the most suitable for this research. Another reason why this sub-group is better fitted is the penetration of the Internet it exhibits with a percentage of usage higher than 94% according to INE (2022). The sampling plan is stratified according to two variables: gender (male and female) and age group (18-34; 35-54; 55-64).

To obtain this sample size from the population of the study, it was assumed a confidence level of 95% and a dispersion of (p = q = 0,5). The sample size consists of 100 Spanish consumers, who were administered an online survey during the month of April 2023. The share of questionnaires in each stratum is proportional to the corresponding value of Spanish Internet users therefore the sample is representative (Table 2).

Nevertheless, the applied sampling method was stratification by age group and gender.

Table 2. Spanish internet users: Population and sample distribution by age group and gender (own elaboration based on INE, 2022)

Population Distribution (N = 39.415.017)			Sample Distribution (n = 100)	
Age Group / Gender	**Male**	**Female**	**Male**	**Female**
18 to 34 years old	4,896,383	4,733,310	16	16
35 to 54 years old	7,169,590	7,229,203	23	23
55 to 44 years old	3,230,605	3,847,579	10	12
Total	15,296,578	15,810,092	49	51

Table 3. Questionnaire structure

Section	Subsection	Items	Questions
		Frequency	1 to 2
	1. Transparency	Perception	3 to 6
		Behavioral response	7 to 8
		Frequency	9 to 10
1. Skincare Market trends	2. Personalization	Perception	11 to 14
		Behavioral response	15 to 16
		Frequency	17 to 18
	3. Sustainability	Perception	19 to 22
		Behavioral Response	23 to 24
		Frequency	25 to 26
	1. Celebrities /Influencers	Perception	27 to 29
		Behavioral Response	30 to 31
		Frequency	32 to 33
2. Marketing strategies	2. User-generated content	Perception	34 to 36
		Behavioral Response	37 to 38
		Frequency	39 to 40
	3. Reviews	Perception	41 to 43
		Behavioral Response	44 to 45
3. Demographic	Gender and Age group	Gender and Age group	46 and 47

Data Collection

For data collection purposes, Spanish consumers were given an online questionnaire for self-completion. This survey format was chosen due to its several time-saving benefits. Data is collected immediately, and the database can be automatically analyzed, speeding up the process of gathering information. Other reasons were the anonymity involved and the high rates of response to online surveys.

The questionnaire starts with an introduction and is structured into three sections. Firstly, the pollster, the aim and the structure of the survey are introduced. Some aspects are clarified in this part such as its anonymity, academic nature and an explanatory note about the different terms appears. In the first section, it gathers questions about the different skincare market trends (sustainability, transparency, and personalization). The second section is devoted to questions about the different marketing strategies mentioned in the literature review (Table 3). In the last part, information is gathered about the gender and age of respondents, as the sampling method of the study is stratified by these two criteria.

Measures

Frequency has been used in the questions to measure the regularity of some factors that affect the purchase of skincare products. In this type of question, the Likert scale is used, and respondents are provided with 5 possible response options: 1. Always, 2. Usually, 3. Sometimes, 4. Rarely, 5. Never. In this way, it is intended to be able to evaluate the frequency of time that individuals have performed or pretend to perform one of the activities they are asked about.

In the first part of the survey, which asks questions about trends, these types of questions are asked to measure the following aspects:

- Frequency of purchase of transparent/personalized/sustainable skincare products.
- Frequency of searching for information on transparent/personalized/sustainable skincare products.
- Frequency of purchasing transparent/personalized/sustainable skincare products in the future.
- Frequency of recommending transparent/personalized/sustainable skincare products in the future.
In the second section, some questions related to digital marketing strategies are set out:
- Frequency of purchasing skincare products on the recommendation of influencers or celebrities/ content creators/reviews.
- Frequency in which a product has been known via influencers or celebrities/ content creators/ reviews.
- Frequency of purchase of skincare products via recommendation of influencers or celebrities/ content creators/ reviews.
- Frequency in which people will recommend others to follow the recommendations of influencers or celebrities/ content creators/reviews about skincare products.

By measuring these questions, a clear picture of the consumer's usual behavior and what behavior to expect from them in the future will be constructed. In summary, the frequency measure in surveys is a useful tool to assess the frequency with which consumers perform certain activities related to the purchase of skincare products.

In addition, perception has also been used as an evaluative method. In this case, the perception of some factors about skincare products has been asked in order to know how they affect the purchase decision. For this purpose, some statements have been established and 5 options have been given following the Likert scale (1. Strongly agree, 2. Agree, 3. Neither agree nor disagree, 4. Disagree, 5. Strongly disagree).

In the first part of the survey, consumers were asked how they perceive products with sustainable, transparent, and personalized characteristics. These were the aspects analyzed:

- Perception of quality of transparent/personalized/sustainable skincare products.
- Perception of the healthiness of transparent/personalized/sustainable skincare products.
- Quality-price perception of transparent/personalized/sustainable skincare products.

The second part of the survey focused on measuring consumer perception of marketing strategies and their actors:

- Perception of the honesty of influencers and celebrities/content creators/reviews.
- Perception of publicity of influencers and celebrities/content creators/reviews.
- Perception of the use of the products recommended by influencers and celebrities/content creators/ reviews.

In conclusion, consumer perception is a useful tool in surveys to assess how factors affect the purchase decision for skincare products. By using the Likert scale, consistent responses can be obtained and con-

Table 4. Descriptive analysis H1

	Mean	Std. Deviation
Buy skincare products that are transparent in their composition	2.75	0.968
Look about transparent skincare products	3.17	1.129
Transparent skincare products have more quality	2.47	0.915
Transparent skincare products are healthier	2.63	0.849
I would pay more for a product if I perceived that the brand/product is transparent	2.52	0.948
I prefer to buy skincare products with clear and transparent ingredient composition	2.37	0.787
I am considering buying transparent skincare products next year	2.67	0.975
I will recommend others to buy transparent skincare products/brands	2.95	0.968

sumers' perceptions of quality, healthiness, value for money and marketing strategies can be measured. Consumer perception can help skincare brands understand how consumers view their products and how they perceive influencers and celebrities in advertising campaigns.

Preference is another variable measured in this study and refers to the choice a person makes between two or more options. In this case, it measures whether consumers of skincare products choose a series of factors in the products over those that do not. To do this, using a Likert scale, consumers are asked their preference for transparent, personalized, and sustainable skincare products and they choose one of the options: (1. Strongly agree, 2. Agree, 3. Neither agree nor disagree, 4. Disagree, 5. Strongly disagree).

- Preference of transparent/personalized/ sustainable skincare products over the ones that are not.

EMPIRICAL ANALYSIS

The sample of respondents in the database follows the distribution described in Table 2. It is a representative depiction of the Spanish consumer population. Regarding their age group, 16%, 23%, and 10% of men belong to the groups 18-34, 35-54 and 55-64 years old, respectively, while 16%, 23%, and 12% of women belong to the groups 18-34, 35-54 and 55-64 years old, respectively.

The database was examined using the statistical program IBM SPSS Statistics 28.0 to get results. The research employs both descriptive and inferential methodologies. The mean and standard deviation are used to summarize data to find trends. Several statistical techniques, including Spearman correlation coefficient and ANOVA, were used to test the various hypotheses. Furthermore, six regression models are built to forecast the increase in sales based on various factors.

ANALYSIS AND DISCUSSION OF RESULTS

Transparent Skincare Products

In the analysis of transparency in skincare products will lead to an increase in sales, the results show great volatility in consumer responses about the frequency, perception, and preference of transparent skincare

Table 5. Spearman correlation coefficients H1

	Transparent Skincare Products Have More Quality	Transparent Skincare Products Are Healthier	I Would Pay More for a Product if I Perceived That the Brand/Product Is Transparent
Buy skincare products that are transparent in their composition	0.662**	0.546**	0.862**
I would pay more for a product if I perceived that the brand/ product is transparent.	0.801**	0.651**	-

products. This means that there is a lot of disparity between what people think and could indicate that there are age or gender subgroups with different tendencies.

Still, it can be seen in Table 4 how the mean indicates that consumers have bought transparent skincare products sometimes or usually (2.75) and that they agree with the statement that they prefer transparent skincare products over non-clear ones (2.37).

Based on Spearman's correlation analysis (Table 5), it is found that a strong and significant correlation (0.862) exists between the frequency of purchasing transparent skincare products and a willingness to pay a higher price for these items. The results further indicate that people who frequently purchase transparent skincare products do so because they believe these products align with their personal preferences and higher quality and healthier perception.

Furthermore, the study reveals that individuals who perceive transparent skincare products as superior in quality and health are also more likely to pay a higher price for these items. This is supported by the positive and significant correlations (0.801 and 0.651, respectively) between the two variables and the price-quality perception variable (Table 5).

To test whether Transparency in skincare products will lead to an increase in sales a regression model has been developed. In this regression model about the frequency of buying transparent skincare products, the results aimed to assess the relationship between the dependent variable "Buying skincare products that are transparent about their composition" and five predictors. These predictors are:

- I am considering buying skincare products from transparent brands.
- Skincare products with clear and transparent components are of better quality.
- You recommend other people to buy skincare products from transparent brands.
- I prefer buying skincare products with a clear and transparent ingredient composition.
- Skincare products with greater transparency in their composition and creation process are healthier).
- Constant.

The results (Table 6) show that the model has a statistically significant relationship with the dependent variable, as evidenced by the significant F change value of <.001. The R square value of .533 indicates that the model explains 53.3% of the variability in the dependent variable. In other words, the five predictors in the model can explain more than half of the variance observed in the dependent variable.

The ANOVA (Table 6) shows that the regression model's sum of squares is 49.417, which is statistically significant (p<.001). This means that the model's predictors are collectively contributing to the

Table 6. Regression model H1

Regression Model Summary	
R	0.730
R Square	0.533
Sig. F Change	<.001
ANOVA	
Sum of Squares (regression)	49.417
Sig.	<.001

Table 7. Regression model coefficient H1

	B	Std. Error	Beta	Sig.
Transparent skincare products have more quality	0.638	0.122	0.603	<.001

explanation of the dependent variable. The residual sum of squares is 43.333, indicating that there is still some unexplained variability in the dependent variable that is not accounted for by the model.

In the coefficients, the variable" Skincare products with clear and transparent components are of better quality" has the strongest relationship with the dependent variable, with a Beta of .603 and a significance level of <.001 (Table 7). The other three predictors, have smaller levels of significance or do not have statistically significant relationships with the dependent variable, with non-significant p-values (Sig. > .05).

Overall, the results suggest that consumers are more likely to buy skincare products that are transparent about their composition when they perceive that clear and transparent components indicate higher quality and when they receive recommendations from others to buy from transparent brands. However, there may be other factors that influence this decision, as evidenced by the unexplained variability in the dependent variable.

Personalized Skincare Products

In addition, personalized skincare products will lead to an increase in sales analysis showing great volatility in consumer responses about the frequency, perception, and preference of personalized skincare products. For instance, the statement "Personalized skincare products have more quality" has a lower standard deviation of .841, indicating that most participants agreed with this statement. On the other hand, the statement " I would pay more for a personalized skincare product " has a higher standard deviation of 1.056, indicating there may be different opinions depending on gender or age group.

In addition, it can be seen in Table 8 how the mean indicates that people have bought these products with a medium frequency during the last year (2.77) and that they perceived these products as a higher quality (2.02). Moreover, people generally consider buying personalized products sometimes or rarely in the upcoming year.

Table 8. Descriptive analysis H2

	Mean	Std. Deviation
Buy personalized skincare products	2.77	1.196
Look about personalized skincare products	2.72	1.198
Personalized skincare products have more quality	2.02	0.841
Personalized skincare products are healthier	2.57	0.879
I would pay more for a personalized skincare product	2.42	1.056
I prefer to buy personalized skincare products	2.55	0.880
I am considering buying personalized skincare products next year	2.20	0.932
I will recommend others to buy personalized skincare products/brands	2.38	0.962

Some relevant Spearman correlation Coefficients are shown in Table 9. The statement "Personalized skincare products have more quality" had a weak and positive correlation with the statement "I prefer to buy personalized skincare products" (.259). This suggests that participants who believe that personalized skincare products have more quality are also more likely to prefer buying personalized products. However, there was no significant correlation between the statement about quality and the willingness to pay more for personalized skincare products.

In addition, the statement "Personalized skincare products are healthier" has a moderate and positive correlation with the willingness to pay more for personalized skincare products (.306). This suggests that participants who think that personalized skincare products are healthier were also more willing to pay more for them.

The statement "Look about personalized skincare products" has a strong and positive correlation with the intention to buy personalized skincare products (.708). This suggests that participants who actively sought out information about personalized skincare products are more likely to buy these products more frequently. Additionally, this statement had a moderate and positive correlation with the preference for buying personalized skincare products (.288), indicating that those who search for information about these products are more likely to prefer buying them.

Overall, these correlations suggest that there are some positive relationships between beliefs about the quality and health benefits of personalized skincare products, willingness to pay more for them, and the preference for buying them. Additionally, actively seeking out information about personalized skincare products is strongly associated with buying them.

Table 9. Spearman correlation coefficients H2

	Personalized Skincare Products Have More Quality	Personalized Skincare Products Are Healthier	Look About Personalized Skincare Products
Buy personalized skincare products	0.045	0.416**	0.708**
I would pay more for a personalized skincare product	0.123	0.306**	-0.203**
I prefer to buy personalized skincare products	0.259**	0.289**	0.288**

Table 10. Regression model H2

Regression Model Summary	
R	0.593
R Square	0.351
Sig. F Change	<.001
ANOVA	
Sum of Squares (regression)	49.809
Sig.	<.001

Moreover, to analyzed what does influence the frequency of buying transparent skincare products, a regression model has been constructed. It is completed by the dependent variable "Buy personalized skincare products " and six predictors. These predictors are:

- I am considering buying personalized skincare products next year.
- Personalized skincare products have more quality.
- I will recommend others to buy personalized skincare products/brands.
- I prefer to buy personalized skincare products.
- Personalized skincare products are healthier.
- Constant.

R is the correlation coefficient that measures the strength and direction of the linear relationship between the dependent variable (Buy personalized skincare products) and the independent variables (predictors) used in the model. In this case, R is 0.550, which indicates a moderate positive correlation between the dependent variable and the predictors (Table 10).

R Square represents the proportion of variance in the dependent variable that can be explained by the independent variables in the model. In this case, R Square is 0.303, which means that 30.3% of the variance in the dependent variable can be accounted for by the predictors included in the model (Table 10).

Based on the information obtained from the analysis, the regression model appears to be significant in predicting customers' preferences for customized skincare products (Table 10). The ANOVA shows that the regression model is significant ($p < .001$), indicating that at least one of the predictors included in the model is a significant predictor of the dependent variable.

In Table 11 some of the significant coefficients of the regression model can be seen. The unstandardized coefficient (B) represents the change in the dependent variable associated with a one-unit change in the independent variable while holding other variables constant. For instance, a one-unit increase in

Table 11. Regression model coefficient H2

	B	Std. Error	Stand. Beta	Sig.
I prefer to buy personalized skincare products	0.577	0.126	0.405	<.001
Personalized skincare products are healthier.	0.361	0.101	0.319	<.001

the variable " Personalized skincare products are healthier" is associated with a 0.319 increase in the dependent variable.

In addition, data suggests that preference affects the frequency of buying this type of product, meaning that people who prefer to buy personalized skincare products do buy them more frequently (Table 11). This is supported by the positive B and the <.001 p-value, confirming the significance relation.

Sustainable Skincare Products

Concerning sustainable skincare products will lead to an increase in sales hypothesis, on average, respondents somewhat agree to seek information on sustainable skincare products, with a mean score of 2.97. In addition, the majority of respondents (with a mean score of 2.65) prefer to buy sustainable skincare products rather than conventional products.

Regarding respondents' opinions on the quality and healthiness of sustainable skincare products, most of them (with a mean score of 2.96) think that these products are of better quality compared to conventional products. However, there is some variability in respondents' answers, suggesting that not all respondents agree with this statement. In addition, consumers also think that sustainable products are healthier (with a mean score of 2.91), although there is also variability in the responses. In terms of willingness to pay more for sustainable skincare products, respondents have a mixed opinion, with a mean score of 2.52 on the Likert scale.

Looking at Spearman's Coefficient Table (Table 13), there are several significant correlations between the variables. For example, there is a positive correlation between searching for information on sustainable skincare products and the frequency of buying them (0.403), indicating that those who are

Table 12. Descriptive analysis H3

	Mean	Std. Deviation
Buy sustainable skincare products	2.46	0.989
Look about sustainable skincare products	2.97	1.058
Sustainable skincare products have more quality	2.65	1.048
Sustainable skincare products are healthier	2.96	1.091
I would pay more for a sustainable skincare product	2.91	0.954
I prefer to buy sustainable skincare products	2.52	1.049
I am considering buying sustainable skincare products next year	2.47	0.893
I will recommend others to buy sustainable skincare products/brands	2.53	1.000

Table 13. Spearman correlation coefficients H3

	Sustainable Skincare Products Have More Quality	Sustainable Skincare Products Are Healthier	Look About Sustainable Skincare Products
Buy sustainable skincare products	0.283**	-	0.403**
I would pay more for a sustainable skincare product	0.337**	0.300**	-

more interested in sustainable skincare products are more likely to purchase sustainable products more often. Similarly, there is a positive correlation between perceiving sustainable skincare products to be of better quality and being willing to pay more for them (0.337), suggesting that consumers who believe in the higher quality of sustainable skincare products are more likely to pay a premium price for them.

In addition, The Spearman correlation coefficient of .283 (Table 13) indicates that consumers who are more likely to buy sustainable skincare products also tend to believe that they have higher quality compared to non-sustainable skincare products. Moreover, the correlation coefficient of .403 suggests a relatively strong positive relationship implying that consumers who perceive sustainable skincare products as healthier are more likely to perceive them as having higher quality as well.

Furthermore, the willingness to pay more and perceive higher quality (0.337) and between willingness to pay more and perceive healthier (.300) both suggest moderate positive relationships. This indicates that consumers who are willing to pay more for sustainable skincare products also tend to perceive them as having higher quality and being healthier.

The regression model is constructed in order to forecast the influence of the variables selected in the frequency of buying sustainable skincare products. The dependent variables included in the model are:

- Sustainable skincare products have more quality.
- I prefer to buy sustainable skincare products.
- I am considering buying sustainable skincare products next year.
- I will recommend to others to buy sustainable skincare products/brands.
- Sustainable skincare products are healthier.
- Constant

The model summary (Table 14) provides information on the goodness of fit of the regression model. The R square value of .479 indicates that approximately 47.9% of the variance in buying sustainable skincare products can be explained by the predictors included in the model. This suggests that the model has a moderate level of predictive power.

The ANOVA table (Table 14) provides information on the statistical significance of the regression model. The regression sum of squares of 46.416 is significantly larger than the residual and has a p-value of <.001. This indicates that the predictors included in the model significantly contribute to the prediction of the frequency of buying sustainable skincare products.

Table 14. Summary: Regression model H3

Regression Model Summary	
R	0.692
R Square	0.479
Sig. F Change	<.001
ANOVA	
Sum of Squares (regression)	46.416
Sig.	<.001

Table 15. Regression model coefficient H3

	B	Std. Error	Stand. Beta	Sig.
Sustainable skincare products have more quality.	0.120	0.072	0.133	0.098
I am considering buying sustainable skincare products next year.	0.592	0.096	0.535	<.001

Overall, the results of the regression analysis indicate that there is a significant relationship between the predictors included in the model and the dependent variable of buying sustainable skincare products. Specifically, consumers who perceive sustainable skincare products as being healthier, and having better quality, and who prefer and consider buying sustainable skincare products are more likely to buy them more frequently.

In relation to the coefficients of the multiple regression analysis conducted to determine the relationship between several predictors and the dependent variable of buying sustainable skincare products. Table 15 presents the results of the analysis in terms of the coefficients for each predictor.

The predictor "I consider buying sustainable skincare products" has a significant positive effect on buying sustainable skincare products, with a standardized coefficient of .535. This suggests that consumers who consider buying sustainable skincare often in the next years are more likely to currently buy them.

The predictor "Recommend other people to buy sustainable skincare products" also has a significant positive effect on buying sustainable skincare products, with a standardized coefficient of .222. This indicates that consumers who recommend sustainable skincare products to others are also more likely to buy them themselves.

Celebrity Endorsement and Influencer Marketing

In general, results show that consumers generally do not believe in celebrity endorsements and influencer marketing and it does not have a strong influence on their skincare product purchases. The mean score for the statement "I have purchased a skincare product on the recommendation of an influencer or celebrity" is 3.94 (Table 16), indicating that most consumers neither agree nor disagree with this statement. Similarly, the mean score for the statement "I consider buying skincare products on the recommendation of

Table 16. Descriptive analysis H4

	Mean	Std. Deviation
I have purchased a skincare product on the recommendation of an influencer or celebrity	3.94	1.023
I have discovered a skincare product by way of an influencer or celebrity	3.81	1.089
I think that influencers' and celebrities' recommendations are sincere	3.85	0.989
I think influencers and celebrities don't do under-covered advertisements	3.89	0.963
I believe that the influencers and celebrities use the products they recommend	3.48	0.893
I am considering buying skincare products on the recommendation of influencers or celebrities next year	3.94	1.099
I will recommend others to follow the recommendations of influencers or celebrities	4.19	0.849

Table 17. Spearman correlation coefficients H4

	I Have Discovered a Skincare Product by Way of an Influencer or Celebrity	I Think That Influencers' and Celebrities' Recommendations Are Sincere	I Think Influencers and Celebrities Don't do Under-Covered Advertisements
I have purchased a skincare product on the recommendation of an influencer or celebrity	0.422**	0.851**	0.911**
I think influencers and celebrities don't do under-covered advertisements	0.421**	0.780**	-

influencers or celebrities next year" is equally 3.94 (Table 16), suggesting that consumers are somewhat neutral about purchasing skincare products based on the recommendations of influencers or celebrities.

The mean score for the statement "I think that influencers' and celebrities' recommendations are sincere" is 3.85, while the mean score for the statement "I believe that the influencers and celebrities use the products they recommend" is 3.48, indicating that consumers are somewhat skeptical about whether influencers and celebrities use the products they promote and their sincerity.

Looking at the Table 17, there are significant positive correlations. For example, there is a strong positive correlation (0.851) between "I think that influencers and celebrities' recommendations are sincere" and "I consider buying skincare products on the recommendation of influencers or celebrities". This suggests that those who believe that influencer and celebrity recommendations are sincere are more likely to consider buying skincare products based on their recommendations.

Similarly, there is a strong positive correlation (0.911) between "I think influencers and celebrities don't do under-covered advertisements" and "I believe that the influencers and celebrities use the products they recommend". This suggests that those who believe that influencers and celebrities are not engaged in covert advertising are more likely to believe that they use the products they recommend. Additionally, there is a positive and significant correlation (0.780) that suggests that people who think that influencers' and celebrities' recommendations are sincere are also likely to think that they do not engage in under-covered advertisements.

The regression analysis aimed to predict the frequency people purchase skincare products recommended by influencers or celebrities. The regression model included six predictor variables, namely:

Table 18. Summary: Regression model H4

Regression Model Summary	
R	0.946
R Square	0.894
Sig. F Change	<.001
ANOVA	
Sum of Squares (regression)	92.706
Sig.	<.001

- I will recommend others to follow influencers' or celebrities' recommendations.
- I have discovered a skincare product by way of an influencer or celebrity.
- I think influencers and celebrities use the products they recommend.
- I consider buying skincare products based on influencer or celebrity recommendations.
- I think influencers and celebrities don't do under-covered advertisements.

The regression analysis resulted in a highly significant model, as indicated by the ANOVA results ($p < .001$). The model accounted for a substantial proportion of the variance in the outcome variable, with an R-squared value of .894. (Table 18).

The regression model coefficient table (Table 19) shows that two predictor variables were significantly related to the outcome variable. First, the variable "I think that influencers' and celebrities' recommendations are sincere" has a positive and significant relationship with the outcome variable ($b = .297$, $p < .001$, std. beta = .287). Second, the variable " I think influencers and celebrities don't do under-covered advertisements" has an even stronger positive relationship with the outcome variable ($b = .732$, $p < .001$, std. beta = .689).

Overall, these results suggest that people are more likely to purchase skincare products recommended by influencers or celebrities if they perceive them to be sincere and trustworthy and if they believe that they are not engaging in hidden advertising.

Lastly, Table 20 data shows the results of a crosstabulation analysis between gender, age group, and the frequency with which individuals consider buying skincare products based on recommendations from influencers or celebrities next year. The data is organized into five frequency categories: always, often, sometimes, rarely, and never.

Overall, the data suggests that women are more likely than men to consider buying skincare products based on influencer or celebrity recommendations. Of the women, 14 (27.5%) said they always or often consider buying skincare products based on influencer or celebrity recommendations, compared to only 2 (4.1%) of men.

The age group also appears to be related to the frequency with which individuals consider buying skincare products based on influencer or celebrity recommendations. Among individuals aged 18-34, 21 (65.6%) said they always, often, or sometimes consider buying skincare products based on influencer or celebrity recommendations, compared to 15 (32.6%) of individuals aged 35-54, and 5 (22.7%) of individuals aged 55-64.

Breaking down the data by both gender and age group reveals further insights. Among women aged 18-34, 6 (37.5%) said they always consider buying skincare products based on influencer or celebrity recommendations, compared to 0 men in the same age group. Among women aged 35-54, 7 (38.9%) said they often consider buying skincare products based on influencer or celebrity recommendations, compared to only 1 (9.1%) man in the same age group.

Table 19. Regression model coefficient H4

	B	Std. Error	Stand. Beta	Sig.
I think that influencers' and celebrities' recommendations are sincere	0.297	0.057	0.287	<.001
I think influencers and celebrities don't do under-covered advertisements	0.732	0.061	0.689	<.001

Table 20. Gender and age sub-groups H4

I Am Considering Buying Skincare Products on the Recommendation of Influencers or Celebrities Next Year							
		Always	**Often**	**Sometimes**	**Rarely**	**Never**	**Total**
18-34 years	Men	0	0	5	4	7	16
	Women	1	5	3	4	3	16
	Total	1	5	8	8	10	32
35-54 years	Men	1	1	4	5	12	23
	Women	1	1	5	9	7	23
	Total	2	2	9	14	19	46
55-34 years	Men		0	3	2	5	10
	Women		1	1	4	6	12
	Total		1	4	6	11	22
Total	Men	1	1	12	11	24	49
	Women	3	7	9	17	16	51
	Total	4	8	21	28	40	100

In contrast, among men aged 35-54, 5 (41.7%) said they rarely consider buying skincare products based on influencer or celebrity recommendations, compared to only 1 (6.3%) woman in the same age group. Similarly, among men aged 55-64, 5 (50%) said they never consider buying skincare products based on influencer or celebrity recommendations, compared to only 2 (16.7%) women in the same age group.

Overall, these findings suggest that women, especially those aged 18-34, are more likely than men to consider buying skincare products based on influencer or celebrity recommendations. However, age group plays a role in this relationship, as older individuals, especially men, are less likely to be influenced by such recommendations.

Table 21. Descriptive analysis H5

	Mean	**Std. Deviation**
I have purchased skincare products on the recommendation of a content creator	3.88	1.113
I have discovered skincare products via content creators	3.93	1.085
I think content creators' recommendations are sincere	3.9	0.98
I believe that content creators use the products they recommend	3.85	0.978
I believe that content creators don't make under-covered advertisements	3.77	1.033
I will consider buying skincare products on the recommendation of content creators	3.55	0.869
I will recommend others to follow skincare product recommendations from content creators	3.88	1.113

User-Generated Content

In addition, the descriptive analysis in Table 21 shows that there is much variation in the opinion of different individuals regarding user-generated content. All the means appear to be in a neutral position, providing complexity in the interpretation of the data. That's why, this could mean there are different tendencies depending on subgroups of age or gender.

Table 22 shows the Spearman correlation coefficients between different variables related to skincare products and content creators. The highest correlation coefficient is 0.864 between "I have purchased skincare products on the recommendation of a content creator" and "I believe that content creators don't make undercover advertisements". This suggests a strong positive correlation between these two variables, meaning that those who have purchased skincare products on the recommendation of a content creator are more likely to believe that the creators don't make undercover advertisements.

Another notable correlation is 0.815 between "I have purchased skincare products on the recommendation of a content creator" and "I believe that content creators use the products they recommend". This suggests a strong positive correlation between these two variables, meaning that those who have purchased skincare products on the recommendation of a content creator are more likely to believe that the creators use the products they recommend.

The correlation coefficients for "I have discovered skincare products via content creators" are also high, indicating a positive correlation with other variables. Specifically, this variable shows a strong positive correlation with "I have purchased skincare products on the recommendation of a content creator" (0.852) and "I believe that content creators use the products they recommend" (0.815).

Overall, Table 22 suggests that there is a positive relationship between discovering and purchasing skincare products through content creators and trusting their recommendations and beliefs about the products they use and endorse.

Table 23 presents the results of a regression analysis that explores the relationship between several predictor variables and the dependent variable "I have purchased skincare products on the recommendation of a content creator". The predictors included in the model have been:

- I will recommend others to follow skincare product recommendations from content creators.
- I think content creators' recommendations are sincere.
- I have discovered skincare products via content creators.

Table 22. Spearman correlation coefficients H5

	I Have Discovered Skincare Products via Content Creators	I Think Content Creators' Recommendations Are Sincere	I Believe That Content Creators Use the Products They Recommend	I Believe That Content Creators Don't Make Under-Covered Advertisements
I have purchased skincare products on the recommendation of a content creator	0.852**	0.576**	0.815**	0.864**
I believe that content creators don't make under-covered advertisements	0.864**	0.705**	0.473**	-

Table 23. Summary: Regression model H5

Regression Model Summary	
R	0.946
R Square	0.895
Sig. F Change	<.001
ANOVA	
Sum of Squares (regression)	109.709
Sig.	<.001

- I am considering buying skincare products on the recommendation of influencers or celebrities next year.
- I believe that content creators don't make under-covered advertisements.
- I believe that content creators use the products they recommend.
- Constan

The model summary (Table 23) shows that the regression model has a high level of explanatory power, with an R-squared value of .895, indicating that 89.5% of the variance in the dependent variable can be explained by the predictor variables included in the model.

The ANOVA results show that the regression model is statistically significant (p<.001), indicating that at least one of the predictor variables is significantly related to the dependent variable. The sum of squares for the regression (109.709) is much larger than the sum of squares for the residual, indicating that the predictor variables are jointly contributing to explaining the variance in the dependent variable.

Overall, this analysis suggests that there is a strong relationship between the predictor variables and the frequency of purchasing skincare products on the recommendation of a content creator. The results suggest that these predictor variables can be used to predict whether an individual is likely to make a purchase based on a content creator's recommendation.

For further analysis, Table 24 shows that the predictor variables "I have discovered skincare products via content creators," "I believe that content creators use the products they recommend," and "I believe that content creators don't make under covered advertisements" all have significant positive beta coefficients. This means that as each of these predictor variables increases, there is a corresponding increase in the frequency that the individual has purchased skincare products on the recommendation of a content creator.

Table 24. Regression model coefficient H5

	B	Std. Error	Stand. Beta	Sig.
I have discovered skincare products via content creators	0.279	0.049	0.272	<.001
I believe that content creators use the products they recommend	0.277	0.068	0.244	<.001
I believe that content creators don't make under-covered advertisements	0.490	0.064	0.455	<.001

The beta coefficient for "I have discovered skincare products via content creators" is .272, which is statistically significant ($p < .001$). This suggests that individuals who have discovered skincare products via content creators are more likely to make a purchase frequently based on their recommendations.

Similarly, the beta coefficient for "I believe that content creators use the products they recommend" is .244, which is also statistically significant ($p < .001$). This suggests that individuals who believe that content creators use the products they recommend are more likely to trust their recommendations and make a purchase.

Finally, the beta coefficient for "I believe that content creators don't make under-covered advertisements" is .455, which is statistically significant ($p < .001$). This suggests that individuals who believe that content creators are not engaging in under-covered advertisements are more likely to trust their recommendations and make a purchase.

In general, these results suggest that trust and credibility are important factors in individuals' decisions to purchase skincare products based on the recommendations of content creators. The more individuals trust content creators and believe in their sincerity and transparency, the more likely they are to make a purchase based on their recommendations.

Moreover, the cross-tabulation (Table 25) shows the relationship between respondents' age and gender with their tendency to consider buying skincare products based on content creators' recommendations in the future. Looking at the table, it can be seen that the majority of respondents who considered buying skincare products based on content creators' recommendations were female (35 out of 56 or 62.5%).

In terms of age groups, the largest group of respondents were between 35-54 years old (46 out of 100 or 46%), followed by 18-34 years old (32 out of 100 or 32%) and 55-64 years old (22 out of 100 or 22%). Among the 18-34 age group, both males and females reported considering buying skincare products based on content creators' recommendations.

For the 35-54 age group, more females reported considering buying skincare products based on content creators' recommendations, with 8 reporting "often" and 9 reporting "sometimes". Among males

Table 25. Gender and age groups H5

I Will Consider Buying Skincare Products on the Recommendation of Content Creators						
		Often	**Sometimes**	**Rarely**	**Never**	**Total**
18-34 years	Men	5	6	3	2	16
	Women	7	7	2	0	16
	Total	12	13	5	2	32
35-54 years	Men	1	9	13	0	23
	Women	8	9	3	3	23
	Total	9	18	16	3	46
55-34 years	Men	1	1	4	4	10
	Women	0	4	3	5	12
	Total	1	5	7	9	22
Total	Men	7	16	20	6	49
	Women	15	20	8	8	51
	Total	22	36	28	14	100

in this age group, the majority reported "rarely" or "never". In addition, in the 55-64 age group, only one male reported considering buying skincare products based on content creators' recommendations, while all five females reported "sometimes", "rarely", or "never".

Overall, the cross-tabulation suggests that gender may play a role in the tendency to consider buying skincare products based on content creators' recommendations, with females more likely to do so. Age also seems to have an impact, with younger respondents more likely to consider buying skincare products based on content creators' recommendations compared to older respondents.

Reviews

Finally, the results of the skincare product reviews increase sales have been obtained. The mean values for all statements fall between 3.34 and 3.93, indicating that the respondents generally have a slightly negative to neutral attitude towards skincare product reviews (Table 26). However, the standard deviations show that there is some variability in the responses.

The statement "I will consider buying skincare products based on their reviews" with a mean of 3.34, indicates that most respondents are somewhat hesitant to buy skincare products solely based on reviews. The statement with the higher mean value is "I have purchased skincare products after reading product reviews" with a mean of 3.93, suggesting that most respondents have not purchased skincare products based on reviews (Table 26).

According to Spearman's Correlation Coefficients (Table 27), the highest correlation coefficient is between "I believe that the people who leave reviews have actually used those products" and "I believe that the reviews do not hide hidden advertising" with a coefficient of 0.687, indicating a strong positive correlation. This suggests that respondents who believe that the reviewers have actually used the products are more likely to believe that the reviews are not influenced by hidden advertising.

There is also a strong positive correlation between "I discovered skincare products through reviews" and "I think the recommendations/opinions left in skincare product reviews are sincere" with a coefficient of 0.749, indicating that respondents who discovered skincare products through reviews are more likely to believe that the recommendations/opinions left in skincare product reviews are sincere.

Finally, there is a moderate positive correlation between "I have purchased skincare products after reading product reviews" and all other statements with correlation coefficients ranging from 0.245 to 0.649. This suggests that respondents who have purchased skincare products after reading product re-

Table 26. Descriptive analysis H6

	Mean	Std. Deviation
I discovered skincare products through reviews	3.88	1.113
I have purchased skincare products after reading product reviews	3.93	1.085
I think the recommendations/opinions left in skincare product reviews are sincere.	3.90	0.980
I believe that the people who leave reviews have actually used those products.	3.85	0.978
I believe that the reviews do not hide hidden advertising.	3.77	1.033
I will consider buying skincare products based on their reviews:	3.34	0.977
I will recommend others to follow the recommendations/opinions of skincare product reviews	3.55	0.869

Table 27. Table Spearman correlation coefficients H6

	I Believe That the Reviews Do Not Hide Hidden Advertising.	I Believe That the People Who Leave Reviews Have Actually Used Those Products	I Discovered Skincare Products Through Reviews	I Think the Recommendations/ Opinions Left in Skincare Product Reviews Are Sincere.
I have purchased skincare products after reading product reviews	0.649**	0.687**	0.245**	0.749 **
I think the recommendations/opinions left in skincare product reviews are sincere.	0.510**	0.547**	0.137	-

views are more likely to believe that the reviewers have used the products, that the reviews do not hide hidden advertising, and that the recommendations/opinions left in skincare product reviews are sincere.

Overall, these results suggest that there is a positive relationship between the belief that skincare product reviews are sincere, trustworthy, and not influenced by hidden advertising and the likelihood of purchasing skincare products after reading reviews more often. This highlights the importance of transparency and authenticity in product reviews for building consumer trust and influencing purchasing decisions.

In addition, the Model Summary table (Table 28) provides information on the goodness of fit of the regression model used to analyze the relationship between various predictors and the dependent variable "I have purchased skincare products after reading product reviews". The predictors used were the following:

- I discovered skincare products through reviews.
- I have purchased skincare products after reading product reviews.
- I think the recommendations/opinions left in skincare product reviews are sincere.
- I believe that the people who leave reviews have actually used those products.
- I believe that the reviews do not hide hidden advertising.
- Constant.

Table 28. Summary: Regression model H6

Regression Model Summary	
R	0.862
R Square	0.743
Sig. F Change	<.001
ANOVA	
Sum of Squares (regression)	51.837
Sig.	<.001

Table 29. Regression model coefficient H6

	B	Std. Error	Stand. Beta	Sig.
I think the recommendations/opinions left in skincare product reviews are sincere.	0.44	0.069	0.428	<.001
I believe that the people who leave reviews have actually used those products.	0.304	0.066	0.306	<.001
I believe that the reviews do not hide hidden advertising.	0.271	0.067	0.262	<.001

The table shows that the multiple R is 0.862, indicating a strong positive correlation between the predictors and the dependent variable. The R-square value of 0.743 indicates that 74.3% of the variance in the dependent variable can be explained by the predictors in the model (Table 28). Furthermore, the ANOVA results show that the regression model is significant ($p<0.001$) and that it explains a significant amount of variance in the dependent variable.

In general, these results suggest that the predictors used in the model have a significant positive impact on the likelihood of purchasing skincare products after reading product reviews. These predictors may be useful in guiding marketing strategies for skincare products and in building consumer trust and confidence in product reviews.

More specifically, the regression model coefficient table (Table 29) indicates that the three predictor variables are significant predictors of the outcome variable. The predictor variable "I think the recommendations/opinions left in skincare product reviews are sincere" has the strongest relationship with the outcome variable ($B = 0.440$, $p < .001$, Stand. Beta = .428), followed by "I believe that the people who leave reviews have actually used those products" ($B = 0.304$, $p < .001$, Stand. Beta = .306) and "I believe that the reviews do not hide hidden advertising" ($B = 0.271$, $p < .001$, Stand. Beta = .262). These

Table 30. Gender and age groups H6

I Am Considering Buying Skincare Products Based on Their Reviews							
		Always	Often	Sometimes	Rarely	Never	Total
18-34 years	Men	3	9	4	0		16
	Women	0	9	5	2		16
	Total	3	18	9	2		32
35-54 years	Men		14	7	2		23
	Women		13	8	2		23
	Total		27	15	4		46
55-74 years	Men	0	6	2	1	1	10
	Women	3	7	2	0	0	12
	Total	3	13	4	1	1	22
Total	Men	3	26	13	3	1	49
	Women	3	29	15	4	0	51
	Total	6	58	28	7	1	100

results suggest that the more people believe in the sincerity of product reviews and the authenticity of reviewers, the more likely they are to purchase skincare products many times based on those reviews.

Finally, according to data obtained depending on the gender and age groups (Table 30), we can see that overall, 6% of respondents said they will always consider buying skincare products based on reviews, 58% said they often consider it, 28% said they sometimes consider it, 7% said they rarely consider it, and 1% said they never consider it.

In terms of age groups, it seems that younger people are more likely to consider buying skincare products based on reviews, with 50% of respondents in the 18-34 age group saying they often or always consider it, compared to 23% in the 35-54 age group and 14% in the 55-64 age group.

In terms of gender, there doesn't seem to be a significant difference, with both men and women having similar percentages across all response categories. Overall, it appears that most people consider buying skincare products based on reviews, and this trend is more prevalent among younger age groups. Gender doesn't seem to play a significant role in this decision-making process.

CONCLUSION

The skincare product industry is highly competitive and constantly changing due to new technological breakthroughs and changing client demands. As a result, organizations must remain informed on industry advances and make efficient use of digital marketing technologies in order to remain competitive.

Customers place high importance on transparency in skincare products, according to one of the study's key findings. Clients are becoming more interested in the ingredients in the skincare products they use, and companies who are upfront about the composition of their skincare products are more likely to gain consumer trust and loyalty. They perceive transparent skincare products to be of higher quality and healthier, thus companies must emphasize their quality. Companies may differentiate themselves and increase sales in the competitive skincare sector by focusing on transparency and quality.

Another important factor to consider is sustainability. The public is increasingly concerned about the environmental effect of their purchasing decisions and is seeking environmentally friendly alternatives. The study discovered a significant relationship between sustainable skincare products and higher sales; however, firms must carefully examine pricing strategies because not all consumers are willing to pay a premium for sustainable products. Therefore, companies may benefit from this trend by offering sustainable skincare products and advertising them to emphasize their sustainability, health benefits, and higher quality when compared to standard cosmetics.

According to this study, businesses should take precautions when relying solely on influencer marketing and celebrity endorsements for their marketing strategies. According to the results, the majority of the consumers are neutral or indifferent about whether they buy skincare products based on advice from influencers or celebrities, suggesting that it has little impact on their choice. Nevertheless, younger women are more likely to be influenced by such advice. The age and gender demographics of a company's target audience should be considered while developing marketing strategies.

Instead of relying on influencer marketing, the study found that reviews and user-generated content can be effective marketing tools if perceived as sincere, reliable, and unaffected by covert advertising. If consumers feel these methods are authentic and trustworthy, they are more inclined to purchase those skincare goods. Companies may encourage consumers to post reviews by delivering exceptional customer service and offering incentives like discounts. In addition, they should boost their clients to create content.

It is noteworthy that the opinions of customers about skincare products differ according to gender and age. Social media and marketing are more likely to convince younger women than elderly people, especially males, who are less likely to be persuaded by such strategies. Companies must be conscious of these demographic variations and adjust their marketing plans appropriately.

Finally, due to constraints, this work has certain limitations that should be addressed since they may impair its reliability. A bigger sample size would be preferred, even if the sample size is representative. The study acknowledges considerable limitations, such as a lack of investigation into the possible impact of other factors on customer behavior, such as price. Furthermore, future research should investigate employing objective measurements of consumer behavior, such as sales data. Furthermore, the research should be expanded globally.

REFERENCES

Age, Ad. (2020, December 21). *The 12 smartest brand-celebrity pairings of 2020*. https://adage.com/article/year-review/12-smartest-brand-celebrity-pairings-2020/2299341

Al Mamun, A., Nawi, N. C., Hayat, N., & Zainol, N. R. B. (2020). Predicting the purchase intention and behaviour towards green skincare products among Malaysian consumers. *Sustainability (Basel)*, *12*(24), 10663. doi:10.3390u122410663

Aramendia-Muneta, M. E. (2017). Spread the word – The effect of word of mouth in e-marketing. In G. Siegert, M. B. Von Rimscha, & S. Grubenmann (Eds.), *Commercial Communication in the Digital Age* (pp. 227–245). De Gruyter. doi:10.1515/9783110416794-013

Bernays, E. L. (1928). *Propaganda*. Horace Liveright.

Chin, J., Jiang, B., Mufidah, I., Persada, S., & Noer, B. (2018). The investigation of consumers' behavior intention in using green skincare products: A pro-environmental behavior model approach. *Sustainability (Basel)*, *10*(11), 3922. doi:10.3390u10113922

Deloitte. (2019). Made-to-order: The rise of mass personalization: Consumer review. *Deloitte*. https://www2.deloitte.com/content/dam/Deloitte/ch/Documents/consumer-business/ch-en-consumer-business-made-to-order-consumer-review.pdf

Dominguez, L. (2022, January 21). Skin care AI: L'Oréal decoding the future of beauty. *Consumer Goods Technology*. https://consumergoods.com/skin-care-ai-loreal-decoding-future-beauty

European Commission. (2022). *Cosmetics legislation*. European single market. https://single-market-economy.ec.europa.eu/sectors/cosmetics/legislation_en

García, P. (2021, July 9). *Las mujeres usan más las redes sociales que los hombres*. Cadena SER. https://cadenaser.com/emisora/2021/07/09/ser_madrid_sur/1625826613_464505.html

González, M. (2019). *La cosmética ya no solo tiene que ver con la estética*. Forbes España. https://forbes.es/empresas/43235/la-cosmetica-ya-no-solo-tiene-que-ver-con-la-estetica/

INE. (2022). *Encuesta de población activa*. https://www.ine.es/ss/Satellite?L=es_ES&c=INESeccion_C&cid=1259925528782&p=1254735110672&pagename=ProductosYServicios%2FPYSLayout

Infosecurity Magazine. (2019, June 10). Consumers unaware of AI impact on data privacy. *Infosecurity Magazine*. https://www.infosecurity-magazine.com/news/consumers-ai-impact-data-privacy/

Kotler, P., Keller, K. L., Brady, M., Goodman, M., & Hansen, T. (2017). Marketing management (3rd European ed.). Academic Press.

Label Insight. (2016). *Transparency ROI study: The business case for more transparency*. Retrieved from https://www.labelinsight.com/hubfs/PDF/Transparency-ROI-Study

Lastra, E. (2022, October 3). La credibilidad de los influencers hace aguas. *Marketing Directo*. https://www.marketingdirecto.com/digital-general/social-media-marketing/credibilidad-influencers-hace-aguas

Latana. (2021, March 4). Lush: A Deep Dive into Their Brand and Marketing Strategy. *Latana*. https://latana.com/post/lush-deep-dive/

Lee, J. E., Goh, M. L., & Mohd Noor, M. N. Bin. (2019). Understanding purchase intention of university students towards skin care products. *PSU Research Review, 3*(3), 161–178.

Levitt, T. (1960). Marketing myopia. *Harvard Business Review*, *38*(4), 45–56. PMID:15252891

Marketing News. (2018, March 5). *Las mujeres utilizan las redes sociales un 7% más que los hombres*. https://www.marketingnews.es/investigacion/noticia/1113054031605/mujeres-utilizan-redes-sociales-7-mas-hombres.1.html

Martín, R. (2021, August 26). Alexia Putellas, nueva embajadora de MartiDerm. *Grazia Magazine*. https://graziamagazine.com/es/articles/alexia-putellas-nueva-embajadora-de-martiderm/

McKinsey & Company. (2021, September 7). *Consumers care about sustainability—and back it up with their wallets*. McKinsey & Company. https://www.mckinsey.com/industries/consumer-packaged-goods/our-insights/consumers-care-about-sustainability-and-back-it-up-with-their-wallets

Mena Roa, M. (2021). Personas que afirman haber comprado productos porque los anunciaban famosos o influencers en España en 2021. *Statista*. https://es.statista.com/grafico/24907/personas-que-afirman-haber-comprado-productos-porque-los-anunciaban-famosos-o-influencers/

Montemayor, C. (2021, September 2). The Ordinary's anti-clean beauty revolution: How beauty brands are fighting back. *BeautyMatter*. https://beautymatter.com/articles/the-ordinary-s-anti-clean-beauty-revolution-how-beauty-brands-are-fighting-back

Morgan, B. (2020, February 24). 11 fashion companies leading the way in sustainability. *Forbes*. https://www.forbes.com/sites/blakemorgan/2020/02/24/11-fashion-companies-leading-the-way-in-sustainability/?sh=2da530666dba

Oladipo, T. (2022, June 6). What is user-generated content? *Buffer*. https://buffer.com/resources/what-is-user-generated-content/

QQGrand View Research. (2021). Personalized skin care products market worth $48.65 billion by 2030 | Grand View Research, Inc. *PR Newswire*. https://www.prnewswire.com/news-releases/personalized-skin-care-products-market-worth-48-65-billion-by-2030-grand-view-research-inc-301752845.html

Rice, B. (2019, June 13). How to use user-generated content to drive sales for your brand. *Jilt*. https://jilt.com/blog/ugc-brands/

Stanpa. (2021). Cosmetic sector in Spain. *Stanpa*. Retrieved from https://www.stanpa.com/en/industry-figures/cosmetic-sector-spain/

Twenge, J. M., & Martin, G. N. (2020). Gender differences in associations between digital media use and psychological well-being: Evidence from three large datasets. *Journal of Adolescence*, *79*(1), 91–102. doi:10.1016/j.adolescence.2019.12.018 PMID:31926450

Velasco, C. (2019, December 12). Los influencers españoles deberán indicar cuáles de sus publicaciones son publicitarias desde el 1 de enero. *Marketing4ecommerce*. https://marketing4ecommerce.net/los-influencers-espanoles-deberan-indicar-cuales-de-sus-publicaciones-son-publicitarias-desde-el-1-de-enero/

Xiong, L., Cho, V., Law, K. M. Y., & Lam, L. (2021). A study of KOL effectiveness on brand image of skincare products. *Enterprise Information Systems*, *15*(10), 1483–1500. doi:10.1080/17517575.2021.1924864

ADDITIONAL READING

Adnan, K., Amjad, N., Iftikhar, A., & Nisar, A. (2023). Study of the Effect of Influencer Marketing on Consumer Purchase Intention with Medators Brand Awareness and Brand Reputation: Organic Skin Care Products in Pakistan. *Journal of Policy Research*, *9*(2), 124–133.

Nurniati, N., Savitri, C., & Faddila, S. P. (2023). Electronic Word of Mouth (e-WoM) and Influencer Marketing Strategy on Purchase Decision of Skincare Products in Marketplace. *International Journal of Economics Development Research*, *4*(2), 290–304.

Oulee, A., Norden, A., Javadi, S. S., & Wu, J. J. (2022). Skincare influencers and skin problems in social media. *Journal of the European Academy of Dermatology and Venereology*, *36*(10), e819–e821. doi:10.1111/jdv.18305 PMID:35686632

Pawestriningrum, W., & Roostika, R. (2022). The The Effect of Beauty Influencer Trust on Brand Credibility, Advertising Credibility, Corporate Credibility and Purchase Intention of Local Skincare Products. Selekta Manajemen. *Jurnal Mahasiswa Bisnis & Manajemen*, *1*(1), 65–80.

KEY TERMS AND DEFINITIONS

Celebrities: Individuals who are widely recognized and admired for their achievements or fame in various fields such as entertainment, sports, politics, or social media.

Influencer: Individual who has established credibility and a significant following in a specific niche or industry, often on social media platforms.

Reviews: Assessments or evaluations of products, services, or experiences shared by individuals to provide feedback or opinions to other.

Skincare Products: Topical formulations designed to cleanse, moisturize, and treat the skin to maintain its health and appearance.

Sustainability: The practice of creating and using skincare products and processes that minimize their negative impact on the environment, while also considering social and ethical aspects

Transparency: The quality of being open, honest, and readily sharing information or actions without concealment or deception.

User-Generated Content: Any form of content, such as text, images, videos, or reviews, that is created and shared by individuals, rather than by professional content creators or organizations.

Chapter 12
Digital Influencers and the Restaurant Sector

Alvaro Díaz Casquero
Universidad de Málaga, Spain

Eva María González Robles
https://orcid.org/0000-0002-6266-3710
Universidad de Málaga, Spain

Benjamín del Alcázar
Universidad de Málaga, Spain

ABSTRACT

This chapter delves into digital influencers' influential role in reshaping restaurant industry communication, dissecting their evolution, categorizing types, and their pivotal role in gastronomic communication. Exploring strategies for optimizing influencer collaborations, scrutinizing trends, and spotlighting key platforms, it equips readers with a comprehensive understanding. Furthermore, it investigates influencers' profound impact on consumer behavior, serving as a practical guide with data-driven insights and examples. In today's digital age, this chapter underscores influencer collaborations' indispensable nature in the restaurant sector, emphasizing their potential for business success. Understanding and harnessing influencer power remains crucial for industry stakeholders as the culinary world evolves.

INTRODUCTION

In the digital age, where technological evolution is advancing by leaps and bounds, the influence and persuasive power of social networks have revolutionized the way in which companies relate to their customers and promote their products and services (Smith, 2018). The commercial impact of influencers has reached all sectors, but it stands out in the restaurant sector, where they have become a key element for the promotion of establishments and products (Johnson & Brown, 2020). Influencers, individuals

DOI: 10.4018/979-8-3693-0551-5.ch012

with a large following on platforms like Instagram, YouTube, and TikTok, have become key players in restaurant marketing around the world (White & Davis, 2019).

This chapter of the book aims to explore and analyze in-depth the role of influencers in the restaurant sector. We will examine how these digital influencers have transformed the traditional marketing dynamics in the restaurant industry (Jones & Green, 2017), how they have impacted consumer decision-making (Clark & Turner, 2021), and how hospitality businesses can take advantage of this commercial figure to improve their visibility and increase their revenue (Robinson et al., 2020).

The importance of addressing this issue lies in the growing relevance of influencers in the promotion of restaurants. As technology and social media have become ubiquitous in everyday life (Anderson, 2019), the way people discover, choose, and share their dining experiences has evolved significantly. Influencers, with their ability to reach massive audiences and influence the opinions of their followers (Adams & Wilson, 2018), play a key role in this shift, which has caused them to become a widely used source of recommendations for consumers seeking the most up-to-date experiences safe and memorable as possible (Smith & Johnson, 2022).

This analysis is relevant both for professionals in the marketing sector and for restaurant managers, since the information reported is used to take advantage of the influence and repercussion offered by influencers in an increasingly competitive market, such as the restaurant sector (Brown & Davis, 2021).

OBJECTIVES AND METHODOLOGY

Objectives

Analyze the role of digital influencers in the restaurant sector. This involves examining how digital influencers affect culinary consumer behavior, the marketing strategies that restaurants employ in collaboration with influencers, and the influence of influencers on restaurant promotion.

Understand how these collaborations affect the restaurant industry and provide recommendations for effective food influencer marketing, all collected in what is known as a best practices manual that will be useful both for future research and for companies in the sector. of the restaurants.

Methodology

The methodology used in this research is based on an exhaustive study of the existing literature on the topic to further conceptualize the topic, identify previous trends and patterns, and establish a solid theoretical framework for the study.

After this review, a good practices manual is proposed that allows hospitality businesses to make more optimal decisions when hiring and implementing a digital influencer.

BACKGROUND

Evolution of the Phenomenon of Digital Influencers

The phenomenon of digital influencers has undergone a significant evolution over the years, from humble beginnings to becoming a dominant force in digital marketing. First of all, we must understand that the concept of digital influencer refers to people or profiles that have gained a large number of followers on platforms such as Instagram, YouTube or TikTok, due to the content generated that is usually based on experiences, lifestyle or particular skills (Kaplan and Haenlein, 2010). At first, the phenomenon of digital influencers focused on sectors such as fashion and beauty, but as time has progressed, it has spread to all sectors, including gastronomy.

In order to understand this phenomenon we are going to analyze the evolution of these from the origin to the present time.

Beginning of the Influencer Phenomenon (2000s)

The rise of digital influencers can be traced back to the 2000s with the popularization of personal blogs. "Bloggers" began sharing their personal experiences online, including product reviews and recommendations. At this time, blogs became influential platforms to promote products and services (Hsu & Lin, 2015), the fashion, beauty and tourism sectors stood out. The latter began to make special mention of the gastronomic recommendations, where they commented on the gastronomic establishments that any tourist should not miss on their tourist route.

The YouTube Explosion (2010s)

It was in the 2010s, where those known as "Youtubers" appeared and continued to be influencers on the YouTube channel. These content creators began to use the platform to generate videos to share their experiences, tutorials, even those known as personal vlogs (blogs in video format). At that time, YouTube was becoming the main platform for content creation and influencer marketing. Content in the gastronomic sector was characterized by a much longer duration than what we are currently used to, where influencers could afford to generate audiovisual content that exceeded 5 minutes in length.

Rise of Instagrammers (2010s - Present)

Instagram, the social network par excellence for digital influencers today, burst onto the market in the 2010s, giving rise to what is known in the marketing sector as "Instagrammers."

This platform, which at first was only based on non-interactive visual content (photographs and images) accompanied by text, popularized product reviews. (Phua, Jin, & Kim, 2017). This social network has not stopped evolving, advancing more dynamic and interactive content, currently allowing publications to be accompanied by videos, audios, surveys, locations, music... allowing influencers to create more attractive content and not lose their dominance in the sector of influence.

In the gastronomic sector, profiles designed solely to generate content on restaurant recommendations in different destinations are breaking out.

Diversification of Platforms and Sectors (Present)

Currently, the phenomenon of digital influencers has diversified into a wide range of platforms, including LinkedIn for a more business profile, Twitch, the network par excellence for esports and gamers, and TikTok, a network that exploded during the pandemic of Covid-19 and is currently the social network that puts the most pressure on Instagram. Subsequently, the consumption of each of the social networks in the sector will be analyzed. Additionally, a variety of influential niches have emerged, from food and beauty to technology and travel. Digital influencers have gained online celebrity status and collaborate with global brands (O'Brien, 2021).

The evolution of the phenomenon of digital influencers has been notable and has greatly influenced consumer behavior and marketing strategies in the digital era. From their modest beginnings on personal blogs to their current diversification across multiple platforms and niches, digital influencers continue to play an essential role in online communication and purchasing decisions.

Types of Digital Influencer

In the field of restoration, several types of digital influencers can be identified (Voorveld, van Noort, Muntinga, & Bronner, 2018), this is interesting in view of the digital marketing strategy that you want to carry out, since each one of them can help us achieve a different goal.

Food Bloggers: These influencers specialize in food critics and share in-depth reviews of restaurants, dishes, and culinary experiences on their blogs and social media. His followers rely on his opinions to make decisions about where to eat.

Some prominent examples of Food Bloggers are as follows:

- Joy Wilson (Joy the Baker): Joy is a food blogger and cookbook author known for her delicious recipes and laid-back style. Among his multiple recipes and gastronomic inventions, he offers reviews about the different establishments he visits.
- David Lebovitz: Author of several cookbooks, his blog is a reference for French pastry and cuisine. It is common to find reviews on its pages about the gastronomic spaces to which it goes.
- Deb Perelman (Smitten Kitchen): Her Smitten Kitchen blog is known for its accessible recipes and impressive photos.

Amateur Chefs: Some digital influencers are not professional chefs, but rather foodies who share recipes, cooking tips, and cooking techniques online. His interest in gastronomy attracts followers interested in learning and improving their culinary skills.

Some examples for this type of influencer are the following:

- Laura in the Kitchen: Laura Vitale, a passionate home cook, has a YouTube channel with easy-to-follow recipes.
- Sally's Baking Addiction: Sally McKenney shares baking and home cooking recipes on her blog and social media.

Foodies: These influencers are passionate foodies who document their dining experiences on social media. They share photos and opinions about restaurants and dishes, influencing the decisions of their followers.

For foodies we can highlight the following social profiles:

- Gordon Ramsay: The celebrity chef and TV personality is a passionate lover of food and shares his passion on his social media.
- Chrissy Teigen: The model and author is known for her food adventures and homemade recipes on Instagram and Twitter.
- Eddie Huang: The chef and author is known for his love of Asian food and his culinary explorations on social media and television shows.

Lifestyle content creators: Some digital influencers integrate food into their lifestyle, creating content that shows how gastronomy relates to other aspects of daily life, such as travel, health, and culture.

- Martha Stewart: Influencer Martha Stewart shares lifestyle content, including cooking, home décor, and gardening, on her social media and TV shows.
- Ina Garten (Barefoot Contessa): Cookbook author and TV presenter combines cooking with lifestyle in her shows and books.
- Tasty Japan: This YouTube channel offers recipes and lifestyle content with a Japanese perspective, appealing to lovers of Japanese food and culture.

These are just a few examples of notable influencers in the food industry, each with their own approach and style, but all have influenced the way people explore, cook and enjoy food and the lifestyle related to gastronomy.

The Importance of Digital Influencers in the Communication of the Gastronomic Sector

The importance of digital influencers in the gastronomy sector is undeniable and has become a key factor in consumer decision-making. Consumers, especially millennials and centennials, are increasingly looking for authentic and trusted recommendations before choosing a restaurant to dine in or order food (Phua, Jin, & Kim, 2017). Influencers on digital platforms, such as Instagram, YouTube, and food blogs, have become trusted sources of information that help consumers in their purchasing decision process.

Digital influencers allow restaurants to reach broader and more specific audiences effectively. Their ability to create engaging and authentic content in the form of images, videos, and reviews provides restaurants with valuable exposure on social media (Smith, Fischer, & Yongjian, 2012). In addition, the digital word of mouth, also known as e-wom (electronic word-of-mouth), that they generate can have a significant impact on consumer purchasing decisions. When influencers share their positive experiences at a restaurant, they are directly influencing the audience's perception of that establishment, which can translate into increased reservations and sales.

In summary, digital influencers play an essential role in promotion and communication in the gastronomic sector. They offer restaurants the opportunity to connect with their audience authentically and effectively in the digital information age. By providing credible recommendations and engaging content, these influencers have become powerful agents in influencing consumer purchasing decisions and restaurant reputations.

DIGITAL INFLUENCER MARKETING STRATEGIES

Content Creation

The creation of high-quality content is the core of the marketing strategies of digital influencers but it is especially relevant in the restaurant sector. Influencers stand out for their ability to produce visually engaging and compelling content that resonates with their audience. Authentic and appetizing content, in the form of images, videos and detailed reviews of dishes and dining experiences, is essential to maintain the interest of followers and attract the attention of new consumers. (Phua, Jin and Kim, 2017). As the digital age has evolved, the importance of content has increased, becoming a determining factor for the success of online businesses (Kaplan & Haenlein, 2010).

Evolution of the Importance of Content

In the last decade, we have witnessed a significant change in the way companies communicate with their customers. Before, traditional advertising dominated the landscape, but with the arrival of social networks and digital marketing, content has become the main core. Companies have had to adapt to this new reality, where the quality and authenticity of content are essential to attract and retain consumers.

Quality content has become essential due to several reasons:

Engagement: Authentic and relevant content creates an emotional connection with consumers. When digital influencers share their culinary experiences in the form of photos, videos, and reviews, followers feel more involved and connected to the brand and the restaurant. There are many influencers who create their own claim, allowing them to be associated with specific values and business models.

Visibility and reach: Search engines and social media algorithms favor fresh and valuable content. Quality content helps posts become more visible to a broader audience, increasing a restaurant's reach and exposure (Voorveld, van Noort, Muntinga, & Bronner, 2018).

Credibility and trust: Consumers look for informative and trustworthy content. Influencers who share honest and transparent content build credibility and trust with their followers. When they recommend a restaurant or a dish, their followers are more inclined to trust those recommendations (Phua, Jin, & Kim, 2017).

Content has become so important in the digital marketing sector that many companies have developed platforms and tools to generate content. Among the essential tools or elements that stand out to generate visually attractive and convincing content, the following stand out:

High-quality cameras and/or phones: Image quality is essential in visual content. Influencers often use DSLR cameras or smartphones with high-resolution cameras to capture high-quality images.

Photo and video editors: Photo and video editing apps and software allow influencers to enhance and personalize their images and videos. This includes color adjustments, cropping, and special effects. The applications in the Adobe package stand out for more personalized and professional work, but applications like Canva make the work easier for any user who does not have design or editing knowledge.

Content scheduling platforms: Influencers plan and schedule their posts using social media management tools like Hootsuite or Buffer. This allows them to maintain a constant presence online. Currently, platforms like Meta allow you to program content on your own social networks such as Facebook or Instagram, without having to resort to external platforms.

These tools help influencers maintain quality and consistency in their content, which is essential to attracting and maintaining their audience.

Co-Branding (Restaurants and Influencer)

Co-branding between restaurants and influencers has become a very effective strategy to increase visibility and credibility. In this collaboration, influencers promote restaurants on their platforms, sharing their experiences and recommendations, generally through audiovisual content. This may include restaurant visits, food tasting and real-time reviews. Kaplan and Haenlein (2010) point out that this partnership can be mutually beneficial, as influencers get fresh and authentic content, while restaurants expand their reach in the digital world.

There are several types of collaborations that can occur between influencers and restaurants:

Reviews and recommendations: In this type of collaboration, the influencer visits the restaurant and shares an honest review about their experience. This may include photos, videos, and comments about the establishment's food, service, and atmosphere. (Neeley & Qaqish, 2020). This collaboration is effective in increasing the restaurant's visibility and building trust among the influencer's followers. (Phua, Jin, & Kim, 2017)

Events and tastings: Restaurants can invite influencers to special events, exclusive tastings or openings. Influencers can share their experience in real time through live broadcasts or social media posts. This creates expectation in the user and excitement among your audience (Peters, 2020).

Custom content creation: In this collaboration, the restaurant asks the influencer to create specific custom content, such as unique recipes using the restaurant's ingredients or dishes. This can generate interest and desire among the influencer's followers to try the products or visit the restaurant. (Guo & Saxton, 2014).

Draws: An increasingly common practice is the generation of contests. Influencers in collaboration with the establishment organize raffles and contests on their social networks. This, in addition to increasing visibility, is usually a good strategy to increase the audience of both parties. The most common prizes are usually free meals or discounts. (Dall'Olmo Riley et al., 2018).

Long-term collaborations: Some influencers establish long-term relationships with restaurants, becoming brand ambassadors. This involves ongoing collaborations where the influencer regularly promotes the restaurant in their content. (Xu & Du, 2020).

Participation in special menus and dishes: Restaurants can name dishes after the influencer or create special menus inspired by their culinary style or preferences. This not only promotes the restaurant, but also increases the influencer's notoriety.

Charity collaborations: Some collaborations go beyond marketing and focus on charitable causes. Influencers and restaurants can come together to raise funds or awareness for social issues.

These are some examples of how cobranding can be carried out between digital influencers and restaurants. Choosing the type of collaboration depends on the restaurant's marketing goals, the style of the influencer, and the target audience. The key to success lies in authenticity and alignment between both parties to offer unique value to followers and customers.

New Trends

Digital influencer marketing strategies in the restaurant sector must also be attentive to new trends. Social media dynamics and consumer preferences are constantly evolving. Therefore, it is essential for influencers and restaurants to be aware of the latest food and marketing trends. This can include embracing emerging content formats, such as Instagram Stories or live video, as well as incorporating elements of sustainability and health into promotional strategies. It should be noted that the size of the content published in the Instagram feed has recently been changed, which has meant an adaptation of the content to this new format in order to get more out of it.

Below are examples of some of the most recent trends that have impacted this area:

Virtual Gastronomic Experiences

With the rise of virtual reality (VR) and augmented reality (AR) technology, food influencers are taking their followers on virtual culinary experiences. For example, some influencers have created VR tours of popular restaurants or even hosted virtual dinner parties where followers can join from the comfort of their homes for an immersive dining experience.

Signature Cuisine at Home

In response to the COVID-19 pandemic and movement restrictions, influencers have begun sharing "signature home cooking" recipes. This involves recreating sophisticated dishes from high-end restaurants in the home environment. Influencers offer step-by-step instructions and tips so their followers can enjoy exceptional culinary experiences without leaving home.

Sustainability and Food Awareness

Sustainability and food awareness have gained relevance in influencer marketing strategies. Influencers are promoting restaurants and dishes that adhere to sustainable practices, such as using local and organic ingredients, reducing food waste, and healthier menu options. This reflects consumers' growing concern for personal and planetary health.

Collaborations With Charities

Some influencers have begun collaborating with charities related to food and food safety. They organize charitable events, raise funds and promote awareness about the importance of fighting hunger and food waste. These collaborations allow influencers to use their platform for noble causes and generate a positive impact on society.

Educational Content

Along with traditional visual posts, influencers are creating content in an educational format. This includes YouTube videos with detailed cooking tutorials, explanations of cooking techniques, and extensive restaurant reviews. Followers are looking for more informative and educational content to help them improve their cooking skills and food knowledge.

These trends represent the constant adaptation of food influencers to the changing preferences and needs of their audience. By incorporating these trends into their marketing strategies, influencers can stay relevant and continue to influence consumer decisions in the restaurant industry.

Main Platforms

Choosing an appropriate platform is essential in digital influencer marketing strategies in the restaurant sector. Instagram, YouTube and TikTok are some of the main platforms used by food influencers to reach their audiences. However, the ideal platform may vary depending on the target audience and the type of content you want to share. The importance of understanding the distinctive characteristics of each platform and adapting the content is one of the main elements that must be taken into account when choosing the channel or platform to choose (Smith, Fischer and Yongjian, 2012).

In the context of digital influencer marketing strategies in the restaurant sector, it is essential to understand the reach and consumption of the main platforms used by these influencers. Below is a ranking of the most relevant platforms, supported by usage and consumption data:

Instagram: Instagram leads the ranking as the most popular platform for gastronomic influencers. According to data from Statista (2021), this platform has more than one billion monthly active users around the world. Its focus on visual content, such as photos and short videos, makes it especially suitable for promoting attractive restaurants and dishes. In addition to its ability to interact with the audience through audio, surveys and visual material such as gifs. The age of its target is young but every day it covers a more adult audience.

YouTube: YouTube ranks second in terms of use and consumption. With over two billion monthly users (Statista, 2021), YouTube is a platform where influencers can create longer-form content, such as in-depth reviews, cooking tutorials, and culinary vlogs.

TikTok: TikTok has seen explosive growth since the Covid-19 pandemic and has become a major player in the world of food influencers. According to Oberlo (2021), TikTok reached one billion monthly active users in 2021, with a mostly young target looking for creative and entertaining content.

Facebook: Although Facebook has been surpassed by other platforms in terms of growth, it is still relevant for digital influencers in the restaurant industry. According to Statista (2021), it has 2.8 billion monthly active users, which provides a diverse audience. It stands out for being the social network that has the greatest capacity to reach a more adult audience.

Twitter or X: Twitter or Food influencers often use Twitter to share updates, short reviews, and food trends. In the influencers sector, this network is created mainly to maintain active communication with its community.

Pinterest: Although Pinterest is less known as an influencer platform, it is relevant for promoting recipes and dishes. With 459 million monthly active users (Statista, 2021), Pinterest focuses on creating and sharing visual boards that can be useful for influencers in the food industry.

Twitch: Possibly the least exploited social network for the use of digital influencers in the gastronomic sector. Its live video model allows brands to create collaborations with influencers both during a live visit to the establishment and at the time of the broadcast to consume products from the establishment. Large franchises are currently doing this type of collaboration, as it is a very global social network.

These usage and consumption data reflect the importance of choosing the appropriate platforms based on the target audience and the type of content you want to promote. Digital influencers in the restaurant industry should carefully consider these platforms to maximize their reach and effectiveness in their marketing strategies.

Relationship Between Influencer Marketing Strategies and Traditional Marketing Strategies

Influencer marketing strategies can complement and enhance various traditional marketing strategies. This strategic collaboration between the world of digital influencers and conventional marketing can generate impressive results. Some of the traditional strategies that can be related to influencer marketing strategies are explored below:

1. Mass media advertising

Advertising in mass media, such as television and radio, continues to be an effective strategy for reaching broad audiences. However, integrating influencers into traditional ads can improve authenticity and audience connection. According to Gupta and Dogra (2018), influencers can provide credibility to advertising messages. Large restaurant chains and franchises is one of the practices that is being carried out the most, since it is also attractive for influencers to reach traditional channels far from their social networks.

2. Content marketing

Content marketing is a strategy that focuses on creating and distributing valuable content to attract and retain an audience. Influencers can play a key role in creating compelling, authentic content that resonates with your audience. This content can be used in direct marketing strategies. Content marketing is essential for brand building and consumer engagement. (Martin, 2018)

3. Event marketing and sponsorships

Event and sponsorship marketing is a strategy that involves participation in major events or sponsorship of brand-related activities. Influencers can be invited to events or be part of sponsorship campaigns. This collaboration can increase the visibility and reach of the event (Gonçalves and Branco, 2020).

4. Public relations and reputation management

Public relations and reputation management strategies are crucial to maintaining a positive brand image. Influencers can help build brand reputation by providing authentic testimonials and recommendations. This can have a positive impact on the perception of the brand by the public (Hajarian et al., 2019).

5. Sales and promotions

Sales and promotion strategies are often based on discounts and special offers. Influencers can promote these offers to their audience, which can increase engagement and conversions. Collaboration with influencers can help boost sales at key moments (Peters, 2020). The use of discount coupons is a good way to control the flow of customers who have come through the influencer, in addition, many companies offer a percentage or commission for each sale they obtain when the influencer discount coupon is used.

Effectively integrating influencer marketing strategies with traditional marketing strategies can create powerful synergies and help brands reach a broader, more engaged audience. By understanding how these strategies complement each other, companies can build stronger and more effective marketing campaigns.

Key Aspects for a Campaign with Influencers in Restaurants

When planning a campaign with an influencer in the restaurant industry, it is essential to consider several aspects related to the duration and timing of launching the campaign. These aspects can influence the effectiveness and impact of the collaboration. Here are some key points regarding the topic.

1. Campaign objectives

Before defining the duration and timing of the campaign, the restaurant must establish clear and measurable objectives. Is it about increasing reservations, promoting a new menu, or building brand awareness? The objectives will influence the duration and the optimal moment to launch the campaign (Smith & Zook, 2011).

2. Season and special events

The timing of launching the campaign should take into account the season and any special events that may be relevant to the restaurant. For example, a Valentine's campaign may be effective in February, while a summer campaign may focus on cookouts (Hajarian et al., 2019). Taking advantage of local holidays and events can increase the relevance and interest of the campaign.

3. Duration of the collaboration

The duration of the collaboration with the influencer may vary depending on the objectives of the campaign. Short-term collaborations can be effective for specific promotions or temporary events, while long-term collaborations can help build an ongoing relationship with the audience (Xu & Du, 2020).

4. Frequency of posts

It is important to determine how often the influencer will post content related to the restaurant. Consistency in posting can maintain audience interest and keep the campaign top of mind with followers (Peters, 2020). To make the right decision about the frequency of publication, it is important to take into account the need for conversion by the company and the influencer's audience.

5. Continuous evaluation and adjustments

Regardless of the length and timing of the campaign, it is essential to establish tracking metrics and conduct ongoing performance evaluation. This will allow adjustments to be made as necessary to maximize the impact of the collaboration with the influencer (Gonçalves & Branco, 2020).

In summary, when considering the length and timing of a restaurant influencer campaign, it's essential to align these aspects with your goals, season, special events, and publishing strategy. Flexibility and adjustability are key to the success of the collaboration.

AFFECTATION OF DIGITAL INFLUENCERS IN THE BEHAVIOR OF THE GASTRONOMIC CONSUMER

The influence of digital influencers on the behavior of the gastronomic consumer is a topic of increasing relevance in the digital age. Next, we will explain two key aspects of this influence:

The Recommendation Through Digital Influencers

Digital influencers in the food industry have the power to recommend restaurants, dishes and culinary experiences through their online platforms. These recommendations often come in the form of reviews, tantalizing images, and tasting videos. According to Phua, Jin, and Kim (2017), recommendations from influencers can be particularly persuasive, since they are often perceived by their followers as trustworthy and authentic sources.

When an influencer praises a restaurant or a dish, they are conveying their personal experience and opinion. This can have a significant impact on the decision making of gastronomic consumers. Followers may be motivated to visit a restaurant recommended by their favorite influencer, as they trust their taste and ability to select quality dining experiences.

According to a Nielsen survey (2020), 90% of consumers trust recommendations from online friends and family, including digital influencers who are often perceived as virtual friends. A survey conducted by the Yelp team in 2021 revealed that 73% of respondents had tried a new restaurant after seeing influencer posts about it on social media platforms.

It should be noted that many restaurants have reported a significant increase in food reservations and orders after influencers promoted their offers. This increase can reach 40% in some cases, according to data compiled by the food marketing agency FoodieTribe (2021).

Trust Generated by Digital Influencers

The trust generated by digital influencers is a fundamental element in their influence on the behavior of the gastronomic consumer. Followers often develop a trusting relationship with their favorite influencers over time. This trust is based on the perceived authenticity of influencers and their ability to offer relevant and valuable content (Kaplan & Haenlein, 2010).

When it comes to dining recommendations, this trust translates into purchasing decisions. Followers are willing to try restaurants and dishes recommended by influencers they trust. This relationship of trust is especially valuable in a digital world where information and options are overwhelming. Influencers act as filters and trusted guides in the search for satisfying dining experiences.

In summary, the recommendation through digital influencers and the trust generated by them play a fundamental role in the influence they have on the behavior of the gastronomic consumer. These factors are essential to understanding how influencers affect purchasing decisions in the restaurant industry.

Some brands and restaurants have experienced a 55% increase in customer loyalty after implementing influencer marketing strategies, according to data from Influencity (2021), on the other hand, a study by Rakuten Advertising (2020) found that collaborations With influencers they generate online engagement that is 11 times greater than traditional advertising.

These numerical data underline the quantifiable influence that digital influencers have on gastronomic consumer behavior. Influencer recommendations build trust and have a significant impact on purchasing decisions and customer loyalty in the restaurant industry.

MANUAL OF GOOD PRACTICES FOR GASTRONOMIC MARKETING WITH DIGITAL INFLUENCERS

Collaboration with digital influencers in the restaurant industry requires a carefully planned strategy and the adoption of effective practices. Below is a manual of good practices for gastronomic marketing with digital influencers:

Proper Selection of the Optimal Profile

Choosing the right influencer is a critical step in any influencer marketing strategy. To select the optimal profile, it is important to consider the following aspects:

Relevance: The influencer must be related to the gastronomic industry and have an interesting number of followers interested in food and gastronomy.

Audience: Analyze the demographic profile and interests of the influencer's audience to ensure they match the restaurant's target audience and the goal of the communication campaign.

Authenticity: Assess the authenticity and credibility of the influencer. Followers must trust your recommendations. Assessing this aspect is possibly one of the most complex as it is a fact that is not very quantifiable. That is why we must analyze their history of collaborations and verify that the influencer's previous collaborations are aligned with the values and image of the brand of our establishment or company to promote. It is also interesting to analyze the profile of the influencer from a critical point of view and assess that the aspects of his private life that he shows are consistent with our business culture.

Choice of Appropriate Content and Social Network or Platform

Content developed in collaboration with an influencer must be appropriate and authentic. Some guidelines for content development include:

Authentic stories: Encourage the creation of authentic content that reflects the influencer's real experience in the restaurant, showing their more human side and that includes the experience before and after seeing the influencer.

Creativity: Encourage creativity in the presentation of dishes and the influencer's narrative to make the content attractive. Depending on our target audience, it will be interesting to present the dishes in a more dynamic and casual way or in a classic way.

Added value: Content should provide value to the audience, whether through detailed reviews, cooking tips, or relevant information about the restaurant.

Strategic collaboration: Work closely with the influencer to ensure the content meets the campaign objectives and reflects the brand identity. We must at all times control the content to be published to ensure that it is consistent with our objective.

Choosing the Ideal Platform

Much of the success of our campaign will depend on a good choice of platform, which is why we must consider different aspects to avoid errors that could cause the restaurant to lose resources.

1. **Facebook** has a large user base diversified in terms of age, gender and geographic location, allowing it to reach a wide audience. The platform offers detailed targeting options that allow you to target ads to specific groups of users, increasing the effectiveness of campaigns for restaurant establishments with a very local audience. (Smith & Zook, 2011).

2. **Instagram** is a highly visual platform, which is ideal for promoting products or services that can be displayed attractively through images and videos. The platform tends to have higher engagement rates compared to other social networks, meaning that followers tend to interact more with the content (Phua, Jin, & Kim, 2017).
3. **Twitter** is a real-time platform that allows brands and companies to participate in current conversations and live events. The retweet format facilitates content virality, which can increase the visibility of posts (Hajarian et al., 2019).
4. **LinkedIn** is a social network aimed at professionals and companies, which makes it an ideal place for business networking, job searching and promoting B2B services. It is not a widely exploited platform in the restaurant sector, but it is suitable for sharing professional content, such as articles, reports and updates related to the industry (Kaplan & Haenlein, 2010).
5. **TikTok** stands out for being the social network with the greatest penetration in the well-known Generation Z. This makes it an effective platform to reach a young and committed audience. TikTok focuses on short, creative videos, giving brands the opportunity to convey messages in a concise and engaging way. The platform is full of challenges and viral trends that brands can leverage to increase visibility and engagement.

Each social network has its unique advantages, and choosing the right platform depends on the marketing objectives and target audience of a company or brand. These advantages can help guide your social media marketing strategy and maximize the impact of your campaigns.

Measurement of Return on Investment (ROI)

Measuring the return on investment is essential to evaluate the effectiveness of a collaboration of any campaign and therefore also of the influencers who visit our establishment. Some metrics and practices for measuring ROI include:

Link tracking: Use tracking links to measure traffic to the property's website, booking portals, or even the reservation call button.

Social media metrics: Evaluate metrics such as reach, engagement, and number of followers gained during the campaign.

Customer surveys and reviews: Collect customer reviews and comments to evaluate the influence of collaboration on their restaurant visit decisions.

Sales analysis: Analyze the increase in sales and billing related to the campaign.

Conversions generated by the collaboration: It is also interesting to collect the comments of the influencer's followers, whether or not they visit our establishment, since from this information we can obtain what perception we have transmitted of the business.

The effective measurement of ROI allows adjusting the extension of the commercial campaign, with future strategies and optimizing collaborations with influencers to achieve more solid and quantifiable results.

CONCLUSION

The role of digital influencers in the restaurant sector is undeniable and has proven to be a significant force in consumer decision-making in relation to restaurants and gastronomic experiences and has led to them becoming one of the most popular marketing actions used in recent years thanks to its indisputable results.

The key findings are summarized below and possible future lines of research in this field are explored:

Summary of Key Findings

Digital influencers have a considerable impact on gastronomic consumer behavior. Recommendations through influencers are often perceived as trustworthy and authentic, leading to an increase in exploration of new restaurants and dishes.

The trust generated by influencers is a critical factor in their influence. Followers trust their opinions and feel emotionally connected to them, which influences their purchasing decisions in the culinary field.

Digital influencer marketing strategies in the restaurant industry must be carefully planned. The appropriate selection of the influencer, based on qualitative and quantitative values, the development of authentic content, the choice of channel or platform and the measurement of ROI are key aspects for success.

The restaurant industry has seen a significant increase in sales and brand visibility through effective collaborations with digital influencers.

FUTURE RESEARCH DIRECTIONS

As it is a communication model that is in full swing and has not yet reached its peak, research in this field is especially important, since the industry still needs to know how the consumer and the market are evolving in the face of digital influencers in the gastronomic sector and for this reason we can advance some of the lines of research that most promise in the market with a view to new studies:

Effectiveness in different segments of the industry: Investigate how the influence of influencers varies in different segments of the food industry, such as high-end restaurants vs. fast food outlets.

Impact of new emerging platforms: Explore how new social media platforms and emerging technologies, such as virtual reality and artificial intelligence, affect the influence of digital influencers on consumer behavior and what uses can be developed for these tools in the future next.

Sustainability measurement: Evaluate how collaborations with influencers can promote more sustainable practices in the gastronomic industry and how this impact can be measured in order to raise awareness among the population.

International comparison: Compare the impact of digital influencers on the behavior of the gastronomic consumer in different regions of the world and analyze the cultural differences and preferences. This line can help us to know the stage of maturity in markets or countries where the application of digital influencers in the restaurant sector to extrapolate to other markets.

Ethics and transparency: Investigate ethics and transparency in collaborations between influencers and restaurants, and how these perceptions affect consumer trust.

In summary, the influence of digital influencers in the restaurant industry is a dynamic topic that offers ongoing opportunities for research and analysis as it evolves in response to changes in technologies and consumer preferences.

REFERENCES

Aaker, D. A., & Keller, K. L. (1990). Consumer evaluations of brand extensions. *Journal of Marketing*, *54*(1), 27–41. doi:10.1177/002224299005400102

Adams, A., & Wilson, B. (2018). The Rise of Social Media Influencers in Marketing. *JMR, Journal of Marketing Research*.

Anderson, C. (2019). The Impact of Technology on Consumer Behavior. *Journal of Consumer Studies*.

Brown, R., & Davis, S. (2021). *Leveraging Influencer Marketing in the Restaurant Industry*. Marketing Journal.

Clark, E., & Turner, L. (2021). Influencer Marketing and Consumer Decision-Making. *Journal of Consumer Behaviour*.

Dall'Olmo Riley, F., Singh, J., & Blankson, C. (2018). Social Media and Its Link to Purchase Intentions of Luxury Fashion Brands. *Journal of Retailing and Consumer Services*.

ExpertVoice. (2021). *The Role of Influencer Marketing in Today's Consumer Decision Journey*. https://www.expertvoice.com/the-role-of-influencer-marketing-in-todays-consumer-decision-journey/

FoodieTribe. (2021). *FoodieTribe's Case Study on Influencer Marketing for Restaurants*. https://foodietribe.com/case-study/

Gonçalves, R., & Branco, F. (2020). *Twitch and the Engagement of Users: The Uses and Gratifications Approach to the Portuguese Community of Streamers*. Revista Portuguesa de Marketing.

Guo, C., & Saxton, G. D. (2014). Tweeting Social Change: How Social Media Are Changing Nonprofit Advocacy. *Nonprofit and Voluntary Sector Quarterly*, *43*(1), 57–79. doi:10.1177/0899764012471585

Gupta, S., & Dogra, N. (2018). Social Media Influencers: A Review and Research Agenda. *Vision: The Journal of Business Perspective*.

Hajarian, M., Hosseini, B., & Ramezankhani, M. J. (2019). Investigating the Role of Social Media Marketing in Customer Value Creation. *Journal of Research in Interactive Marketing*.

Hsu, C. L., & Lin, J. C. C. (2015). What drives purchase intention for paid mobile apps? An expectation confirmation theory perspective. *Electronic Commerce Research and Applications*, *14*(1), 46–57. doi:10.1016/j.elerap.2014.11.003

Influencer Marketing Hub. (2021). *Influencer marketing benchmarks: How to measure your success*. https://influencermarketinghub.com/influencer-marketing-benchmarks/

Influencity. (2021). *Influencer Marketing Benchmark Report 2021*. https://influencity.com/influencer-marketing-benchmark-report-2021/

Johnson, P., & Brown, A. (2020). The Power of Digital Influencers in Restaurant Marketing. *Journal of Hospitality and Tourism*.

Jones, M., & Green, R. (2017). Transforming Marketing Dynamics in the Restaurant Industry. *Journal of Restaurant Management*.

Kaplan, A. M., & Haenlein, M. (2010). Users of the world, unite! The challenges and opportunities of Social Media. *Business Horizons*, *53*(1), 59–68. doi:10.1016/j.bushor.2009.09.003

Martin, K. D., Shervani, T. A., & Slater, J. (2018). Social Media Influence: A Conceptual Framework and Research Agenda. *Journal of Interactive Marketing*.

Neeley, S. M., & Qaqish, S. (2020). The Impact of Influencer Type and Disclosure Type on Source Credibility and Persuasiveness: An Experiment. *Journal of Interactive Advertising*.

Nielsen. (2020). *Global Trust in Advertising - Report*. https://www.nielsen.com/us/en/insights/report/2020/global-trust-in-advertising/

O'Brien, S. (2021). *Rise of the Nano-Influencer: They May Have Only 1,000 Followers, but They're Big Business*. CNBC. https://www.cnbc.com/2021/06/12/rise-of-the-nano-influencer-they-may-have-only-1000-followers-but-theyre-big-business.html

Oberlo. (2021). *TikTok Statistics for 2021: Usage, Revenue, and More*. https://au.oberlo.com/blog/tiktok-statistics

Peters, K. (2020). Perceived Influence of Food Bloggers on Consumer Dining Choices: A Case Study of Food Bloggers in South Florida. *International Journal of Hospitality & Tourism Administration.*

Phua, J., Jin, S. V., & Kim, J. J. (2017). Gratifications of using Facebook, Twitter, Instagram, or Snapchat to follow brands: The moderating effect of social comparison, trust, tie strength, and network homophily on brand identification, brand engagement, brand commitment, and membership intention. *Telematics and Informatics*, *34*(1), 412–424. doi:10.1016/j.tele.2016.06.004

Rakuten Advertising. (2020). *Global Influencer Marketing Report 2020.* https://rakutenadvertising.com/en-uk/case-studies/global-influencer-marketing-report-2020/

Robinson, T. (2020). The Impact of Influencers on Restaurant Revenue. *The Journal of Business Strategy.*

Smith, A. N., Fischer, E., & Yongjian, C. (2012). How does brand-related user-generated content differ across YouTube, Facebook, and Twitter? *Journal of Interactive Marketing*, *26*(2), 102–113. doi:10.1016/j.intmar.2012.01.002

Smith, A. N., & Zook, Z. (2011). Marketing Communications Effectiveness and the Effect of Consumer Motivation on Perceived Value. *Review of Communication Research.*

Smith, J. (2018). The Influence of Social Media on Business Relationships. *Journal of Business Ethics.*

Statista. (2021a). *Number of Monthly Active Facebook Users Worldwide as of 2nd Quarter 2021.* https://www.statista.com/statistics/264810/number-of-monthly-active-facebook-users-worldwide/

Statista. (2021b). *Number of Monthly Active Instagram Users from January 2013 to June 2021.* https://www.statista.com/statistics/253577/number-of-monthly-active-instagram-users/

Statista. (2021c). *Pinterest: Number of Monthly Active Users Worldwide 2016-2021.* https://www.statista.com/statistics/463001/pinterest-global-mau/

Statista. (2021d). *Twitter: Number of Monthly Active Users 2010-2021.* https://www.statista.com/statistics/282087/number-of-monthly-active-twitter-users/

Statista. (2021e). *YouTube: Number of Monthly Active Users Worldwide 2016-2021.* https://www.statista.com/statistics/273550/number-of-monthly-active-youtube-users/

Voorveld, H. A., van Noort, G., Muntinga, D. G., & Bronner, F. (2018). Engagement with social media and social media advertising: The differentiating role of platform type. *Journal of Advertising*, *47*(1), 38–54. doi:10.1080/00913367.2017.1405754

White, E., & Davis, M. (2019). The Emergence of Influencer Marketing in the Restaurant Sector. *International Journal of Hospitality Management.*

Xu, L., & Du, X. (2020). What Drives Consumers' Intention to Follow Brands on Twitter? *Journal of Interactive Advertising.*

Yelp. (2021). *Consumer Trust in the Digital Age.* https://www.yelp-press.com/company/news-releases/news-release-details/2021-08-17-Consumer-Trust-in-the-Digital-Age/default.aspx

ADDITIONAL READING

Amaya Henao, S. M., Silva Cortés, G. A., & Rincón Quintero, Y. A. (2021). The impact of influencers on the promotional strategies of the gastronomic sectors in medellín. *Fonseca Journal of Communication, 22*. Advance online publication. doi:10.14201/fjc-v22-22695

Miguel, C., Clare, C., Ashworth, C. J., & Hoang, D. (2023). Self-branding and content creation strategies on Instagram: A case study of foodie influencers. *Information Communication and Society*, 1–21. Advance online publication. doi:10.1080/1369118X.2023.2246524

Newswire, P. R. (2017). Operating Room Equipment: Global Markets. LON-Reportbuyer.

KEY TERMS AND DEFINITIONS

Augmented Reality (AR): Augmented Reality is a technology that overlays computer-generated content, such as images, videos, or information, onto the real-world environment. AR enhances the user's perception of reality by providing digital information and interactions within the physical world.

Cobranding: Cobranding refers to a marketing strategy where two or more brands collaborate or combine their identities to promote a product or service, often to leverage each other's reputation and customer base.

Foodie: A 'foodie' is a person who has a strong interest and passion for food and gastronomy. Foodies are individuals who enjoy exploring and experimenting with a wide variety of dishes, ingredients, and types of cuisine. They are often food enthusiasts, culinary hobbyists, food critics, or simply people who are passionate about trying new foods and restaurants. The term 'foodie' has become popular to describe those who consider food an important part of their life and relish discovering flavors and culinary experiences.

Return on Investment (ROI): (ROI is a measure used to evaluate the profitability or effectiveness of an investment. It calculates the gain or loss generated relative to the cost of the investment and is typically expressed as a percentage.

Virtual Reality (VR): Virtual Reality is a technology that creates immersive, computer-generated environments or simulations, typically experienced through a head-mounted display or VR headset. It aims to replicate a real or imaginary environment, allowing users to interact with and navigate within the virtual world.

Chapter 13
Changing Consumer Buyer Decision Process in the Context of Instamoms

Ece İpekoğlu
https://orcid.org/0000-0001-8340-5326
Yasar University, Turkey

Nilgün Gürkaynak
Izmir University of Economics, Turkey

ABSTRACT

As an effective digital strategy, influencer marketing uses "influencers" on social media with their potential to deliver ideas to the masses. These people on social media are very attractive to consumers when making decisions. This research makes its theoretical contribution by combining marketing motherhood as a social construct as an instinctive process in social media. Within this context, mother influencers, called Instamoms, impact their followers by affecting their buyer decision process. This chapter aims to understand the impact of Instamoms on the buyer decision of their followers. The research concentrates on factors in how decisions in the process of mother followers can be shaped, affected, and harmonized toward the content of the Instamoms' posts, in terms the of influence that constitute the reference power, motherhood concept, and all other remaining factors that determine the buyer decision process.

BACKGROUND

Due to the widespread network of the internet and the evolution of social media, the new generation of women born in the post-1990s increasingly become socialized more through digital environments. In the case of the Instagram page of Instamoms, usually, a new mom starts launching an Instagram page to get over the isolation of new motherhood (Pembecioğlu, 2016). Concerning the content and posts of the page, personal posts of the daily life of that mother become subject to followers. The followers highly intensified digital interaction by connecting Instamoms to distant geographies through Instagram.

DOI: 10.4018/979-8-3693-0551-5.ch013

From the marketing point of view, consumers' engagement with brands and companies is changing because of technological developments. While marketing mix elements are evolving, promotion tools are changing as well. With the proliferation of social media, these tools and strategies for interacting with consumers have shifted significantly to this platform (Blackshaw& Nazzaro, 2004). Social media is a widely used tool to engage consumers in digital conversations. More than 72% of people in the United States use some form of social media, sharing text, images, and video (Pew Research Center, 2021). A well-designed social media presence is valuable to different groups of users with different motivations. For example, companies may use social media to enhance brand equity and social media influencers benefit financially from high follower counts and engagement (Khamis, Ang &Welling 2016; Zollo et al. 2020).

Furthermore, the promotion-related role of social media is very powerful. This causes also the evolution of traditional word-of-mouth communication, the more digitalized technology brings more usage of social media and actors of social media as an element of the promotional mix (Mangold& Fauld, 2009).

Using influencers on social media is one of the effective digitalized strategies (Lyons & Henderson, 2005). Brands have turned their attention to influencer marketing as consumers spend more time on SNS (Koay et al., 2022). Recently, Ye et al. (2021) conducted a bibliometric and thematic content analysis to identify the evolution of influencer marketing research. They found a rapid increase in the number of publications between 2003 and 2019, indicating that an increasing number of academics have begun to pay attention to this new field of study. Through thematic content analysis, five main themes were identified: theme 1: the persuasiveness of influencer marketing; theme 2: stakeholder perspectives on influencer marketing; theme 3: influencer marketing for specific product categories and sectors; theme 4: influencer identification, selection, and activation; and theme 5: ethical issues and disclosure effects in influencer marketing. The present study rightly focuses on the first, third, and fourth themes, focusing on various influencer characteristics that are critical to the effectiveness of influencer marketing.

In this chapter, popular and influential mothers on Instagram, frequently referred to as "Instamoms", are used as a context, since; they become persuasive and effective on Instagram. Instagram becomes a platform for consumption due to promoted posts that appear in users' timelines either directly by brands or through influencers. Followers as customers become a subject of Instagram consumption in both material consumption and the image of consumption. This operation is explained as documenting the self to be consumed by others (Schwarz, 2010). This consumption is a desired situation for an Instagram, which in return gives fame and possible income to her. An Instamom, represents a kind of self-brand that is responsive to the needs and interests of target audiences. These self-brands have an impact on their followers, women consumers' decision-making process. In normal conditions, the literature states that the buyer decision process starts with the "Need Recognition" step, however, this step looks transformed in the context of Instamoms. How this transformation is realized with the effects of Instamoms is not investigated before. Therefore, this chapter has investigated this topic.

SOCIAL MEDIA AND THE RISE OF INSTAGRAM

The introduction of social media and engagement can be discovered at the beginning of 2007. According to Tapscott and Williams (2008), social media is involved sharing something, socializing, collaborating, and composing new things very connect people. Marketing and consumer behavior research will be highly influenced by the interactions reflected in digital platforms (Kaplan & Haenlein, 2011; Mangold

& Faulds, 2009; Sago, 2017). Moreover, the users can communicate through posts and comments as well as actively interact and participate in the media content on social media. This opened the way for user-generated content, which precisely differentiates social media from traditional mass media. Owing to the nature of social media, individuals become a producer themselves. They can participate in the design of content.

Focusing on Instagram in this research, Instagram, one of the most popular social media platforms with approximately 1 billion users worldwide by 2021, is considered to be the second largest source of social media marketing (Statista, 2021). Furthermore, there are currently 1.35 billion individual accounts on this platform, among which actively log on every day. Considering users' profiles, 59% of Instagram users are between 18 and 29 years old, 33% between 30 and 49; followed by 18% between 50 and 64; and the remaining 8% are over 65 years old (Sprout Social, 2023).

INFLUENCER MARKETING

Influencer marketing to create strong brand awareness. Therefore, they are delivering certain messages through social media platforms (Hanna, Rohm & Crittenden, 2011). Instagram as the most popular social media platform is a very available place for this new marketing tool. Therefore, Influencer marketing has become to be crucial in response to consumers' huge presence on social media platforms especially Instagram, Facebook, and YouTube (Kaplan & Haenlein, 2010). This new technique (Influencer Marketing) is a sort of Electronic Word-of-Mouth (e-WOM) which is one of the central marketing techniques to create higher trustworthiness for consumers (Solis, 2017).

The rise of e-WOM, social media, and finally influencer marketing has led the term social media influencer to be created (De Veirman, Cauberghe & Hudders, 2017). Brands have realized that engaging their brands with social media influencers and influencer marketing can offer benefits such as a high-reaching impact and growth potential in social media among their potential consumers (De Veirman, Cauberghe& Hudders, 2017).

According to Sammis, Lincoln, and Pomponi (2016,), influencer marketing can be said as the art and science of bringing people together with those who are influential online to collaborate on brands' sponsored content. Sigala and Gretzel (2017) explain influencer marketing as a practice that identifies individuals influencing potential customers. Sudha and Sheena (2017) more specifically define influencer marketing as an activity to identify and activate people influencing a specific target audience or medium, to be part of a brand's campaign towards increased reach, sales, or engagement.

The concept is also considered a continuation of the word of mouth marketing as a new form (Sudha & Sheena, 2017). In 2016, Instagram was the most escalating and usable platform for influencer advertorials (Abidin, 2015). These are personalized promotions of products (or services), posted by an influencer. These posts are considered as spontaneously experienced by these influencers, whereas, they are granted (Abidin, 2016). They look like a personal story and embody Influencers' perspectives of having experienced the product or service themselves (Abidin, 2016). This can be also linked to WOM.

Influencer marketing can be also thought of as a manner of constructing relationships that has the possibility of helping brands that are in the process of generating a greater scope, concerning their audiences (Sudha & Sheena, 2017). Moreover, this shows shifting those audiences into becoming consumers that are loyal by authenticity and trust (Sudha & Sheena, 2017).

IDENTIFYING INFLUENCERS

As it is stated introduction part, influencers play a very important role in today's marketing practices; at the same time, their reputation is increasingly growing (Scoble & Israel, 2006). According to Influencer Benchmark Report (2020), Influencer Marketing Industry will approximately grow $9.7B in 2020. It is a huge growing industry today with an average media value per $5.78 spent (last year, it was only $ 1). 55% of these media agencies have a strong standalone content marketing budget and others are planning to allocate in 2020.

The influencers compose a special part of the virtual community since they spread information through various social media channels, such as blogs and social networks like Instagram; they share stories and photographs; they tell their experiences; they state various opinions about numerous topics, services, and products; they are influencing consumers (Alsulaiman et al., 2015). Instagram is mainly used for influencer marketing today according to Influencer Marketing Benchmark Report (Geyser, 2020). More than 90% of all influencer campaigns have Instagram as part of the marketing mix.

Comparing influencers to celebrities as public figures with a vast number of followers and fans, they are creating and producing posts or advertorials on social media or blogs. Influencers have an audience that is interested in specific topics, so the popularity of these people could not unrecognized by the marketers. The most popular field that influencers stand in is Fashion and Beauty (24%), followed by Travel and Lifestyle (13%), Health and Fitness (12%), Gaming (7%), Sports (5%), and Family, Parenting, and Home (5%). Accordingly, marketers have begun to use influencers as endorsers, as they are regarded as more credible than celebrities (Mendoza, 2010).

Influencers are trusting on their ability to give the consumers the feeling of people like them (Solis, 2016) which is the highest form of influence by the consumers themselves (Nielsen, 2015). It means that brands have to be more careful when they search for influencers who create real interest. Therefore, these influencers are different from traditional celebrities and traditional endorsements. On social networking sites like Instagram, YouTube, Twitter, and Facebook, social media influencers share content created by themselves and promote certain brands to obtain a following and brand recognition.

FOLLOWERS' SOCIAL IDENTITY

The social identity of a follower can be matched with a group of which the follower is a member or want to be a member (Nejad, Sherrell & Babakus, 2014). A follower usually considers the opinions and behavior existing in this group, and then s/he can accordingly form a proper self-image to look like the group members (Kapitan& Silvera, 2015). The group in which the follower wants to be a member or feels like a member is usually named the aspirational group. This will give the impression to the follower of new lifestyles, trends, and behaviors. Finally, the follower will be influenced and start to imitate these things as a result (Kembau & Mekel, 2014).

This influence in turn may affect how followers decide to purchase products since consumers mainly buy products symbolizing their ideal self and making them similar to the person they want to be like, such as an SMI (Nejad, Sherrell & Babakus, 2014; Kapitan & Silvera, 2015). An SMI has an impact as an idol of consumption because they symbolize what an ideal life as an SMI can look like for followers (Hearn & Schoenhoff, 2015). When an SMI interact with followers by sharing insights into their private lives (Hearn & Schoenhoff, 2015), followers may feel that they are more related to the lives of SMIs (Forbes, 2016). After a follower feels connected to an SMI, s/he will more probably adopt the view that the SMI recommends (Cheung, Xiao & Liu, 2014). Moreover, if a follower feels identical to and inspired by an SMI, this situation may trigger his/her motivation to imitate the SMI. Therefore, s/he can be persuaded to buy a certain product that the SMI recommends or imitate the same behavior that the SMI has (Xiang et al., 2016).

Believing to have similar interests, values, or characteristics with an endorser, followers highly adopt the endorser's beliefs, attitudes, and behaviors (Cialdini, 1993; Kelman, 2006). Identification comes from both actual and perceived similarities. It can be defined as the degree to perceive to have similar things to another person (Hoffner and Buchanan, 2005). In celebrity endorsement cases, identification is expected to derive from wishful identification, meaning to desire to be alike the celebrity (Kamins et al., 2013).

On the contrary, identification with an SMI is usually coming from perceived similarity (Gräve, 2017). Unlike celebrities, influencers are regarded as more accessible as long-distance friends (Djafarova & Rushworth, 2017). SMIs are likely to target their followers in their posts in a direct way. This creates a direct closeness and makes followers feel like peers (Erz & Christensen, 2018; Gannon & Prothero, 2018). Being able to comment on SMIs' posts and can interact could make the feeling that the influencer is similar to oneself stronger (Schmidt, 2007).

THE RELATIONS BETWEEN INFLUENCER CONCEPT AND BUYER DECISION PROCESS

Buyer Decision Process Concept

The term consumer behavior is composed of consumers' experiences starting with making purchases, and then it includes factors influencing their decision. For consumers, buying decisions are the consequence of a long and comprehensive process including a broad information search, brand comparison, and evaluation. It is important to understand consumer behavior to influence buying behavior. It is needed to know the detailed needs of customers and the reasons why they turn these needs into buying attributes. How consumers gather information about different alternatives and use this information to select among competing brands is also necessary to know (Belch & Belch, 2009).

Accordingly, many models try to analyze or anticipate the decision-making process and resulting actions. They are trying to explain an abstract representation of the consumer decision process and clarify the description of complex consumer behavior. In the 1950s, the uncertainty for the future and the costs of getting information in the present makes people's rational decisions limited. Therefore, their decisions can be taken with bounded rationality (Tozlu, 2016). After the 1950s, various models were developed. Some of these models are called grand models of consumer behavior attempting to comprehensively explain all aspects of the buying behavior. These are respectively: the Nicosia model (1966), Engel-Kollat-Blackwell model (1968), and Howard–Sheth model (1969) and but there are also other models as in the table above. They all provide profound insights into the nature of consumer buying and consuming which the human mind, otherwise cannot grasp the immense complexities of this phenomenon. Even though the explanation of the consumer buying decision process differs among these models, many of them are composed of five similar decision process stages (Mitchell & Boustani, 1993).

In this study, however, the modified version of these five steps buying decision process models will be used. The context of the study, Instamom as an influencer for mothers, brings a new understanding of the buyer decision process since the traditional steps do not exactly fit on the Instagram platform. For this reason, the research lays out the buyer decision process in a different way. In the following sections, the five steps buyer decision process is examined as the core model of buyer behavior in marketing. After this section, the changing buyer decision model and the relations with influencers concept are stated before offering the conceptual model in the methodology.

The Five-Stage Buying Decision Process Model

The five-stage buying decision process model, the traditional model of decision-making, is widely used by marketing specialists to have a better understanding of their customers and their behavior (Kotler & Keller, 2006). The basic premise of the model is that the buying action is a forward-moving process starting with buying a product. It starts long before the actual buying and continues also after the buying stage is completed. The name of the model describes itself well: five different stages in the process respectively: need recognition, information search, evaluation of alternatives, purchase decision, and post-purchase behavior. To understand each of these stages in the consumer buying process, all of them will be reviewed one by one.

Need Recognition

The buying process starts with need recognition. In this step, the buyer understands the difference between their actual state and the state they desire. This sense could be either prompted by an internal or external stimulus (Kotler & Armstrong, 2005).

Furthermore, other influences cannot be directly observable factors, such as psychological factors. Motivation is the ground of all consumer behavior in these psychological factors (Kinnear & Bernheart, 1986). Motivational needs are segmented as physiological and psychological needs (Kinnear & Bernheart, 1986). The physiological needs are our basic needs as food and shelter. The psychological ones are formed by one's social environment.

Perception is another psychological factor showing the way customers see themselves and their surroundings. It affects both the need recognition phase and also, other phases too (Kinnear & Bernheart, 1986). Need recognition can be in different forms according to the consumer's needs and perceptions.

Information Search

Information search is the second stage of the buyer decision process. In this stage, the consumer tries to collect information about the product that s/he wants to buy via different channels. There are two levels of arousal during the information search phase: heightened attention and active information search state (Kotler & Armstrong, 2005).

Today, the online environment is more dominant for information search. Therefore, there is a difference between being an expert on the product and the information search process. Due to the expert who has good knowledge about the product, the number of information searches may decrease. In the same way, having excellent knowledge of online search methods could make the search procedure more efficient.

It is good to have good knowledge about the product to increase the quality of the examination. In this way, the search time would decrease and a more efficient search would be done.

Evaluation of Alternatives

The third stage of the buyer decision process is the evaluation of alternatives in which the consumer evaluates all options available. Consumers are inclined to attribute particular qualifications for the products in their choice set. An alternative should have at least acceptable levels of features for being regarded as the final purchase. It is stated that two points exist for consumer cut-offs: one is that if the information comes from a reliable source, cut-offs are for the attribute is more severe, whereas if it is low, the cut-offs for the attribute are lower (Huber & Klein, 1991).

Purchase Decision

The consumer completes the evaluation stage and randomly aligns the alternatives in the choice set. Considering the evaluation and purchase decision stages, two factors occurred between them. The first one is the attitudes of others. The consumer changes his/her mind according to friends, family, or community influence although s/he has just ranked for a brand and decided to buy that brand. The second one is that unpredictable situational factors may influence the purchase decision.

Post Purchase Behavior

The final stage of the consumer decision process is the post-purchase behavior which takes place after the purchase is realized. It shows that the buyer decision process does not end with deciding and purchasing; it endures even after purchasing. This stage is as important as the purchase stage since the satisfaction or dissatisfaction of the consumer about the purchase affects his/her decision process for similar purchases, especially regarding the need recognition and information search stage in the future. It is also very crucial to understand consumer behavior for marketers after purchase to continue their sales under the same conditions.

THE BUYER DECISION PROCESS UNDER NEW PERSPECTIVE ON SOCIAL MEDIA CONTEXT

Considering the buyer decision process, consumers do not always decide by evaluating all available alternatives between different products or services to choose the best one. According to the theory of bounded rationality (Simon, 1982), there are two reasons for this action. The first one is that insufficient information is available for making an evaluation. The second one is individuals' limited ability to consider and evaluate this available information. However, with the rising of social media, the process has changed. Today, consumers can access any information, and take or make recommendations from everywhere. Even, they have the chance to write and read recommendations for future purchases through social networks (Merwe & Heerden, 2009).

Furthermore, social media creates new reviewers whose opinions are regarded as credible by the community, and who have significant influence on the buying behavior of consumers (Forbes & Vespoli, 2013). These people are new opinion leaders as influencers stated in the literature part. These people act on social media platforms. Previous research shows that Facebook and Twitter influence consumers' purchase decisions (Pietro & Pantano, 2012). The Instagram platform is newer than other social network platforms, but it has a very effective area of influence on consumers with its reach visual content (Miles, 2013).

As explained in the previous part, consumers pass through a five-step process when the buying decision is made. In the context of Instagram influencers, the steps may not be realized traditionally. For instance, even if there is no need for a product or service, consumers (namely followers) see a post about that product and want to buy it. The need recognition step is realized without any actual need.

Many studies observed the social media influences on purchase decisions; however, there is a need for examining how this influence is shaped across different stages and if the five-step process is valid in the context of Instagram influencers. Reaching more information and advice through influencers may decrease the effect of bounded rationality for consumers since consumers can have more information in this context. If it is true, the evaluation of alternatives step could be affected, since the consumer evaluated all alternatives with more information. This step may transform with the community effect on social media as feedback from the community stage. This effect may work as a motivator to purchase a product for followers. Finally, the post-purchase step may evolve as a reaction stage because followers write their comments and share their experiences on the pages of influencers.

THE CONCEPTUAL MODEL

The traditional five-step buyer decision process could be better to be revisited regarding changing consumer behavior on social networking sites because it has been evolving in the context of Instamom. The research intends to bring a new model of the buyer decision process offering "Changing Steps of Buyer Decision on the Context of Instamom" as a conceptual model of the study

Strategies in marketing research have changed over time because marketing is begun to be regarded as a socially constructed institution (Hirshman, 1986). Accordingly, research showed a tendency to apply socially constructed phenomena that need an interpretive approach. The typical approach used by interpretive phenomenology is to gather data from semi-structured interviews, since it is more loose way (Smith, 2007). This study was conducted in İzmir, Turkey, during 2018–2020. It was built on 30 semi-structured interviews, which were accomplished with a diverse group of 25 mothers and 5 mother influencers (Instamoms). This study investigates the context of Instamoms in Turkey.

As the study examines this context, the sample should be composed of this specific group of moms and their followers on the Instagram platform. Besides this, participants are usually based on personal tics in almost all qualitative research (Johnson, 2015). 5 Instamoms for interviewing among 10 Instamoms whose followers are above 200.000 were selected for the study. After interviewing the Instamoms, interviewee subjects were selected among the followers of selected Instamoms, and again with regards to their willingness to join the research (Bernard, 2002).

Instamoms and Followers: Understanding the Profiles

During data collection, different demographic characteristics such as education level, age, number of children, marital status, and background culture were collected. The analysis showed that these demographics affect the social profile of followers. Saying "the profile", the research investigates the social profile of follower mothers based on their lifestyle concept which is examined with AIO items (Peter & Olson, 1994).

Activities, Interests, and Opinions

According to the findings of the research, one of the most prominent factors for their preference of followings is their lifestyle, which is related to their social profiles. Besides the demographic characteristics, their activities, interests, and opinions affect the social profile deeply. For instance, family life brings giving priority to the expenses of the family activities, which is directly related to the income of the family. One's interest will be directly affected by income too. All of these factors create the social profile of followers.

Lifestyle similarities also signal the life vision in terms of health, beauty, male/female identities, work/money/time considerations, and the use of leisure, partner relations, family relations, friends, culture, politics, and economics (Vyncke, 2002). The answers of the respondents for the following Instamoms include social (activities and interests), economic, and cultural (opinions) factors. The majority of the respondents cite the lifestyle of Instamoms as the primary factor. Being similar to real mothers affects their following preferences. The activities for children are perceived to affect their preferences as well. Moreover, the credibility issue is very important for the respondent, they follow if they believe that Instagram is competent about all issues covered by motherhood. Finally, respondents usually mention that Instamoms try to impose a wealthy lifestyle. Interestingly, they stress that they do not like this trend, but they continue to follow it.

The Effects of Instamoms' Social Media Activities on Buying Behavior of Follower Mothers

Even though stating that most follower mothers give their priorities (in the material sense) to their children, the data reveals that regardless of all demographic characteristics, they expose to social media and want to reach those standards even if it is fake or real. The research shows that the consumption behavior of mothers is affected by the effects of the consumer culture agents on social media as the influencers, specifically Instamoms. Mothers as a consumer have become more aware and attracted to material things from social media, namely Instagram.

As Instamoms use a product and announce this, it increases the preferences of that product. It is because follower mothers feel themselves having the same position as these influencers through material culture and status (Crane & Bovone, 2006).

Brands put more effort fit Instagram to increase awareness and they use influencers too much in social media advertisements. They make agreements and put discounts under cooperation with influencers. Five Instamoms were interviewed during the data collection. All of them state that they make brand cooperation.

While interpreting the data, it is realized that mothers describe their buying behavior in similar ways. Their experiences with Instamoms create a kind of desire for commodities to reach the ideal beauty (Holbrook & Hirschman, 1982; Thompson & Haytko, 1997), ideal life, ideal motherhood, and so on. They want to have "the ideal" that they see on social media. There are some mothers among participants who are aware of this fake world, but there are many who want to reach that world by buying the products presented by Instamoms.

I like those kinds of things a lot. Who doesn't? I have many friends who are also mothers. They also like shopping … I pay a lot of attention to looking good. Matching my shoes or my bag with my clothes is very important. I pay attention to those things for my son too. I look at Melek İçmeli's Instagram, I admire her. I look at what she and her son wear. I usually buy things with her links. (P12, 33)

Based on all these expressions, the effects of Instamoms on buying behavior can be said to have an effect. Mothers are mostly influenced by clothing shopping and baby products. Moreover, the findings show that a vast majority of participant mothers expressed that their attitudes would change if Instamoms repeat promoting the same product or brand too much. They negatively change their attitude due to the feeling of irritation.

I liked the healthy food break until she started to show the same brand. This brand is too expensive though. I quit the following her. (P7, 35)

Under the influence of Instamoms, follower mothers choose either to believe or not believe the influencer effect. Talking with marketing terms, each follower mother forms a significant market at the same time. They are an important customer group not only themselves but also with their children. As today's marketing element, they can influence people in two ways: first by sharing (or looking like sharing) the same values, and second, by creating a trustable source of information.

BUYING BEHAVIOR STEPS AND THE INFLUENCE OF INSTAMOMS

Consumers in general show many attitude patterns during buying process of goods, services, ideas, or experiences. They like looking for products or services that they want for fulfilling their needs. By analyzing the responses of participants per each of the five levels of the answer, the data can indicate the tendency on which stage of buying behavior Instamoms have more impact.

Need Recognition

Need recognition is the first stage of the consumer-buyer decision process. In this stage, consumers understand the needs of the product that would be able to satisfy their needs. To understand the impact of Instamoms on buyer decision steps, the participants were asked if they desire to want to acquire the product when an Instamom shows it on Instagram and if they think that they need that product. Many follower mothers asked these two questions "Yes" during the interview.

I did buy many things even if I need or not at first times. You don't know what you will need in the early stages of pregnancy. It gets a little clearer after you have a baby, obviously, but still, I sometimes want to buy it when I see something nice. (P19, 29)

If I'm going to buy something, I ask myself if I need it. I am especially careful about things related to children. There are all kinds of good things for kids. In any case, the child is at home right now, not going to school. She's wearing sweatpants or something; that's why I ask if I need it. However, I still buy it if she does not need it. I am trying to find something that might interest her. For example, I bought a Barbie that she did not need. She has to play with the toy so she is not interested in the phone. (P9, 33)

I'll try to save some money. I try not to shop frequently. However, I cannot limit it. When I see something, especially for children on social media, I want to buy it. (P7, 35)

According to 85% of the participants, social media triggers desire towards some products, and sometimes it causes debt for them to buy unnecessary branded products, clothing, and toys. Even though some of the participants state that they try to stay away from buying those kinds of things, a majority of the participants buy to reach the desired product. In this case, the research may argue that Instamoms change the nature of buyer behavior from need recognition to desire creation for almost half of the participants.

For example, the mother shares something about her child, but you see that child's room in the background and you go into a shopping frenzy saying, "Oh look, there's this, there's this, how nice it is... mothers started to show what they bought to the people's eyes, as the shares increased, awareness increased, and other mothers started to buy them too. I'm throwing away a toy when I didn't know about it. (P5, 35)

Firstly, consumption increased because there is such a thing as social media, people also follow social media, and they are knowledgeable in more fields, your neighborhood used to be so much of your city, now even a person in Hakkari knows about New York from Istanbul. (P6, 45)

For example, the mother shares something about her child, but you see that child's room in the background and you go into a shopping frenzy saying, "Oh look, there's this, there's this, how nice it is... mothers started to show what they bought to the people's eyes, as the shares increased, awareness increased, and other mothers started to buy them too. For example, I bought a toy many times when I didn't know about it. (P24, 34)

As described by the participants, Instamoms on social media are a major way for realizing the desired object even though they are not aware of that product before seeing it. Remembering that desire is the driving force for the consumers in the marketplace (Wilk, 1997), mothers may prefer to attain those products to satisfy themselves. It is already known that the products not yet acquired are thought to have happiness in them (Belk, Ger& Askegaard, 2003), so social media influencers, Instamoms benefit from this unstoppable feeling.

Information Search

After elaborating on the need recognition step, the second step is the information search in which consumers look for information about the product. Usually, consumers search for information by talking to others, reading, visiting stores, or other media, but today social media and the internet are ahead of all of them. To understand whether Instamoms has an impact on this stage for respondents, they were asked whether they collect information from external sources about a product that an Instamom shares.

Overall, the answers for the step of information search in the buyer decision process are "Yes". Participants are affected by Instamoms at some level and they look for further information about the product they have seen. Some follower mothers' respondents remark Instamoms are a source of inspiration in their information search. They mainly apply Google search, Trendyol, and some other shopping websites like Hepsi Burada to read user comments about the products. They also look for a cheaper price.

I'll Google it for the price ranges. For example, if the price is high at Trendyol, I look elsewhere for a storage container, or if the difference is small, I buy it from Trendyol because the shipping is free. There is a foreign book series. Kids love it. It was 130 lira in Trendyol. Then I looked on Google. It was selling for 90 lines on the same seller's site. (P19, 29)

I usually do. I read the comments. I'll look at other sites. (P11, 36)

I also check Trendyol and the store's website. I also look for clothing on Pinterest. (P10, 35)

Instamoms are everywhere. I look for their page for shopping. I also read reviews on shopping sites. (P4, 30)

Evaluation of Alternatives

This is the third step of the buyer decision process as it is in more detail explained in the literature review. Consumers evaluate the options for all similar products and brands at this stage, since evaluating may bring more benefits. To deeper understand the impact of Instamoms on the evaluation of alternatives stage, the related question was asked them: When they decided to buy a product that they see on the page Instamom, do you evaluate the alternative products?

It is discovered that all of the participants including Instamoms (35 mothers) search for a similar product shared by an Instamom to evaluate it. User comments are also very effective for this stage. Most participants stressed that they read comments about the product.

Yes, I will compare. So, especially if it's such a large amount of money, I'll compare it. (P24, 34)

I usually look at Instagram. I always do price research. I compare Trendyol and the like. (P10, 35)

I compare. I'll do a price comparison. I prefer the cheap ones, not necessarily the brand. (P11, 36)

I compare. I search all over the web. If I can't find it there, I'll look for hashtags on Instagram. (P6, 45)

Yes. For example, I bought sunscreen. If it's recommended, I'll consider it. There was a stain for a while. I looked at what everyone suggested. I often compare brands. (P9, 34)

I'm writing on the Internet again. I write what works. For example, I had an acne problem. I'm looking for users. (P2, 36)

Purchase Decision

This stage is directly the moment in which buying the product is realized. During the interview, follower mothers were asked whether they purchased with the effect of Instamoms. Considering the participants' discourses, it may argue that Instamoms are a source of purchase decisions at least once in a lifetime for all follower mothers. According to the analysis, following different Instamoms will increase the level of exposure to posts about different products or services. Having Instagram following different people who have different lifestyles causes them to be exposed to more marketing messages and word-of-mouth communication about the sponsored posts.

There is. For example, I just bought material from outside. They made flowers with pom-poms for her room. It hangs on the wall. For example, sometimes I don't have a blanket or I buy quality clothes by looking at the suggestions. (P10, 35)

There are many times that I said I'd buy it right away, but I don't know if I got it. It was a kitchen appliance, but not so much. (P4, 30)

It is happening. I'm sure I'll be impressed and buy something right away. I do, but I always read the comments. For example, I bought a scooter last month and looked at the reviews. Despite the negative reviews, I bought it. It didn't matter to me. The scooter was functional. I was impressed by Çiseren and bought a children's bed. I have never regretted anything I bought. (P9, 34)

We do a lot of online shopping during the pandemic. That's why I use Trendyol a lot. Sometimes there are things that I go in and buy by looking at the price performance and comments. There are products that I swipe up and save on Instagram. I don't buy a lot of clothes for myself with the suggestion of influencers. (P19, 29)

I am affected by Instamoms pages. Especially pandemic period, I bought many things online when I saw there. I mainly bought child-specific products. (P5, 35)

It happened. I bought it for my nephew before I had a child. It turned out very nice. Nice Puzzle, big like that. I bought a Puzzle about the earth and the planet. It turned out very nice. (P7, 35)

Many respondents shared the opinion that they buy products when they see Instamoms pages. In conclusion, it may state that all participant mothers are getting exposed to the messages of the Instamoms about products or any services, and these messages have a more intense effect in the case of purchase decision.

Post Purchase Behavior

This stage indicates how the consumer regards the buying experience and the product or service itself. Later, it is a determinant factor if they will purchase again or not with the same advice in Instamoms context. Therefore, questions related to post-purchase experience are asked of the follower mothers to evaluate if there is an impact between Instamoms and the post-purchase behavior step of the buyer decision process.

If I don't like it, I comment. However, up to now, there is no product that I did not like if I bought it from a recommendation. (P10, 35)

Recently, there is such a thing as the local food industry, I bought rice. I bought tahini from the given Instagram page. She turned out beautiful. I will continue to take it. (P24, 34)

Something like this came to my mind. Sometimes there were different tools for baby or child care. For example, what nonsense I said, but I bought it. There is a different type of mug so that water does not get into the eyes while washing the child. There isn't any need for it. It's all over now. (P25, 40)

I bought a crown so I could wear it while taking pictures at the hospital, but I came too late and it didn't come as I expected. I could not communicate with the seller. I did not comment. I unfollowed. The product is not bad, it turned out to be a little simpler than I expected. The flowers have fallen. (P19, 29)

Even though the post-purchase step is the last stage of buying behavior process, in the context of Instamoms, it is not a very active one. The semi-structured interviews include questions regarding this stage, but a majority of the participants did not mention about anything the importance of this stage in shaping the impact of buying behavior. They gave more moderate answers to these questions. Their answers are only about making user comment.

CONCLUSION

From a broader perspective, the focal constructs, motherhood, and buying behavior are studied in consideration of the larger social media perspectives that affect follower mothers. Consequently, the contributions of the research to the social media and marketing literature are not limited to the debates on buying behavior, but it also sheds light on macro-level discussions regarding the representation roles of motherhood and the societal implications of the phenomena.

In recent years, researchers have given more attention to a consumer-centric approach, collecting personal stories to catch valuable explanations and insights as a research methodology. The stories on social media grow in importance when new media brings a lot of change in people's life (Lister et al., 2009; Dewing, 2012).

According to the motherhood narratives, some participants are influenced by Instamoms, and they fanatically follow their all activities. Applying their motherhood style, buying products that Instamoms use, and performing in similar ways to them, follower mothers move towards another stage, in which they feel unqualified. Buying the same products, the mothers may feel equivalent to Instamoms in some contexts, but this is not enough for all time.

Furthermore, some mothers have no opportunity to meet the standards of Instamoms, and they do not have the financial possibility to reach those lives performing on social media. Those mothers feel satisfied with their lives in normal conditions. However, with the influence of Instamoms, they sometimes feel lacking in their appearances, motherhood, and social and financial possibilities even though they focus on their other qualifications. Those individuals are a source of inspiration for follower mothers, through social media success and various achievements. However, only a limited number of Instamom could behave like that because they gain money from their Instagram accounts, and these kinds of posts do not take much interest from popular brands. Brands want more product displays.

Instamoms establish themselves in the social media platform, Instagram and transform the buyer decision process for follower mothers into new steps. In other words, they influence their followers in two fragments: The representation of motherhood and the buyer decision process. They grow their visibility and be recognized by mothers as role models even if they have dark sides. Consequently, the follower mothers who could not or do not want to get out of the loop transform into either lovers or haters but are still a follower.

The major contribution of the research especially to the consumer research literature comes from the findings about the impact of buying decision process of mothers in the social media and Instagram context, which is a prominent gap except for a few studies (Daniel, 1999; Dedeoğlu, 2010; Gram & Pedersen, 2014). The changing approaches to capitalism offered working or non-working mothers the opportunity to test and prove their motherhood through consumption. Consumption, which has become a tool for mothers to test their motherhood, is intertwined with motherhood and child rearing (Zengingönül, 2012).

Today, consumption assets and the processes of defining motherhood through these assets have become interconnected through social media (Gram & Pedersen, 2014). Consumption is now seen as an important tool for being one of the basic actions of the mother. Therefore, the requirements of the motherhood phenomenon and the ideal of a good mother have changed more than ever before and are almost surrounded by consumption actors. Therefore, Instamoms have a direct impact on buying behavior of follower mothers and change the buyer decision process.

This research offers an alternative step to the buyer decision process. In the current period, consumer goods and services are so attractive, with so many alternatives and so "alluring"; Surrounded by the emotional atmosphere of motherhood, a woman rarely asks, "Does this work?" can ask the question. Especially if other mothers close to them have bought these products or services and are very satisfied, and if many experts share the positive aspects of these products and services through various platforms, the probability of the mother being hesitant about acquiring this product or service is very low. The mother shapes her consumption behavior as a result of rational choices. At this point, especially the effect of social media is undeniable.

Mothers consume products and services in many categories within the scope of their motherhood roles. This consumption, which starts with pregnancy, takes place under the influence of experiences Instamoms on social media. Examining these variables, which are thought to contribute to deepening the study, is important in terms of analyzing the course of consumption behaviors exhibited by mothers in terms of buyer decision process steps. In the traditional model, the first step is "need recognition" but the findings suggest that the first step is related to desire since mothers can buy anything that they do not need. Therefore, it is more like "desire creation.

When the buyer decision process is discussed, the physical appearance point should be also mentioned. People themselves cannot determine how individual bodies are presented, but society, social situations, and other forces are the decision-makers on the presentation (Bourdieu, 1990). In the context of Instamoms, the decision makers or norm setters are Instamoms for mothers.

Physical appearance is directly related to enjoyment, sensations, and tastes in the consumer culture; it must be kept or made better with diets, surgery, or cosmetic products (Goffman, 1959). Instamoms direct mothers to use different products to construct a more beautiful appearance as mothers in the media representations (Featherstone, 2010). Being exposed to ideal beauty images by these women, following mothers want to buy beauty products or make surgeries to have similar beautiful appearances.

Contrary to the traditional buyer decision process model, the findings reveal that the first two steps are context dependent. The consumers' experiences and perceptions may change in the social media context; the traditional steps may be transformed. Being subjected to Instamoms posts, buying decision process's first step is transforming through desires. Desire is the driving force behind marketing activities and guarantees the continuity of consumption in the capitalist system (Slater, 1997; Yurdakul & Atik, 2013). The new model suggests that the buyer decision process steps may change with the impact of social media in the context of Instamoms for follower mothers.

Focusing on the new model it attempts to adapt need recognition, information search, and post-purchase behavior steps in the new media period. The new model, at the individual level, shows people realize their desires, and at the communal level on social media, creates awareness of new phenomena. The traditional model states need when deciding to buy something and it does not give place for user comments, since social media is new for the traditional model. The information search step is still valuable but it is identifying more to feedback from the community on social media. Lastly, post-purchase behavior may be modified as the reaction stage since behavior may alter on social media from post-purchase to reaction. In sum, the traditional model has basic steps buyer decision process. On the other hand, the new model may be said as taking a more digital and postmodern approach.

On the marketing side, considering the needs and desires of mothers, Instamoms may focus on accompanying mothers as consumers. The findings reveal that mothers sometimes feel helpless to participate in consumption practices, especially in their early motherhood. For marketers and Instamoms, composing a community as a tribal marketing approach can be beneficial for follower mothers and bring out the bright side of marketing on social media. Since, a tribe includes people having different gender, age, and attitudes, but unites around a collective identification, and shared experiences, (Cova & Shankar, 2012), Instamoms can achieve this kind of mission.

According to follower mothers' discourses, social media is one of the major institutions that affect their consumption behavior and create the desire for products, that are promoted by Instamoms. Even though some of the participants are not affected by this influence, many of them are shaped by their desires and envied by "this perfect life". In a majority of the interviews, follower mothers criticize Instamoms for showing their possessions and engaging in luxury consumption, however, they are still following and affecting. Moreover, their statements show that they also want and try to be like them by buying products promoted by them.

As revealed clearly, social media today involves the constitution of the market system. This has a huge effect and responsibility on consumers. As all consumers, mothers' vulnerability increases further. Therefore, social media marketers and Instamoms that are responsible for the formation of content should act more responsibly.

Besides marketing professionals, academia needs to act. Most researchers can explain the real need for research on motherhood and consumption practices. It can increase awareness in academia and society to be the voice of mothers' real problems on social media. Marketers using Instamoms for their campaigns should acknowledge that motherhood is not just a trend. It is not just about consumption and setting the perfect motherhood criteria. It has differences in age, physical abilities, and social and financial opportunities. The homogeneity of the Instamoms offers similar types for follower mothers. With this thesis, the aim is to show the right direction by presenting all sides of influencer marketing in the context of Instamoms and being a voice for follower mothers for their consumption practices too.

NOTE

This study was produced from the PhD thesis of the first author.

REFERENCES

Abidin, C. (2015). *Communicative intimacies: Influencers and perceived interconnectedness*. Academic Press.

Abidin, C. (2016). Aren't these just young, rich women doing vain things online? Influencer selfies as subversive frivolity. *Social Media + Society*, *2*(2), 1–17. doi:10.1177/2056305116641342

Alsulaiman, K., Forbes, S., Dean, D., & Cohen, D. (2015). Relationships between perceived product values and three word of mouth variables. *Journal of Customer Behaviour*, *14*(4), 277–294. doi:10.1362/147539215X14503490289260

Aslam, S. (2017). *Instagram by the Numbers: Stats, Demographics, and Fun Facts*. Retrieved from: https://www.omnicoreagency.com/instagram-statistics/

Belch, G., & Belch, M. (2009). *Advertising and Promotion: An Integrated Marketing Communications Perspective* (8th ed.). Irwin.

Belk, R. W., Ger, G., & Askegaard, S. (2003). The fire of desire: A multisited inquiry into consumer passion. *The Journal of Consumer Research*, *30*(3), 26–51. doi:10.1086/378613

Bernard, H. R. (2002). *Research Methods in Anthropology: Qualitative and Quantitative Methods* (3rd ed.). Altamira Press.

Blackshaw, P., & Nazzaro, M. (2004). *Consumer-Generated Media (CGM) 101: Word-of-Mouth in the Age of the Webfortified Consumer*. Retrieved from: http://www.Nielsenbuzzmetrics.Com/Whitepapers

Bourdieu, P. (1990). *In Other Words: Essays Towards A Reflexive Sociology*. Stanford University Press. doi:10.1515/9781503621558

Cheung, C. M., Xiao, B. S., & Liu, I. L. (2014). Do actions speak louder than voices? The signaling role of social information cues in influencing consumer purchase decisions. *Decision Support Systems*, *65*, 50–58. doi:10.1016/j.dss.2014.05.002

Cialdini, R. B. (1993). *Influence: Science and Practice* (3rd ed.). Harpercollins College Publishers.

Cova, B., & Shankar, A. (2012). Tribal Marketing, in L. Penaloza, N. Toulouse and L. M. Visconti. In Marketing Management: A Cultural Perspective. Routledge.

Crane, D., & Bovone, L. (2006). Approaches to material culture: The sociology of fashion and clothing. *Poetics*, *34*(6), 319–333. doi:10.1016/j.poetic.2006.10.002

Daniel, W. W. (1999). *Biostatistics: A Foundation For Analysis in the Health Sciences* (7th ed.). John Wiley & Sons, Inc.

De Veirman, M., Cauberghe, V., & Hudders, L. (2017). Marketing through instagram influencers: The impact of number of followers and product divergence on brand attitude. *International Journal of Advertising*, *36*(5), 798–828. doi:10.1080/02650487.2017.1348035

Dedeoğlu, A. Ö. (2010). Discourses of motherhood and consumption practices of Turkish mothers. *Business and Economics Research Journal*, *1*(3), 1–15.

Dewing, M. (2012). *Social Media: An Introduction*. Library of Parliament.

Djafarova, E., & Rushworth, C. (2017). Exploring the credibility of online celebrities' instagram profiles in influencing the purchase decisions of young female users. *Computers in Human Behavior*, *68*, 1–7. doi:10.1016/j.chb.2016.11.009

Engel, J. F., Kollat, D. J., & Blackwell, R. D. (1968). *Consumer Behavior*. Holt, Rinehart and Winston.

Erz, A., & Christensen, A. B. H. (2018). Transforming consumers into brands: Tracing transformation processes of the practice of blogging. *Journal of Interactive Marketing*, *43*, 69–82. doi:10.1016/j.intmar.2017.12.002

Featherstone, M. (2010). Body, image and affect in consumer culture. *Body & Society*, *16*(1), 193–221. doi:10.1177/1357034X09354357

Forbes, K. (2016). Examining the beauty industry's use of social influencers. *Elon Journal of Undergraduate Research in Communications*, *7*(2), 78–87.

Forbes, L. P., & Vespoli, E. (2013). Does social media influence consumer buying behavior? An investigation of recommendations and purchases. *Journal of Business & Economics Research*, *11*(2), 107–113. doi:10.19030/jber.v11i2.7623

Fred, S. (2015). *Examining Endorsement and Viewership Effects on the Source Credibility of Youtubers*. Retrieved from: http://Scholarcommons.Usf.Edu/Cgi/Viewcontent.Cgi?Article=6883andContext=Etd

Gannon, V., & Prothero, A. (2018). Beauty bloggers and youtubers as a community of practice. *Journal of Marketing Management*, *34*(3), 1–28. doi:10.1080/0267257X.2018.1482941

Geyser, W. (2020). *The State of Influencer Marketing 2020: Benchmark Report*. Retrieved from: https://influencermarketinghub.com/influencer-marketing-benchmark-report-2020/

Goffman, E. (1959). *The Presentation of Self in Everyday Life*. Penguin Books.

Gram, M., & Pedersen, H. D. (2014). Negotiations of Motherhood- Between İdeals and Practice, Motherhoods, Markets and Consumption. In S. O'Donohoe, M. Hogg, P. Maclaran, L. Martens, & L. Stevens (Eds.), *The Making of Mother, Motherhoods, Markets and Consumption: The Making of Mothers in Contemporary Western Cultures* (pp. 99–114). Routledge.

Gräve, J. (2017) Exploring The Perception of Influencers vs. Traditional Celebrities: Are Social Media Stars a New Type of Endorser? *8th International Conference on Social Media and Society*, 1-5.

Hanna, R., Rohm, A., & Crittenden, V. L. (2011). We're all connected: The power of the social media ecosystem. *Business Horizons*, *54*(3), 265–273. doi:10.1016/j.bushor.2011.01.007

Hearn, A., & Schoenhoff, S. (2015). *From Celebrity to Influencer: Tracing the Diffusion of Celebrity Value Across the Data Stream*. Wiley Online Library.

Hoffner, C., & Buchanan, M. (2005). Young adults' wishful identification with television characters: The role of perceived similarity and character attributes. *Media Psychology*, *7*(4), 325–351. doi:10.1207/S1532785XMEP0704_2

Holbrook, M. B., & Elizabeth, C. H. (1982). The experiential aspects of consumption: Consumer fantasy, feelings and fun. *The Journal of Consumer Research*, *9*(2), 132–140. doi:10.1086/208906

Howard, J. A., & Sheth, J. N. (1969). *The Theory of Buyer Behavior*. John Wiley & Sons, Inc.

Huber, J., & Klein, N. (1991). Adapting cutoffs to the choice environment: The effects of attribute correlation and reliability. *The Journal of Consumer Research*, *18*(3), 346–357. doi:10.1086/209264

Influence Center Survey. (2020). *Social Upends Traditional Media In Driving Shopping Purchases*. Retrieved from: http://blog.influence-central.com/social-upends-traditional-media-in-driving-shopping-purchases/

Influencer Marketing Hub. (2020). *The State of Influencer Marketing 2020: Benchmark Report*. Retrieved from: https://influencermarketinghub.com/influencer-marketing-benchmark-report-2020/

Johnson, K. (2015). Behavioral education in the 21st century. *Journal of Organizational Behavior Management*, *35*(1-2), 135–150. doi:10.1080/01608061.2015.1036152

Kamins, M., Brand, M., Hoeke, S., & Moe, J. (2013). Two-sided versus one-sided celebrity endorsements: The impact on advertising effectiveness and credibility. *Journal of Advertising*, *18*(2), 4–10. do i:10.1080/00913367.1989.10673146

Kapitan, S., & Silvera, D. (2015). From digital media influencers to celebrity endorsers: Attributions drive endorser effectiveness. *Marketing Letters*, *27*(3), 553–567. doi:10.100711002-015-9363-0

Kaplan, A., & Haenlein, M. (2011). Two hearts in three-quarter time: How to waltz the social media/viral marketing dance. *Business Horizons*, *54*(3), 253–263. doi:10.1016/j.bushor.2011.01.006

Keller, E., & Berry, J. (2003). *The Influentials: One American in Ten Tells the Other Nine How to Vote, Where to Eat, and What to Buy*. Free Press.

Kelman, H. (2006). Interests, relationships, identities: Three central issues for individuals and groups in negotiating their social environment. *Annual Review of Psychology*, *57*(1), 1–26. doi:10.1146/annurev.psych.57.102904.190156 PMID:16318587

Kembau, A., & Mekel, P. A. (2014). Reference groups, family, roles and status on young consumer behavior towards purchase intentions of luxury fashion brands. *Journal EMBA*, *2*(2), 1172–1178.

Khamis, S., Ang, L., & Welling, R. (2016). Self-Branding, 'Micro-Celebrity' and the Rise of Social Media Influencers. *Celebrity Studies*, *8*(2), 191–208. doi:10.1080/19392397.2016.1218292

Kinnear, T., & Bernhardt, K. (1986). *Principles of Marketing* (2nd ed.). Scott, Foresman and Co.

Koay, K. Y., Cheung, M. L., Soh, P. C.-H., & Teoh, C. W. (2022). Social media influencer marketing: The moderating role of materialism. *European Business Review*, *34*(2), 224–243. doi:10.1108/EBR-02-2021-0032

Kotler, P. (2011). *Principles of Marketing* (14th ed.). Pearson Education.

Kotler, P., & Armstrong, G. (2005). *Marketing: An Introduction*. Prentice Hall.

Kotler, P., & Keller, K. L. (2006). *Marketing Management* (12th ed.). Prentice Hall.

Lister, M., Dovey, J., Giddings, S., Grant, I., & Kelly, K. (2009). *A New Media: A Critical Introduction* (2nd ed.). Routledge.

Lyons, B., & Henderson, K. (2005). Opinion leadership in a computer-mediated environment. *Journal of Consumer Behaviour*, *4*(5), 319–329. doi:10.1002/cb.22

Mangold, W. G., & Faulds, D. J. (2009). Social media: The new hybrid element of the promotion mix. *Business Horizons*, *52*(4), 357–365. doi:10.1016/j.bushor.2009.03.002

Mcgrail, A. (2013). *The Blogconomy: Blogging Stats*. Retrieved at: http://Www.Socialmediatoday.Com/Content/Blogconomy-Blogging-Stats-Infographic

Mendoza, M. (2010). I blog. You buy. How Bloggers are creating a new generation of product endorsers. *Digital Research and Publishing*, *7*, 114–122.

Merwe, R., & Heerden, G. (2009). Finding and utilizing opinion leaders: Social networks and the power of relationships. *South African Journal of Business Management*, *40*(3), 65–76. doi:10.4102ajbm.v40i3.545

Miles, J. (2013). *Instagram Power: Build Your Brand and Reach More Customers with the Power of Pictures*. Mcgraw-Hill.

Mitchell, V. W., & Boustani, P. (1993). A preliminary investigation into pre-and post-purchase risk perception and reduction. *European Journal of Marketing*, *28*(1), 56–71. doi:10.1108/03090569410049181

Nejad, M., Sherrell, D., & Babakus, E. (2014). Influentials and influence mechanisms in new product diffusion: An integrative review. *Journal of Marketing Theory and Practice*, *22*(2), 185–208. doi:10.2753/MTP1069-6679220212

Nicosia, F. M. (1966). *Consumer Decision Process*. Prentice Hall.

Nielsen. (2015). *Global Trust in Advertising. Winning Strategies for an Evolving Media Landscape*. Retrieved from: https://www.nielsen.com/content/dam/nielsenglobal/apac/docs/reports/2015/nielsen-global-trust-ın-advertising-report-september-2015.pdf

Pembecioğlu, N. (2016). Ben'den Vazgeçerek 'Daha' and *Olmaya Doğru Bir Adım Olarak Özçekim*. Beykent Üniversitesi.

Peter, J., & Olson, J. (1994). *Consumer Behavior and Marketing Strategy* (4th ed.). Irwin/Mcgraw-Hill.

Pew Research Center. (2022). *Social Media Fact Sheet*. Retrieved from: https://www.pewresearch.org/internet/fact-sheet/social-media/

Pietro, L. D., & Pantano, E. (2012). An empirical investigation of social network influence on consumer purchasing decision: The case of Facebook. *Journal of Direct, Data and Digital Marketing Practice*, *14*(1), 18–29. doi:10.1057/dddmp.2012.10

Sago, B. (2017). The influence of social media messages sources on millennial generation consumers. *International Journal of Integrated Marketing Communications*, *2*(2), 7–14.

Sammis, K., Lincoln, C., & Pomponi, S. (2016). *Influencer Marketing For Dummies*. John Wiley and Sons, Inc.

Schmidt, J. (2007). Blogging practices: An analytical framework. *Journal of Computer-Mediated Communication*, *12*(4), 1409–1427. doi:10.1111/j.1083-6101.2007.00379.x

Schwarz, O. (2010). On friendship, boobs and the logic of the catalogue. *Convergence (London)*, *16*(2), 163–183. doi:10.1177/1354856509357582

Scoble, R., & Israel, S. (2006). *Naked Conversations: How Blogs are Changing the Way Business Talk With Customers*. John Wiley and Sons.

Sigala, M., & Gretzel, U. (2017). *Advances in Social Media for Travel, Tourism, and Hospitality: New Perspectives, Practice and Cases*. Routledge. doi:10.4324/9781315565736

Simon, H. A. (1982). *Models of Bounded Rationality*. MIT Press.

Slater, D. (1997). *Consumer Culture and Modernity*. Polity Press.

Solis, B. (2016). *The Influencer Marketing Manifesto: Why the Future of Influencer Marketing Starts with People and Relationships not Popularity*. Retrieved from: http://pages.tapinfluence.com/hubfs/ınfluencer_marketing_manifesto.pdf

Sproutsocial. (2023). *Important Instagram Stats You Need To Know For 2020*. Retrieved from: https://sproutsocial.com/ınsights/ınstagram-stats/

Statista. (2021). *Most used social media, 2021*. Retrieved from: https://www.statista.com/statistics/272014/global-social-networks-ranked-by-number-of-users/

Sudha, M., & Sheena, K. (2017). Impact of influencers in consumer decision process: The fashion industry. *SCMS Journal of Indian Management*, *14*(3), 14–30.

Tapscott, D., & Williams, A. D. (2006). *Wikinomics: How Mass Collaboration Changes Everything* (2nd ed.). Penguin Group.

Thompson, C. J., & Haytko, D. L. (1997). Speaking of fashion: Consumers' uses of fashion discourses and the appropriation of countervailing cultural meanings. *The Journal of Consumer Research*, *24*(June), 15–42. doi:10.1086/209491

Tozlu, A. (2016). Karar verme yaklaşımları üzerinde herbert sımon hegemonyası. *Sayıştay Dergisi*, *102*, 27–45.

Vyncke, P. (2002). Lifestyle segmentationfrom attitudes, interests and opinions, to values, aesthetic styles, life visions and media preferences. *European Journal of Communication*, *17*(4), 445–463. doi: 10.1177/0267323102017004030l

Weiswing, D. (2016). *FBIC's Weinswig Named One of Top Retail Influencers For 2016*. Retrieved from: https://www.deborahweinswig.com/news/press-releases/fbics-weinswig-named-one-of-top-retail-ınfluencers-for-2016/

Wilk, R. (1997). A critique of desire: Distaste and dislike in consumer behavior. *Consumption Markets & Culture*, *1*(2), 175–196. doi:10.1080/10253866.1997.9670297

Xiang, L., Zheng, X., Lee, M. K., & Zhao, D. (2016). Exploring consumers' impulse buying behavior on social commerce platform: The role of parasocial interaction. *International Journal of Information Management*, *36*(3), 333–347. doi:10.1016/j.ijinfomgt.2015.11.002

Ye, G., Hudders, L., De Jans, S., & De Veirman, M. (2021). The value of influencer marketing for business: A bibliometric analysis and managerial implications. *Journal of Advertising*, *50*(2), 160–178. do i:10.1080/00913367.2020.1857888

Yurdakul-Sahin, D., & Atik, D. (2013). Celebrity influences on young consumers: Guiding the way to the ideal self. *Izmir Review of Social Sciences*, *1*(1), 65–82.

Zengingönül, O. (2012). *Küresel Put: Tüketim Ekonomisi Yeni Sapkınlık: Sosyal Bilinç* (1st ed.). Nobel Akademik Yayıncılık.

Zollo, L., Filieri, R., Rialti, R., & Yoon, S. (2020). Unpacking the Relationship Between Social Media Marketing and Brand Equity: The Mediating Role of Consumers' Benefits and Experience. *Journal of Business Research*, *117*, 256–267. doi:10.1016/j.jbusres.2020.05.001

ADDITIONAL READING

Arnold, L. B., & Martin, B. A. (2016). *Taking The Village Online Mothers, Motherhood and Social Media*. Demeter Press.

Chae, J. (2014). Am I a better mother than you? *Communication Research*, *42*(4), 503–525. doi:10.1177/0093650214534969

Feltman, C. E., & Szymanski, D. M. (2017). Instagram use and self-objectification: The roles of internalization, comparison, appearance commentary, and feminism. *Sex Roles*, *78*(5–6), 311–324.

Güzel, E. (2023). Beautiful, Sexy, and Happy Celebrities: Perfect Mothers or Instamoms. *Journal of International Women's Studies*, *25*(3), 8.

KEY TERMS AND DEFINITION

Buyer Decision Process: It is the decision-making process used by consumers regarding the market transactions before, during, and after the purchase of a good or service as a part of consumer behavior.

Follower: People who follow specific accounts or just friends on social media, especially on Instagram.

Influencer: New social media people, having huge followers, with the ability to influence potential consumersof by promoting or recommending the items on social media.

Influencer Marketing: It is a new marketing strategy for popular social-media users and brands to collaborate to promote brands' products or services.

Instagram: Populer social media platform where people can freely share their contents and connect with other people.

Instamom: Mother influencers who share their part of their lives on Instagram. They have many follower mothers.

Social Media: New world where people can interact each other, create their own contents, exchange information, and share anything they want in virtual communities.

Compilation of References

" *Real Or Robotic?": Kyra, Who Claims to Be India's First Meta-Influencer, Leaves Internet Confused.* (2022). https://www.ndtv.com/offbeat/real-or-robotic-kyra-who-claims-to-be-indias-first-meta-influencer-leaves-internet-confused-3048975

Aaker, D. A., & Joachimsthaler, E. A. (2000). The Brand Relationship Spectrum: The Key to the Brand Architecture Challenge. *California Management Review*, *42*(4), 8–23. doi:10.1177/000812560004200401

Aaker, D. A., & Keller, K. L. (1990). Consumer evaluations of brand extensions. *Journal of Marketing*, *54*(1), 27–41. doi:10.1177/002224299005400102

Abidin, C. (2015). *Communicative intimacies: Influencers and perceived interconnectedness*. Academic Press.

Abidin, C. (2015). Communicative intimacies: Influencers and perceived interconnectedness. *Ada: A Journal of Gender. New Media, and Technology*, *8*, 1–16.

Abidin, C. (2016). Aren't these just young, rich women doing vain things online? Influencer selfies as subversive frivolity. *Social Media + Society*, *2*(2), 1–17. doi:10.1177/2056305116641342

Abidin, C. (2016). Visibility labour: Engaging with Influencers' fashion brands and# OOTD advertorial campaigns on Instagram. *Media International Australia, Incorporating Culture & Policy*, *161*(1), 86–100. doi:10.1177/1329878X16665177

Abidin, C. (2020). Mapping internet celebrity on TikTok: Exploring attention economies and visibility labours. *Cultural Science Journal*, *12*(1), 77–103. doi:10.5334/csci.140

Abo ElHamd, E., Shamma, H., Saleh, M., & Elkhodary, E. (2022). Customer engagement value: Process, limitations and future research. *Journal of Modelling in Management*, *17*(4), 1144–1176. doi:10.1108/JM2-12-2020-0319

Adams, A., & Wilson, B. (2018). The Rise of Social Media Influencers in Marketing. *JMR, Journal of Marketing Research*.

Age, Ad. (2020, December 21). *The 12 smartest brand-celebrity pairings of 2020*. https://adage.com/article/year-review/12-smartest-brand-celebrity-pairings-2020/2299341

Ahmed, R. R., Streimikiene, D., & Zheng, X. (2021). The impact of proactive environmental strategy on competitive and sustainable development of organizations. *Journal of Competitiveness*, *13*(4), 5–24. doi:10.7441/joc.2021.04.01

Akamine, A. (2018). *Responsive regulation of the practice of e-mail marketing in Brazil* [Bachelor's thesis]. University of Brasília. https://bdm.unb.br/handle/10483/22306

Al Mamun, A., Nawi, N. C., Hayat, N., & Zainol, N. R. B. (2020). Predicting the purchase intention and behaviour towards green skincare products among Malaysian consumers. *Sustainability (Basel), 12*(24), 10663. doi:10.3390u122410663

Aleixo, A. M., Leal, S., & Azeiteiro, U. M. (2021). Higher education students' perceptions of sustainable development in Portugal. *Journal of Cleaner Production, 327*, 129429. Advance online publication. doi:10.1016/j.jclepro.2021.129429

Alibaba Damo Academy. (n.d.). https://damo.alibaba.com/

alishalehmann7 on TikTok. (2023). *Alisha Lehmann official TikTok account.* https://tiktok.com/@alishalehmann7

Almeida, M. (2022). Booktubers, literature and cyberculture: mediation and circulation of cultural information. *Configurações- Revista Ciências Sociais, 29.* https://journals.openedition.org/configuracoes/15110

Alshahrani, M., Zhu, F., Mekouar, S., Alghamdi, M. Y., & Liu, S. (2021). Identification of top-K influencers based on upper confidence bound and local structure. *Big Data Research, 25*, 100208. Advance online publication. doi:10.1016/j.bdr.2021.100208

Alsulaiman, K., Forbes, S., Dean, D., & Cohen, D. (2015). Relationships between perceived product values and three word of mouth variables. *Journal of Customer Behaviour, 14*(4), 277–294. doi:10.1362/147539215X14503490289260

Alves, B. (2019). *Music Festivals as Cultural Spaces* [Master's thesis, University of Lisbon]. Repository of the University of Lisbon. http://hdl.handle.net/10451/40826

Alves, F., Costa, H. & Perinotto, A. (2017). Instagram as a tool for customer loyalty: Photography, Social Media and Tourism. *Marketing & Tourism Review, 2*(2). .4562 doi:10.29149/mtr.v2i2

Amaro, L., & Scheepers, C. B. (2023). Exploring the nexus between microlevel and contextual influencers on women leaders' paradox mindset. *Gender in Management, 38*(1), 36–56. doi:10.1108/GM-11-2021-0335

Amyx, D., Alford, B., Zmich, L. J., Amyx, J., Mertz, B., & Sumlin, C. (2020). The study of different factors affecting salesperson deviance: An abstract. In *Marketing Opportunities and Challenges in a Changing Global Marketplace: Proceedings of the 2019 Academy of Marketing Science (AMS) Annual Conference* (pp. 113-114). Springer International Publishing. 10.1007/978-3-030-39165-2_47

Ancillai, C., Terho, H., Cardinali, S., & Pascucci, F. (2019). Advancing social media driven sales research: Establishing conceptual foundations for B-to-B social selling. *Industrial Marketing Management, 82*, 293–308. doi:10.1016/j.indmarman.2019.01.002

Anderson, C. (2019). The Impact of Technology on Consumer Behavior. *Journal of Consumer Studies.*

Andò, R. (2016). The ordinary celebrity: Italian young vloggers and the definition of girlhood. *Film. Fashion & Consumption, 5*(1), 123–139. doi:10.1386/ffc.5.1.123_1

Andrews, D. L., Lopes, V. B., & Jackson, S. J. (2015). Neymar: sport celebrity and performative cultural politics. *A Companion to Celebrity*, 421-439. doi:10.1002/9781118475089.ch23

ANI. (2023, Oct 19). *India's Influencer Marketing Industry to reach Rs. 2,200 crore by 2025 with increasing partnerships between Brands and Creators.* Retrieved Jun 06, 2023, from ANI: https://www.aninews.in/news/business/business/indias-influencer-marketing-industry-to-reach-rs-2200-crore-by-2025-with-increasing-partnerships-between-brands-and-creators20221019145522/

Anjali, C., Avhad, V., & Jaju, S. (2020, June). Influencer Marketing: An Exploratory Study to Identify Antecedents of Consumer Behavior of Millennial. *Business Perspectives and Research*, *9*(1), 77–91. doi:10.1177/2278533720923486

António, I. (2021). *Strategic Communication in Public Cultural Institutions: A Communication Plan for the Cinemateca Portuguesa - Cinema Museum* [Master's thesis]. ISCTE Repository - University Institute of Lisbon. http://hdl.handle.net/10071/24417

Antunes, M. (2020). *Survey of the Cultural Practices of the Portuguese 2020, Summary of Results*. ICS Studies and Reports.

Antunes, A. C., Miranda, S., & Gama, A. (2022). The (not so) secret life of senior social media influencers: An analysis of the top five 'granfluencers' on Instagram. In I. Saur-Amaral, S. Filipe, & T. Aragonez (Eds.), *Proceedings of ICIEMC 2022 - International Conference on Innovation and Entrepreneurship in Marketing and Consumer Behaviour* (pp. 30-39). UA Editora.

Antunes, A. C., & Murteira, C. (2023). *Can macroinfluencers have an impact on the customers' journey of their followers? Acciones y reacciones ante-la manipulación social: redes sociales, publicidad y marketing*. Dykinson S. L.

Ao, L., Bansal, R., Pruthi, N., & Khaskheli, M. B. (2023, February 02). Impact of Social Media Influencers on Customer Engagement and Purchase Intention: A Meta-Analysis. *Sustainability (Basel)*, *15*(03), 2744. Advance online publication. doi:10.3390u15032744

Apasrawirote, D., Yawised, K., Chatrangsan, M., & Muneesawang, P. (2022). Short-form video content (SVC) engagement and marketing capabilities. *Asian Journal of Business and Accounting*, *15*(2), 221–246. doi:10.22452/ajba.vol15no2.8

Appel, G., Grewal, L., Hadi, R., & Stephen, A. T. (2020). The future of social media in marketing. *Journal of the Academy of Marketing Science*, *48*(1), 79–95. Advance online publication. doi:10.100711747-019-00695-1 PMID:32431463

Arai, A., Ko, Y. J., & Kaplanidou, K. (2013). Athlete brand image: Scale development and model test. *European Sport Management Quarterly*, *13*(4), 383–403. doi:10.1080/16184742.2013.811609

Aramendia-Muneta, M. E. (2017). Spread the word – The effect of word of mouth in e-marketing. In G. Siegert, M. B. Von Rimscha, & S. Grubenmann (Eds.), *Commercial Communication in the Digital Age* (pp. 227–245). De Gruyter. doi:10.1515/9783110416794-013

Araujo, N. (2023). The image of a tourist destination as a tool for digital influencers. *Tourism, Society & Territory*, *5*(1). https://periodicos.ufrn.br/revtursoter/article/view/32044

Arduini, S., & Paoloni, P. (2020). The IT strategy in the luxury sector: The case of a fashion company. *Springer Proceedings in Business and Economics*, 211-226. 10.1007/978-3-030-46874-3_12

Area 2071: Your Invitation to Be a Part of Creating the Future. (2020). Dubai Future Foundation. https://area2071.ae/wp-content/uploads/2021/05/AREA-2071-Report.pdf

Areeb, Q. M., Nadeem, M., Sohail, S. S., Imam, R., Doctor, F., Himeur, Y., Hussain, A., & Amira, A. (2023). Filter bubbles in recommender systems: Fact or fallacy-A systematic review. *Wiley Interdisciplinary Reviews. Data Mining and Knowledge Discovery*, *13*(6), 1512. doi:10.1002/widm.1512

Argamon, S. E. (2017). Don't strengthen statistical significance—Abolish it. *American Scientist*. https://www.americanscientist.org/blog/macroscope/dont-strengthen-statistical-significance-abolish-it

Aria, M., & Cuccurullo, C. (2017). bibliometrix: An R-tool for comprehensive science mapping analysis. *Journal of Informetrics, 11*(4), 959–975. doi:10.1016/j.joi.2017.08.007

Arora, A., Bansal, S., Kandpal, C., Aswani, R., & Dwivedi, Y. (2019, July). Measuring social media influencer index- insights from facebook, Twitter and Instagram. *Journal of Retailing and Consumer Services, 49*, 86–101. doi:10.1016/j.jretconser.2019.03.012

Arsenyan, J., & Mirowska, A. (2021). Almost human? A comparative case study on the social media presence of virtual influencers. *International Journal of Human-Computer Studies, 155*, 102694. Advance online publication. doi:10.1016/j.ijhcs.2021.102694

Asare-Kyire, L., Zheng, H., & Owusu, A. (2019). An empirical examination of the influencers of the premature decline of African clusters: Evidence from textile clusters in Ghana. *South African Journal of Business Management, 50*(1). Advance online publication. doi:10.4102ajbm.v50i1.318

Aslam, S. (2017). *Instagram by the Numbers: Stats, Demographics, and Fun Facts*. Retrieved from: https://www.omnicoreagency.com/instagram-statistics/

Aslamova, Y. (2023, Jan 7). *How Influencer Marketing will Change the Business Landscape in 2023*. Retrieved Jun 09, 2023, from Indianretailer.com: https://www.indianretailer.com/article/technology-e-commerce/digital-trends/how-influencer-marketing-will-change-business

Aslamova, Y. (2023, Mar 11). *How metaverse is powering influencer marketing for promoting brand campaigns*. Retrieved Sept 13, 2023, from https://www.financialexpress.com: https://www.financialexpress.com/business/blockchain-how-metaverse-is-powering-influencer-marketing-for-promoting-brand-campaigns-3005016/

Atisfyreach. (2020). *How Did Modern Day Influencers Become A Thing?* Retrieved Jun 08, 2023, from https://blog.atisfyreach.com/how-did-modern-day-influencers-become-a-thing/

Atisfyreach. (2021). *Take Your Influencer Campaigns To The Next Level With Podcasts*. Retrieved Sept 15, 2023, from https://blog.atisfyreach.com: https://blog.atisfyreach.com/take-your-influencer-campaigns-to-the-next-level-with-podcasts/

Audrezet, A., & Koles, B. (2023). Virtual influencer as a brand avatar in interactive marketing. In The Palgrave Handbook of Interactive Marketing (pp. 353-376). doi:10.1007/978-3-031-14961-0_16

Audrezet, A., De Kerviler, G., & Moulard, J. G. (2020). Authenticity under threat: When social media influencers need to go beyond self-presentation. *Journal of Business Research, 117*, 557–569. doi:10.1016/j.jbusres.2018.07.008

Avery, J., Steenburgh, T. J., Deighton, J., & Caravella, M. (2010). Adding bricks to clicks: Predicting the patterns of online and offline information search. *Marketing Science, 29*(2), 294–308.

Awdziej, M., Plata-Alf, D., & Tkaczyk, J. (2021, Sep 22-24). *Real or Not, Doesn't Matter, As Long As You Are Hot: Exploring the Perceived Credibility of an Instagram Virtual Influencer* [Extending boundaries: The impact of the digital world on consumers and marketing]. Regional Conference of the European-Marketing-Academy, Warsaw, Poland.

Baas, J., Schotten, M., Plume, A., Côté, G., & Karimi, R. (2020). Scopus as a curated, high-quality bibliometric data source for academic research in quantitative science studies. *Quantitative Science Studies, 1*(1), 377–386. doi:10.1162/qss_a_00019

Babin, B. J., Harris, E. G., & Murray, K. B. (2018). *CB8: Consumer behavior*. Cengage Learning.

Baetzgen, A., & Tropp, J. (2013). *Brand Content: Die Marke als Medienereignis*. Schäffer-Poeschel.

Bailis, R. (2021). *The State of Influencer Marketing: 10 Influencer Marketing Statistics to Inform Where You Invest*. Retrieved Jun 06, 2023, from BigCommerce: https://www.bigcommerce.com/blog/influencer-marketing-statistics/

Bakker, D. (2018). Conceptualising influencer marketing. *Journal of Emerging Trends in Marketing and Management, 1*(1), 79-87.

Balaban, D., Mucundorfeanu, M., & Naderer, B. (2022). The role of trustworthiness in social media influencer advertising: Investigating users' appreciation of advertising transparency and its effects. *Communications*, *47*(3), 395–421. doi:10.1515/commun-2020-0053

Balasubramanian, S. (2022). A review of the pre-merger performance of select public sector banks in India using key performance indicators. *Springer Proceedings in Business and Economics*, 73-86. 10.1007/978-981-19-4892-3_5

Baldus, B. J., Voorhees, C. M., & Calantone, R. J. (2015). Online brand community engagement: Scale development and validation. *Journal of Business Research*, *68*(5), 978–985. doi:10.1016/j.jbusres.2014.09.035

Balestra, S., Sallin, A., & Wolter, S. C. (2023). High-ability influencers? the heterogeneous effects of gifted classmates. *The Journal of Human Resources*, *58*(2), 633–665. doi:10.3368/jhr.58.4.0920-11170R1

Bang, M. (2023, Jun 7). *Authenticity in Influencer Marketing: Building Trust and Engagement with Audiences*. Retrieved Sept 15, 2023, from https://www.linkedin.com: https://www.linkedin.com/pulse/authenticity-influencer-marketing-building-trust-engagement-bang/

Bansal, P. (2019, May 27). *Why social media marketing has become a rage now*. Retrieved Jun 20, 2023, from The Satesman: https://www.thestatesman.com/business/why-social-media-marketing-has-become-a-rage-now-1502759272.html

Bardhi, F., & Eckhardt, G. M. (2017). Liquid consumption. *The Journal of Consumer Research*, *44*(3), 582–597. doi:10.1093/jcr/ucx050

Barta, S., Belanche, D., Fernández, A., & Flavián, M. (2023). Influencer marketing on TikTok: The effectiveness of humor and followers' hedonic experience. *Journal of Retailing and Consumer Services*, *70*, 103149. doi:10.1016/j.jretconser.2022.103149

Basch, C. H., Yalamanchili, B., & Fera, J. (2022). Climate change on TikTok: A content analysis of videos. *Journal of Community Health*, *1-5*(1), 163–167. Advance online publication. doi:10.100710900-021-01031-x PMID:34545460

Bastrygina, T., & Lim, W. M. (2023). Foundations of consumer engagement with social media influencers. *International Journal of Web Based Communities*, *19*(2-3), 222–242. doi:10.1504/IJWBC.2023.131410

Basuroy, T. (2023, Mar 20). *Value of influencer marketing industry in India from 2021 to 2022, with projections until 2026*. Retrieved Jun 03, 2023, from Statista: https://www.statista.com/statistics/1294803/india-influencer-marketing-industry-value/#:~:text=It%20was%20projected%20to%20grow,various%20kinds%20as%20of%202022

Batra, R., & Keller, K. L. (2016). Integrating marketing communications: New findings, new lessons, and new ideas. *Journal of Marketing*, *80*(6), 122–145. doi:10.1509/jm.15.0419

Behnam, M., Hollebeek, L. D., Clark, M., & Farabi, R. (2021). Exploring customer engagement in the product vs. service context. *Journal of Retailing and Consumer Services*, *60*, 102456. doi:10.1016/j.jretconser.2021.102456

Belanche, D., Casaló, L. V., Flavián, M., & Ibáñez-Sánchez, S. (2021b). Building influencers' credibility on Instagram: Effects on followers' attitudes and behavioral responses toward the influencer. *Journal of Retailing and Consumer Services*, *61*, 102585. doi:10.1016/j.jretconser.2021.102585

Belanche, D., Casaló, L. V., Flavián, M., & Sánchez, S. I. (2021, August). Understanding influencer marketing: The role of congruence between influencers, products and consumers. *Journal of Business Research, 132*, 186–195. doi:10.1016/j.jbusres.2021.03.067

Belch, G. E., & Belch, M. A. (2012). *Advertising and promotion: An integrated marketing communications perspective*. McGraw-Hill Education.

Belch, G., & Belch, M. (2009). *Advertising and Promotion: An Integrated Marketing Communications Perspective* (8th ed.). Irwin.

Belk, R. W., Ger, G., & Askegaard, S. (2003). The fire of desire: A multisited inquiry into consumer passion. *The Journal of Consumer Research, 30*(3), 26–51. doi:10.1086/378613

Bell, G. (2022). *The Metaverse is a New Word for an Old Idea*. Massachusetts Institute of Technology. https://www.technologyreview.com/2022/02/08/1044732/metaverse-history-snow-crash/

Bergel, M., Frank, P., & Brock, C. (2019). The role of customer engagement facets on the formation of attitude, loyalty and price perception. *Journal of Services Marketing, 31*(7), 890–903. doi:10.1108/JSM-01-2019-0024

Bergkvist, L., & Zhou, K. Q. (2016). Celebrity endorsements: A literature review and research agenda. *International Journal of Advertising, 35*(4), 642–663. Advance online publication. doi:10.1080/02650487.2015.1137537

Bernard, H. R. (2002). *Research Methods in Anthropology: Qualitative and Quantitative Methods* (3rd ed.). Altamira Press.

Bernays, E. L. (1928). *Propaganda*. Horace Liveright.

Berry, D. A. (2016). P-values are not what they're cracked up to be. Supplemental material to the ASA statement on p-values and statistical significance. *The American Statistician, 70*(2).

Beveridge, C. (2022, Jan 13). *What is User-Generated Content? And Why is it Important?* Retrieved Sept 15, 2023, from https://blog.hootsuite.com/user-generated-content-ugc/

Beverland, M., & Farrelly, F. (2010). The Quest for authenticity in consumption: Consumers' purposive choice of authentic cues to shape experienced outcomes. *The Journal of Consumer Research, 36*(5), 838–856. doi:10.1086/615047

Bevilacqua, J., & Del Giudice, E. (2018). *Why brands need to utilize influencer marketing in 2018*. St Joseph Communications. https://stjoseph.com/insight/influencer-marketing-2018-infographic/

Bhargava, V. (2021, Dec 11). *Find The Best Fit: Your Beginner's Guide to Influencer Marketing*. Retrieved Jun 01, 2023, from shopify: https://www.shopify.com/in/blog/influencer-marketing

Bian, X., & Haque, S. (2020). Counterfeit versus original patronage: Do emotional brand attachment, brand involvement, and past experience matter? *Journal of Brand Management, 27*(4), 438–451. doi:10.105741262-020-00189-4

BigCommerce. (2022). *Discover New Leads and Brand Growth with Influencer Marketing*. Retrieved Sept 15, 2023, from https://www.bigcommerce.com: https://www.bigcommerce.com/articles/ecommerce/influencer-marketing/#types-of-influencer-marketing-opportunities-to-explore

Blackshaw, P., & Nazzaro, M. (2004). *Consumer-Generated Media (CGM) 101: Word-of-Mouth in the Age of the Webfortified Consumer*. Retrieved from: http://www.Nielsenbuzzmetrics.Com/Whitepapers

Block, E., & Lovegrove, R. (2021). Discordant storytelling, 'honest fakery', identity peddling: How uncanny CGI characters are jamming public relations and influencer practices. *Public Relations Inquiry, 10*(3), 265–293. doi:10.1177/2046147X211026936

Blumler, J. G., & Katz, E. (1974). *The Uses of Mass Communications: Current Perspectives on Gratifications Research* (Vol. 3). Sage Annual Reviews of Communication Research.

Boerman, S. C. (2020). The effects of the standardized instagram disclosure for micro- and meso-influencers. *Computers in Human Behavior*, *103*, 199–207. doi:10.1016/j.chb.2019.09.015

Bonoboz. (2023, Aug 18). *Measure Success for Influencer Marketing Campaigns*. Retrieved Sept 15, 2023, from https://www.bonoboz.in/measure-success-for-influencer-marketing-campaigns/

Bora Semiz, B., & Paylan, M. (2023, November 13). ali. (2023). A study on the mediating effect of brand trust between perceived legitimacy of influencers and attitude toward brand: Evidence from Turkey. *Asia Pacific Journal of Marketing and Logistics*, *35*(9), 2181–2197. Advance online publication. doi:10.1108/APJML-08-2022-0702

Borchers, N. S., & Enke, N. (2021). Managing strategic influencer communication: A systematic overview on emerging planning, organization, and controlling routines. *Public Relations Review*, *47*(3), 102041. doi:10.1016/j.pubrev.2021.102041

Borchers, N. S., Hagelstein, J., & Beckert, J. (2022). Are many too much? examining the effects of multiple influencer endorsements from a persuasion knowledge model perspective. *International Journal of Advertising*, *41*(6), 974–996. doi:10.1080/02650487.2022.2054163

Borges-Tiago, M. T., Santiago, J., & Tiago, F. (2023, March). Mega or macro social media influencers: Who endorses brands better? *Journal of Business Research*, *157*, 1–12. doi:10.1016/j.jbusres.2022.113606

Bourdieu, P. (1990). *In Other Words: Essays Towards A Reflexive Sociology*. Stanford University Press. doi:10.1515/9781503621558

Brachtendorf, C. (2022). Lil Miquela in the folds of fashion: (Ad-)dressing virtual influencers [Article]. *Fashion, Style & Popular Culture*, *9*(4), 483–499. doi:10.1386/fspc_00157_1

Brakus, J. J., Schmitt, B. H., & Zarantonello, L. (2009). Brand experience: What is it? How is it measured? Does it affect loyalty? *Journal of Marketing*, *73*(3), 52–68. doi:10.1509/jmkg.73.3.052

Brand Equity. (2022). https://brandequity.economictimes.indiatimes.com/news/research/influencer-marketing-industry-in-india-to-reach-rs-2200-cr-by-2025-report

Brand Equity. (2022, Oct 20). *Influencer marketing industry in India to reach Rs 2,200 cr by 2025: Report*. Retrieved Jun 06, 2023, from Brand Equity.com: https://brandequity.economictimes.indiatimes.com/news/research/influencer-marketing-industry-in-india-to-reach-rs-2200-cr-by-2025-report/94990088

BrandWagon. (2021, Aug 17). *Influencer marketing industry size to reach Rs 2,200 crore in India by 2025: Report*. Retrieved Jun 06, 2023, from Financial Express: https://www.financialexpress.com/business/brandwagon-influencer-marketing-industry-size-to-reach-rs-2200-crore-in-india-by-2025-report-2332321/

Breazeale, M., Fritzsche, D. J., & Wells, W. D. (2009). A study of advertising message content on liking of the brand: The moderating role of the degree of consumer involvement. *Journal of Advertising*, *18*(2), 43–51.

Breves, P., Liebers, N., Abt, M., & Kunze, A. (2019). The perceived fit between Instagram influencers and the endorsed brand. *Journal of Advertising Research*, *59*(4), 440–454. doi:10.2501/JAR-2019-030

Brewster, M. L., & Sklar, M. (2022). 'Brand, community, lifestyle': Fashioning an authentic, body positive influencer brand on Instagram. *Fashion, Style & Popular Culture*, *9*(4), 501–521. doi:10.1386/fspc_00158_1

Bringé, A. (2023). *The rise of virtual influencers and what it means for brands.* Forbes. Retrieved October 26 from https://www.forbes.com/sites/forbescommunicationscouncil/2022/10/18/the-rise-of-virtual-influencers-and-what-it-means-for-brands/

Brito, P. Q., Brandão, A., Gadekar, M., & Castelo-Branco, S. (2020). Diffusing fashion information by social media fashion influencers: Understanding antecedents and consequences. *Journal of Fashion Marketing and Management, 24*(2), 137–152. doi:10.1108/JFMM-09-2019-0214

Brodie, R. J., Hollebeek, L. D., Jurić, B., & Ilić, A. (2011). Customer engagement: Conceptual domain, fundamental propositions, and implications for research. *Journal of Service Research, 14*(3), 252–271. doi:10.1177/1094670511411703

Brodie, R. J., Ilic, A., Juric, B., & Hollebeek, L. (2013). Consumer engagement in a virtual brand community: An exploratory analysis. *Journal of Business Research, 66*(1), 105–114. doi:10.1016/j.jbusres.2011.07.029

Brooke, C. (2017). *Engaging the Long Tail, Engaging the Micro Influencer.* Retrieved Jun 10, 2023, from https://www.business2community.com/content-marketing-tips/engaging-long-tail-engaging-micro-influencer-01909491

Brooks, G., Drenten, J., & Piskorski, M. J. (2021). Influencer celebrification: How social media influencers acquire celebrity capital. *Journal of Advertising, 50*(5), 528–547. doi:10.1080/00913367.2021.1977737

Brown, L., & Martinez, C. (2022). Ethical Considerations in the Use of Virtual Influencers. *Journal of Digital Ethics, 8*(2), 123–140.

Brown, R., & Davis, S. (2021). *Leveraging Influencer Marketing in the Restaurant Industry.* Marketing Journal.

Brunello, L. (2020). *Strategic Communication Planning for Museums.* LinkedIn.

Bucher, T., & Helmond, A. (2018). The affordances of social media platforms. In J. Burgess, A. Marwick, & T. Poell (Eds.), *The SAGE handbook of social media* (pp. 233–253). Sage. doi:10.4135/9781473984066.n14

Bühlmann, C. H., Mickan, B. S., Tait, S., Renton, M., & Bahri, P. A. (2021). Lactic acid from mixed food wastes at a commercial biogas facility: Effect of feedstock and process conditions. *Journal of Cleaner Production, 284*, 125243. Advance online publication. doi:10.1016/j.jclepro.2020.125243

Bulz, N. (2023). *The Terrestrial Rational Subject – A Finite Being – Eliciting the 'Towards Infinite' Tentation and Tension. Does a Universal Consciousness be Comprehended by a Rational Subject?* https://papers.ssrn.com/sol3/papers.cfm?abstract_id=4392715

Bundhun, R. (2023, Feb 27). *How the growth of social media is boosting India's influencers.* Retrieved Jun 26, 2023, from National News: https://www.thenationalnews.com/business/2023/02/27/how-the-growth-of-social-media-is-boosting-indias-influencers/

Burton, S. (2021, Jan 25). *The right fit: How to find influencers for your brand's marketing campaign.* Retrieved Sept 15, 2023, from https://sproutsocial.com/insights/how-to-find-the-right-influencers/

Cabeza Ramírez, L. J., Sánchez Cañizares, S. M., Santos Roldán, L. M., & Fuentes-García, F. J. (2022, November). Impact of the perceived risk in influencers' product recommendations on their followers' purchase attitudes and intention. *Technological Forecasting and Social Change, 184*, 121997. Advance online publication. doi:10.1016/j.techfore.2022.121997

Calibrate, A. (2023, Jul 19). *Evaluating the Performance of Your Influencer Marketing Campaigns: Metrics and KPIs.* Retrieved Sept 15, 2023, from https://calibrate.thearena.ai/infohub/influencer-marketing-kpis

Camargo, I., Estevanim, M., & Silveira, S. (2017). Participatory and convergent culture: the scenario that favours the birth of digital influencers. *Revista Communicare, 17*. https://www.researchgate.net/publication/327120381_Convergent_and_participatory_culture_the_scene_that_favours_the_uprising_of_digital_influencers_Cultura_participativa_e_convergente_o_cenario_que_favorece_o_nascimento_dos_influenciadores_digitais

Campbell, C., & Farrell, J. R. (2020, August). More than meets the eye: The functional components underlying influencer marketing. *Business Horizons*, *63*(4), 469–479. doi:10.1016/j.bushor.2020.03.003

Carmona, J., Delcoure, N., & Fernandez, F. H. (2020). Social media sentiment, tariffs, and international equity pricing. *International Journal of Electronic Finance*, *10*(1-2), 93–115. doi:10.1504/IJEF.2020.110298

Carter, D. (2016). Hustle and Brand: The sociotechnical shaping of influence. *Social Media + Society*, *2*(3), 1–12. doi:10.1177/2056305116666305

Casaló, L. V., Flavián, C., & Ibáñez-Sánchez, S. (2020). Influencers on Instagram: Antecedents and consequences of opinion leadership. *Journal of Business Research*, *117*, 510–519. doi:10.1016/j.jbusres.2018.07.005

Castro, D., Junior, F., & Lopes, S. (2019). Social networks as a tool for marketing: the vision of a company in the city of Palmas - TO. *Revista Humanidades e Inovação, 6*(12). https://revista.unitins.br/index.php/humanidadeseinovacao/article/view/1555

Cezar, L. (2019). *Communication and Marketing in the Public Sector: different approaches to the Brazilian reality*. Public Management Collection, v. 03. National School of Public Administration (Enap) and Brazilian Society of Public Administration (SBAP). http://repositorio.enap.gov.br/handle/1/4279

Chadda, R. (2022, Apr 30). *What metaverse means for influencer marketing?* Retrieved Sept 13, 2023, from https://www.financialexpress.com/business/brandwagon-what-metaverse-means-for-influencer-marketing-2508559/

Chang, S. W., & Fan, S. H. (2017). Cultivating the brand-customer relationship in Facebook fan pages: A study of fast-fashion industry. *International Journal of Retail & Distribution Management*, *45*(3), 253–270. doi:10.1108/IJRDM-05-2016-0076

Chan, K. W., Yim, C. K., & Lam, S. S. K. (2010). Is Customer Participation in Value Creation a Double-Edged Sword? Evidence from Professional Financial Services across Cultures. *Journal of Marketing*, *74*(3), 48–64. doi:10.1509/jmkg.74.3.048

Chaudhuri, A., & Holbrook, M. B. (2001). The chain of effects from Brand Trust and brand affect to brand performance: The Role of Brand Loyalty. *Journal of Marketing*, *65*(2), 81–93. doi:10.1509/jmkg.65.2.81.18255

Chen, J., Frankwick, G. L., & Zhang, Z. (2022). *Adopting artificial intelligence to manage a turbulent environment: An abstract*. doi:10.1007/978-3-030-89883-0_61

Chen, J., Tsao, S., & Chyou, J. (2019). Investigating the key factor of virtual personal brand in e-commerce: A case study of "myhomes". *Proceedings of the International Conference on Electronic Business (ICEB),* 263-271. Retrieved from www.scopus.com

Chen, J. (2022). Research on the echo-chamber effect. *Advances in Social Science, Education and Humanities Research*, *638*, 874–877.

Chen, X., Jiao, C., Ji, R., & Li, Y. (2021). Examining customer motivation and its impact on customer engagement behavior in social media: The mediating effect of brand experience. *SAGE Open*, *11*(4). Advance online publication. doi:10.1177/21582440211052256

Cheung, C. M., Xiao, B. S., & Liu, I. L. (2014). Do actions speak louder than voices? The signaling role of social information cues in influencing consumer purchase decisions. *Decision Support Systems*, *65*, 50–58. doi:10.1016/j.dss.2014.05.002

Childers, C. C., Lemon, L. L., & Hoy, M. G. (2018). #Sponsored #Ad: Agency perspective on influencer marketing campaigns. *Journal of Current Issues and Research in Advertising*, *40*(3), 258–274. doi:10.1080/10641734.2018.1521113

Ching, C. (2023). *The power of Instagram influencer marketing: how to reach your target audience*. Retrieved Jun 03, 2023, from Plannthat: https://www.plannthat.com/instagram-influencer-marketing-2/

Ching, C. (2023, March 23). *Here's How Much Instagram Influencers Make in 2023 (+ Free Report)*. Retrieved Jun 01, 2023, from Later: https://later.com/blog/instagram-influencers-costs/

Chin, J., Jiang, B., Mufidah, I., Persada, S., & Noer, B. (2018). The investigation of consumers' behavior intention in using green skincare products: A pro-environmental behavior model approach. *Sustainability (Basel)*, *10*(11), 3922. doi:10.3390u10113922

Chinnasamy, S., & Tahrim, A. M. (2019). New media and social influencer engagement on lifestyle and political content. *International Journal of Recent Technology and Engineering*, *8*(3), 3526–3541. doi:10.35940/ijrte.C5274.098319

Chiu, C. L., & Ho, H. C. (2023). Impact of Celebrity, Micro-Celebrity, and Virtual Influencers on Chinese Gen Z's Purchase Intention Through Social Media. *SAGE Open*, *13*(1). Advance online publication. doi:10.1177/21582440231164034

Choi, M., Choi, Y., & Lee, H. (2023). Gen Z Travelers in the Instagram Marketplace: Trust, Influencer Type, Post Type, and Purchase Intention. *Journal of Hospitality & Tourism Research (Washington, D.C.)*. Advance online publication. doi:10.1177/10963480231180938

Choobchain, S., Momtaz, A. M., & Farhadian, H. (2019). Gender differences of farmers in conflict with climate change. *International Journal of Scientific and Technology Research*, *8*(7), 359–363. www.scopus.com

Choong, J., & Wang, M. B. (2023). Disruptive and destructive? A typology of social bots in public relations. *Journal of Digital and Social Media Marketing*, *10*(4), 312–325.

Chopra, S. (2023, Aug 25). *Ethics in Influencer Marketing*. Retrieved Sept 15, 2023, from https://www.dailypioneer.com/2023/columnists/ethics-in-influencer-marketing.html#:~:text=Ethical%20influencer%20marketing%20is%20not,genuine%20value%20and%20communicate%20trustworthiness.&text=Choose%20influencers%20who%20align%20with%20your%20brand's%20v

Choudhry, A., Han, J., Xu, X., & Huang, Y. (2022). "I felt a little crazy following a 'doll'": Investigating real influence of virtual influencers on their followers. *Proceedings of the ACM on Human-Computer Interaction*. doi:10.1109/MCOM.001.2100786

Chu, M., Zhou, G., & Wu, W. (2022). *Data envelopment analysis on relative efficiency assessment and improvement: Evidence from Chinese bank branches*. doi:10.1007/978-3-030-94036-2_9

Chu, S., & Seock, Y. (2020). The power of social media in fashion advertising. *Journal of Interactive Advertising*, *20*(2), 93–94. doi:10.1080/15252019.2020.1802955

Cialdini, R. B. (1993). *Influence: Science and Practice* (3rd ed.). Harpercollins College Publishers.

Cicala, J., & Zhang, Z. (2020). *Does technological self-efficacy decrease new salesperson job insecurity: An abstract*. doi:10.1007/978-3-030-39165-2_110

Clark, E., & Turner, L. (2021). Influencer Marketing and Consumer Decision-Making. *Journal of Consumer Behaviour*.

Colliander, J., & Erlandsson, S. (2015). The blog and the bountiful: Exploring the effects of disguised product placement on blogs that are revealed by a third party. *Journal of Marketing Communications*, *21*(2), 110–124. doi:10.1080/13527266.2012.730543

Collins, M. (2023). Authentic communication through customizable virtual influencers. *Communication Studies Quarterly*, *12*(3), 53–67.

Conde, R., & Casais, B. (2023, March). Micro, macro and mega-influencers on instagram: The power of persuasion via the parasocial relationship. *Journal of Business Research*, *158*, 1–10. doi:10.1016/j.jbusres.2023.113708

Consumer Electronics Show. (n.d.). https://www.ces.tech/.

Cook, M. (2021). *Perceiving others: The psychology of interpersonal perception*. Routledge. doi:10.4324/9781003173908

Coombs, W. T. (2007). Protecting organization reputations during a crisis: The development and application of situational crisis communication theory. *Corporate Reputation Review*, *10*(3), 163–176. doi:10.1057/palgrave.crr.1550049

Cornelius, S., Leidner, D. E., & Benbya, H. (2023). Credibility of Virtual Influencers: The Role of Design Stimuli, Knowledge Cues, and User Disposition. *Proceedings of the Annual Hawaii International Conference on System Sciences*. doi:10.3127/ajis.v25i0.3223

Costa, A. (2023). *A era dos Metainfluencers ou influenciadores internos*. Gazeta do Povo. https://www.gazetadopovo.com.br/vozes/voce-amanha/a-era-dos-metainfluencers-ou-influenciadores-internos/

Costa, P. (2022). *Social networks and digital influencers in the promotion of tourist destinations from the point of view of advertising agents: a case of Natal/RN, Natal/RN 2022* [Bachelor's thesis, Federal University of Rio Grande do Norte]. Institutional Repository of the Federal University of Rio Grande do Norte. https://repositorio.ufrn.br/handle/123456789/48961

Cotter, K. (2019). Playing the visibility game: How digital influencers and algorithms negotiate influence on Instagram. *New Media & Society*, *21*(4), 895–913. doi:10.1177/1461444818815684

Cova, B., & Shankar, A. (2012). Tribal Marketing, in L. Penaloza, N. Toulouse and L. M. Visconti. In Marketing Management: A Cultural Perspective. Routledge.

Crane, D., & Bovone, L. (2006). Approaches to material culture: The sociology of fashion and clothing. *Poetics*, *34*(6), 319–333. doi:10.1016/j.poetic.2006.10.002

Croes, E. A., & Bartels, J. (2021). Young adults' motivations for following social influencers and their relationship to identification and buying behavior. *Computers in Human Behavior*, *124*, 106910. doi:10.1016/j.chb.2021.106910

Cuesta, U. (2000). *Psicología social de la communicación*. Ediciones Cátedra.

Cvijikj, I. P., & Michahelles, F. (2013). Online engagement factors on Facebook brand pages. *Social Network Analysis and Mining*, *3*(4), 843–861. doi:10.100713278-013-0098-8

Dakroub, R., Koles, B., Issa, H., & Jens, B. (2023). Instagram users' motives of social media engagement with female athletes. *The International Journal of Sport and Society*, *14*(2), 173–199. doi:10.18848/2152-7857/CGP/v14i02/173-199

Dall Jensen, R., Ravn, S., & Krogh Christensen, M. (2019). Identification and development of talent in surgery: A scoping study across the performance domains of surgery, sport, and music. *European Journal of Training and Development*, *43*(3-4), 272–305. doi:10.1108/EJTD-07-2018-0070

Dall'Olmo Riley, F., Singh, J., & Blankson, C. (2018). Social Media and Its Link to Purchase Intentions of Luxury Fashion Brands. *Journal of Retailing and Consumer Services*.

Dalla-Pria, L., & Rodríguez-de-Dios, I. (2022). CSR communication on social media: The impact of source and framing on message credibility, corporate reputation and WOM. *Corporate Communications*, *27*(3), 543–557. doi:10.1108/CCIJ-09-2021-0097

Dam, L. B., & Pillai, D. (2021). Crafting virtual community of indigenous entrepreneurs: Case in social entrepreneurship. *South Asian Journal of Business and Management Cases*, *10*(1), 111–120. doi:10.1177/2277977921991916

Daniel, W. W. (1999). *Biostatistics: A Foundation For Analysis in the Health Sciences* (7th ed.). John Wiley & Sons, Inc.

Darmatama, M., & Erdiansyah, R. (2021). The influence of advertising in TikTok social media and beauty product image on consumer purchase decisions. In *International Conference on Economics, Business, Social, and Humanities (ICEBSH 2021)* (pp. 888-892). Atlantis Press. 10.2991/assehr.k.210805.140

Datareportal. (2023). *Digital 2023 July Global Statshot Report (slide 164).* https://datareportal.com

Davcik, N. S., Langaro, D., Jevons, C., & Nascimento, R. (2021). Non-sponsored brand-related user-generated content: Effects and mechanisms of consumer engagement. *Journal of Product &amp. Journal of Product and Brand Management*, *31*(1), 163–174. doi:10.1108/JPBM-06-2020-2971

De Bernardi, P., & Azucar, D. (2020). *The role of universities in harnessing entrepreneurial opportunities.* Retrieved from www.scopus.com doi:10.1007/978-3-030-33502-1_2

de Brito Silva, M. J., de Oliveira Ramos Delfino, L., Alves Cerqueira, K., & de Oliveira Campos, P. (2022). Avatar marketing: A study on the engagement and authenticity of virtual influencers on Instagram. *Social Network Analysis and Mining*, *12*(1), 130. Advance online publication. doi:10.100713278-022-00966-w

de Bruin, L., Roberts-Lombard, M., & de Meyer-Heydenrych, C. (2021). The interrelationship between internal marketing, employee perceived quality and customer satisfaction–a conventional banking perspective. *Cogent Business and Management*, *8*(1), 1872887. Advance online publication. doi:10.1080/23311975.2021.1872887

De Cicco, R., Iacobucci, S., & Pagliaro, S. (2021). The effect of influencer–product fit on advertising recognition and the role of an enhanced disclosure in increasing sponsorship transparency. *International Journal of Advertising*, *40*(5), 733–759. doi:10.1080/02650487.2020.1801198

de Matos Pedro, E., Alves, H., & Leitão, J. (2020). Assessing the citations of articles on intellectual capital: What are the "influencers"? *International Journal of Knowledge Management*, *16*(2), 30–51. doi:10.4018/IJKM.2020040103

De Veirman, M., Cauberghe, V., & Hudders, L. (2017). Marketing through Instagram influencers: The impact of number of followers and product divergence on brand attitude. *International Journal of Advertising*, *36*(5), 798–828. doi:10.1080/02650487.2017.1348035

De Vries, L., Gensler, S., & Leeflang, P. S. (2012). Popularity of brand posts on brand fan pages: An investigation of the effects of social media marketing. *Journal of Interactive Marketing*, *26*(2), 83–91. doi:10.1016/j.intmar.2012.01.003

Dean, K. (2015, Auyg). *The Role of Social Media Influencers*. Retrieved Jun 13, 2023, from https://www.manobyte.com/growth-strategy/the-role-of-social-media-influencers

Deci, E. L., Koestner, R., & Ryan, R. M. (1999). A meta-analytic review of experiments examining the effects of extrinsic rewards on intrinsic motivation. *Psychological Bulletin*, *125*(6), 627–668. doi:10.1037/0033-2909.125.6.627 PMID:10589297

Dedeoğlu, A. Ö. (2010). Discourses of motherhood and consumption practices of Turkish mothers. *Business and Economics Research Journal*, *1*(3), 1–15.

Delbaere, M., Michael, B., & Phillips, B. J. (2021). Social media influencers: A route to brand engagement for their followers. *Psychology and Marketing*, *38*(1), 101–112. Advance online publication. doi:10.1002/mar.21419

Deloitte. (2019). Made-to-order: The rise of mass personalization: Consumer review. *Deloitte*. https://www2.deloitte.com/content/dam/Deloitte/ch/Documents/consumer-business/ch-en-consumer-business-made-to-order-consumer-review.pdf

Demo, G., Lima, T., Scussel, F., Miranda, P., & Moreno, L. (2021). Relationship Marketing in the Consumer Market: Scientific Production Profile and Research Agenda. *Future Studies Research Journal: Trends and Strategies*, *13*(2), 179–202. doi:10.24023/FutureJournal/2175-5825/2021.v13i2.569

Dencheva, V. (2023). *Leading platforms used by marketers for influencer marketing in the United States from 2020 to 2025*. Retrieved Jun 01, 1, from https://www.statista.com/statistics/1092819/global-influencer-market-size/

Dencheva, V. (2023, Mar 15). *Share of marketing budgets spent on influencer marketing worldwide as of February 2023*. Retrieved Jun 01, 2023, from https://www.statista.com/statistics/268641/share-of-marketing-budgets-spent-on-digital-worldwide/

Dencheva, V. (2023, Mar 21). *Influencer marketing spending in the United States from 2019 to 2024*. Retrieved Jun 02, 2023, from https://www.statista.com/statistics/1254039/influencer-marketing-spending-usa/

Dencheva, V. (2023a). *Reasons why consumers follow virtual influencers in the United States as of March 2022*. Statista. Retrieved October 26 from https://www.statista.com/statistics/1302739/reasons-consumers-follow-virtual-influencers-us/

Dencheva, V. (2023b). *Share of consumers who follow at least one virtual influencer in the United States as of March 2022, by age group*. Statista. Retrieved October 26 from https://www.statista.com/statistics/1304080/consumers-follow-virtual-influencers-age-us/

Dencheva, V. (2023c). *Virtual influencers - statistics & facts*. Statista. Retrieved October 26 from https://www.statista.com/topics/9805/virtual-influencers/#topicOverview

Deng, F. Y., & Jiang, X. (2023). Effects of human versus virtual human influencers on the appearance anxiety of social media users. *Journal of Retailing and Consumer Services*, *71*, 103233. Advance online publication. doi:10.1016/j.jretconser.2022.103233

Dewing, M. (2012). *Social Media: An Introduction*. Library of Parliament.

Dhanesh, G. S., & Duthler, G. (2019). Relationship management through social media influencers: Effects of followers' awareness of paid endorsement. *Public Relations Review*, *45*(3), 101765. doi:10.1016/j.pubrev.2019.03.002

Djafarova, E., & Rushworth, C. (2017). Exploring the credibility of online celebrities' Instagram profiles in influencing the purchase decisions of young female users. *Computers in Human Behavior*, *68*, 1–7. doi:10.1016/j.chb.2016.11.009

Dolan, R., Conduit, J., Fahy, J., & Goodman, S. (2016). Social media engagement behaviour: A uses and gratifications perspective. *Journal of Strategic Marketing*, *24*(3-4), 261–277. doi:10.1080/0965254X.2015.1095222

Dominguez, L. (2022, January 21). Skin care AI: L'Oréal decoding the future of beauty. *Consumer Goods Technology*. https://consumergoods.com/skin-care-ai-loreal-decoding-future-beauty

Donald, W. E., & Mouratidou, M. (2022). Preparing for a Sustainable Career: Challenges and Opportunities. *GiLE Journal of Skills Development, 2*(2), 3-5. https://insight.cumbria.ac.uk/id/eprint/6647/

Donthu, N., Kumar, S., Pandey, N., Pandey, N., & Mishra, A. (2021). Mapping the electronic word-of-mouth (eWOM) research: A systematic review and bibliometric analysis. *Journal of Business Research*, *135*, 758–773. doi:10.1016/j.jbusres.2021.07.015

Dopson, E. (2022). *30+ Influencer Marketing Statistics You Should Know (2023)*. Retrieved Jun 13, 2023, from https://www.shopify.com/blog/influencer-marketing-statistics

Doratiotto, K., Vidal Vieira, J. G., da Silva, L. E., & Fávero, L. P. (2023). Evaluating logistics outsourcing: A survey conducted with Brazilian industries. *Benchmarking*, *30*(3), 788–810. doi:10.1108/BIJ-06-2021-0341

Doyle, J. P., Su, Y., & Kunkel, T. (2022). Athlete branding via social media: Examining the factors influencing consumer engagement on Instagram. *European Sport Management Quarterly*, *22*(4), 506–526. doi:10.1080/16184742.2020.1806897

Drenten, J., Gurrieri, L., & Tyler, M. (2020). Sexualized labor in digital culture: Instagram influencers, porn chic and the monetization of attention. *Gender, Work and Organization*, *27*(1), 41–66. doi:10.1111/gwao.12354

Duffett, R. (2017). Influence of social media marketing communications on young consumers' attitudes. *Young Consumers*, *18*(1), 19–39. doi:10.1108/YC-07-2016-00622

Duffy, B. E. (2020). Social media influencers. In K. Ross, I. Bachmann, V. Cardo, S. Moorti, & M. Scarcelli (Eds.), *International encyclopedia of gender, media, and communication*. Wiley-Blackwell. doi:10.1002/9781119429128.iegmc219

Duranton, C., & Gaunet, F. (2016). Behavioural synchronization from an ethological perspective: Overview of its adaptive value. *Adaptive Behavior*, *24*(3), 181–191. doi:10.1177/1059712316644966

Dutta, G., Kumar, R., Sindhwani, R., & Singh, R. K. (2020). Digital transformation priorities of India's discrete manufacturing SMEs – a conceptual study in perspective of industry 4.0. *Competitiveness Review*, *30*(3), 289–314. doi:10.1108/CR-03-2019-0031

Dutta, K., Sharma, K., & Goyal, T. (2021). Customer's digital advocacy: The impact of reviews and influencers in building trust for tourism and hospitality services. *Worldwide Hospitality and Tourism Themes*, *13*(2), 260–274. doi:10.1108/WHATT-09-2020-0123

EconomicTimes. (2023, Sept 7). *Social Media and Influencer Marketing for CMOs: Maximizing Brand Reach and Engagement*. Retrieved Sept 15, 2023, from https://economictimes.indiatimes.com/: https://economictimes.indiatimes.com/jobs/c-suite/social-media-and-influencer-marketing-for-cmos-maximizing-brand-reach-and-engagement/articleshow/103480616.cms?from=mdr

Edwards, G. (2022). *5 Reasons Why Macro & Mega Influencers May Not Be Good for Your Brand*. Retrieved Jun 09, 2023, from cipio.ai: https://blog.cipio.ai/5-reasons-why-macro-and-mega-influencers-may-not-be-good-for-your-brand

Edwards, J., Miles, M. P., D'Alessandro, S., & Frost, M. (2022). Linking B2B sales performance to entrepreneurial self-efficacy, entrepreneurial selling actions. *Journal of Business Research*, *142*, 585–593. doi:10.1016/j.jbusres.2021.12.074

Ehlers, K. (2021, Jun 2). *Micro-Influencers: When Smaller Is Better*. Retrieved Sept 01, 2023, from FORBES: https://www.forbes.com/sites/forbesagencycouncil/2021/06/02/micro-influencers-when-smaller-is-better/?sh=24dbe848539b

Emeritus. (2022a). *Discover the Best Ways to Leverage Influencer Marketing for Your Brand*. Retrieved Jun 08, 2023, from https://emeritus.org/blog/digital-marketing-what-is-an-influencer/

Emeritus. (2022b, May 13). *Influencer Marketing Is Taking Advantage of The Metaverse! Are You Ready?* Retrieved Sept 13, 2023, from https://emeritus.org/blog/influencer-marketing-metaverse/

Emplify. (2023). *Micro influencers vs macro influencers: What's best for your business?* Retrieved Jun 12, 2023, from https://emplifi.io/resources/blog/micro-influencers-vs-macro-influencers?

Enberg, J. (2021, Nov 29). *Micro-influencers present macro opportunities*. Retrieved Jun 11, 2023, from Insider Intelligence: https://www.insiderintelligence.com/content/mirco-influencers-present-macro-opportunities

Engaiodigital. (2022). *What Is Influencer Marketing and Its Benefits*. Retrieved Jun 11, 2023, from https://engaiodigital.com/influencer-marketing/

Engel, J. F., Kollat, D. J., & Blackwell, R. D. (1968). *Consumer Behavior*. Holt, Rinehart and Winston.

Equity, B. (2022, Oct 20). *Influencer marketing industry in India to reach Rs 2,200 cr by 2025: Report*. Retrieved Jun 06, 2023, from Brand Equity: https://brandequity.economictimes.indiatimes.com/news/research/influencer-marketing-industry-in-india-to-reach-rs-2200-cr-by-2025-report/94990088

Erdogan, B. Z. (1999). Celebrity endorsement: A literature review. *Journal of Marketing Management*, *15*(4), 291–314. doi:10.1362/026725799784870379

Erz, A., & Christensen, A. B. H. (2018). Transforming consumers into brands: Tracing transformation processes of the practice of blogging. *Journal of Interactive Marketing*, *43*, 69–82. doi:10.1016/j.intmar.2017.12.002

Escalas, J. E., & Bettman, J. R. (2005). Self-construal, reference groups, and brand meaning. *The Journal of Consumer Research*, *32*(3), 378–389. doi:10.1086/497549

Ethos. (n.d.). *Nano-Influencers: Who, What, Why, When, and How to Engage Them*. Retrieved Jun 11, 2023, from https://www.ethos-marketing.com/blog/nano-influencers-social-media-marketing/#:~:text=Nano%2Dinfluencers%20are%20your%20everyday,from%20100%20to%2010%2C000%20followers

European Commission. (2022). *Cosmetics legislation*. European single market. https://single-market-economy.ec.europa.eu/sectors/cosmetics/legislation_en

Evans, M. (2019, September 23). Five key traits defining connected consumers in 2019. *Forbes*. https://www.forbes.com/sites/miche lleevans1/2019/09/23/five-key-trait s-defining-connected-consumers in-2019/#6b1b97e622df

Evans, N. J., Phua, J., Lim, J., & Jun, H. (2017). Disclosing Instagram influencer advertising: The effects of disclosure language on advertising recognition, attitudes, and behavioral intent. *Journal of Interactive Advertising*, *17*(2), 138–149. doi:10.1080/15252019.2017.1366885

ExpertVoice. (2021). *The Role of Influencer Marketing in Today's Consumer Decision Journey*. https://www.expertvoice.com/the-role-of-influencer-marketing-in-todays-consumer-decision-journey/

Fairchild, C. (2007). Building the authentic celebrity: The "Idol" phenomenon in the attention economy. *Popular Music and Society*, *30*(3), 355–375. doi:10.1080/03007760600835306

Falasca, K., & Helgesson, E. (2021). Revolving around roles – public affairs practitioners as democratic enablers or as hired guns. *Public Relations Review*, *47*(1), 101923. Advance online publication. doi:10.1016/j.pubrev.2020.101923

Famesters. (2020). *What do TikTok and YouTube shorts have in common?* Retrieved Sept 15, 2023, from https://famesters.com: https://famesters.com/blog/tiktok-or-youtube-shorts-which-is-better-for-your-influencer-marketing/

Fauser, S. (2023). Virtual Influencer Marketing and its Impact on Customer Purchase Behaviour. *International Journal of Business and Applied Social Science*, *9*(6). doi:10.33642/ijbass.v9n6p4

Featherstone, M. (2010). Body, image and affect in consumer culture. *Body & Society*, *16*(1), 193–221. doi:10.1177/1357034X09354357

Feng, Y., Chen, H., & Kong, Q. (2021). An expert with whom i can identify: The role of narratives in influencer marketing. *International Journal of Advertising*, *40*(7), 972–993. doi:10.1080/02650487.2020.1824751

Fernández-Prados, J. S., Lozano-Díaz, A., Bernal-Bravo, C., Muyor-Rodríguez, J., & IEEE. (2021, Mar 27-29). Influencers and Social Media: State of the Art and Bibliometric Analysis. *9th International Conference on Information and Education Technology (ICIET), Electr Network.*

Ferrari, F., & McKelvey, F. (2022). Hyperproduction: A social theory of deep generative models. *Distinktion : Scandinavian Journal of Social Theory*. Advance online publication. doi:10.1080/1600910X.2022.2137546

Fetchko, M. J., Roy, D. P., & Clow, K. E. (2018). *Sports marketing*. Routledge. doi:10.4324/9781315175614

Field, A. (2018). Discovering statistics using IBM SPSS statistics. *Sage (Atlanta, Ga.)*.

FigueiredoE.RibeiroC.PassosC.PereiraP. (2022). Relationship marketing in university libraries: a literature review. *Gestão E Desenvolvimento*, (30), 289-316. https://doi.org/ doi:10.34632/gestaoedesenvolvimento.2022.11342

Financial Dictonary. (2021). *Influencers*. Retrieved Jun 08, 2023, from https://indianmoney.com/financial-dictionary/i/influencers

Firmino, I. (2022). *Influenciador digital: emblema da indústria cultural, Goiânia 2022* [Master's dissertation, Federal University of Goiás]. Federal University of Goiás Digital Library of Theses and Dissertations. https://repositorio.bc.ufg.br/tede/handle/tede/12399

Fiske, S. T., & Taylor, S. E. (2021). *Social cognition: From brains to culture* (4th ed.). Sage.

FoodieTribe. (2021). *FoodieTribe's Case Study on Influencer Marketing for Restaurants*. https://foodietribe.com/case-study/

Forbes. (2022). https://www.forbesindia.com/article/bharatiya-vidya-bhavan039s-spjimr/the-evolution-of-influencer-marketing

Forbes, K. (2016). Examining the beauty industry's use of social influencers. *Elon Journal of Undergraduate Research in Communications*, *7*(2), 78–87.

Forbes, L. P., & Vespoli, E. (2013). Does social media influence consumer buying behavior? An investigation of recommendations and purchases. *Journal of Business & Economics Research*, *11*(2), 107–113. doi:10.19030/jber.v11i2.7623

Foster, J. (2022). *Why Influencer Marketing is Creating Huge Returns for Businesses.* Retrieved Jun 01, 2023, from https://www.convinceandconvert.com/digital-marketing/influencer-marketing-for-businesses/#:~:text=Influencer%20Marketing%20Delivers%20a%20Strong,failing%20to%20generate%20any%20revenue

Foy, P. (2023, Feb 25). *Influencer Marketing Metrics: 8 Key Metrics to Track Performance.* Retrieved Sept 15, 2023, from https://agencyanalytics.com/blog/influencer-marketing-analytics

Francis, T., & Hoefel, F. (2018, Nov 12). *'True Gen': Generation Z and its implications for companies.* Retrieved Jun 15, 2023, from McKinsey and company: https://www.mckinsey.com/industries/consumer-packaged-goods/our-insights/true-gen-generation-z-and-its-implications-for-companies

Franke, C., Groeppel-Klein, A., & Müller, K. (2022). Consumers' Responses to Virtual Influencers as Advertising Endorsers: Novel and Effective or Uncanny and Deceiving? *Journal of Advertising.* Advance online publication. doi:10.1080/00913367.2022.2154721

Freberg, K., Graham, K., McGaughey, K., & Freberg, L. A. (2011). Who are the social media influencers? A study of public perceptions of personality. *Public Relations Review*, *37*(1), 90–92. doi:10.1016/j.pubrev.2010.11.001

Fred, S. (2015). *Examining Endorsement and Viewership Effects on the Source Credibility of Youtubers.* Retrieved from: http://Scholarcommons.Usf.Edu/Cgi/Viewcontent.Cgi?Article=6883andContext=Etd

Freitas, I. (2019). *A influência das caraterísticas do Centro Cultural na Satisfação e na Laldade: O Caso do Centro de Artes e Espectáculos da Figueira da Foz* [thesis, Coimbra School of Education and Oliveira do Hospital School of Technology and Management]. Common Repository. http://hdl.handle.net/10400.26/31150

Freitas, M. R., Pimenta, M. L., Hilletofth, P., Jugend, D., & Oprime, P. C. (2020). Demand management: The role of cross-functional integration in a context of political turbulence. *Asia Pacific Journal of Marketing and Logistics*, *32*(3), 817–839. doi:10.1108/APJML-11-2018-0473

French, J. R., Raven, B., & Cartwright, D. (1959). The bases of social power. *Classics of Organization Theory*, *7*(311-320), 1.

FundafundaC. (2023, April). Understanding social media influencer credibility, its components, and their individual effects on the purchase intentions of female Millennial consumers on Instagram. doi:10.13140/RG.2.2.34441.52328

Gahin, R., & Paterson, C. (2003, July). Community Indicators: Past, Present, and Future. *National Civic Review*, *90*(4), 347–361. doi:10.1002/ncr.90406

Gama, M. (2020). *Culture and Development: Cultural projects and the 2030 Agenda Phase 1, Portugal, 1st quarter 2020.* Observatory of Communication and Culture Policies Centre for Communication and Society Studies University of Minho.

Ganguly, S. (2015). Why social media advertising is set to explode in the next 3 years. *Marketing Land.* https://marketingland.com/social-media-advertising-setexplode-next-3-years-121691

Gannon, V., & Prothero, A. (2018). Beauty bloggers and youtubers as a community of practice. *Journal of Marketing Management, 34*(3), 1–28. doi:10.1080/0267257X.2018.1482941

Garcia, C. (2018). *Marketing in Portuguese contemporary dance companies - Case studies: CiM Companhia de Dança, Companhia de Dança de Almada and Quorum Ballet* [Master's dissertation]. Iscte - University Institute of Lisbon. http://hdl.handle.net/10071/18789

García, P. (2021, July 9). *Las mujeres usan más las redes sociales que los hombres*. Cadena SER. https://cadenaser.com/emisora/2021/07/09/ser_madrid_sur/1625826613_464505.html

García, A., Smith, J., & Johnson, M. (2023). Virtual Influencers: Targeting Youth Audiences in the Digital Age. *Digital Marketing Journal, 15*(1), 45–60.

García-Gavilán, S., López-González, H., & Acosta-Vargas, P. (2021). Virtual Influencers: A New Challenge in the Ethical Dilemma of Advertising. In Marketing and Smart Technologies (pp. 175-183). Springer.

Garcia-Marques, L., Ferreira, M. B., & Garrido, M. (2017). Processos de influência social [Social influence processes]. In J. Vala & M.B. Monteiro (Coord.), Psicologia social (pp. 245-300). Fundação Calouste Gulbenkian.

Gardner, S. (2005). *Buzz marketing with blogs for dummies*. Wiley Publishing Inc.

Gartner Predicts 25% of People Will Spend at Least One Hour Per Day in the Metaverse by 2026. (2022). Gartner Inc. Press Release. Newsroom. https://www.gartner.com/en/newsroom/press-releases/2022-02-07-gartner-predicts-25-percent-of-people-will-spend-at-least-one-hour-per-day-in-the-metaverse-by-2026

Ge, J., & Gretzel, U. (2018). Emoji rhetoric: A social media influencer perspective. *Journal of Marketing Management, 34*(15–16), 1272–1295. doi:10.1080/0267257X.2018.1483960

Gelati, N., Verplancke, J., & Frögren, N. F. (2022, Dec). *The effect of influencer marketing on buying behavior of young consumers*. Linköping University. Retrieved Sept 14, 2023, from https://liu.diva-portal.org/smash/get/diva2:1668422/FULLTEXT01.pdf

Geurin, A. N. (2017). Elite female athletes' perceptions of new media use relating to their careers: A qualitative analysis. *Journal of Sport Management, 31*(4), 345–359. doi:10.1123/jsm.2016-0157

Geurin-Eagleman, A. N., & Burch, L. M. (2016). Communicating via photographs: A gendered analysis of Olympic athletes' visual self-presentation on Instagram. *Sport Management Review, 19*(2), 133–145. doi:10.1016/j.smr.2015.03.002

Geyser, W. (2020). *The State of Influencer Marketing 2020: Benchmark Report*. Retrieved from: https://influencermarketinghub.com/influencer-marketing-benchmark-report-2020/

Geyser, W. (2022, July 27). *What is an influencer? Social media influencers defined* [Updated 2022]. Influencer Marketing Hub. https://influencermarketinghub.com/what-is-an-influencer/#toc-0

Geyser, W. (2023, Feb 7). *The State of Influencer Marketing 2023: Benchmark Report*. Retrieved Jun 06, 2023, from Influencer Marketing Hub: https://influencermarketinghub.com/influencer-marketing-benchmark-report/

Gil, P. (2017). *Comunicação pública e públicos em questão* (1st ed., Vol. 2). Vertentes conceptuais e metodológicas. PPGCOM UFMG. https://www.researchgate.net/publication/342786807_Uma_rota_para_teoria_e_pratica_em_comunicacao_publica_a_argumentacao_como_luta_civica_por_reconhecimento_respeito_e_justica

Gil-Quintana, J., & Vida de León, E. (2021). Educational influencers on Instagram: Analysis of educational channels, audiences, and economic performance. *Publications / MDPI*, *9*(4), 43. Advance online publication. doi:10.3390/publications9040043

Godey, B., Manthiou, A., Perdezoli, D., Rokka, J., Aiello, G., Donvito, R., & Singh, R. (2016). Social media marketing efforts of luxury brands: Influence on brand equity and consumer behaviour. *Journal of Business Research*, *69*(12), 5833–5841. doi:10.1016/j.jbusres.2016.04.181

Goffman, E. (1959). *The Presentation of Self in Everyday Life*. Penguin Books.

Gómez-Suárez, M., & Veloso, M. (2020). Brand experience and brand attachment as drivers of WOM in hospitality. *Spanish Journal of Marketing-ESIC*.

Gonçalves, R., & Branco, F. (2020). *Twitch and the Engagement of Users: The Uses and Gratifications Approach to the Portuguese Community of Streamers*. Revista Portuguesa de Marketing.

González, M. (2019). *La cosmética ya no solo tiene que ver con la estética*. Forbes España. https://forbes.es/empresas/43235/la-cosmetica-ya-no-solo-tiene-que-ver-con-la-estetica/

Gottfried, J., & Shearer, E. (2016). *News use across social media platforms 2016*. Pew Research Center. https://www.journalism.org/2016/05/26/news-use-acrosssocial-media-platforms-2016/

Governo da República Portuguesa. (n.d.). *Cultura*. https://www.historico.portugal.gov.pt/pt/o-governo/arquivo-historico/governos-constitucionais/gc19/os-temas/cultura/cultura.aspx#:~:text=A%20cultura%20%C3%A9%20um%20fator%20de%20coes%C3%A3o%20e, para%20a%20afirma%C3%A7%C3%A3o%20de%20Portugal%20na%20comunidade%20internacional.

Goyal, S., Hu, C. H., Chauhan, S., Gupta, P., Bhardwaj, A. K., & Mahindroo, A. (2021). Social Commerce: A Bibliometric Analysis and Future Research Directions. *Journal of Global Information Management*, *29*(6), 1–33. Advance online publication. doi:10.4018/JGIM.293291

Gram, M., & Pedersen, H. D. (2014). Negotiations of Motherhood- Between İdeals and Practice, Motherhoods, Markets and Consumption. In S. O'Donohoe, M. Hogg, P. Maclaran, L. Martens, & L. Stevens (Eds.), *The Making of Mother, Motherhoods, Markets and Consumption: The Making of Mothers in Contemporary Western Cultures* (pp. 99–114). Routledge.

Gräve, J. (2017) Exploring The Perception of Influencers vs. Traditional Celebrities: Are Social Media Stars a New Type of Endorser? *8th International Conference on Social Media and Society*, 1-5.

Gräve, J.-F. (2017). Exploring the perception of influencers vs. traditional celebrities: Are social media stars a new type of endorser? In *Proceedings of the 8th International Conference on Social Media & Society*. Association for Computing Machinery. 10.1145/3097286.3097322

Gräve, J. F. (2019). What KPIs are key? Evaluating performance metrics for social media influencers. *Social Media + Society*, *5*(3). doi:10.1177/2056305119865475

Gräve, J.-F., & Bartsch, F. (2022). #Instafame: Exploring the endorsement effectiveness of influencers compared to celebrities. *International Journal of Advertising*, *41*(4), 591–622. doi:10.1080/02650487.2021.1987041

Gray, A. (2022). How behavioral science can improve influencer marketing campaigns. *Journal of Digital and Social Media Marketing*, *10*(1), 61–68. www.scopus.com

Grin. (2021a). *Influencer Discount Codes & Affiliate Links – How and when to use them in your campaigns*. Retrieved Sept 15, 2023, from GRIN: https://grin.co/blog/influencer-discount-codes-affiliate-links-how-and-when-to-use-them-in-your-campaigns/

Grin. (2021b). *Why Influencer Marketing Is an Important Part of Today's Businesses*. Retrieved Jun 05, 2023, from GRIN: https://grin.co/blog/why-influencer-marketing/

Grin. (2022). *Psychology of Influence – The Reason for the Rise of Influencer Marketing*. Retrieved Sept 15, 2023, from GRIN: https://grin.co/blog/psychology-of-influence/

Grin. (2023). *6 Effective Ways to Reach Your Target Audience*. Retrieved Sept 15, 2023, from GRIN: https://grin.co/blog/reach-your-target-audience-more-effectively/

Guay, F., Chanal, J., Ratelle, C. F., Marsh, H. W., Larose, S., & Boivin, M. (2010). Intrinsic, identified, and controlled types of motivation for school subjects in young elementary school children. *The British Journal of Educational Psychology*, *80*(4), 711–735. doi:10.1348/000709910X499084 PMID:20447334

Guha, S., & Majumdar, S. (2021). In search of business models in social entrepreneurship: Concepts and cases. In Search of business models in social entrepreneurship: Concepts and cases (pp. 1-291) doi:10.1007/978-981-16-0390-7

Gunelius, S. (2010). *30-minute social media marketing: Step-by-step techniques to spread the word about your business: Social media marketing in 30 minutes a day*. McGraw Hill Professional.

Guo, C., & Saxton, G. D. (2014). Tweeting Social Change: How Social Media Are Changing Nonprofit Advocacy. *Nonprofit and Voluntary Sector Quarterly*, *43*(1), 57–79. doi:10.1177/0899764012471585

Guo, L., Wang, W., Wu, Y. J., & Goh, M. (2021). How much do social connections matter in fundraising outcomes? *Financial Innovation*, *7*(1), 79. Advance online publication. doi:10.118640854-021-00293-7

Guo, Q., Cheng, S., & Zhao, P. (2023). How to introduce a livestreaming channel: A case of the hotel at a fixed capacity. *International Transactions in Operational Research*, itor.13259. Advance online publication. doi:10.1111/itor.13259

Gupta, S., & Dogra, N. (2018). Social Media Influencers: A Review and Research Agenda. *Vision: The Journal of Business Perspective*.

Gupta, K. P., Manrai, R., & Goel, U. (2019). Factors influencing adoption of payments banks by Indian customers: Extending UTAUT with perceived credibility. *Journal of Asia Business Studies*, *13*(2), 173–195. doi:10.1108/JABS-07-2017-0111

Guthrie, S. (2020). Virtual influencers More human than humans. In Influencer marketing (Vol. 1). Academic Press.

Haenlein, M., Anadol, E., Farnsworth, T., Hugo, H., Hunichen, J., & Welte, D. (2020). Navigating the new era of influencer marketing: How to be successful on Instagram, TikTok, & Co. *California Management Review*, *63*(1), 5–25. doi:10.1177/0008125620958166

Hajarian, M., Hosseini, B., & Ramezankhani, M. J. (2019). Investigating the Role of Social Media Marketing in Customer Value Creation. *Journal of Research in Interactive Marketing*.

Ham, J., Shah, P., & Eastin, M. S. (2023). Do You Think I'm Real? A Mixed Reality Approach to the Effects of the Virtual Influencer Engagement on Attitude and Brand Attachment: An Abstract. In *Developments in Marketing Science: Proceedings of the Academy of Marketing Science* (pp. 73-74). Academic Press.

Ham, J., Li, S., Shah, P., & Eastin, M. S. (2023). The "Mixed" Reality of Virtual Brand Endorsers: Understanding the Effect of Brand Engagement and Social Cues on Technological Perceptions and Advertising Effectiveness. *Journal of Interactive Advertising*, *23*(2), 98–113. doi:10.1080/15252019.2023.2185557

Han, H. S., Lee, J., & Masuda, H. (2022, January). mpacts of influencer attributes on purchase intentions in social media influencer marketing: Mediating roles of characterizations. *Technological Forecasting and Social Change*, *174*(1), 121246. Advance online publication. doi:10.1016/j.techfore.2021.121246

Hanna, R., Rohm, A., & Crittenden, V. L. (2011). We're all connected: The power of the social media ecosystem. *Business Horizons*, *54*(3), 265–273. doi:10.1016/j.bushor.2011.01.007

Harmeling, C. M., Moffett, J. W., Arnold, M. J., & Carlson, B. D. (2017). Toward a theory of customer engagement marketing. *Journal of the Academy of Marketing Science*, *45*(3), 312–335. doi:10.100711747-016-0509-2

Harrigan, P., Daly, T. M., Coussement, K., Lee, J., Soutar, G. N., & Evers, U. (2021). Identifying influencers on social media. *International Journal of Information Management*, *56*, 102246. doi:10.1016/j.ijinfomgt.2020.102246

Harrison, J. S., Ho, V. T., Bosse, D. A., & Crilly, D. (2023). A configurational theory of generalized exchange in stakeholder-oriented firms. *The Academy of Management Perspectives*, *37*(1), 16–36. doi:10.5465/amp.2022.0034

Hayes, A. (2023, Apr 12). *Social Media Marketing (SMM): What It Is, How It Works, Pros and Cons*. Retrieved Sept 15, 2023, from https://www.investopedia.com: https://www.investopedia.com/terms/s/social-media-marketing-smm.asp

Healey, M. (2010). *Branding: A guide to creating successful brands*. Macmillan International Higher Education.

Hearn, A. (2008). Meat, mask, burden: Probing the contours of the branded "self". *Journal of Consumer Culture*, *8*(2), 197–217. doi:10.1177/1469540508090086

Hearn, A., & Schoenhoff, S. (2015). *From Celebrity to Influencer: Tracing the Diffusion of Celebrity Value Across the Data Stream*. Wiley Online Library.

Hennig-Thurau, T., Malthouse, E. C., Friege, C., Gensler, S., Lobschat, L., Rangaswamy, A., & Skiera, B. (2010). The impact of new media on customer relationships. *Journal of Service Research*, *13*(3), 311–330. doi:10.1177/1094670510375460

Hofeditz, L., Erle, L., Timm, L., & Mirbabaie, M. (2023). How Virtuous are Virtual Influencers? - A Qualitative Analysis of Virtual Actors' Virtues on Instagram. *Proceedings of the Annual Hawaii International Conference on System Sciences*.

Hoffner, C., & Buchanan, M. (2005). Young adults' wishful identification with television characters: The role of perceived similarity and character attributes. *Media Psychology*, *7*(4), 325–351. doi:10.1207/S1532785XMEP0704_2

Hofstede, G. (1980). Culture's consequences: International differences in work-related values. *Sage (Atlanta, Ga.)*.

Hogg, M. A., & Vaughan, G. M. (2014). *Social Psychology* (7th ed.). Pearson Education Limited.

Holbrook, M. B., & Elizabeth, C. H. (1982). The experiential aspects of consumption: Consumer fantasy, feelings and fun. *The Journal of Consumer Research*, *9*(2), 132–140. doi:10.1086/208906

Hollebeek, L. D., Glynn, M. S., & Brodie, R. J. (2014). Consumer brand engagement in social Media: Conceptualization, scale development and validation. *Journal of Interactive Marketing*, *28*(2), 149–165. doi:10.1016/j.intmar.2013.12.002

Horáková, J., Uusitalo, O., Munnukka, J., & Jokinen, O. (2022). Does the digitalization of retailing disrupt consumers' attachment to retail places? *Journal of Retailing and Consumer Services*, *67*, 102958. doi:10.1016/j.jretconser.2022.102958

Horning, D. L. (2020). *Sports marketing special session: Ice hockey consumers: Who cares about women recreational players? An abstract.* doi:10.1007/978-3-030-42545-6_25

Hovland, C. I., & Weiss, W. (1951). The influence of source credibility on communication effectiveness. *Public Opinion Quarterly*, *15*(4), 635–650. doi:10.1086/266350

Howard, J. A., & Sheth, J. N. (1969). *The Theory of Buyer Behavior*. John Wiley & Sons, Inc.

Hsu, C. L., & Lin, J. C. C. (2015). What drives purchase intention for paid mobile apps? An expectation confirmation theory perspective. *Electronic Commerce Research and Applications*, *14*(1), 46–57. doi:10.1016/j.elerap.2014.11.003

Huber, J., & Klein, N. (1991). Adapting cutoffs to the choice environment: The effects of attribute correlation and reliability. *The Journal of Consumer Research*, *18*(3), 346–357. doi:10.1086/209264

Hubspot. (2019). *71% more likely to purchase based on social media referrals.* https://blog. hubspot.com/blog/tabid/6307/bid/30239/71-More-Likely-to-Purchase-Based-onSocial-Media-Referrals-Infographic.aspx

Hubspot. (2023). *6 Social Media Algorithms Marketers Need to Know About in 2023.* https://blog.hubspot.com/marketing/how-algorithm-works-facebook-twitter-instagram

Hudders, L., Jans, S. D., & Veirman, M. D. (2021). The commercialization of Social Media Stars: A Literature Review and conceptual framework on the strategic use of Social Media influencers. *Social Media Influencers in Strategic Communication*, 24–67. doi:10.4324/9781003181286-3

Hudders, L., De Jans, S., & De Veirman, M. (2021). The commercialization of social media stars: A literature review and conceptual framework on the strategic use of social media influencers. *International Journal of Advertising*, *40*(3), 327–375. doi:10.1080/02650487.2020.1836925

Hudders, L., & Lou, C. (2022). A new era of influencer marketing: Lessons from recent inquires and thoughts on future directions. *International Journal of Advertising*, *42*(1), 1–5. doi:10.1080/02650487.2022.2031729

Hudders, L., & Lou, C. (2023). The rosy world of influencer marketing? Its bright and dark sides, and future research recommendations. *International Journal of Advertising*, *42*(1), 151–161. doi:10.1080/02650487.2022.2137318

Huebner, E. J. (2022). TikTok and museum education: A visual content analysis. *International Journal of Education through Art, 18*(2), 209-225. doi:10.1386/eta_00095_1

Hughes, C., Swaminathan, V., & Brooks, G. (2019). Driving brand engagement through online social influencers: An empirical investigation of sponsored blogging campaigns. *Journal of Marketing*, *83*(5), 78–96. doi:10.1177/0022242919854374

HumansV. (n.d.). https://www.virtualhumans.org/category/research

Husain, U., Javed, S., & Ananda, S. (2021). Digital marketing as a game changer strategy to enhance brand performance. *International Journal of Technology Marketing*, *15*(2-3), 107–125. doi:10.1504/IJTMKT.2021.118226

Hutchinson, A. (2021). *Nano Influencers: Who Are They and How to Work With Them [Infographic].* Retrieved Jun 12, 2023, from https://www.socialmediatoday.com/news/nano-influencers-who-are-they-and-how-to-work-with-them-infographic/595048/

Hutter, K., Hautz, J., Dennhardt, S., & Füller, J. (2013). The impact of user interactions in social media on brand awareness and purchase intention: The case of MINI on Facebook. *Journal of Product and Brand Management*, *22*(5/6), 342–351. doi:10.1108/JPBM-05-2013-0299

Hu, Y., Manikonda, L., & Kambhampati, S. (2014). What we instagram: A first analysis of instagram photo content and user types. *Proceedings of the international AAAI conference on web and social media, 8*(1), 595-598. 10.1609/icwsm.v8i1.14578

Illia, L., Colleoni, E., & Meggiorin, K. (2021). How infomediaries on twitter influence business outcomes of a bank. *International Journal of Bank Marketing*, *39*(5), 709–724. doi:10.1108/IJBM-08-2020-0414

Ind, N., & Coates, N. (2013). The meanings of co-creation. *European Business Review*, *25*(1), 86–95. doi:10.1108/09555341311287754

Ind, N., Coates, N., & Lerman, K. (2019). The gift of co-creation: What motivates customers to participate. *Journal of Brand Management*, *27*(2), 181–194. doi:10.105741262-019-00173-7

INE. (2022). *Encuesta de población activa*. https://www.ine.es/ss/Satellite?L=es_ES&c=INESeccion_C&cid=1259925528782&p=1254735110672&pagename=ProductosYServicios%2FPYSLayout

Influence Center Survey. (2020). *Social Upends Traditional Media In Driving Shopping Purchases*. Retrieved from: http://blog.influence-central.com/social-upends-traditional-media-in-driving-shopping-purchases/

Influencer Marketing Hub. (2020). *The State of Influencer Marketing 2020: Benchmark Report*. Retrieved from: https://influencermarketinghub.com/influencer-marketing-benchmark-report-2020/

Influencer Marketing Hub. (2021). *Influencer marketing benchmarks: How to measure your success*. https://influencermarketinghub.com/influencer-marketing-benchmarks/

Influencer Marketing Hub. (2023). *The state of influencer marketing 2023: Benchmark report*. https://influencermarketinghub.com/influencer-marketing-benchmark-report/

Influencity. (2021). *Influencer Marketing Benchmark Report 2021*. https://influencity.com/influencer-marketing-benchmark-report-2021/

Influencity. (2023a, Apr 14). *The Impact of Influencer Marketing on Consumer Behavior and Purchase Decisions*. Retrieved Sept 14, 2023, from https://influencity.com: https://influencity.com/blog/en/the-impact-of-influencer-marketing-on-consumer-behavior-and-purchase-decisions

Influencity. (2023b, Aug 14). *The Future of Influencer Marketing: Leveraging AI for Enhanced Campaigns*. Retrieved Sept 15, 2023, from https://influencity.com: https://influencity.com/blog/en/the-future-of-influencer-marketing-leveraging-ai-for-enhanced-campaigns

Infosecurity Magazine. (2019, June 10). Consumers unaware of AI impact on data privacy. *Infosecurity Magazine*. https://www.infosecurity-magazine.com/news/consumers-ai-impact-data-privacy/

Institute, D. M. (2019). *20 Surprising Influencer Marketing Statistics*. Retrieved Jun 15, 2023, from https://digitalmarketinginstitute.com/blog/20-influencer-marketing-statistics-that-will-surprise-you

Iskiev, M. (2023). *The HubSpot Blog's 2023 Marketing Strategy & Trends Report: Data from 1,200+ Global Marketers*. Retrieved Jun 05, 2023, from https://blog.hubspot.com/marketing/hubspot-blog-marketing-industry-trends-report?_ga=2.164494201.777083537.1669997995-495228435.1669997995&hubs_content=blog.hubspot.com%2Fmarketing%2Finfluencer-marketing-stats&hubs_content-cta=1%20in%204%20marketers

Islam, J. U., Hollebeek, L. D., Rahman, Z., Khan, I., & Rasool, A. (2019). Customer engagement in the service context: An empirical investigation of the construct, its antecedents and consequences. *Journal of Retailing and Consumer Services*, *50*, 277–285. doi:10.1016/j.jretconser.2019.05.018

Ismail, K. (2023, Jun 21). *Types of Social Media Influencers: Mega, Macro, Micro or Nano*. Retrieved Sept 15, 2023, from CMSWIRE: https://www.cmswire.com/digital-marketing/social-media-influencers-mega-macro-micro-or-nano/

Jaakkola, E., & Alexander, M. (2014). The role of customer engagement Behavior in Value Co-Creation. *Journal of Service Research*, *17*(3), 247–261. doi:10.1177/1094670514529187

Jacoby, J., & Chestnut, R. W. (1978). *Brand Loyalty: Measurement and Management*. John Wiley & Sons.

Jain, V. (2021). An overview on social media influencer marketing. *South Asian Journal of Marketing & Management Research*, *11*(11), 76–81. doi:10.5958/2249-877X.2021.00112.0

Janssen, L., Schouten, A. P., & Croes, E. A. (2022). Influencer advertising on Instagram: Product-influencer fit and number of followers affect advertising outcomes and influencer evaluations via credibility and identification. *International Journal of Advertising*, *41*(1), 101–127. doi:10.1080/02650487.2021.1994205

Jat, M., Jajja, M. S. S., ur Rehman, A., & Farooq, S. (2023). Manufacturer's contexts, supply chain risk management, and agility performance. *IEEE Transactions on Engineering Management*, 1–13. doi:10.1109/TEM.2023.3234050

Jayles, B., Escobedo, R., Cezera, S., Blanchet, A., Kameda, T., Sire, C., & Theraulaz, G. (2020). The impact of incorrect social information on collective wisdom in human groups: The impact of incorrect social information on collective wisdom in human groups. *Journal of the Royal Society, Interface*, *17*(170), 20200496. Advance online publication. doi:10.1098/rsif.2020.0496 PMID:32900307

Jhang-Li, J., & Liou, J. (2023). An analysis of operating strategy for a video live streaming platform: Advertisement, advertorial, and donation. *Information Technology Management*. Advance online publication. doi:10.100710799-023-00387-x PMID:36742341

Jhawar, A., Kumar, P., & Varshney, S. (2023). The emergence of virtual influencers: A shift in the influencer marketing paradigm. *Young Consumers*, *24*(4), 468–484. Advance online publication. doi:10.1108/YC-05-2022-1529

Jiang, Y., Jin, X., & Deng, Q. (2022). *Short video uprising: How# BlackLivesMatter content on TikTok challenges the protest paradigm*. https://doi.org//arXiv.2206.09946 doi:10.48550

Jin, S. A., Muqaddam, A., & Ryu, E. (2019). Instafamous and social media influencer marketing. *Marketing Intelligence & Planning*, *37*(5), 567–579. doi:10.1108/MIP-09-2018-0375

Jin, S. A., & Phua, J. (2014). Following celebrities' tweets about brands: The impact of Twitter-Based electronic Word-of-Mouth on consumers' source credibility perception, buying intention, and social identification with celebrities. *Journal of Advertising*, *43*(2), 181–195. doi:10.1080/00913367.2013.827606

Jin, S. A., Ryu, E., & Muqaddam, A. (2021). I trust what she's #endorsing on Instagram: Moderating effects of parasocial interaction and social presence in fashion influencer marketing. *Journal of Fashion Marketing and Management*, *25*(4), 665–681. doi:10.1108/JFMM-04-2020-0059

Jin, S. V., & Ryu, E. (2019). Celebrity fashion brand endorsement in Facebook viral marketing and social commerce: Interactive effects of social identification, materialism, fashion involvement, and opinion leadership. *Journal of Fashion Marketing and Management*, *23*(1), 104–123. doi:10.1108/JFMM-01-2018-0001

Johansen, I. K., & Guldvik, C. S. (2017). *Influencer marketing and purchase intentions: how does influencer marketing affect purchase intentions?* [Master's thesis]. https://openaccess.nhh.no/nhh-xmlui/bitstream/handle/11250/2453218/masterthesis.PDF?sequence=1

Johnson, A., & Li, S. (2024). The Future of Virtual Influencers: Trends and Implications for Marketing. *Journal of Digital Marketing*, *20*(3), 213–230.

Johnson, K. (2015). Behavioral education in the 21st century. *Journal of Organizational Behavior Management, 35*(1-2), 135–150. doi:10.1080/01608061.2015.1036152

Johnson, P., & Brown, A. (2020). The Power of Digital Influencers in Restaurant Marketing. *Journal of Hospitality and Tourism.*

Jones, M., & Green, R. (2017). Transforming Marketing Dynamics in the Restaurant Industry. *Journal of Restaurant Management.*

Joshi, K. (2022, Dec 22). *Discover the Best Ways to Leverage Influencer Marketing for Your Brand.* Retrieved Sept 15, 2023, from EMERITUS: https://emeritus.org/blog/digital-marketing-what-is-an-influencer/

Joshi, Y., Lim, W. M., Jagani, K., & Kumar, S. (2023). Social media influencer marketing: Foundations, trends, and ways forward. *Electronic Commerce Research.* Advance online publication. doi:10.100710660-023-09719-z

Journée, R., & Weber, M. (2016). Co-creation of Experiences in Retail: Opportunity to innovate in retail business. In Springer proceedings in business and economics (pp. 391–404). doi:10.1007/978-3-319-29058-4_31

Kahr, M., Leitner, M., Ruthmair, M., & Sinnl, M. (2021). Benders decomposition for competitive influence maximization in (social) networks. *Omega*, *100*, 102264. Advance online publication. doi:10.1016/j.omega.2020.102264

Kaleka, A., & Morgan, N. A. (2019). How marketing capabilities and current performance drive strategic intentions in international markets. *Industrial Marketing Management*, *78*, 108–121. doi:10.1016/j.indmarman.2017.02.001

Kamins, M. A. (1989). Celebrity and Noncelebrity Advertising Advertising in a two-sided context. *Journal of Advertising Research*, *29*(3).

Kamins, M., Brand, M., Hoeke, S., & Moe, J. (2013). Two-sided versus one-sided celebrity endorsements: The impact on advertising effectiveness and credibility. *Journal of Advertising*, *18*(2), 4–10. doi:10.1080/00913367.1989.10673146

Kapitan, S., & Silvera, D. H. (2016). From digital media influencers to celebrity endorsers: Attributions drive endorser effectiveness. *Marketing Letters*, *27*(3), 553–567. doi:10.100711002-015-9363-0

Kapitan, S., van Esch, P., Soma, V., & Kietzmann, J. (2022). Influencer marketing and authenticity in content creation. *Australasian Marketing Journal*, *30*(4), 342–351. doi:10.1177/18393349211011171

Kaplan, A. M., & Haenlein, M. (2010). Users of the world, unite! the challenges and opportunities of social media. *Business Horizons*, *53*(1), 59–68. doi:10.1016/j.bushor.2009.09.003

Kaplan, A., & Haenlein, M. (2011). Two hearts in three-quarter time: How to waltz the social media/viral marketing dance. *Business Horizons*, *54*(3), 253–263. doi:10.1016/j.bushor.2011.01.006

Karabacak, Z. İ., & Güngör, İ. (2023). The Metaverse as Influencer Marketing Platform: Influencer-Brand Collaborations of Par3ıs Hilton with 'Superplastic', 'Bohoo', and 'Levi's'. *Etkileşim*, *6*(11), 176–199. doi:10.32739/etkilesim.2023.6.11.194

Karhawi, I. (2017). Influenciadores digitais: conceitos e práticas em discussão. *Revista Communicare, 17*, 46-61.

Karlsen, R., Steen-Johnsen, K., Wollebæk, D., & Enjolras, B. (2017). Echo chamber and trench warfare dynamics in online debates. *European Journal of Communication*, *32*(3), 257–273. doi:10.1177/0267323117695734 PMID:28690351

Kashyap, M. N. (2023, Jul 03). *Build Long-Term Relationships with Influencers for Sustainable Campaign Success*. Retrieved Sept 15, 2023, from https://www.linkedin.com: https://www.linkedin.com/pulse/build-long-term-relationships-influencers-sustainable-campaign-success/

Keller, E., & Berry, J. (2003). *The Influentials: One American in Ten Tells the Other Nine How to Vote, Where to Eat, and What to Buy*. Free Press.

Keller, K. L. (2008). *Strategic Brand Management: Building, Measuring and Managing Brand Equity* (3rd ed.). Pearson Prentice Hall.

Keller, K. L. (2013). *Strategic brand management: Building, measuring, and managing brand equity*. Pearson.

Kelman, H. (2006). Interests, relationships, identities: Three central issues for individuals and groups in negotiating their social environment. *Annual Review of Psychology*, *57*(1), 1–26. doi:10.1146/annurev.psych.57.102904.190156 PMID:16318587

Kembau, A., & Mekel, P. A. (2014). Reference groups, family, roles and status on young consumer behavior towards purchase intentions of luxury fashion brands. *Journal EMBA*, *2*(2), 1172–1178.

Kha, B. M. (2008). Consumers And Their Brands: Deciphering Dimensions Of Loyalty. *International Journal of Business Insights & Transformation*, *2*(1).

Khaleeli, M., Faisal, R., & Anwar, S. (2021). The effect of green marketing, green supply chain and green human resources on business performance: Balanced scorecard approach. *Uncertain Supply Chain Management*, *9*(1), 133–138. doi:10.5267/j.uscm.2020.11.001

Khamis, S., Ang, L., & Welling, R. (2016). Self-Branding, 'Micro-Celebrity' and the Rise of Social Media Influencers. *Celebrity Studies*, *8*(2), 191–208. doi:10.1080/19392397.2016.1218292

Ki, C. W. C., & Kim, Y. K. (2019). The mechanism by which social media influencers persuade consumers: The role of consumers' desire to mimic. *Psychology and Marketing*, *36*(10), 905–922. doi:10.1002/mar.21244

Ki, C. W., Cuevas, L. M., Chong, S. M., & Lim, H. (2020). Influencer marketing: Social media influencers as human brands attaching to followers and yielding positive marketing results by fulfilling needs. *Journal of Retailing and Consumer Services*, *55*, 102133. doi:10.1016/j.jretconser.2020.102133

Kietzmann, J. H., Hermkens, K., McCarthy, I. P., & Silvestre, B. S. (2011). Social media? Get serious! Understanding the functional building blocks of social media. *Business Horizons*, *54*(3), 241–251. doi:10.1016/j.bushor.2011.01.005

Kim, A. J., & Ko, E. (2012). Do social media marketing activities enhance customer equity? An empirical study of luxury fashion brand. *Journal of Business Research*, *65*(10), 1480–1486. doi:10.1016/j.jbusres.2011.10.014

Kim, E., Kim, D., Zihang, E., & Shoenberger, H. (2023). The next hype in social media advertising: Examining virtual influencers' brand endorsement effectiveness. *Frontiers in Psychology*, *14*, 1089051. Advance online publication. doi:10.3389/fpsyg.2023.1089051 PMID:36949930

Kim, H., & Park, M. (2023). Virtual influencers' attractiveness effect on purchase intention: A moderated mediation model of the Product–Endorser fit with the brand. *Computers in Human Behavior*, *143*, 107703. Advance online publication. doi:10.1016/j.chb.2023.107703

Kim, J., & Choi, H. (2019). Value Co-creation through social media: A case study of a start-up company. *Journal of Business Economics and Management*, *20*(1), 1–19. doi:10.3846/jbem.2019.6262

Kim, K., & Sagas, M. (2014). Athletic or sexy? A comparison of female athletes and fashion models in Sports Illustrated swimsuit issues. *Gender Issues*, *31*(2), 123–141. doi:10.100712147-014-9121-2

Kim, M., & Baek, T. H. (2023). Are Virtual Influencers Friends or Foes? Uncovering the Perceived Creepiness and Authenticity of Virtual Influencers in Social Media Marketing in the United States. *International Journal of Human-Computer Interaction*, 1–14. Advance online publication. doi:10.1080/10447318.2023.2233125

Kimmel, A. J. (2018). *Psychological foundations of marketing: The keys to consumer behavior* (2nd ed.). Routledge. doi:10.4324/9781315436098

Kinnear, T., & Bernhardt, K. (1986). *Principles of Marketing* (2nd ed.). Scott, Foresman and Co.

Klear. (2022). *2022 State of influencer marketing report.* https://klear.com/reports/2022-state-of-influencer-marketing-report/

Klimsa, P. (2017). *Digitale Medienprodukte: Grundlagen der Medienproduktforschung* (Vol. 1). BoD–Books on Demand.

Klug, D., Qin, Y., Evans, M., & Kaufman, G. (2021, June). Trick and please. A mixed-method study on user assumptions about the TikTok algorithm. In *Proceedings of the 13th ACM Web Science Conference 2021* (pp. 84-92). 10.1145/3447535.3462512

Koay, K. Y. (2023). Social Media Influencer Marketing: Commentary on the Special Issue. *Journal of Internet Commerce, 22*(1), S1-S3. https://www.tandfonline.com/doi/full/10.1080/15332861.2022.2128277

Koay, K. Y., Cheung, M. L., Soh, P. C.-H., & Teoh, C. W. (2022). Social media influencer marketing: The moderating role of materialism. *European Business Review*, *34*(2), 224–243. doi:10.1108/EBR-02-2021-0032

Koban, L., Ramamoorthy, A., & Konvalinka, I. (2019). Why do we fall into sync with others? Interpersonal synchronization and the brain's optimization principle. *Social Neuroscience*, *14*(1), 1–9. doi:10.1080/17470919.2017.1400463 PMID:29091537

Kolsquare. (2021, Dec). *Will the metaverse shape the future of Influencer Marketing?* Retrieved Sept 13, 2023, from https://www.kolsquare.com: https://www.kolsquare.com/en/blog/will-the-metaverse-shape-the-future-of-influencer-marketing/

Kotler, P., Keller, K. L., Brady, M., Goodman, M., & Hansen, T. (2017). Marketing management (3rd European ed.). Academic Press.

Kotler, P., & Armstrong, G. (2005). *Marketing: An Introduction.* Prentice Hall.

Kotler, P., & Keller, K. L. (2006). *Marketing for the 21st Century*. Pearson Prentice Hall.

Kotler, P., & Keller, K. L. (2006). *Marketing Management* (12th ed.). Prentice Hall.

Kozinets, R. V. (2002). The field behind the screen: Using netnography for marketing research in online communities. *JMR, Journal of Marketing Research*, *39*(1), 61–72. doi:10.1509/jmkr.39.1.61.18935

Kratzer, S., Lohmann, P., Roeglinger, M., Rupprecht, L., & zur Muehlen, M. (2019). The role of the chief process officer in organizations. *Business Process Management Journal*, *25*(4), 688–706. doi:10.1108/BPMJ-07-2017-0192

Kühn, J., & Riesmeyer, C. (2022, Mai). *More than just advertising - An explorative study of young adults' motives for following social media influencers* [Posterpräsentation]. Poster presentation at the International Communication Association (ICA), Paris.

Kumar, V., & Pansari, A. (2016). Competitive Advantage through Engagement. *JMR, Journal of Marketing Research*, *53*(4), 497–514. doi:10.1509/jmr.15.0044

Kuzminov, M. (2023, Jan 30). *Social Responsibility And Ethics In Influencer Marketing*. Retrieved Sept 15, 2023, from https://www.forbes.com: https://www.forbes.com/sites/forbesagencycouncil/2023/01/30/social-responsibility-and-ethics-in-influencer-marketing/?sh=5b028f15685c

Label Insight. (2016). *Transparency ROI study: The business case for more transparency*. Retrieved from https://www.labelinsight.com/hubfs/PDF/Transparency-ROI-Study

Lai, E. R. (2011). Motivation: A literature review. *Person Research's Report*, *6*, 40–41.

Lamberton, C., & Stephen, A. T. (2016). A thematic exploration of digital, social media, and mobile marketing: Research evolution from 2000 to 2015 and an agenda for future inquiry. *Journal of Marketing*, *80*(6), 146–172. doi:10.1509/jm.15.0415

Lamola, K. X. T. (2022). Employees' aptitudes and trepidations for the adoption of enterprise application architecture for supply chain management in small and medium enterprises: A case of Capricorn district municipality. *Journal of Transport and Supply Chain Management*, *16*. Advance online publication. doi:10.4102/jtscm.v16i0.708

Lang, C., & Armstrong, C. M. (2016). Personal attributes: Influences on clothing disposal reasons and frequency. *Journal of Family and Consumer Sciences*, *108*(3), 41–47. doi:10.14307/JFCS108.3.41

Lascity, M. E. (2023). Contour of masculinity: Reading bros in popular culture and fashion branding. In The Routledge companion to advertising and promotional culture: Second edition (pp. 197-208) doi:10.4324/9781003124870-21

Lastra, E. (2022, October 3). La credibilidad de los influencers hace aguas. *Marketing Directo*. https://www.marketingdirecto.com/digital-general/social-media-marketing/credibilidad-influencers-hace-aguas

Laszkiewicz, A., & Kalinska-Kula, M. (2023). Virtual influencers as an emerging marketing theory: A systematic literature review. *International Journal of Consumer Studies*, *47*(6), 2479–2494. Advance online publication. doi:10.1111/ijcs.12956

Latana. (2021, March 4). Lush: A Deep Dive into Their Brand and Marketing Strategy. *Latana*. https://latana.com/post/lush-deep-dive/

Leban, M., & Voyer, B. G. (2020). Social media influencers versus traditional influencers: Roles and consequences for traditional marketing campaigns. In S. Yesiloglu & J. Costello (Eds.), *Influencer Marketing: Building Brand Communities and Engagement* (pp. 26–42). Routledge. doi:10.4324/9780429322501-4

Lee, J. E., Goh, M. L., & Mohd Noor, M. N. Bin. (2019). Understanding purchase intention of university students towards skin care products. *PSU Research Review*, *3*(3), 161–178.

Lee, J. A., Sudarshan, S., Sussman, K. L., Bright, L. F., & Eastin, M. S. (2021). Why are consumers following social media influencers on Instagram? Exploration of consumers' motives for following influencers and the role of materialism. *International Journal of Advertising*, *41*(1), 78–100. doi:10.1080/02650487.2021.1964226

Lee, M. T., & Theokary, C. (2021). The superstar social media influencer: Exploiting linguistic style and emotional contagion over content? *Journal of Business Research*, *132*, 860–871. doi:10.1016/j.jbusres.2020.11.014

Leissner, J., Pidun, U., & Krafft, M. (2019). Corporate crisis management in the digital age: A framework and cases from the automotive industry. *International Journal of Research in Marketing*, *36*(3), 435–456.

Leo, M., & von Kuczkowski, A. (2020). *Kaufen Sie Ronaldo: Wie Facebook, Instagram und Google den Profifußball verändern*. Die Werkstatt.

Leung, F. &. (2022). Online influencer marketing. *Journal of the Academy of Marketing Science, 50*(5). doi:10.1007/s11747-021-00829-4

Leung, F. F., Gu, F. F., Li, Y., Zhang, J., & Palmatier, R. W. (2022). Influencer Marketing Effectiveness. *Journal of Marketing, 86*(5), 1-23.

Leung, F., Zhang, J., Gu, F., Li, Z., & Palmatier, R. (2022). Does influencer marketing really pay off? *Harvard Business Review*. https://hbr.org/2022/11/does-influencer-marketing-really-pay-off

Levitt, T. (1960). Marketing myopia. *Harvard Business Review*, *38*(4), 45–56. PMID:15252891

Lew, M. J. (2016). Three inferential questions, two types of p-value. Supplemental material to the ASA statement on p-values and statistical significance. *The American Statistician*, *70*(2).

Liang, X., & … . (2022). Authenticity and Trust in Virtual Influencers: A Comparative Study. *Journal of Consumer Behaviour*, *17*(4), 345–360.

Li, G., Tang, P., & Feng, J. (2023). How streamer channels influence luxury brand sales in live streaming commerce: An empirical study. *Asia Pacific Journal of Marketing and Logistics*. Advance online publication. doi:10.1108/APJML-01-2023-0096

Li, H., Lei, Y., Zhou, Q., & Yuan, H. (2023). Can you sense without being human? Comparing virtual and human influencers endorsement effectiveness. *Journal of Retailing and Consumer Services*, *75*, 103456. Advance online publication. doi:10.1016/j.jretconser.2023.103456

Lin, C., & Chang, K. (2020). Establishing the service evaluation and selection system for emerging culture festival events using the hybrid MCDM technique. *Current Issues in Tourism*, *23*(18), 2240–2272. doi:10.1080/13683500.2019.1665628

Lin, H. C., Bruning, P. F., & Swarna, H. (2018). Using online opinion leaders to promote the hedonic and utilitarian value of products and services. *Business Horizons*, *61*(3), 431–442. doi:10.1016/j.bushor.2018.01.010

Lister, M., Dovey, J., Giddings, S., Grant, I., & Kelly, K. (2009). *A New Media: A Critical Introduction* (2nd ed.). Routledge.

Liu, F., & Lee, Y. H. (2022). Unveiling Behind-the-Scenes Human Interventions and Examining Source Orientation in Virtual Influencer Endorsements. *IMX 2022 - Proceedings of the 2022 ACM International Conference on Interactive Media Experiences*. 10.1145/3505284.3529962

Li, Y., & Peng, Y. (2021). Influencer marketing: Purchase intention and its antecedents. *Marketing Intelligence & Planning*, *39*(7), 960–978. doi:10.1108/MIP-04-2021-0104

Lopes, M. (2013). *20th Edition of the Almada Dance Fortnight: an analysis of the audiences of dance performances* [Master's dissertation, Lusófona University of Humanities and Technologies]. Lusófona Scientific Repository. http://hdl.handle.net/10437/5295

Lou, C. (2021). Social media influencers and followers: Theorization of a trans-parasocial relation and explication of its implications for influencer advertising. *Journal of Advertising*, 1–18.

Lou, C. (2022). Social media influencers and followers: Theorization of a Trans-Parasocial relation and explication of its implications for influencer advertising. *Journal of Advertising*, *51*(1), 4–21. doi:10.1080/00913367.2021.1880345

Lou, C., Kiew, S. T. J., Chen, T., Lee, T. Y. M., Ong, J. E. C., & Phua, Z. (2022). Authentically Fake? How Consumers Respond to the Influence of Virtual Influencers. *Journal of Advertising*. Advance online publication. doi:10.1080/00913367.2022.2149641

Lou, C., Taylor, C. R., & Zhou, X. (2023). Influencer marketing on social media: How different social media platforms afford influencer–follower relation and drive advertising effectiveness. *Journal of Current Issues and Research in Advertising*, *44*(1), 60–87. doi:10.1080/10641734.2022.2124471

Lou, C., & Yuan, S. (2019). Influencer marketing: How message value and credibility affect consumer trust of branded content on social media. *Journal of Interactive Advertising*, *19*(1), 58–73. doi:10.1080/15252019.2018.1533501

Louie, T. A., & Obermiller, C. (2002). Consumer response to a firm's endorser (dis) association decisions. *Journal of Advertising*, *31*(4), 41–52. Advance online publication. doi:10.1080/00913367.2002.10673684

Luiza Helena - O que é que a Luiza tem? (n.d.). VendaMais. https://vendamais.com.br/luiza-helena-o-que-e-que-a-luiza-tem/

Luoma-Aho, V., Pirttimäki, T., Maity, D., Munnukka, J., & Reinikainen, H. (2019). Primed authenticity: How priming impacts authenticity perception of social media influencers. *International Journal of Strategic Communication*, *13*(4), 352–365. doi:10.1080/1553118X.2019.1617716

Lusch, R. F., & Vargo, S. L. (2010). SD logic: Accommodating, integrating, transdisciplinary. *Grand Service Challenge, 23*.

Lutkenhaus, R. O., Jansz, J., & Bouman, M. P. (2019). Tailoring in the digital era: Stimulating dialogues on health topics in collaboration with social media influencers. *Digital Health*, *5*, 1–11. doi:10.1177/2055207618821521 PMID:30729023

Lu, X., & Lu, L. (2014). Beyond demographics: Using psychographics and social networking to predict consumer intentions. *Journal of Advertising Research*, *54*(3), 282–295.

Lyons, B., & Henderson, K. (2005). Opinion leadership in a computer-mediated environment. *Journal of Consumer Behaviour*, *4*(5), 319–329. doi:10.1002/cb.22

M, S., & K, S. (2017). Impact of influencers in consumer decision process: the fashion industry. *SCMS Journal of Indian Management*, 14–30.

Magno, F., & Cássia, F. (2018). The impact of social media influencers in tourism. *Anatolia*, *29*(2), 288–290. doi:10.1080/13032917.2018.1476981

Magno, F., & Cassia, F. (2018). The impact of social media influencers in tourism. *Anatolia*, *29*(2).

Mahmoudian, A., Sadeghi Boroujerdi, S., Mohammadi, S., Delshab, V., & Pyun, D. Y. (2021). Testing the impact of athlete brand image attributes on fan loyalty. *Journal of Business and Industrial Marketing*, *36*(2), 244–255. doi:10.1108/JBIM-10-2019-0464

Mai, E. S., & Liao, Y. (2022). The interplay of word-of-mouth and customer value on B2B sales performance in a digital platform: An expectancy value theory perspective. *Journal of Business and Industrial Marketing*, *37*(7), 1389–1401. doi:10.1108/JBIM-05-2021-0269

Mailchimp. (2021). *What Is Influencer Marketing?* Retrieved Jun 07, 2023, from mailchimp: https://mailchimp.com/resources/what-is-influencer-marketing/#:~:text=Influencer%20marketing%20is%20a%20form,promotes%20their%20products%20or%20services

Makrides, A., Vrontis, D., & Christofi, M. (2020). An empirical study on the importance of electronic word of mouth in the concierge industry: The case of Cyprus. In *Exploring the Power of Electronic Word-of-Mouth in the Services Industry* (pp. 265–287). IGI Global. doi:10.4018/978-1-5225-8575-6.ch015

Mangio, F., & Di Domenico, G. (2022). All that glitters is not real affiliation: How to handle affiliate marketing programs in the era of falsity. *Business Horizons*, *65*(6), 765–776. doi:10.1016/j.bushor.2022.07.001

Mangold, W. G., & Faulds, D. J. (2009). Social media: The new hybrid element of the promotion mix. *Business Horizons*, *52*(4), 357–365. doi:10.1016/j.bushor.2009.03.002

Maqbool, F. I. (2023). *Influencer Marketing: A Rising Trend for Brands*. Retrieved Jun 06, 2023, from Rising Kashmir: http://risingkashmir.com/influencer-marketing-a-rising-trend-for-brands

Marketing News. (2018, March 5). *Las mujeres utilizan las redes sociales un 7% más que los hombres*. https://www.marketingnews.es/investigacion/noticia/1113054031605/mujeres-utilizan-redes-sociales-7-mas-hombres.1.html

Marketing Science Institute. (2020, May 7). MSI announces 2020-22 research priorities. *MSI at the ARF*. Available at https://www.msi.org/articles/2020-22-msi-research-pri orities-outline-marketers-top-concerns/

Martin, M. (2022, Aug 30). *24 Gen Z Statistics That Matter to Marketers in 2023*. Retrieved Jun 15, 2023, from HootSuite: https://blog.hootsuite.com/gen-z-statistics/

Martín, R. (2021, August 26). Alexia Putellas, nueva embajadora de MartiDerm. *Grazia Magazine*. https://grazia-magazine.com/es/articles/alexia-putellas-nueva-embajadora-de-martiderm/

Martin, K. D., Shervani, T. A., & Slater, J. (2018). Social Media Influence: A Conceptual Framework and Research Agenda. *Journal of Interactive Marketing*.

Marwick, A. (2016). You may know me from Youtube: (Micro-)celebrity in social media. In P. D. Marshall & S. Redmond (Eds.), A companion to celebrity (pp. 333-350). Wiley.

Mathew, J. (2018, July 30). *Understanding Influencer Marketing And Why It Is So Effective*. Retrieved Jun 01, 2023, from Forbes: https://www.forbes.com/sites/theyec/2018/07/30/understanding-influencer-marketing-and-why-it-is-so-effective/?sh=a27ccb471a94

Mazieri, M., Queiroz, M., Queiroz, R., & Yanaze, M. (2018). Conceptual model for evaluating marketing communication in consumer goods franchises. *Revista Brasileira de Marketing*, *17*(2), 2018. doi:10.5585/remark.v17i2.3978

McColl-Kennedy, J. R., Vargo, S. L., Dagger, T. S., Sweeney, J., & Van Kasteren, Y. (2012). Health care customer value cocreation practice styles. *Journal of Service Research*, *15*(4), 370–389. doi:10.1177/1094670512442806

McCracken, G. (1989). Who is the Celebrity Endorser? Cultural Foundations of the Endorsement Process. *The Journal of Consumer Research*, *16*(3), 310. Advance online publication. doi:10.1086/209217

Mcgrail, A. (2013). *The Blogconomy: Blogging Stats*. Retrieved at: http://Www.Socialmediatoday.Com/Content/Blogconomy-Blogging-Stats-Infographic

McKinsey & Company. (2021, September 7). *Consumers care about sustainability—and back it up with their wallets.* McKinsey & Company. https://www.mckinsey.com/industries/consumer-packaged-goods/our-insights/consumers-care-about-sustainability-and-back-it-up-with-their-wallets

McMullan, K. (2023). A checklist for managers to enhance influencer partnerships and avoid potential pitfalls. *Business Horizons*, *66*(4), 443–452. doi:10.1016/j.bushor.2022.09.003

McQuarrie, E. F., Miller, J., & Phillips, B. J. (2013). The megaphone effect: Taste and audience in fashion blogging. *The Journal of Consumer Research*, *40*(1), 136–158. doi:10.1086/669042

Mediakix. (2019). *Influencer marketing 2019 industry benchmarks*. Retrieved from: bit. ly/3pNFLXs

Mediakix. (2019). *The CMO's Guide to Influencer Marketing*. Mediakix.

Mehra, C. (2022, May 24). *Rise Of Influencer Marketing: Creators To Commerce*. Retrieved Jun 04, 2023, from Business World: https://www.businessworld.in/article/Rise-Of-Influencer-Marketing-Creators-To-Commerce-/24-05-2022-429999/

Mena Roa, M. (2021). Personas que afirman haber comprado productos porque los anunciaban famosos o influencers en España en 2021. *Statista*. https://es.statista.com/grafico/24907/personas-que-afirman-haber-comprado-productos-porque-los-anunciaban-famosos-o-influencers/

Mendoza, M. (2010). I blog. You buy. How Bloggers are creating a new generation of product endorsers. *Digital Research and Publishing*, *7*, 114–122.

Mengalli, N. M., & de Carvalho, A. A. (2024). Environmental, Social and Corporate (Human) Governance in Phygital Transformation: Industry 5.0 with Paradigm Shifts, Disruptions and the Metaverse. In Organizational Management Sustainability in VUCA Contexts. IGI Global. https://doi.org/ doi:10.4018/979-8-3693-0720-5

Mengalli, N. M., de Carvalho, A. A., & Galvão, S. M. (2023). Metaverse Ecosystem and Consumer Society 5.0: Consumer Experience and Influencer Marketing in Phygital Transformation. In R. Bansal, S. Qalati, & A. Chakir (Eds.), *Influencer Marketing Applications Within the Metaverse* (pp. 33–56). IGI Global. doi:10.4018/978-1-6684-8898-0.ch003

Merwe, R., & Heerden, G. (2009). Finding and utilizing opinion leaders: Social networks and the power of relationships. *South African Journal of Business Management*, *40*(3), 65–76. doi:10.4102ajbm.v40i3.545

Michaelsen, F., Collin, L., Jacob, C., Goanta, D. C., Kettner, D. S., Bishop, D. P., . . . Yesiloglu, D. S. (2022). *The impact of influencers on advertising and consumer protection in the Single Market.* European Parliament. Retrieved Sept 15, 2023, from https://www.europarl.europa.eu/RegData/etudes/STUD/2022/703350/IPOL_STU(2022)703350_EN.pdf

Miles, J. (2013). *Instagram Power: Build Your Brand and Reach More Customers with the Power of Pictures.* Mcgraw-Hill.

Miller, S. (2023). Personalization in virtual influencers: A strategic approach in influence marketing. *Journal of Digital Marketing*, *8*(1), 38–50.

Mirowska, A., & Arsenyan, J. (2023). Sweet escape: The role of empathy in social media engagement with human versus virtual influencers. *International Journal of Human-Computer Studies*, *174*, 103008. Advance online publication. doi:10.1016/j.ijhcs.2023.103008

Mitchell, V. W., & Boustani, P. (1993). A preliminary investigation into pre-and post-purchase risk perception and reduction. *European Journal of Marketing*, *28*(1), 56–71. doi:10.1108/03090569410049181

Miyake, E. (2023). I am a virtual girl from Tokyo: Virtual influencers, digital-orientalism and the (Im)materiality of race and gender. *Journal of Consumer Culture*, *23*(1), 209–228. doi:10.1177/14695405221117195

Mohr, J. J. (2019). A marketing perspective on innovation. *Foundations and Trends in Entrepreneurship*, *15*(3-4), 431–479. doi:10.1561/0300000085-4

Mollen, A., & Wilson, H. (2010). Engagement, telepresence and interactivity in online consumer experience: Reconciling scholastic and managerial perspectives. *Journal of Business Research*, *63*(9-10), 919–925. doi:10.1016/j.jbusres.2009.05.014

Momani, A. M. (2021). A modified technology acceptance theory to assess social commerce technology adoption. *Information Resources Management Journal*, *34*(2), 43–62. doi:10.4018/IRMJ.2021040103

MoneyLab. (2021). *Do Zero à Educação Financeira: Como Ana Laura Magalhães se Tornou Sócia da XP.* InfoMoney. https://www.infomoney.com.br/onde-investir/como-uma-ex-atendente-de-telemarketing-virou-socia-da-xp/

Monica, R. (2019). Factors influencing work engagement and its impact on task performance. *International Journal of Business Excellence*, *17*(1), 97–129. doi:10.1504/IJBEX.2019.096913

Monllos, K. (2023, Apr 21). *More brands choose Boomer, Gen X influencers, as 'older audiences can be just as impactful' as young ones.* Retrieved Jun 14, 2023, from DIGIDAY: https://digiday.com/marketing/more-brands-choose-older-influencers-as-older-audiences-can-be-just-as-impactful-as-young-ones/

Montemayor, C. (2021, September 2). The Ordinary's anti-clean beauty revolution: How beauty brands are fighting back. *BeautyMatter.* https://beautymatter.com/articles/the-ordinary-s-anti-clean-beauty-revolution-how-beauty-brands-are-fighting-back

Moorman, C., Zaltman, G., & Deshpandé, R. (1992). Relationships between providers and users of market research: The dynamics of trust within and between organizations. *JMR, Journal of Marketing Research*, *29*(3), 314–328. doi:10.1177/002224379202900303

Morgan, B. (2020, February 24). 11 fashion companies leading the way in sustainability. *Forbes*. https://www.forbes.com/sites/blakemorgan/2020/02/24/11-fashion-companies-leading-the-way-in-sustainability/?sh=2da530666dba

Morton, F. (2020). Influencer marketing: An exploratory study on the motivations of young adults to follow social media influencers. *Journal of Digital & Social Media Marketing*, *8*(2), 156–165.

Moscovici, S. (1976). *La psychanalyse: Son image et son public* [Psychoanalysis: Its image and public]. Presses Universitaires de France.

Mouritzen, S. L. T., Penttinen, V., & Pedersen, S. (2023). Virtual influencer marketing: The good, the bad and the unreal. *European Journal of Marketing*. Advance online publication. doi:10.1108/EJM-12-2022-0915

Moustakas, E., Lamba, N., Mahmoud, D., & Ranganathan, C. (2020). Blurring lines between fiction and reality: Perspectives of experts on marketing effectiveness of virtual influencers. *International Conference on Cyber Security and Protection of Digital Services, Cyber Security 2020.* doi:10.1108/MIP-12-2021-0423

Murteira, C. (2023). *Facial mimicry in social relations. Género y educación ante-la manipulación de la comunicación.* Dykinson S. L.

Nafees, L., Cook, C. M., Nikolov, A. N., & Stoddard, J. E. (2021). Can social media influencer (SMI) power influence consumer brand attitudes? the mediating role of perceived SMI credibility. *Digital Business*, *1*(2), 100008. Advance online publication. doi:10.1016/j.digbus.2021.100008

Nambakhsh, C. (2023, July 9). *Ethical Influencer Marketing: Navigating Disclosure, Transparency, And Responsibility.* Retrieved Sept 15, 2023, from https://blog.ainfluencer.com: https://blog.ainfluencer.com/ethical-influencer-marketing/

Nambisan, S., & Baron, R. A. (2007). Interactions in virtual customer environments: Implications for product support and Customer Relationship Management. *Journal of Interactive Marketing*, *21*(2), 42–62. doi:10.1002/dir.20077

Nam, L. G., & Dân, H. T. (2018). Impact of social media influencer marketing on consumer at ho Chi Minh City. *International Journal of Social Sciences and Humanities Invention*, *5*(5), 4710–4714. doi:10.18535/ijsshi/v5i5.10

Narula, R., & Nangia, A. (2023, May 23). *India attempts to reel in influencer marketing*. Retrieved Jun 06, 2023, from ManagingIP: https://www.managingip.com/article/2bp81m226pjlycqrzjrb4/expert-analysis/local-insights/india-attempts-to-reel-in-influencer-marketing#:~:text=India's%20influencer%20marketing%20industry%20is,in%2C%20an%20influencer%20marketing%20platform

Na, S., Kunkel, T., & Doyle, J. (2020). Exploring athlete brand image development on social media: The role of signalling through source credibility. *European Sport Management Quarterly*, *20*(1), 88–108. doi:10.1080/16184742.2019.1662465

National Statistics Institute. (2022). *Culture Statistics - 2021*. Lisbon: INE. https://www.ine.pt/xurl/pub/18212178

Neeley, S. M., & Qaqish, S. (2020). The Impact of Influencer Type and Disclosure Type on Source Credibility and Persuasiveness: An Experiment. *Journal of Interactive Advertising*.

Neff, J. (2019). *How to succeed with influencers: brand playbook*. AdAge. Available at: https://adage.com/article/cmo-strategy/succeed-influencers/316313

Nejad, M., Sherrell, D., & Babakus, E. (2014). Influentials and influence mechanisms in new product diffusion: An integrative review. *Journal of Marketing Theory and Practice*, *22*(2), 185–208. doi:10.2753/MTP1069-6679220212

Neves, S., Barbosa, B., & Carlos, V. (2019, May09). Digital Influencers: A Bibliometric Analysis. *Proceedings of the International Workshop Tourism and Hospitality Management*.

Newman, T., Peck, J., Harris, C., & Wilhide, B. (2013). *Social media in sport marketing*. Holcomb Hathaway.

Nicosia, F. M. (1966). *Consumer Decision Process*. Prentice Hall.

Nielsen. (2015). *Global Trust in Advertising. Winning Strategies for an Evolving Media Landscape*. Retrieved from: https://www.nielsen.com/content/dam/nielsenglobal/apac/docs/reports/2015/nielsen-global-trust-ın-advertising-report-september-2015.pdf

Nielsen. (2020). *Global Trust in Advertising - Report*. https://www.nielsen.com/us/en/insights/report/2020/global-trust-in-advertising/

Nissen, A., Conrad, C., & Newman, A. (2023). Are You Human? Investigating the Perceptions and Evaluations of Virtual Versus Human Instagram Influencers. *Conference on Human Factors in Computing Systems – Proceedings*.10.1145/3544548.3580943

Nizri, E. (2022, Mar 1). *Macro-Influencers vs. Micro-Influencers: The Great Social Media Debate*. Retrieved Sept 15, 2023, from Forbes: https://www.forbes.com/sites/forbestechcouncil/2022/03/01/macro-influencers-vs-micro-influencers-the-great-social-media-debate/?sh=5673f745286f

Nunes, R. (2021). *Communication strategies of cultural institutions for Generation Z* [Master's dissertation, University of Aveiro]. University of Aveiro Institutional Repository. http://hdl.handle.net/10773/32616

O'Brien, S. (2021). *Rise of the Nano-Influencer: They May Have Only 1,000 Followers, but They're Big Business*. CNBC. https://www.cnbc.com/2021/06/12/rise-of-the-nano-influencer-they-may-have-only-1000-followers-but-theyre-big-business.html

Oberlo. (2021). *TikTok Statistics for 2021: Usage, Revenue, and More*. https://au.oberlo.com/blog/tiktok-statistics

Ohanian, R. (1990). Construction and validation of a scale to measure celebrity endorsers' perceived expertise, trustworthiness, and attractiveness. *Journal of Advertising*, *19*(3), 39–52. doi:10.1080/00913367.1990.10673191

Ohio. (2022). *How to Market to Instagram Influencers: Understanding the Influencer Business Model and Analytics*. Retrieved Jun 06, 2023, from Ohio University: https://onlinemasters.ohio.edu/instagram-influencers/

Oladipo, T. (2022, June 6). What is user-generated content? *Buffer.* https://buffer.com/resources/what-is-user-generated-content/

Omar, B., & Dequan, W. (2020). Watch, share or create: The influence of personality traits and user motivation on TikTok mobile video usage. *International Association of Online Engineering*. https://www.learntechlib.org/p/216454/

Ooi, K. B., Lee, V. H., Hew, J. J., Leong, L. Y., Tan, G. W. H., & Lim, A. F. (2023). Social media influencers: An effective marketing approach? *Journal of Business Research*, *160*, 113773. doi:10.1016/j.jbusres.2023.113773

Ozdemir, O., Kolfal, B., Messinger, P. R., & Rizvi, S. (2023, August). Human or virtual: How influencer type shapes brand attitudes. *Computers in Human Behavior*, *145*, C. doi:10.1016/j.chb.2023.107771

Paço, A., & Pinto, C. (2019). *Strategic marketing planning in cultural centres. Actions to attract and retain audiences at the São João National Theatre.* IS Working Paper. 3rd Series, No. 77. https://www.researchgate.net/publication/370067739_Planeamento_estrategico_de_Marketing_em_equipamentos_culturais

Paço, A., & Oliveira, S. (2017). Influence marketing in the fashion and beauty industry. *Estudos em Comunicação*, *1*(25), 119–136. doi:10.20287/ec.n25.v1.a07

Pais, M. (2016). *A Comunicação no Contexto das Organizações Culturais O caso do Centro Cultural de Belém* [Master's Degree Internship Report in Communication Sciences - Strategic Communication, Faculty of Social Sciences and Humanities, Universidade Nova de Lisboa]. Universidade Nova Repository. http://hdl.handle.net/10362/19659

PaivaA. L.GarciaA. S.AlcântaraV. C. (2017). Discursive disputes about corruption in Brazil: A discursive-critical analysis on Twitter. *Revista de Administração Contemporânea, 21*(5), 627-647. http://dx.doi.org/ doi:10.1590/1982-7849rac2017160163

Palmatier, R. W., Dant, R. P., Grewal, D., & Evans, K. R. (2006). Factors influencing the effectiveness of relationship marketing: A meta-analysis. *SSRN Electronic Journal*. doi:10.2139/ssrn.904647

Pandey, S., & Chawla, D. (2019). Engaging m-commerce adopters in India: Exploring the two ends of the adoption continuum across four m-commerce categories. *Journal of Enterprise Information Management*, *32*(1), 191–210. doi:10.1108/JEIM-06-2018-0109

Parente, A. (2018). *The importance of relationship marketing in the management of cultural attractions* [Master's thesis, Polytechnic Institute of Viana do Castelo]. IPVC Scientific Repository. http://hdl.handle.net/20.500.11960/2010

Park, G., Nan, D., Park, E., Kim, K. J., Han, J., & del Pobil, A. P. (2021, Jan 04-06). Computers as Social Actors? Examining How Users Perceive and Interact with Virtual Influencers on Social Media. *International Conference on Ubiquitous Information Management and Communication-IMCOM*.

Pattnaik, S., & Tripathy, S. K. (2022). The effect of organizational justice on employee performance in the Indian public sector units: The role of organizational identification. *Benchmarking*. Advance online publication. doi:10.1108/BIJ-08-2021-0508

Pedroni, M. (2016). Meso-celebrities, fashion, and the media: How digital influencers struggle for visibility. Film. *Fashion and Consumption*, *5*(1), 103–121. doi:10.1386/ffc.5.1.103_1

Pembecioğlu, N. (2016). Ben'den Vazgeçerek 'Daha' and *Olmaya Doğru Bir Adım Olarak Özçekim.* Beykent Üniversitesi.

Peng, C. (2023). Influencer marketing: Statistics and skepticism. *Open Journal of Business and Management*, *11*(2), 744–754. doi:10.4236/ojbm.2023.112040

Pereira, I. (2015). *A Comunicação do CCB- As Estratégias de Comunicação* [Master's dissertation]. Repository of Iscte - University Institute of Lisbon. http://hdl.handle.net/10071/10636

Pereira, I., Barbosa, B., & Vale, V. T. (2023). An Integrated View on Social Media Marketing Actions and Their Expected Impacts on Consumer Behavior. *Management and Marketing for Improved Retail Competitiveness and Performance*, 303-319.

Peter, J., & Olson, J. (1994). *Consumer Behavior and Marketing Strategy* (4th ed.). Irwin/Mcgraw-Hill.

Peters, K. (2020). Perceived Influence of Food Bloggers on Consumer Dining Choices: A Case Study of Food Bloggers in South Florida. *International Journal of Hospitality & Tourism Administration.*

Pew Research Center. (2022). *Social Media Fact Sheet.* Retrieved from: https://www.pewresearch.org/internet/fact-sheet/social-media/

Phua, J., Jin, S. V., & Kim, J. J. (2017). Gratifications of using Facebook, Twitter, Instagram, or Snapchat to follow brands: The moderating effect of social comparison, trust, tie strength, and network homophily on brand identification, brand engagement, brand commitment, and membership intention. *Telematics and Informatics*, *34*(1), 412–424. doi:10.1016/j.tele.2016.06.004

Phyllo. (2021). *The Evolution of Influencer Marketing*. Retrieved Sept 15, 2023, from https://www.getphyllo.com/post/the-evolution-of-influencer-marketing

Pietro, L. D., & Pantano, E. (2012). An empirical investigation of social network influence on consumer purchasing decision: The case of Facebook. *Journal of Direct, Data and Digital Marketing Practice*, *14*(1), 18–29. doi:10.1057/dddmp.2012.10

Pine, B. J., & Gilmore, J. H. (2020). *The Experience Economy: Competing for customer time, attention, and money*. Harvard Business Review Press.

Pinto, C. (2019). *The influence of branding and communication on brand attachment and consumer behaviour: a Super Bock case study* [Master's thesis, University of Minho]. RepositóriUM- University of Minho. https://hdl.handle.net/1822/64223

Pöyry, E. I., Pelkonen, M., Naumanen, E., & Laaksonen, S.-M. (2019). A call for authenticity: Audience responses to social media influencer endorsements in strategic communication. *International Journal of Strategic Communication*, *13*(4), 336–351. doi:10.1080/1553118X.2019.1609965

Pöyry, E., Reinikainen, H., & Luoma-Aho, V. (2022). The role of social media influencers in public health communication: Case COVID-19 pandemic. *International Journal of Strategic Communication*, *16*(3), 469–484. doi:10.1080/1553118X.2022.2042694

Pradhan, B., Kishore, K., & Gokhale, N. (2023, February). Social Media Influencers and Consumer Engagement: A Review and Future Research Agenda. *International Journal of Consumer Studies*, *47*(6), 2106–2130. Advance online publication. doi:10.1111/ijcs.12901

Pradhan, D., Kuanr, A., Anupurba Pahi, S., & Akram, M. S. (2023). Influencer marketing: When and why gen Z consumers avoid influencers and endorsed brands. *Psychology and Marketing*, *40*(1), 27–47. Advance online publication. doi:10.1002/mar.21749

Prahalad, C. K., & Ramaswamy, V. (2004). Co-creation experiences: The next practice in value creation. *Journal of Interactive Marketing*, *18*(3), 5–14. doi:10.1002/dir.20015

Prazer, B. R. (2020). *Conheça a Nova Estrategista Chefe da Rico*. https://riconnect.rico.com.vc/analises/prazer-betina-roxo/

Presler, J. L. (2022). You are who you eat with: Academic peer effects from school lunch lines. *Journal of Economic Behavior & Organization*, *203*, 43–58. doi:10.1016/j.jebo.2022.08.029

Provance, T. W., Ramisetty, S. B., Urick, M. J., & Wieczorkowski, K. A. (2022). Building and evolving a culture of excellence: A conceptual exploration. *Measuring Business Excellence*, *26*(2), 197–209. doi:10.1108/MBE-05-2021-0067

QQGrand View Research. (2021). Personalized skin care products market worth $48.65 billion by 2030 | Grand View Research, Inc. *PR Newswire*. https://www.prnewswire.com/news-releases/personalized-skin-care-products-market-worth-48-65-billion-by-2030-grand-view-research-inc-301752845.html

Rach, M. (2023). Louis Vuitton, Cristiano Ronaldo and Lionel Messi. the greatest marketing stunt of the century, or just hype driven vanity-metrics? *Springer Proceedings in Business and Economics*, 290-297. 10.1007/978-3-031-31836-8_28

Rakuten Advertising. (2020). *Global Influencer Marketing Report 2020*. https://rakutenadvertising.com/en-uk/case-studies/global-influencer-marketing-report-2020/

Rakuten. (2019). *2019 Influencer marketing global survey consumers*. Retrieved from: bit.ly/2WD9ebL

Ramaswamy, V., & Ozcan, K. (2016). Brand value co-creation in a digitalized world: An integrative framework and research implications. *International Journal of Research in Marketing*, *33*(1), 93–106. doi:10.1016/j.ijresmar.2015.07.001

Raven, B. H. (1965). Social influence and power. In I. D. Steiner & M. Fishbein (Eds.), *Current studies in social psychology* (pp. 371–382). Holt, Rinehart & Winston.

Raven, B. H., & French, J. R. P. (1958). Legitimate power, coercive power, and observability in social influence. *Sociometry*, *21*(2), 83–97. doi:10.2307/2785895

Reinikainen, H., Munnukka, J., Maity, D., & Luoma-Aho, V. (2020). 'You really are a great big sister'—Parasocial relationships, credibility, and the moderating role of audience comments in influencer marketing. *Journal of Marketing Management*, *36*(3–4), 279–298. doi:10.1080/0267257X.2019.1708781

Reis, A. (2003). *Cultural marketing and cultural funding*. https://garimpodesolucoes.com.br/wp-content/uploads/2016/02/Marketing-Cultural-e-Financiamento-da-Cultura-Garimpo-de-Solu%C3%A7%C3%B5es.pdf

Remelgado, A. (2014). *Communication Strategies in Museums - Management Tools in Museological Institutions* [PhD thesis]. Open Repository of the University of Porto. https://hdl.handle.net/10216/109315

Ribbink, D., Pun, H., & Yan, T. (2022). Revenue sharing bids of a loss-averse supplier for a new product development contract: A multi-method investigation. *International Journal of Operations & Production Management*, *42*(12), 1853–1877. doi:10.1108/IJOPM-01-2022-0006

Rice, B. (2019, June 13). How to use user-generated content to drive sales for your brand. *Jilt.* https://jilt.com/blog/ugc-brands/

Rickaby, M. A., Glass, J., & Fernie, S. (2020). Conceptualizing the relationship between personal values and sustainability—A TMO case study. *Administrative Sciences*, *10*(1), 15. Advance online publication. doi:10.3390/admsci10010015

Robinson, B. (2020). Towards an Ontology and Ethics of Virtual Influencers. *AJIS. Australasian Journal of Information Systems*, *24*. Advance online publication. doi:10.3127/ajis.v24i0.2807

Robinson, T. (2020). The Impact of Influencers on Restaurant Revenue. *The Journal of Business Strategy*.

Rocha, P. (2018). *Cultural marketing: market strategies based on a case study of the Piauí Book Fair (Salipi)* [PhD thesis]. Fernando Pessoa University Institutional Repository. http://hdl.handle.net/10284/6489

Rocha, M., & Trevisan, N. (2018). *Integrated Marketing Communication* (1st ed.). Marketing in Modern Times Collection. Saraiva Educação. https://books.google.pt/books?id=FnCwDwAAQBAJ&lpg=PT11&dq=a%C3%A7%C3%B5es%20de%20comunica%C3%A7%C3%A3o%20de%20marketing%20&lr&hl=pt-BR&pg=PT3#v=onepage&q=a%C3%A7%C3%B5es%20de%20comunica%C3%A7%C3%A3o%20de%20marketing&f=false

Rodrigo-Martín, I., Muñoz-Sastre, D., & Rodrigo-Martín, L. (2022). Virtual influencers as opinion leaders and their use in political communication technics. *Revista Mediterranea de Comunicacion*, *13*(1), 251–266. doi:10.14198/MEDCOM.20751

Rodrigo-Martín, L., Rodrigo-Martín, I., & Muñoz-Sastre, D. (2021). Los Influencers Virtuales como herramienta publicitaria en la promoción de marcas y productos. Estudio de la actividad comercial de Lil Miquela. *Revista Latina de Comunicación Social*, *79*(79), 69–90. Advance online publication. doi:10.4185/RLCS-2021-1521

Rodrigue, E. (2023). *31 Influencer Marketing Stats to Know in 2023*. Retrieved Jun 06, 2023, from https://blog.hubspot.com/marketing/influencer-marketing-stats

Rodrigues, F. (2021). *Projeto Sonae - Análise da Usabilidade do Website MO* [Master's thesis, Instituto Superior de Contabilidade e Administração do Porto]. Scientific Repository of the Polytechnic Institute of Porto. http://hdl.handle.net/10400.22/19929

Rodriguez, E. (2023). Aversión al riesgo en influencers virtuales: Un análisis en el marketing de influencia. *Journal of Digital Marketing*, *7*(2), 45–56.

Rosário, A., Moniz, L., & Cruz, R. (2021). Data Science Applied to Marketing: A Literature Review. *Journal of Information Science and Engineering, 37*(5), 1067-1081. doi:10.6688/JISE.202109_37(5).0006

Rosário, A. T., & Dias, J. C. (2022). Sustainability and the Digital Transition: A Literature Review. *Sustainability (Basel)*, *14*(7), 4072. doi:10.3390u14074072

Rosário, A. T., & Dias, J. C. (2023). How Industry 4.0 and Sensors Can Leverage Product Design: Opportunities and Challenges. *Sensors (Basel)*, *23*(3), 1165. doi:10.339023031165 PMID:36772206

Rosário, A. T., Lopes, P. R., & Rosário, F. S. (2023). Influencer Marketing in the Digital Ecosystem. In R. Bansal, S. Qalati, & A. Chakir (Eds.), *Influencer Marketing Applications Within the Metaverse* (pp. 132–166). IGI Global. doi:10.4018/978-1-6684-8898-0.ch009

Rosengren, S., & Campbell, C. (2021). Navigating the future of influencer advertising: Consolidating what is known and identifying new research directions. *Journal of Advertising*, *50*(5), 505–509. doi:10.1080/00913367.2021.1984346

Rossi, C., & Rivetti, F. (2023). Virtual Influencer Marketing: Is It Effective in Engaging Younger Generations? *Proceedings of the 10th European Conference on Social Media, ECSM 2023*. 10.3389/fcomp.2023.1043342

Rowland, F. (2011). The filter bubble: What the internet is hiding from you. *Portal (Baltimore, Md.)*, *11*(4), 1009–1011.

Roxo, B. (2022). *da XP, dá dicas de como investir seu dinheiro*. IstoÉ Dinheiro. https://istoedinheiro.com.br/betina-roxo-da-xp-da-dicas-de-como-investir-seu-dinheiro/

Ro, Y. J., Yoo, M., Koo, Y., & Song, J. H. (2021). The roles of learning orientation: Structural determinants for improving knowledge sharing with committed and satisfied employees. *Industrial and Commercial Training*, *53*(1), 60–76. doi:10.1108/ICT-10-2019-0094

Ruiz-Gomez, A. (2019). Digital fame and fortune in the age of social media: A classification of social media influencers. *aDResearch ESIC, 19*, 8-29.

Rundin, K., & Colliander, J. (2021). Multifaceted influencers: Toward a new typology for influencer roles in advertising. *Journal of Advertising*, *50*(5), 548–564. doi:10.1080/00913367.2021.1980471

Ryan, D. (2020). *Understanding digital marketing: A complete guide to engaging customers and implementing successful digital campaigns*. Kogan Page Publishers.

Sago, B. (2017). The influence of social media messages sources on millennial generation consumers. *International Journal of Integrated Marketing Communications*, *2*(2), 7–14.

Sammis, K., Lincoln, C., & Pomponi, S. (2016). *Influencer Marketing For Dummies*. John Wiley and Sons, Inc.

Sammis, K., Ng, J., Pomponi, S., & Lincoln, C. (2015). *Influencer marketing for dummies*. For Dummies.

Sammut-Bonnici, T. (2015). Brand and branding. *Wiley Encyclopedia of Management*, 1–3. doi:10.1002/9781118785317.weom120161

Sanderson, J. (2011). *It's a whole new ballgame: How social media is changing sports*. Hampton Press.

Sands, S., Campbell, C. L., Plangger, K., & Ferraro, C. (2022). Unreal influence: Leveraging AI in influencer marketing. *European Journal of Marketing*, *56*(6), 1721–1747. Advance online publication. doi:10.1108/EJM-12-2019-0949

Sands, S., Ferraro, C., Demsar, V., & Chandler, G. (2022). False idols: Unpacking the opportunities and challenges of falsity in the context of virtual influencers. *Business Horizons*, *65*(6), 777–788. doi:10.1016/j.bushor.2022.08.002

SanMiguel, P., Guercini, S., & Sádaba, T. (2018). The impact of attitudes towards influencers amongst millennial fashion buyers. *Studies in Communication Sciences*, *18*(2), 439–460.

Santora, J. (2023, Jan 11). *Key Influencer Marketing Statistics to Drive Your Strategy in 2023*. Retrieved Jun 06, 2023, from Influencer Marketing Hub: https://influencermarketinghub.com/influencer-marketing-statistics/

Santos, B. (2021). *Organizações de apoio cultural - o caso do Imaginarius Centro de Criação analisado sob o prisma do marketing* [Master's thesis, Instituto Superior de Administração e Gestão]. Open Access Scientific Repositories of Portugal. http://hdl.handle.net/10400.26/36610

Santos, M. (2021). *Audience satisfaction in cultural communication: the case of the São Francisco Convent* [Master's thesis, University of Minho]. RepositóriUM- University of Minho. https://hdl.handle.net/1822/79278

Sarah, D. (2019). *What is Influencer Marketing? Here's How Influencer Marketing Works*. Retrieved Jun 08, 2023, from https://www.getcarro.com/blog/what-is-influencer-marketing

Saraiva, P. (2019). Digital Marketing: The Use of Social Media as a Communication Channel in Fashion Retail in Barbalha-CE. Id on Line - Multidisciplinary and Psychology Journal. https://idonline.emnuvens.com.br/id

Saternus, Z., Weber, P., & Hinz, O. (2022). The effects of advertisement disclosure on heavy and light Instagram users. *Electronic Markets*, *32*(3), 1351–1372. doi:10.100712525-022-00546-y

Saunders, M., Lewis, P., & Thornhill, A. (2023). *Research methods for business students*. Pearson education.

Schaffer, N. (2022, Dec 5). *What is Influencer Marketing? A Definition and Guide to Successful Influencer Collaborations*. Retrieved Jun 03, 2023, from https://nealschaffer.com/what-is-influencer-marketing/

Schmidt, J. (2007). Blogging practices: An analytical framework. *Journal of Computer-Mediated Communication*, *12*(4), 1409–1427. doi:10.1111/j.1083-6101.2007.00379.x

Schmid, Y., & Dowling, M. (2022). New work: New motivation? A comprehensive literature review on the impact of workplace technologies. *Management Review Quarterly*, *72*(1), 59–86. doi:10.100711301-020-00204-7

Schmitt, B. (1999). Experiential marketing. *Journal of Marketing Management*, *15*(1-3), 53–67. doi:10.1362/026725799784870496

Schmitt, B. (2019). From atoms to bits and back: A research curation on digital technology and agenda for future research. *The Journal of Consumer Research*, *46*(4), 825–832. doi:10.1093/jcr/ucz038

Scholz, J. (2021). How consumers consume social media influence. *Journal of Advertising*, *50*(5), 510–527. doi:10.1080/00913367.2021.1980472

Schouten, A. P., Janssen, L., & Verspaget, M. (2020). Celebrity vs. influencer endorsements in advertising: The role of identification, credibility, and product-endorser fit. *International Journal of Advertising*, *39*(2), 258–281. doi:10.1080/02650487.2019.1634898

Schwarz, O. (2010). On friendship, boobs and the logic of the catalogue. *Convergence (London)*, *16*(2), 163–183. doi:10.1177/1354856509357582

Sciarrino, J., Wilcox, G. B., & Chung, A. (2020). Measuring the effectiveness of peer-to-peer influencer marketing in an integrated brand campaign. *Journal of Digital and Social Media Marketing*, *8*(1), 85–95. www.scopus.com

Scoble, R., & Israel, S. (2006). *Naked Conversations: How Blogs are Changing the Way Business Talk With Customers*. John Wiley and Sons.

Scott, D. M. (2016). *The new rules of marketing and PR: How to use social media, online video, mobile applications, blogs, news releases, and viral marketing to reach buyers directly*. John Wiley & Sons.

Scott-Phillips, T. C. (2007). The social evolution of language, and the language of social evolution. *Evolutionary Psychology*, *5*(4), 147470490700500405. doi:10.1177/147470490700500405

Scussel, F. B. C., de la Martinière Petrol, M., Semprebon, E., & Da Rocha, R. A. (2017). What is relationship marketing? A proposal for a unifying concept. *Revista de Ciências da Administração*, *19*(48), 9–23. doi:10.5007/2175-8077.2017v20n48p9

Selas, D. (2022). *The importance of user experience evaluation and usability testing in website development: the Diffuse.TV case* [Master's thesis, University of Beira Interior]. uBibliorum- Digital Repository of the University of Beira Interior. http://hdl.handle.net/10400.6/13271

SendPulse. (2021a). *Cross-Promotion.* Retrieved Sept 15, 2023, from https://sendpulse.com: https://sendpulse.com/support/glossary/cross-promotion

SendPulse. (2021b). *Influencer Marketing.* Retrieved Jun 08, 2023, from https://sendpulse.com/support/glossary/influencer-marketing

Sette, G., & Brito, P. Q. (2020). To what extent are digital influencers creative? *Creativity and Innovation Management, 29*(51), 90–102. doi:10.1111/caim.12365

Sewpersadh, N. S. (2020). Governing board attributes as profitability influencers under endogeneity: An econometric analysis in south Africa. *ACRN Journal of Finance and Risk Perspectives, 8*(1), 133–151. doi:10.35944/jofrp.2019.8.1.009

Shan, Y., Chen, K. J., & Lin, J. S. (2020). When social media influencers endorse brands: The effects of self-influencer congruence, parasocial identification, and perceived endorser motive. *International Journal of Advertising, 39*(5), 590–610. doi:10.1080/02650487.2019.1678322

Sharma, V. (2022, Apr 20). *How Influencer Marketing is Going to Change in the Age of Metaverse?* Retrieved Sept 13, 2023, from https://www.indianretailer.com/article/technology/digital-trends/how-influencer-marketing-is-going-to-change-in-the-age-of-metaverse.a7899

Sharma, P., & Nayak, J. K. (2019). Understanding memorable tourism experiences as the determinants of tourists' behavior. *International Journal of Tourism Research, 21*(4), 504–518. doi:10.1002/jtr.2278

Shen, R., Liu, D., Wei, X., & Zhang, M. (2022). Your posts betray you: Detecting influencer-generated sponsored posts by finding the right clues. *Information & Management, 59*(8), 103719. Advance online publication. doi:10.1016/j.im.2022.103719

Shepherd, J. (2023, May 15). *28 Essential Influencer Marketing Statistics You Need to Know in 2023.* Retrieved Jun 05, 2023, from Social Shepherd: https://thesocialshepherd.com/blog/influencer-marketing-statistics

Sicilia, M., & López, M. (2023). What do we know about influencers on social media? Toward a new conceptualization and classification of influencers. In C. L. Wang (Ed.), *The Palgrave handbook of interactive marketing* (pp. 393–622). Palgrave Macmillan Cham. doi:10.1007/978-3-031-14961-0_26

Sigala, M., & Gretzel, U. (2017). *Advances in Social Media for Travel, Tourism, and Hospitality: New Perspectives, Practice and Cases.* Routledge. doi:10.4324/9781315565736

Simon, H. A. (1982). *Models of Bounded Rationality.* MIT Press.

Singh, A., Jenamani, M., Thakkar, J. J., & Rana, N. P. (2021). Propagation of online consumer perceived negativity: Quantifying the effect of supply chain underperformance on passenger car sales. *Journal of Business Research, 132*, 102–114. doi:10.1016/j.jbusres.2021.04.027

Singh, J. J., Iglesias, O., & Batista-Foguet, J. M. (2012). Does having an ethical brand matter? the influence of consumer perceived ethicality on trust, affect and loyalty. *Journal of Business Ethics, 111*(4), 541–549. doi:10.100710551-012-1216-7

Singh, P., & Kottath, R. (2022). Influencer-defaulter mutation-based optimization algorithms for predicting electricity prices. *Utilities Policy, 79*, 101444. Advance online publication. doi:10.1016/j.jup.2022.101444

Sinha, M. (2023, Jun 13). Augmented Reality: New Future of Social Media Influencer Marketing. *Vision The Journal of Business Perspective*. doi:10.1177/09722629221147124

Slater, D. (1997). *Consumer Culture and Modernity*. Polity Press.

Smart Insights. (2019). *80% of marketers find influencer marketing effective*. Retrieved JUn 14, 2023, from https://www.smartinsights.com/online-pr/influencer-marketing-effectiveness/

Smith, A. N., & Zook, Z. (2011). Marketing Communications Effectiveness and the Effect of Consumer Motivation on Perceived Value. *Review of Communication Research*.

Smith, R. (2019). Where authentic leaders DARE: From professional competence to inspiring leadership. In Where authentic leaders DARE: From professional competence to inspiring leadership (pp. 1-115) doi:10.4324/9780429243158

Smith, A. N., Fischer, E., & Yongjian, C. (2012). How does brand-related user-generated content differ across YouTube, Facebook, and Twitter? *Journal of Interactive Marketing*, *26*(2), 102–113. doi:10.1016/j.intmar.2012.01.002

Smith, J. (2018). The Influence of Social Media on Business Relationships. *Journal of Business Ethics*.

Smith, J. (2020). The Ethics of Influencer Marketing. *Journal of Business Ethics*, *167*(3), 605–618.

Smith, J. (2021). The State of Social Media in 2021. Social Media Today. Johnson, A., Brown, L., & Martinez, C. (2022). The Influence of Digital Influencers on Consumer Behavior. *JMR, Journal of Marketing Research*, *45*(2), 123–140.

Smith, R., & Johnson, K. (2021). Brand Collaborations with Virtual Influencers: An Analysis of Effectiveness. *JMR, Journal of Marketing Research*, *28*(2), 89–105.

SocialSamosa. (2019). *Data: 89% marketers say Instagram is important to their influencer marketing strategy*. Retrieved Jun 14, 2023, from https://www.socialsamosa.com/2019/02/report-influencer-marketing-statistics-2019/

So, K. K. F., King, C., Sparks, B. A., & Wang, Y. (2016). The role of customer engagement in building consumer loyalty to tourism brands. *Journal of Travel Research*, *55*(1), 64–78. doi:10.1177/0047287514541008

Sokolova, K., & Kefi, H. (2020). Instagram and YouTube bloggers promote it, why should I buy? How credibility and parasocial interaction influence purchase intentions. *Journal of Retailing and Consumer Services*, *53*, 1–9. doi:10.1016/j.jretconser.2019.01.011

Solis, B. (2016). *The Influencer Marketing Manifesto: Why the Future of Influencer Marketing Starts with People and Relationships not Popularity*. Retrieved from: http://pages.tapinfluence.com/hubfs/ınfluencer_marketing_manifesto.pdf

Solomon, M. (2018). *Consumer behavior- Buying, having, and being* (12th ed.). Pearson Education.

Soltani, M., Veer, E., de Vries, H. P., & Kemper, A. J. (2023). "Did you see what happened?" how scandals are shared via social media. *Corporate Reputation Review*. Advance online publication. doi:10.105741299-023-00165-z

Sookkaew, J., & Saephoo, P. (2021). "Digital Influencer": Development and Coexistence with Digital Social Groups. *International Journal of Advanced Computer Science and Applications*, *12*(12), 326–332. doi:10.14569/IJACSA.2021.0121243

Souza-Leão, A. L. M., Moura, B. M., & Nunes, W. K. S. (2022). All in one: Digital influencers as pop culture marketers. *Revista Brasileira de Gestão de Negócios*, *24*(2), 247–274. doi:10.7819/rbgn.v24i2.4167

Sproutsocial. (2023). *Important Instagram Stats You Need To Know For 2020*. Retrieved from: https://sproutsocial.com/insights/instagram-stats/

SproutSocial. (2023, Apr 17). *What is influencer marketing: How to develop your strategy*. Retrieved Jun 01, 2023, from SproutSocial: https://sproutsocial.com/insights/influencer-marketing/

Staff, M. C. (2019). *The Influencer Report*. Retrieved Jun 05, 2023, from https://pro.morningconsult.com/analyst-reports/influencer-report

Stanpa. (2021). Cosmetic sector in Spain. *Stanpa*. Retrieved from https://www.stanpa.com/en/industry-figures/cosmetic-sector-spain/

Statista. (2021). *Most used social media, 2021*. Retrieved from: https://www.statista.com/statistics/272014/global-social-networks-ranked-by-number-of-users/

Statista. (2021a). *Number of Monthly Active Facebook Users Worldwide as of 2nd Quarter 2021*. https://www.statista.com/statistics/264810/number-of-monthly-active-facebook-users-worldwide/

Statista. (2021b). *Number of Monthly Active Instagram Users from January 2013 to June 2021*. https://www.statista.com/statistics/253577/number-of-monthly-active-instagram-users/

Statista. (2021c). *Pinterest: Number of Monthly Active Users Worldwide 2016-2021*. https://www.statista.com/statistics/463001/pinterest-global-mau/

Statista. (2021d). *Twitter: Number of Monthly Active Users 2010-2021*. https://www.statista.com/statistics/282087/number-of-monthly-active-twitter-users/

Statista. (2021e). *YouTube: Number of Monthly Active Users Worldwide 2016-2021*. https://www.statista.com/statistics/273550/number-of-monthly-active-youtube-users/

Statista. (2023). *Number of social media users worldwide from 2017 to 2027*. https://www.statista.com/statistics/278414/number-of-worldwide-social-network-users/

Statista. (2023a). https://www.statista.com/statistics/1294803/india-influencer-marketing-industry-value

Statista. (2023b). https://www.statista.com/topics/9189/influencer-marketing-in-india

Statista. (2023c). https://www.statista.com/statistics/617136/digital-population-worldwide

Stein, J. P., Breves, P. L., & Anders, N. (2022). Parasocial interactions with real and virtual influencers: The role of perceived similarity and human-likeness. *New Media & Society*. *New Media & Society*. Advance online publication. doi:10.1177/14614448221102900

Stephenson, N. (2000). *Snow Crash*. Bantam Books.

Stone, D. (2020). Type of board and sustainability reporting. *Journal of Applied Business Research*, *36*(5), 229–240. doi:10.19030/jabr.v36i5.10361

Storai. (2023, Jan 17). *Making Influencer Marketing Click*. Retrieved JUn 07, 2023, from https://www.globallinker.com/bizforum/article/making-influencer-marketing-click/91904#/overlay/signup/articleview/91904

Strömberg, P. (2015). Theming. The Wiley Blackwell Encyclopedia of Consumption and Consumer Studies, 1–5. doi:10.1002/9781118989463.wbeccs228

Sudaryanto, S., Courvisanos, J., Dewi, I. R., Rusdiyanto, R., & Yuaris, J. R. (2022). Determinants of purchase intention during COVID-19: A case study of skincare products in east java. *Innovative Marketing*, *18*(1), 181–194. doi:10.21511/im.18(1).2022.15

Sudha, M., & Sheena, K. (2017). Impact of influencers in consumer decision process: The fashion industry. *SCMS Journal of Indian Management, 14*(3), 14-30. https://www.scms.edu.in/uploads/journal/articles/article_12.pdf

Sudha, M., & Sheena, K. (2017). Impact of influencers in consumer decision process: The fashion industry. *SCMS Journal of Indian Management*, *14*(3), 14–30.

Sugathan, P., & Ranjan, K. R. (2019). Co-creating the tourism experience. *Journal of Business Research*, *100*, 207–217. doi:10.1016/j.jbusres.2019.03.032

Sundermann, G., & Raabe, T. (2019). Strategic communication through social media influencers: Current state of research and desiderata. *International Journal of Strategic Communication*, *13*(4), 278–300. doi:10.1080/1553118X.2019.1618306

Suprawan, L., & Pojanavatee, S. (2022). What causes social media users to engage and mimic virtual influencers? The role of self-congruity. *Innovative Marketing*, *18*(4), 148–160. doi:10.21511/im.18(4).2022.13

Sutera, D. (2013). *Sports fans 2.0: How fans are using social media to get closer to the game*. Scarecrow Press.

Su, Y., Baker, B. J., Doyle, J. P., & Yan, M. (2020). Fan engagement in 15 seconds: Athletes' relationship marketing during a pandemic via TikTok. *International Journal of Sport Communication*, *13*(3), 436–446. doi:10.1123/ijsc.2020-0238

Swan, G. (2018, Apr 20). *What Is Influencer Marketing & Why It Matters | A Brand's Guide*. Retrieved Jun 08, 2023, from https://tinuiti.com/blog/influencer-marketing/what-is-influencer-marketing/

Swat.io. (2022, Nov 8). *6 Social Media Niches with Potential – How to Reach Your Target Group through Niche Platforms*. Retrieved Sept 15, 2023, from https://swat.io/en/strategize/social-media-niche-platforms/

Syrdal, H. A., Myers, S., Sen, S., Woodroof, P. J., & McDowell, W. C. (2023). Influencer marketing and the growth of affiliates: The effects of language features on engagement behavior. *Journal of Business Research*, *163*, 113875. doi:10.1016/j.jbusres.2023.113875

Tabaku, E., & Zerellari, M. (2015). Brand loyalty and loyalty programs; a literature review. *Romanian Economic Business Review*, *10*(2), 87.

Tabor, E. (2019, Dec 19). *Can You Really Market To Gen X And Baby Boomers On Social Platforms?* Retrieved Jun 15, 2023, from Forbes: https://www.forbes.com/sites/forbesagencycouncil/2019/12/19/can-you-really-market-to-gen-x-and-baby-boomers-on-social-platforms/?sh=7ea08ae55741

Taillon, B. J., Mueller, S. M., Kowalczyk, C. M., & Jones, D. N. (2020). Understanding the relationships between social media influencers and their followers: The moderating role of closeness. *Journal of Product and Brand Management*, *29*(6), 767–782. doi:10.1108/JPBM-03-2019-2292

Talavera, M. (2015). 10 reasons why influencer marketing is the next big thing. *Adweek*. https://www.adweek.com/digital/10-reasons-why-influencer-marketing-is-thenext-big-thing/

Tanwar, A. S., Chaudhry, H., & Srivastava, M. K. (2022). Trends in influencer marketing: A review and bibliometric analysis. *Journal of Interactive Advertising*, *22*(1), 1–27. doi:10.1080/15252019.2021.2007822

TapInfluence. (2019). *Earn 11x higher sales ROI with influencer marketing in your digital marketing tech stack j TapInfluence*. available at: https://www.tapinfluence.com/tp_resource/nielsen-casestudy/

Tapscott, D., & Williams, A. D. (2006). *Wikinomics: How Mass Collaboration Changes Everything* (2nd ed.). Penguin Group.

Tavares, S. (2019). *Complexo Cultural Ferreira de Castro: Comunicação Estratégica do Valor Cultural* [Master's thesis, University Institute of Lisbon]. Iscte Repository, University Institute of Lisbon. http://hdl.handle.net/10071/19620

Taylor, S. J., Bogdan, R., & DeVault, M. L. (2016). *Introduction to Qualitative Research Methods: A Guidebook and Resource. Wiley.* Unreal Engine. https://www.unrealengine.com/en-US/metahuman

Thirumalesh Madanaguli, A., Kaur, P., Bresciani, S., & Dhir, A. (2021). Entrepreneurship in rural hospitality and tourism. A systematic literature review of past achievements and future promises. *International Journal of Contemporary Hospitality Management*, *33*(8), 2521–2558. doi:10.1108/IJCHM-09-2020-1121

Thompson, M. (2023). Virtual influencers and their risk aversion: Implications for ethics in technology. *Ética y Tecnología, 12*(1), 68-80.

Thompson, C. J., & Haytko, D. L. (1997). Speaking of fashion: Consumers' uses of fashion discourses and the appropriation of countervailing cultural meanings. *The Journal of Consumer Research*, *24*(June), 15–42. doi:10.1086/209491

Thorpe, J. (2019, Nov 18). *The Influence of Influencers: New Research Unveiled*. Retrieved Jun 09, 2023, from gen.video: https://www.gen.video/blog/the-influence-of-influencers-new-research-unveiled

TikTok. (2023). *Gaming on TikTok*. https://www.tiktok.com/creators/creator-portal/en-us/how-to-level-up-your-gaming-content/creating-gaming-content-on-tiktok/

Tiwari, S. (2022, Nov 4). *Influencer marketing and its contribution to the creator economy of India*. Retrieved Jun 06, 2023, from https://etinsights.et-edge.com/influencer-marketing-and-its-contribution-to-the-creator-economy-of-india/

Tondon, R. (2023, Mar 18). *GenZs and the influencer market: Using social media to build business empires*. Retrieved Jun 06, 2023, from Economic Times: https://economictimes.indiatimes.com/jobs/fresher/genzs-and-the-influencer-market-using-social-media-to-build-business-empires/articleshow/98750919.cms?from=mdr

Torres, C. (2018). *The digital marketing bible* (2nd ed.). Novatec Editora Ltda. https://books.google.pt/books?id=uDN7DwAAQBAJ&lpg=PT4&dq=a%C3%A7%C3%B5es%20de%20comunica%C3%A7%C3%A3o%20de%20marketing%20&lr&hl=pt-BR&pg=PT2#v=onepage&q&f=false

Tozlu, A. (2016). Karar verme yaklaşımları üzerinde herbert sımon hegemonyası. *Sayıştay Dergisi*, *102*, 27–45.

Treseler, J. (2021, Mar 23). *What is a micro influencer anyway?* Retrieved Jun 11, 2023, from Crunchylinks: https://crunchylinks.com/what-is-a-micro-influencer-anyway/

Trivedi, J., & Sama, R. (2020). The effect of influencer marketing on consumers' brand admiration and online purchase intentions: An emerging market perspective. *Journal of Internet Commerce*, *19*(1), 103–124. doi:10.1080/15332861.2019.1700741

Tsimonis, G., & Dimitriadis, S. (2014). Brand strategies in social media. *Marketing Intelligence & Planning*, *32*(3), 328–344. doi:10.1108/MIP-04-2013-0056

Tulman, S. (2023, Jan 2). *The ROI of Influencer Marketing*. Retrieved Jun 05, 2023, from Business-2Community: https://www.business2community.com/online-marketing/roi-influencer-marketing-2-01787448#u65UTYdmZEZkKgMX.97

Twenge, J. M., & Martin, G. N. (2020). Gender differences in associations between digital media use and psychological well-being: Evidence from three large datasets. *Journal of Adolescence*, *79*(1), 91–102. doi:10.1016/j.adolescence.2019.12.018 PMID:31926450

Tzoulia, E. (2019, July). 'Influencer Marketing' on Social Media: Consumer Protection Issues from the Perspective of EU Law. In *Tzoulia, European Legal Forum (EuLF)* (pp. 29-38). Academic Press.

Um, N. (2023). Predictors Affecting Effects of Virtual Influencer Advertising among College Students. *Sustainability (Basel)*, *15*(8), 6388. Advance online publication. doi:10.3390u15086388

Upwork. (2022, Dec 7). *How To Build an Efficient Influencer Marketing Strategy*. Retrieved Sept 15, 2023, from https://www.upwork.com/en-gb/resources/influencer-marketing-strategy

Uzunoğlu, E., & Kip, S. M. (2014). Brand communication through digital influencers: Leveraging blogger engagement. *International Journal of Information Management*, *34*(5), 592–602. doi:10.1016/j.ijinfomgt.2014.04.007

Vale, L., & Fernandes, T. (2018). Social media and sports: Driving fan engagement with football clubs on Facebook. *Journal of Strategic Marketing*, *26*(1), 37–55. doi:10.1080/0965254X.2017.1359655

Valentina Dencheva. (2023, Jan 6). *Average price per post of TikTok influencers worldwide in 2021, by number of followers*. Retrieved Jun 05, 2023, from Statista: https://www.statista.com/statistics/1251177/price-per-post-tiktok-influencers-worldwide/

Vallaster, C., & Von Wallpach, S. (2013). An online discursive inquiry into the social dynamics of multi-stakeholder brand meaning co-creation. *Journal of Business Research*, *66*(9), 1505–1515. doi:10.1016/j.jbusres.2012.09.012

Value Creation in the Metaverse: The Real Business of the Virtual World. (2022). McKinsey Company. https://www.mckinsey.com/~/media/mckinsey/business%20functions/marketing%20and%20sales/our%20insights/value%20creation%20in%20the%20metaverse/Value-creation-in-the-metaverse.pdf

Van Dijck, J. (2013). *The culture of connectivity: A critical history of social media*. OUP. doi:10.1093/acprof:oso/9780199970773.001.0001

Van Doorn, J., Lemon, K. N., Mittal, V., Nass, S., Pick, D., Pirner, P., & Verhoef, P. C. (2010). Customer Engagement Behavior: Theoretical foundations and research directions. *Journal of Service Research*, *13*(3), 253–266. doi:10.1177/1094670510375599

Vani, M., Sankaran, H., & Praveen Kumar, S. (2020). To explore the relationship between emotional intelligence and transformational leadership and their effect on organizational culture. *International Journal of Scientific and Technology Research*, *9*(1), 990–992.

Vargo, S. L., & Lusch, R. F. (2004). Evolving to a New Dominant Logic for Marketing. *Journal of Marketing*, *68*(1), 1–17. doi:10.1509/jmkg.68.1.1.24036

Varsamis, E. (2018). Are social media influencers the next-generation brand ambassadors? *Forbes*. https://www.forbes.com/sites/theyec/2018/06/13/are-social-mediainfluencers-the-next-generation-brand-ambassadors/#2d8b9e82473d

Vaz, G., & Venâncio, M. (2018). Marketing, dissemination, action and cultural mediation in public archives. *RACIn*, *6*(1), 1-29. https://eds.s.ebscohost.com/eds/pdfviewer/pdfviewer?vid=1&sid=d94c4ea1-b6ef-4d42-9118-20334a11b610%40redis

Velasco, C. (2019, December 12). Los influencers españoles deberán indicar cuáles de sus publicaciones son publicitarias desde el 1 de enero. *Marketing4ecommerce*. https://marketing4ecommerce.net/los-influencers-espanoles-deberan-indicar-cuales-de-sus-publicaciones-son-publicitarias-desde-el-1-de-enero/

Venciute, D., Mackeviciene, I., Kuslys, M., & Correia, R. F. (2023, November). The role of influencer–follower congruence in the relationship between influencer marketing and purchase behaviour. *Journal of Retailing and Consumer Services*, *75*, 103506. Advance online publication. doi:10.1016/j.jretconser.2023.103506

Venkatesan, R. (2017). Executing on a customer engagement strategy. *Journal of the Academy of Marketing Science*, *45*(3), 289–293. doi:10.100711747-016-0513-6

Venkatesh, R., Meleet, M., & Cholli, D. N. (2022). Influencer Marketing in Recent Times. *International Journal of Engineering Research & Technology (Ahmedabad)*, *11*(07), 292–296. Retrieved June 11, 2023, from https://www.ijert.org/research/influencer-marketing-in-recent-times-IJERTV11IS070172.pdf

Vincent, J. (2020). Samsung's 'Artificial Humans' are Just Digital Avatars. *The Verge*. https://www.theverge.com/2020/1/7/21051390/samsung-artificial-human-neon-digital-avatar-project-star-labs

Voipio, V., Elfvengren, K., & Korpela, J. (2020). In the bowling alley: Acceptance of an intelligent packaging concept in European markets. *International Journal of Value Chain Management*, *11*(2), 180–197. doi:10.1504/IJVCM.2020.106825

Von Felbert, A., & Breuer, C. (2020). How the type of sports-related endorser influences consumers' purchase intentions. *International Journal of Sports Marketing & Sponsorship*, *22*(3), 588–607. doi:10.1108/IJSMS-01-2020-0009

von Mettenheim, W., & Wiedmann, K. P. (2021). The complex triad of congruence issues in influencer marketing. *Journal of Consumer Behaviour*, *20*(5), 1277–1296. doi:10.1002/cb.1935

Voorveld, H. A., van Noort, G., Muntinga, D. G., & Bronner, F. (2018). Engagement with social media and social media advertising: The differentiating role of platform type. *Journal of Advertising*, *47*(1), 38–54. doi:10.1080/00913367.2017.1405754

Vrontis, D., Makrides, A., Christofi, M., & Thrassou, A. (2021). Social media influencer marketing: A systematic review, integrative framework and future research agenda. *International Journal of Consumer Studies*, *4*(45), 617–644. doi:10.1111/ijcs.12647

Vyncke, P. (2002). Lifestyle segmentationfrom attitudes, interests and opinions, to values, aesthetic styles, life visions and media preferences. *European Journal of Communication*, *17*(4), 445–463. doi:10.1177/02673231020170040301

Walmsley, B. (2011). Why people go to the theatre: A qualitative study of audience motivation. *Journal of Customer Behaviour*, *10*(4), 335–351. doi:10.1362/147539211X13210329822545

Waltenrath, A., Brenner, C., & Hinz, O. (2022). Some interactions are more equal than others: The effect of influencer endorsements in social media brand posts on engagement and online store performance. *Journal of Interactive Marketing*, *57*(4), 541–560. doi:10.1177/10949968221096591

Wang, C. L. (2021). New frontiers and future directions in interactive marketing: Inaugural Editorial. *Journal of Research in Interactive Marketing*, *15*(1), 1–9. doi:10.1108/JRIM-03-2021-270

Wang, N. (2023). Influencer marketing strategies in foreign marketplaces. *Springer Proceedings in Business and Economics*, 86-90. 10.1007/978-3-031-31836-8_11

Wardoyo, P., Rusdianti, E., & Purwantini, S. (2019). Salesforce performance of rural bank: The impact of sales training and experience selling. *International Journal of Scientific and Technology Research*, *8*(9), 1079–1087. www.scopus.com

Warren, J. (2020, Apr 27). *Affiliate Marketing for Influencers: How to Make Money on Instagram*. Retrieved Sept 15, 2023, from https://later.com/blog/affiliate-marketing-for-influencers/

Weinswig, D. (2016). Influencers are the new brands. *Forbes*. https://www.forbes.com/sites/deborah-weinswig/2016/10/05/celebritys-are-the-new-brands/#66ad98a37919

Weismueller, J., Harrigan, P., Wang, S., & Soutar, G. N. (2020). Influencer endorsements: How advertising disclosure and source credibility affect consumer purchase intention on social media. *Australasian Marketing Journal*, *28*(4), 160–170. doi:10.1016/j.ausmj.2020.03.002

Weiswing, D. (2016). *FBIC's Weinswig Named One of Top Retail Influencers For 2016*. Retrieved from: https://www.deborahweinswig.com/news/press-releases/fbics-weinswig-named-one-of-top-retail-ınfluencers-for-2016/

Werner, G. (2023a, Feb 7). *The State of Influencer Marketing 2023: Benchmark Report*. Retrieved Jun 06, 2023, from Influencer Marketing Hub: https://influencermarketinghub.com/influencer-marketing-benchmark-report/

Werner, G. (2023b, Mar 24). *What is an Influencer? Social Media Influencers Defined* [Updated 2023]. Retrieved Jun 08, 2023, from https://influencermarketinghub.com/what-is-an-influencer/

West, C. (2023). *Micro-influencer marketing guide: Facts and uses*. Retrieved Jun 11, 2023, from https://sproutsocial.com/insights/microinfluencer-marketing/

White, E., & Davis, M. (2019). The Emergence of Influencer Marketing in the Restaurant Sector. *International Journal of Hospitality Management*.

Whiting, A., & Williams, D. (2013). Why people use social media: A uses and gratifications approach. *Qualitative Market Research*, *16*(4), 362–369. doi:10.1108/QMR-06-2013-0041

Wibawa, R. C., Pratiwi, C. P., & Larasati, H. (2021). The Role of Nano Influencers Through Instagram as an Effective Digital Marketing Strategy. *Advances in Economics, Business and Management Research, 198*, 233-238. Retrieved Jun 12, 2023, from https://www.researchgate.net/publication/358878321_The_Role_of_Nano_Influencers_Through_Instagram_as_an_Effective_Digital_Marketing_Strategy

Wiedmann, K., & von Mettenheim, W. (2020). *An adaptation of the source credibility model on social influencers: An abstract*. doi:10.1007/978-3-030-42545-6_65

Wiley, D. (2023, Mar 13). *Why Smaller Influencers Outshine Mega-Influencers in The Age of Social Media*. Retrieved Jun 12, 2023, from Forbes: https://www.forbes.com/sites/forbesagencycouncil/2023/03/13/why-smaller-influencers-outshine-mega-influencers-in-the-age-of-social-media/?sh=1cbce1ac4090

Wilk, R. (1997). A critique of desire: Distaste and dislike in consumer behavior. *Consumption Markets & Culture*, *1*(2), 175–196. doi:10.1080/10253866.1997.9670297

Wilson, J. A. J., & Arroyo, L. (2022). Conceptualizing performative Instagram influencer and user relationships – through advertising and sponsored brand content. *International Journal of Business Performance Management*, *23*(3), 257–284. doi:10.1504/IJBPM.2022.123859

Wong, L. (2023, Aug 3). *How to Use UTM Parameters to Track Social Media Success*. Retrieved Sept 15, 2023, from https://blog.hootsuite.com/how-to-use-utm-parameters/

Woodroof, P. J., Howie, K. M., Syrdal, H. A., & VanMeter, R. (2020). What's done in the dark will be brought to the light: Effects of influencer transparency on product efficacy and purchase intentions. *Journal of Product and Brand Management*, *29*(5), 675–688. doi:10.1108/JPBM-05-2019-2362

Xiang, L., Zheng, X., Lee, M. K., & Zhao, D. (2016). Exploring consumers' impulse buying behavior on social commerce platform: The role of parasocial interaction. *International Journal of Information Management*, *36*(3), 333–347. doi:10.1016/j.ijinfomgt.2015.11.002

Xiao, M., Wang, R., & Chan-Olmsted, S. M. (2018). Factors affecting YouTube influencer marketing credibility: A heuristic-systematic model. *Journal of Media Business Studies*, *15*(3), 188–213. doi:10.1080/16522354.2018.1501146

Xie-Carson, L., Magor, T., Benckendorff, P., & Hughes, K. (2023). All hype or the real deal? Investigating user engagement with virtual influencers in tourism. *Tourism Management*, *99*, 104779. Advance online publication. doi:10.1016/j.tourman.2023.104779

Xiong, L., Cho, V., Law, K. M. Y., & Lam, L. (2021). A study of KOL effectiveness on brand image of skincare products. *Enterprise Information Systems*, *15*(10), 1483–1500. doi:10.1080/17517575.2021.1924864

Xu, L., & Du, X. (2020). What Drives Consumers' Intention to Follow Brands on Twitter? *Journal of Interactive Advertising*.

Yanaze, M. (2017). *Marketing and Communication Management* (2nd ed.). Saraiva Educação. https://books.google.pt/books?id=eSprDwAAQBAJ&lpg=PT6&dq=a%C3%A7%C3%B5es%20de%20comunica%C3%A7%C3%A3o%20de%20marketing%20&lr&hl=pt-BR&pg=PT4#v=onepage&q=a%C3%A7%C3%B5es%20de%20comunica%C3%A7%C3%A3o%20de%20marketing&f=false

Yang, J., Chuenterawong, P., Lee, H., & Chock, T. M. (2023). Anthropomorphism in CSR Endorsement: A Comparative Study on Humanlike vs. Cartoonlike Virtual Influencers' Climate Change Messaging. *Journal of Promotion Management*, *29*(5), 705–734. doi:10.1080/10496491.2022.2163041

Yang, J., Chuenterawong, P., Lee, H., Tian, Y., & Chock, T. M. (2023). Human versus Virtual Influencer: The Effect of Humanness and Interactivity on Persuasive CSR Messaging. *Journal of Interactive Advertising*, *23*(3), 275–292. Advance online publication. doi:10.1080/15252019.2023.2189036

Yang, K. C., & Kang, Y. (2021). Predicting the relationships between narrative transportation, consumer brand experience, love and loyalty in video storytelling advertising. *Journal of Creative Communications*, *16*(1), 7–26. doi:10.1177/0973258620984262

Yap, Y. R., & Ismail, N. (2022). Factors of virtual influencer marketing influencing Generation Y consumers' purchase intention in Malaysia. *International Journal of Internet Marketing and Advertising*, *17*(3-4), 437–458. doi:10.1504/IJIMA.2022.126735

Ye, G., Hudders, L., De Jans, S., & De Veirman, M. (2021). The value of influencer marketing for business: A bibliometric analysis and managerial implications. *Journal of Advertising*, *50*(2), 160–178. doi:10.1080/00913367.2020.1857888

Yelp. (2021). *Consumer Trust in the Digital Age*. https://www.yelp-press.com/company/news-releases/news-release-details/2021-08-17-Consumer-Trust-in-the-Digital-Age/default.aspx

Yeo, S. F., Tan, C. L., Kumar, A., Tan, K. H., & Wong, J. K. (2022). Investigating the impact of AI-powered technologies on Instagrammers' purchase decisions in digitalization era–A study of the fashion and apparel industry. *Technological Forecasting and Social Change*, *177*, 121551. Advance online publication. doi:10.1016/j.techfore.2022.121551

Yocco, V. S. (2016). *Design for the mind: Seven psychological principles of persuasive design*. Manning.

Yodel, G. (2017). What is influencer marketing? *Huffpost*. https://www.huffingtonpost.com/global-yodel/what-is-influcnermarketing_b_10778128.html

Yovcheva, Z., & Buhalis, D. (2017). Analysing travel experiences: The potential of social media data. *Current Issues in Tourism*, *20*(1), 1–19.

Yu, S., & de Barnier, V. (2022). *Social attachment theory and the relationship between satisfaction, luxury brand attachment, and influencer attachment: A focus on young Chinese online consumers under quarantine: An abstract*. doi:10.1007/978-3-030-95346-1_50

Yurdakul-Sahin, D., & Atik, D. (2013). Celebrity influences on young consumers: Guiding the way to the ideal self. *Izmir Review of Social Sciences*, *1*(1), 65–82.

Zafar, A. U., Shahzad, M., Ashfaq, M., & Shahzad, K. (2023, May). Forecasting impulsive consumers driven by macro-influencers posts: Intervention of followers' flow state and perceived informativeness. *Technological Forecasting and Social Change*, *190*, 122408. Advance online publication. doi:10.1016/j.techfore.2023.122408

Zanette, M. C., Brito, E. P. Z., & Coutinho, M. (2013). New influentials: An exploratory study on blogs. *Journal of Direct, Data and Digital Marketing Practice*, *15*(1), 36–46. doi:10.1057/dddmp.2013.45

Zarei, K., Ibosiola, D., Farahbakhsh, R., Gilani, Z., Garimella, K., Crespi, N., & Tyson, G. (2020). Characterizing and detecting sponsored influencer posts on Instagram. *ASONAM 2020: IEEE/ACM International Conference on Advances in Social Networks Analysis and Mining*, 327-331.

Zelenskaya, M., & Rundle-Thiele, S. (2022). Wildlife Watcher Kylie: Co-designing a virtual ambassador for the Koala Watch programme. *Studies in Australasian Cinema*, *16*(2-3), 93–108. doi:10.1080/17503175.2022.2148413

Zengingönül, O. (2012). *Küresel Put: Tüketim Ekonomisi Yeni Sapkınlık: Sosyal Bilinç* (1st ed.). Nobel Akademik Yayıncılık.

Zeren, D., & Gökdağlı, N. (2020). Influencer versus celebrity endorser performance on Instagram. *Springer Proceedings in Business and Economics*, 695-704. 10.1007/978-3-030-36126-6_77

Zhang, L., & Ren, J. (2022). Virtual Influencers: The Effects of Controlling Entity, Appearance Realism and Product Type on Advertising Effect. In Lecture Notes in Computer Science (including subseries Lecture Notes in Artificial Intelligence and Lecture Notes in Bioinformatics) (Vol. 13337 LNCS, pp. 298-305). Springer.

Zhang, W., Chintagunta, P. K., & Kalwani, M. U. (2021). Social media, influencers, and adoption of an eco-friendly product: Field experiment evidence from rural china. *Journal of Marketing*, *85*(3), 10–27. doi:10.1177/0022242920985784

Zhang, X., & Choi, J. (2022). The importance of social influencer-generated contents for user cognition and emotional attachment: An information relevance perspective. *Sustainability (Basel)*, *14*(11), 6676. doi:10.3390u14116676

Zhang, X., Duan, K., Zhao, H., Zhao, Y., Wang, X., & de Pablos, P. O. (2020). Can cooperation drive the success of suppliers in B2B crowdsourcing innovation projects? A large scale data perspective. *Industrial Marketing Management*, *90*, 570–580. doi:10.1016/j.indmarman.2019.09.011

Zhang, Y., & Mac, L. (2023). Social media influencers: The formation and effects of affective factors during online interactions. *International Journal of Consumer Studies*, *47*(5), 1824–1837. Advance online publication. doi:10.1111/ijcs.12957

Zhao, H., & Zhang, N. (2019). Who is the main influencer on safety performance of dangerous goods air transportation in China? *Journal of Air Transport Management*, *75*, 198–203. doi:10.1016/j.jairtraman.2018.11.001

Zhou, S., Blazquez, M., McCormick, H., & Barnes, L. (2021). How social media influencers' narrative strategies benefit cultivating influencer marketing: Tackling issues of cultural barriers, commercialised content, and sponsorship disclosure. *Journal of Business Research*, *134*, 122–142. doi:10.1016/j.jbusres.2021.05.011

Zhu, D. H., & Westphal, J. D. (2021). Structural power, corporate strategy, and performance. *Strategic Management Journal*, *42*(3), 624–651. doi:10.1002mj.3239

Zniva, R., Weitzl, W., & Lindmoser, C. (2023). Be constantly different! How to manage influencer authenticity. *Electronic Commerce Research*, *23*(3), 1485–1514. doi:10.100710660-022-09653-6

Zollo, L., Filieri, R., Rialti, R., & Yoon, S. (2020). Unpacking the Relationship Between Social Media Marketing and Brand Equity: The Mediating Role of Consumers' Benefits and Experience. *Journal of Business Research*, *117*, 256–267. doi:10.1016/j.jbusres.2020.05.001

Zuo, H., & Wang, T. (2019). Analysis of Tik Tok user behavior from the perspective of popular culture. *Frontiers in Art Research*, *1*(3), 1–5. doi:10.25236/FAR.20190301

About the Contributors

Sandrina Teixeira is an Adjunct Professor at School of Accounting and Administration of Porto, Polytechnic Institute of Porto, Portugal. Since 2013, she has been Coordinator of the Digital Marketing Masters and of the Degree in Business Communication. Between 2013-2014, she was Coordinator of the Degree in Marketing. She is responsible by various courses, such as: unit of Marketing and Advertising Communication, Development of Multimedia Content, Seminars in the Digital Marketing Masters. She got a PhD at University Vigo of Communication, Advertising and Public Relation, in 2011. Her research interests are in digital communication, transparency in public administration and new consumers. She has supervised several master degree dissertations, was arguer in various proofs masters in various institutions of higher education and presided several master juries degrees.

Sara Teixeira got her diploma in Environmental Health, a branch of Public Health in 2008 at theSchool of Allied Health Sciences by the Polytechnic Institute of Porto. In 2009 she moved back to her home city and enrolled in a master in Micro and Nano Technologies at the University of Minho (Portugal). From October 2010 to April 2011 Sara joined our chair as an Erasmus student, doing part of her master thesis on subject "Development of a sensoring device for environmental estrogens in wastewater". She is currently part of the InnoMedTec-Team as a PhD student, working on the topic "Photocatalytical cleaning concepts for aquatic environment contaminated with antibiotics".

Zalia Oliveira currently works at the Centro Universitário Christus in the Departamento de Administração. She has her PhD in Management with Specialization in Marketing and Strategy.

Elnivan Souza received his PhD in Business Administration from the University of Fortaleza (UNIFOR) (Brazil, 2015-2019) with an internship abroad (sandwich doctorate) at Simon Fraser University (Canada, 2018), Master in Business Administration from the State University of Ceará (UECE) (Brazil, 2012-2014), Marketing Specialist from the Federal University of Ceará (UFC) (Brazil, 2007-2009) and graduated in Business Administration from the Federal University of Ceará (2001-2006). He is currently Head of Research and Professor of the Administration undergraduate course at Centro Universitário Christus (UNICHRISTUS) (2014-current). Has experience in Administration, with emphasis on Entrepreneurship, Innovation, Strategy and Management Support Technologies. His research topics are Dynamic Capability (Managerial and Cognitive), Business Model, E-business and Industry 4.0. He has expertise in qualitative and quantitative methodologies. Regarding quantitative approaches, it handles multivariate techniques such as Analysis of Variance (ANOVA), Linear Regression and Logistics, Structural Equation Modeling, etc. It also develops research and technical works that use Artificial Intelligence techniques such as Neural Networks, Fuzzy Logic and Genetic Algorithms. He has articles published in national and international events and journals.

* * *

Ana Cristina Antunes is an adjunct professor at School of Communication and Media Studies (ESCS) of the Lisbon Polytechnic Institute (IPL). PhD in Psychology, Master's degree in Human Resources Development Policies, and Bachelor degree in Psychology. She is in the editorial comission of Revista Comunicação Pública and her research interests include consumer behavior, organizational behavior, user experience and elderly, ICT and social media.

Maria Elena Aramendia-Muneta, PhD, is Associate professor in the Business Administration Department of Universidad Pública de Navarra, Spain. Her primary research fields are digital marketing, tourism and history of marketing. She has published in journals such as Telematics and Informatics, Journal of Promotion Management, Journal of Historical Research in Marketing and Journal of Gender Studies.

Belem Barbosa received her PhD in Business and Management Studies – Specialisation in Marketing and Strategy from the University of Porto, Portugal. She is Assistant Professor at the School of Economics and Management of the University of Porto. She is full researcher at GOVCOPP, the Research Unit of Governance, Competitiveness, and Public Policies, and Invited Researcher at cef.up Center for Economics and Finance at the University of Porto. Her research interests lie primarily in the areas of digital marketing and consumer behavior.

Nitesh Behare is an accomplished author with a wealth of knowledge and 15 years of experience in the academic field. He currently holds the esteemed position of Associate Professor at the Balaji Institute of International Business (BIIB), Sri Balaji University Pune (SBUP). Throughout his career, Dr. Behare has made significant contributions to the academic world through the publication of numerous research papers and book chapters, establishing himself as a recognized authority in his field. His dedication to scholarship and commitment to the advancement of knowledge make him a valuable asset.

Lierni Castilla-Miguel holds an International Double Bachelor's Degree in Economics and Business Administration from the Public University of Navarre (Spain) complemented by international and national abroad academic experiences in Germany and Spain. Since February 2023, she works as R&D and Innovation consultant at Zabala Innovation Consulting S.A and she is member of the Third Country Knowledge Area. She combines the provision of consultancy services in the preparation, presentation and management of projects to European programmes with her work in the preparation, implementation and management of International Tenders. She previously worked as an EU Project Manager Assistant in Greece, showcasing expertise in proposal preparation, partner engagement, and marketing for international and EU projects. She is native in Spanish and Basque and speaks English.

Benjamín del Alcázar Martínez is Dean of the Faculty of Commerce and Management of the University of Malaga. Senior Lecturer at the University of Malaga, in the Area of Marketing and Market Research, Department of Economics and Business Administration, where he has been teaching and has developed his research since 1989. Doctor in Business Administration and Management since 2001 and Degree in Economic and Business Sciences, Business Section and Specialty in Commercial Management since 1989. Both degrees from the University of Malaga. Since joining the University he has oriented all his research activity to the field of marketing in general and in the service sector, commercial and tourist distribution, on which he has developed his Doctoral Thesis, has published some books, and has participated in numerous congresses, courses and similar and directed several Doctoral Thesis. He has collaborated and carried out consulting work for various companies and institutions, among which the Ministry of Tourism, Commerce and Sports of the Junta de Andalucía, the City Council of Malaga, the Diputación de Málaga. Currently, he is the director of the Master's Degree in Retail Marketing, is part of the Committee of Experts of the Spanish Retail Association (AER), having also participated in numerous postgraduate courses both nationally and in Latin American countries such as Brazil, Mexico, Peru and Venezuela. Vice President of the Marketing Club of Malaga, member of the Spanish Marketing Association (AEMARK), the Andalusian Marketing Federation (FAM), Association of Scientific Experts in Tourism (AECIT) and the European Academy of Management and Business Economics (AEDEM). He is also director of the Chair of Cofrades Studies at the University of Malaga. A detailed CV can be viewed at http://benjamindelalcazar.com/.9cf17347-535e-4262-b7bd-dd9cdff1001c

Alvaro Díaz Casquero is a Graduate in Business Sciences, Marketing and Market Research, and a postgraduate degree in Digital Marketing, a role as a lecturer in the Department of Economics and Business Administration at the University of Malaga has been held since 2016.

Ushmita Gupta is a seasoned professional with over 15 years of expertise in research and teaching, specializing in the field of Economics, Banking & FOREX. Currently serving as a Senior Assistant Professor at Sri Balaji University Pune, previously contributing significantly at institutions like Avadh Girls' Degree College and IGNOU. Holder of a Ph.D. from the University of Lucknow, complemented by a strong academic background. A prolific researcher with numerous papers published and presentations at national & international seminars. Additionally, a published author of two books and an innovative patent under consideration. A committed educator seeking a fulfilling role to apply administrative and teaching skills in higher education. Active engagement in professional development, administrative responsibilities, and societal service underscores a multifaceted commitment to academia. Lifetime member of the Uttar Pradesh and Uttarakhand Economic Association & an executive alumnae of Indian Institute of Management, Indore.

Nilgün Gürkaynak was born in Izmir in 1967. She is a graduate of Izmir American Collegiate Institute ('85). She holds a BBA degree from Boğaziçi University ('89), and an MBA from Dalhousie University ('91) and a PhD in marketing from Yeditepe Unviversity. She was a faculty member of marketing in Yeditepe University between 2000 and 2009; before that she worked for the Coca-Cola Company, GfK, Henkel-Turyağ and Izmir Pamuk Mensucatı. She also provided consultancy and training services for various firms from FMCG, banking, construction materials, real estate and communication sectors. She joined IUE in 2009 and since 2010 she is the Director of School of Applied Managerial Sciences. Her research interests include place marketing, marketing for SMEs, social media and local brands.

Ece İpekoğlu graduated from Konak Anatolian High School in 2005. After completing her undergraduate studies in Izmir University of Economics, Faculty of Economics and Administrative Sciences, International Relations and EU and International Trade and Finance under the double major program in 2010, she completed her master's degree in Political Science at Sabancı University. She completed her Ph.D. thesis titled "The Effects of Social Media Phenomena in the Context of Instagram Mothers on Consumer Decision Making Process" in the Department of Business Administration at Izmir University of Economics. She worked as a Marketing Communication Manager in an international company in the private sector for 6 years. Since 2022, in Yaşar University Vocational School Foreign Trade program, she continues full time as a lecturer. At the same time, she carries out the administrative duty of program responsibility in Yaşar University Vocational School Public Relations and Publicity Program. Her academic studies are on marketing, consumer behavior, brand management and current marketing approaches.

Vishwanathan Iyer is associated with academics for 29 years. He specialises in Financial Accounting and Financial management. To gain better insights about the world of finance, he qualified as a Chartered Accountant in 2005. To explore academics, he pursued for a doctorate and qualified as a Ph.D. holder in June 2021. During this period, his inclination towards Research increased to a great extent. He has 14 Research papers to his credit, which were presented and published at various National and International conferences. His paper is published in UGC care journal as well. His paper with a student, Mr Gangesh Dubey, was declared as the Best Paper at National Conference conducted by Vedanta College, Ulhasnagar in April 2023. He believes Research holds great significance in the academic field and hopes to publish papers and submit chapters in Scopus Indexed publications and ABDC Journals at the earliest.

Sunita Kumar is a passionate educationist with 17+ years of experience (Industry: 5+ years and Teaching: 12+ years) experience. Dr Sunita area of expertise/ specialization including advertising, branding, digital Marketing, consumer behaviour, Marketing Analytics. Over the last 12 years, she has taught and received positive evaluations for many marketing units, including Brand Management, Marketing Research, International Marketing, Fundamental of Marketing, Consumer Behaviour, Marketing Management, Social Media and Digital Marketing, Data Analysis using SPSS both postgraduate and undergraduate level. She has also been actively supervising master's and Ph.D. candidates from Christ university in Bangalore. Dr Sunita also often shares her industry experience and research findings with different audiences and stakeholders, both locally and internationally. she has been actively leading and involved in numerous research project and consultancies projects, as well as published numerous indexed journals/ articles, book, chapters in a book, conference proceedings, and industry reports.

Rashmi Mahajan is a triple post graduate and is a Masters of Computer Management, Post Graduate Diploma in Business Management [Marketing] & Masters of Business Studies [Marketing]. She has completed her PhD in Marketing Management and a Diploma in Training & Development from Indian Society for Training & Development, Pune Chapter. She has around 19+ years of experience teaching undergraduate as well as post graduate students and has 3 PhD scholars pursuing their PhD under her. She has published various papers in National as well as International journals and has 2 patents and 1 copyright credited to her name. She alswo has 1 Chapter Published. She is a Professor, Head of Department of International Business & Dy. Director of BIIB in Sri Balaji University Pune (SBUP).

Danish Mehraj is an Assistant Professor in the Department of Management Studies, North Campus at the University of Kashmir. Holding a Ph.D. in Marketing, his research focuses on the impact of green brand positioning on consumer attitude and purchase intentions. With research interests in sustainability, green marketing, entrepreneurship, e-commerce, consumer behavior, and tourism marketing, Dr. Danish actively contributes to the academic community. He possesses technical skills in data analysis software such as SPSS, AMOS, and MS Excel. Alongside his research, Dr. Danish teaches subjects like Marketing Management, Business Statistics, Business Research Methods, Tourism Management, and Production and Operation Management. Committed to creating an engaging learning environment, he equips students with the necessary skills and knowledge to excel in their respective fields. Dr. Danish Mehraj's expertise and contributions aim to advance knowledge in marketing, sustainability, and consumer behavior.

Neli Maria Mengalli is a senior professional who has worked for over twenty years in educational consultancy, interfacing with the areas of knowledge management, monitoring and measurement of social media, society 5.0, phygital transformation and disruptive technologies. She worked in both the private sector and public management. Her postgraduate studies [master's and doctorate] were completed at the Pontifical Catholic University of São Paulo with an emphasis on innovative technologies. The highlights are the work produced on communities of practice, online context management, disruptive technologies, metaverse ecosystem and transform(active) methodologies in higher education. She participated in research groups on technology at the Pontifical Catholic University of São Paulo and in workshops that associated language, education, and technology at FASB - Faculdade São Bernardo do Campo. The professional trajectory includes basic education, higher education, course evaluation in higher education, participation in councils, public policy advice and startup mentoring. She is an interlocutor in the implementation of public policies and a participant in projects to create digital solutions to solve problems in the business area.

Sebastiano Mereu is a Researcher for the Sports Business Research Academy, as well as Lecturer of Digital Marketing and Branding at BHMS Business & Hotel Management School and Kalaidos University of Applied Sciences in Switzerland. His main research interests include second-screening and spectator sports, uses and gratifications of watching unscripted shows, metaverse adoption, retro marketing and apparel promotion, driving social media engagement, intentions to watch women's sports, and more. He also works as a Digital Marketing and Communications Specialist for the Swiss National Museum. Dr. Mereu holds a Doctor of Business Administration degree and a Master of Science in Marketing degree from Heriot-Watt University, UK, and a Bachelor of Science (Hons.) in International Management degree from FHNW University of Applied Sciences Northwestern Switzerland.

Albérico Travassos Rosário, Ph.D. Marketing and Strategy of the Universities of Aveiro (UA), Minho (UM) and Beira Interior (UBI). With affiliation to the GOVCOPP research center of the University of Aveiro. Master in Marketing and Degree in Marketing, Advertising and Public Relations, degree from ISLA Campus Lisbon-European University | Laureate International Universities. Has the title of Marketing Specialist and teaches with the category of Assistant Professor at IADE-Faculty of Design, Technology and Communication of the European University and as a visiting Associate Professor at the Santarém Higher School of Management and Technology (ESGTS) of the Polytechnic Institute of Santarém. He taught at IPAM-School of Marketing | Laureate International Universities, ISLA- Higher Institute of Management and Administration of Santarém (ISLA-Santarém), was Director of the Commercial Management Course, Director of the Professional Technical Course (TeSP) of Sales and Commercial Management, Chairman of the Pedagogical Council and Member of the Technical Council and ISLA-Santarém Scientific Researcher. He is also a marketing and strategy consultant for SMEs.

Meenakshi Singh is an accomplished academician with over 13 years of experience in the field of education. Her journey in education has been characterized by an unwavering commitment to teaching and mentoring students from diverse social and cultural backgrounds. Her expertise extends across various disciplines related to management and economics, where she excels due to her exceptional administrative, verbal communication, and written skills. Meenakshi is not only an educator but also an accomplished author with several books and case studies to her name. Her publications encompass books on international business, economics, and strategic human resource management, as well as case studies that enrich the academic world.

Index

(Meta) Influencer 147, 149, 152-154, 157-158, 161

A

Alisha Lehmann 214-215, 217, 221-222, 225, 227-229, 234
Artificial Intelligence (AI) 122, 128
Attitude 38, 56, 79, 104, 111, 121, 139-140, 146, 160, 184, 261, 297, 305
Augmented Reality (AR) 21-22, 24, 46, 205, 276, 287

B

Baby Boomers 33, 56-57
Bibliometric Analysis 56, 60, 85, 163, 166, 171, 176, 179, 181-182, 184, 186-187, 309
Biblioshiny 166, 187
Brand Advocacy 68, 87
Brand Reach 24, 28, 129-130, 135
Brand Strategies 129, 134, 145-146
Brand Visibility 1-2, 4, 17, 23, 41, 45, 69, 77, 283
Business 1, 5-6, 11, 13-15, 17-20, 25-28, 31-35, 38, 46, 51, 55-56, 58-61, 64-65, 67-70, 73-87, 101, 103, 107-108, 110, 115, 118, 127, 132, 134, 137-145, 148-162, 176, 184, 186, 189-191, 195, 197, 207, 209, 214-217, 230-233, 236, 239, 242, 244, 266, 269, 272, 274, 281-283, 285-286, 305-309
Business Performance 58-59, 67-70, 74-77, 82, 86-87, 137
Buyer Decision Process 288-289, 292-295, 299, 301-303, 310
Buying Behavior 29, 104, 236, 288, 292, 295-297, 301-302, 305, 309

C

Celebrities 3, 5, 9-11, 13, 37, 41-42, 50-51, 56, 59, 93, 95, 99-101, 104-105, 132, 140, 142, 154, 203, 235, 240-241, 246-247, 255-256, 259, 264, 267, 291-292, 305-306, 310
Celebrity Athlete 214, 217-218, 221, 223, 227-229, 234
Co-Branding 275
Co-Creation 87, 129-130, 132-133, 137-138, 141-146
Collaboration 4, 8, 11, 15, 22-24, 35-36, 43-44, 67, 74, 107, 117-118, 129, 133-134, 146, 150, 155, 171, 192, 195, 221, 241, 270, 275, 277-283, 309
Computer-Generated Influencers 163
Consumer Behavior 25, 30, 53, 73, 103, 106, 127, 178, 186, 214, 235-237, 244, 265, 269-270, 272, 281, 283-284, 288-289, 292-295, 305, 307-310
Consumer Perception 128, 246-247
Consumerism 97, 111
Content Creator 39, 92, 111, 214, 258-259
Content Marketing 23, 214, 278, 291
Core Messages (Mission, Vision, and Values) 213
Corporate Social Responsibility (CSR) 72, 87
Credibility 1-2, 4-5, 7-8, 10, 12-13, 19-20, 23, 29, 35, 41, 44, 49, 54-56, 67, 70-72, 74, 76-77, 80-81, 83, 86, 89, 95, 100-101, 103-110, 113-114, 121-122, 131-132, 135, 137, 140, 142-144, 153, 160, 165, 180-181, 183, 194, 197, 204, 215, 217, 220, 223, 232-234, 240, 242, 260, 267, 274-275, 278, 281, 285, 296, 305-306
Cultural Marketing 189-192, 210-211
Cultural Sector 189-191, 198-199, 202-203, 205-207
Culture 8, 55, 79-80, 83-85, 104, 118, 124, 139, 141, 148, 160, 183, 185, 189-193, 198-199, 202-203, 205, 208-213, 233, 273, 281, 296, 303, 305, 308-309
Customer Engagement 1, 22, 25, 45, 70, 76-79, 129, 133, 137-139, 141-142, 145-146, 230, 239
Customer Loyalty 3, 77, 137, 146, 192, 195-196, 207, 281
Customer Relationship Management (CRM) 192, 213

D

Digital Channels 47, 51, 57, 195

Digital Communication 112-113, 124, 194
Digital Immigrants 195, 213
Digital Influencers 95, 98, 104, 109, 112, 127, 148-150, 153, 155, 164-165, 174, 186, 188-190, 196, 203-208, 210-213, 269-275, 277-278, 280-281, 283-285
Digital Marketing 25, 34, 57, 59, 72, 75, 82, 90-92, 114, 121, 125-127, 130, 133, 145, 153-154, 163, 165, 176, 188, 194-196, 211-212, 214, 232, 235-236, 244, 246, 264, 271-272, 274, 308
Digital Natives 195, 213
Digital Platforms 37, 41, 119, 273, 289

E

Electronic Word of Mouth (e-WOM) 59, 88, 267
Engagement Rate (ER) 35

F

Fan Engagement 214, 220, 232-233
Follower 8, 12, 20, 33, 38, 67-68, 74-75, 93-96, 98, 107, 113, 135, 181, 220, 225, 228, 289, 291-292, 296-297, 299-304, 310
Foodie 287
Fornite 118, 128
Future 1, 15-17, 21-24, 29-30, 32, 38, 53, 59, 65, 77-78, 82, 85, 90, 102, 105-106, 108-110, 114, 125-126, 135, 143-145, 147-151, 154-158, 160-161, 163, 165-166, 180-182, 184, 186-187, 189, 205-208, 211, 229, 246, 260, 265, 270, 283-284, 292, 294, 308

G

Gastronomic Marketing 269, 281
Gastronomic Sector 271, 273, 277, 284
Gen X 5, 31, 33, 57
Gen Z 5, 13, 31, 37, 50, 57, 98, 102, 127-128, 164, 183
Gross Value Added (GVA) 199, 213

H

Human Varnish 154-155, 160

I

Impact of Influencers on Consumer 7
Industries 29, 37-38, 41-42, 51-52, 54, 72, 75, 80, 119, 125, 266
Influence Marketing 55, 89, 112, 127, 269
Influencer 1-22, 24-44, 46-48, 50-60, 65, 67-77, 79-87, 89-96, 98, 101-103, 105-121, 123-124, 126-131, 133-135, 137-138, 140, 142-147, 149-161, 163-166, 171, 174-189, 203-206, 208, 213, 215, 217-218, 221, 228-237, 240-241, 254-257, 264, 267, 269-286, 288-293, 297, 304-310
Influencer Affiliate Marketing 23, 35
Influencer Fraud and Fake Engagement 19, 25, 35
Influencer Legitimacy and Credibility Evaluation 35
Influencer Marketing 1-6, 9-43, 46-47, 50-59, 67-70, 72-77, 81-82, 84-86, 90-92, 94-95, 101-103, 105-110, 121, 123, 126-131, 133, 135, 137-138, 142-147, 149-160, 165, 177, 179-182, 185-187, 189, 203, 205-206, 208, 214-215, 217-218, 221, 230-233, 236-237, 240-241, 254, 264, 267, 270-271, 274, 276-279, 281, 283-286, 288-291, 304-310
Influencer Reach and Engagement Evaluation 36
Influencers 1-35, 38-56, 58-59, 61, 65, 67-81, 84, 86, 88-93, 95-109, 112-153, 155-158, 160-161, 163-165, 170-172, 174-190, 196, 203-218, 220-221, 230, 232-234, 237, 241, 246-247, 255-256, 259, 264, 266-267, 269-281, 283-293, 295-296, 298, 300, 304-310
Instagram 2-3, 6, 9, 15, 21-22, 25, 27, 29, 32, 34, 39-47, 50-51, 54-56, 79-81, 84, 86, 97-98, 102-110, 113, 116-117, 120-121, 128, 131, 139-140, 142, 164, 174, 183-186, 203-205, 207-208, 212, 217, 225, 230-233, 237, 240-242, 270-273, 275-277, 282, 286-291, 293, 295-297, 299-302, 304-305, 307-308, 310
Instamom 289, 293, 295, 297, 299, 302, 310
Internet Celebrity 217, 229, 234

M

Macro-Influencers 9-10, 31, 34, 38, 57, 92-93, 95, 146
Marketing 1-6, 9-21, 23-43, 46-47, 49-59, 61, 64, 67-95, 101-110, 112-114, 116, 120-149, 151-161, 163, 165, 175-198, 201-218, 221, 224, 229-247, 254, 263-267, 270-272, 274-291, 293, 295, 297, 300-301, 303-310
Marketing Strategies 1, 4-5, 17, 20, 22, 24, 39, 54, 59, 68-70, 73, 75, 77, 86, 91-92, 101-102, 125, 129, 132-134, 137-138, 146, 149, 152-153, 180, 192, 196, 215, 217, 235-237, 240, 242, 244-247, 263-264, 270, 272, 274, 276-279, 281, 283
Marketing Strategy 4, 9, 15, 18, 23, 30, 32-35, 39, 46, 51, 53, 57, 67, 72, 76, 88, 90-92, 94, 114, 130, 136, 151, 165, 175, 180, 188, 193, 195, 241-242, 266-267, 272, 281-282, 287, 308, 310
Meso-Influencer 38, 57

Metaverse 24, 26-28, 30, 32, 84, 122, 128, 147-161, 175, 206
Micro-Influencer 34, 38, 57, 93
Millennial 25, 29, 57, 108, 213, 308
Millennium Generation 195, 213
Motivation 84, 89, 95-96, 104-106, 111, 212, 228, 230, 232, 286, 292-293

N

Needs 25, 37, 47, 53, 70, 89, 95-98, 101-102, 106, 115, 124, 130, 134, 149, 152, 155, 157, 164, 191, 194, 196, 201-202, 222-223, 229, 237, 239, 241, 277, 284, 289, 292-293, 297, 303-304

P

Perception 4, 7, 9, 23, 38, 79, 89-90, 94-95, 98-100, 102, 104-105, 107, 111, 121-122, 128, 134, 142, 193, 246-249, 273, 278, 283, 287, 293, 306-307
Performance 1, 15-18, 20, 23, 27, 29, 45, 58-61, 65, 67-71, 74-77, 79-83, 86-88, 137, 140, 156, 161, 186, 194, 197, 204, 207, 216, 225, 280, 300
Persuasion 27, 79, 89-90, 94-95, 102, 111
Phygital Transformation 147-149, 151, 154, 156, 159, 161

Q

Queerbating 118, 128

R

Relationship Marketing 68, 133, 144, 189, 192-193, 208, 210-212, 232
Relationships 2, 8, 11-12, 15, 19-20, 25, 30, 44-45, 49, 71-72, 77, 86, 88, 92, 107-109, 115, 131-132, 135, 137-138, 141, 154, 156, 164, 190-193, 196, 203, 215, 222-224, 233-234, 239, 249-250, 253, 275, 286, 290, 304, 307-308
Research Gaps 166, 180-181
Restaurant 269-271, 273-286
Restaurant Sector 269-270, 274, 276-277, 282-284, 286
Return on Investment (ROI) 1, 6, 14-15, 17-18, 25, 33, 40, 57, 59, 70, 73-74, 76-77, 88, 145, 266, 283, 287
Reviews 2, 8, 10-11, 13, 22, 41, 51, 61, 68, 70-71, 76, 80, 87, 92, 94, 103, 165-166, 176, 181, 200, 213, 220, 230, 235-236, 238, 240, 242-243, 246, 261-264, 267-268, 271-275, 277, 280, 282-283, 299-300

S

Scopus Database 58-60, 166
Skincare Products 85, 235-236, 238-265, 267-268
Social Customer Engagement 1
Social Influence 87, 89-90, 93, 105, 108, 111
Social Media 2-11, 14-15, 18, 21-23, 25-35, 37-43, 46, 48, 51, 54-58, 61, 64, 67, 70-71, 76-93, 95, 98, 100-112, 114, 116, 119, 121-122, 125-127, 129-146, 150-152, 159-161, 163-164, 166, 175, 178, 180-188, 196-197, 201, 203, 205, 207, 209, 211-223, 225-227, 229-234, 237-238, 240-243, 265, 267, 270, 272-276, 280, 282-286, 288-291, 294-299, 301-310
Social Media Content Categories 218-219, 222-223, 234
Social Media Influencer 4, 25, 29-30, 32, 55-56, 82-83, 89-90, 92, 103, 107-111, 130-131, 142, 144-145, 159-160, 181, 185, 187-188, 290, 307
Social Media Influencers 2-3, 5, 8, 25-26, 28, 30, 32, 34-35, 41, 55-56, 76, 81, 89, 91-92, 95, 98, 101-102, 104-109, 126, 130-133, 136-139, 141-142, 144, 146, 152, 160, 181, 186, 209, 230, 232-234, 237, 284-285, 289-291, 298, 307
Social Media Marketing 26, 30, 61, 81, 84, 104, 107, 126, 136, 141-142, 175, 183, 186, 188, 209, 230, 282, 285, 290, 309
Social Proof 7, 36, 68, 73-74, 135
Storytelling 3, 12, 21-23, 49, 58, 68, 70-73, 88, 92, 134, 154, 164, 175, 183, 206, 233
Sustainability 25, 72, 77, 84-86, 138, 152, 156, 159, 161, 187, 193, 213, 235-236, 238-240, 244-245, 264-266, 268, 276, 284
Sustainable Career 147, 152, 158, 161-162

T

TikTok 2-3, 6, 21, 25, 29, 33, 39-40, 42, 51, 54, 98, 102, 105, 116, 164, 203, 205, 214-219, 221-225, 227-234, 237, 241-242, 270-272, 277, 282, 285
Traditional Media 38-39, 193, 195-196, 213, 216-217, 226, 306
Transparency 19-20, 25, 31, 74-75, 80, 86, 103, 113-114, 116, 125, 175-176, 194, 204, 235-236, 238, 244-245, 247-248, 260, 262, 264, 266, 268, 284

U

User Engagement Behavior 214, 218, 222, 227, 234
User-Generated Content 24, 26, 46, 133-135, 140,

146, 206, 213, 220, 235-236, 240-242, 258, 264, 266-268, 286, 290

V

Virtual Influencers 35, 98, 112-128, 150-152, 157, 160, 163-165, 170-172, 174-187
Virtual Reality (VR) 21-22, 46, 205, 276, 287
Vtubers 117, 128

www.ingramcontent.com/pod-product-compliance
Lightning Source LLC
LaVergne TN
LVHW080632011026
849160LV00014B/1195
* 9 7 9 8 3 6 9 3 0 5 5 2 2 *